Lecture Notes in Computer Science 13505

More information about this series at https://link.springer.com/bookseries/558

Ahmed Bouajjani · Lukáš Holík ·
Zhilin Wu (Eds.)

Automated Technology for Verification and Analysis

20th International Symposium, ATVA 2022
Virtual Event, October 25–28, 2022
Proceedings

Editors
Ahmed Bouajjani 🆔
Université Paris Diderot
Paris, France

Lukáš Holík 🆔
Brno University of Technology
Brno, Czech Republic

Zhilin Wu
Chinese Academy of Sciences
Beijing, China

ISSN 0302-9743   ISSN 1611-3349 (electronic)
Lecture Notes in Computer Science
ISBN 978-3-031-19991-2   ISBN 978-3-031-19992-9 (eBook)
https://doi.org/10.1007/978-3-031-19992-9

This Springer imprint is published by the registered company Springer Nature Switzerland AG
The registered company address is: Gewerbestrasse 11, 6330 Cham, Switzerland

Preface

This volume contains the papers presented at the 20th International Symposium on Automated Technology for Verification and Analysis (ATVA 2022). ATVA intends to promote research in theoretical and practical aspects of automated analysis, verification, and synthesis by providing a forum for interaction between regional and international research communities and industry in related areas.

ATVA 2022 was planned to be hosted in Beijing, China, in late October 2022. However, due to the COVID-19 pandemic and travel restrictions, the Steering Committee decided to host the conference virtually. ATVA 2022 received 81 submissions covering theory and applications in automated verification and analysis techniques. Each paper was reviewed by at least three reviewers, and the Program Committee accepted 21 regular papers and five tool papers, leading to a high-quality and attractive scientific program.

This edition of ATVA was blessed by the presence of five prestigious keynote speakers, who gave talks covering current hot research topics and revealing many new and interesting research directions:

- Mohamed Faouzi Atig from Uppsala University, Sweden, spoke about string constraint solving by flattening regular constraints,
- Xinyu Feng from Nanjing University, China, addressed compositional reasoning about concurrent randomized programs,
- Shaz Qadeer from Meta, USA, gave a talk on the Civl verifier, a new approach to the construction of verified concurrent programs and their proofs by layered refinement,
- Jean-François Raskin from Université Libre de Bruxelles, Belgium, spoke about the subgame perfect equilibrium for games of infinite duration played on graphs, and
- Sanjit A. Seshia from the University of California at Berkeley, USA, addressed runtime assurance for verified AI-based autonomy. Sanijit A. Seisha also contributed an invited paper.

The conference was preceded by tutorials on important topics given by two renowned experts:

- Constantin Enea from Ecole Polytechnique, France, gave a tutorial on verifying the consistency of large-scale storage systems and applications.
- Mahesh Viswanathan from the University of Illinois at Urbana-Champaign, USA, gave a tutorial on verifying the privacy and accuracy of algorithms for differential privacy.

ATVA 2022 would not have been successful without the involvement of the Program Committee members and the external reviewers who contributed to the review process (with 254 reviews) and the selection of the best papers. This event would not exist if authors and contributors did not submit their work. We address our thanks to every person, reviewer, author, Program Committee member, and organizer involved in the success of ATVA 2022. The EasyChair system was set up for the management of ATVA 2022, supporting the submission, review, and volume preparation processes. It proved to be a powerful framework.

Although ATVA 2022 was hosted virtually, the local host and sponsor, the Institute of Software, Chinese Academy of Sciences, provided financial support and tremendous help with registration and online facilities. The other sponsors, Springer, contributed in different forms to help the conference run smoothly. Many thanks to all the local organizers and sponsors.

We wish to express our special thanks to the General Chair, Huimin Lin, and steering committee members, particularly Yu-Fang Chen, for their valuable support.

October 2022   Ahmed Bouajjani
                                                                          Lukáš Holík
                                                                          Zhilin Wu

Organization

General Chair

Huimin Lin   Institute of Software, Chinese Academy of Sciences, China

Program Co-chairs

Ahmed Bouajjani   IRIF, Paris Cité University, France
Lukáš Holík   Brno University of Technology, Czech Republic
Zhilin Wu   Institute of Software, Chinese Academy of Sciences, China

Steering Committee

Yu-Fang Chen   Institute of Information Science, Academia Sinica, Taiwan
Yunja Choi   Kyungpook National University, South Korea
Ichiro Hasuo   National Institute of Informatics, Japan
Jie-Hong Roland Jiang   National Taiwan University, Taiwan
Doron A Peled   Bar Ilan University, Israel

Advisory Committee

E. Allen Emerson   University of Texas at Austin, USA
Teruo Higashino   Osaka University, Japan
Oscar H. Ibarra   University of California, Santa Barbara, USA
Insup Lee   University of Pennsylvania, USA
Farn Wang   National Taiwan University, Taiwan
Hsu-Chun Yen   National Taiwan University, Taiwan

Program Committee

Eugene Asarin   IRIF, Paris Cité University, France
Christel Baier   TU Dresden, Germany
Supratik Chakraborty   IIT Bombay, India
Yu-Fang Chen   Institute of Information Science, Academia Sinica, Taiwan
Taolue Chen   Birkbeck, University of London, UK
Yunja Choi   Kyungpook National University, South Korea
Alessandro Cimatti   Fondazione Bruno Kessler, Italy
Hung Dang Van   UET, Vietnam National University, Vietnam

Cezara Dragoi	Inria Paris, ENS, France
Michael Emmi	Amazon Web Services, USA
Bernd Finkbeiner	CISPA Helmholtz Center for Information Security, Germany
Hongfei Fu	Shanghai Jiao Tong University, China
Vijay Ganesh	University of Waterloo, Canada
Ichiro Hasuo	National Institute of Informatics, Japan
Fei He	Tsinghua University, China
Zhe Hou	Griffith University, Australia
Jie-Hong Roland Jiang	National Taiwan University, Taiwan
Orna Kupferman	Hebrew University, Israel
Anthony Widjaja Lin	TU Kaiserslautern, Germany
Roland Meyer	TU Braunschweig, Germany
Kedar Namjoshi	Nokia Bell Labs, USA
K. Narayan Kumar	Chennai Mathematical Institute, India
Mizuhito Ogawa	Japan Advanced Institute of Science and Technology, Japan
Doron Peled	Bar Ilan University, Israel
Andreas Podelski	University of Freiburg, Germany
Pavithra Prabhakar	Kansas State University, USA
Andrew Reynolds	University of Iowa, USA
Adam Rogalewicz	Brno University of Technology, Czech Republic
Philipp Ruemmer	Uppsala University, Sweden
Cesar Sanchez	IMDEA Software Institute, Spain
Arnaud Sangnier	IRIF, Paris Cité University CNRS, France
Sven Schewe	University of Liverpool, UK
Mihaela Sighireanu	LMF, ENS Paris-Saclay, Université Paris-Saclay, and CNRS, France
Fu Song	ShanghaiTech University, China
Jiří Srba	Aalborg University, Denmark
B. Srivathsan	Chennai Mathematical Institute, India
Jun Sun	Singapore Management University, Singapore
Margus Veanes	Microsoft, USA
Chao Wang	University of Southern California, USA
Bow-Yaw Wang	Institute of Information Science, Academia Sinica, Taiwan

Additional Reviewers

Roman Andriushchenko	Benedikt Bollig
Souheib Baarir	Vishnu Bondalakunta
Haniel Barbosa	Guillaume Bonfante
Sebastien Bardin	Marco Bozzano
Jan Baumeister	Thomas Chatain
Anna Becchi	Xin Chen

Yuqi Chen
Spandan Das
Michel De Rougemont
Aldric Degorre
Yizhak Elboher
Shenghua Feng
Paul Gastin
Martijn Goorden
Felipe Gorostiaga
Matthew Hague
Vojtěch Havlena
Yu-Shan Huang
Peter Gjøl Jensen
Piyush Jha
Nai-Ning Ji
Takashi Kitamuta
Ondrej Lengal
Chunxiao Li
Jiaxiang Liu
Wanwei Liu
Florian Lorber
John Lu
Oliver Markgraf
Stephan Mennicke
Niklas Metzger
Yasuhiko Minamide
Srinidhi Nagendra
Van Anh Nguyen
Andres Noetzli
Hyeyoung Park
Noemi Passing

Jiří Pavela
Jakob Piribauer
Hernan Ponce-De-Leon
Davide Prandi
M. Praveen
Andoni Rodriguez
Christian Schilling
Frederik Schmitt
Thiago D. Simão
Jeremy Sproston
Yoshiaki Takata
Yann Thierry-Mieg
Nikolaj Jensen Ulrik
Sören van der Wall
Pierre Vandenhove
Chang-Jun Wang
Hao-Ren Wang
Amalee Wilson
Ye Xin
Jhou Yan-Ru
Pengfei Yang
Peisen Yao
Fang Yu
Shoji Yuen
Bohua Zhan
Leping Zhang
Min Zhang
Yedi Zhang
Hengjun Zhao
Zhe Zhao

Abstracts of Invited Talks

Compositional Reasoning about Concurrent Randomized Programs (Extended Abstract)

Xinyu Feng

State Key Laboratory for Novel Software Technology
Nanjing University, Nanjing, Jiangsu, China
xyfeng@nju.edu.cn

It is challenging to reason about concurrent randomized programs because there are two sources of non-determinism—one comes from the coin-flip operations introduced for randomization, and the other from the scheduling and the corresponding interference between concurrent threads. Moreover, instead of considering properties of every individual program state or execution trace (e.g. the value of x at the end must be greater than 0), we now care about the probabilistic properties of all the possible behaviors of the program (e.g. the expectation of the value of x at the end of the program is 0.5, or the probability that different threads see different values of x must be smaller than certain value). As a result, the properties can be very sensitive to the scheduling policy.

Algorithm designers do introduce *adversary models* to describe scheduling policies. From the currently running thread's point of view, an adversary decides which thread to run next. A *strong* adversary can make the decision based on the full knowledge of the program execution, including the current machine configuration and all the historical steps, while an oblivious adversary has *no* knowledge and must fix the schedule before the program execution. There have been algorithms proposed to take advantage of the oblivious adversary model for better results that cannot be easily achieved in the strong adversary model. On the other hand, correctness of these algorithms can be sensitive to the program structure and the number of execution steps since they rely on the prefixed schedules. This poses great challenges for compositional reasoning using Hoare-style program logics.

This talk introduces a program logic for concurrent randomized programs under the oblivious adversary model. We consider programs in the form of $C_1 \| \ldots \| C_n$. Each thread C_i is a sequential program and may contain the *probabilistic choice statement* $\langle C_1 \rangle \oplus_p \langle C_2 \rangle$, which executes the *atomic* statement $\langle C_1 \rangle$ with probability p, and $\langle C_2 \rangle$ with probability $1 - p$. The atomic statement $\langle C \rangle$ executes C atomically, which cannot be interrupted by other threads. The execution of the multi-threaded program is

Work reported in this talk is done jointly with Weijie Fan and Hongjin Liang from Nanjing University, and Hanru Jiang from Yanqi Lake Beijing Institute of Mathematical Sciences and Applications (BIMSA).

parameterized with a schedule φ, which is chosen non-deterministically at the beginning of the execution.

To see the challenges for reasoning about concurrent randomized programs under the oblivious adversary model, we consider the following two programs:

$$C_1 \stackrel{\text{def}}{=} \textbf{if } (c = 0) \textbf{ then } s := 0 \textbf{ else } s := 2$$
$$C_2 \stackrel{\text{def}}{=} \textbf{if } (c = 0) \textbf{ then } (\textbf{skip}; s := 0) \textbf{ else } s := 2$$

Suppose the value of c is assigned in a probabilistic choice, which is either 0 or 1, each with probability 0.5. In the oblivious adversary model, the concurrent programs $C_1 \| s := 1$ and $C_2 \| s := 1$ actually generate different results.

For $C_1 \| s := 1$, the expectation of s at the end must be 1. This is because the right thread either executes at the end of C_1, or executes before the execution of the **then** and **else** branches of C_1. In the oblivious adversary model, it is impossible for the two threads to have different interleaving in the **then** and **else** branches. However, for $C_2 \| s := 1$, since the **then**-branch has two statements, it is possible to execute $s := 1$ before $s := 0$ (if **then**-branch is taken) but after $s := 2$ (if **else**-branch is taken). The expectation of s at the end is no longer 1.

This example shows that the behavior of programs in the oblivious adversary model may depend on the program structures and the number of execution steps. Also, to reason about probabilistic properties, we may need to consider the execution of different branches altogether. More specifically, we need to consider the correspondence of different statements in different branches according to the number of steps taken to reach them. This is almost impossible when we consider **while**-loops that may execute different rounds (thus different number of steps) with different probability. These problems pose great challenges to design structural logic rules for Hoare-style compositional reasoning.

To address this problem, we focus on proving *closed* properties of programs. An assertion is closed if, to prove it holds over a distribution, it is sufficient to prove there exists a partition of the distribution such that the assertion holds over every partition. We observe the correctness of many algorithms designed for the oblivious adversary model can be expressed as closed properties. To prove them, we do not need to prove they hold over the whole state distribution, which contains states resulting from different branches. Instead, we can split the state distribution according to the branches and prove the properties hold over every partition.

Based on this intuition, we propose a novel proof technique called *split* for compositional reasoning. By splitting the state distribution into smaller ones, we can reason about each branch of the program independently. We provide a light instrumentation mechanism so that the user can insert auxiliary **split** statements at proper positions of the program to guide the proof. We then develop the first program logic for compositional reasoning under the oblivious adversary model. With the split technique, the structural logic rules for sequential composition, **if**-statements and **while**-loops can be viewed as natural extensions of their classical (non-probabilistic) counterparts. We also show how typical algorithms designed in the oblivious adversary model can be verified using the program logic.

Flattening String Constraints

Mohamed Faouzi Atig

Uppsala University, Uppsala, Sweden
mohamed_faouzi.atig@it.uu.se

Abstract. String data type is present in all modern programming and is a part of the core semantics of programming languages such as JavaScript and Python. The testing and verification of such programs require a decision procedure for string constraints. The types of constraints include: (1) *equality constraints* of the form $t_1 = t_2$ where t_1 and t_2 consist of a sequence of string variables and constants, (2) *regular constraints* of the form $x \in R$ where x is a string variable and R is a regular language, and (3) *integer constraints* which are linear arithmetic formulas over the length of the string variables. In this keynote talk, we will present our recent decision procedure for string constraints. We will focus on the decision procedure that uses the Counter-Example Guided Abstraction Refinement (CEGAR) framework which contains both an under- and an over-approximation module running in an alternating manner. The flow of information between these modules is used to increase their precision in an automatic manner.

This talk will be based on join work with Parosh Aziz Abdulla, Yu-Fang Chen, Bui Phi Diep, Julian Dolby, Lukáš Holík, Denghang Hu, Petr Janku, Hsin-Hung Lin, Ahmed Rezine, Philipp Rümmer, Wei-Lun Tsai, Wei-Cheng Wu, Zhillin Wu and Di-De Yen.

1 Summary

The string data type is very present in almost all modern programming languages. This is especially the case with scripting languages (e.g., JavaScript and Python) where strings are part of their core semantics. The testing and verification of programs manipulating strings are important and challenging problems. In fact, many security vulnerabilities such as injection and cross-site scripting attacks can be the result of malicious string inputs. Software (bounded) model checking (e.g., [7, 8, 11–13, 16]), symbolic execution techniques [6, 9, 15] and concolic testing (e.g., [14, 17]) are the most used techniques to test and verify programs manipulating strings. Such techniques are usually based on symbolic encodings of executions into a formula, and use constraint solvers for computing on such encodings. The types of constraints to be solved depend on the manipulated data types. These constraints include at least the following basic string operations:

- *regular* membership constraints (e.g., $x \in [0,9]^+$, that says that x is in the regular language $[0,9]^+$),

- *integer* constraints (e.g., $|x| = |y| - 1$, that says the length of the string variable x is equal to the length of the string variable y minus one),
- *equality* constraints (e.g., $x = y \cdot z$ which states that the string vairable x is equal to the concatenation of the string variables y and z), and
- *transduction* (e.g., $y = T(x)$, that means that the string variable y is the output of the transducer T when the input is the string variable x).

In this keynote talk, we will present a framework that efficiently handles different combination of string constrains [1, 2, 3, 4, 5]. Since the satisfiability problem of string constraints is undecidable in general [10], our framework uses the Counter-Example Guided Refinement (CEGAR) schema which combines an under- and an over-approximation module in an alternating manner: the under- approximation module is used to establish the satisfiability of the given set of constraints; and the over-approximation module is used to show the unsatisfiability of the set of constraints. Moreover, these two modules will be refined on demand by letting information flow between them. More precisely, if the under-approximation module fails to find a solution in a search space predefined using a set of patterns, then this information will be used to exclude this search space when running the over-approximation module during the next phase. Furthermore, if the over-approximation module finds a solution then it can be used to adjust the search space of the under-approximation module (which should also cover the found solution). Observe that running the under-approximation module on this new predefined search space will also check if the solution returned by the over-approximation module is a spurious or genuine solution. In the framework presented in [1, 2, 3, 4, 5], we restrict the search space of each string variable to strings belonging to flat languages (i.e., languages consisting of the set of strings of the form $w_1^* w_2^* \cdots w_n^*$, where $w_1, w_2, \ldots, w_n$ are finite words). This has resulted in an effective decision procedure for solving string constraints. This procedure has been implemented in our string solver Trau [4], which is among the most efficient string solvers. Our framework covers most of commonly used string constraints such as *equality constrains, integer constrains, transduction, context-free membership, string-number conversion constraints*, and *not-substring constraints*.

References

1. Abdulla, P.A., et al.: Efficient handling of string-number conversion. In: PLDI, pp. 943–957. ACM (2020)
2. Abdulla, P.A., et al.: Solving not-substring constraint withFlat abstraction. In: Oh, H. (ed.) Programming Languages and Systems. APLAS 2021. Lecture Notes in Computer Science(), vol. 13008, pp. 305–320. Springer, Cham (2021). https://doi.org/10.1007/978-3-030-89051-3_17
3. Abdulla, P.A., et al.: Flatten and conquer: a framework for efficient analysis of string constraints. In: PLDI. ACM (2017)
4. Abdulla, P.A., et al.: Trau: SMT solver for string constraints. In: FMCAD. IEEE (2018)

5. Abdulla, P.A., Atig, M.F., Diep, B.P., Holík, L., Janků, P.: Chain-free string constraints. In: Chen, Y.F., Cheng, C.H., Esparza, J. (eds.) Automated Technology for Verification and Analysis. ATVA 2019. Lecture Notes in Computer Science(), vol. 11781, pp. 277–293. Springer, Cham (2019). https://doi.org/10.1007/978-3-030-31784-3_16
6. Baldoni, R., Coppa, E., D'Elia, D.C., Demetrescu, C., Finocchi, I.: A survey of symbolic execution techniques. ACM Comput. Surv. 51(3), 50:1–50:39 (2018)
7. Biere, A.: Bounded model checking. In: Handbook of Satisfiability, Frontiers in Artificial Intelligence and Applications, vol. 185, pp. 457–481. IOS Press (2009)
8. Biere, A., Cimatti, A., Clarke, E.M., Zhu, Y.: Symbolic model checking without BDDs. In: Cleaveland, W.R. (ed.) Tools and Algorithms for the Construction and Analysis of Systems. TACAS 1999, LNCS, vol. 1579, pp. 193–207. Springer, Berlin, Heidelberg (1999). https://doi.org/10.1007/3-540-49059-0_14
9. Cadar, C., Sen, K.: Symbolic execution for software testing: three decades later. Commun. ACM 56(2), 82–90 (2013)
10. Chen, T., Hague, M., Lin, A.W., Rümmer, P., Wu, Z.: Decision procedures for path feasibility of string-manipulating programs with complex operations. In: Proceedings of the ACM Program. Lang. 3(POPL) (2019)
11. Clarke, E., Kroening, D., Lerda, F.: A tool for checking ANSI-C programs. In: Jensen, K., Podelski, A. (eds.) Tools and Algorithms for the Construction and Analysis of Systems. TACAS 2004. Lecture Notes in Computer Science, vol. 2988, pp. 168–176. Springer, Berlin, Heidelberg (2004). https://doi.org/10.1007/978-3-540-24730-2_15
12. Clarke, E.M., Emerson, E.A.: Design and synthesis of synchronization skeletons using branching-time temporal logic. In: Kozen, D. (eds.) Logics of Programs, Workshop, Yorktown Heights, New York, USA, May 1981. LNCS, vol. 131, pp. 52–71. Springer, Berlin, Heidelberg (1981). https://doi.org/10.1007/BFb0025774
13. D'Silva, V., Kroening, D., Weissenbacher, G.: A survey of automated techniques for formal software verification. IEEE Trans. Comput. Aided Des. Integr. Circ. Syst. 27(7), 1165–1178 (2008)
14. Godefroid, P., Klarlund, N., Sen, K.: DART: directed automated random testing. In: PLDI, pp. 213–223. ACM (2005)
15. King, J.C.: Symbolic execution and program testing. Commun. ACM 19(7), 385–394 (1976)
16. Queille, J., Sifakis, J.: Specification and verification of concurrent systems in CESAR. In: Dezani-Ciancaglini, M., Montanari, U. (eds.) International Symposium on Programming. LNCS, vol. 137, pp. 337–351. Springer, Berlin, Heidelberg (1982). https://doi.org/10.1007/3-540-11494-7_22
17. Sen, K., Marinov, D., Agha, G.: CUTE: a concolic unit testing engine for C. In: ESEC/SIGSOFT FSE, pp. 263–272. ACM (2005)

Runtime Assurance for Verified AI-Based Autonomy

Sanjit A. Seshia

University of California at Berkeley, USA

Abstract. Verified artificial intelligence (AI) is the goal of designing AI-based systems that have strong, verified assurances of correctness with respect to mathematically-specified requirements. This goal is particularly important for autonomous and semi-autonomous systems. In this talk, I will review the progress towards Verified AI from the perspective of formal methods with a special focus on autonomy. The talk will focus mainly on the use of formal methods for run-time assurance, which is especially important as many AI-based autonomous systems are designed to operate in unknown and uncertain environments. The presented research will be illustrated with examples from the domain of intelligent cyber-physical systems, with a particular focus on deep neural network-based autonomy in transportation systems.

The Civl Verifier

Shaz Qadeer

Meta, USA
shaz.qadeer@gmail.com

Abstract. The Civl verifier introduces layered refinement, a new approach to the construction of verified concurrent programs and their proofs. This approach simplifies and scales (human and automated) reasoning by enabling a concurrent program to be represented and manipulated at multiple layers of abstraction. These abstraction layers are chained together via simple program transformations; each transformation is justified by a collection of automatically-checked verification conditions. Civl proofs are maintainable and reusable, specifically eliminating the need to write complex invariants on the low-level encoding of the concurrent program as a flat transition system. Civl has been used to construct verified low-level implementations of complex systems such as a concurrent garbage collector, a consensus protocol, and shared-memory data structures.

Civl is jointly developed with Bernhard Kragl and publicly available at https://civl-verifier.github.io/.

Subgame Perfect Equilibrium
with an Algorithmic Perspective

Jean-François Raskin

Université Libre de Bruxelles, Brussels, Belgium
`jraskin@ulb.ac.be`

Abstract. In this invited talk, we will recall the notion of subgame perfect equilibrium (SPE) for games of infinite duration played on graph. We will introduce new algorithmic ideas in this context. In particular, we will provide an effective characterization of all the SPEs in infinite duration games played on finite graphs for the case of parity objectives and for the case of mean-payoff objectives. To this end, we will introduce the notion of requirement and the notion of negotiation function. We will establish that the set of plays that are supported by SPEs are exactly those that are consistent with the least fixed point of the negotiation function. By studying the properties of the least fixed point of the negotiation function, we will provide provably optimal algorithms to solve relevant decision problems related to SPEs. This talk will be based on the following publications [1–3].

References

1. Brice, L., Raskin, J.-F., van den Bogaard, M.: Subgame-perfect equilibria in mean-payo games. In: Haddad, S., Varacca, D. (eds.) 32nd International Conference on Concurrency Theory, CONCUR 2021, 24–27 August 2021, Virtual Conference, volume 203 of LIPIcs, pp. 8:1–8:17. Schloss Dagstuhl - Leibniz-Zentrum für Informatik (2021)
2. Brice, L., Raskin, J.-F., van den Bogaard, M.: The complexity of spes in mean-payo games. In: Bojanczyk, M., Merelli, E., Woodru, D.P. (eds.) 49th International Colloquium on Automata, Languages, and Programming, ICALP 2022, 4–8 July 2022, Paris, France, volume 229 of LIPIcs, pp. 116:1–116:20. Schloss Dagstuhl - Leibniz-Zentrum für Informatik (2022)
3. Brice, L., Raskin, J.-F., van den Bogaard, M.: On the complexity of spes in parity games. In: Manea, F., Simpson, A., (eds.) 30th EACSL Annual Conference on Computer Science Logic, CSL 2022, 14–19 February 2022, Göttingen, Germany (Virtual Conference), volume 216 of LIPIcs, pp. 10:1–10:17. Schloss Dagstuhl - Leibniz-Zentrum für Informatik (2022)

Contents

Synthesis and Repair

Verification of Neural Networks

Invited Paper

Learning Monitorable Operational Design Domains for Assured Autonomy

Hazem Torfah[1]([✉]), Carol Xie[1], Sebastian Junges[2], Marcell Vazquez-Chanlatte[1], and Sanjit A. Seshia[1]

[1] University of California at Berkeley, Berkeley, USA
torfah@berkeley.edu
[2] Radboud University, Nijmegen, The Netherlands

Abstract. AI-based autonomous systems are increasingly relying on machine learning (ML) components to perform a variety of complex tasks in perception, prediction, and control. The use of ML components is projected to grow and with it the concern of using these components in systems that operate in safety-critical settings. To guarantee a safe operation of autonomous systems, it is important to run an ML component in its operational design domain (ODD), i.e., the conditions under which using the component does not endanger the safety of the system. Building safe and reliable autonomous systems which may use machine-learning-based components, calls therefore for automated techniques that allow to systematically capture the ODD of systems.

In this paper, we present a framework for learning runtime monitors that capture the ODDs of black-box systems. A runtime monitor of an ODD predicts based on a sequence of monitorable observations whether the system is about to exit the ODD. We particularly investigate the learning of optimal monitors based on counterexample-guided refinement and conformance testing. We evaluate the applicability of our approach on a case study from the domain of autonomous driving.

Keywords: AI-based autonomy · Runtime assurance · Operational design domains · Black-box models

1 Introduction

In recent years, there has been an increase in using autonomous systems in various safety-critical applications such as in transport, medicine, manufacturing, and space. Considering the complexity of the environments these systems are being deployed in, autonomous systems rely on machine learning (ML) techniques to solve complex tasks in perception, prediction and control. The use of

This work is partially supported by NSF grants 1545126 (VeHICaL), 1646208 and 1837132, by the DARPA contracts FA8750-18-C-0101 (AA) and FA8750-20-C-0156 (SDCPS), by Berkeley Deep Drive, by C3DTI, by the Toyota Research Institute, and by Toyota under the iCyPhy center.

A. Bouajjani et al. (Eds.): ATVA 2022, LNCS 13505, pp. 3–22, 2022.
https://doi.org/10.1007/978-3-031-19992-9_1

complex, black-box ML components raises concerns regarding the safe operation of ML-based systems [2,10,40]. ML models such as deep neural networks are unpredictable; unanticipated changes in the environment may cause a neural network to produce faulty outcomes that could endanger the safety of the system [1,14,22]. To raise the level of assurance in autonomous systems, it is therefore crucial to provide designers with the necessary tools that help them understand and further capture the *operational design domain (ODD)* of such systems. In autonomous driving, the SAE J3016 standard for driving automation systems, [36], defines an ODD as the

> *operating conditions under which a given driving automation system or feature thereof is specifically designed to function, including, but not limited to, environmental, geographical, and time-of-day restrictions, and/or the requisite presence or absence of certain traffic or roadway characteristics.*

In general, from a user or authority perspective, the ODD can be seen as the operating environment in which a system should operate safely. To assure the safety of the system, the boundaries defined by an ODD must be monitored during system operation and the system should only operate (autonomously) when these boundaries are met.

However, not every ODD can be monitored at run time. First and foremost, some aspects of the ODD may not be reliably observable or are too expensive to observe. A monitor relying on these aspects is not (efficiently) implementable. Furthermore, we are interested in obtaining monitors that are *predictive* – we optimally want to raise an alarm *before* the system leaves its ODD. Lastly, we emphasize that a powerful ODD needs to be specified over runs of the system, as the history of observable features allows us to approximate hidden system states.

In this paper, we introduce a framework for learning *monitorable operational design domains* of black-box systems, in particular for systems with critical ML components. We define a monitorable ODD to be one that is defined over an observable feature space and that can be implemented as a runtime monitor that predicts whether the system will exit the ODD. This stands in contrast to general definitions of ODDs [26,36] that do not assume their executability. A monitorable ODD in our framework is learned in terms of a system-level specification that defines a general ODD over a possible non-observable abstract feature space, and a desired class of programs defined over the observable feature space. For a system-level specification, our framework can be used to learn a monitorable ODD from the class of programs that predicts whether the system will violate the specification.

We are particularly interested in learning monitorable ODDs for *temporal system-level* specifications, i.e., where the safe operation conditions bounded by an ODD are defined in terms of timed sequences of observations. Compared to conditions that only rely on non-temporal features such as the type of a road, the state of the system, the weather conditions, or the current traffic situation, the ODDs in our setting incorporate the change of features over time. Consider a perception module in an autonomous vehicle used for lane keeping. While the perception module accurately computes the distance from the edge of a lane, continuous interruptions of the side markings, for example, due to a line of parking cars or obstacles, may cause the module to produce values triggering a faulty steering behavior by the controller of the vehicle. In general, this should not endanger the vehicle if it happens at a low frequency. An occurrence over a large period of time, may, however, lead to steering the vehicle away from the lane. A runtime monitor learned by our framework may decide to switch to a more safe controller (or manual control) if the latter scenario is detected, and may issue a switch back to using the neural network when the line of obstacles is passed.

Our framework is based on a *quantitative* approach for learning monitors. Since monitors for ODDs are constricted to a specific class of programs and to an observable feature space possibly different from that of the system-level feature space, finding a monitor that exactly captures the ODD of a system may not be feasible: First, the program class may not include enough programs that can cover the entire concept class of functions defined over the observable feature space. Furthermore, a sequence of observations over the observable feature space may correspond to several executions over the system-level feature space. Some of these executions may satisfy the system-level specification and some may violate it. Depending on whether the corresponding sequence of observation is to be classified as part or not included in the ODD will result in a mismatch between the monitorable ODD and the system-level specification. In this case, given a quantitative measure over the system level executions, our approach will learn the optimal monitor over the observable feature space from the class of programs with respect to the given optimality objective. Particularly, our optimality objective is defined in terms of the quantitative measure and the rates of false positives and negatives.

The framework follows a data-driven counterexample-guided refinement approach for learning monitors. Data used for learning are generated via simulation-based runtime verification techniques. Specifically, we use VERIFAI, an open-source toolkit for the formal design and analysis of systems that include AI or ML components [13]. VERIFAI allows us to analyze ML-based components using system-level specifications. To scale to complex high-dimensional feature spaces, VERIFAI operates on an abstract semantic feature space. This space is typically represented using SCENIC, a probabilistic programming language for modeling environments [19]. Using SCENIC, we can define scenarios, distributions over spatial and temporal configurations of objects and agents, in which we want to deploy and analyze a system. Once the training data has been generated, it is forwarded to an algorithm for learning monitors from the class of interest (e.g., neural networks, decision trees, automata, etc.). The learned monitor is then checked by a conformance tester. The conformance tester relies again on the simulation-based testing techniques provided by VERIFAI to check whether a monitor satisfies a given quantitative objective. If this is the case, a monitor is returned. Otherwise, counterexamples found during testing are used in the next learning cycle. We demonstrate the applicability of our framework using a case study from the domain of autonomous driving. We show that our counterexample-guided approach can be used to learn a monitorable ODD for an image-based neural network used for lane keeping. Our example is inspired by several real case studies VERIFAI has been applied in including with industrial partners (e.g., see [18,21,46]).

We summarize our contributions as follows:

– We formalize the notion of operational design domains by introducing the problem of finding monitorable operational design domains of systems with respect to system-level specifications.
– We present a framework for learning monitorable operational designs domains based on a quantitative counterexample-guided refinement approach.
– We present a case study that demonstrates the applicability of our framework and that points out the challenges in learning monitorable ODDs for black-box (ML) models.

2 Motivating Example: Autonomous Lane Keeping

Fig. 1. Example input images to the neural network, rendered in CARLA, showing a variety of orientation, weather, and road conditions.

Consider a scenario of an autonomous vehicle driving through a city. The car is equipped with a camera-based perception module using a convolutional neural network that based on images captured by a camera (cf. Fig. 1) estimates the *cross-track error (CTE)*, i.e., the lateral offset of the car from the centerline of the road. The estimated values are forwarded to a controller that adjusts the steering angle of the car. The perception module is a black box. In particular, we do not have access to (any statistics of) the images used to train the network nor any knowledge about potential gaps in the training set.

Our goal is to learn a monitor that captures the conditions under which using the neural network does not result in large CTE values that endanger the safety of the car. The monitor should alert in time, to refrain from using the network and maybe switch to a more trustworthy safe controller, e.g. to human control or one that is less optimal but uses more trustworthy sensors.

The behavior of the neural network may be influenced by many factors, some of that may not have been sufficiently covered during training. For example, while the network was trained on images, its behavior may depend on other parameters not accounted for in the input to the network such as weather conditions (like precipitation or cloudiness), the sun angle, thus, determining the time of day and shadowing effects, the position and heading on the road, its velocity, and other objects on the road. We refer to these factors as *semantic features*. For our goal, these features must be observable and monitorable at run time.

Once we fix the observable semantic features, which we intend to use to monitor the system, the next step is to establish a connection between the values of these semantic features and a general system-level safety specification (e.g., leaving the lane). A monitor that implements this connection is one that captures the ODD of the neural network with respect to the above-mentioned semantic features and predicts whether the system will leave the ODD. For example, under rainy weather conditions, at certain turns, or after observing certain landmarks on the road, the monitor might predict that the system will likely deviate too far from the centerline or even exits its lane.

We present a systematic approach to capturing the connection between the system-level specification and the sequences of values of observable features. Our approach is based on exploring the diverse set of scenarios possible under different instantiations of the aforementioned semantic features and analyzing the executions of the system with respect to a system-level specification. Based on data generated by the exploration and analysis processes, our approach learns a monitor that predicts a faulty behavior of the system, or in other words, leaving the ODD of the neural network.

3   Optimal Monitors for Operational Design Domains

In this section, we introduce the problem of learning a monitorable operational design domain of a system. We first establish some key definitions. We then define the learning problem, and finally state some of the challenges in constructing matching monitors for operational design domains.

3.1   Learning Monitors for ODDs

Notation. For an (possibly infinite) alphabet Σ, we define the set of traces over Σ by the set of finite words Σ^*. We define the set of traces of a fixed-length $d \in \mathbb{N}$ over Σ by the set Σ^d. A language over Σ is any set $L \subseteq \Sigma^*$. A language of d-length traces is any set $L \subseteq \Sigma^d$.

For a (discrete-time) black-box system with inputs $\mathcal{I}$ and outputs $\mathcal{O}$, we capture its behavior as a discrete sequence of input-output pairs. Formally, we use $\Sigma_{sys} = (\mathcal{I} \times \mathcal{O})$. The system behavior is then a language $C \subseteq \Sigma_{sys}^*$. We make no further assumptions over the system, in particular, we allow for the system to be nondeterministic, i.e., the system may provide different outputs for the same sequence of inputs. The system-level specification, encoding a correct system behavior, can be captured as set of traces over input-output pairs that the system's behavior should not deviate from. Formally, a system-level specification is a language $\varphi \subseteq \Sigma_{sys}^*$. A system $C \subseteq \Sigma_{sys}^*$ satisfies a specification $\varphi \subseteq \Sigma_{sys}^*$ if $C \subseteq \varphi$. We denote the satisfaction relation of systems and specifications by $C \models \varphi$.

For a specification φ and a system C, the *operational design domain* of C with respect to φ, captures the set of "behavioral conditions" where the system C is guaranteed to satisfy the specification φ. In a discrete-time model, we define a behavioral condition as a sequence of observations that can be observed off the system. Formally, we define the operational design domain D of C and φ as the tuple $D_{C,\varphi} = (\Sigma_{obs}, obs, d)$, where Σ_{obs} defines a set of observable inputs and actions, $obs \colon \Sigma_{sys}^* \to \Sigma_{obs}^*$ defines the relation between the system-level inputs and actions and the observations of interest, and $d \in \mathbb{R}^+$ is the prediction horizon. An operational design domain D defines a set $[\![D]\!] = \{\sigma \mid \forall \tau \in \Sigma_{sys}^*.\ obs(\tau) = \sigma \to \forall \tau' \in \Sigma_{sys}^d.\ \tau \cdot \tau' \notin \overline{\varphi}\}$. Intuitively, $[\![D]\!]$ defines the set of sequences of observations that cannot be mapped to a trace of the system C that violates the specification φ in d steps. We highlight that our definition of ODDs allows us to distinguish temporal interactions of the system with its environment, e.g. that driving over road marks for a short time is not problematic, but that driving over such an area for a prolonged time is problematic.

Our goal is synthesize a runtime monitor that captures the ODD of a system and a specification with respect to a set of observations. A runtime monitor M for an ODD D over observations Σ_{obs} is a program that implements a function $f_M \colon \Sigma_{obs}^* \to \mathbb{B}$, such that, for every trace $\tau \in \Sigma_{obs}^*$, $f_M(\tau)$ if and only if $\tau \in [\![D]\!]$[1]. In the rest of the paper will use f_M to also denote the set of traces τ for which $f_M(\tau) = true$. We formalize the monitor synthesis problem for ODD as follows.

Problem 1 (Synthesizing Monitors for ODDs) *For an operational design domain $D_{C,\varphi} = (\Sigma_{obs}, obs, d)$ and a class of monitors $\mathcal{M}$ over Σ_{obs}, find a monitor $M \in \mathcal{M}$, such that $f_M = [\![D]\!]$, or report that there does not exist such monitor.*

The ODD definition and the monitor extraction problem described above is idealized. In the following, we give some details on why this idealized problem statement is not well suited in practice and present a quantitative more practical version of the problem.

---

[1] We choose a Boolean codomain for monitors for simplicity reasons. Our approach can be extended easily to quantitative domains, i.e., monitors with a robustness semantics [9,11].

3.2   Challenges in Learning Monitorable ODDs

The problem statement above yields monitors that are too conservative. In particular, it assumes the possibility of absolute safety: An observation trace is excluded from the ODD if any system-level traces that violates the specification may yield this observation trace. In line with safety standards, a practical formulation of the problem relaxes the safety requirements to a more quantitative setting. We observe that the occurrence of system-level traces which match a particular observation trace may be rare. In this case, including their corresponding observations in the operational design domain may be admissible, even in safety-critical domains. Furthermore, the class of monitors may not always include a monitor for the exact ODD. Semantically speaking, the monitors within a class typically cover only a subset of monitors over Σ_{obs}. In this case, our goal would be to search for an optimal monitor, e.g., one with the lowest misclassification rate. The optimality of a monitor can be defined in terms of a measure $\nu\colon \mathcal{P}(\Sigma_{obs}^*) \to \mathbb{R}^+$ over sets of observation traces. In this case, the monitor learning problem is converted to the following optimization problem. For a system C, a specification φ, and a class of monitors $\mathcal{M}$, find a monitor $M \in \mathcal{M}$, such that,

$$M \in \arg\min_{M' \in \mathcal{M}} \nu(f_{M'} \triangle [\![D]\!]),$$

where $\triangle$ denotes the symmetric difference.

While the latter formulation overcomes the mismatch in Problem 1, by searching for the optimal monitor, practically solving the problem is still faced with some issues. First, the usage of a *symmetric* difference treats *false positives* and *false negatives* equivalently. False positives are given as the set of traces of C that satisfy φ, but that are mistakenly identified by the monitor to be executions that lead to a violation of the ODD. False negatives are traces of C that violate φ but are not captured by the monitor as erroneous. In safety-critical settings, this is inadequate, and in general, we want the ability to find monitors that favor false positives over false negatives whenever possible. Another shortcoming of the formulation above is that it requires defining correctness/optimality on sets of traces over Σ_{obs}, which is often troublesome, as correctness/optimality is defined in our setting as a system-level specification, i.e., on traces over Σ_{sys}.

To address these challenges, in the next section, we present a quantitative variant of the monitor learning problem for ODDs. It is based on a correctness definition with respect to the traces over Σ_{sys}, and thus transforms the problem to minimizing a measure μ on languages over Σ_{sys}. This variant allows us to search for optimal monitors within a given class of monitors and with respect to given quantitative measure on the sets of system-level traces.

3.3 Quantitative Monitor Learning

Considering the challenges discussed above, a practical definition of the problem of learning optimal monitorable ODDs needs to define optimality with respect to

1. system-level traces, i.e., traces over Σ_{sys}
2. the rates of and biases towards false positives and negatives

One consequence of transforming the definition to measures over system-level traces is the matter of predictiveness. To remind the reader, an ODD is defined in terms of a prediction horizon d. The value of a monitor f_M for a trace τ_{obs}, depends the value of φ on system-level trace τ_{sys} of length $|\tau_{obs}|+d$. The problem definition should take this prediction horizon into account when defining the measure over system-level traces. To accommodate for this difference in length, we cut off all suffixes of length d of all traces in $(C \cap \varphi)$ and $(C \cap \overline{\varphi})$. In the problem definition, we will make use of the following notation: for a language L, we let L^{-d}, for $d \in \mathbb{N}$, denote $L^{-d} = \{\alpha_0\alpha_1 \ldots \alpha_{k-d} \mid \alpha_0\alpha_1 \ldots \alpha_k \in L, k \in \mathbb{N} \text{ s.t. } k - d \geq 0\}$.

Problem 2 (Optimal Monitor Synthesis for ODDs) *Given an operational design domain* $D = (\Sigma_{obs}, obs, d)_{C,\varphi}$ *of a system* C *and a specification* φ *over* Σ_{sys}^*, *a class of monitors* $\mathcal{M}$ *over* Σ_{obs}, *and a measure* $\mu \colon \mathcal{P}(\Sigma_{sys}^*) \to \mathbb{R}^+$, *find a monitor* $M \in \mathcal{M}$, *such that,*

$$M \in \underset{M' \in \mathcal{M}}{\arg\min} \ \mu(T_p \setminus obs^{-1}(f_{M'})) + w_{fn} \cdot \mu(T_n \cap obs^{-1}(f_{M'}))$$

for fixed values $w_{fn} \in \mathbb{R}^+$ *and where* $T_p = (C \cap \varphi)^{-d}$ *and* $T_n = (C \cap \overline{\varphi})^{-d}$.

The problem statement above defines a monitor as optimizing a kind of loss function with respect to system-level traces. The left side of the sum in the objective function defines a measure over the false positives. The false-negatives side of the objective function is weighted by w_{fn}, that allows us to bias the search towards false positives or false negatives.

Example 1. A system C we are interested in capturing its ODD, could be the image-based neural network from our motivating example. A monitor for the ODD in this case can be defined over values of the weather, time of the day, location, and road properties, representing a projection of general system-level values, such as the state of the car, or the images received by the neural network as well as its output. On top of system-level traces we define a measure μ that for a set Γ returns the ratio of Γ to the entire set of system-level traces.

Remark 1 (Relation between Problem 1 and Problem 2). In cases where the ODD can be captured by a monitor in a given class and where absolute safety is realizable, a solution to Problem 2 will indeed solve Problem 1.

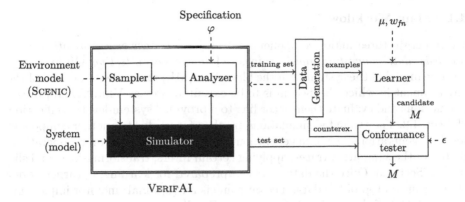

Fig. 2. Extension of VERIFAI with the monitor learning framework

3.4 Black-Box vs. White-Box Settings

Problem 2 defines the optimality with respect to a system C, i.e., a set of traces. In a white-box setting, one can assume access to a model defining the entire set of traces and thus extract models for the sets T_p and T_n by evaluating φ over C. In a black-box setting, this is in general infeasible. Obtaining an exhaustive set of samples from a black-box model is not practical, considering the large (potentially infinite) inputs domains autonomous systems are defined over. The question that we need to raise at this point is how to sample from the black box and how large this sample set must be to obtain monitors that do not overfit the set of samples. Depending on the class of monitors at hand, we can rely on theories from the field of *probably approximate correct learning (PAC)* [42] to construct monitors that are closest to optimal with high confidence. In practice this requires a large number of samples, considering that the class of monitors needed to obtain good monitors is usually very large. In this paper, we suggest a different approach based on conformance testing Here we rely on learning monitor from a small set of samples performing a conformance test to check the quality of the monitor (A testing PAC guarantee using theories such as the Hoeffding's inequality [24]). Relating this to Problem 2, the sets T_p and T_n are then defined with respect to the sample set and the monitors learned are optimal with respect to these sets. Conformance testing is done with respect to the measure μ and the sample sets are extended based on counterexamples obtained during testing. A framework implementing this workflow is given next.

4 Framework

We present of counterexample-guided learning framework. We sketch the overall architecture given in Fig. 2 and give details on the individual components in separate sections.

4.1 Main Workflow

We integrate three major components into a joint framework: *simulation-based analysis, data generation and learning,* and *conformance testing*. Given an executable model of the system with the black-box (ML) component, a model of the environment in which the system is to be executed, we use VERIFAI [13] to run simulations and evaluate them according to a provided system-level specification, cf. Sect. 4.2. The evaluated simulations are then forwarded to another component for data generation. The data generation component performs several operations on top of the simulation traces, applying certain filters, transformations, and slicing, cf. Sect. 4.3. Once the data has been prepared for learning, a learner of our choice runs on top of the data. The outcome is an (optimal) monitor implementing the ODD of the black-box component. Finally, a conformance tester checks the quality of the monitor, cf. Sect. 4.4. Here, the conformance tester may use further simulation runs, using VERIFAI, to search for any counterexamples. If conformance testing succeeds, the framework terminates and returns the so-far learned monitor. Otherwise, counterexamples found during testing are passed to the data generating process to compute a new set of data over which a new monitor is learned.

4.2 Simulation-Based Analysis Using VERIFAI and SCENIC

VERIFAI is an open-source toolkit for the formal design and analysis of systems that include AI or ML components [13]. VERIFAI follows a paradigm of *formally-driven simulation*, using formal models of a system, its environment, and its requirements to guide the generation of testing and training data. The high-level architecture of VERIFAI is shown in Fig. 2. To use VERIFAI, one first provides an environment model which defines the space of environments that the system should be tested or trained against. Environment models can be specified using the SCENIC probabilistic modeling language [19]. A SCENIC program defines a distribution over configurations of physical objects and their behaviors over time. For example, Fig. 3 shows a SCENIC program for the lane keeping scenario used in our case study. This program specifies a variety of semantic features including time of day, weather, and the position and orientation of the car, giving distributions for all of them. SCENIC also supports modeling dynamic behaviors of objects, with syntax for specifying temporal relationships between events and composing individual scenarios into more complex ones [20]. Finally, SCENIC is also simulator- and application-agnostic, being successfully used in a variety of CPS domains including autonomous driving [21], aviation [18], robotics [19], and reinforcement learning agents for simulated sports [3]. In all these applications, the formal semantics of SCENIC programs allow them to serve as precise models of a system's environment. For more examples we refer the reader to [19].

Once the abstract feature space has been defined, VERIFAI can search the space using a variety of sampling algorithms suited to different applications (e.g., these include passive samplers which seek to evenly cover the space, such as low-discrepancy (Halton) sampling, as well as active samplers which use the history

```
param weather = Uniform('ClearNoon', 'CloudyNoon',
                        'WetNoon', 'MidRainyNoon'
                        'ClearSunSet')

lane = Uniform(*network.lanes)
start = OrientedPoint on lane.centerline

ego = Car at start,
    with visibleDistance 60,
    with behavior EgoBehavior(10)
```

Fig. 3. A SCENIC program specifying the environment for the lane keeping scenario

of past tests to identify parts of the space more likely to yield counterexamples). Each point sampled from the abstract feature space defines a concrete test case which we can execute in the simulator. During the simulation, VERIFAI monitors whether the system has satisfied or violated its specification, which can be provided as a black-box monitor function or in a more structured representation such as a formula of Metric Temporal Logic [31,34]. VERIFAI uses the quantitative semantics of MTL [9,11], allowing the search algorithms to distinguish between safe traces which are closer or farther from violating the specification. The results of each test can be used to guide future tests as mentioned above, and are also saved in a table for offline analysis, including monitor generation.

4.3 Data Generation

In this section, we discuss the training data generation process. Training data is generated from the execution runs of several simulations through a process consisting of two phases, *mapping* and *segmentation*.

Mapping. The role of the mapper is to establish the connection between the sequence of events collected during a simulation and the inputs to the monitor. In general, the mapper consists of a *projection* and a *filtering* phase.

Projection involves *mapping a sequence of simulation events to a (sub)set of events that can be reliably observed at runtime*. A monitor must be defined over inputs that are observable by the system during runtime. Properties of other entities in the environment may be known during simulation, but not during runtime. Thus, the data collected at simulation must be projected to a stream of observable data. We especially want to project the data onto *reliable* and *trustable* data. Some data may be observable, but should not be used by a monitor. For example, a monitor for validating the confidence in using the camera-based neural network, can be based on the data of the weather condition and the time of day, radar values, whereas it might be better to refrain from using the images captured by the camera.

Filtering involve *mapping traces to other traces using transformation functions that may have an internal state (based on the history of events)*. Beyond projecting, we may use the data available at runtime to estimate an unobservable system or environment state by means of filtering approaches and then use this system state (or statistics of this state) as an additional observable entity. For example, to validate the conditions for our neural network, we may want to use data computed based on an aggregate model that evaluates the change in the heading of the car.

At all times, mappers should preserve the order of events as received from the evaluator and maintain the valuations of the system-level specification on the original system-level trace.

Segmentation. Rather than considering traces from the initial (simulation) state, a sliding window approach can be used to generate traces σ of fixed length starting in any state encountered during the simulation. This approach is important to avoid generating monitors that overly depend on the initial situation or monitors that (artificially) depend on outdated events For example, the behavior of the car in our lane keeping example, may depend on the frequency of obstacles along the side of the road. Short-period occurrences may not cause major errors in the CTE values or perhaps only for a short recoverable period of time. Frequent occurrences may however cause a series of errors that could lead the car to exit the lane. Therefore, the monitor does not need the entire history of data, as the car will recover from small patches, but the monitor should switch from using the neural network-based controller to manual control when the a long series of obstacles on the side of the road is observed. In general, the length of segments needs to be tuned based on the application at hand and the frequency in which data is received. We remark that the loss of information due to ignoring events earlier in the history can be partially alleviated by adding a state estimate to the trace using an appropriate filter in the mapping phase.

After the table of training data is created by the segmentation process it can be forwarded to any learning algorithm that generates a suitable artifact for the monitor. We feed the traces that we obtain in a trace *warehouse*. From that warehouse, we select traces to feed into the learner.

4.4   Conformance Testing

The goal of conformance testing is to test the quality of our learned monitors. This is done by testing the monitor on new independent simulation runs using VERIFAI and checking whether a hypothesis with respect to the optimality objective is met. If we pass the hypothesis, we have found a monitor. If not, we augment our warehouse with the counterexamples found during testing. We particularly look for cases, where the monitor failed to issue an alert, and the specification was violated d steps later, where d is the prediction horizon, i.e., false negatives. We also look for cases, where the monitor issued false alerts, triggering unnecessary switches to manual control, i.e., false positives.

The result of the conformance tester is given relative to the set of sampled traces in VERIFAI. For high confidence in the result of the conformance tester, we need to make sure to test the monitor on a sufficient number of simulations. For example, assuming that we sampled the simulation traces i.i.d. from the actual distribution, and assuming that we are using a quantitative measure over a σ-algebra over traces, then using Hoeffding's inequality, we can determine the number of samples for given error and confidence measures. For more details on this we refer the reader to [24].

5 Experiments

We used our framework in an experiment for learning a monitor for the ODD of the system with the image-based perception module used for lane keeping as described in Sect. 2. The perception module is a convolutional neural network (CNN) that for a given snapshot taken by a camera mounted at the front of the car returns the estimated cross-track error to the centerline of the road. We are interested in learning a monitor that based on features such as precipitation, cloudiness, the sun angle, and location determines whether the system will be safe in the presence of these conditions. In our experiment, we evaluate the latter based on whether the car exits its lane. In the following, we provide some details on the experimental setup and results.

5.1 Experimental Setup

Our setup uses VERIFAI's interface to the CARLA simulator [12]. The perception module was executed as part of a closed-loop system whose computations were sent to a client running inside CARLA. These are named values that represent the simulator state, such as the position of the car, its velocity, heading, weather conditions, other objects on the road, etc.

The environment is modelled by the SCENIC program depicted in Fig. 3. The sampler was able to choose simulations in different weather conditions, different roads and initial positions on the road, and different sun angle, thus sampling different times of the day and their shadowing effects. The behavior of the ego car was implemented as a call to an external function OncCarAction, which depending on the setting either used the perception-based controller for steering or switched between perception-based control and a safe controller (mimicking manual control) if we were testing a learned monitor.

To evaluate simulation runs we used a built-in CARLA specification for detecting lane invasions. Initially, we started with 100 simulations. In each conformance testing round, we used ca. 160 i.i.d sampled scenes from SCENIC. The number of samples were computed using Hoeffding's inequality [24] for confidence value $\alpha = 0.05$ and error-margin $\epsilon = 0.07$. Lastly, we fixed the class of decision trees as the class of our monitors and used a decision-tree learning procedure provided by the sci-kit learning library[2].

---

[2] https://scikit-learn.org/.

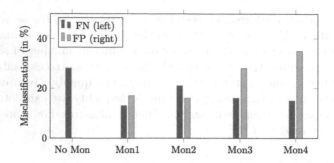

Fig. 4. Results using only static features

5.2 Results

We perform two experiments. The first is solely on static features, such as weather and time of the day (using the sun angle attribute of CARLA), The second additionally considers dynamic features such as the location and road information. The results show the importance of dynamic features in capturing adequate and monitorable ODDs.

We executed our framework for several iterations. In the initial iteration, referred to by *No Mon* in Fig. 4 and Fig. 5, referring to one where we did not use a monitor (or using a monitor that does not issue alerts), we evaluated the performance of the network by calculating the rate of lane invasions over the number of steps performed in 163 simulation runs. Each run included 250 simulation steps. We use the value as a reference for later iterations to determine how the learned monitors in each iteration increase the safety of the system. The initial lane invasion rate was 21%.

In each iteration that follows, a new monitor is learned (indicated by Mon 1 to Mon 4). For each monitor, we calculated the false negatives rate and the false positives rate. The false negatives rate determines the lane invasion rate in the presence of the monitor. We compare this value to the initial reference rate to determine the increase in safety after using the monitor. To determine the quality of the monitor we also looked at the false positives cases where the monitor issued an unnecessary switch to the safe controller.

Results for Static Features. In this first experiment, we only use values of the static features of precipitation, cloudiness, and sun angle to train the monitor.

In the first iteration, while the monitor can reduce to rate of lane invasions by 8%, the false positives rate of that monitor is very high. We apply another round of learning, this time amending the warehouse with counterexamples, both false positives, and negatives examples, collected during conformance testing. In the second iteration, the process managed to learn a monitor with a lower false positives rate, at the cost of increasing the false negatives rate. With further iterations, the misclassification rate increased, due to an increase in the false

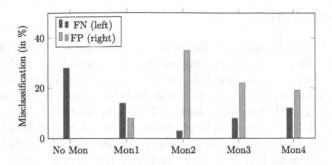

Fig. 5. Results using static and dynamic features

positives rate. From then on, the rates kept fluctuating aggressively. In Fig. 4 we present the first five iterations.

The aggressive fluctuation is an indication that we have exhausted the role of the given semantic features in learning an optimal monitor with respect to these features. This in turn means that we need to extend the set of features with ones that allow us to construct monitors that can distinguish more cases than with the smaller set of features. For example, we noticed in some cases, that while the monitors constructed in the above experiments captured well the weather conditions where the CNN will mostly keep the system safe, in some corner cases such as entering a junction or a sharp turn, a lane invasion was occurring even when adequate weather conditions were present. In the next experiment, we show that we can improve on this, by adding location information, which will allow our framework to distinguish these cases from the general weather cases and return better quality monitors.

Results for Dynamic Features. In this experiment, in addition to the features of precipitation, cloudiness, and sun angle, we used features defining the road id and the location of the car on this road. The latter two indirectly capture dynamic features such as being at the end of the road or passing by certain landmarks. Using the new additional features we were able to learn monitors with lower false negatives and false positives rates than monitors solely based on static features. While the rates fluctuate at the beginning, they start to stabilize after the third iteration.

By looking at simulations using some of the monitors above, we did indeed encounter situations where the monitor triggered an alert shortly before arriving at a junction or sharp turn. These scenarios would not have been able to be detected using the monitors from the previous experiment. Scenarios that could still be not handled by the new monitors, were cases where driveways had a similar texture and curvature as the roads. This emphasizes the importance of feature engineering in the learning process of monitors. In the future, we plan to build on our findings to further investigate this problem.

6   Related Work

Operational Design Domains. A key aspect in assuring the safety of AI-based autonomous systems is to clearly understand their capabilities and limitations. It is therefore important to establish the operational design domains of the system and its components and to communicate this information to the different stakeholders [5,29,30]. Several works have been dedicated to investigating ways of describing ODDs. Some of them are textual and follow a structured natural language format for describing ODDs [36,47]. Others include a tabular description defining a checklist of rules and functional requirements that need to be checked to guarantee a safe operation of the system [44]. A generic taxonomy of the different ODD representation formats is presented in BSI PAS 1883 standard [25].

While the approaches above concentrate on the design of languages for describing ODDs, many works have concluded that there also is a necessity for ODDs to be executable, e.g., to enable the construction of monitors that can be used at runtime [7]. To this end, there has been a focus on developing machine-readable domain-specific languages for implementing ODD, to enable specification, verification, and validation of the ODD, both at design and runtime [26]. In contrast to previous work, we go one step further and present a framework for the automated construction of ODDs, i.e., for a given system component we learn the ODD which is initially unknown. We especially introduce a formal definition of monitorable ODD. Based on this definition we present a new quantitative formalization of the problem learning optimal ODDs for black-box models and solve the problem using a counterexample-guided learning approach.

Runtime Verification. Runtime verification and assurance techniques aim to ensure that a system meets its (safety) specification at runtime [8,15,38]. A large body of work in the runtime verification community has been dedicated to the development of specification languages for monitoring and investigating efficient monitoring algorithms for these languages. Most of the work on formal runtime monitoring is based on temporal logics [17,32,37]. The approaches vary between inline methods that realize a formal specification as assertions added to the code to be monitored [37], and outline approaches that separate the implementation of the monitor from the system under investigation [17]. Based on these approaches and with the rise of real-time temporal logics such as MTL [31] and STL [34], a series of works introduced new algorithms and tools for the monitoring of real-time properties [4,9,16,45]. Neural networks themselves may be used as monitors [6]. All these monitoring can be adopted in our framework and can be used as monitoring tools for evaluating runtime properties during simulation. Runtime monitoring techniques can also be applied to investigate whether the input to a known neural network is within its support [33].

Furthermore, the literature also includes a list of frameworks for designing systems with integrated runtime assurance modules that are guaranteed to satisfy these criteria. An example of such a framework is SOTER [8,43], a runtime assurance framework for building safe distributed mobile robots. A SOTER program is a collection of asynchronous processes that interact with each other using a publish-subscribe model of communication. A runtime assurance module in SOTER is based on the famous Simplex architecture [41] and consists of a safe controller, an advanced controller, and a decision module. A key advantage of SOTER is that it also allows for straightforward integration of many monitoring frameworks. Another approach based on Simplex is the ModelPlex framework [35]. ModelPlex combines design-time verification of CPS models with runtime validation of system executions for compliance with the model to build correct by construction runtime monitors which validate at runtime any assumption on the model collected at design time, i.e., whether or not the behavior of the system complies with the verified model and its assumptions. In case an error is detected, a fail-safe fallback procedure is initiated.

Counterexample-Guided Synthesis. Our learning and conformance testing loop is a quantitative extension of the general line of work of inductive synthesis [27,28]. We particularly use a quantitative extension of counterexample-guided synthesis to learn a monitorable ODD by querying an oracle, in our case the conformance tester. Inductive synthesis is heavily used in the context of programming languages but can also be used for perception modules and control [23]. Rather than learning a program, we learn a monitor. The main idea here is that rather than learning a complete monitor, we have a skeleton of the monitor that may be extracted from domain-specific knowledge or learned.

Another direction for monitor synthesis is the paradigm of introspective environment modeling (IEM) [39,40]. In IEM, one considers the situation where the agents and objects in the environment are substantially unknown, and thus the environment variables are not all known. In such cases, we cannot easily define a SCENIC program for the environment. The only information one has is that the environment is sensed through a specified sensor interface. One seeks to synthesize an assumption on the environment, monitorable on this interface, under which the desired specification is satisfied. While very preliminary steps on IEM have been taken [39], significant work remains to be done to make this practical, including efficient algorithms for monitor synthesis and the development of realistic sensor models that capture the monitorable interface.

7   Conclusion

We presented a formal definition of monitorable operational design domains and a formalization of the problem of learning monitors for the operational design domains of black-box (ML) components. We discussed the need for a quantitative version of the problem and presented a quantitative counterexample-guided learning framework for solving the problem. Our experiments show, how the introduced framework can be used to learn monitors on a monitorable feature space that prevent the system from using a critical component when the system exits its ODD. Learning monitors of high quality requires a lot of effort on the feature engineering side. Furthermore, learning monitors may be subject to different objectives, e.g., accuracy vs efficiency. In the future we plan on investigating the latter problems further with the goal of providing the user with adequate feedback that helps in the selection process of monitors.

Acknowledgments. The authors are grateful to Daniel Fremont for his contributions to the VERIFAI and SCENIC projects, and assistance with these tools for this paper. The authors also want to thank Johnathan Chiu, Tommaso Dreossi, Shromona Ghosh, Francis Indaheng, Edward Kim, Hadi Ravanbakhsh, Ameesh Shah and Kesav Viswanadha for their valuable feedback and contributions to the VERIFAI project.

References

1. Abdar, M., et al.: A review of uncertainty quantification in deep learning: techniques, applications and challenges. Inf. Fusion **76**, 243–297 (2021)
2. Amodei, D., Olah, C., Steinhardt, J., Christiano, P., Schulman, J., Mané, D.: Concrete problems in AI safety. CoRR, abs/1606.06565 (2016)
3. Azad, A.S., et al.: Scenic4rl: programmatic modeling and generation of reinforcement learning environments. CoRR, abs/2106.10365 (2021)
4. Basin, D., Klaedtke, F., Müller, S., Zălinescu, E.: Monitoring metric first-order temporal properties. J. ACM **62**(2), 1–45 (2015)
5. Blumenthal, M.S., Fraade-Blanar, L., Best, R., Irwin, J.L.: Safe Enough: Approaches to Assessing Acceptable Safety for Automated Vehicles. RAND Corporation, Santa Monica, CA (2020)
6. Bortolussi, L., Cairoli, F., Paoletti, N., Smolka, S.A., Stoller, S.D.: Neural predictive monitoring and a comparison of frequentist and bayesian approaches. Int. J. Softw. Tools Technol. Transf. **23**(4), 615–640 (2021). https://doi.org/10.1007/s10009-021-00623-1
7. Colwell, I., Phan, B., Saleem, S., Salay, R., Czarnecki, K.: An automated vehicle safety concept based on runtime restriction of the operational design domain. In: 2018 IEEE Intelligent Vehicles Symposium (IV), pp. 1910–1917 (2018)
8. Desai, A., Ghosh, S., Seshia, S.A., Shankar, N., Tiwari, A.: SOTER: a runtime assurance framework for programming safe robotics systems. In: IEEE/IFIP International Conference on Dependable Systems and Networks (DSN) (2019)
9. Deshmukh, J.V., Donzé, A., Ghosh, S., Jin, X., Juniwal, G., Seshia, S.A.: Robust online monitoring of signal temporal logic. Formal Meth. Syst. Des. **51**(1), 5–30 (2017). https://doi.org/10.1007/s10703-017-0286-7
10. Dietterich, T.G., Horvitz, E.: Rise of concerns about AI: reflections and directions. Commun. ACM **58**(10), 38–40 (2015)
11. Donzé, A., Maler, O.: Robust satisfaction of temporal logic over real-valued signals. In: Chatterjee, K., Henzinger, T.A. (eds.) FORMATS 2010. LNCS, vol. 6246, pp. 92–106. Springer, Heidelberg (2010). https://doi.org/10.1007/978-3-642-15297-9_9
12. Dosovitskiy, A., Ros, G., Codevilla, F., Lopez, A., Koltun, V.: CARLA: an open urban driving simulator. In: Proceedings of the 1st Annual Conference on Robot Learning, pp. 1–16 (2017)
13. Dreossi, T., et al.: VERIFAI: a toolkit for the formal design and analysis of artificial intelligence-based systems. In: Dillig, I., Tasiran, S. (eds.) CAV 2019. LNCS, vol. 11561, pp. 432–442. Springer, Cham (2019). https://doi.org/10.1007/978-3-030-25540-4_25

14. Dreossi, T., Jha, S., Seshia, S.A.: Semantic adversarial deep learning. In: Chockler, H., Weissenbacher, G. (eds.) CAV 2018. LNCS, vol. 10981, pp. 3–26. Springer, Cham (2018). https://doi.org/10.1007/978-3-319-96145-3_1

15. Falcone, Y., Mounier, L., Fernandez, J.-C., Richier, J.-L.: Runtime enforcement monitors: composition, synthesis, and enforcement abilities. Formal Meth. Syst. Des. **38**(3), 223–262 (2011). https://doi.org/10.1007/s10703-011-0114-4

16. Faymonville, P., et al.: StreamLAB: stream-based monitoring of cyber-physical systems. In: Dillig, I., Tasiran, S. (eds.) CAV 2019. LNCS, vol. 11561, pp. 421–431. Springer, Cham (2019). https://doi.org/10.1007/978-3-030-25540-4_24

17. Finkbeiner, B., Sipma, H.: Checking finite traces using alternating automata. Formal Meth. Syst. Des. **24**(2), 101–127 (2004). https://doi.org/10.1023/B:FORM.0000017718.28096.48

18. Fremont, D.J., Chiu, J., Margineantu, D.D., Osipychev, D., Seshia, S.A.: Formal analysis and redesign of a neural network-based aircraft taxiing system with VERIFAI. In: Lahiri, S.K., Wang, C. (eds.) CAV 2020. LNCS, vol. 12224, pp. 122–134. Springer, Cham (2020). https://doi.org/10.1007/978-3-030-53288-8_6

19. Fremont, D.J., et al.: Scenic: a language for scenario specification and scene generation. In: PLDI, pp. 63–78. ACM (2019)

20. Fremont, D.J., et al.: Scenic: a language for scenario specification and data generation (2020)

21. Fremont, D.J., et al.: Formal scenario-based testing of autonomous vehicles: from simulation to the real world. In: ITSC (2020)

22. Gawlikowski, J., et al.: A survey of uncertainty in deep neural networks. CoRR, abs/2107.03342 (2021)

23. Ghosh, S., Pant, Y.V., Ravanbakhsh, H., Seshia, S.A.: Counterexample-guided synthesis of perception models and control. In: American Control Conference (ACC), pp. 3447–3454. IEEE (2021)

24. Hoeffding, W.: Probability inequalities for sums of bounded random variables. J. Am. Stat. Assoc. **58**(301), 13–30 (1963)

25. The British Standards Institution. Operational design domain (odd) taxonomy for an automated driving system (ads) - specification. BSI PAS 1883 (2020)

26. Irvine, P., Zhang, X., Khastgir, S., Schwalb, E., Jennings, P.: A two-level abstraction ODD definition language: part i*. In: 2021 IEEE International Conference on Systems, Man, and Cybernetics (SMC), pp. 2614–2621. IEEE Press (2021)

27. Jha, S., Gulwani, S., Seshia, S.A., Tiwari, A.: Oracle-guided component-based program synthesis. In: ICSE, vol. 1, pp. 215–224. ACM (2010)

28. Jha, S., Seshia, S.A.: A theory of formal synthesis via inductive learning. Acta Informatica **54**(7), 693–726 (2017). https://doi.org/10.1007/s00236-017-0294-5

29. Khastgir, S., Birrell, S.A., Dhadyalla, G., Jennings, P.A.: Calibrating trust through knowledge: introducing the concept of informed safety for automation in vehicles. In: Transportation Research Part C: Emerging Technologies (2018)

30. Khastgir, S., Brewerton, S., Thomas, J., Jennings, P.: Systems approach to creating test scenarios for automated driving systems. Reliab. Eng. Syst. Saf. **215**, 107610 (2021)

31. Koymans, R.: Specifying real-time properties with metric temporal logic. Real-Time Syst. **2**(4), 255–299 (1990)

32. Lee, I., Kannan, S., Kim, M., Sokolsky, O., Viswanathan, M.: Runtime assurance based on formal specifications. In: Arabnia, H.R. (ed.) Proceedings of the International Conference on Parallel and Distributed Processing Techniques and Applications, PDPTA 1999, June 28 - Junlly 1 1999, Las Vegas, Nevada, USA, pp. 279–287. CSREA Press (1999)

33. Lukina, A., Schilling, C., Henzinger, T.A.: Into the unknown: active monitoring of neural networks. In: Feng, L., Fisman, D. (eds.) RV 2021. LNCS, vol. 12974, pp. 42–61. Springer, Cham (2021). https://doi.org/10.1007/978-3-030-88494-9_3

34. Maler, O., Nickovic, D.: Monitoring temporal properties of continuous signals. In: Lakhnech, Y., Yovine, S. (eds.) FORMATS/FTRTFT -2004. LNCS, vol. 3253, pp. 152–166. Springer, Heidelberg (2004). https://doi.org/10.1007/978-3-540-30206-3_12

35. Mitsch, S., Platzer, A.: Modelplex: verified runtime validation of verified cyber-physical system models. Formal Meth. Syst. Des. **49**(1–2), 33–74 (2016). https://doi.org/10.1007/s10703-016-0241-z

36. SAE on Road Automated Driving Committee et al. SAE J3016. taxonomy and definitions for terms related to driving automation systems for on-road motor vehicles. Technical report

37. Roşu, G., Chen, F., Ball, T.: Synthesizing monitors for safety properties: this time with calls and returns. In: Leucker, M. (ed.) RV 2008. LNCS, vol. 5289, pp. 51–68. Springer, Heidelberg (2008). https://doi.org/10.1007/978-3-540-89247-2_4

38. Sánchez, C., et al.: A survey of challenges for runtime verification from advanced application domains (beyond software). Formal Meth. Syst. Des. **54**(3), 279–335 (2019). https://doi.org/10.1007/s10703-019-00337-w

39. Seshia, S.A.: Introspective environment modeling. In: Finkbeiner, B., Mariani, L. (eds.) RV 2019. LNCS, vol. 11757, pp. 15–26. Springer, Cham (2019). https://doi.org/10.1007/978-3-030-32079-9_2

40. Seshia, S.A., Sadigh, D.: Towards verified artificial intelligence. CoRR, abs/1606.08514 (2016)

41. Sha, L.: Using simplicity to control complexity. IEEE Softw. **18**(4), 20–28 (2001)

42. Shalev-Shwartz, S., Ben-David, S.: Understanding Machine Learning: From Theory to Algorithms. Cambridge University Press, USA (2014)

43. Shivakumar, S., Torfah, H., Desai, A., Seshia, S.A.: SOTER on ROS: a run-time assurance framework on the robot operating system. In: Deshmukh, J., Ničković, D. (eds.) RV 2020. LNCS, vol. 12399, pp. 184–194. Springer, Cham (2020). https://doi.org/10.1007/978-3-030-60508-7_10

44. Thorn, E., Kimmel, S. C., Chaka, M..: A framework for automated driving system testable cases and scenarios (2018)

45. Torfah, H.: Stream-based monitors for real-time properties. In: Finkbeiner, B., Mariani, L. (eds.) RV 2019. LNCS, vol. 11757, pp. 91–110. Springer, Cham (2019). https://doi.org/10.1007/978-3-030-32079-9_6

46. Torfah, H., Junges, S., Fremont, D.J., Seshia, S.A.: Formal analysis of AI-based autonomy: from modeling to runtime assurance. In: Feng, L., Fisman, D. (eds.) RV 2021. LNCS, vol. 12974, pp. 311–330. Springer, Cham (2021). https://doi.org/10.1007/978-3-030-88494-9_19

47. Zhang, X., Khastgir, S., Jennings, P.: Scenario description language for automated driving systems: a two level abstraction approach. In: 2020 IEEE International Conference on Systems, Man, and Cybernetics (SMC), pp. 973–980 (2020)

Reinforcement Learning

Dynamic Shielding for Reinforcement Learning in Black-Box Environments

Masaki Waga[1]([⊠])[iD], Ezequiel Castellano[2][iD], Sasinee Pruekprasert[3][iD],
Stefan Klikovits[2][iD], Toru Takisaka[4][iD], and Ichiro Hasuo[2,5][iD]

[1] Graduate School of Informatics, Kyoto University, Kyoto, Japan
mwaga@fos.kuis.kyoto-u.ac.jp
[2] National Institute of Informatics, Tokyo, Japan
[3] National Institute of Advanced Industrial Science and Technology, Tokyo, Japan
[4] University of Electronic Science and Technology of China, Chengdu, China
[5] The Graduate University for Advanced Studies, Tokyo, Japan

Abstract. It is challenging to use reinforcement learning (RL) in cyber-physical systems due to the lack of safety guarantees during learning. Although there have been various proposals to reduce undesired behaviors during learning, most of these techniques require prior system knowledge, and their applicability is limited. This paper aims to reduce undesired behaviors during learning without requiring *any* prior system knowledge. We propose *dynamic shielding*: an extension of a model-based safe RL technique called *shielding* using *automata learning*. The dynamic shielding technique constructs an approximate system model in parallel with RL using a variant of the RPNI algorithm and suppresses undesired explorations due to the shield constructed from the learned model. Through this combination, potentially unsafe actions can be foreseen before the agent experiences them. Experiments show that our dynamic shield significantly decreases the number of undesired events during training.

Keywords: Reinforcement learning · Shielding · Automata learning

1 Introduction

Reinforcement learning (RL) [27] is a powerful tool for learning optimal (or near-optimal) controllers, where the performance of controllers is measured by their long-term cumulative rewards. An agent in RL explores the environment by taking actions at each visited state, each of which yields a corresponding reward: RL aims for an efficient exploration by prioritizing actions that maximize the subsequent cumulative reward. RL is particularly advantageous when the system model is unavailable [20] or too large for an exhaustive search [26].

Since an RL agent learns a controller through trial and error, the exploration can lead to undesired behavior. For instance, when the learning is conducted

---

S. Pruekprasert and T. Takisaka—The work was done during the employment of S.P. and T.T. at NII, Tokyo.

A. Bouajjani et al. (Eds.): ATVA 2022, LNCS 13505, pp. 25–41, 2022.
https://doi.org/10.1007/978-3-031-19992-9_2

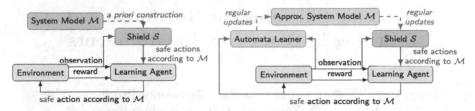

(a) Conventional shielding [1] based on a system model $\mathcal{M}$ given by a user. The shield is constructed before starting RL.

(b) Our *dynamic* shielding. An approximate model $\mathcal{M}$ is learned and updated in parallel with RL, and the shield is regularly updated.

Fig. 1. Comparison of the conventional shielding and our dynamic shielding.

on a cyber-physical system, such undesired behaviors can be harmful because they can damage the hardware, e. g., by crashing into a wall. *Shielding* [1][1] is actively studied to address this problem. A shield is an external component that suggests a set of safe actions to an RL agent so that the agent can explore the environment with fewer encounters with undesired behaviors (Fig. 1a).

Example 1 (WATERTANK). Consider a 100 liter water tank with valves to control the water inflow. The *controller* opens and closes the valve, and tries to prevent the water tank from becoming empty or full. The exact inflow cannot be controlled but can be observed, s.t. inflow $\in \{0, 1, 2\}$. The tank also has a random outflow, s.t. outflow $\in \{0, 1\}$. A good shield prevents opening (resp. closing) the valve when the water tank is almost full (resp. empty). Moreover, there must be at least three time steps between two consecutive valve position changes to prevent hardware failure. Hence, the shield should also prevent changing the valve position when the last change was too recent.

Most of the existing shielding techniques [1,2,8,12,14] for RL assume that the system model is at least partially available, and its formal analysis is feasible. Thus, with few exceptions (e. g., [11]), black-box systems have been beyond existing techniques. However, this assumption of conventional shielding techniques limits the high applicability of RL, which is one of the major strengths of RL.

Dynamic Shielding. To improve the applicability of shielding for RL, we propose the dynamic shielding scheme (Fig. 1b). Our goal is to *prevent actions similar to those ones that led to undesired behavior in previous explorations.* In our dynamic shielding scheme, the shield is constructed and regularly updated using an approximate system model learned by a variant of *the RPNI algorithm* [21] for passive automata learning [17]. Since the RPNI algorithm generates a system model consistent with the agent's experience, a dynamic shield can prevent previously experienced undesired actions. Moreover, since the RPNI algorithm can deem some of the actions similar, a dynamic shield can prevent undesired actions even without experiencing if the action is deemed unsafe.

---

[1] The shield we use in this paper is the variant called *preemptive shield* in [1]. It is straightforward to apply our framework to the classic shield called *post-posed shield*.

It is, however, not straightforward to use a system model constructed by the original RPNI algorithm for shielding. At the beginning of the learning, our knowledge of the system is limited, and the RPNI algorithm often deems a safe action as unsafe, which prevents necessary exploration for RL. To infer the (un)safety of unexplored actions with higher accuracy, we introduce a novel variant of the RPNI algorithm tailored for our purpose. Intuitively, our algorithm deems two actions in the training data similar only if there is a long example supporting it, while the original RPNI algorithm deems two actions similar unless there is an explicit counter example. We also modified the shield construction to optimistically enable not previously seen actions, as otherwise, necessary explorations are also prevented.

We implemented our dynamic shielding scheme in Python and conducted experiments to evaluate its performance compared to two baselines: the plain RL without shielding and safe padding [11], one of the shielding techniques applicable to black-box systems. Our experiments suggest that dynamic shielding prevents undesired exploration during training and often improves the quality of the resulting controller. Although the construction and the use of dynamic shielding require some extra time, it is not prohibitive.

Contributions. The following list summarizes our contributions.

- We introduce the dynamic shielding scheme (Fig. 1b) using a variant of the RPNI algorithm for passive automata learning.
- We modify the RPNI algorithm and the shield construction so that the shield does not prevent necessary exploration, even if our prior system knowledge is limited.
- We experimentally show that our dynamic shielding scheme significantly reduces the number of undesired explorations during training.

1.1   Related Works

The notion of shield is originally proposed in [5] as an approach for *runtime enforcement*. In this line of research [3,4,28], a shield takes the role of an *enforcer* that overwrites the output of the system when the specification is violated at runtime. Shielding in this context is fundamentally different from ours, where shields are used to block system inputs that incur unsafe outputs of the system.

Shielding for RL (or simply shielding) is categorized as a technique of *safe RL*. Using the taxonomy of [10], shielding is an instance of "teacher provides advice"; i.e., a shield as a teacher giving additional information to the learning agent to prevent unsafe exploration. Such a use of a shield is first proposed in [1], and several probabilistic variants are also proposed [2,6,14]; they assure that the learning is safely done with high probability (but not necessarily with full certainty). In these works, a system model is necessary to construct a shield. Some works propose shielding for inaccurate models [8,12,23], but they still require some prior knowledge of the system (e. g., the nominal dynamics of the system).

To the best of our knowledge, the existing work closest to ours is *cautious RL* [11]: it is also a shielding-based safe RL that does not require a system model

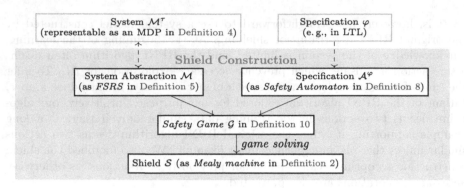

Fig. 2. Shield construction schema. Our main contribution is the system abstraction's inference through automata learning techniques.

(but can perform better with a system model). To avoid unsafe events under uncertainty, cautious RL learns an MDP in parallel with the RL process, and its *safe padding* blocks actions that let the agent come too close to an area where an action may lead to undesired behavior according to the learned MDP. That strong blocking policy works as a safety buffer against unexpected transitions.

A major difference between our technique and safe padding is in the approximate model learning: in safe padding, the observation space is directly used as the state space of the learned MDP, while we merge some of them based on similarity of the suffixes to generalize observations. In experiments, we demonstrate that generalization by automata learning effectively reduces safety violations.

2   Preliminaries

For a set X, we denote the set of probability functions over X by $\mathscr{D}X$. For a set Σ, let Σ^* be the set of finite sequences over Σ. We denote the empty sequence by ε. For any $w \in \Sigma^*$, the length is denoted by $|w|$.

We use *Mealy machines* to formalize an abstract system model and a shield.

Definition 2 (Mealy machine). *A* Mealy machine *is a 6-tuple* $\mathcal{M} = (S, s_0, \Sigma_{\text{in}}, \Sigma_{\text{out}}, E, \Lambda)$, *where:* S *is a finite set of states,* $s_0 \in S$ *is the initial state,* Σ_{in} *and* Σ_{out} *are finite alphabets for inputs and outputs,* $E \colon S \times \Sigma_{\text{in}} \nrightarrow S$ *is a partial transition function, and* $\Lambda \colon S \times \Sigma_{\text{in}} \nrightarrow \Sigma_{\text{out}}$ *is a partial output function such that* $\Lambda(s, a)$ *is defined if and only if* $E(s, a)$ *is defined.*

Definition 3 (path, run, output). *Let* $\mathcal{M} = (S, s_0, \Sigma_{\text{in}}, \Sigma_{\text{out}}, E, \Lambda)$ *be a Mealy machine and let* $w_{\text{in}} = a_1, a_2, \ldots a_n \in \Sigma_{\text{in}}^*$ *be an input word. For a state* $s \in S$ *of* $\mathcal{M}$, *the* path ρ *of* $\mathcal{M}$ *from* s *over* w_{in} *is the alternating sequence* $\rho = s, a_1, s_1, a_2, \ldots, a_n, s_n$ *of states* $s_i \in S$ *and input actions* $a_i \in \Sigma_{\text{in}}$ *satisfying* $E(s, a_1) = s_1$ *and* $E(s_{i-1}, a_i) = s_i$ *for each* $i \in \{2, \ldots, n\}$. *A* run *of a Mealy machine* $\mathcal{M}$ *is a path of* $\mathcal{M}$ *from the initial state* s_0. *For a state* $s \in S$ *of* $\mathcal{M}$, *we write* $E(w_{\text{in}}, s)$ *to denote the last state* s_n *of the path* $\rho = s, a_1, s_1, a_2, \ldots, a_n, s_n$

*of $\mathcal{M}$ from s over w_{in}. The output $\mathcal{M}(w_{\text{in}}, s) \in \Sigma_{\text{out}}$ of a Mealy machine $\mathcal{M}$
is defined by $\mathcal{M}(w_{\text{in}}, s) = \Lambda(s_{n-1}, a_n)$, where $s_{n-1} = E(w_{\text{in}}', s)$ and $w_{\text{in}}' = a_1, a_2, \ldots, a_{n-1}$. We write $E(w_{\text{in}}) = E(w_{\text{in}}, s_0)$ and $\mathcal{M}(w_{\text{in}}) = \mathcal{M}(w_{\text{in}}, s_0)$.*

2.1 Automata and Games for System Modeling

As shown in Fig. 2, we assume that the system is representable as a *Markov decision process* (MDP), and we use *finite-state reactive systems* (FSRSs) [1] to abstract the MDP. More precisely, an FSRS is a two-player deterministic game of the controller (Cont) and the environment (Env), where MDP's probabilistic transitions are represented by Env transitions. Note that MDPs are only used for the theoretical discussion in this paper.

Definition 4 (Markov decision process (MDP)). *An MDP is a 5-tuple $(S, s_0, \Sigma_{\text{in}}, \Sigma_{\text{out}}, \Delta)$ such that: S is a finite set of states, $s_0 \in S$ is the initial state, Σ_{in} and Σ_{out} are the finite set of input and output alphabets, respectively, and $\Delta \colon S \times \Sigma_{\text{in}} \nrightarrow \mathscr{D}(S \times \Sigma_{\text{out}})$ is the probabilistic transition function.*

Definition 5 (finite-state reactive system (FSRS)). *An FSRS is a Mealy machine $\mathcal{M} = (S, s_0, \Sigma_{\text{in}}, \Sigma_{\text{out}}, E, \Lambda)$ that satisfies the following: $\Sigma_{\text{in}} = \Sigma_{\text{in}}^1 \times \Sigma_{\text{in}}^2$, where $\Sigma_{\text{in}}^1 (resp. \Sigma_{\text{in}}^2)$ is the set of actions of Cont (resp. Env); for each $s \in S$ and $a^1 \in \Sigma_{\text{in}}^1$, there is $a^2 \in \Sigma_{\text{in}}^2$ for which $E(s, (a^1, a^2))$ is defined.*

Definition 6 (strategy). *For an FSRS $\mathcal{M} = (S, s_0, \Sigma_{\text{in}}^1 \times \Sigma_{\text{in}}^2, \Sigma_{\text{out}}, E, \Lambda)$, strategies of Cont and Env are functions $\sigma \colon \Pi_{\mathcal{M}} \to \mathscr{D}\Sigma_{\text{in}}^1$ and $\tau \colon \Pi_{\mathcal{M}} \times \Sigma_{\text{in}}^1 \to \mathscr{D}\Sigma_{\text{in}}^2$, respectively, where $\Pi_{\mathcal{M}}$ is the set of runs of $\mathcal{M}$. For strategies τ of Env, we also require that $\tau(\rho, a^1)(\{a^2\}) > 0$ holds only if $E(\rho_{\text{last}}, (a^1, a^2))$ is defined, where ρ_{last} is the last state of ρ. A strategy is memoryless if it is independent of the run except for the last state.*

We use an FSRS as an abstraction of an MDP because for an FSRS $\mathcal{M}$ and a memoryless strategy τ of Env, there is a canonical MDP $\mathcal{M}^\tau$, where the actions of Env are chosen by τ. Formally, for $\mathcal{M} = (S, s_0, \Sigma_{\text{in}}^1 \times \Sigma_{\text{in}}^2, \Sigma_{\text{out}}, E, \Lambda)$ and τ, $\mathcal{M}^\tau$ is $\mathcal{M}^\tau = (S, s_0, \Sigma_{\text{in}}^1, \Sigma_{\text{out}}, \Delta)$, where for each $s, s' \in S$, $a^1 \in \Sigma_{\text{in}}^1$, and $b \in \Sigma_{\text{out}}$, $\Delta(s, a^1)$ is such that

$$(\Delta(s, a^1))(s', b) = (\tau(s, a^1))(\{a^2 \in \Sigma_{\text{in}}^2 \mid E(s, (a^1, a^2)) = s' \wedge \Lambda(s, (a^1, a^2)) = b\}).$$

By fixing both Cont and Env strategies σ and τ of an FSRS $\mathcal{M}$, we obtain a stochastic structure $\mathcal{M}^{\sigma,\tau}$. We define the language $\mathcal{L}(\mathcal{M}^{\sigma,\tau}) \subseteq ((\Sigma_{\text{in}}^1 \times \Sigma_{\text{in}}^2) \times \Sigma_{\text{out}})^*$ of $\mathcal{M}^{\sigma,\tau}$ as the set of sequences of input/output actions $((a_i^1, a_i^2), b_i) \in (\Sigma_{\text{in}}^1 \times \Sigma_{\text{in}}^2) \times \Sigma_{\text{out}}$ in the runs of $\mathcal{M}^{\sigma,\tau}$.

Example 7 (WATERTANK FSRS). The Water Tank in Example 1 is formalized as an FSRS $\mathcal{M} = (S, s_0, \Sigma_{\text{in}}^1 \times \Sigma_{\text{in}}^2, \Sigma_{\text{out}}, E, \Lambda)$, where: $S = \{0, 1, \ldots, 100\}$; $\Sigma_{\text{in}}^1 = \{\text{open}, \text{close}\}$; $\Sigma_{\text{in}}^2 = \text{inflow} \times \text{outflow}$, where inflow $= \{0, 1, 2\}$ and outflow $= \{0, 1\}$; $\Sigma_{\text{out}} = \{\text{low}, \text{safe}, \text{high}\}$; $\Delta(s, (a^1, (n, m)))$ is defined if either $a^1 = \text{open}$

and $n \in \{1, 2\}$ or $a^1 = $ close and $n = 0$; $\Delta(s, (a^1, (n, m))) = \max\{0, \min\{s + n - m, 100\}\}$; For any $(a^1, (n, m)) \in \Sigma_{\text{in}}^1 \times \Sigma_{\text{in}}^2$, we have $\Lambda(0, (a^1, (n, m))) = $ low, $\Lambda(100, (a^1, (n, m))) = $ high, and $\Lambda(s, (a^1, (n, m))) = $ safe otherwise.

The probabilistic behavior of the WATERTANK environment (i.e., Env) is such that i) the inflow of water is randomly chosen from $\{1, 2\}$ when $a^1 = $ open, and ii) the outflow of the water is randomly chosen from $\{0, 1\}$. Such a behavior is formalized by a Env strategy τ such that: $\tau(s, \text{open})(\{(n, m)\}) = 0.25$ for each $(n, m) \in \{1, 2\} \times \{0, 1\}$, and $\tau(s, \text{close})(\{(0, m)\}) = 0.5$ for each $m \in \{0, 1\}$.

2.2 Safety Automata for Specifications

In the shielding methodology, the shield's specification is given as a *safety automaton*. As shown in Fig. 2, typically, this automaton is automatically generated from a temporal logic formula, e.g., *linear temporal logic* (LTL). See, e.g., [15] for the construction of an automaton from an LTL formula.

Definition 8 (Safety Automata). *A* safety automaton *is a 5-tuple* $\mathcal{A} = (Q, q_0, F, \Sigma, N)$, *where:* Q *is a finite set of states,* $q_0 \in Q$ *is the initial state,* $F \subseteq Q$ *is the set of safe states,* Σ *is the finite set of alphabet, and* $N : Q \times \Sigma \to Q$ *is the* transition function *satisfying* $N(q, a) \in F$ *only if* $q \in F$.

A run of a safety automaton is defined similarly to that of a Mealy machine. For a safety automaton $\mathcal{A}$, the *language* $\mathcal{L}(\mathcal{A}) \subseteq \Sigma^*$ of $\mathcal{A}$ is the set of words $w = a_1, a_2, \ldots, a_n$ such that the run $q_0, a_1, q_1, \ldots, a_n, q_n$ over w satisfies $q_n \in F$. By the definition of N and F, $\mathcal{L}(\mathcal{A})$ is prefix-closed. We call $\varphi \subseteq \Sigma^*$ a *satefy specification* if there is a safety automaton recognizing it. For an FSRS $\mathcal{M}$ over Σ_{in} and Σ_{out}, a Cont strategy σ of $\mathcal{M}$, and a specification $\varphi \subseteq (\Sigma_{\text{in}} \times \Sigma_{\text{out}})^*$, we say $\mathcal{M}$ satisfies φ under σ if for any Env strategy τ, we have $\mathcal{L}(\mathcal{M}^{\sigma,\tau}) \subseteq \varphi$.

2.3 Shielding for Safe Reinforcement Learning

We use an FSRS and a safety automaton to define a *safety game* which we use to create a shield for safe RL. First, we show the formal definition of shields.

Definition 9 ((Preemptive) Shield [1]). *Let* $\mathcal{M}$ *be an FSRS as above. A* shield *for* $\mathcal{M}$ *is a Mealy machine* $\mathcal{S} = (S_{\mathcal{S}}, s_{0,\mathcal{S}}, \Sigma_{\text{in}}^1 \times \Sigma_{\text{in}}^2, 2^{\Sigma_{\text{in}}^1}, \Delta_{\mathcal{S}}, \Lambda_{\mathcal{S}})$ *s.t. for any* $s_{\mathcal{S}} \in S_{\mathcal{S}}$ *and input actions* $a, a' \in \Sigma_{\text{in}}^1 \times \Sigma_{\text{in}}^2$, *we have* $\Lambda_{\mathcal{S}}(s_{\mathcal{S}}, a) = \Lambda_{\mathcal{S}}(s_{\mathcal{S}}, a')$.

For any input word $w_{\text{in}} \in (\Sigma_{\text{in}}^1 \times \Sigma_{\text{in}}^2)^*$, the shield $\mathcal{S}$ returns $\Lambda_{\mathcal{S}}(w_{\text{in}})$ as the set of safe actions for Cont after w_{in} is processed in $\mathcal{M}$. A shield $\mathcal{S}$ canonically induces a strategy σ for an MDP $\mathcal{M}^\tau$ generated by any τ, namely a strategy σ such that $\sigma(\hat{s}_0, a_1, \hat{s}_1, \ldots, a_k, \hat{s}_k)$ is the discrete uniform distribution over $\Lambda_{\mathcal{S}}(w_{\text{in}})$.

Given an FSRS $\mathcal{M}$ and a specification φ realized by a safety automaton $\mathcal{A}^\varphi$ (i.e., $\mathcal{L}(\mathcal{A}^\varphi) = \varphi$), our goal is to construct a shield $\mathcal{S}$ such that for any Env strategy τ, the MDP $\mathcal{M}^\tau$ satisfies φ under any Cont strategy σ compatible with $\mathcal{S}$. To this end, we consider a *safety game* constructed by $\mathcal{M}$ and $\mathcal{A}^\varphi$.

Definition 10 (Safety Game). *A* 2-player safety game *is an FSRS* $\mathcal{G} = (G, g_0, \Sigma_{\text{in}}^1 \times \Sigma_{\text{in}}^2, \{0,1\}, E^G, F^G)$.

For an FSRS $\mathcal{M}$ and a safety automaton $\mathcal{A}^\varphi$, the parallel composition $\mathcal{M} \parallel \mathcal{A}^\varphi$ is the safety game $\mathcal{M} \parallel \mathcal{A}^\varphi = (G, (s, q), \Sigma_{\text{in}}^1 \times \Sigma_{\text{in}}^2, \{0,1\}, E^G, F^G)$, where $G = S \times Q$, $E^G((s,q), (a^1, a^2)) = (s', q')$, $s' = E(s, (a^1, a^2))$, $q' = N(q, (a, \Lambda(s, (a^1, a^2))))$, and F^G is such that $F^G((s, q), (a^1, a^2)) = 1$ if and only if $N(q, ((a^1, a^2), \Lambda(s, (a^1, a^2)))) \in F$.

We say $g \in G$ is a *safe state* if there is a Cont strategy σ such that, for any Env strategy τ and $w = ((a_1^1, a_1^2), b_1), ((a_2^1, a_2^2), b_2), \ldots, ((a_n^1, a_n^2), b_n) \in \mathcal{L}(\mathcal{M}^{\sigma, \tau})$, the unique run $g_0, (a_1^1, a_1^2), g_1, \ldots, (a_n^1, a_n^2), g_n$ of $\mathcal{M}$ over w satisfies $g_n \in F^G$. Intuitively, a state g is safe if there is a Cont strategy σ such that the run always remains in safe states, regardless of the Env actions.

We utilize the shield construction algorithm in [1] to the above safety game $\mathcal{G}$. Namely, the shield generated from $\mathcal{G}$ is an FSRS $\mathcal{S} = (G, g_0, \Sigma_{\text{in}}^1 \times \Sigma_{\text{in}}^2, 2^{\Sigma_{\text{in}}^1}, E^G, \Lambda_{\mathcal{S}})$, where for each state $s \in G$, $\Lambda_{\mathcal{S}}$ assigns the set of Cont actions such that for any Env strategy, we remain in the safe states forever.

2.4 The RPNI Algorithm for Passive Automata Learning

We use a variant of the RPNI algorithm [21] to learn an approximate system model in parallel with RL. See, e.g., [17] for the detail. Given a finite training data $D \subseteq \Sigma_{\text{in}}^* \times \Sigma_{\text{out}}$, the RPNI algorithm constructs a Mealy machine $\mathcal{M}$ that is *consistent* with the training data D, i.e., for any $(w_{\text{in}}, b) \in D$, we have $\mathcal{M}(w_{\text{in}}) = b$. For simplicity, we assume that the training data is prefix-closed, i.e., if D contains (w_{in}, b), for any prefix w_{in}' of w_{in} and for some $b' \in \Sigma_{\text{out}}$, D contains (w_{in}, b'). This assumption holds in our dynamic shielding scheme and does not harm its applicability. Since we learn a Mealy machine, we assume that the output in the training data is uniquely determined by the input word, i.e., for each $(w_{\text{in}}, b), (w_{\text{in}}', b') \in D$, $w_{\text{in}} = w_{\text{in}}'$ implies $b = b'$.

The RPNI algorithm creates the *prefix tree Mealy machine* (PTMM) $\mathcal{M}_D$ from the training data D and constructs a Mealy machine $\mathcal{M}$ by merging the states of $\mathcal{M}_D$. The PTMM $\mathcal{M}_D$ is the Mealy machine such that the states are the input words in the training data, and the transition and output functions are $E(w_{\text{in}}, a) = w_{\text{in}} \cdot a$ and $\Lambda(w_{\text{in}}, a) = b$ if $(w_{\text{in}} \cdot a, b) \in D$ for some $b \in \Sigma_{\text{out}}$, and otherwise, undefined. When merging states s and s' of $\mathcal{M}_D$, we require them to be *compatible*, i.e., the merging of s and s' must not cause any nondeterminism to make the learned Mealy machine the consistent with the training data. The RPNI algorithm greedily merges states s and s' of $\mathcal{M}_D$ as far as they are compatible.

3 Dynamic Shielding with Online Automata Inference

Here, we introduce our dynamic shielding scheme in Fig. 1b, where the shield is constructed from the FSRS inferred in parallel with the RL process. Since our dynamic shielding scheme does not require the system model, we can apply it to black-box systems.

3.1 Dynamic Shielding Scheme

In conventional shielding (Fig. 1a), the shield is constructed from the system model and provides safe actions to the learning agent. See also Fig. 2 for the shield creation schema. By shielding, we can ensure the safety of the exploration in RL if the given system model correctly abstracts the actual system. However, the use of a predefined system model limits the applicability of shielding. Specifically, we cannot use the conventional shielding scheme for black-box systems.

In dynamic shielding (Fig. 1b), using the RPNI algorithm, we learn a system model in parallel with RL, and prevent exploring undesired actions according to the learned model. More precisely, all the inputs and the outputs in RL are given to the RPNI algorithm, and we obtain an FSRS $\mathcal{M}$ in Fig. 2. From $\mathcal{M}$ and the given specification φ, we generate a shield $\mathcal{S}$, and prevent undesired exploration using $\mathcal{S}$. We continuously reconstruct the shield along with the RL process. Since we learn FSRS from observations, the learned FSRS may be incomplete or inconsistent with the actual system, which causes the following challenges.

3.2 Challenge 1: Incompleteness of the Learned FSRS

Since the RPNI algorithm is based on merging of nodes of the prefix tree representing the training data, the inferred FSRS $\mathcal{M}$ has partial transitions when there are unexplored actions from some of the states of $\mathcal{M}$. Specifically, there may be a state $s \in S$ of the FSRS $\mathcal{M}$ and a Cont action a^1 such that $E(s, (a^1, a^2))$ is undefined for any Env action a^2. If we construct a shield from such an FSRS by the algorithm in [1], the shield prevents the Cont action a^1 because there is no transition labeled with a^1 to stay in the safe states. However, since we have no evidence of safety violation by the Cont action a^1, this interference is against the "minimum interference" policy of shielding [1]. Moreover, such interference can harm the performance of the synthesized controller because it limits the exploration in RL.

To minimize the interference, we modify the safety game construction so that the undefined destinations in the FSRS are deemed safe. More precisely, we create a fresh sink state $s_\perp$ that is safe in the safety game, and make it the destination of the undefined transitions in the FSRS. We remark that the use of such an additional sink state does not allow any Cont action with evidence of safety violation because even if a Cont action a^1 leads to a safe state for one Env action a^2, the Cont action a^1 is prevented if there is another Env action $\tilde{a}^2$ leading to a violation of the specification φ.

The safety game construction is formalized as follows.

Definition 11. *For an FSRS* $\mathcal{M} = (S, s_0, \Sigma_{\text{in}}^1 \times \Sigma_{\text{in}}^2, \Sigma_{\text{out}}, E, \Lambda)$ *and a safety automaton* $\mathcal{A}^\varphi = (Q^\varphi, q_0^\varphi, F, \Sigma_{\text{out}}, N^\varphi)$, *their compositions is the safety game* $\mathcal{G} = (G, g_0, \Sigma_{\text{in}}^1 \times \Sigma_{\text{in}}^2, \{0, 1\}, E^G, F^G)$ *such that:* $G = (S \cup \{s_\perp\}) \times Q^\varphi$; $g_0 = (s_0, q_0^\varphi)$; E^G *is* $E^G((s, q^\varphi), (a^1, a^2)) = (E(s, (a^1, a^2)), N^\varphi(q^\varphi, \Lambda(s, (a^1, a^2))))$ *if* $E(s, (a^1, a^2))$, *is defined, and otherwise,* $E^G((s, q^\varphi), (a^1, a^2)) = (s_\perp, N^\varphi(q^\varphi, \Lambda(s, (a^1, a^2))))$; $F^G = (S \times F) \cup (\{s_\perp\} \times Q^\varphi)$.

3.3   Challenge 2: Precision in Automata Learning

In the RPNI algorithm, the generalization of the training data is realized by the state merging. Such generalization allows a dynamic shield to foresee potentially unsafe actions before the learning agent experiences them.

Since the RPNI algorithm aims to construct a minimal FSRS, it greedily merges the states as long as there is no evidence of inconsistency. However, when the training data is limited, there may not be evidence of the inconsistency of states, even if they must be distinguished according to the (black-box) ground truth. In such a case, the greedy merging in the RPNI algorithm may decrease the precision of the learned FSRS. This is especially the case at the beginning of the training because the training data D is small. Moreover, such an imprecise dynamic shield may even harm the quality of the controller synthesized by RL because the dynamic shield may prevent necessary exploration when it deems a safe action to be unsafe.

To prevent such too aggressive merging, we require additional evidence in the state merging. Namely, we modify the RPNI algorithm so that states s and s' can be merged only if there are paths from s and s' over a common word $w \in (\Sigma_{\text{in}} \times \Sigma_{\text{out}})^*$ longer than a threshold MINDEPTH. This idea is related to the *evidence-driven state merging* (EDSM) [16], where similar evidence is used in prioritizing the merged states. In our implementation, we adaptively decide MINDEPTH so that MINDEPTH is large when the mean length of the episodes is short. This typically makes the merging more aggressive through the learning process. Nevertheless, further investigation of MINDEPTH is future work.

3.4   Theoretical Validity of Our Dynamic Shielding

We show that our dynamic shielding scheme assures the safety of RL when the training data is large enough to construct an *abstraction* of the actual system.

Definition 12 (abstraction). *For FSRSs* $\mathcal{M} = (S, s_0, \Sigma_{\text{in}}^1 \times \Sigma_{\text{in}}^2, \Sigma_{\text{out}}, E, \Lambda)$ *and* $\mathcal{M}' = (S', s_0', \Sigma_{\text{in}}^1 \times \Sigma_{\text{in}}^2, \Sigma_{\text{out}}, E', \Lambda')$, $\mathcal{M}'$ *abstracts* $\mathcal{M}$ *if for each* $w \in (\Sigma_{\text{in}}^1 \times \Sigma_{\text{in}}^2)^*$ *if* $E(w)$ *is defined,* $E'(w)$ *is also defined, and* $\Lambda(w) = \Lambda'(w)$ *holds.*

Theorem 13 (safety assurance by a dynamic shield). *Let* $\mathcal{M}$ *be an FSRS, let* $\mathcal{M}'$ *be its abstraction, let* φ *be a specification realized by* $\mathcal{A}^\varphi$, *and let* $\mathcal{S}$ *be a shield generated by* $\mathcal{M}'$ *and* $\mathcal{A}^\varphi$. *For any strategy* τ *of* Env *in* $\mathcal{M}$, *the MDP* $\mathcal{M}^\tau$ *satisfies* φ *under any strategy* σ *generated by* $\mathcal{S}$.

Proof (sketch). Let σ be a Cont strategy of $\mathcal{M}' \times \mathcal{A}^\varphi$, and let σ' be a Cont strategy of $\mathcal{M}'$ obtained by taking the obvious projection of σ. It is well known that if a state (s, q) of the product game is winning for Cont under σ, in $\mathcal{M}'$, any path from s satisfies φ under σ'. Since $\mathcal{M}'$ is an abstraction of $\mathcal{M}$, if any path from the initial state s_0' of $\mathcal{M}'$ satisfies φ under σ', any path from the initial state s_0 of $\mathcal{M}$ also satisfies φ under σ'. Therefore, for any Env strategy τ, the MDP $\mathcal{M}^\tau$ satisfies φ under any strategy σ generated by $\mathcal{S}$.   □

Let $\mathcal{M}^\tau$ be the MDP representing the actual system in Fig. 2, where $\mathcal{M}$ is an FSRS and τ is a Env strategy in $\mathcal{M}$. By Theorem 13, if the learned FSRS $\mathcal{M}'$ abstracts $\mathcal{M}$, the dynamic shield S assures the safety of the exploration in $\mathcal{M}^\tau$. When the training data is large and includes a certain set of words called *characteristic* set, the RPNI algorithm is guaranteed to learn the abstraction correctly [17]. However, in our dynamic shielding scheme, the training data may not be a superset of the characteristic set even in the limit because the dynamic shield interferes with the exploration. Nevertheless, suppose the learning algorithm eventually explores all available actions, and the maximum length of each episode in RL is long enough to cover all states of $\mathcal{M}$. In that case, the training data eventually includes the characteristic set of $\mathcal{M}$ restricted to the safe actions according to the dynamic shield S. Since the dynamic shield constructed from such training data prohibits all the unsafe actions, our dynamic shielding assures the safety in the limit.

4   Experimental Evaluation

To show the applicability of dynamic shielding and the viability of our approach, we conducted a series of experiments. The following research questions guided our experiments on our dynamic shielding scheme for RL.

RQ1 Does dynamic shielding reduce the number of undesired behaviors?
RQ2 How does dynamic shielding affect the quality of the controller synthesized by RL?
RQ3 What is the computational overhead of dynamic shielding, and is it prohibitively large?

4.1   Implementation and Experiments

We implemented our dynamic shielding scheme in Python 3 and Java using LearnLib [13] for the RPNI algorithm[2]. For deep RL, we used Stable Baselines 3 [24] (for *proximal policy optimization algorithm* (PPO) [25]) and Keras-RL [22] (for *deep Q learning* (DQN) [19]). We used two libraries and learning algorithms to demonstrate that dynamic shielding is independent of the RL algorithm.

To answer the research questions, we compared the performance of RL with dynamic shielding (denoted as SHIELDING) with the standard RL process without shielding (denoted as PLAIN) and the RL process with safe padding [11] (denoted as SAFEPADDING).

Learning of each controller consists of the *training* and the *test* phases. The training phase is the main part of the learning, and the testing phase is invoked once every 10,000 training steps to evaluate the learned controller and choose the resulting one. We finish the learning when the total number of steps in the training phase exceeds the predetermined bound, which is one of the commonly used criteria. See Table 1 for the bounds for each benchmark.

---

[2] The artifact is publicly available at https://doi.org/10.5281/zenodo.6906673.

Table 1. Summary of the benchmarks we used. MLP and CNN are abbreviations of "multilayer perceptron" and "convolutional neural network".

	Benchmark's origin	Observation space (size)	Network	Learning algorithm	# of steps
WATERTANK	Alshiekh et al. [1]	Discrete (714)	MLP	PPO	500,000
GRIDWORLD	Our original	Discrete (625)	MLP	PPO	100,000
TAXI	OpenAI Gym [7]	Discrete (500)	MLP	PPO	200,000
CLIFFWALK	OpenAI Gym [7]	Discrete (48)	MLP	PPO	200,000
SELFDRIVINGCAR	Alshiekh et al. [1]	Continuous ($[-1,1]^4$)	MLP	DQN	200,000
SIDEWALK	MiniWorld [9]	Image ($80 \times 60 \times 3 \times 256$)	CNN	PPO	100,000
CARRACING	OpenAI Gym [7]	Image ($96 \times 96 \times 3 \times 256$)	CNN	PPO	200,000

To evaluate the RL training, we measure the total number of training episodes with undesired behaviors and the total execution time, including both training and testing phases. To evaluate each controller, we run it for 30 episodes and measure the *mean reward* and the *safe rate*, i. e., the rate of the episodes without undesired behaviors in the 30 episodes.

We ran experiments on a GPU server with AMD EPYC 7702P, NVIDIA GeForce RTX 2080 Ti, 125GiB RAM, and Ubuntu 20.04.3 LTS. We used eight CPUs and one GPU for each execution. We ran each instance of the experiment 30 times, i. e., we trained $7 \times 3 \times 30$ controllers in total. For each metric, we report the mean of the 30 executions, i. e., we have 7×3 reported values.

4.2 Benchmarks

We chose seven benchmarks for our experiments. Table 1 summarizes them. Most of them are common and openly available. We modified them to fit to dynamic shielding: randomness except for those observable as Env actions are removed; the actions are discretized; the observations for the RL agent is not changed, while the observation for the dynamic shield is discretized. We used CNN for the benchmarks with graphical observation and MLP for the others.

WATERTANK implements the benchmark already used for shielding in [1]. Example 1 and 7 show the details of the system. The undesired behavior used in the shield construction is: *i*) to make the water tank empty or full, or *ii*) to change the status of the switch too often.

GRIDWORLD is a high-level robot control example of two robots in a 5×5 grid arena. One of them is the ego robot we control, and the other robot randomly moves. The objective of the ego robot is to reach the goal area, without touching the arena walls or the other robot.

TAXI is a benchmark to pick up passengers and drop them off at another place in a 5×5 grid arena. As criteria of a safety violation, we measured the number of episodes where the taxi is broken, which randomly occurs when it hits the wall. The undesired behavior used in the shield construction is hitting the wall, picking up or dropping off the passenger at an inappropriate location.

CLIFFWALK is a benchmark to move ego to the goal area without stepping off the cliff in a 3×12 grid arena. The undesired behavior used in the shield construction is to step off the cliff.

Table 2. Mean of 1) the number of episodes with undesired behavior in training phases and 2) the execution time (in seconds), including both training and testing phases. The cells with the best results are highlighted.

	Undesired episodes			Total time		
	PLAIN	SAFEPADDING	SHIELDING	PLAIN	SAFEPADDING	SHIELDING
WATERTANK	1883.67	1892.40	177.13	1860.46	1947.09	6080.89
GRIDWORLD	6996.40	7322.23	5623.43	177.18	1487.10	4548.70
CLIFFWALK	1493.20	1528.67	478.20	355.18	365.54	839.06
TAXI	8723.13	2057.33	37.77	336.04	349.78	611.87
SELFDRIVINGCAR	6403.07	6454.60	5662.40	865.55	4919.13	10087.18
SIDEWALK	373.60	427.93	273.37	762.67	1734.66	6395.73
CARRACING	180.13	141.17	41.73	7650.38	16694.63	12532.04

SELFDRIVINGCAR is a benchmark to drive a car in a 480×480 arena around a blocked area in a clockwise direction without hitting the walls. The undesired behavior used in the shield construction is to hit the walls in the arena.

SIDEWALK is a benchmark for 3D robot simulation. Its objective is to reach the goal area on the sidewalk without entering the roadway. The undesired behavior used in the shield construction is to enter the roadway.

CARRACING is a benchmark to drive a car on a predetermined racing course. As criteria of a safety violation, we measured the number of episodes with *spin behavior*, i.e., ego drives off the road and keeps rotating indefinitely. The undesired behavior used in the shield construction is to deviate from the road for any consecutive steps, which is not yet a safety violation but tends to lead to it.

4.3 RQ1: Safety by Dynamic Shielding in the Training Phase

To evaluate the safety by dynamic shielding, we measured the number of training episodes with undesired behaviors ("Undesired episodes" columns in Table 2), and the relationship between the number of undesired training episodes before each testing phase and the highest mean reward by the testing phase (Fig. 3).

In Table 2, we observe that, for all benchmarks, the training episodes with undesired behavior were, on average, the lowest when we used dynamic shielding. For example, for CARRACING, the mean number of the training episodes with undesired behavior was reduced by about 77% compared to PLAIN and about 70% compared to SAFEPADDING. In Fig. 3, we observe that for all benchmarks, the curve of SHIELDING is growing faster than the curves of PLAIN and SAFEPADDING. This suggests that dynamic shielding decreased the number of undesired explorations to obtain a controller with similar performance.

> **Answer to RQ1:** Overall, we conclude that dynamic shielding can significantly reduce undesired behaviors during exploration.

Compared to PLAIN, SHIELDING decreases such undesired training episodes because it prevents exploration of actions known to cause undesired behavior,

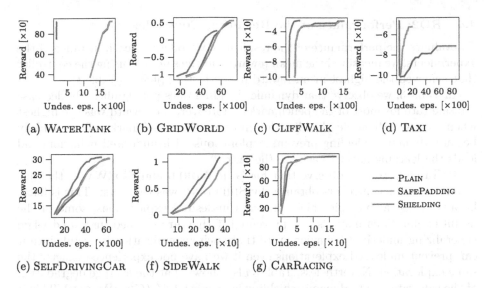

Fig. 3. The mean of the number of undesired episodes before each testing phase and the reward of the best controller obtained in the testing phase.

Table 3. Mean of the performance of the best controllers obtained in the 30 executions. The cells with the best results are highlighted.

	Mean reward			Safe rate		
	PLAIN	SAFEPADDING	SHIELDING	PLAIN	SAFEPADDING	SHIELDING
WATERTANK	918.89	919.81	921.81	1.00	1.00	1.00
GRIDWORLD	0.37	0.46	0.07	0.80	0.85	0.73
CLIFFWALK	-69.13	-66.00	-65.93	1.00	1.00	1.00
TAXI	-147.61	-139.62	-92.93	0.57	0.67	1.00
SELFDRIVINGCAR	28.83	28.86	29.81	1.00	1.00	1.00
SIDEWALK	0.93	0.90	0.67	0.93	0.89	0.89
CARRACING	375.53	509.25	622.07	1.00	1.00	1.00

while the plain RL may repeatedly explore such actions. Although SAFEPADDING also prevents such an undesired exploration, the number of the undesired training episodes of SHIELDING was smaller than that of SAFEPADDING. This is because, with SHIELDING, the undesired explorations are generalized by state merging in the RPNI algorithm, while in SAFEPADDING, the state space of the learned MDP is identical to the observation space in the RL, and the undesired explorations are not often generalized.

4.4 RQ2: Performance of the Resulting Controller

To evaluate the performance of the resulting controller, for each instance of the experiments, we measured the mean reward and the safe rate using the controller that achieved the highest mean reward in the testing phases (Table 3).

In Table 3, we observe that dynamic shielding does not significantly decrease the safe rate for most of the benchmarks. Moreover, the reward was the highest when we used dynamic shielding for most of the benchmarks. This is likely because dynamic shielding prevents explorations with undesired behaviors and leads the learning agent to achieve the task.

In Table 3, we also observe that for GRIDWORLD and SIDEWALK, the performance of the controllers obtained by SHIELDING was the worst. This is likely because when a dynamic shield prevents undesired explorations, some of the useful explorations may also be prevented if they are deemed undesired when generalizing undesired behavior. Note that such generalization is useful since it can prevent undesired explorations even if we have not experienced exactly the same exploration. Nevertheless, Table 3 also shows that the average degradation of the safe rate due to dynamic shielding is at most 12% (GRIDWORLD). This is not prohibitively large considering the reduction of undesired explorations (e. g., from 6996.40 to 5623.43 for GRIDWORLD in Table 3).

> **Answer to RQ2:** Overall, we conclude that dynamic shielding usually improves the performance of the resulting controller.

4.5 RQ3: Time Efficiency of Dynamic Shielding

To evaluate the overhead of dynamic shielding, we measured the execution time, including both training and testing phases ("Total time" columns in Table 2).

In Table 2, we observe that PLAIN was the fastest on average for all benchmarks. This is mainly because of the computation cost to construct the set of safe actions. We also observe that SAFEPADDING is usually faster than SHIELDING. This is due to the combinatorial exploration in the RPNI algorithm to choose the merged states, while SAFEPADDING does not conduct such state merging and directly uses the observation space in the RL as the state space of the learned MDP. We again remark that the generalization by the state merging contributes to the safety of SHIELDING.

In Table 2, we also observe that the overhead of SHIELDING is at most about 2.5 h (153.7 min in SELFDRIVINGCAR). This is not negligible but still acceptable for many common usage scenarios, e. g., learning a controller during non-working hours. Moreover, Table 2 also shows that the overhead is not very sensitive to the cost of each execution and the observation space. For example, the overhead of SHIELDING for WATERTANK was close to that for CARRACING. This indeed makes the relative overhead for CARRACING small.

> **Answer to RQ3:** Overall, we conclude that the overhead of dynamic shielding is not prohibitively large, especially when the RL is time-consuming even without shielding.

5 Conclusions and Perspectives

Based on passive automata learning, we proposed a new shielding scheme called *dynamic shielding* for RL. Since dynamic shielding does not require a predetermined system model, it is applicable to black-box systems. The experiment results suggest that *i*) dynamic shielding prevents undesired exploration during training, *ii*) dynamic shielding often improves the quality of the resulting controller, and *iii*) the overhead of dynamic shielding is not prohibitively large.

In dynamic shielding, we assume that the system behaves deterministically once the actions of the controller and the environment are fixed. Extending our approach, for example, utilizing a probabilistic model identification [18] to support probabilistic systems is a future direction.

Acknowledgements. This work is partially supported by JST ERATO HASUO Metamathematics for Systems Design Project (No. JPMJER1603). Masaki Waga is also supported by JST ACT-X Grant No. JPMJAX200U. Stefan Klikovits is also supported by JSPS Grant-in-Aid No. 20K23334. Sasinee Pruekprasert is also supported by JSPS Grant-in-Aid No. 21K14191. Toru Takisaka is also supported by NSFC Research Fund for International Young Scientists No. 62150410437.

References

1. Alshiekh, M., Bloem, R., Ehlers, R., Könighofer, B., Niekum, S., Topcu, U.: Safe reinforcement learning via shielding. In: McIlraith, S.A., Weinberger, K.Q. (eds.) Proceedings of the AAAI 2018, pp. 2669–2678. AAAI Press (2018)
2. Avni, G., Bloem, R., Chatterjee, K., Henzinger, T.A., Könighofer, B., Pranger, S.: Run-time optimization for learned controllers through quantitative games. In: Dillig, I., Tasiran, S. (eds.) CAV 2019. LNCS, vol. 11561, pp. 630–649. Springer, Cham (2019). https://doi.org/10.1007/978-3-030-25540-4_36
3. Bharadwaj, S., Bloem, R., Dimitrova, R., Könighofer, B., Topcu, U.: Synthesis of minimum-cost shields for multi-agent systems. In: Proceedings of the ACC 2019, pp. 1048–1055. IEEE (2019)
4. Bloem, R., Jensen, P.G., Könighofer, B., Larsen, K.G., Lorber, F., Palmisano, A.: It's time to play safe: shield synthesis for timed systems. CoRR abs/2006.16688 (2020)
5. Bloem, R., Könighofer, B., Könighofer, R., Wang, C.: Shield synthesis: runtime enforcement for reactive systems. In: Baier, C., Tinelli, C. (eds.) TACAS 2015. LNCS, vol. 9035, pp. 533–548. Springer, Heidelberg (2015). https://doi.org/10.1007/978-3-662-46681-0_51
6. Bouton, M., Karlsson, J., Nakhaei, A., Fujimura, K., Kochenderfer, M.J., Tumova, J.: Reinforcement learning with probabilistic guarantees for autonomous driving. CoRR abs/1904.07189 (2019)
7. Brockman, G., et al.: OpenAI Gym. CoRR abs/1606.01540 (2016)
8. Cheng, R., Orosz, G., Murray, R.M., Burdick, J.W.: End-to-end safe reinforcement learning through barrier functions for safety-critical continuous control tasks. In: Proceedings of the AAAI 2019, pp. 3387–3395. AAAI Press (2019)

9. Chevalier-Boisvert, M.: Gym-MiniWorld Environment for OpenAI Gym (2018). https://github.com/maximecb/gym-miniworld
10. García, J., Fernández, F.: A comprehensive survey on safe reinforcement learning. J. Mach. Learn. Res. **16**, 1437–1480 (2015)
11. Hasanbeig, M., Abate, A., Kroening, D.: Cautious reinforcement learning with logical constraints. In: Seghrouchni, A.E.F., Sukthankar, G., An, B., Yorke-Smith, N. (eds.) Proceedings of the AAMAS 2020, pp. 483–491. IFAAMS (2020)
12. Hunt, N., Fulton, N., Magliacane, S., Hoang, T.N., Das, S., Solar-Lezama, A.: Verifiably safe exploration for end-to-end reinforcement learning. In: Bogomolov, S., Jungers, R.M. (eds.) Proceedings of the HSCC 2021, pp. 14:1–14:11. ACM (2021)
13. Isberner, M., Howar, F., Steffen, B.: The open-source LearnLib - a framework for active automata learning. In: Kroening, D., Păsăreanu, C.S. (eds.) CAV 2015. LNCS, vol. 9206, pp. 487–495. Springer, Cham (2015). https://doi.org/10.1007/978-3-319-21690-4_32
14. Jansen, N., Könighofer, B., Junges, S., Serban, A., Bloem, R.: Safe reinforcement learning using probabilistic shields (invited paper). In: Konnov, I., Kovács, L. (eds.) Proceedings of the CONCUR 2020. LIPIcs, vol. 171, pp. 3:1–3:16. Schloss Dagstuhl - Leibniz-Zentrum für Informatik (2020)
15. Kupferman, O., Lampert, R.: On the construction of fine automata for safety properties. In: Graf, S., Zhang, W. (eds.) ATVA 2006. LNCS, vol. 4218, pp. 110–124. Springer, Heidelberg (2006). https://doi.org/10.1007/11901914_11
16. Lang, K.J., Pearlmutter, B.A., Price, R.A.: Results of the Abbadingo one DFA learning competition and a new evidence-driven state merging algorithm. In: Honavar, V., Slutzki, G. (eds.) ICGI 1998. LNCS, vol. 1433, pp. 1–12. Springer, Heidelberg (1998). https://doi.org/10.1007/BFb0054059
17. López, D., García, P.: On the inference of finite state automata from positive and negative data. In: Heinz, J., Sempere, J.M. (eds.) Topics in Grammatical Inference, pp. 73–112. Springer, Heidelberg (2016). https://doi.org/10.1007/978-3-662-48395-4_4
18. Mao, H., Chen, Y., Jaeger, M., Nielsen, T.D., Larsen, K.G., Nielsen, B.: Learning Markov decision processes for model checking. In: Fahrenberg, U., Legay, A., Thrane, C.R. (eds.) Proceedings of the QFM 2012. EPTCS, vol. 103, pp. 49–63 (2012)
19. Mnih, V., et al.: Playing Atari with deep reinforcement learning. CoRR abs/1312.5602 (2013)
20. Mnih, V., et al.: Human-level control through deep reinforcement learning. Nature **518**(7540), 529–533 (2015)
21. Oncina, J., García, P.: Identifying regular languages in polynomial time. Series in Machine Perception and Artificial Intelligence, pp. 99–108 (1993)
22. Plappert, M.: Keras-RL (2016). https://github.com/keras-rl/keras-rl
23. Pranger, S., Könighofer, B., Tappler, M., Deixelberger, M., Jansen, N., Bloem, R.: Adaptive shielding under uncertainty. In: Proceedings of the ACC 2021, pp. 3467–3474. IEEE (2021)
24. Raffin, A., Hill, A., Ernestus, M., Gleave, A., Kanervisto, A., Dormann, N.: Stable baselines3 (2019). https://github.com/DLR-RM/stable-baselines3
25. Schulman, J., Wolski, F., Dhariwal, P., Radford, A., Klimov, O.: Proximal policy optimization algorithms. CoRR abs/1707.06347 (2017)

26. Silver, D., et al.: Mastering the game of go without human knowledge. Nature **550**(7676), 354–359 (2017)
27. Sutton, R.S., Barto, A.G.: Reinforcement Learning - An Introduction. Adaptive Computation and Machine Learning. MIT Press (1998)
28. Wu, M., Wang, J., Deshmukh, J., Wang, C.: Shield synthesis for real: Enforcing safety in cyber-physical systems. In: Barrett, C.W., Yang, J. (eds.) Proceedings of the FMCAD 2019, pp. 129–137. IEEE (2019)

An Impossibility Result in Automata-Theoretic Reinforcement Learning

Ernst Moritz Hahn[1] (ID), Mateo Perez[2] (ID), Sven Schewe[3] (ID), Fabio Somenzi[2](✉) (ID), Ashutosh Trivedi[2] (ID), and Dominik Wojtczak[3] (ID)

[1] University of Twente, Enschede, The Netherlands
[2] University of Colorado Boulder, Boulder, USA
fabio@colorado.edu
[3] University of Liverpool, Liverpool, UK

Abstract. The expanding role of reinforcement learning (RL) in safety-critical system design has promoted ω-automata as a way to express learning requirements—often non-Markovian—with greater ease of expression and interpretation than scalar reward signals. When ω-automata were first proposed in model-free RL, deterministic Rabin acceptance conditions were used in an attempt to provide a direct translation from ω-automata to finite state "reward" machines defined over the same automaton structure (a memoryless reward translation). While these initial attempts to provide faithful, memoryless reward translations for Rabin acceptance conditions remained unsuccessful, translations were discovered for other acceptance conditions such as suitable, limit-deterministic Büchi acceptance or more generally, good-for-MDP Büchi acceptance conditions. Yet, the question "whether a *memoryless* translation of Rabin conditions to scalar rewards exists" remained unresolved.

This paper presents an impossibility result implying that any attempt to use Rabin automata directly (without extra memory) for model-free RL is bound to fail. To establish this result, we show a link between a class of automata enabling memoryless reward translation to closure properties of its accepting and rejecting infinity sets, and to the insight that both the property and its complement need to allow for positional strategies for such an approach to work. We believe that such impossibility results will provide foundations for the application of RL to safety-critical systems.

1 Introduction

The empirical success of reinforcement learning (RL, [26]) in solving challenging problems, even in the absence of an explicit model of the environment, has

* ■ This project has received funding from the European Union's Horizon 2020 research and innovation programme under grant agreements 864075 (CAESAR), and 956123 (FOCETA). This work is supported in part by the National Science Foundation (NSF) grant CCF-2009022 and by NSF CAREER award CCF-2146563.

A. Bouajjani et al. (Eds.): ATVA 2022, LNCS 13505, pp. 42–57, 2022.
https://doi.org/10.1007/978-3-031-19992-9_3

made its application to the design of safety-critical systems inevitable. However, traditional RL relies on expert inputs in the form of scalar reward signals that are often designed in intuitive, empirical fashion. A rigorous approach to the design of safety-critical systems demands formal specifications at every stage of the design process. Consequently, there is an increased interest in formal languages that express learning requirements and in their automatic translation to reward signals for model-free RL. *This paper concerns an impossibility result on the automatic reward translations when requirements are specified using an important class of formal languages: the ω-regular objectives.*

Omega-regular languages [21,27] have been used to specify high level objectives in the safety-critical system-design community for decades—often in the form of declarative specifications in Linear Temporal Logic [23]. Omega-regular objectives express qualitative properties for infinite-horizon behaviors, extending what regular languages do for finite-horizon behaviors: they are expressive, robust, and support efficient, automatic analysis. However, unlike regular languages, for which deterministic finite automata provide a *de facto* canonical machine model, the machine models for ω-regular objectives are characterized by infinitary *acceptance conditions* to be satisfied by the infinite-horizon behavior. Widely adopted acceptance conditions include Büchi, parity, Rabin, and Streett conditions [2], and the name of the acceptance condition customarily precedes "automata" to specify the kind of ω-automata. Deterministic parity, Rabin, Streett, and nondeterministic Büchi automata capture the same class of languages and characterize the class of ω-regular languages; while, deterministic Büchi automata are strictly less expressive.

It is known that unrestricted nondeterminism is not compatible with the computation of optimal strategies when they are used to express the properties of probabilistic systems modeled as Markov decision processes (MDPs). This has motivated the study of a restricted form of nondeterminism formalized as the *good-for-MDPs automata* [9,15,30]. Notably, good-for-MDPs Büchi automata are expressive enough to represent all ω-regular objectives. The optimal control problem for MDPs against ω-automata based specifications has been studied extensively [1,6,22]. These solution methods, however, require a model of the environment dynamics. In the RL framework, the system, specified as an MDP, is unknown. Model-free RL algorithms synthesize a strategy without creating an explicit model of the dynamics. Thus, when designing a model-free translation from an ω-automaton to rewards, the rewards should not depend directly on the unknown transition structure of the MDP. Model-free reward translations for good-for-MDPs Büchi automata [5,13] and parity automata [16] have been demonstrated; they assign reward from the transitions of the automaton.

When choosing a type of ω-automata to use for a model-free reward translation, one must consider that there are optimal positional strategies in MDPs for discounted and average reward RL [24]. This means that, if a model-free reward translation results in an MDP where optimal strategies for the ω-regular objective require additional memory, then this construction is incorrect. For instance, if one forms the synchronous product between a deterministic Streett automaton and an MDP, optimal policies in the resulting product MDP may require finite memory, so there is no faithful reward assignment on this product MDP. Good-for-MDPs Büchi, deterministic parity, and deterministic Rabin automata admit positional optimal strategies in the product MDP.

Since good-for-MDPs Büchi and deterministic parity automata are known to have faithful model-free reductions, one may consider if a faithful model-free reduction exists for Rabin automata with no additional memory. Attempts at this [25] have later been shown to be incorrect [13]. We show that no such reduction exists. This somewhat surprising result explains why no attempt at using Rabin automata in RL has been successful. We observe connections between the existence of a model-free reward translation and the closure sets of Muller automata. We also show how the positional nature of optimal strategies for the complement of an automaton affects the existence of a model-free reward translation.

We begin the technical discussion by introducing ω-automata (Sect. 2) and their closure properties (Sect. 3). Section 4 formalizes MDPs and the RL framework with both automata-theoretic rewards and non-Markovian scalar rewards. Section 5 introduces the idea of "memoryless" translations and associated impossibility theorems for Rabin. Section 6 provides concluding remarks.

2   Omega-Automata

A finite word over an alphabet Σ is a finite concatenation of symbols from Σ. Similarly, an ω-word w over Σ is a function $w : \omega \to \Sigma$ from the natural numbers to Σ. We write Σ^* and Σ^ω for the set of finite and ω-strings over Σ. We write $\mathbb{B}$ for the binary alphabet $\{0, 1\}$.

Definition 1. *An ω-automaton $\mathcal{A} = \langle \Sigma, Q, q_0, \delta, \alpha \rangle$ consists of a finite alphabet Σ, a finite set of states Q, an initial state $q_0 \in Q$, a transition function $\delta :$ $Q \times \Sigma \to 2^Q$, and an acceptance condition $\alpha \subseteq Q^\omega$. A deterministic automaton is such that $\delta(q, \sigma)$ is a singleton for every state q and alphabet letter σ. For deterministic automata, we write $\delta(q, \sigma) = q'$ instead of $\delta(q, \sigma) = \{q'\}$.*

A *run* of an automaton $\mathcal{A} = \langle \Sigma, Q, q_0, \delta, \alpha \rangle$ on word $w \in \Sigma^\omega$ is a function $\rho : \omega \to Q$, such that $\rho(0) = q_0$ and $\rho(i + 1) \in \delta(\rho(i), w(i))$ holds. A run ρ is *accepting* if $\rho \in \alpha$. A word w is accepted by $\mathcal{A}$ if there exists an accepting run of $\mathcal{A}$ on w. The language of $\mathcal{A}$, written $L(\mathcal{A})$, is the set of words accepted by $\mathcal{A}$.

The set of states that appear infinitely often in ρ is written $\mathrm{Inf}(\rho)$. A deterministic automaton $\mathcal{D}$ has exactly one run for each word in Σ^ω. We write $\mathrm{Inf}^{\mathcal{D}}(w)$ for the set of states that appear infinitely often in the unique run of $\mathcal{D}$ on w. When the deterministic automaton $\mathcal{D}$ is clear from the context, we drop the superscript and simply write $\mathrm{Inf}(w)$.

Definition 2 (Acceptance Conditions). *Several ways to give finite presentations of α acceptance conditions[1] are in use. We recall the most common ones so as to fix notation. They are all defined in terms of $\mathrm{Inf}(\rho)$.*

---

[1] Abusing notation, we sometimes use α to denote the indicator function $\alpha : Q^\omega \to \mathbb{B}$.

- A Büchi *acceptance condition is specified by a set* $F \subseteq Q$ *such that*

$$\alpha = \{\rho \in Q^\omega : \mathrm{Inf}(\rho) \cap F \neq \emptyset\}.$$

- A co-Büchi *acceptance condition is specified by a set* $F \subseteq Q$ *such that*

$$\alpha = \{\rho \in Q^\omega : \mathrm{Inf}(\rho) \cap F = \emptyset\}.$$

- A generalized Büchi *condition is specified by a set of sets* $\mathcal{F} \subseteq 2^Q$ *such that*

$$\alpha = \{\rho \in Q^\omega : \forall F \in \mathcal{F}. \mathrm{Inf}(\rho) \cap F \neq \emptyset\}.$$

- A generalized co-Büchi *condition is specified by a set of sets* $\mathcal{F} \subseteq 2^Q$ *such that*

$$\alpha = \{\rho \in Q^\omega : \exists F \in \mathcal{F}. \mathrm{Inf}(\rho) \cap F = \emptyset\}.$$

- A parity *acceptance condition of index* k *is specified by a function* $\pi : Q \to \{0,\dots,k-1\}$ *that assigns a priority to each state of the automaton, so that*

$$\alpha = \{\rho \in Q^\omega : \pi(\mathrm{Inf}(\rho)) \text{ is odd}\},$$

where $\pi(S) = \max\{\pi(s) : s \in S\}$ *is the maximum priority of states in* $S \subseteq Q$.
- A Rabin *acceptance condition of index* k *is specified by* k *pairs of sets of states,* $\{\langle R_i, G_i\rangle\}_{1 \le i \le k}$. *Intuitively, a run should visit at least one set of Red (ruinous) states finitely often and its matching Green (good) set of states infinitely often. Formally,*

$$\alpha = \{\rho \in Q^\omega : \exists i . 1 \le i \le k \text{ and } \mathrm{Inf}(\rho) \cap R_i = \emptyset \text{ and } \mathrm{Inf}(\rho) \cap G_i \neq \emptyset\}.$$

- A Streett *acceptance condition of index* k *is specified by* k *pairs of sets of states,* $\{\langle G_i, R_i\rangle\}_{1 \le i \le k}$. *Intuitively, a run should visit each Red set of states finitely often or its matching Green set of states infinitely often. Formally,*

$$\alpha = \{\rho \in Q^\omega : \forall i . 1 \le i \le k \to \mathrm{Inf}(\rho) \cap R_i = \emptyset \text{ or } \mathrm{Inf}(\rho) \cap G_i \neq \emptyset\}.$$

- A Muller *acceptance condition is specified by a collection of sets of states* $\mathcal{C} \subseteq 2^Q$ *such that*

$$\alpha = \{\rho \in Q^\omega : \mathrm{Inf}(\rho) \in \mathcal{C}\}.$$

The name of the acceptance condition customarily precedes automata to specify the kind of ω-automata, e.g. ω-automata with Büchi acceptance conditions are called Büchi automata. A Büchi (or co-Büchi) automaton where, in every strongly connected component (SCC) of the automaton, either all or none of the states is in F, is called *weak*.

3   Closure Properties of Acceptance Conditions

Definition 3 (Eventual Sets). *An* eventual set *of a deterministic automaton* $\mathcal{A} = \langle \Sigma, Q, q_0, \delta, \alpha \rangle$ *is a set of states* $E \subseteq Q$ *such that* $E = \mathrm{Inf}(w)$ *for some* $w \in \Sigma^\omega$. *An eventual set is* accepting *if it satisfies the acceptance condition* α; *otherwise, it is* rejecting. *We denote the set of all eventual sets of* $\mathcal{A}$ *by* $\mathcal{E}^{\mathcal{A}}$. *The set of accepting (rejecting) eventual sets of* $\mathcal{A}$ *is written* $\mathcal{E}_a^{\mathcal{A}}$ ($\mathcal{E}_r^{\mathcal{A}}$). *Note that* $\mathcal{E}_a^{\mathcal{A}} \cup \mathcal{E}_r^{\mathcal{A}} = \mathcal{E}^{\mathcal{A}}$ *and* $\mathcal{E}_a^{\mathcal{A}} \cap \mathcal{E}_r^{\mathcal{A}} = \emptyset$. *When the automaton* $\mathcal{A}$ *is clear from the context, we drop the superscript and simply write,* $\mathcal{E}$, $\mathcal{E}_a$, $\mathcal{E}_r$.

For a Muller automaton with acceptance condition $\mathcal{C}$, for example, $\mathcal{E}_a = \mathcal{E} \cap \mathcal{C}$ and $\mathcal{E}_r = \mathcal{E} \setminus \mathcal{C}$. For a Büchi automaton with acceptance condition F, $\mathcal{E}_a = \{ E \in \mathcal{E} : E \cap F \neq \emptyset \}$ and so on.

Definition 4 (Upward-Closure and Closure under Union). *A set* $S \subseteq \mathcal{E}$ *of eventual sets is* upward-closed *if, whenever* $E_1 \in S$, $E_2 \in \mathcal{E}$, *and* $E_1 \subseteq E_2$, *it is also the case that* $E_2 \in S$. *The set* S *is* closed under union *if, whenever* $E_1, E_2, \ldots, E_n$ *are in* S, *and* $E_1 \cup E_2 \cup \cdots \cup E_n \in \mathcal{E}$, *then it is also the case that* $E_1 \cup E_2 \cup \cdots \cup E_n \in S$. *Note that upward closure implies closure under union because* $E_1 \cup E_2 \cup \cdots \cup E_n \supseteq E_1$.

We define "closure under union" in terms of union of n sets instead of just pairs to account for cases like this: we have rejecting eventual sets E_1, E_2, E_3 such that their pairwise unions are not in $\mathcal{E}$, but the union of all three is. We still want the union to be in $\mathcal{E}_r$. E_1, E_2, E_3 may form a ring that is only strongly connected when all three are taken together.

Table 1 summarizes the requirements that $\mathcal{E}_a$ and $\mathcal{E}_r$ must satisfy for the acceptance condition of a *deterministic* Muller automaton to be translated into an equivalent acceptance condition of different type for the same transition structure. Dual types of acceptance condition (e.g., Streett and Rabin) must satisfy dual requirements. A weak automaton may be regarded as both a Büchi automaton and a co-Büchi automaton. Hence, it has the most restrictive conditions. Likewise, a parity automaton may be seen as both a Rabin automaton and a Streett automaton. Hence the constraints imposed on parity conditions combine those of Rabin and Streett conditions.

Remark 1. The result for generalized Büchi acceptance extends [18, Theorem 4.2], because it says that, with generalized Büchi acceptance, one is not only guaranteed the existence of a deterministic Büchi automaton equivalent to the given Muller automaton, but is also told that one exists with the same transition structure as long as a generalized acceptance condition is used. Any standard technique to "degeneralize" that automaton may be applied to recover an automaton with plain Büchi acceptance.

As an example of how Table 1 is arrived at, we prove the following result. Analogous results are in [32, Lemma 13] and [21, Proposition 4.4.5].

Table 1. Closure conditions that $\mathcal{E}_a$ and $\mathcal{E}_r$ must satisfy for a Muller condition to be expressed as another type of condition. Positional and co-positional refer to the (guaranteed) existence of positional optimal policies for maximizing the chance that a run in $\mathcal{E}_a$ and $\mathcal{E}_r$, respectively, is produced. The final column lists which of these target types permit memoryless reward translations (MRT) to scalar values with convex aggregator functions, which allows for using them in reinforcement learning.

Target type	$\mathcal{E}_a$	$\mathcal{E}_r$	Positional	Co-positional	MRT
weak	upward	upward	yes	yes	yes
Büchi	upward	union	yes	yes	yes
co-Büchi	union	upward	yes	yes	yes
generalized Büchi	upward		no	yes	no
generalized co-Büchi		upward	yes	no	no
parity	union	union	yes	yes	yes
Streett	union		no	yes	no
Rabin		union	yes	no	no

Theorem 1 (Muller to Rabin). *A Muller condition is expressible in Rabin form if, and only if, $\mathcal{E}_r$ is closed under union.*

Proof. To see that, in a Rabin condition $\{\langle R_i, G_i \rangle\}_{1 \le i \le k}$, $\mathcal{E}_r$ is closed under union, let, for $j = 1, \ldots, n$, E_j be an element of $\mathcal{E}_r$. Then, for every $i \in \{1, \ldots, k\}$, $E_j \cap R_i \ne \emptyset$ or $E_j \cap G_i = \emptyset$ holds. If any E_j intersects G_i, so does $E_1 \cup E_2 \cup \cdots \cup E_n$. In the remaining case, no E_j intersects R_i, but then neither does $E_1 \cup E_2 \cup \cdots \cup E_n$.

To prove the other direction, i.e., that closure under union of $\mathcal{E}_r$ guarantees the existence of an equivalent Rabin condition, we observe that closure under union of $\mathcal{E}_r$ implies that, for $E \in \mathcal{E}_a$, the set

$$S_E = \bigcup \{S \in \mathcal{E}_r : S \subseteq E\}$$

is a proper subset of E. (Otherwise, E would belong to both $\mathcal{E}_a$ and $\mathcal{E}_r$.) Therefore, a Rabin condition equivalent to the given Muller condition such that $\mathcal{E}_r$ is closed under union consists of one pair $\langle Q \setminus E, E \setminus S_E \rangle$ for each element E of $\mathcal{E}_a$. Every set $E \in \mathcal{E}_a$ is accepting in the Rabin automaton thanks to the pair $\langle Q \setminus E, E \setminus S_E \rangle$ because $E \setminus S_E$ is not empty. For a set $D \in \mathcal{E}_r$ and a generic pair $\langle Q \setminus E, E \setminus S_E \rangle$ of the Rabin condition, we consider two cases. If $D \subset E$, then $D \cap (E \setminus S_E) = \emptyset$. If, however, $D \not\subseteq E$, given that $D \ne E$ and $D \ne \emptyset$, it must be $D \cap (Q \setminus E) \ne \emptyset$. Hence, no pair in the Rabin condition makes D accepting. □

Example 1. For the deterministic Muller automaton of Fig. 1,

$$\mathcal{E}_a = \{\{q_0\}, \{q_1\}\}$$
$$\mathcal{E}_r = \{\{q_0, q_1\}\}.$$

The automaton accepts the language $L = (\Sigma^* a^\omega) \cup (\Sigma^* b^\omega)$. Since $\mathcal{E}_r$ is (trivially) closed under union, the acceptance condition can be written in Rabin form.

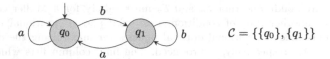

Fig. 1. A deterministic Muller automaton on the alphabet $\Sigma = \{a, b\}$.

The construction of Theorem 1 yields $\{\langle \{q_1\}, \{q_0\}\rangle, \langle \{q_0\}, \{q_1\}\rangle\}$. Since $\mathcal{E}_a$ is not closed under union, the automaton of Fig. 1 cannot be equipped with a parity condition so that it still accepts L.

A deterministic Muller automaton for L that may be equipped with a parity acceptance condition is shown in Fig. 2. State q_0 is given priority 2, while the other two states are given priority 1.

Remark 2. If acceptance is defined in terms of transitions instead of states, the smallest deterministic Rabin automaton for the language L of Example 1 has one state, while the smallest deterministic parity automaton has two states. In general, translation from Rabin to parity may incur a factorial blow-up [19].

4   Markov Decision Processes

Let $\mathbb{R}$ be the set of real numbers. Let $\mathcal{D}(S)$ be the set of distributions over the set S. A Markov decision process (MDP) $\mathcal{M}$ is a tuple (S, s_0, A, T, AP, L), where S is a finite set of states, $s_0 \in S$ is the initial state, A is a finite set of *actions*, $T : S \times A \to \mathcal{D}(S)$ is the probabilistic transition function, AP is the set of *atomic propositions*, and $L : S \to 2^{AP}$ is the *labeling function*.

For any state $s \in S$, $A(s)$ denotes the set of actions that may be selected in state s. An MDP is a Markov chain if $A(s)$ is singleton for all $s \in S$. For states $s, s' \in S$ and $a \in A(s)$, $T(s, a)(s')$ equals $p(s'|s, a)$, that is, the probability that the MDP moves from state s to state s' if action a is chosen. A *run* of $\mathcal{M}$ is an ω-word $\langle s_0, a_1, s_1, \ldots\rangle \in S \times (A \times S)^\omega$ such that $p(s_{i+1}|s_i, a_{i+1}) > 0$ for all $i \geq 0$. A finite run is a finite such sequence $(\langle s_0, a_1, s_1, \ldots\rangle \in S \times (A \times S)^*)$. For a *run* $r = \langle s_0, a_1, s_1, \ldots\rangle$ we define the corresponding labeled run as $L(r) = \langle L(s_0), L(s_1), \ldots\rangle \in (2^{AP})^\omega$. We write $Runs^{\mathcal{M}}(FRuns^{\mathcal{M}})$ for the set of runs (finite runs) of the MDP $\mathcal{M}$ from its initial state and $Runs^{\mathcal{M}}(s)(FRuns^{\mathcal{M}}(s))$ for the set of runs (finite runs) of the MDP $\mathcal{M}$ starting from the state s. When

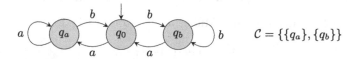

Fig. 2. A deterministic Muller automaton, equivalent to the one of Fig. 1, that may be equipped with a parity condition.

the context resolves ambiguity, we drop the superscript and simply write *Runs* and *FRuns*. We write $last(r)$ for the last state of a finite run r.

A *strategy* for $\mathcal{M}$ is a function $\sigma : FRuns^{\mathcal{M}} \to \mathcal{D}(A)$ such that $supp(\sigma(r)) \subseteq A(last(r))$, where $supp(d)$ denotes the support of the distribution d. A strategy σ is *pure* if $\sigma(r)$ is a point distribution for all runs $r \in FRuns^{\mathcal{M}}$ and is *mixed* otherwise. Let $Runs_\sigma^{\mathcal{M}}(s)$ denote the subset of runs $Runs^{\mathcal{M}}(s)$ that are possible under strategy σ from state s. We say that σ is *stationary* if $last(r) = last(r')$ implies $\sigma(r) = \sigma(r')$ for all runs $r, r' \in FRuns^{\mathcal{M}}$. A stationary strategy can be given as a function $\sigma : S \to \mathcal{D}(A)$. A strategy is *positional* if it is both pure and stationary. We write $\Sigma_{\mathcal{M}}$ for the set of all strategies on $\mathcal{M}$ and $\Pi_{\mathcal{M}}$ for the set of positional strategies on $\mathcal{M}$.

An MDP $\mathcal{M}$ under a strategy σ results in a Markov chain $\mathcal{M}_\sigma$. If σ is a finite memory strategy, then $\mathcal{M}_\sigma$ is a finite-state Markov chain. The behavior of an MDP $\mathcal{M}$ under a strategy σ and starting state $s \in S$ is defined on a probability space $(Runs_\sigma^{\mathcal{M}}(s), \mathcal{F}_{Runs_\sigma^{\mathcal{M}}(s)}, \Pr_\sigma^{\mathcal{M}}(s))$ over the set of infinite runs of σ with starting state s. Given a random variable $f : Runs^{\mathcal{M}} \to \mathbb{R}$, we denote by $\mathbb{E}_\sigma^{\mathcal{M}}(s)\{f\}$ the expectation of f over the runs of $\mathcal{M}$ from s under strategy σ.

4.1 Optimal Strategies Against ω-Automata

Given an MDP $\mathcal{M} = (S, s_0, A, T, AP, L)$ and deterministic automaton $\mathcal{A} = \langle \Sigma, Q, q_0, \delta, \alpha \rangle$ with $\Sigma = 2^{AP}$, a strategy σ determines sequences X_i, Q_i, and Y_i of random variables denoting the ith state of the MDP, state of the automaton, and action, respectively, where $Q_0 = q_0$ and, for $i > 0$, $Q_i = \delta(Q_{i-1}, L(X_{i-1}))$. We define the optimal satisfaction probability $\mathsf{PSem}_{\mathcal{A}}^{\mathcal{M}}(s)$ as

$$\mathsf{PSem}_{\mathcal{A}}^{\mathcal{M}}(s) = \sup_{\sigma \in \Sigma_{\mathcal{M}}} \mathbb{E}_\sigma^{\mathcal{M}}(s)\{\alpha(\langle Q_0, Q_1, \ldots \rangle)\}.$$

We say that a strategy $\sigma \in \Sigma_{\mathcal{M}}$ is optimal for $\mathcal{A}$ if

$$\mathsf{PSem}_{\mathcal{A}}^{\mathcal{M}}(s) = \mathbb{E}_\sigma^{\mathcal{M}}(s)\{\alpha(\langle Q_0, Q_1, \ldots \rangle)\}.$$

4.2 Optimal Strategies Against Scalar Rewards

Reinforcement learning [26] is a sequential optimization approach where a decision maker learns to optimally resolve a sequence of choices from feedback provided by an unknown or partially known environment. This feedback takes the form of rewards and punishments with strength proportional to the fitness of the decisions taken by the agent as judged by the environment towards some higher-level objectives. RL is inspired by the way dopamine-driven organisms latch on to past rewarding actions. Historically, RL paradigms integrated a myopic way of looking at the reward sequences in the form of discounted reward, with additional notions such as average reward being introduced more recently.

For simplicity, we take an abstract interpretation of RL as a sampling-based optimization approach that asymptotically converges to the optimal values and policies for a given cost objective Agg. We will make some assumptions on RL that are known to hold for popular RL algorithms based on total reward, discounted reward, multi-discounted reward, and average reward RL.

A *rewardful* MDP is a tuple $\mathcal{M} = (S, s_0, A, T, \rho, \mathsf{Agg})$ where S, s_0, A, and T are defined in a similar way as for MDPs, $\rho : S \times A \times S \to \mathcal{D}(\mathcal{C})$ is a (stochastic) reward function with values in a given set $\mathcal{C}$ of colors, and the *aggregator* function $\mathsf{Agg} : \mathcal{C}^\omega \to \mathbb{R}$ is a real-valued optimization objective that converts infinite sequences of colors to real numbers. Traditionally, the set of colors $\mathcal{C}$ is often the set of real numbers encoding a scalar reward signal; however permitting more general sets of colors has paved the way for more expressive reward aggregations, such as state-dependent discounting, reachability reward, and average reward-per-cost objectives. We extend ρ from transitions to runs by $\hat{\rho} : Runs \to \mathcal{D}(\mathcal{C})^\omega$ in a straightforward manner. Some common aggregator functions are listed below.

– The *reachability-sum* (also, stochastic shortest path [3]) aggregator Reach : $(\mathbb{R} \times \{0, 1\})^\omega \to \mathbb{R}$ is defined as

$$\mathsf{Reach} : \langle (r_0, b_0), (r_1, b_1), \ldots \rangle \mapsto \liminf_{n \to \infty} \sum_{0 \le i < \min\{j \le n : b_j = 1\}} r_i,$$

and provides the sum of rewards until the first appearance of $b_i = 1$ (reachability). If $b_i = 0$ for all i, one obtains the *total-sum* aggregator Total : $\mathbb{R}^\omega \to \mathbb{R}$.
– The *variable-discounted-sum* (also, state-dependent discounted) [11] aggregator $D : (\mathbb{R} \times [0, 1))^\omega \to \mathbb{R}$ is defined as

$$D : \langle (r_0, \lambda_0), (r_1, \lambda_1), \ldots \rangle \mapsto \lim_{n \to \infty} \sum_{i < n} \left[\prod_{0 \le j < i} \lambda_j \right] r_i.$$

When the discount is a constant λ, variable-discounted-sum recovers the classical discounted-sum aggregator $D_\lambda : \mathbb{R}^\omega \to \mathbb{R}$.
– The *reward-per-cost* [4] aggregator RpC : $(\mathbb{R} \times \mathbb{R})^\omega \to \mathbb{R}$ is defined as

$$\mathsf{RpC} : \langle (r_0, c_0), (r_1, c_1) \ldots \rangle \mapsto \liminf_{n \to \infty} \frac{\sum_{0 \le i < n} r_i}{\sum_{0 \le i < n} c_i},$$

with suitable assumptions on the cost sequence $\langle c_0, c_1, \ldots \rangle$ to avoid division by zero. For the cost sequence $\langle 1, 1, \ldots \rangle$, reward-per-cost reduces to the *average* aggregator Avg : $\mathbb{R}^\omega \to \mathbb{R}$.
– The *limit inferior* [8] LimInf : $\mathbb{R}^\omega \to \mathbb{R}$ is defined as

$$\mathsf{LimInf} : \langle r_0, r_1, \ldots \rangle \mapsto \liminf_{n \to \infty} r_i.$$

The *limit superior* aggregator LimSup : $\mathbb{R}^\omega \to \mathbb{R}$ is defined analogously.

Since an optimization problem over an MDP is specified by a reward function and an aggregator, we refer to aggregators as optimization objectives (or simply objectives). A rewardful MDP $\mathcal{M}$ under a strategy σ determines a sequence of random colors $\rho(X_{i-1}, Y_i, X_i)_{i \geq 1}$, where X_i and Y_i are the random variables denoting the ith state and action, respectively. For an objective Agg and an initial state s, we define the optimal reward as

$$\mathsf{Agg}_*^{\mathcal{M}}(s) = \sup_{\sigma \in \Sigma} \mathbb{E}_{\sigma}^{\mathcal{M}}(s)\left\{\mathsf{Agg}(\hat{\rho}(\langle X_0, Y_1, X_1, \ldots \rangle))\right\}.$$

We say that a strategy σ is optimal for the objective Agg if, for all $s \in S$,

$$\mathsf{Agg}_*^{\mathcal{M}}(s) = \mathbb{E}_{\sigma}^{\mathcal{M}}(s)\left\{\mathsf{Agg}(\hat{\rho}(\langle X_0, Y_1, X_1, \ldots \rangle))\right\}.$$

Definition 5 (Positional objectives). *An optimization objective Agg is positional if, for every MDP $\mathcal{M}$, there exists a positional optimal strategy for Agg.*

Definition 6 (Convex combination of strategies). *We say that a strategy $\sigma \in \Sigma$ is a convex combination of strategies $\sigma_1, \sigma_2 \in \Sigma$ if, for some $\beta \in [0,1]$, for every run $r \in FRuns$ and every $a \in A$, $\sigma(r)(a) = \beta\sigma_1(r)(a) + (1-\beta)\sigma_2(r)(a)$.*

Definition 7 (Convex objectives). *An objective Agg is convex, if the set of optimal stationary strategies, for every MDP $\mathcal{M}$, is convex. In particular, an objective Agg is convex if any convex combination of positional optimal strategies for Agg is a stationary optimal strategy.*

The objectives listed above are both positional and convex. (See, e.g., [24] for the discounted and average objectives.)

5 Memoryless Reward Translations for RL

We are interested in memoryless reward translation from ω-regular acceptance conditions to optimization problems with various aggregation semantics. Our notion of a memoryless reward translation is similar in spirit to the notion of Blackwell optimality [24] in reducing the average reward to discounted-reward that continues to operate on the same MDP state space, but accommodates the presence of a hyperparameter (the discount factor). Another example of such memoryless translation is the reduction of [13] from limit-deterministic Büchi automata to average-reward objectives with an unknown hyperparameter ζ.

5.1 Memoryless Reward Translation

To compute strategies that maximize the probability that an MDP $\mathcal{M}$ satisfies an ω-regular objective by reinforcement learning, one defines a rewardful MDP $\mathcal{M}^{\times}$ such that, from the optimal strategies for $\mathcal{M}^{\times}$, strategies may be derived for $\mathcal{M}$ that maximize the probability that a run of $\mathcal{M}$ satisfies the objective. The construction of $\mathcal{M}^{\times}$ that we consider builds a product of the transition structures of the MDP $\mathcal{M}$ and the automaton $\mathcal{A}$ that accepts the objective. The reward for a state-action pair of $\mathcal{M}^{\times}$ depends on the state of the automaton and, possibly, on a fixed set of parameters whose values depend on $\mathcal{M}$. Finally, a suitable objective must be chosen. This way of converting an ω-regular objective into an RL objective is quite general and encompasses the approaches adopted in the literature, e.g., [5,13,16,25]. The fixed set of parameters stand for the hyperparameters of reinforcement learning.

With this scheme, even if the strategies computed for $\mathcal{M}^\times$ are positional, the strategies for $\mathcal{M}$ require the memory supplied by the transition structure of the automaton. Since the reward only depends on the state of the automaton, and on no other memory, we call this translation *memoryless*.

In detail, let $\mathcal{A} = \langle \Sigma, Q, q_0, \delta, \alpha \rangle$ be an automaton and P a set of parameter values. A *reward assignment function* for $\mathcal{A}$ and P is a function $f : Q \times \Sigma \times Q \times P \to \mathcal{D}(\mathcal{C})$. Given an MDP $\mathcal{M}$, an automaton $\mathcal{A}$, a reward assignment function f, values for the parameters $\hat{P}$, and an aggregator Agg, we define the *rewardful product* MDP

$$\mathcal{M}^\times = (S \times Q, (s_0, q_0), A \times Q, T^\times, \rho^\times, \text{Agg}),$$

where $T^\times : (S \times Q) \times (A \times Q) \to \mathcal{D}(S \times Q)$ is such that

$$T^\times((s,q),(a,q'))((s',q')) = T(s,a)(s')$$

if $q' \in \delta(q, L(s))$ and 0 otherwise. This definition of $T^\times$ delegates to the strategy for $\mathcal{M}^\times$ the resolution of nondeterminism for nondeterministic automata. The reward function $\rho^\times : (S \times Q) \times (A \times Q) \times (S \times Q) \to \mathcal{D}(\mathcal{C})$ is defined by

$$\rho^\times((s,q),(a,q'),(s',q')) = f(q,a,q',\hat{P})$$

if $q' \in \delta(q, L(s))$ and 0 otherwise.

Definition 8 (Memoryless Translation). *Given $\mathcal{A} = \langle 2^{AP}, Q, q_0, \delta, \alpha \rangle$ and payoff Agg, we say that a memoryless translation exists from the acceptance condition α to the aggregator function Agg, and we write $\alpha \hookrightarrow \text{Agg}$, when there exists a reward function $f : Q \times 2^{AP} \times Q \times P \to \mathcal{D}(\mathcal{C})$ such that, for any MDP $\mathcal{M}$ with atomic propositions AP and for any two strategies $\sigma_1, \sigma_2 \in \Sigma_\mathcal{M}$,*

$$\mathbb{E}_{\sigma_1}^{\mathcal{M}^\times}(s)\{\alpha(\langle Q_0, Q_1, \ldots \rangle)\} < \mathbb{E}_{\sigma_2}^{\mathcal{M}^\times}(s)\{\alpha(\langle Q_0, Q_1, \ldots \rangle)\}$$

if, and only if, for every $\varepsilon > 0$ there exists $\hat{P} \in P$ (that may depend on the MDP) such that

$$\mathbb{E}_{\sigma_1}^{\mathcal{M}^\times}(s)\{\text{Agg}(\hat{\rho}^\times(\langle X_0, Y_1, X_1 \ldots \rangle))\} < \mathbb{E}_{\sigma_2}^{\mathcal{M}^\times}(s)\{\text{Agg}(\hat{\rho}^\times(\langle X_0, Y_1, X_1 \ldots \rangle))\} + \varepsilon$$

on the product $\mathcal{M}^\times$ defined by $\mathcal{M}$, $\mathcal{A}$, and $f(\cdot, \cdot, \cdot, \hat{P})$.

Theorem 2. *The following translations are memoryless:*

1. *good-for-MDPs Büchi objective to reachability-sum aggregator [13];*
2. *good-for-MDPs Büchi objective to variable-discounted-sum aggregator [5];*
3. *good-for-MDPs Büchi objective to average aggregator [14];*
4. *good-for-MDPs Büchi objective to total-sum aggregator [14]; and*
5. *parity objective to reachability-sum aggregator [16].*

Note that, although the reduction of [25] for Rabin automata does not use additional memory, it is incorrect [13], so it is not a memoryless translation. We will show in the next subsection that a memoryless translation for deterministic Rabin automata is impossible if the aggregator is convex.

5.2   Conditions for Memoryless Reductions

We are now in a position to discuss what the properties of acceptance conditions of ω-automata discussed in Sect. 2 entail for a memoryless translation to exist.

Definition 9 (Test MDP). *A test MDP for the set of atomic propositions AP is*

$$\mathcal{M}_{AP} = (2^{AP}, s_0, 2^{AP}, T, AP, L),$$

with one state and one action for each subset of AP, such that, for all states, $L(s) = s$, and $p(s'|s, s') = 1$. The initial state s_0 is a subset of AP.

All sequences of labels in 2^{AP} that start with s_0 may be produced by this *test* MDP.

Theorem 3. *Let $\mathcal{A} = \langle 2^{AP}, Q, q_0, \delta, \alpha \rangle$ be a deterministic automaton and let Agg be a convex objective. Then $\alpha \hookrightarrow$ Agg implies that $\mathcal{E}_a^{\mathcal{A}}$ and $\mathcal{E}_r^{\mathcal{A}}$ are closed under union.*

Proof. Suppose $E_1, \ldots, E_n \in \mathcal{E}_a$ (resp. $\in \mathcal{E}_r$) are accepting (resp. rejecting) eventual sets of $\mathcal{A}$ such that their union is in $\mathcal{E}$. Let $\mathcal{M}_T$ be a test MDP for $\mathcal{A}$ such that $\bigcup_i E_i$ is reachable from $\delta(q_0, s_0)$. Such an s_0 exists because all eventual sets are reachable from the automaton's initial state. Let $\mathcal{M}^{\times}$ be the rewardful product defined by $\mathcal{M}_T$, $\mathcal{A}$, and a reward function f for which $\alpha \hookrightarrow$ Agg.

For each E_i there exists a stationary strategy ξ_i such that a run from any state in $2^{AP} \times (\{q_0\} \cup \bigcup_i E_i)$ eventually dwells in E_i. Since $\alpha \hookrightarrow$ Agg and Agg is convex, $\xi_1, \ldots, \xi_n$ are ε-maximal (resp. ε-minimal), so are their convex combination, and such combination strategies also maximize (resp. minimize) the probability of satisfying α. Since there are combination strategies that visit all states in $E_1 \cup \cdots \cup E_n$ infinitely often, $\mathcal{E}_a$ (resp. $\mathcal{E}_r$) is closed under union. $\square$

Corollary 1. *There exist a Rabin automaton with acceptance conditions α such that, if $\alpha \hookrightarrow$ Agg, then Agg is not convex.*

Proof. The deterministic Rabin automaton in Fig. 3 is such that $\mathcal{E}_a$ is not closed under union. Application of Theorem 3 yields the desired result. $\square$

Remark 3. Note that the complement of α for the Rabin automaton in Fig. 3—a Streett condition that requires that both q_1 and q_2 be visited infinitely often—is not positional. Since $\mathcal{E}_a$ is not closed under union and $\mathcal{E}_r = \{\{q0, q1, q2\}\}$ is upward closed, the acceptance condition of the automaton of Fig. 3 may be expressed as a generalized co-Büchi condition, but not as a plain co-Büchi condition. Correspondingly, the complementary condition may be expressed as a generalized Büchi condition, but not as a plain Büchi condition for the transition structure of Fig. 3.

$$R_1 = \{q_2\}, G_1 = \{q_0, q_1\}$$
$$R_2 = \{q_1\}, G_2 = \{q_0, q_2\}$$

Fig. 3. A Rabin automaton on the alphabet $\Sigma = 2^{\{p\}}$.

The connection between closure under union of *both* $\mathcal{E}_a$ and $\mathcal{E}_r$ (a property called '$\mathcal{E}_a$ has no splits' there) and the existence of positional optimal strategies for *both* players was first established in [20, Theorem 6.2].

To be self-contained, we provide a proof for the direction we need, namely that closedness under union of $\mathcal{E}_r$ entails memoryless strategies for a maximizer, while closedness under union of $\mathcal{E}_a$ entails memoryless strategies for a minimizer.

Lemma 1. *Let $\mathcal{A} = \langle 2^{AP}, Q, q_0, \delta, \alpha \rangle$ be a deterministic automaton and let $\mathcal{A}^c$ be the automaton obtained from $\mathcal{A}$ by complementing the acceptance condition (so that $\mathcal{E}_a^{\mathcal{A}} = \mathcal{E}_r^{\mathcal{A}^c}$ and $\mathcal{E}_r^{\mathcal{A}} = \mathcal{E}_a^{\mathcal{A}^c}$). If no strategy to produce an accepting word on $\mathcal{A}$ ($\mathcal{A}^c$) is positional, then $\mathcal{E}_r^{\mathcal{A}}$ ($\mathcal{E}_a^{\mathcal{A}}$) is not closed under union.*

Proof. Suppose that there is no positional strategy for $\mathcal{A}$ ($\mathcal{A}^c$). Then, for every $E \in \mathcal{E}_a^{\mathcal{A}}$ ($E \in \mathcal{E}_a^{\mathcal{A}^c}$), there exist states in E for which a pure strategy that visits all of E chooses different successors depending on the run up to that point. For at least one such state, the strategy depends on memory essentially, in the sense that, if the strategy is made positional at that state by choosing one successors among all successors chosen by the strategy, the resulting eventual set is a proper subset of E that belongs to $\mathcal{E}_r^{\mathcal{A}}$ ($\mathcal{E}_r^{\mathcal{A}^c}$). Moreover, depending on which successor is chosen, there must be more than one distinct restriction of E that is contained in $\mathcal{E}_r^{\mathcal{A}}$ ($\mathcal{E}_r^{\mathcal{A}^c}$), and the union of all such restrictions must be E. This shows that $\mathcal{E}_r^{\mathcal{A}}$ ($\mathcal{E}_r^{\mathcal{A}^c}$) is not closed under union. Observing that $\mathcal{E}_a^{\mathcal{A}^c} = \mathcal{E}_r^{\mathcal{A}}$ ($\mathcal{E}_a^{\mathcal{A}} = \mathcal{E}_r^{\mathcal{A}^c}$) completes the proof. $\square$

Together with Lemma 1, we obtain the following corollary.

Corollary 2. *Let $\mathcal{A} = \langle 2^{AP}, Q, q_0, \delta, \alpha \rangle$ be a deterministic automaton, let* Agg *be a convex objective, and let $\mathcal{A}^c$ be the automaton obtained from $\mathcal{A}$ by complementing the acceptance condition (so that $\mathcal{E}_a^{\mathcal{A}} = \mathcal{E}_r^{\mathcal{A}^c}$ and $\mathcal{E}_r^{\mathcal{A}} = \mathcal{E}_a^{\mathcal{A}^c}$). Then $\mathcal{A}$ and $\mathcal{A}^c$ have optimal positional strategies.*

Lemma 1 shows that a memoryless translation with a convex aggregator does not exist for deterministic Rabin and Streett automata. Lemma 1 provides a sufficient condition to check for the application of Theorem 3. Intuitively, if we could compute the strategy for Rabin automata with RL, then we could compute positional strategies for the complement of the Rabin condition by maximizing the negative reward. Since the complement of a Rabin condition does not admit positional strategies in general, this is impossible. This impossibility also applies to generalized co-Büchi automata, as observed in Remark 3, as well as to their duals (Streett as the dual to Rabin and generalized Büchi automata as the dual to generalized co-Büchi), with the dual argument: here, it is the strategy of the maximizer itself that requires memory.

Theorem 3, and Corollary 2 provide the entries for the last three columns of Table 1.

6 Conclusion

The study of ω-regular specifications for systems modeled as Markov decision processes was initiated in [30] and [9] resulting in a thriving research community (probabilistic model checking) developing principled techniques [2] and analysis tools [17] for the analysis of probabilistic systems. Reinforcement learning is a classical area of machine learning undergoing remarkable transformation under the deep learning revolution [12,26] provide a snapshot of both classical and recent results.

A combination of ω-regular specifications with RL has potential to positively impact both research fields: for probabilistic model checking, RL offers the twinned advantages of scalability and an ability to reason with system without an explicit model; while for RL, ω-regular objectives provide a rich specification language to express learning requirements instead of scalar rewards. As a result, the study of integrating formal requirements in RL in a way that is correct and efficient has attracted considerable interest [5,13,16]. At the same time, the machine learning community has advocated the need for non-Markovian reward signals in RL [10,28]. These representations often take the form of weighted automata called reward machines [28]. Automata-based rewards also serve as a memory mechanism for reasoning over partially observable environments [29], are useful for defining reward shaping functions to mitigate sparse reward signals [7], and can facilitate explanations of RL systems [31].

When ω-regular objectives were first used in model checking MDPs, deterministic Rabin automata were used to represent the objectives. The same was attempted by the reinforcement learning community when they first turned to ω-regular objectives: they tried the tested route through deterministic Rabin [25], but that translation fails as shown in [13]. This paper answers why any translation of Rabin conditions, even from a deterministic automaton, directly into scalar values is not possible for common reward aggregators used in reinforcement learning, like discounted and average reward. In a broader sense, this paper highlights the existence of positional optimal strategies that may not be computed by reinforcement learning. In so doing, the paper underscores the need for theoretical machine learning research at the promising intersection of the overlapping fields of probabilistic model checking and reinforcement learning.

References

1. de Alfaro, L.: Formal verification of probabilistic systems. Ph.D. thesis, Stanford University (1998)
2. Baier, C., Katoen, J.P.: Principles of Model Checking (Representation and Mind Series). The MIT Press (2008)

3. Bertsekas, D.: Reinforcement Learning and Optimal Control. Athena Scientific (2019)
4. Bouyer, P., Brinksma, E., Larsen, K.G.: Optimal infinite scheduling for multi-priced timed automata. Formal Methods Syst. Des. **32**(1), 3–23 (2008)
5. Bozkurt, A.K., Wang, Y., Zavlanos, M.M., Pajic, M.: Control synthesis from linear temporal logic specifications using model-free reinforcement learning. In: International Conference on Robotics and Automation (ICRA), pp. 10349–10355 (2020)
6. Buhrke, N., Lescow, H., Vöge, J.: Strategy construction in infinite games with Streett and Rabin chain winning conditions. In: Margaria, T., Steffen, B. (eds.) TACAS 1996. LNCS, vol. 1055, pp. 207–224. Springer, Heidelberg (1996). https://doi.org/10.1007/3-540-61042-1_46
7. Camacho, A., Toro Icarte, R., Klassen, T.Q., Valenzano, R.A., McIlraith, S.A.: LTL and beyond: formal languages for reward function specification in reinforcement learning. In: IJCAI, vol. 19, pp. 6065–6073 (2019)
8. Chatterjee, K., Doyen, L., Henzinger, T.A.: A survey of stochastic games with limsup and liminf objectives. In: Albers, S., Marchetti-Spaccamela, A., Matias, Y., Nikoletseas, S., Thomas, W. (eds.) ICALP 2009. LNCS, vol. 5556, pp. 1–15. Springer, Heidelberg (2009). https://doi.org/10.1007/978-3-642-02930-1_1
9. Courcoubetis, C., Yannakakis, M.: The complexity of probabilistic verification. J. ACM **42**(4), 857–907 (1995)
10. Gaon, M., Brafman, R.: Reinforcement learning with non-Markovian rewards. In: Proceedings of the AAAI Conference on Artificial Intelligence, vol. 34–04, pp. 3980–3987 (2020)
11. Gimbert, H., Zielonka, W.: Limits of multi-discounted Markov decision processes. In: Symposium on Logic in Computer Science (LICS 2007), pp. 89–98 (2007)
12. Goodfellow, I., Bengio, Y., Courville, A., Bengio, Y.: Deep Learning, vol. 1. MIT Press (2016)
13. Hahn, E.M., Perez, M., Schewe, S., Somenzi, F., Trivedi, A., Wojtczak, D.: Omega-regular objectives in model-free reinforcement learning. In: Vojnar, T., Zhang, L. (eds.) TACAS 2019. LNCS, vol. 11427, pp. 395–412. Springer, Cham (2019). https://doi.org/10.1007/978-3-030-17462-0_27
14. Hahn, E.M., Perez, M., Schewe, S., Somenzi, F., Trivedi, A., Wojtczak, D.: Faithful and effective reward schemes for model-free reinforcement learning of omega-regular objectives. In: Hung, D.V., Sokolsky, O. (eds.) ATVA 2020. LNCS, vol. 12302, pp. 108–124. Springer, Cham (2020). https://doi.org/10.1007/978-3-030-59152-6_6
15. Hahn, E.M., Perez, M., Schewe, S., Somenzi, F., Trivedi, A., Wojtczak, D.: Good-for-MDPs automata for probabilistic analysis and reinforcement learning. In: TACAS 2020. LNCS, vol. 12078, pp. 306–323. Springer, Cham (2020). https://doi.org/10.1007/978-3-030-45190-5_17
16. Hahn, E.M., Perez, M., Schewe, S., Somenzi, F., Trivedi, A., Wojtczak, D.: Model-free reinforcement learning for stochastic parity games. In: CONCUR: International Conference on Concurrency Theory. LIPIcs, vol. 171, pp. 21:1–21:16 (2020)
17. Kwiatkowska, M., Norman, G., Parker, D.: PRISM 4.0: verification of probabilistic real-time systems. In: Gopalakrishnan, G., Qadeer, S. (eds.) CAV 2011. LNCS, vol. 6806, pp. 585–591. Springer, Heidelberg (2011). https://doi.org/10.1007/978-3-642-22110-1_47
18. Landweber, L.H.: Decision problems for ω-automata. Math. Syst. Theory **3**(4), 376–384 (1969)

19. Löding, C.: Optimal bounds for transformations of ω-automata. In: Rangan, C.P., Raman, V., Ramanujam, R. (eds.) FSTTCS 1999. LNCS, vol. 1738, pp. 97–109. Springer, Heidelberg (1999). https://doi.org/10.1007/3-540-46691-6_8

20. McNaughton, R.: Infinite games played on finite graphs. Ann. Pure Appl. Logic **65**, 149–184 (1993)

21. Perrin, D., Pin, J.É.: Infinite Words: Automata, Semigroups, Logic and Games. Elsevier (2004)

22. Piterman, N., Pnueli, A.: Faster solutions of Rabin and Streett games. In: Symposium on Logic in Computer Science, pp. 275–284 (2006)

23. Pnueli, A.: The temporal logic of programs. In: IEEE Symposium on Foundations of Computer Science, pp. 46–57 (1977)

24. Puterman, M.L.: Markov Decision Processes: Discrete Stochastic Dynamic Programming. Wiley, New York (1994)

25. Sadigh, D., Kim, E., Coogan, S., Sastry, S.S., Seshia, S.A.: A learning based approach to control synthesis of Markov decision processes for linear temporal logic specifications. In: Conference on Decision and Control (CDC), pp. 1091–1096 (2014)

26. Sutton, R.S., Barto, A.G.: Reinforcement Learning: An Introduction, 2nd edn. MIT Press, Cambridge (2018)

27. Thomas, W.: Automata on infinite objects. In: Handbook of Theoretical Computer Science, pp. 133–191. The MIT Press/Elsevier (1990)

28. Toro Icarte, R., Klassen, T., Valenzano, R., McIlraith, S.: Using reward machines for high-level task specification and decomposition in reinforcement learning. In: International Conference on Machine Learning, pp. 2107–2116 (2018)

29. Toro Icarte, R., Waldie, E., Klassen, T., Valenzano, R., Castro, M., McIlraith, S.: Learning reward machines for partially observable reinforcement learning. In: Advances in Neural Information Processing Systems, vol. 32, pp. 15523–15534 (2019)

30. Vardi, M.Y.: Automatic verification of probabilistic concurrent finite state programs. In: Foundations of Computer Science, pp. 327–338 (1985)

31. Xu, Z., Wu, B., Ojha, A., Neider, D., Topcu, U.: Active finite reward automaton inference and reinforcement learning using queries and counterexamples. In: Holzinger, A., Kieseberg, P., Tjoa, A.M., Weippl, E. (eds.) CD-MAKE 2021. LNCS, vol. 12844, pp. 115–135. Springer, Cham (2021). https://doi.org/10.1007/978-3-030-84060-0_8

32. Zielonka, W.: Infinite games on finitely coloured graphs with applications to automata on infinite trees. Theor. Comput. Sci. **200**(1–2), 135–183 (1998)

Reusable Contracts for Safe Integration of Reinforcement Learning in Hybrid Systems

Julius Adelt[✉], Daniel Brettschneider, and Paula Herber[✉]

University of Münster, Einsteinstr. 62, 48149 Münster, Germany
{julius.adelt,daniel.brettschneider,paula.herber}@uni-muenster.de

Abstract. Deductive verification is a powerful approach for establishing crucial safety properties of intelligent hybrid systems. However, deductive verification requires abstract formal descriptions, e.g. properties, contracts, and invariants. Defining these requires a high level of expertise and an enormous amount of manual effort, in particular if the system contains intelligent components such as reinforcement learning agents. In this paper, we propose reusable contract patterns for the safe integration of reinforcement learning in hybrid systems. Our key ideas are threefold: First, we identify recurring verification problems for intelligent hybrid systems that contain reinforcement learning agents. Second, we provide a set of contract patterns that ease the definition of contracts for the safe integration of reinforcement learning agents. Third, we indicate how to derive invariants from the contract patterns. Our contract patterns together with the invariant derivation enable systematic reuse of manually defined hybrid contracts and invariants and reduce the manual effort of the deductive verification process for intelligent hybrid systems.

Keywords: Hybrid systems · Reinforcement learning · Formal verification · Theorem proving · Reusability

1 Introduction

Embedded or cyber-physical systems are often *hybrid systems* (HS), i.e., they combine discrete and continuous behavior, for example, a discrete controller is embedded into a continuous environment. The complexity of HS is ever growing, and they are more and more embedded into highly dynamic environments. To make good control decisions in unexpected situations, HS increasingly use machine learning techniques such as reinforcement learning. At the same time, these systems are often safety-critical, for example, because an autonomous robot may harm pedestrians or a reactor may overheat. This makes it highly desirable to formally verify their correct behavior under all circumstances. One possible solution for this problem is provided by deductive verification [2,8,9]. However, deductive verification typically requires manual definitions of specifications, contracts, and invariants to guide the verification process, which requires a high expertise and a substantial amount of manual time and effort. This is especially true if learning components are used within HS.

A. Bouajjani et al. (Eds.): ATVA 2022, LNCS 13505, pp. 58–74, 2022.
https://doi.org/10.1007/978-3-031-19992-9_4

In this paper, we propose reusable contract patterns for the safe integration of reinforcement learning (RL) in HS. Our key ideas are threefold: First, we identify recurring verification problems for intelligent HS that contain RL agents. Such verification problems often concern crucial properties such as safety and resilience, e.g. they require the RL agent to maintain a minimal safety threshold or to adapt to external disruptions. Second, we provide a set of contract patterns that ease the definition of hybrid contracts (HC) for the safe integration of RL agents. These contracts formally define the safe behavior of the RL agent with respect to the previously identified verification problems. Third, and finally, we indicate how to derive invariants from the contract patterns. These invariants capture conditions that are necessary to maintain safe behavior until the next discrete control decision. Our contract patterns together with the derived invariants enable the reuse of manually defined HC and invariants and thus have the potential to significantly reduce the manual effort for deductive verification.

We illustrate the applicability of our approach with five illustrating examples that use RL for discrete control decisions in continuous or hybrid environments: a temperature control system, a water tank, a water distribution system, an adaptive cruise control and an autonomous factory robot. All of these examples are inspired by existing Simulink models. Simulink [22] is a widely used modeling language and has become the de facto standard for the design of HS in industry. With the RL Toolbox [21], it enables the integration of RL agents. We have translated the Simulink models into formal models in differential dynamic logic (d$\mathcal{L}$) using an automated transformation [17], and carried out all correctness proofs using the interactive theorem prover KeYmaera X [8]. Our experimental results demonstrate the applicability of the proposed contract patterns. For the considered examples, the derived invariants play a key role for verifying the safe integration of RL agents. We deduce from this that they have the potential to significantly reduce the required effort and expertise for deductive verification.

The rest of this paper is structured as follows: In Sect. 2, we introduce preliminaries. In Sect. 3, we summarize related work. In Sect. 4, we introduce our approach for reusable contract patterns. We conclude in Sect. 5.

2 Preliminaries

In this section, we introduce RL, Simulink, the RL Toolbox, d$\mathcal{L}$, and our previously proposed transformation from Simulink to d$\mathcal{L}$.

2.1 Reinforcement Learning

Reinforcement learning is a class of machine learning methods for learning in a trial and error approach by interacting with an environment through actions [30]. The mathematical basis for most RL algorithms are Markov decision processes (MDPs) [30]. An MDP is a tuple (S, A, R, p), where S is a set of possible states, A a set of possible actions, $R \subset \mathbb{R}$ a set of rewards, and p a probability distribution. In an MDP, an agent and an environment interact in discrete time steps. At each

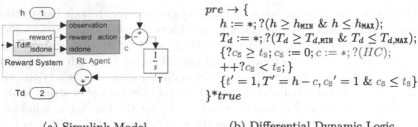

$$pre \rightarrow \{$$
$$h := *; ?(h \geq h_{\text{MIN}} \ \& \ h \leq h_{\text{MAX}});$$
$$T_d := *; ?(T_d \geq T_{d,\text{MIN}} \ \& \ T_d \leq T_{d,\text{MAX}});$$
$$\{?c_s \geq t_s; c_s := 0; c := *; ?(IIC);$$
$$++?c_s < t_s;\}$$
$$\{t' = 1, T' = h - c, c_s' = 1 \ \& \ c_s \leq t_s\}$$
$$\}*true$$

(a) Simulink Model   (b) Differential Dynamic Logic

Fig. 1. Simulink and d$\mathcal{L}$

step t, the agent receives a current state $s_t \in S$ from the environment and chooses an action $a_t \in A$ to interact with it. The environment reacts with a new state $s_{t+1} \in S$ resulting from the action and a numeric reward $r_{t+1} \in R$. The goal of an RL algorithm is to optimize the reward over time by learning a policy $\pi(a|s)$ that determines which actions to take in which states.

2.2 Simulink and the RL Toolbox

Simulink [22] is an industrially well established, graphical modeling language for HS. Simulink models consist of blocks that are connected by discrete or continuous signals. The Simulink block library provides a large set of predefined blocks, from arithmetics over control flow blocks to integrators and complex transformations. The RL Toolbox [21] provides an RL agent block, which samples observations and rewards and chooses actions in fixed intervals.

Figure 1a shows a Simulink model of an intelligent temperature control system, e.g., for cooling a motor or a reactor. The model has two input ports for the current heating value (h) and a desired temperature T_d. The system features an *RL Agent* block, which decides on a cooling value (c) in discrete sample times. The current temperature T is computed in an integrator block by integrating $h - c$ over time. The reward system supplies the RL agent with numeric rewards for keeping the temperature T close to T_d and may terminate the simulation.

2.3 Deductive Verification with the Differential Dynamic Logic

Differential dynamic logic (d$\mathcal{L}$) [26] is a logic for formally specifying and reasoning about properties of HS, which are described as hybrid programs.

The syntax is as follows: $\alpha; \beta$ models a sequential composition of two hybrid programs α and β. $\alpha \cup \beta$ (or $\alpha ++ \beta$) models a non-deterministic choice. A non-deterministic loop α^* executes α zero or more times. The hybrid program $x := e$ evaluates the term e and assigns it to the variable x. $x := *$ denotes a non-deterministic assignment. $?\mathcal{Q}$ is a test formula. A continuous evolution $\{x_1' = \eta_1, x_2' = \eta_2, \ ... \ x_n' = \eta_n \ \& \ \mathcal{Q}\}$ evolves a set of variables x_i with a set of differential equations $x_i' = \eta_i$. A continuous evolution may progress as long as the evolution domain $\mathcal{Q}$ is satisfied. d$\mathcal{L}$ provides two modalities for reasoning about reachable states of hybrid programs. $[\alpha]\phi$ states that a formula ϕ holds in every state reachable by α. $\langle\alpha\rangle\phi$ states that there exists a state reachable by α in which ϕ holds. Specifications are defined as $pre \rightarrow [\alpha]post$.

A d$\mathcal{L}$ specification can be deductively verified with the interactive theorem prover KeYmaera X [8]. Proofs in KeYmaera X are based on the d$\mathcal{L}$ sequent calculus, which enables applying inference rules to simplify d$\mathcal{L}$ formulas into subgoals. One of the central proof rules is the *loop* rule:

$$\frac{(1.)\ \Gamma \vdash J, \Delta \quad (2.)\ J \vdash [\alpha]J \quad (3.)\ J \vdash P}{\Gamma \vdash [\alpha^*]P, \Delta}$$

The rule enables verifying non-deterministic loops using an invariant, namely a set of properties J, which (1.) holds initially, (2.) holds before and after each repetition, and (3.) implies the postcondition P. By proving all three subgoals, the sequent $\Gamma \vdash [\alpha^*]P$ is proven (within an arbitrary context Δ).

2.4 Transformation from Simulink to d$\mathcal{L}$

In [17], we have presented an automated transformation of hybrid Simulink models into d$\mathcal{L}$. To integrate RL agents safely into the transformation, we have proposed to define the safe behavior of RL agents with hybrid contracts (HC), which specify assumptions on the inputs and guarantees on the outputs [2,18].

A simplified illustrating example is shown in Fig. 1b. The d$\mathcal{L}$ model corresponds to the intelligent temperature control system in Fig. 1a. The inputs h and T_d are captured by non-deterministic assignments with constraining tests, i.e., an arbitrary value from the given input range can be assigned at any time. The integrator block for the temperature T is captured by a continuous evolution $T' = h - c$. The agent selects a cooling value as an action (c) restricted by the HC in discrete sampling steps, i.e. whenever the time since the last decision c_S reaches the sample time t_S. Otherwise, it does nothing. The clock variable c_S is evolved in the continuous evolution and $c_S \leq t_S$ is added to the evolution domain to ensure that no discrete sampling step is missed. A non-deterministic repetition models the global simulation loop.

3 Related Work

In the last decade, a variety of approaches have been proposed for the formal verification of hybrid systems that are modeled in Simulink. For example, in [23], Simulink is translated into hybrid automata. However, the models are verified by exploring the state space via reachability analysis, which does not scale for larger systems. In [5,32], the authors present an approach to automatically transform Simulink models into Hybrid CSP and enable verification with hybrid Hoare logic in the HHL Prover. They thereby inherit compositionality from a

62   J. Adelt et al.

highly expressive process algebra. However, both the property specification and
the verification process with Hybrid CSP require a very high level of expertise.
Formal methods to ensure safety of RL have seen increasing interest in the last
years. A common approach is the use of a formally synthesised shield [3,14],
which substitutes unsafe for safe actions. In [9], the safety of an RL controller
is ensured via verified runtime monitors that are automatically generated from
d$\mathcal{L}$ models. In [25] the authors ensure contracts for complex system components
using a simplex architecture. All of these approaches, however, require formal
specifications, but do not provide any guidance on how to define these.

There exists a broad body of work on reusability in deductive verification,
and techniques to enable proof reuse have been incorporated in many verification
systems, including KeY [4] and KeYmaera X [8]. An overview over the reuse
of specifications, intermediate representations, and verification tools is given in
[11]. However, all of these approaches address reusability from a perspective
of building proofs technically, and not from an application point of view, i.e.,
they do not address the question how we can reuse specifications or contracts
we have specified for one application to similar applications. The same holds
for the broad spectrum of approaches for automated invariant generation, for
example, [13,27]: they tend to focus on technology for building proofs and not
on leveraging knowledge about the application [11].

Some application-specific specification patterns have been proposed for complex verification problems, for example, for structured arrays in [10], or for the
parallel prefix sum in [28]. In [6], a contract-based approach to analyze systems
from various application domains is proposed, in [12], abstract method calls for
structured reuse are proposed, and in [31], the reuse of proofs for variants of software product lines. However, to the best of our knowledge, none of the existing
approaches proposes contract patterns that are derived from recurring verification problems in intelligent hybrid systems and their requirements and ease the
specification and verification of similar systems.

4   Reusable Hybrid Contracts

In intelligent hybrid systems (HS), an intelligent discrete controller typically controls a continuous environment. This approach follows the classical architecture
of HS [15] with a controller that takes discrete control decisions, and a plant,
whose continuous behavior is described by differential equations. In this paper,
we consider intelligent HS where the discrete controller is implemented as an RL
agent (for example with the RL Toolbox), and the plant is modeled in Simulink.
For the safe integration of RL in HS, we have proposed to define the safe behavior
of RL agents with hybrid contracts (HC) in [2]. HC precisely define the safety-
relevant behavior of an RL component and abstract from the concrete behavior
learned during execution. For example, for an autonomous robot, a contract
may describe collision avoidance, but omit navigation and planning. HC can be
enforced at run-time, e.g., with automatically generated run-time monitors [9].
For system verification, we replace RL agents with their HC, and deductively

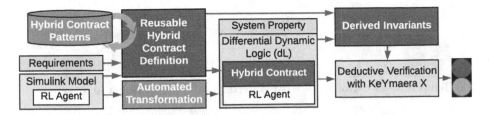

Fig. 2. Deductive Verification with Reusable Hybrid Contracts

verify safety properties under the assumption that the agent adheres to its contract with the interactive theorem prover KeYmaera X. However, the process of defining contracts and their use for system verification is time-intensive and requires a high level of expertise.

In this paper, we propose reusable HC patterns for recurring verification problems of intelligent HS. We have identified the following kinds of properties that are crucial for many intelligent HS with RL agents:

- *Threshold properties.* Many control systems have to maintain minimal or maximal values of a process variable, e.g., a maximal temperature to avoid overheating, or a minimal distance between two cars [15].
- *Range properties.* Often, process variables have to be kept within a lower and an upper limit. For example, the temperature must be kept within a certain range, or the fluid in a tank should neither overflow nor run dry [15].
- *Recovery properties.* One of the major strengths of intelligent HS is their ability to function in dynamic environments. A recurring verification problem in this context is to recover from unexpected disruptions, i.e., if the process variable falls below a certain threshold due to external stressors, e.g., a pump failure, the system should recover in a timely manner [7].
- *Resilience properties.* The ability of a system to recover from external disruptions is an important step towards resilient system design. To increase resilience, systems are often required to remain operational in the presence of stressors and to dynamically adapt their functioning in case stressors persist [16]. To achieve this, many resilient systems offer a degraded service level [29]. A crucial property for such systems is that they maintain safety properties while always providing at least the degraded service level.

For each of these kinds of properties, we identify the elements that are relevant to precisely capture the safety-relevant behavior of an RL discrete controller and its interplay with the continuous environment. From these elements, we build an HC pattern, which can be used to construct HC for RL agents. The pattern involves the relevant state variables together with actions and reactions, and their timing behavior. Our pattern-based approach enables the designer to define HC from a template and helps to identify relevant variables and relations. This eases the deductive verification process and reduces the required expertise.

The overarching goal of our method is shown in Fig. 2. The HC patterns we define are embedded into our deductive verification process presented in

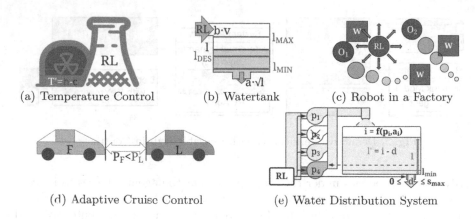

(a) Temperature Control   (b) Watertank   (c) Robot in a Factory

(d) Adaptive Cruise Control   (e) Water Distribution System

Fig. 3. Illustrating Examples

[17,18]. The key idea is to derive reusable HC definitions from Simulink models (which may contain an RL agent) and their requirements. By identifying reusable patterns in these contract definitions, we incrementally build a library of HC design patterns, which a designer can select from for the verification of other systems. These HC design patterns significantly ease the definition of HC. A major challenge in deductive verification is finding invariants, properties which hold throughout all runs of a system and which imply the system property. Invariants are closely related to the HC and typically contain similar elements, e.g., relevant state variables and actions. As a consequence, they can often be derived from HC design patterns. Together with our previously proposed transformation from Simulink to d$\mathcal{L}$, the invariant derivation significantly reduces the effort for the deductive verification of intelligent HS with KeYmaera X.

In the following, we first introduce five case studies as illustrating examples. All of these are inspired by existing Simulink models and demonstrate how HS that use RL are typically modeled [20]. Then, we define HC patterns and indicate how to derive invariants for the four kinds of properties defined above: threshold properties, range properties, recovery properties and resilience properties. For each pattern, we discuss the recurring elements constituting the pattern as well as the invariant derivation, and illustrate its application with our case studies.

4.1   Illustrating Examples

To illustrate the applicability of our approach, we present a set of illustrating examples, which represent typical HS that use RL.

Temperature Control. In the temperature control system in Fig. 3a, an RL agent controls the temperature T in a reactor by applying a cooling value c. At the same time, the reactor temperature can heat up with a heating value $h \in [h_{MIN}, h_{MAX}]$. The change in temperature is described by the differential equation $T' = h - c$. Furthermore, a sudden disruption, e.g. overheating due to a coolant leakage, is possible. This changes the temperature suddenly, possibly to unsafe values.

Water Tank. Figure 3b depicts a Simulink water tank example from the RL Toolbox [21]. The RL agent is tasked with keeping the water level l in a certain range $[l_{\text{MIN}}, l_{\text{MAX}}]$. The agent can change the inflow into the tank by setting a voltage v. The outflow out of the tank is dependant on the square root of the current water height. b and a are proportional constants for the in- an outflow respectively. The water level follows the differential equation $l' = b \cdot v - a \cdot \sqrt{l}$.

Autonomous Robot. Figure 3c depicts our case study from [2], which is inspired by [19]. It consists of multiple robots, i.e., an RL robot (RL) and two opponents (A,B) in an abstract factory setting. The RL robot is tasked with reaching workstations (W) while avoiding opponents. The collision avoidance concept of this example is inspired by [24]. If the distance of an opponent to the robot ($d(p_r, p_o)$) falls below a safety threshold θ_o, the opponent evades. To ensure that the opponent evades successfully, we require the RL robot to stop in time to not surpass the safety threshold θ_o of the opponent. The position of each robot $Rob \in \{RL\} \cup \{A, B\}$ is a vector $p_{Rob} = (x_{Rob}, y_{Rob})$. Robots move with $x'_{Rob} = v_{x,Rob}$ and $y'_{Rob} = v_{y,Rob}$. The overall velocity of a robot is $v_{Rob} = \|(v_{x,Rob}, v_{y,Rob})\|$.

Adaptive Cruise Control (ACC). Figure 3d depicts an adaptive cruise control system inspired by [21]. A follower car controlled by an RL agent (F) has to keep a minimum distance to a leading car (L) $p_F < p_L$. The cars change positions with $p'_{car} = v_{car}$ and $v'_{car} = a_{car}$. Accelerations (a_{car}) are constant between decisions.

Water Distribution System (WDS). Figure 3e depicts a water distribution system. It is based on another Simulink example [21], and we have extended it with pump failures and with varying service levels in [1]. The system features four pumps ($p_1 - p_4$) that pump fluid from a reservoir into a water tank. Pumps can fail during usage and can be repaired. The systems RL agent can activate three of the pumps (actions $a_1 - a_3$), and it can limit the outflow to a maximum supply s. The fourth pump is a backup pump, which is automatically activated if the water falls below a certain threshold. If a pump is turned on by the RL agent and is functional, it pumps fluid with a constant rate r into the tank. The overall inflow i is determined by the activated pumps. The fluid in the tank is used to satisfy a consumer demand $d \in [0, s]$. The water level l evolves with $l' = i - d$.

4.2 Recurring Elements

To define HC patterns, we have first identified a set of recurring elements that are needed to capture the safety-relevant behavior of RL agents for the verification problems we consider in this paper. From these elements, HC can be systematically constructed using the HC patterns we define in the following subsections.

1. *Critical Variable (var_{sc}).* The process variable that should be kept above or below a threshold or in a certain range.
2. *Current State (state).* The current system state (including the values of variables and system parameters).

3. *Controller Action (*action*)*. The action chosen by an RL controller.
4. *Maximum Effect Time (t_E)*. The maximum time for which we need to consider the effect of a chosen action.
5. *Worst-Case Reaction (*wcreaction*)*. The worst case reaction of the overall hybrid system in the current state with the currently chosen action.
6. *Relation ($\sim$)*. A relation to a threshold or bound with $\sim \in \{\geq, >, <, \leq\}$.
7. *Threshold (θ)*. A lower or upper bound on a critical variable.
8. *Degraded Service Level (*$service_{deg}$*)*. A degraded service level an RL agent may choose to dynamically adapt to persisting stressors.

4.3 Threshold Pattern

If an RL agent has to keep a critical variable above or below a threshold, this means that it has to be ensured that for each system state and for each control decision in which a new action is chosen, the worst case reaction of the overall system still maintains the threshold. The worst case reaction depends on the current state and chosen action. The maximum effect time is the time between control decisions , i.e., one sample time (t_S). Often, *wcreaction* can be divided into the effect of the RL agents action and the worst case reaction of the environment. For example, for the temperature control, the worst case reaction is a combination of the effect of the cooling action chosen by the RL agent and the heating by the environment. For simple differential equations, whose solutions can be represented in d$\mathcal{L}$, *wcreaction* corresponds to this solution with worst case assumptions applied for one sample time. For more complex differential equations, over-approximations may be necessary (e.g. for the water tank).

Definition 1: Threshold Pattern

$$var_{sc} \sim \theta \rightarrow var_{sc} + wcreaction(state, action, t_S) \sim \theta$$

Invariant Derivation. To verify threshold properties, we need to establish that the controllers actions are safe in every reachable state, including intermediate states between control decisions. Thus, we can derive loop invariants that capture safe behavior at arbitrary time steps by replacing the worst case reaction or sample time t_S by the remaining time $t_S - c_S$, where c_S is the time since the last decision (cf. Sect. 2.4), and use this for loop induction.

Illustrating Examples. Table 1 shows threshold properties, hybrids contracts, and derived invariants that are built from the threshold contract pattern for our illustrating examples. For brevity, assumptions are omitted here. To avoid overheating, the *Temperature Control* system has to keep $T \leq T_{MAX}$. The controller chooses a cooling value c (*action*). The worst case reaction of the environment is the maximum possible heating h_{MAX}, which leads to a worst case change in temperature of $+h_{MAX} \cdot t_S - c \cdot t_S$ until the next sample time. The *Water Tank* has to ensure $l > l_{MIN}$, i.e., the tank may never run empty. The controller chooses a voltage v, which determines the inflow $v \cdot b$ until the next sample time t_S. The

Table 1. Threshold Properties, Contracts, and Invariants

	Pattern	var_{sc}	$+wcreaction(state, action, t_s)$	$\sim$	θ
Temp Ctrl	Property	$pre \to [\alpha]$	$T \leq T_{MAX}$		
	Contract	T	$+(h_{MAX} - c) \cdot t_s$	$\leq$	T_{MAX}
	Invariant	T	$+(h_{MAX} - c) \cdot (t_s - c_s)$	$\leq$	T_{MAX}
Water Tank	Property	$pre \to [\alpha]$	$l > l_{MIN}$		
	Contract	l	$+(v \cdot b - a \cdot \sqrt{l}) \cdot t_s$	$>$	l_{MIN}
	Invariant	l	$+(v \cdot b - a \cdot \sqrt{l}) \cdot (t_s - c_s)$	$>$	l_{MIN}
Robot	Property	$pre \to [\alpha]$	$d(p_r, p_o) > \theta_o$		
	Contract	$d(p_r, p_o)$	$-(v_r + v_{o,MAX}) \cdot t_s$	$>$	θ_o
	Invariant	$d(p_r, p_o)$	$-(v_r + v_{o,MAX}) \cdot (t_s - c_s)$	$>$	θ_o
ACC	Property	$pre \to [\alpha]$	$p_F < p_L$		
	Contract	$p_L - p_F$	$-(v_F \cdot t_s + \frac{a_F \cdot (t_s)^2}{2})$	$>$	$\frac{(v_F + a_F \cdot t_s)^2}{2 \cdot b}$
	Invariant	$p_L - p_F$	$-(v_F \cdot (t_s - c_s) + \frac{a_F \cdot ((t_s - c_s))^2}{2})$	$>$	$\frac{(v_F + a_F \cdot (t_s - c_s))^2}{2 \cdot b}$
WDS	Property	$pre \to [\alpha]$	$l > l_{MIN}$		
	Contract	l	$+(0 \cdot r - s) \cdot t_s$	$>$	l_{MIN}
	Invariant	l	$+(0 \cdot r - s) \cdot (t_s - c_s)$	$>$	l_{MIN}

flow of the tank is described by the differential equation $l' = b \cdot v - a \cdot \sqrt{l}$. The differential equations solution cannot be defined in KeYmaera X. Because of this, we use a linear over-approximation of the flow where $\sqrt{l}$ is treated as a constant value until the next sample time. The RL *Robot* has to maintain a safety distance to the opponent $d(p_r, p_o) > \theta_o$. In the contract, we omit directions. Thus, as a worst case reaction, the agent decreases distance with its velocity v_r and the opponent with maximum velocity $v_{o,MAX}$ for one sample time t_s. In the *ACC*, the follower may not crash into the lead car. For this, the distance to the lead car must always be greater than the followers maximum braking distance, which can be calculated from the current velocity, chosen acceleration and maximal braking force b ($\theta = (v_F + a_F \cdot t_s)^2 / (2 \cdot b)$). The effect of choosing an acceleration $a_F \geq 0$ is a reduction of the current distance ($p_L - p_F$) by $v_F \cdot t_s + a_F \cdot t_s^2 / 2$. The worst case reaction of the environment is that the opponent stopps instantly, i.e., $v_L = a_L = 0$. In the *WDS*, the RL agent also has to keep the water level above a minimum $l > l_{MIN}$. As an action, the agent may limit the outflow s_{MAX} and activate pumps ($a_1 - a_3$). The worst case reaction of the environment is a demand that fully exploits the supply limit (i.e. $d = s$) together with a failure of all three pumps, which sets the inflow to zero independent of pump activations.

4.4 Range Pattern

An HC pattern for keeping a critical variable var_{sc} inside a range $[\theta_{MIN}, \theta_{MAX}]$ can be constructed by combining two threshold patterns for staying above θ_{MIN} and below θ_{MAX}. Note that $\geq$ and $\leq$ can be replaced with $>$ and $<$.

Table 2. Additional Properties, Contracts, and Invariants for Ranges

	Pattern	var_{sc}	$+wcreaction(state, action, t_{\mathrm{S}})$	$\sim \theta$
Temp Ctrl	Property	$pre \rightarrow [\alpha]\ T{\geq}T_{\mathtt{MIN}}$		
	Contract	T	$+(h_{\mathtt{MIN}} - c) \cdot t_{\mathrm{S}}$	$\geq T_{\mathtt{MIN}}$
	Invariant	T	$+(h_{\mathtt{MIN}} - c) \cdot (t_{\mathrm{S}} - c_{\mathrm{S}})$	$\geq T_{\mathtt{MIN}}$
WDS	Property	$pre \rightarrow [\alpha]\ l{<}l_{\mathtt{MAX}}$		
	Contract	l	$+((a_1 + a_2 + a_3) \cdot r) - 0) \cdot t_{\mathrm{S}}$	$< l_{\mathtt{MAX}}$
	Invariant	l	$+((a_1 + a_2 + a_3) \cdot r) - 0) \cdot (t_{\mathrm{S}} - c_{\mathrm{S}})$	$< l_{\mathtt{MAX}}$

Definition 2: Range Pattern

$$var_{sc} \geq \theta_{\mathtt{MIN}} \rightarrow var_{sc} + wcreaction_{\mathtt{MIN}}(state, action, t_{\mathrm{S}}) \geq \theta_{\mathtt{MIN}}$$
$$var_{sc} \leq \theta_{\mathtt{MAX}} \rightarrow var_{sc} + wcreaction_{\mathtt{MAX}}(state, action, t_{\mathrm{S}}) \leq \theta_{\mathtt{MAX}}$$

Invariant Derivation. Analogously to the threshold properties, invariants for range properties can be derived by replacing t_{S} by $t_{\mathrm{S}} - c_{\mathrm{S}}$.

Illustrating Examples. The applicability of the range pattern is illustrated by the additional properties, threshold contracts and invariants for the temperature control, the water tank, and the WDS shown in Table 2. For the *Temperature Control* system, the temperature is now kept in a range $[T_{\mathtt{MIN}}, T_{\mathtt{MAX}}]$. To achieve this, we add a second threshold contract for $T_{\mathtt{MIN}}$. Note that the worst case reactions $wcreaction_{\mathtt{MIN}}$ and $wcreaction_{\mathtt{MAX}}$ are dependant on the respective thresholds, i.e. while the worst-case reaction for the upper bound involves the maximum possible heating value $h_{\mathtt{MAX}}$, the contract for the lower bound involves the minimal possible heating value $h_{\mathtt{MIN}}$. The range patterns for the water tank and the ACC example work analogously and are omitted here for brevity. In the *WDS*, the water level should be kept in $(l_{\mathtt{MIN}}, l_{\mathtt{MAX}})$. The worst case reaction w.r.t. the upper bound is a maximum possible inflow (i.e. none of the pumps activated by the RL agent fail) combined with a minimal possible outflow ($d = 0$).

4.5 Range Recovery Pattern

If a safety-critical variable changes its value unexpectedly because of a disruption, the system should recover back into a safe range within a given maximum recovery time. To achieve this, the RL agent needs to ensure that whenever the process variable is out of the safe range, an action is chosen that guarantees that the process variable reaches the safe range within the maximum recovery time, even if the system shows worst case behavior. After recovery or without disruptions, the variable should be kept inside the safe range.

Our Range recovery pattern consists of two parts. The upper two lines describe recovery. The effect of the action and worst case reaction takes place during the whole revocery time. Thus, the *wcreaction* that may be permitted by the contract depends on the remaining recovery time (t_R), which can be calculated from the time of the last disruption ($t_{D,LAST}$) and the maximum recovery time ($t_{R,MAX}$). The recovery part states that whenever out of range $\neg(var_{sc} \sim \theta)$, the agent chooses an action which brings var_{sc} back into the safe range within the remaining recovery time (t_R), even with a worst case system reaction. The lower two lines (analogous to the range pattern) ensure that the safety critical variable is kept in the safe range after recovery or as long as no disruptions occur.

Definition 3: Range Recovery Pattern

$$\neg(var_{sc} \geq \theta_{\text{MIN}}) \rightarrow var_{sc} + wcreaction_{\text{MIN}}(state, action, t_R) \geq \theta_{\text{MIN}}$$
$$\neg(var_{sc} \leq \theta_{\text{MAX}}) \rightarrow var_{sc} + wcreaction_{\text{MAX}}(state, action, t_R) \leq \theta_{\text{MAX}}$$
$$var_{sc} \geq \theta_{\text{MIN}} \quad \rightarrow var_{sc} + wcreaction_{\text{MIN}}(state, action, t_S) \geq \theta_{\text{MIN}}$$
$$var_{sc} \leq \theta_{\text{MAX}} \quad \rightarrow var_{sc} + wcreaction_{\text{MAX}}(state, action, t_S) \leq \theta_{\text{MAX}}$$

Invariant Derivation. For the deductive verification of range recovery patterns, an invariant can be used that states that a disruption either just occured within the current sample time ($t - t_{D,LAST} \leq c_S$), or that the recovery contract is maintained. The recovery part of the contract (upper two lines) is already strong enough as it reasons about the remaining time and can thus directly be used in the invariant. For the range part (lower two lines), analogously to range properties, invariants can be derived by replacing t_S by $t_S - c_S$.

Illustrating Examples. In Table 3, the application of the range recovery pattern is illustrated for the temperature control system and the water tank. As desired properties, we require the system to always keep the temperature resp. water level within a certain range if the time since the last disruption is greater than the maximal recovery time. The HC for the RL agents can directly be constructed from our HC pattern. For the temperature control, if the temperature is too low, the worst case reaction is minimal heating together with the chosen cooling value. The effect must be strong enough to reach or exceed T_{MIN} within the remaining recovery time $t_R = t_{D,LAST} + t_{R,MAX} - t$. The range patterns are applied as before, and the contract for the water tank is built analogously.

4.6 Resilience Contracts

If external stressors persist, e.g., components of a model fail permanently, recovery may not be possible. Resilient systems can dynamically adapt to such persisting stressors by, e.g., switching to a degraded service level. In the WDS, a degraded service level is modeled by limiting the maximum supply, and a backup pump ensures that the limited supply can always be provided even if all other pumps fail. For the autonomous robot, an external stressor might lead to opponents getting closer to the RL robot than expected, and the RL robot provides a degraded service level where it just stops as long as this stressor persists.

Table 3. Range Recovery Properties, Contracts, and Invariants

	Pattern	$var_{sc} \sim_a \theta \;\rightarrow\; var_{sc} + wcreaction(, action, t_R)$	$\sim_g$	θ
Temp Ctrl	Property	$pre \rightarrow [\alpha]\,(t - t_{D,LAST} > t_{R,MAX} \rightarrow T_{MIN} \leq T \leq T_{MAX})$		
	$\text{Recovery}_{T_{MIN}}$	$T < T_{MIN} \quad\rightarrow\quad T + (h_{MIN} - c) \cdot (t_{D,LAST} + t_{R,MAX} - t)$	$\geq$	T_{MIN}
	$\text{Recovery}_{T_{MAX}}$	$T > T_{MAX} \quad\rightarrow\quad T + (h_{MAX} - c) \cdot (t_{D,LAST} + t_{R,MAX} - t)$	$\leq$	T_{MAX}
	$\text{Range}_{T_{MIN}}$	$T \geq T_{MIN} \quad\rightarrow\quad T + (h_{MIN} - c) \cdot t_S$	$\geq$	T_{MIN}
	$\text{Range}_{T_{MAX}}$	$T \leq T_{MAX} \quad\rightarrow\quad T + (h_{MAX} - c) \cdot t_S$	$\leq$	T_{MAX}
	Invariant	$t - t_{D,LAST} \leq c_S \vee ((\text{Recovery}_{T_{MIN}}) \wedge (\text{Recovery}_{T_{MAX}}) \wedge$ $(T \geq T_{MIN} \rightarrow T + (h_{MIN} - c) \cdot (t_S - c_S) \geq T_{MIN}) \wedge$ $(T \leq T_{MAX} \rightarrow T + (h_{MAX} - c) \cdot (t_S - c_S) \leq T_{MAX}))$		
Water Tank	Property	$pre \rightarrow [\alpha]\,(t - t_{D,LAST} > t_{R,MAX} \rightarrow l_{MIN} < l < l_{MAX})$		
	$\text{Recovery}_{l_{MIN}}$	$l \leq l_{MIN} \quad\rightarrow\quad l + (v \cdot b - a \cdot \sqrt{l}) \cdot (t_{D,LAST} + t_{R,MAX} - t)$	$>$	l_{MIN}
	$\text{Recovery}_{l_{MAX}}$	$l \geq l_{MAX} \quad\rightarrow\quad l + (v \cdot b - a \cdot \sqrt{l}) \cdot (t_{D,LAST} + t_{R,MAX} - t)$	$<$	l_{MAX}
	$\text{Range}_{l_{MIN}}$	$l > l_{MIN} \quad\rightarrow\quad l + (v \cdot b - a \cdot \sqrt{l}) \cdot t_S$	$>$	l_{MIN}
	$\text{Range}_{l_{MAX}}$	$l < l_{MAX} \quad\rightarrow\quad l + (v \cdot b - a \cdot \sqrt{l}) \cdot t_S$	$<$	l_{MAX}
	Invariant	$t - t_{D,LAST} \leq c_S \vee ((\text{Recovery}_{l_{MIN}}) \wedge (\text{Recovery}_{l_{MAX}}) \wedge$ $(l > l_{MIN} \rightarrow l + (v \cdot b - a \cdot \sqrt{l}) \cdot (t_S - c_S) > l_{MIN} \wedge$ $(l < l_{MAX} \rightarrow l + (v \cdot b - a \cdot \sqrt{l}) \cdot (t_S - c_S) < l_{MAX}))$		

A crucial property of resilient systems is that they are always safe, e.g., safety thresholds are maintained, while at least the degraded service level $service_{deg}$ is always provided. For the HC of an RL agent controlling a resilient system, this means that it may only choose an action with a higher service level than $service_{deg}$ if it can guarantee to provide this service level until the next control decision, even with a worst case system reaction. If threshold properties are considered, this means that we can only choose a higher service level if the safety threshold θ_{safe} is not yet tight ($var_{sc} \sim \theta_{safe} \pm \Delta_{MIN}$). If the process variable is to close to the safety threshold, the RL agent provides the degraded service level.

Definition 4: Resilience Pattern

$$var_{sc} \sim \theta_{safe} \pm \Delta_{MIN} \;\rightarrow\; \frac{action \geq service_{deg} \wedge}{var_{sc} + wcreaction(state, action, t_S) \sim \theta_{safe}}$$

$$\neg(var_{sc} \sim \theta_{safe} \pm \Delta_{MIN}) \rightarrow action = service_{deg}$$

Invariant Derivation. An invariant can be derived from the HC pattern by using a disjunction of the case where the agent is able to provide a higher service level for the remaining sample time and the case where the agent provides the degraded service level. For the former, we can again replace t_S by $t_S - c_S$. In addition, we explicitly state that the agent provides at least degraded service.

Illustrating Example. The resilience properties, contracts, and invariants for the WDS and the autonomous robot are shown in Table 4. In the *WDS*, the RL agent

Table 4. Resilience Properties, Contracts, and Invariants

Pattern	$v_{sc} \sim \theta_{safe} \pm \Delta_{MIN} \quad \rightarrow \quad act \geq serv_{deg} \wedge v_{sc} + wcr(, act, t_S) \sim \theta_{safe}$	
	$\neg(v_{sc} \sim \theta_{safe} \pm \Delta_{MIN}) \quad \rightarrow \quad act = serv_{deg}$	
WDS Property	$pre \rightarrow [\alpha] \, l > l_{MIN} \wedge s \geq s_{deg}$	
Serv$_{W,high}$	$l > l_{MIN} + \Delta_{suff} \quad \rightarrow \quad s \geq s_{deg} \quad \wedge \quad l + (0 \cdot r - s) \cdot t_S > l_{MIN}$	
Serv$_{W,deg}$	$l \leq l_{MIN} + \Delta_{suff} \quad \rightarrow \quad s = s_{deg}$	
Invariant	$(l + (0 \cdot r - s) \cdot (t_S - c_S) > l_{MIN} \vee s = s_{deg}) \wedge s \geq s_{deg}$	
Robot Property	$pre \rightarrow [\alpha] \, (d(p_r, p_o) > \theta_o \vee v_r = 0) \wedge v_r \geq 0$	
Serv$_{R,high}$	$d(p_r, p_o) > \theta_o \quad \rightarrow \quad v_r \geq 0 \quad \wedge \quad d(p_r, p_o) - (v_r + v_{MAX,o}) \cdot t_S > \theta_o$	
Serv$_{W,deg}$	$d(p_r, p_o) \leq \theta_o \quad \rightarrow \quad v_r = 0$	
Invariant	$(d(p_r, p_o) - (v_{RL} + v_{MAX,o}) \cdot (t_S - c_S) > \theta_o \vee v_r = 0) \wedge v_r \geq 0$	

may limit the service level by setting the maximum water supply s provided to consumers. For the worst case, in which all pumps fail, the system features a backup pump, which ensures that a minimum amount of water can be supplied to critical consumers (degraded service s_{deg}). A crucial system property is that the tank never runs dry while the degraded service can always be provided. To verify this property, we ensure that the RL agent only chooses $s \geq s_{deg}$ if a sufficient amount of water $l > l_{MIN} + \Delta_{suff}$ is available. Otherwise, s_{deg} must be chosen. For the autonomous *Robot*, a degraded service level is to just stop ($v_r = 0$). A crucial safety property of the robot is to maintain a safety distance or to stop. For the RL agent, this means that if the distance to the opponent is big enough ($d(p_r, p_o) > \theta_o + 0$), it may choose any velocity $v_r \geq 0$ which maintains the safety distance. If the distance is violated, the RL agent stops.

4.7   Deductive Verification in KeYmaera X

We have deductively verified most of the properties used as illustrating examples in KeYmaera X, namely threshold properties for all of our case studies, range properties for the temperature control and the water tank, range recovery for the temperature control, and resilience for the WDS and the autonomous robot. The proof files can be found at https://www.uni-muenster.de/EmbSys/research/Simulink2dL.html. To define the necessary invariants, the derived invariants mainly needed to be supplemented by simple variable relations in all of our case studies, e.g., non-negativity conditions and relations between clocks. This shows that the derived invariants play a key role for deductive verification and significantly ease the verification process.

5   Conclusion

In this paper, we have proposed an approach for making hybrid contracts for the safe integration of reinforcement learning into hybrid systems reusable. Our main contribution is a set of HC patterns, which are derived from recurring verification problems in such systems. In addition, for each contract pattern, we have discussed how invariants that play a key role for deductive verification can be derived from the resulting HC. Our HC patterns help the designer to construct HC from predefined elements. The derived invariants help the designer to perform deductive system verification, i.e., to verify that the overall system satisfies safety and resilience properties under the assumption that the RL components adhere to their HC. Together, the HC patterns and derived invariants have the potential to significantly decrease the time and effort for deductive verification of intelligent HS that use RL. We have illustrated the applicability of our approach with several case studies that were designed in Simulink together with the RL Toolbox, namely an intelligent temperature control system, a water tank controlled by an RL controller, an autonomous factory robot, an adaptive cruise control, and an intelligent water distribution system. To further demonstrate the applicability of our approach, we have deductively verified at least one case study for each contract pattern in KeYmaera X.

In future work, we plan to investigate further contract patterns. In particular, the dynamic adaptation to a degraded service level only constitutes a small part of what makes a system resilient. We plan to investigate further system adapations and requirements in the context of resilience.

References

1. Adelt, J., Herber, P., Niehage, M., Remke, A.: Towards safe and resilient hybrid systems in the presence of learning and uncertainty. In: International Symposium On Leveraging Applications of Formal Methods, Verification and Validation (ISoLA). LNCS, vol. 13701. Springer (2022)
2. Adelt, J., Liebrenz, T., Herber, P.: Formal verification of intelligent hybrid systems that are modeled with simulink and the reinforcement learning toolbox. In: Huisman, M., Păsăreanu, C., Zhan, N. (eds.) FM 2021. LNCS, vol. 13047, pp. 349–366. Springer, Cham (2021). https://doi.org/10.1007/978-3-030-90870-6_19
3. Alshiekh, M., Bloem, R., Ehlers, R., Könighofer, B., Niekum, S., Topcu, U.: Safe reinforcement learning via shielding. In: AAAI Conference on Artificial Intelligence, vol. 32 (2018)
4. Beckert, B., Klebanov, V.: Proof reuse for deductive program verification. In: Proceedings of the Second International Conference on Software Engineering and Formal Methods, 2004. SEFM 2004, pp. 77–86. IEEE (2004)
5. Chen, M., et al.: MARS: a toolchain for modelling, analysis and verification of hybrid systems. In: Hinchey, M.G., Bowen, J.P., Olderog, E.-R. (eds.) Provably Correct Systems. NMSSE, pp. 39–58. Springer, Cham (2017). https://doi.org/10.1007/978-3-319-48628-4_3
6. Cimatti, A., Dorigatti, M., Tonetta, S.: OCRA: a tool for checking the refinement of temporal contracts. In: IEEE/ACM International Conference on Automated Software Engineering (ASE), pp. 702–705. IEEE (2013)
7. Cloth, L., Haverkort, B.R.: Model checking for survivability! In: International Conference on the Quantitative Evaluation of Systems (QEST), pp. 145–154. IEEE (2005)
8. Fulton, N., Mitsch, S., Quesel, J.-D., Völp, M., Platzer, A.: KeYmaera X: an axiomatic tactical theorem prover for hybrid systems. In: Felty, A.P., Middeldorp,

A. (eds.) CADE 2015. LNCS (LNAI), vol. 9195, pp. 527–538. Springer, Cham (2015). https://doi.org/10.1007/978-3-319-21401-6_36

9. Fulton, N., Platzer, A.: Safe reinforcement learning via formal methods: toward safe control through proof and learning. In: AAAI Conference on Artificial Intelligence, vol. 32 (2018)

10. Genestier, R., Giorgetti, A., Petiot, G.: Sequential generation of structured arrays and its deductive verification. In: Blanchette, J.C., Kosmatov, N. (eds.) TAP 2015. LNCS, vol. 9154, pp. 109–128. Springer, Cham (2015). https://doi.org/10.1007/978-3-319-21215-9_7

11. Hähnle, R., Huisman, M.: Deductive software verification: from pen-and-paper proofs to industrial tools. In: Steffen, B., Woeginger, G. (eds.) Computing and Software Science. LNCS, vol. 10000, pp. 345–373. Springer, Cham (2019). https://doi.org/10.1007/978-3-319-91908-9_18

12. Hähnle, R., Schaefer, I., Bubel, R.: Reuse in software verification by abstract method calls. In: Bonacina, M.P. (ed.) CADE 2013. LNCS (LNAI), vol. 7898, pp. 300–314. Springer, Heidelberg (2013). https://doi.org/10.1007/978-3-642-38574-2_21

13. Hoder, K., Kovács, L., Voronkov, A.: Invariant generation in vampire. In: Abdulla, P.A., Leino, K.R.M. (eds.) TACAS 2011. LNCS, vol. 6605, pp. 60–64. Springer, Heidelberg (2011). https://doi.org/10.1007/978-3-642-19835-9_7

14. Könighofer, B., Lorber, F., Jansen, N., Bloem, R.: Shield synthesis for reinforcement learning. In: Margaria, T., Steffen, B. (eds.) ISoLA 2020. LNCS, vol. 12476, pp. 290–306. Springer, Cham (2020). https://doi.org/10.1007/978-3-030-61362-4_16

15. Koutsoukos, X.D., Antsaklis, P.J., Stiver, J.A., Lemmon, M.D.: Supervisory control of hybrid systems. Proc. IEEE **88**(7), 1026–1049 (2000)

16. Laprie, J.C.: From dependability to resilience. In: IEEE/IFIP International Conference on Dependable Systems and Networks (DSN), pp. G8–G9 (2008)

17. Liebrenz, T., Herber, P., Glesner, S.: Deductive verification of hybrid control systems modeled in Simulink with KeYmaera X. In: Sun, J., Sun, M. (eds.) ICFEM 2018. LNCS, vol. 11232, pp. 89–105. Springer, Cham (2018). https://doi.org/10.1007/978-3-030-02450-5_6

18. Liebrenz, T., Herber, P., Glesner, S.: A service-oriented approach for decomposing and verifying hybrid system models. In: Arbab, F., Jongmans, S.-S. (eds.) FACS 2019. LNCS, vol. 12018, pp. 127–146. Springer, Cham (2020). https://doi.org/10.1007/978-3-030-40914-2_7

19. MathWorks: Control and Simulate Multiple Warehouse Robots

20. MathWorks: Reinforcement Learning Examples

21. MathWorks: Reinforcement Learning Toolbox

22. MathWorks: Simulink

23. Minopoli, S., Frehse, G.: SL2SX Translator: from Simulink to SpaceEx models. In: International Conference on Hybrid Systems: Computation and Control, pp. 93–98. ACM (2016)

24. Mitsch, S., Ghorbal, K., Vogelbacher, D., Platzer, A.: Formal verification of obstacle avoidance and navigation of ground robots. Int. J. Robot. Res. **36**(12), 1312–1340 (2017)

25. Phan, D., et al.: A component-based simplex architecture for high-assurance cyber-physical systems. In: 2017 17th International Conference on Application of Concurrency to System Design (ACSD), pp. 49–58. IEEE (2017)

26. Platzer, A.: Differential dynamic logic for hybrid systems. J. Autom. Reason. **41**(2), 143–189 (2008)

27. Rodríguez-Carbonell, E., Kapur, D.: Automatic generation of polynomial invariants of bounded degree using abstract interpretation. Sci. Comput. Program. **64**(1), 54–75 (2007)
28. Safari, M., Oortwijn, W., Joosten, S., Huisman, M.: Formal verification of parallel prefix sum. In: Lee, R., Jha, S., Mavridou, A., Giannakopoulou, D. (eds.) NFM 2020. LNCS, vol. 12229, pp. 170–186. Springer, Cham (2020). https://doi.org/10.1007/978-3-030-55754-6_10
29. Smith, P., Hutchison, D., Sterbenz, J.P., Schöller, M., Fessi, A., Karaliopoulos, M., Lac, C., Plattner, B.: Network resilience: a systematic approach. IEEE Commun. Mag. **49**(7), 88–97 (2011)
30. Sutton, R.S., Barto, A.G.: Reinforcement Learning: An Introduction, 2nd edn. The MIT Press Cambridge, Massachusetts London, England (2018)
31. Thüm, T., Schaefer, I., Apel, S., Hentschel, M.: Family-based deductive verification of software product lines. In: International Conference on Generative Programming and Component Engineering, pp. 11–20. ACM (2012)
32. Zou, L., Zhan, N., Wang, S., Fränzle, M.: Formal verification of Simulink/Stateflow diagrams. In: Finkbeiner, B., Pu, G., Zhang, L. (eds.) ATVA 2015. LNCS, vol. 9364, pp. 464–481. Springer, Cham (2015). https://doi.org/10.1007/978-3-319-24953-7_33

Program Analysis and Verification

SISL: Concolic Testing of Structured Binary Input Formats via Partial Specification

Sören Tempel[1]([✉])[ID], Vladimir Herdt[1,2][ID], and Rolf Drechsler[1,2][ID]

[1] Institute of Computer Science, University of Bremen, 28359 Bremen, Germany
{tempel,vherdt,drechsler}@uni-bremen.de
[2] Cyber-Physical Systems, DFKI GmbH, 28359 Bremen, Germany

Abstract. Automatically generating test inputs for input handling routines which implement highly structured input formats is challenging. Existing input generation approaches (e.g. fuzzing) address this problem by requiring verification engineers to create input specifications based on which new inputs are generated. However, depending on the input format, creating such input specifications can be cumbersome and error-prone. We propose simplifying the creation of input specifications by allowing input formats to be only partially specified. This is achieved by utilizing concolic testing (a combination of concrete random testing and symbolic execution) as an input generation technique and thereby allowing parts of the input format to remain unspecified (i.e. unconstrained) symbolic values. For this purpose, we present SISL, a domain-specific language for creating partial input specifications for structured binary input formats.

Keywords: Concolic testing · Software verification · Network protocols

1 Introduction

Input handling routines are a known source of potentially exploitable bugs in existing software [4]. An emerging dynamic testing technique to uncover these sorts of bugs is concolic testing, a combination of concrete random testing (i.e. fuzzing) and symbolic execution. Employment of concolic testing is limited by the fact that input handling routines often expect inputs to satisfy a complex predefined structured input format (e.g. JSON). As such, invalid inputs are rejected early by the software without performing interesting input processing. Since concolic testing is largely performed with a given time budget, critical

This work was supported in part by the German Federal Ministry of Education and Research (BMBF) within the project Scale4Edge under contract no. 16ME0127 and within the project VerSys under contract no. 01IW19001.

A. Bouajjani et al. (Eds.): ATVA 2022, LNCS 13505, pp. 77–82, 2022.
https://doi.org/10.1007/978-3-031-19992-9_5

bugs remain unnoticed if deeper parts of the software are not reached within that budget.

The outlined problem is of central importance in the fuzzing context. Contrary to symbolic execution, fuzzing performs no formal reasoning and instead relies solely on randomly generated values to create test inputs, thus requiring even more time to satisfy complex input formats. Prior work on fuzzing attempts to address this problem by randomizing individual rules of a specified grammar [1, 6, 9] or individual fields of specified input blocks [3, 7]. Due to the lack of formal reasoning, it is necessary in both cases to manually provide a detailed description of the utilized input format, which can be cumbersome and error-prone. Errors in the provided input specification will cause the software to consider generated inputs as invalid. We propose using concolic testing (which combines fuzzing and symbolic execution) to ease the creation of input format specifications by allowing verification engineers to only partially specify the targeted structured input format. That is, unspecified parts of the input format can be treated as unconstrained symbolic values, thereby allowing an SMT solver—used in symbolic execution for formal reasoning—to automatically fill in the leftover gaps based on extracted program constraints.

We present SISL, a *Domain-Specific Language* (DSL) to partially specify structured binary input formats which are often used in security critical domains (such as the Internet of Things). Furthermore, we illustrate that our proposed language can be easily integrated into existing concolic testing frameworks by proposing an exemplary integration for SYMEX-VP [8], a concolic testing engine for embedded RISC-V software. Lastly, we evaluate our DSL by providing evidence that the minimal effort, required to create partial specifications, is outweighed by the gain in coverage and that our proposed DSL is expressive enough to describe a wide range of structured binary input formats. To the best of our knowledge, SISL is the first input format specification language designed explicitly for concolic testing. The SISL tooling is open source and can be obtained from https://agra-uni-bremen.github.io/sisl/.

2   Scheme-Based Input Specification Language

The *Scheme-based Input Specification Language* (SISL) is a DSL for partially specifying parametrisable binary input formats for concolic software testing. As the name suggests, SISL is based on the Scheme programming language which, in turn, is a Lisp dialect. We choose Scheme as the basis for our language since it supports hygienic macros which allow defining custom syntactic constructs within the language framework, thereby easing the creation of DSLs [2].

Similar to block-based fuzzers [3, 7], SISL allows specifying binary input formats as a sequence of variable-width bit blocks. Contrary to existing work on fuzzing, SISL targets concolic testing and therefore supports distinct block types to distinguish concrete and symbolic values in the specified input format. Symbolic field values can optionally be constrained with symbolic expressions, hence allowing expressing the relationship between different symbolic fields (e.g. $X < Y$

```
1   (define-input-format (ipv6-packet next-hdr &encapsulate payload)
2     (make-uint 'version-field 4 ipv6-version-value)
3     (make-uint 'traffic-class 8 0)
4     (make-uint 'flow-label 20 0)
5     (make-uint 'payload-length 16 (input-format-bytesize payload))
6     (make-uint 'next-header 8 next-hdr)
7     (make-uint 'hop-limit 8 42)
8     (make-symbolic 'src-addr 128)
9     (make-symbolic 'dst-addr 128))
10
11  (define-input-format (icmpv6-packet &encapsulate body)
12    (make-symbolic 'type 8 '((Or
13                               (Eq type ,icmpv6-nbr-sol)
14                               (Eq type ,icmpv6-nbr-adv))))
15    (make-symbolic 'code 8)
16    (make-symbolic 'checksum 16))
17
18  (write-format
19    (ipv6-packet
20      icmpv6-next-header
21      (icmpv6-packet
22        (make-input-format
23          (make-symbolic 'body (bytes->bits 32))))))
```

Fig. 1. Excerpt of an example SISL input specification for the ICMPv6 message format.

must hold for two symbolic fields X and Y). Unconstrained symbolic fields can be used to leave parts of the input format unspecified, therefore allowing the concolic testing engine to fill in these gaps based on program execution and thus easing the creation of input format specifications. Defined input formats can also be nested, e.g. to express encapsulation in the network protocol context.

An example SISL input specification is provided in Fig. 1 were a specification for the ICMPv6 message format is presented. ICMPv6 is a binary network protocol implemented on top of IPv6. For this reason, the SISL specification in Fig. 1 defines two input formats. First, the IPv6 message format is defined in Line 1–Line 9 using SISL's **define-input-format** keyword. This keyword defines a new input format and requires specifying the input format name, optional input format parameters, and the input format fields. In Line 1 the input format name is given as **ipv6-packet**, an optional **next-hdr** parameter is defined, and the special **&encapsulate** keyword is used to denote that the format encapsulates an additional **payload** format. In Line 2–Line 9 the fields of the IPv6 packet format are defined. Each field definition takes at least two parameters: A field name (expressed as a Scheme symbol) and a field size in bits. Fields can either be concrete or symbolic. Concrete fields require the field value as a third argument. Symbolic fields support an optional third parameter to express symbolic constraints. For **ipv6-packet**, six concrete fields are defined in Line 2–Line 7. The majority of these fields (Line 3, Line 4, Line 6, and Line 7) use an integer literal as field value. The **version** field (Line 2) uses a predefined variable as a field value and the value of the **payload-length** field depends on the byte size of the **payload** parameter. Furthermore, the **ipv6-packet** definition also uses two symbolic fields for the source and destination address of the IPv6 header format (Line 8–Line 9). IPv6 addresses have a complex internal structure which

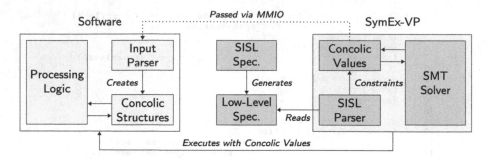

Fig. 2. Overview of our SISL-based concolic testing setup using SYMEX-VP.

is cumbersome to express, by declaring them as symbolic the correct value for these fields will be inferred by the concolic testing engine during execution.

The second input format, defined in Fig. 1, is the ICMPv6 message format (Line 11–Line 16) This definition is analog to the `ipv6-packet` definition, with the exception that it only consists of symbolic fields (Line 12–Line 16). Furthermore, the symbolic `type` field (Line 12–Line 14) demonstrates the expression of symbolic constraints on a symbolic field values. Symbolic constraints are expressed as a list of KQuery expressions, a textual representation of symbolic constraints from prior work [5]. In Line 12–Line 16, the `type` field is constrained so that it either has the value of the variable `icmpv6-nbr-sol` or `icmpv6-nbr-adv`. These two variables refer to constants from the IPv6 *Neighbor Discovery Protocol* (NDP) specification, thereby enabling targeted concolic testing of an NDP implementation with this SISL specification.

To enable such tests, the two described input formats are instantiated in Line 18–Line 23 of Fig. 1 with specific parameters. In this case, the `next-hdr` of the `ipv6-packet` is instantiated with the value of the variable `icmpv6-next-header` and the `payload` parameter is set to an instance of an `icmpv6-packet` which itself has its `body` parameter set to an input format with 32 unconstrained symbolic bytes.

3 Overview and Implementation

We have integrated our proposed DSL with SYMEX-VP, an existing open source concolic testing engine for RISC-V embedded software [8]. An overview of the interaction between SISL, the tested software, and SYMEX-VP is provided in Fig. 2. The central component of Fig. 2 is the high-level SISL specification. As discussed in Sect. 3, this specification is created manually by a verification engineer. Based on the human-readable SISL input specification, a machine-readable low-level specification is automatically generated. This low-level specification is then provided to and read by SYMEX-VP which constrains utilized concolic values according to the specification. Since SYMEX-VP targets embedded RISC-V software in binary form, the constrained concolic input values are passed to the

Table 1. Comparison of concolic testing with SISL and the original SYMEX-VP.

Application	SISL				SYMEX-VP	
Name	ALOC	SLOC	#Paths	ST	#Paths	ST
Zephyr-CoAP	25383	24	23411	226 min	22999	232 min
Zephyr-IPv6-NDP	31066	30	15122	338 min	1736	453 min
Zephyr-MDNS	31238	35	19585	242 min	2287	452 min

executed software via *Memory-Mapped I/O* (MMIO) peripheral interfaces (e.g. via a network peripheral) [8]. The software binary is then explored by SYMEX-VP based on these input values. Figure 2 (left side) shows a schematic representation of relevant software components performing input processing. Conceptually, the input parser of the software will process the concolic inputs and create data structures based on them. Since the inputs are concolic, the created data structures will also contain concolic values. Based on these concolic values, execution paths through both the input parser and the software processing logic (which processes data structures created by the input parser component) will be enumerated by SYMEX-VP. For this purpose, SYMEX-VP employs a standard *Dynamic Symbolic Execution* (DSE) concolic testing technique where branches in the software are tracked and negated by an SMT solver to discover new assignments for concolic input values.

By constraining concolic input values prior to execution using SISL, we can (a) reduce the amount of generated input values which are rejected by the software's input parser early on and do not reach the processing logic and (b) reduce the amount of time spend in the SMT solver by using partially instead of fully symbolic inputs, thus reducing the complexity of SMT queries.

4   Experiments and Conclusion

We evaluate our proposed input specification language by applying it to Zephyr[1]. Zephyr is a popular operating system for programming constrained embedded devices in the Internet of Things. For this reason, Zephyr provides input handling routines for structured binary input formats used by different network protocols in this domain. We performed experiments with three different protocol message formats (CoAP, IPv6 NDP, MDNS) using example Zephyr applications. Generated input values were passed directly to the Zephyr network stack through a network peripheral provided by SYMEX-VP. The results of our experiments are show in Table 1. For each application, we list the amount of RISC-V assembler instructions (ALOC) in the binary and the amount of SISL lines (SLOC), required for the created input format specification, as a complexity metric. We executed each application for 8h using the created input specification with our SISL enhanced version of SYMEX-VP and with the original SYMEX-VP (i.e.

---

[1] https://zephyrproject.org/.

entirely unconstrained symbolic input). For both executions, we list the amount of discovered paths through the program (as a coverage metric, column: #Paths) and the amount of time spend solving constraints on symbolic values (a known bottleneck of concolic testing, column: ST).

The results in Table 1 demonstrate that partial SISL input specifications significantly reduce the amount of solver time, thereby allowing the discovery of more execution paths through a given program in a given time span. The gain in path coverage increases with application complexity (as measured in assembler instructions, column: ALOC). We deem the effort required to create partial input specifications to be comparatively low since complex parts of the input format can be marked as unconstrained symbolic and will thus be inferred during execution. For example, even for a complex input format like MDNS (which is encapsulated in an IPv6 and UDP packet) only 35 lines of SISL specification were required. The utilized SISL specifications and Zephyr applications are available as part of the publication artifacts[2].

In conclusion, we have presented an open source DSL for partial specification of binary input formats in the concolic testing context. Our experiments with Zephyr indicate that our DSL is expressive enough to support different binary input formats and the manual labor required to employ our DSL is outweighed by the benefits in terms of increase in path coverage.

References

1. Aschermann, C., Frassetto, T., Holz, T., Jauernig, P., Sadeghi, A.R., Teuchert, D.: NAUTILUS: fishing for deep bugs with grammars. In: The Network and Distributed System Security Symposium 2019, NDSS, San Diego, California (2019)
2. Ballantyne, M., King, A., Felleisen, M.: Macros for domain-specific languages. Proc. ACM Program. Lang. 4(OOPSLA) (2020)
3. Banks, G., Cova, M., Felmetsger, V., Almeroth, K., Kemmerer, R., Vigna, G.: SNOOZE: toward a stateful NetwOrk prOtocol fuzZEr. In: Katsikas, S.K., López, J., Backes, M., Gritzalis, S., Preneel, B. (eds.) ISC 2006. LNCS, vol. 4176, pp. 343–358. Springer, Heidelberg (2006). https://doi.org/10.1007/11836810_25
4. Bratus, S., Locasto, M.E., Patterson, M.L., Sassaman, L., Shubina, A.: Exploit programming: from buffer overflows to weird machines and theory of computation. Usenix; login 36, 13–21 (2011)
5. Cadar, C., Dunbar, D., Engler, D.: KLEE: unassisted and automatic generation of high-coverage tests for complex systems programs, OSDI 2008, pp. 209–224. USENIX Association (2008)
6. Godefroid, P., Kiezun, A., Levin, M.Y.: Grammar-based whitebox fuzzing. In: PLDI 2008, pp. 206–215. Association for Computing Machinery (2008)
7. Pham, V.T., Böhme, M., Santosa, A.E., Căciulescu, A.R., Roychoudhury, A.: Smart greybox fuzzing. IEEE Trans. Softw. Eng. 47(9) (2021)
8. Tempel, S., Herdt, V., Drechsler, R.: SymEx-VP: an open source virtual prototype for OS-agnostic concolic testing of IoT firmware. J. Syst. Architect. (2022)
9. Wang, J., Chen, B., Wei, L., Liu, Y.: Superion: grammar-aware greybox fuzzing. In: 2019 IEEE/ACM 41st International Conference on Software Engineering (2019)

---

[2] https://doi.org/10.5281/zenodo.6802198.

Fence Synthesis Under the C11 Memory Model

Sanjana Singh[1]([✉]), Divyanjali Sharma[1], Ishita Jaju[2], and Subodh Sharma[1]

[1] Indian Institute of Technology Delhi, Delhi, India
{sanjana.singh,divyanjali,svs}@cse.iitd.ac.in
[2] Uppsala University, Uppsala, Sweden

Abstract. The C/C++11 (*C11*) standard offers a spectrum of ordering guarantees on memory access operations. The combinations of such orderings pose a challenge in developing *correct* and *efficient* weak memory programs. A common solution to preclude those program outcomes that violate the correctness specification is using *C11* synchronization-fences, which establish ordering on program events. The challenge is in choosing a combination of fences that (i) restores the correctness of the input program, with (ii) as little impact on efficiency as possible (*i.e.*, the smallest set of weakest fences). This problem is the *optimal fence synthesis* problem and is NP-hard for straight-line programs. In this work, we propose the first fence synthesis technique for *C11* programs called FenSying and show its optimality. We additionally propose a near-optimal efficient alternative called fFenSying. We prove the optimality of FenSying and the soundness of fFenSying and present an implementation of both techniques. Finally, we contrast the performance of the two techniques and empirically demonstrate fFenSying's effectiveness.

Keywords: *C11* · Fence-synthesis · Optimal

1 Introduction

Developing weak memory programs requires careful placement of fences and memory barriers to preserve ordering between program instructions and exclude undesirable program outcomes. However, computing the correct combination of the type and location of fences is challenging. Too few or incorrectly placed fences may not preserve the necessary ordering, while too many fences can negatively impact the performance. Striking a balance between preserving the correctness and obtaining performance is highly non-trivial even for expert programmers.

This paper presents an automated fence synthesis solution for weak memory programs developed using the C/C++11 standard (*C11*). *C11* provides a spectrum of ordering guarantees called *memory orders*. In a program, a memory access operation is associated with a memory order which specifies how other memory accesses are ordered with respect to the operation. The memory orders range from *relaxed* (rlx) (that imposes no ordering restriction) to *sequentially-consistent* (sc) (that may restore sequential consistency). Understanding all the

A. Bouajjani et al. (Eds.): ATVA 2022, LNCS 13505, pp. 83–99, 2022.
https://doi.org/10.1007/978-3-031-19992-9_6

subtle complexities of *C11* orderings and predicting the program outcomes can quickly become exacting. Consider the program (RWRW) Sect. 2), where the orders are shown as subscripts. When all the memory accesses are ordered rlx, there exists a program outcome that violates the correctness specification (specified as an *assert* statement). However, when all accesses are ordered sc, the program is provably correct.

In addition, the *C11* memory model supports *C11 fences* that serve as tools for imposing ordering restrictions. Notably, *C11* associates fences with memory orders, thus, supporting various degrees of ordering guarantees through fences.

This work proposes an *optimal* fence synthesis technique for *C11* called FenSying. It involves finding solutions to two problems: (i) computing an optimal (minimal) set of locations to synthesize fences and (ii) computing an optimal (weakest) memory order to be associated with the fences (formally defined in Sect. 3). FenSying takes as input *all* program runs that violate user-specified assertions and attempts optimal *C11* fence synthesis to stop the violating outcomes. FenSying reports when *C11* fences alone cannot fix a violation. In general, computing a minimal number of fences with multiple types of fences is shown to be NP-hard for straight-line programs [24]. We note, rather unsurprisingly, that this hardness manifests in the proposed optimal fence synthesis solution even for the simplest *C11* programs. Our experiments (Sect. 7) show an exponential increase in the analysis time with the increase in the program size.

Further, to address scalability, this paper proposes a *near-optimal* fence synthesis technique called fFenSying (fast FenSying) that fixes *one* violating outcome at a time optimally. Note that fixing one outcome optimally may not guarantee optimality across all violating outcomes. In the process, this technique may add a small number of extra fences than what an optimal solution would compute. Our experiments reveal that fFenSying performs exponentially better than FenSying in terms of the analysis time while adding no extra fences in over 99.5% of the experiments.

Both FenSying and fFenSying, compute the solution from a set of combinations of fences that can stop the violating outcomes, also called *candidate solutions*. The candidate solutions are encoded in a *head-cycle-free* CNF SAT query [8]. Computing an optimal solution from candidates then becomes finding a solution to a *min-model finding problem*.

Many prior works have focused on automating fence synthesis (discussed in Sect. 8). However, the techniques presented in this paper are distinct from prior works in the following two ways: (i) prior techniques do not support C11 memory orders, and (ii) the proposed techniques in this paper synthesize fences that are portable and not architecture-specific.

Contributions. To summarize, this work makes the following contributions:

- The paper presents FenSying and fFenSying (Sect. 6). To the best of our knowledge, these are the first fence synthesis techniques for *C11*.
- The paper shows (using Theorems 1 and 2) that the techniques are sound, *i.e.*, if the input program can be fixed by *C11* fences, then the techniques

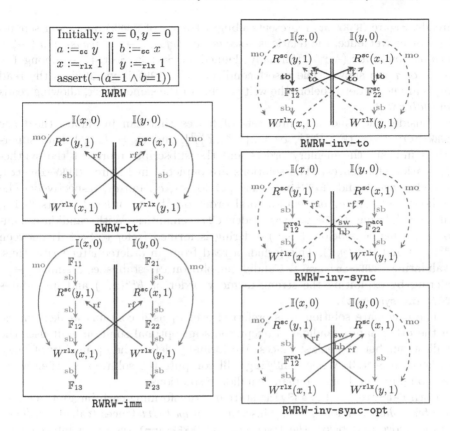

will indeed find a solution. The paper also shows (using Theorem 3) that FenSying produces an optimal result in the number and type of fences.

- Finally, the paper presents an implementation of the said techniques and presents an empirical validation using a set of 1389 litmus tests. Further, the paper empirically shows the effectiveness of fFenSying on a set of challenging benchmarks from prior works. fFenSying performs on an average 67x faster than FenSying.

2 Overview of FenSying and fFenSying

Given a program P, a *trace* τ of P (formally defined in Sect. 3); is considered *buggy* if it violates an assertion of P. FenSying takes *all* buggy traces of P as input. The difference in fFenSying is that the input is a *single* buggy trace of P.

Consider the input program (RWRW), where x and y are shared objects with initial values 0, and a and b are local objects. Let $W^m(o,v)$ and $R^m(o,v)$ represent the write and read of object o and value v with the memory order m. Let $\mathbb{I}(o,v)$ represent the initialization event for object o with value v. The parallel bars ($\parallel$) represent the parallel composition of events from separate

threads. Figure (RWRW-bt) represents a buggy trace τ of (RWRW) under *C11* seman-
tics. For convenience, the relations $-$*sequenced-before* ($\to_\tau^{\text{sb}}$), *reads-from* ($\to_\tau^{\text{rf}}$),
modification-order ($\to_\tau^{\text{mo}}$) (formally defined in Sect. 3, Sect. 4) $-$ among the
events of τ are shown. The assert condition of (RWRW) is violated as the read
events are not ordered before the write events of the same object, allowing reads
from *later* writes.

Consider the following three sets of fences that can invalidate the trace
(RWRW-bt): $c_1 = \{\mathbb{F}_{12}^{\text{sc}}, \mathbb{F}_{22}^{\text{sc}}\}$, $c_2 = \{\mathbb{F}_{12}^{\text{rel}}, \mathbb{F}_{22}^{\text{acq}}\}$ and $c_3 = \{\mathbb{F}_{12}^{\text{rel}}\}$ (the superscripts indicate the memory orders and the subscripts represent the synthe-
sis locations for fences). The solutions are depicted in Figures (RWRW-inv-to),
(RWRW-inv-sync) and (RWRW-inv-sync-opt) for c_1, c_2 and c_3, respectively. The
candidate solution c_1 prevents a total order on the sc ordered events [9,12],
thus, invalidating (RWRW-inv-to) under *C11* semantics. With candidate solu-
tion c_2, a happens-before ($\to_\tau^{\text{hb}}$) ordering is formed (refer to Sect. 4) between
$R^{\text{sc}}(y, 1)$ and $W^{\text{sc}}(y, 1)$. This forbids a read from an ordered-later write, thus,
invalidating (RWRW-inv-sync). Candidate solution c_3 establishes a similar $\to_\tau^{\text{hb}}$
ordering by exploiting the strong memory order of $R^{\text{sc}}(x, 1)$ and invalidates
(RWRW-inv-sync-opt).

The candidate solution c_2 is preferred over c_1 as it contains weaker fences.
On the other hand, candidate c_3 represents an optimal solution as it uses the
smallest number of weakest fences. We formally define the optimality of fence
synthesis in Sect. 3. While FenSying will compute the solution c_3, fFenSying
may compute one from the many candidate solutions.

Both FenSying and fFenSying start by transforming each buggy trace τ to
an *intermediate* version, τ^{imm}, by inserting *untyped C11* fences (called *candidate
fences*) above and below the trace events. (RWRW-imm) shows an intermediate
version corresponding to (RWRW-bt). The addition of fences (assuming they are
of the strongest variety) leads to the creation of new $\to_\tau^{\text{hb}}$ ordering edges. This
may result in cycles in the dependency graph under the *C11* semantics (explained
in Sect. 4). The set of fences in a cycle constitutes a *candidate solution*. For
example, an ordering from $\mathbb{F}_{12}$ to $\mathbb{F}_{22}$ in (RWRW-imm) induces a cyclic relation
$W^{\text{rlx}}(y, 1) \to_\tau^{\text{rf}} R^{\text{sc}}(y, 1) \to_\tau^{\text{hb}} W^{\text{rlx}}(y, 1)$ violating the $\to_\tau^{\text{rf}}; \to_\tau^{\text{hb}}$ irreflexivity
(refer to Sect. 4).

The candidate solutions are collected in a SAT query (Φ). Assuming c_1, c_2
and c_3 are the only candidate solutions for (RWRW-bt), then $\Phi = (\mathbb{F}_{12} \wedge \mathbb{F}_{22}) \vee$
$(\mathbb{F}_{12} \wedge \mathbb{F}_{22}) \vee (\mathbb{F}_{12})$, where for a fence $\mathbb{F}_i^m$, $\mathbb{F}_i$ represents the same fence with
unassigned memory order. fFenSying uses a SAT solver to compute the *min-
model* of Φ, min$\Phi = \{\mathbb{F}_{12}\}$. Further, fFenSying applies the *C11* ordering rules
on fences to determine the weakest memory order for the fences in minΦ. For
instance, $\mathbb{F}_{12}$ in minΦ is computed to have the order rel (explained in Sect. 6).
fFenSying then inserts $\mathbb{F}_{12}$ with memory order rel in (RWRW) at the location
depicted in (RWRW-inv-sync-opt). This process repeats for the next buggy trace.

In contrast, since FenSying works with all buggy traces at once, it requires
the conjunction of the SAT queries Φ_i corresponding to each buggy trace τ_i. The
min-model of the conjunction is computed, which provides optimality.

3   Preliminaries

Consider a multi-threaded *C11* program (*P*). Each thread of *P* performs a sequence of *events* that are runtime instances of memory access operations (reads, writes, and rmws) on shared objects and *C11* fences. Note that an event is uniquely identified in a trace; however, multiple events may be associated with the same program location. The events may be atomic or non-atomic.

***C11* Memory Orders.** The atomic events and fence operations are associated with memory orders that define the ordering restriction on atomic and non-atomic events around them. Let $\mathcal{M} = \{$na, rlx, rel, acq, ar, sc$\}$, represent the orders relaxed (rlx), release (rel), acquire/consume (acq), acquire-release (ar) and sequentially consistent (sc) for atomic events. A non-atomic event is recognized by the na memory order. Let $\sqsubset \subseteq \mathcal{M} \times \mathcal{M}$ represent the relation *weaker* such that $m_1 \sqsubset m_2$ represents that the m_1 is weaker than m_2. As a consequence, annotating an event with m_2 may order two events that remain unordered with m_1. The orders in $\mathcal{M}$ are related as na $\sqsubset$ rlx $\sqsubset$ {rel, acq} $\sqsubset$ ar $\sqsubset$ sc. We also define the relation $\sqsubseteq$ to represent *weaker or equally weak*. Similarly, we define $\sqsupset$ to represent *stronger* and $\sqsupseteq$ to represent *stronger or equally strong*.

We use $\mathcal{E}^{\mathrm{W}} \subseteq \mathcal{E}$ to denote the set of events that perform write to shared memory objects *i.e.*, write events or rmw events. Similarly, we use $\mathcal{E}^{\mathbb{R}} \subseteq \mathcal{E}$ to denote events that read from a shared memory object *i.e.*, read events and rmw events, and $\mathcal{E}^{\mathbb{F}}$ to denote the fence events. We also use $\mathcal{E}^{(m)} \in \mathcal{E}$ (and accordingly $\mathcal{E}^{\mathrm{W}(m)}$, $\mathcal{E}^{\mathbb{R}(m)}$ and $\mathcal{E}^{\mathbb{F}(m)}$) to represent the events with the memory order $m \in \mathcal{M}$; as an example $\mathcal{E}^{\mathbb{F}(\mathrm{sc})}$ represents the set of fences with the memory order sc.

Definition 1 (Trace). A *trace*, τ, of *P* is a tuple $\langle \mathcal{E}_\tau, \rightarrow^{\mathrm{hb}}_\tau, \rightarrow^{\mathrm{mo}}_\tau, \rightarrow^{\mathrm{rf}}_\tau \rangle$, where

$\mathcal{E}_\tau \subseteq \mathcal{E}$ represents the set of events in the trace τ;
$\rightarrow^{\mathrm{hb}}_\tau$ (*Happens-before*) $\subseteq \mathcal{E}_\tau \times \mathcal{E}_\tau$ is a partial order which captures the event interactions and inter-thread synchronizations, discussed in Sect. 4;
$\rightarrow^{\mathrm{mo}}_\tau$ (*Modification-order*) $\subseteq \mathcal{E}^{\mathrm{W}}_\tau \times \mathcal{E}^{\mathrm{W}}_\tau$ is a total order on the writes of an object;
$\rightarrow^{\mathrm{rf}}_\tau$ (*Reads-from*) $\subseteq \mathcal{E}^{\mathrm{W}}_\tau \times \mathcal{E}^{\mathbb{R}}_\tau$ is a relation from a write event to a read event signifying that the read event takes its value from the write event in τ.

Note that, we use $\mathcal{E}^{\mathrm{W}}_\tau$, $\mathcal{E}^{\mathbb{R}}_\tau$ and $\mathcal{E}^{\mathbb{F}}_\tau$ (and also $\mathcal{E}^{\mathrm{W}(m)}_\tau$, $\mathcal{E}^{\mathbb{R}(m)}_\tau$ and $\mathcal{E}^{\mathbb{F}(m)}_\tau$) where $m \in \mathcal{M}$) for the respective sets of events for a trace τ.

Relational Operators. R^{-1} represents the inverse and R^+ represents the transitive closure of a relation R. Further, $R_1; R_2$ represents the composition of relations R_1 and R_2. Let $R|_{\mathrm{sc}}$ represent a subset of a relation R on sc ordered events; *i.e.* $(e_1, e_2) \in R|_{\mathrm{sc}} \iff (e_1, e_2) \in R \land e_1, e_2 \in \mathcal{E}^{(\mathrm{sc})}$. Note that we also use the infix notation $e_1 R e_2$ for $(e_1, e_2) \in R$. Lastly, a relation R has a cycle (or is cyclic) if $\exists e_1, e_2 \in \mathcal{E}$ s.t. $e_1 R e_2 \land e_2 R e_1$.

A Note on Optimality. The notion of optimality may vary with context. Consider two candidate solutions $\{\mathbb{F}^{\mathrm{sc}}_i\}$ and $\{\mathbb{F}^{\mathrm{rel}}_j, \mathbb{F}^{\mathrm{acq}}_k\}$ where the superscripts represent the memory orders. The two solutions are incomparable under *C11*, and their performance efficiency is subject to the input program and the underlying architecture. FenSying chooses a candidate solution c as an optimal solution if: (i) c has the smallest number of candidate fences, and (ii) each fence of c has the weakest memory order compared to other candidate solutions that satisfy (i).

Let $sz(c)$ represent the size of the candidate solution c and given the set of all candidate solutions $\{c_1, ..., c_n\}$ to fix P, let $\underline{sz}(P) = \min(sz(c_1), ..., sz(c_n))$. Further, we assign weights $wt(c)$ to each candidate solution c, computed as the summation of the weights of its fences where a fence ordered rel or acq is assigned the weight 1, a fence ordered ar is assigned 2, and a fence ordered sc is assigned 3. Optimality for FenSying is formally defined as:

Definition 2. Optimality of Fence Synthesis. Consider a set of candidate solutions $c_1, ..., c_n$. A solution c_i (for $i \in [1, n]$) is considered optimal if:

(i) $sz(c_i) = \underline{sz}(P) \land$ (ii) $\forall j \in [1, n]$ s.t. $sz(c_j) = \underline{sz}(P)$, $wt(c_i) \leq wt(c_j)$.

4   Background: C11 Memory Model

The *C11* memory model defines a trace using a set of event relations, described in Definition 1. The most significant relation that defines a *C11* trace τ is the irreflexive and acyclic happens-before relation, $\rightarrow_\tau^{\mathrm{hb}} \subseteq \mathcal{E}_\tau \times \mathcal{E}_\tau$. The $\rightarrow_\tau^{\mathrm{hb}}$ relation is composed of the following relations [12].

$\rightarrow_\tau^{\mathrm{sb}}$ (*Sequenced-before*): total occurrence order on the events of a thread.

$\rightarrow_\tau^{\mathrm{sw}}$ (*Synchronizes-with*) Inter-thread synchronization between a write e_w (ordered $\sqsupseteq$ rel) and a read e_r (ordered $\sqsupseteq$ acq) when $e_w \rightarrow_\tau^{\mathrm{rf}} e_r$.

$\rightarrow_\tau^{\mathrm{dob}}$ (*Dependency-ordered-before*): Inter-thread synchronization between a write e_w (ordered $\sqsupseteq$ rel) and a read e_r (ordered $\sqsupseteq$ acq) when $e_w' \rightarrow_\tau^{\mathrm{rf}} e_r$ for $e_w' \in$ *release-sequence*[1] of e_w in τ [9,12].

$\rightarrow_\tau^{\mathrm{ithb}}$ (*Inter-thread-hb*): Inter-thread relation computed by extending $\rightarrow_\tau^{\mathrm{sw}}$ and $\rightarrow_\tau^{\mathrm{dob}}$ with $\rightarrow_\tau^{\mathrm{sb}}$.

$\rightarrow_\tau^{\mathrm{hb}}$ (*Happens-before*): Inter-thread relation defined as $\rightarrow_\tau^{\mathrm{sb}} \cup \rightarrow_\tau^{\mathrm{ithb}}$.

The $\rightarrow_\tau^{\mathrm{hb}}$ relation along with the $\rightarrow_\tau^{\mathrm{mo}}$ and $\rightarrow_\tau^{\mathrm{rf}}$ relations (Definition 1) is used in specifying the set of six **coherence conditions** [12,17]:

$\rightarrow_\tau^{\mathrm{hb}}$ is irreflexive.   (co-h)

$\rightarrow_\tau^{\mathrm{rf}}; \rightarrow_\tau^{\mathrm{hb}}$ is irreflexive.   (co-rh)

$\rightarrow_\tau^{\mathrm{mo}}; \rightarrow_\tau^{\mathrm{hb}}$ is irreflexive.   (co-mh)

$\rightarrow_\tau^{\mathrm{mo}}; \rightarrow_\tau^{\mathrm{rf}}; \rightarrow_\tau^{\mathrm{hb}}$ is irreflexive.   (co-mrh)

$\rightarrow_\tau^{\mathrm{mo}}; \rightarrow_\tau^{\mathrm{hb}}; \rightarrow_\tau^{\mathrm{rf}^{-1}}$ is irreflexive.   (co-mhi)

$\rightarrow_\tau^{\mathrm{mo}}; \rightarrow_\tau^{\mathrm{rf}}; \rightarrow_\tau^{\mathrm{hb}}; \rightarrow_\tau^{\mathrm{rf}^{-1}}$ is irreflexive.   (co-mrhi)

---

[1] *release-sequence* of e_w in τ: maximal contiguous sub-sequence of $\rightarrow_\tau^{\mathrm{mo}}$ that starts at e_w and contains: (i) write events of $thr(e_w)$, (ii) rmw events of other threads [9,12].

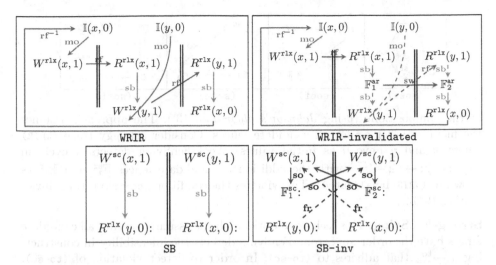

Additionally, *all* sc ordered events in a trace τ must be related by a total order $(\rightarrow_\tau^{\text{to}})$ that concurs with the coherence conditions. We use an irreflexive relation called *from-reads* $(\rightarrow_\tau^{\text{fr}} \triangleq \rightarrow_\tau^{\text{rf}^{-1}}; \rightarrow_\tau^{\text{mo}})$ for ordering reads with *later* writes. Consequently, $\rightarrow_\tau^{\text{to}}$ must satisfy the following condition [12,25], referred to as (to-sc) and formally defined in the extended version [22].

- $\forall e_1^{\text{sc}}, e_2^{\text{sc}} \in \mathcal{E}_\tau^{(\text{sc})}$ if $e_1^{\text{sc}} \rightarrow_\tau^{\text{to}} e_2^{\text{sc}}$ then $(e_2^{\text{sc}}, e_1^{\text{sc}}) \notin \rightarrow_\tau^{\text{hb}} \cup \rightarrow_\tau^{\text{mo}} \cup \rightarrow_\tau^{\text{rf}} \cup \rightarrow_\tau^{\text{fr}}$; *and,*
- an sc read (or any read with an sc fence $\rightarrow_\tau^{\text{sb}}$ ordered before it) must not read from an sc write that is not *immediately* $\rightarrow_\tau^{\text{to}}$ ordered before it.

Conjunction of (coherence conditions) and (to-sc) forms the sufficient condition to determine if a trace τ is valid under *C11* (formally defined in [22]).

HB with *C11* Fences. *C11* fences form $\rightarrow_\tau^{\text{ithb}}$ with other events [9,12]. A fence can be associated with the memory orders rel, acq, ar and sc. An appropriately placed fence can form $\rightarrow_\tau^{\text{sw}}$ and $\rightarrow_\tau^{\text{dob}}$ relation from an $\rightarrow_\tau^{\text{rf}}$ relation between events of different threads (formal described in the extended version [22]).

5 Invalidating Buggy Traces with *C11* Fences

The key idea behind the proposed techniques is to introduce fences such that either (coherence conditions) or (to-sc)are violated. This section introduces two approaches for determining if the trace is rendered invalid with fences.

Consider τ^{imm} of a buggy trace τ. The candidate fences of τ^{imm} inflate $\rightarrow_\tau^{\text{sb}}$, $\rightarrow_\tau^{\text{sw}}$, $\rightarrow_\tau^{\text{dob}}$ and $\rightarrow_\tau^{\text{ithb}}$ relations (fences do not contribute to $\rightarrow_{\tau^{\text{imm}}}^{\text{mo}}$, $\rightarrow_{\tau^{\text{imm}}}^{\text{rf}}$ and $\rightarrow_{\tau^{\text{imm}}}^{\text{fr}}$). The inflated relations are denoted as $\rightarrow_{\tau^{\text{imm}}}^{\text{sb}}$, $\rightarrow_{\tau^{\text{imm}}}^{\text{sw}}$, $\rightarrow_{\tau^{\text{imm}}}^{\text{dob}}$ and $\rightarrow_{\tau^{\text{imm}}}^{\text{ithb}}$. We propose *Weak-FenSying* and *Strong-FenSying* to detect the invalidity of τ^{imm}.

Weak-FenSying. Weak-FenSying computes compositions of relations that correspond to the (coherence conditions). It then checks if there exist cycles

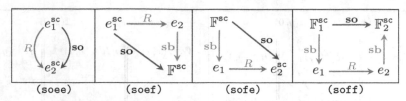

in the compositions (using *Johnson's algorithm* [13]). The approach assumes the memory order ar for all candidate fences. Consider a buggy trace (WRIR) where x and y have 0 as initial values. Weak-FenSying detects a cycle in $\rightarrow_\tau^{mo}; \rightarrow_\tau^{rf}; \rightarrow_\tau^{hb}; \rightarrow_\tau^{rf^{-1}}$ with the addition of candidate fences $\mathbb{F}_1^{ar}$ and $\mathbb{F}_2^{ar}$ as shown in (WRIR-invalidated). This violates the condition (co-mrhi), thus, invalidating (WRIR).

Strong-FenSying. This technique works with the assumption that all candidate fences have the order sc. Strong-FenSying detects the infeasibility in constructing a $\rightarrow_{\tau^{imm}}^{to}$ that adheres to (to-sc). In order to detect violation of (to-sc), Strong-FenSying introduces a possibly reflexive relation on sc-ordered events of τ^{imm}, called sc-*order* ($\rightarrow_{\tau^{imm}}^{so}$). The $\rightarrow_{\tau^{imm}}^{so}$ relation is such that a total order cannot be formed on the sc events of τ^{imm} iff a cycle exists in $\rightarrow_{\tau^{imm}}^{so}$. All sc event pairs ordered by $\rightarrow_{\tau^{imm}}^{hb}$, $\rightarrow_{\tau^{imm}}^{mo}$, $\rightarrow_{\tau^{imm}}^{rf}$ and $\rightarrow_{\tau^{imm}}^{fr}$ are contained in $\rightarrow_{\tau^{imm}}^{so}$. Notably, pairs of sc events that do not have a definite order are not ordered by $\rightarrow_{\tau^{imm}}^{so}$. This is because if such a pair of events is involved in a cycle then we can freely flip their order and eliminate the cycle. Consider the buggy trace (SB), $W^{sc}(x,1)\rightarrow^{to}W^{sc}(y,1)$ and $W^{sc}(y,1)\rightarrow^{to}W^{sc}(x,1)$ are both valid total-orders on the sc events of the trace. The set $\rightarrow_{\tau^{imm}}^{so}$ does not contain either of the two event pairs and would be empty for this example.

As a consequence, pairs of events that do not have definite total order cannot contribute to the reflexivity of $\rightarrow_\tau^{so}$ and can be safely ignored. Thus, $\rightarrow_\tau^{so+} \subseteq \rightarrow_\tau^{to}$ for a trace τ. Further, if a total order cannot be formed on sc ordered events then a corresponding cycle exists in $\rightarrow_{\tau^{imm}}^{so}$. The observations are formally presented with supporting proofs in the extended version [22]).

Definition 3 formally presents $\rightarrow_{\tau^{imm}}^{so}$ based on the above stated considerations.

Definition 3 sc-order ($\rightarrow_{\tau^{imm}}^{so}$).
$\forall e_1, e_2 \in \mathcal{E}_\tau$ s.t. $(e_1, e_2) \in R$, where $R = \rightarrow_\tau^{hb} \cup \rightarrow_\tau^{mo} \cup \rightarrow_\tau^{rf} \cup \rightarrow_\tau^{fr}$

- if $e_1, e_2 \in \mathcal{E}_\tau^{(sc)}$ then $e_1\rightarrow_{\tau^{imm}}^{so}e_2$;   (soee)
- if $e_1 \in \mathcal{E}_\tau^{(sc)}$, $\exists \mathbb{F}^{sc} \in \mathcal{E}_{\tau^{imm}}^{\mathbb{F}(sc)}$ s.t. $e_2\rightarrow_{\tau^{imm}}^{sb}\mathbb{F}^{sc}$ then $e_1\rightarrow_{\tau^{imm}}^{so}\mathbb{F}^{sc}$;   (soef)
- if $e_2 \in \mathcal{E}_\tau^{(sc)}$, $\exists \mathbb{F}^{sc} \in \mathcal{E}_{\tau^{imm}}^{\mathbb{F}(sc)}$ s.t. $\mathbb{F}^{sc}\rightarrow_{\tau^{imm}}^{sb}e_1$ then $\mathbb{F}^{sc}\rightarrow_{\tau^{imm}}^{so}e_2$;   (sofe)
- if $\exists \mathbb{F}_1^{sc}, \mathbb{F}_2^{sc} \in \mathcal{E}_{\tau^{imm}}^{\mathbb{F}(sc)}$ s.t. $\mathbb{F}_1^{sc}\rightarrow_{\tau^{imm}}^{sb}e_1$ and $e_2\rightarrow_{\tau^{imm}}^{sb}\mathbb{F}_2^{sc}$ then $\mathbb{F}_1^{sc}\rightarrow_{\tau^{imm}}^{so}\mathbb{F}_2^{sc}$.   (soff)

The trace depicted in (SB) can be invalidated with strong fences as shown in (SB-inv). The sc events of (SB-inv) cannot be totally ordered and Strong-FenSying detects the same through a cycle in $\rightarrow^{so}$ (formed by @@soee and @@sofe).

Scope of FenSying/fFenSying. Our work synthesizes *C11* fences and stands fundamentally different from techniques that strengthen the memory orders of events. On the one hand, sc fences cannot restore sequential consistency; thus, strengthening memory orders may invalidate buggy traces that the strongest *C11* fences cannot. On the other hand, strengthening may lead to sub-optimal byte-code. The difference is explained in the extended version [22].

6 Methodology

Buggy Traces and Candidate Fences. Algorithms 1 and 2 present FenSying and fFenSying, respectively. The algorithms rely on an external buggy trace generator (BTG) for the buggy trace(s) of P (lines 2,8). The candidate fences are inserted (to obtain τ^{imm}), and the event relations are updated (lines 16–17).

Detecting Violation of Trace Coherence. The algorithms detect possible violations of trace coherence conditions resulting from the candidate fences at lines 18–19 of the function synthesisCore. Figures (RWRW-inv-sync) and (RWRW-inv-sync-opt) represent two instances of violations of (co-rh) detected by Weak-FenSying (through a cycle $W^{\text{rlx}}(y,1) \rightarrow_{\tau^{\text{imm}}}^{\text{rf}} R^{\text{rlx}}(y,1) \rightarrow_{\tau^{\text{imm}}}^{\text{hb}} W^{\text{rlx}}(y,1)$). The candidate solutions corresponding to these cycles (which include only candidate fences) are $\{\mathbb{F}_{12}, \mathbb{F}_{22}\}$ and $\{\mathbb{F}_{12}\}$. Further, for the same example, (RWRW-inv-to) represents a violation detected by Strong-FenSying with the candidate solution $\{\mathbb{F}_{12}, \mathbb{F}_{22}\}$. The algorithms discard all candidate fences other than $\mathbb{F}_{12}$ and $\mathbb{F}_{22}$ from future considerations (assuming no other violations were detected). Now τ can be invalidated as the set of cycles is nonempty (line 20).

The complexity of detecting all cycles for a trace is $\mathcal{O}((|\mathcal{E}_\tau|+\text{E}).(\text{C}+1))$ where C represents the number of cycles of τ and E represents the number of pairs of events in $\mathcal{E}_\tau$. Note that E is in $O(|\mathcal{E}_\tau|^2)$ and C is in $O(|\mathcal{E}_\tau|!)$. Thus, Weak- and Strong-Fensying have exponential complexities in the number of traces and the number of events per trace.

Reduction for Optimality. The algorithms use a SAT solver to determine the optimal number of candidate fences. The candidate fences from each candidate solution of τ are conjuncted to form a SAT query. Further, to retain at least one solution corresponding to τ the algorithms take a disjunction of the conjuncts. The SAT query is represented in the algorithm as $\Phi_\tau :=$ $\mathcal{Q}(\text{weakCycles}_\tau \vee \text{strongCycles}_\tau)$ (line 22) and presented in Eq. 1 (where $\mathbf{W}_\tau$ and $\mathbf{S}_\tau$ represent weakCycles$_\tau$ and strongCycles$_\tau$ and W^{F} and S^{F} represent the set of candidate fences in cycles W and S respectively). Further, FenSying combines the SAT formulas corresponding to each buggy trace via conjunction (line 4), shown in Eq. 2. However, note that for fFenSying $\Phi = \Phi_\tau$.

$$\Phi_\tau = (\bigvee_{\text{W} \in \mathbf{W}_\tau} \bigwedge_{\mathbb{F}_\text{w} \in \text{W}^{\text{F}}} \mathbb{F}_\text{w}) \vee (\bigvee_{\text{S} \in \mathbf{S}_\tau} \bigwedge_{\mathbb{F}_\text{s} \in \text{S}^{\text{F}}} \mathbb{F}_\text{s}) \quad (1) \qquad \Phi = \bigwedge_{\tau \in \text{BT}} \Phi_\tau \quad (2)$$

Algorithm 1: FenSying (P)	**Algorithm 2:** fFenSying (P)
1 $\Phi := \top; \mathcal{C} := \emptyset$	8 **if** $\exists \tau \in$ buggyTraces(P) **then**
2 **forall** $\tau \in$ buggyTraces(P) **do**	9 $\quad$ $\Phi, \mathcal{C} :=$ synthesisCore(τ)
3 $\quad$ $\Phi_\tau, \mathcal{C}_\tau :=$ synthesisCore(τ)	10 $\quad$ min$\Phi :=$ minModel(Φ)
4 $\quad$ $\Phi := \Phi \wedge \Phi_\tau; \mathcal{C} := \mathcal{C} \cup \mathcal{C}_\tau$	11 $\quad$ $\mathcal{F} :=$ assignMO(min$\Phi, \mathcal{C}$)
5 min$\Phi :=$ minModel(Φ)	12 $\quad$ $P' :=$ syn$(P, \mathcal{F})$
6 $\mathcal{F} :=$ assignMO(min$\Phi, \mathcal{C}$)	13 $\quad$ **return** fFenSying (P')
7 **return** syn$(P, \mathcal{F})$	14 **else return** P

---

15 **Function** synthesisCore(τ) /* $\tau = \langle \mathcal{E}_\tau, \xrightarrow[\tau]{\text{hb}}, \xrightarrow[\tau]{\text{mo}}, \xrightarrow[\tau]{\text{rf}} \rangle$ */:

16 $\quad$ $\mathcal{E}_{\tau^{\text{imm}}} := \mathcal{E}_\tau \cup$ candidateFences(τ)

17 $\quad$ $(\xrightarrow[\tau'^{\text{imm}}]{\text{hb}}, \xrightarrow[\tau'^{\text{imm}}]{\text{mo}}, \xrightarrow[\tau'^{\text{imm}}]{\text{rf}}, \xrightarrow[\tau'^{\text{imm}}]{\text{rf}^{-1}}, \xrightarrow[\tau'^{\text{imm}}]{\text{fr}}) :=$ computeRelations$(\tau, \mathcal{E}_{\tau^{\text{imm}}})$

18 $\quad$ weakCycles$_\tau :=$ weakFensying(τ^{imm})

19 $\quad$ strongCycles$_\tau :=$ strongFensying(τ^{imm})

20 $\quad$ **if** weakCycles$_\tau = \emptyset \wedge$ strongCycles$_\tau = \emptyset$ **then**

21 $\quad\quad$ **return**   /* ABORT: cannot stop τ with C11 fences */

22 $\quad$ $\Phi_\tau := \mathcal{Q}($weakCycles$_\tau \vee$ strongCycles$_\tau$); $\mathcal{C}_\tau :=$weakCycles$_\tau \cup$ strongCycles$_\tau$

23 $\quad$ **return** $\Phi_\tau, \mathcal{C}_\tau$

We use a SAT solver to compute the *min-model* (minΦ) of the query Φ (lines 5,10). For instance, the query for (RWRW-bt) is $\Phi = (\mathbb{F}_{12}) \vee (\mathbb{F}_{12} \wedge \mathbb{F}_{22}) \vee (\mathbb{F}_{12} \wedge \mathbb{F}_{22})$ and min-model, min$\Phi = \{\mathbb{F}_{12}\}$. The solution to the SAT query returns the smallest set of fences to be synthesized.

The complexity of constructing the query Φ_τ is $\mathcal{O}(\text{C.F})$, where C is the number of cycles per trace and F is the number of fences per cycle. The structure of the query Φ corresponds to the *Head-cycle-free* (HCF) class of CNF theories; hence, the min-model computation falls in the FP complexity class [8].

Determining Optimal Memory Orders of Fences. The set minΦ gives a sound solution that is optimal only in the number of fences. The function assignMO (lines 6,11) assigns the weakest memory order to the fences in minΦ that is sound. Let min-cycles represent a set of cycles such that every candidate fence in the cycles belongs to minΦ. The assignMO function computes memory order for fences of min-cycles of each trace as follows: If a cycle $c \in$ min-cycles is detected, then its fences must form a $\xrightarrow[\tau^{\text{imm}}]{\text{sw}}$ or $\xrightarrow[\tau^{\text{imm}}]{\text{dob}}$ with an event of τ^{imm} (since, candidate fences only modify $\xrightarrow[\tau]{\text{sb}}$, $\xrightarrow[\tau]{\text{sw}}$ and $\xrightarrow[]{\text{dob}}$). Let $R = \xrightarrow[\tau^{\text{imm}}]{\text{sw}} \cup \xrightarrow[\tau^{\text{imm}}]{\text{dob}}$. The scheme to compute fence types is as follows:

- If a fence $\mathbb{F}$ in a weak cycle c is related to an event e of c by R as $e R \mathbb{F}$, then $\mathbb{F}$ is assigned the memory order acq;
- if an event e in c is related to $\mathbb{F}$ as $\mathbb{F} R e$ then $\mathbb{F}$ is assigned rel;
- if events e, e' of c are related to $\mathbb{F}$ as $e R \mathbb{F} R e'$ then $\mathbb{F}$ is assigned ar.
- All the fences in a strong cycle are assigned the memory order sc.

Consider a cycle $c : e \xrightarrow[\tau'^{\text{imm}}]{\text{sb}} \mathbb{F}_1 \xrightarrow[\tau'^{\text{imm}}]{\text{sw}} \mathbb{F}_2 \xrightarrow[\tau'^{\text{imm}}]{\text{sw}} \mathbb{F}_3 \xrightarrow[\tau'^{\text{imm}}]{\text{sb}} e' \xrightarrow[\tau'^{\text{imm}}]{\text{rf}} e$ representing a violation of $\xrightarrow[\tau'^{\text{imm}}]{\text{rf}}; \xrightarrow[\tau'^{\text{imm}}]{\text{hb}}$ irreflexivity (condition (co-rh)). According to the scheme discussed above, the fences $\mathbb{F}_1$, $\mathbb{F}_2$ and $\mathbb{F}_3$ are assigned the memory orders rel, ar and acq respectively and $wt(c) = 4$ (defined in Sect. 3).

$\tau_1 c_1(4)$: $\mathbb{F}_1^{ar} \wedge \mathbb{F}_2^{ar}$
$\tau_1 c_2(4)$: $\mathbb{F}_1^{rel} \wedge \mathbb{F}_2^{acq} \wedge \mathbb{F}_3^{ar}$
cycles of τ_1
$\tau_2 c_1(3)$: $\mathbb{F}_1^{rel} \wedge \mathbb{F}_2^{acq} \wedge \mathbb{F}_3^{acq}$
cycle of τ_2
$\tau_{12} c_{11}(5)$: $\mathbb{F}_1^{ar} \wedge \mathbb{F}_2^{ar} \wedge \mathbb{F}_3^{acq}$
$\tau_{12} c_{21}(4)$: $\mathbb{F}_1^{rel} \wedge \mathbb{F}_2^{acq} \wedge \mathbb{F}_3^{ar}$

candidate-fences

cycles in τ_1 (C_{τ_1}):
$\{\mathbb{F}_1, \mathbb{F}_2, e_1\}$ and $\{\mathbb{F}_1, \mathbb{F}_3, \mathbb{F}_4\}$
$\Phi_{\tau_1} = (\mathbb{F}_1 \wedge \mathbb{F}_2) \vee (\mathbb{F}_1 \wedge \mathbb{F}_3 \wedge \mathbb{F}_4)$
cycles in τ_2 (C_{τ_2}): $\{\mathbb{F}_3, \mathbb{F}_4\}$
$\Phi_{\tau_2} = (\mathbb{F}_3 \wedge \mathbb{F}_4)$

3-fence

Further, `assignMO` iterates over all buggy traces and detects the sound weakest memory order for each fence across all traces as follows. Assume a cycle c_1 in $\tau_1{}^{imm}$ and a cycle c_2 in $\tau_2{}^{imm}$. The function computes a union of the fences of τ_1 and τ_2 while choosing the stronger memory order for each fence that is present in both the cycles. In doing so, both τ_1 and τ_2 are invalidated. Further, when two candidate solutions have the same set of fences, the function selects the one with the lower weight.

Consider the cycles of buggy traces τ_1 and τ_2 shown in (`candidate-fences`). Let $\min\Phi = \{\mathbb{F}_1, \mathbb{F}_2, \mathbb{F}_3\}$. The memory orders of the fences for each trace are shown with superscripts and the weights of the cycle $\tau_1 c_1$, $\tau_1 c_2$ and $\tau_2 c_1$ are written against the name of the cycles. The candidate solutions $\tau_1 c_1$ and $\tau_1 c_2$ are combined with $\tau_2 c_1$ to form $\tau_{12} c_{11}$ and $\tau_{12} c_{21}$ of weights 5 and 4, respectively. The solution $\tau_{12} c_{11}$ is of higher weight and is discarded. In $\tau_{12} c_{21}$, the optimal memory orders `rel`, `acq` and `ar` are assigned to fences $\mathbb{F}_1$, $\mathbb{F}_2$ and $\mathbb{F}_3$, respectively. It is possible that `min-cycles` may contain fences originally in P. If the process discussed above computes a stronger memory order for a program fence than its original order in P, then the technique strengthens the memory order of the fence to the computed order. Note that this reasoning across traces does not occur in `fFenSying` as it considers only one trace at a time.

Determining the optimal memory orders has a complexity in $\mathcal{O}(\text{BT}.\text{C}.\text{F} + \text{M}^{\text{BT}})$, where BT if the number of buggy traces of P, C and F are defined as before, and M is the number of min-cycles per trace.

In our experimental observation (refer to Sect. 7), the number of buggy traces analyzed by `fFenSying` is significantly less than $|\text{BT}|$. Therefore, in practice, the complexity of various steps of `fFenSying` that are dependent on BT reduces exponentially by a factor of $|\text{BT}|$.

Nonoptimality of `fFenSying`. Consider the example (`3-fence`). It shows cycles in two buggy traces τ_1 and τ_2 of an input program. `FenSying` provides the formula $\Phi_{\tau_1} \wedge \Phi_{\tau_2}$ to the SAT solver and the optimal solution obtained is ($\mathbb{F}_1 \wedge \mathbb{F}_3 \wedge \mathbb{F}_4$). However, `fFenSying` considers the formula Φ_{τ_1} and Φ_{τ_2} in separate iterations and may return a nonoptimal result ($\mathbb{F}_1 \wedge \mathbb{F}_2$) $\wedge$ ($\mathbb{F}_3 \wedge \mathbb{F}_4$).

We prove the soundness of `fFenSying` and `FenSying` with Theorems 1 and 2 respectively and the optimality of `FenSying` with Theorem 3. The theorems are formally presented with proofs in the extended version [22].

Theorem 1. *`fFenSying` is sound. If a buggy trace τ of P can be invalidated using C11 fences then `fFenSying` will invalidate τ.*

Theorem 2. *FenSying is sound. If a buggy program P can be fixed using C11 fences, then FenSying will invalidate all buggy traces of P.*

Theorem 3. *FenSying is optimal. FenSying synthesizes optimal number of fences with optimal memory orders.*

7   Implementation and Results

Implementation Details. The techniques are implemented in Python. Weak-FenSying and Strong-FenSying use *Johnson's* cycle detection algorithm in the *networkx* library. We use Z3 theorem prover to find the *min-model* of SAT queries. As a BTG, we use CDSChecker [20], an open-source model checker, for the following reasons;

1. CDSChecker supports the *C11* semantics. Most other techniques are designed for a variant [15] or subset [1,3,23] of *C11*.
2. CDSChecker returns buggy traces along with the corresponding $\rightarrow_\tau^{\mathrm{hb}}$, $\rightarrow_\tau^{\mathrm{rf}}$ and $\rightarrow_\tau^{\mathrm{mo}}$ relations.
3. CDSChecker does not halt at the detection of the first buggy trace; instead, it continues to provide all buggy traces as required by FenSying.

To bridge the gap between CDSChecker's output and our requirements, we modify CDSChecker's code to accept program location as an attribute of the program events and to halt at the first buggy trace when specified. FenSying and fFenSying are available as an open-source tool that performs fence synthesis for *C11* programs at: https://github.com/singhsanjana/fensying.

Experimental Setup. The experiments were performed on an Intel(R) Xeon(R) CPU E5-1650 v4 @ 3.60 GHz with 32 GB RAM and 32 cores. We collected a set of 1389 litmus tests of buggy *C11* input programs (borrowed from Tracer [3]) to validate the correctness of FenSying and fFenSying experimentally. We study the performance of FenSying and fFenSying on a set of benchmarks borrowed from previous works on model checking under *C11* and its variants [1,3,20,23].

Experimental Validation. The summary of the 1389 litmus tests is shown under *Litmus Tests Summary*, Table 1. The number of buggy traces for the litmus tests ranged between 1–9 with an average of 1.05, while the number of fences synthesized ranged between 2–4. None of the litmus tests contained fences in the input program. Hence, no fences were strengthened in any of the tests.

We present the results of FenSying and fFenSying under *Result Summary*, Table 1. The results have been averaged over five runs for each test. fFenSying timed out (column 'TO') on a fewer number of tests (34 tests) in comparison to FenSying (56 tests). The techniques could not fix 148 tests with *C11* fences ('no fix'). The column 'NO' represents the number of tests where the fences synthesized or strengthened is nonoptimal. To report the values of 'NO', we conducted a sanity test on the fixed program as follows: we create versions

Table 1. Litmus testing summary

Litmus Tests Summary

Tests	min-BT	max-BT	avg-BT	min-syn	max-syn	avg-syn	min-str	max-str	avg-str
1389	1	9	1.05	1	4	2.25	0	0	0

BT: #buggy traces, syn: #fences synthesized, str: # fences strengthened

min: minimum, max: maximum, avg: average

Results Summary

	completed (syn+no fix)	TO	NO	Tbtg (total)	TF (total)	Ttotal
FenSying	1333 (1185+148)	56	0	50453.19	36896.06	87266.09
fFenSying	1355 (1207+148)	34	0	30703.71	49068.61	79772.32

Times in seconds.   TO: 15 min for BTG + 15min for technique

Tbtg: Time of BTG, TF: Time of FenSying or fFenSying, Ttotal: Tbtg+TF

$P_1, ...P_k$ of the fixed program P^{fx} s.t. in each version, one of the fences of P^{fx} is either weakened or eliminated. Each version is then tested separately on BTG. The sanity check is successful if a buggy trace is returned for each version.

Performance Analysis. We contrast the performance of the techniques using a set of benchmarks that produce buggy traces under *C11*. The results are averaged over five runs. Table 2 reports the results where '#BT' shows the number of buggy traces, 'iter' shows the minimum:maximum number of iterations performed by fFenSying over the five runs and, 'FTo' and 'BTo' represent FenSying/fFenSying time-out and BTG time-out, respectively (set to 15 min each). A '?' in '#BT' signifies that BTG could not scale for the test, so the number of buggy traces is unknown. The column ('syn+str') under fFenSying reports the minimum:maximum number of fences synthesized and/or strengthened. We add a '*' against the time when BTG timed out in detecting that the fixed program has no more buggy traces.

The performance of FenSying and fFenSying is diagrammatically contrasted in Fig. 1. It is notable that fFenSying significantly outperforms FenSying in terms of the time of execution and scalability and adds extra fences in only 7 tests with an average of 1.57 additional fences. With the increase in the number of buggy traces, an exponential rise in FenSying's time leading to FTo was observed; except in cases 12, 13, 20, and 25, where FenSying times out with as low as 10 traces. The tests time-out in *Johnson's* cycle detection due to a high density of the number of related events or the number of cycles.

fFenSying analyzes a remarkably smaller number of buggy traces ('iter') in comparison with '#BT' (≤ 2 traces for ~85% of tests). We conclude that a solution corresponding to a single buggy trace fixes more than one buggy traces. As a result, fFenSying can scale to tests with thousands of buggy traces and we witness an average speedup of over 67x, with over 100x speedup in ~41% of tests, against FenSying.

Interesting cases. Consider test 16, where BTG times out in 3/5 runs and completes in ~100s in the remaining 2 runs. A fence is synthesized between two events, e_1

Table 2. Comparative performance analysis

Id	Name	#BT	FenSying				fFenSying				
			syn+str	Tbtg	TF	Ttotal	iter	syn+str	Tbtg	TF	Ttotal
1	peterson(2,2)	30	1+0	2.63	54.31	56.94	1:1	1:1+0:0	0.18	2.07	2.25
2	peterson(2,3)	198	1+0	29.96	594.34	624.3	1:1	1:1+0:0	0.53	3.58	4.11
3	peterson(4,5)	?	−	−	FTo	−	1:1	1:1+0:0	397.51	21.07	418.58
4	peterson(5,5)	?	−	BTo	−	−	1:1	1:1+0:0	BTo	31.52	*931.52
5	barrier(5)	136	1+0	1.09	207.74	208.83	1:1	1:1+0:0	0.13	1.40	1.53
6	barrier(10)	416	1+0	3.37	565.44	568.81	1:1	1:1+0:0	0.2	2.70	2.9
7	barrier(100)	31106	−	−	FTo	−	1:1	1:1+0:0	34.2	198.54	232.74
8	barrier(150)	?	−	−	FTo	−	1:1	1:1+0:0	117.09	399.20	516.29
9	barrier(200)	−	−	−	−	−	−	−	−	FTo	−
10	store-buffer(2)	6	2+0	0.08	0.91	0.99	1:1	2:2+0:0	0.04	0.05	0.09
11	store-buffer(4)	20	2+0	1.61	195.35	196.96	1:1	2:2+0:0	1.20	0.05	1.25
12	store-buffer(5)	30	−	−	FTo	−	1:1	2:2+0:0	14.07	0.22	14.29
13	store-buffer(6)	42	−	−	FTo	−	1:1	2:2+0:0	171.09	0.15	171.24
14	store-buffer(10)	?	−	BTo	−	−	1:1	2:2+0:0	BTo	0.05	*900.05
15	dekker(2)	54	2+0	0.17	0.27	0.44	1:1	2:2+0:0	0.26	0.04	0.3
16	dekker(3)	1596	−	−	FTo	−	1:1	2:2+0:0	586.46	1.34	587.8
17	dekker-fen(2,3)	54	1+1	0.15	0.29	0.44	1:1	1:1+1:1	0.25	0.05	0.3
18	dekker-fen(3,2)	730	−	−	FTo	−	1:1	1:1+1:1	159.84	5.56	165.4
19	dekker-fen(3,4)	3076	−	BTo	−	−	1:1	1:1+1:1	BTo	6.06	*906.06
20	burns(1)	36	−	−	FTo	−	7:8	8:10+2:2	0.61	4.69	5.3
21	burns(2)	10150	−	−	FTo	−	6:7	8:10+0:1	71.53	554.6	626.13
22	burns(3)	?	−	BTo	−	−	−	−	−	FTo	−
23	burns-fen(2)	100708	−	−	FTo	−	5:7	4:6+3:3	329.41	43.96	373.37
24	burns-fen(3)	?	−	BTo	−	−	5:7	4:6+3:3	BTo	70.14	*970.14
25	linuxrwlocks(2,1)	10	−	−	FTo	−	1:1	2:2+0:0	0.13	0.12	0.25
26	linuxrwlocks(3,8)	353	−	−	FTo	−	2:2	3:4+0:0	686.52	0.41	*686.93
27	seqlock(2,1,2)	500	−	−	FTo	−	1:1	1:1+0:0	341.54	2.38	343.92
28	seqlock(1,2,2)	592	−	−	FTo	−	1:2	1:2+0:0	119.88	27.69	147.57
29	seqlock(2,2,3)	?	−	BTo	−	−	1:2	1:2+0:0	BTo	88.52	988.52*
30	bakery(2,1)	6	1+0	0.25	25.42	2.88	1:1	1:1+0:0	0.07	0.18	0.25
31	bakery(4,3)	7272	−	−	FTo	−	1:1	1:1+0:0	166.11	5.68	171.79
32	bakery(4,4)	50402	−	−	FTo	−	1:1	1:1+0:0	BTo	18.17	918.17*
33	lamport(1,1,2)	1	No fix	0.06	0.05	0.11	1:1	No fix	0.04	0.05	0.09
34	lamport(2,2,1)	1	No fix	411.94	0.05	411.99	1:1	No fix	53.34	0.05	53.39
35	lamport(2,2,3)	?	−	BTo	−	−	1:1	No fix	389.77	0.05	389.82
36	flipper(5)	297	2+0	6.22	254.18	260.40	1:1	2+0	2.51	0.02	2.53
37	flipper(7)	4493	−	−	FTo	−	1:1	2+0	119.21	0.02	119.23
38	flipper(10)	?	−	−	FTo	−	1:1	2+0	BTo	0.03	900.03*

Tbtg: Time of BTG, TF: Time of technique (FenSying or fFenSying), Ttotal: Tbtg+TF

and e_2, that are inside a loop. Additionally, e_1 is within a condition. Depending on where the fence is synthesized (within the condition or outside it), BTG either runs out of time or finishes quickly. Similarly, BTG for test 26 times out in 3/5 runs. However, the reason here is the additional nonoptimal fences synthesized that increase the analysis overhead of the chosen BTG (CDSChecker).

Note that, for most benchmarks, fFenSying's scalability is limited by BTo and observably fFenSying's time is much lesser than FTo for such cases. Therefore, an alternative BTG would significantly improve fFenSying's performance.

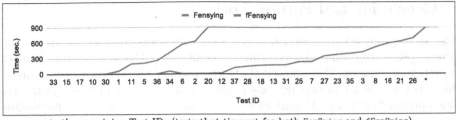

★ represents the remaining Test IDs (tests that timeout for both FenSying and fFenSying)

Fig. 1. Performance comparison between **FenSying** and **fFenSying**

8 Related Work

The literature on fence synthesis is rich with techniques targeting the x86-TSO [2,5–7,10] and sparc-PSO [4,18] memory models or both [14,16,19]. The work in [10] and [16] perform fence synthesis for ARMv7 and RMO memory models. The works in [4,7,11] are proposed for Power memory model, where [11] also supports IA-32 memory model.

Most fence synthesis techniques introduce additional ordering in the program events with the help of fences [5–7,10,11,14,18,19,24]. However, the axiomatic definition of ordering varies with memory models. As a consequence, most existing techniques (such as those for TSO and PSO) may not detect *C11* buggy traces due to a strong implicit ordering. While the techniques [6,7,24] are parametric in or oblivious to the memory model, they introduce ordering between *pairs* of events that is *globally visible* (to all threads). Such an ordering constraint is restrictive for weaker models such as *C11* that may require ordering on a *set* of events that may be *conditionally visible* to a thread. Similarly, [14] proposes a bounded technique applicable to any memory model that supports interleaving with reordering. Program outcomes under *C11* may not be feasible under such a model. Moreover, any existing technique, cannot fix a *C11* input program while conserving its portability.

Some earlier works such as [2,7,11] synthesize fences to restrict outcomes to SC or its variant for store-buffering [5]. Most fence synthesis techniques [4, 14,16,18,19] attempt to remove traces violating a safety property specification under their respective axiomatic definition of memory model. Various works [4,5,10,14,16,19,24] perform optimal fence synthesis where the optimality (in the absence of types of fences) is simply defined as the smallest set of fences. Technique [6] assigns weights to various types of fences (similar to our work) and defines optimality on the summation of fence weights of candidate solutions. However, their definition of optimality is incomparable with ours, and no prior work establishes the advantage of one definition over the other.

Lastly, a recent technique [21] fixes a buggy *C11* program by strengthening memory access events instead of synthesizing fences.

9   Conclusion and Future Work

This paper proposed the first fence synthesis techniques for *C11* programs: an optimal (FenSying) and a near-optimal (fFenSying). The work also presented theoretical arguments that showed the correctness of the synthesis techniques. The experimental validation demonstrated the effectiveness of fFenSying vis-à-vis optimal FenSying. As part of future work, we will investigate extending the presented methods (i) to support richer constructs such as locks and (ii) to include strengthening memory accesses to fix buggy traces.

References

1. Abdulla, P.A., Arora, J., Atig, M.F., Krishna, S.: Verification of programs under the release-acquire semantics. In: Proceedings of the 40th ACM SIGPLAN Conference on Programming Language Design and Implementation, pp. 1117–1132 (2019)
2. Abdulla, P.A., Atig, M.F., Chen, Y.-F., Leonardsson, C., Rezine, A.: Automatic fence insertion in integer programs via predicate abstraction. In: Miné, A., Schmidt, D. (eds.) SAS 2012. LNCS, vol. 7460, pp. 164–180. Springer, Heidelberg (2012). https://doi.org/10.1007/978-3-642-33125-1_13
3. Abdulla, P.A., Atig, M.F., Jonsson, B., Ngo, T.P.: Optimal stateless model checking under the release-acquire semantics. Proc. ACM Program. Lang. **2**(OOPSLA), 1–29 (2018)
4. Abdulla, P.A., Atig, M.F., Lång, M., Ngo, T.P.: Precise and sound automatic fence insertion procedure under PSO. In: Bouajjani, A., Fauconnier, H. (eds.) NETYS 2015. LNCS, vol. 9466, pp. 32–47. Springer, Cham (2015). https://doi.org/10.1007/978-3-319-26850-7_3
5. Abdulla, P.A., Atig, M.F., Ngo, T.-P.: The best of both worlds: trading efficiency and optimality in fence insertion for TSO. In: Vitek, J. (ed.) ESOP 2015. LNCS, vol. 9032, pp. 308–332. Springer, Heidelberg (2015). https://doi.org/10.1007/978-3-662-46669-8_13
6. Alglave, J., Kroening, D., Nimal, V., Poetzl, D.: Don't sit on the fence. In: Biere, A., Bloem, R. (eds.) CAV 2014. LNCS, vol. 8559, pp. 508–524. Springer, Cham (2014). https://doi.org/10.1007/978-3-319-08867-9_33
7. Alglave, J., Maranget, L., Sarkar, S., Sewell, P.: Fences in weak memory models. In: Touili, T., Cook, B., Jackson, P. (eds.) CAV 2010. LNCS, vol. 6174, pp. 258–272. Springer, Heidelberg (2010). https://doi.org/10.1007/978-3-642-14295-6_25
8. Angiulli, F., Ben-Eliyahu-Zohary, R., Fassetti, F., Palopoli, L.: On the tractability of minimal model computation for some CNF theories. Artif. Intell. **210**, 56–77 (2014)
9. Batty, M., Owens, S., Sarkar, S., Sewell, P., Weber, T.: Mathematizing c++ concurrency. ACM SIGPLAN Notices **46**(1), 55–66 (2011)
10. Bender, J., Lesani, M., Palsberg, J.: Declarative fence insertion. ACM SIGPLAN Notices **50**(10), 367–385 (2015)
11. Fang, X., Lee, J., Midkiff, S.P.: Automatic fence insertion for shared memory multi-processing. In: Proceedings of the 17th Annual International Conference on Super-computing, pp. 285–294 (2003)
12. ISO/IEC-JTC1/SC22/WG21: Programming languages - C++ (2013). http://www.open-std.org/jtc1/sc22/wg21/docs/papers/2013/n3690.pdf

13. Johnson, D.B.: Finding all the elementary circuits of a directed graph. SIAM J. Comput. **4**(1), 77–84 (1975)
14. Joshi, S., Kroening, D.: Property-driven fence insertion using reorder bounded model checking. In: Bjørner, N., de Boer, F. (eds.) FM 2015. LNCS, vol. 9109, pp. 291–307. Springer, Cham (2015). https://doi.org/10.1007/978-3-319-19249-9_19
15. Kokologiannakis, M., Raad, A., Vafeiadis, V.: Model checking for weakly consistent libraries. In: Proceedings of the 40th ACM SIGPLAN Conference on Programming Language Design and Implementation, pp. 96–110 (2019)
16. Kuperstein, M., Vechev, M., Yahav, E.: Automatic inference of memory fences. ACM SIGACT News **43**(2), 108–123 (2012)
17. Lahav, O., Vafeiadis, V., Kang, J., Hur, C.K., Dreyer, D.: Repairing sequential consistency in c/c++ 11, vol. 52, pp. 618–632. ACM New York, NY (2017)
18. Linden, A., Wolper, P.: A verification-based approach to memory fence insertion in PSO memory systems. In: Piterman, N., Smolka, S.A. (eds.) TACAS 2013. LNCS, vol. 7795, pp. 339–353. Springer, Heidelberg (2013). https://doi.org/10.1007/978-3-642-36742-7_24
19. Meshman, Y., Dan, A., Vechev, M., Yahav, E.: Synthesis of memory fences via refinement propagation. In: Müller-Olm, M., Seidl, H. (eds.) SAS 2014. LNCS, vol. 8723, pp. 237–252. Springer, Cham (2014). https://doi.org/10.1007/978-3-319-10936-7_15
20. Norris, B., Demsky, B.: CDSchecker: checking concurrent data structures written with C/C++ atomics. In: Proceedings of the 2013 ACM SIGPLAN International Conference on Object Oriented Programming Systems Languages & Applications, pp. 131–150 (2013)
21. Oberhauser, J., et al.: VSync: push-button verification and optimization for synchronization primitives on weak memory models. In: Proceedings of the 26th ACM International Conference on Architectural Support for Programming Languages and Operating Systems, pp. 530–545 (2021)
22. Singh, S., Sharma, D., Jaju, I., Sharma, S.: Fence synthesis under the c11 memory model. arXiv preprint arXiv:2208.00285 (2022)
23. Singh, S., Sharma, D., Sharma, S.: Dynamic verification of c11 concurrency over multi copy atomics. In: 2021 International Symposium on Theoretical Aspects of Software Engineering (TASE), pp. 39–46. IEEE (2021)
24. Taheri, M., Pourdamghani, A., Lesani, M.: Polynomial-time fence insertion for structured programs. In: 33rd International Symposium on Distributed Computing (DISC 2019). Schloss Dagstuhl-Leibniz-Zentrum fuer Informatik (2019)
25. Vafeiadis, V., Balabonski, T., Chakraborty, S., Morisset, R., Zappa Nardelli, F.: Common compiler optimisations are invalid in the c11 memory model and what we can do about it. In: Proceedings of the 42Nd Annual ACM SIGPLAN-SIGACT Symposium on Principles of Programming Languages, pp. 209–220 (2015)

Checking Scheduling-Induced Violations of Control Safety Properties

Anand Yeolekar[1,2(✉)], Ravindra Metta[1,2], Clara Hobbs[3], and Samarjit Chakraborty[3]

[1] TCS Research, Pune, India
{anand.yeolekar,r.metta}@tcs.com
[2] TUM Germany, Munich, Germany
[3] University of North Carolina at Chapel Hill, Chapel Hill, USA
{cghobbs,samarjit}@cs.unc.edu

Abstract. Cyber-physical systems (CPS) are typically implemented as a set of real-time control tasks with periodic activation. When a control task misses it's deadline, policies for handling deadline miss – *e.g.* delayed scheduling of the task instance – may still lead the CPS into an unsafe or sub-optimal state. We present a technique for *exact* checking of such control safety and reachability properties, for a class of CPS, under common deadline miss handling and control update policies. In particular, we propose a joint encoding of control and scheduling behaviour as a satisfiability-modulo-theory formulation and a novel abstraction-refinement procedure with incremental solving to scale the analysis. Case studies with realistic systems show the utility of our approach.

Keywords: Control · Scheduling · Verification · Abstraction · Refinement

1 Introduction

CPS controllers are typically designed as a set of real-time tasks assuming ideal conditions, such as all tasks meet their deadlines, for ease of design, by abstracting away the implementation details. However, when the tasks are finally implemented in software, the control performance might deviate from the expected behaviour due to factors such as control task missing deadlines due to transient overload on the processor. When a control task instance misses its deadline, then depending on how the CPS is configured to handle deadline misses, the corresponding control computation may be *skipped* or *delayed* causing a potential deviation from the expected behaviour. Such intermittent deviation from expected behaviour, depending on when it occurs and by what amount, may in turn lead to control safety or reachability violation.

For example, consider the F1Tenth car model [14], where the controller is designed to steer the car along a predetermined path, without hitting an obstacle. Only some deadline miss patterns, coupled with selected choice of initial state of

A. Bouajjani et al. (Eds.): ATVA 2022, LNCS 13505, pp. 100–116, 2022.
https://doi.org/10.1007/978-3-031-19992-9_7

the car, will result into a collision (see Fig. 5). In this work, we focus on *analysing the interaction* between control and scheduling leading to such violations.

Existing analysis techniques assume a simplified scheduling model, such as bounding the maximum number of *consecutive* deadline misses [10,18], or restrict the scheduling behaviour by not admitting non-determinism in task specification, or non-preemption of tasks. However, a precise bound accounting for all feasible scheduling behaviours may not be easily identifiable for a given task set implementing the CPS. As a result, these techniques tend to be *pessimistic*, meaning the assumed worst-case deadline miss pattern, based on the bound, might never occur for a real system. Further, bugs that occur based on the interaction between control and scheduling layers are often subtle, near-impossible to reproduce by analyzing separately control or scheduling.

Therefore, to establish system correctness with respect to control properties, an analysis that **precisely maps** task runs containing all permitted sequences of deadline misses to control behaviour is needed, especially if the control or task specification admits non-determinism. Such an analysis helps CPS designers (i) to gauge the impact of scheduling parameters on control performance, and (ii) gain insight into the interplay of control evolution, scheduling policy, and strategies for handling deadline misses. Towards this end, we propose an approach to check scheduling-induced violations of control safety and reachability properties.

Summary of Our Approach: Given a (discrete) control system, a set of tasks realizing the controller, and an analysis horizon h indicating length of control evolution, we construct an *abstract* model of the system behaviour (control evolution and runs of the tasks), which admits all feasible system behaviour as well as some infeasible (spurious) behaviour. We check this model for violation of specified control properties using a constraint solver, which reports a *witness* on finding a violation. If the witness is spurious (an infeasible task run or control trajectory), we iteratively *refine* the model to *block* the spurious witnesses, until either a genuine witness is obtained or no more witnesses exist, proving that the control property holds on the original system. Our main contributions are:

Encoding: we propose a Satisfiability-Modulo-Theory (SMT) encoding that *abstracts* control and scheduling by *relaxing* certain constraints on their behaviour, which is then composed together with the property to be checked. Our encoding admits non-determinism at the control layer (arbitrary initial states), and scheduling layer such as delayed release (jitter) and variable execution times.

Refinement: we construct *blocking implications* from spurious witnesses to refine the abstraction, and utilize the *incremental analysis* feature of SMT solvers to efficiently analyze reasonably sized controllers and task sets.

Tool: we implemented the above abstraction and the refinement scheme to check control property violations, supporting four common combinations of deadline miss handling and control update strategies, and one static and one dynamic non-preemptive scheduling policy.

Table 1. Symbolic variables used in the SMT encoding

Notation	Type	Description
$x_{j,k}$	Real	j-th dimension of plant state at k-th time step
u_k	Real	Control update value at k-th step
$r_k^i, s_k^i, e_k^i, d_k^i$	Int	release, start, end, and deadline times of the k-th job of i-th task

Related Work: Encoding of control and schedule to assess and correct impact of scheduling anomalies on control performance has been studied [17] when a set of periodic tasks with implicit deadlines is not schedulable, and to systematically adjust the task periods to achieve schedulablity. [5] combines the control and timing models as hybrid automata and verifies with Space Ex model checker [6].

The impact of timing uncertainty, such as deadline misses, on control has been studied [10,12,18,20], but broadly focused on analysis of control stability *i.e.* whether control trajectories converge to an equilibrium point. However, as observed in [1], a stable control system might still violate safety properties, hence the need for an approach to check safety properties. [15] proposes a rich state-based representation for capturing deadline misses and measure their impact on control performance. [16] presents a static scheduling strategy that guarantees control performance while smartly saving resources. Another approach of automatically adapting the control system to deadline misses to guarantee performance is proposed in [19], along with worst-case stability analysis. However, these approaches need a bound to be specified on the number of consecutive deadline misses possible.

The effect of control trajectories going outside safe regions in CPS has also been studied and remedial actions were proposed [4,21] for fixed priority scheduling and controller co-design. [3] dynamically extends the period of control tasks, based on historical measurements, to reduce power consumption and accommodate increased resource demands from other components.

In most works, a model of deadline misses needs to be provided by user, which may sometimes help scale the analysis better than our approach. However the main limitations of these approaches are: (i) *extracting* the assumed model of deadline misses from the task specification, and (ii) unavoidable pessimism due to worst case assumptions. In contrast, our approach faithfully models task runs and control evolution, for *precise* analysis.

2   System Model and Encoding

2.1   Control System Model and Evolution

A discrete control system describing the plant model is defined as:

$$x_{k+1} = Ax_k + Bu_k \qquad u_k = R - Kx_k \qquad (1)$$

where $x \in \mathbb{R}^{n \times 1}$ is the discrete state vector, $n \geq 1$ is the control system dimension; $k \in \mathbb{N}$ denotes the discrete steps of evolution; $A \in \mathbb{R}^{n \times n}$ and $B \in \mathbb{R}^{n \times 1}$

are matrices specifying the discrete-time plant model with timestep δ. The control input $u \in \mathbb{R}$ is computed using a state feedback vector $K \in \mathbb{R}^{1 \times n}$, and an optional reference value $R \in \mathbb{R}$. The initial state x_0 must lie in a user-specified interval $[\underline{X}_0, \overline{X}_0]$ along each dimension.

Our encoding approach unrolls the closed-loop discrete control system described in Eq. 1 up to the user-specified bound h. To unroll, we introduce symbolic variables $x_{j,k}$ corresponding to the control states, and u_k corresponding to the control action update, where j ranges over the dimension of the control system $1, 2, \ldots, n$, and k ranges over the discrete steps of evolution $0, 1, \ldots, h$. We first construct the constraints on the initial plant state as:

$$\phi_{init} := \forall j : \underline{X}_{j,0} \leq x_{j,0} \leq \overline{X}_{j,0} \tag{2}$$

Then, symbolically encoding the trajectories that could originate from any point in the initial set, we construct constraints on the control state variables as:

$$\phi_{traj} := \bigwedge_{k=0}^{h} \left(\bigwedge_{i=1}^{n} x_{i,k+1} = \sum_{j'=1}^{j} A_{i,j'} x_{j',k} + B_i u_k \right) \tag{3}$$

We defer the explanation of the timing model and associated control update modeling u_k to Sect. 2.4. Given the analysis horizon h, the control safety and reachability properties over the trajectories are:

$$\phi_{prop} := \underline{X}_{j,h} \leq x_{j,h} \leq \overline{X}_{j,h} \quad \text{(reachability)}$$
$$\phi_{prop} := \underline{X}_{j,k} \leq x_{j,k} \leq \overline{X}_{j,k} \, , \, 0 \leq k \leq h \quad \text{(safety)} \tag{4}$$

where $[\underline{X}_{j,h}, \overline{X}_{j,h}]$, $[\underline{X}_{j,k}, \overline{X}_{j,k}]$ denote the user-specified reach and safety intervals (or safety pipes), respectively, for j-th dimension.

2.2   Task Specification

The controller is realized in software via a set of tasks $\mathcal{T}$ that includes the control and auxiliary tasks $e.g.$ loggers, communication, etc. We currently support non-preemptive earliest-deadline-first (NP-EDF) representing dynamic priority scheduling, and rate-monotonic (NP-RM), representing static priority scheduling[1], under unicore setting. A task $\tau_i \in \mathcal{T}$ is defined as $(O, J, \underline{E}, \overline{E}, P)$, where i is a unique task id, O is the task offset, J denotes release jitter faced by task instances, $\underline{E}$ and $\overline{E}$ denote the best- and worst-case execution times of the tasks respectively, and P denotes the period. We assume τ_0 corresponds to the controller task with period set to the discretization timestep: $P^0 = \delta$.

We refer to task instances as $jobs$. Release time of the k-th job spawned by τ_i is denoted by r_k^i. Due to release jitter, the instant of job release lies in the interval $[kP^i + O^i, kP^i + O^i + J^i]$. We denote the start, end and deadline

---

[1] While our method can be adapted to handle preemptions, we focus on NP scheduling for ease of presentation and leave the extension as future work.

time of the job as s_k^i, e_k^i and d_k^i. We assume task deadlines are implicit, thus $d_k^i = O^i + (k+1)P^i$, and a deadline *miss* occurs when $e_k^i > d_k^i$. Under CONTINUE policy, jobs are eventually scheduled even if they miss deadline, and under KILL, jobs are aborted in case of *conservative* deadline miss (*i.e.*, a job is aborted if its execution does not begin by $d_k^i - \overline{E^i}$). Under NP-RM, jobs of the same task are scheduled in the order of release. Finally, jobs are released, scheduled and terminate at *discrete* time points.

Definition 1. *A run of the task set is a timed sequence of jobs, $\langle \ldots, (i, k, s_k^i, e_k^i), \ldots \rangle$, respecting the given scheduling policy and deadline miss strategy.*

We assume the scheduling is *work-conserving i.e.* a ready job must be scheduled as soon as the processor is available. Observe that multiple runs of the task set are possible due to (i) release jitter experienced by each job, (ii) variable execution budget leading to non-deterministic termination time for each job, and (iii) arbitrary selection of equal-priority ready jobs. These runs can have varying impact on the control performance and need to be analyzed rigorously.

2.3   An Abstraction for Task Runs

We explain how to encode the set of runs of the task set. Our approach spawns jobs of all tasks up to the time instant $h \times \delta$ and we encode runs of the task set as a logical formula. There is no explicit modeling of the scheduler; the operational semantics of the scheduling process, *e.g.*, the scheduler's run queue, tasks moving from sleep to ready state, etc. are modeled implicitly in the formula.

From the task specification (Sect. 2.2) we construct constraints on the symbolic variables (Table 1) associated with each spawned job as:

$$\phi_{runs} := \forall\ (i, k):\ r_k^i \leq s_k^i\ \wedge\ kP^i + O^i \leq r_k^i \leq kP^i + O^i + J^i \wedge e_k^i \leq s_{k+1}^i$$
$$\wedge\ \underline{E^i} \leq e_k^i - s_k^i \leq \overline{E^i} \text{ (under CONTINUE)}$$
$$\wedge\ (s_k^i + \overline{E^i} \leq d_k^i \Rightarrow \underline{E^i} \leq e_k^i - s_k^i \leq \overline{E^i}) \wedge (s_k^i + \overline{E^i} > d_k^i \Rightarrow e_k^i = s_k^i) \text{ (under KILL)}$$
$$(5)$$

These constraints restrict the release, start and end times of jobs as per the task specification and deadline miss policy, however, they exclude the scheduling policy and work conservation at this stage of modeling. While this helps to keep the constraints concise and tractable, it introduces an *abstraction* with respect to the set of valid runs of the task set (admits all valid runs as well as spurious ones) as defined in Definition 1. In Sect. 3, we will restore precision by using refinements to prune away the spurious behaviour *i.e* invalid task runs.

2.4   Control Action Update Modeling

We admit ZERO and HOLD policies for control update u, where ZERO signifies applying $u = 0$ when the corresponding control task instance misses deadline, and HOLD signifies applying the previous value. Figure 1 illustrates the simplified logical execution timing (LET) model assumed in this work and the associated control action updates, under HOLD semantics. Plant sensing and actuation happens *instantaneously* at fixed discrete time points $k\delta$, irrespective of the scheduling of tasks[2]. As shown in the figure, job $k-1$, spawned at time $(k-1)\delta$, reads the plant state x_{k-1} at the beginning of its execution, processes the data, and writes an actuation value at termination. This actuation value is applied to the plant at the *next* time step $k\delta$, and corresponds to the control action update u_k. We assume $u_0 = 0$ (open loop for first step). On a deadline miss, *e.g* instance k missing deadline, u_{k+1} is matched to u_k (due to HOLD). Observe that instance k, which missed its deadline, is scheduled in the *next* slot $[(k+1)\delta, (k+2)\delta)$, enabling it to read the relatively *fresher* plant state x_{k+1}. Instance $k+1$ is scheduled in its own slot $[(k+1)\delta, (k+2)\delta)$ but misses its deadline, instance $k+2$ meets its deadline, and both write sequentially to the actuation buffer in the same time slot, corresponding to control action update u_{k+3}. In such a case, we assume the actuation buffer is *overwritten* by the fresher value.

Updates are thus *delayed* when the controller is realized in software. We model this by constructing *conditional control update* constraints as:

$$\phi_u := \forall k : u_k = 0, \text{ if } k = 0$$
$$\wedge\, e_{k-1}^0 \leq d_{k-1}^0 \Rightarrow u_k = R - \sum_{j=1}^{n} K_j x_{j,k-1} \text{ (under CONTINUE)}$$
$$\wedge\, s_{k-1}^0 + \overline{E}^0 \leq d_{k-1}^0 \Rightarrow u_k = R - \sum_{j=1}^{n} K_j x_{j,k-1} \text{ (under KILL)} \qquad (6)$$
$$\wedge\, s_{k-1}^0 + \overline{E}^0 > d_{k-1}^0 \Rightarrow u_k = u_{k-1} \text{ (under HOLD-KILL)}$$
$$\wedge\, s_{k-1}^0 + \overline{E}^0 > d_{k-1}^0 \Rightarrow u_k = 0 \text{ (under ZERO-KILL)}$$

Notice that, under CONTINUE policy, the above constraints enforce control update computation when deadlines are *met*, but leaves the control update *unconstrained* on a deadline miss. This introduces an *abstraction* with respect to control updates. This is necessary at this stage of modeling, as we do not know *statically* how many jobs could miss being *consecutively scheduled* all together in any run of the given task set *i.e.* how much to "look back" from the current step to pick the *preceding* control task instance execution, to use that value as the freshest, when encoding the control update. Additionally, this helps in keeping the control action constraints tractable and concise. In Sect. 3.4, we will restore precision by refining control updates. Note that under KILL policy, control updates are always precisely computed (there is no abstraction).

Definition 2 (Trajectory). *A (discrete) trajectory of the control system is a sequence of values of state variables $\langle \ldots, (k, x_1, \ldots, x_j), \ldots \rangle$, originating from a valid initial state, ordered on the evolution step counter k, respecting the state and control Eqs. 1 and 6.*

---

[2] We assume a time-triggered hardware implementation of sensing/actuation, outside the scheduling purview, with values stored in buffers accessed by the control task.

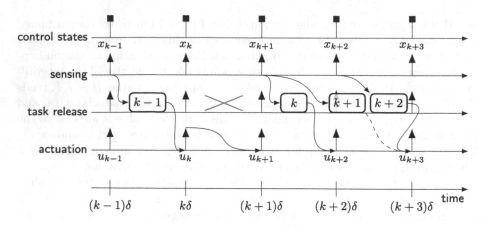

Fig. 1. Timing model illustrating sensing, task release and actuation, under HOLD

2.5 Composing Control and Scheduling Models

From the encodings for the control trajectories from Eqs. 2 and 3, task runs from Eq. 5, control update from Eq. 6, and the control property from Eq. 4, we construct the system composition as:

$$\phi_{sys} := \phi_{init} \wedge \phi_{traj} \wedge \phi_u \wedge \phi_{runs} \wedge \neg\phi_{prop} \tag{7}$$

3 Refining the Abstraction

Consider a solution to ϕ_{sys} reported by an SMT solver, that assigns concrete values to all the symbolic variables in the formula. The solution is parsed to extract (i) the run of the tasks consisting of a sequence of jobs, termed σ_{run}, and (ii) the control trajectory, sorted on the step counter k, termed σ_{traj}. If σ_{run} satisfies Definition 1, we have a run generated from the abstract ϕ_{sys} that precisely maps to a *concrete run* of $\mathcal{T}$. Similarly, if σ_{traj} satisfies Definition 2, we have a control trajectory, generated from the abstract ϕ_{sys}, that precisely maps to a *concrete trajectory* of the control system.

However, if either σ_{run} or σ_{traj} violate their respective definitions, we have a *spurious* trace leading to property violation. To block such a trace from ϕ_{sys}, we identify the causes of non-compliance within the definitions. For Definition 1 the causes can be overlapping jobs, scheduling policy violation, or work conservation violation, and for Definition 2, unconstrained control update due to deadline miss.

3.1 Overlapping Jobs

Suppose job (i, j) overlaps with (i', j') in σ_{run}, with $s_j^i \leq s_{j'}^{i'}$. This is possible as the abstraction does not prevent overlaps *upfront*. Observe that though in this trace (i, j) preceded (i', j'), there can be a run of $\mathcal{T}$ with the precedence reversed. Thus, to block this overlap as witnessed in this trace, we construct:

$$B_{ov} := (s_j^i \leq s_{j'}^{i'} \wedge s_{j'}^{i'} < e_j^i) \Rightarrow e_j^i \leq s_{j'}^{i'} \tag{8}$$

This implication when conjuncted with ϕ_{sys} blocks *this* particular pair of jobs from overlapping again in *any* trace, under the premise that (i, j) precedes (i', j').

3.2 Schedule Violation

Suppose job (i, j) precedes (i', j') in σ_{run}, but this precedence violates the scheduling policy. Under NP-EDF, (i, j) can precede (i', j') if and only if the deadline of (i, j) is *no later than* that of (i', j'), or (i, j) is scheduled strictly before (i', j') is released. Thus we construct the blocking implication[3]:

$$B_{sv} := s_j^i < s_{j'}^{i'} \Rightarrow (d_j^i \leq d_{j'}^{i'} \vee s_j^i < r_{j'}^{i'}) \qquad \text{(under NP-EDF)} \tag{9}$$

Conjuncting B_{sv} with ϕ_{sys} blocks the scheduling violation caused by *this* pair of jobs in *any* trace, under the premise that (i, j) precedes (i', j').

3.3 Work Conservation Violation

Here, the processor cannot idle in the presence of a ready job. We assume that σ_{run} is free of overlapping jobs, easily achieved by repeatedly refining ϕ_{sys} with B_{ov} implications. There are two cases to analyze: (a) processor idling immediately after release of job (i, j), implying that $s_j^i = r_j^i$, and (b) idling post termination of some job (i', j') within the waiting time of (i, j), implying $s_j^i = e_{j'}^{i'}$.

Observe, however, there can be runs of $\mathcal{T}$ with different jobs preceding (i, j), which raises the question: what is the set of jobs preceding (i, j) across all runs? This set, denoted $prec_j^i$, is *conservatively* estimated as follows: Intuitively, jobs released earlier *and* having higher priority will *always* precede (i, j) in all runs, and vice versa. Importantly, this set of jobs can be identified *statically* based on their period and deadline. Then, the complement of this set, characterized by a lack of static precedence guarantee, forms $prec_j^i$. Formally, consider job $(i', j'), i' \neq i$. If $d_{j'}^{i'} < d_j^i \wedge j'P^{i'} + O^{i'} + J^{i'} <= jP^i + O^i$ (and vice-versa) *does not hold* (under NP-EDF)[4], then $(i', j') \in prec_j^i$. Observe that $prec$ sets need to be computed only once per job violating work conservation.

The concrete starting instant of the processor idle interval, which is r_j^i in case (a), serves to *partition* the set of jobs $prec_j^i$, as witnessed in σ_{run}, into: (i) a *prefix* subset of jobs scheduled prior to r_j^i, and (ii) a *suffix* subset of jobs scheduled post r_j^i. Since there are no job overlaps in σ_{run}, we are guaranteed that *prefix* and *suffix* are mutually exclusive. Thus, we construct the blocking implication for case (a) to preventing processor idling as:

---

[3] Under NP-RM, priority (period) must be higher (lower): $P_i \leq P_{i'} \vee s_j^i < r_{j'}^{i'}$.

[4] Under NP-RM, this is $P^{i'} < P^i$.

$$B_{wc\_a} := (\ r_j^i < s_j^i \wedge \bigwedge_{(i',j') \in prefix} e_{j'}^{i'} < r_j^i \wedge \bigwedge_{(i',j') \in suffix} s_{j'}^{i'} > r_j^i\ ) \Rightarrow s_j^i = r_j^i \qquad (10)$$

Here, the antecedent captures the context witnessed in σ_{run} that: (i) job (i, j) had a non-zero waiting time, (ii) some jobs that could precede (i, j) were scheduled prior to r_j^i, (iii) the remaining jobs that could precede (i, j) were scheduled post r_j^i . Under these premises, the consequent enforces work conservation.

Similarly for case (b), $e_{j'}^{i'}$ partitions $prec$, changing the consequent to $s_j^i = e_{j'}^{i'}$.

3.4   Unconstrained Control Updates

The basic idea for refining unconstrained control updates is to locate the latest control job that was scheduled in σ_{run}, compute the control update issued by this job (if not already done), and use this as the freshest value. Observe that we cannot always pick the control update issued by the *preceding* job: From Fig. 1, job $k + 1$ missed its deadline, leading to an unconstrained u_{k+2}. However, here, we cannot pick u_{k+1} to match u_{k+2}, as job k did get scheduled and successfully terminated before the instant $(k + 2)\delta$, thereby issuing a *fresher* control update that must be matched with u_{k+2}. We discuss the various cases below.

Case 1: Suppose job $(0, n)$ missed its deadline d_n^0 in σ_{run}, enabling a spurious assignment to u_{n+1} in σ_{traj}. Then, suppose examining σ_{run} leads us to a job $(0, m), m < n$, as the closest control job that was scheduled (and thus terminated) prior to the instant d_n^0. Then, u_{n+1} should have matched u_{m+1}, based on HOLD. Now, if job $(0, m)$ has met its deadline in σ_{run}, then u_{m+1} is already computed (and the concrete value is reflected in σ_{traj}). This allows us to build the blocking implication for this first case as:

$$B_{uu\_a} := (\ e_n^0 > d_n^0 \wedge e_m^0 \leq d_m^0 \wedge e_{m+1}^0 > d_n^0\ ) \Rightarrow u_{n+1} = u_{m+1} \qquad (11)$$

Here, the antecedent captures the context that (i) job $(0, n)$ missed deadline, (ii) job $(0, m)$ is the closest preceding job to the time instant d_n^0 (through $e_{m+1}^0 > d_n^0$) and met deadline . This case is illustrated in Fig. 1 with job k missing deadline and job $k - 1$ meeting its deadline, enforcing u_{k+1} to match u_k.

Case 2: Consider that the preceding job $(0, m)$ too missed its deadline in σ_{run}, and hence u_{m+1} is not computed, as defined in Eq. 6. We have to locate the "scheduling slot" in which $(0, m)$ started execution, encode computation of the the corresponding control update, and match with u_{n+1}. Recall that control task instances read the control state at the beginning of their execution. Suppose, by examining σ_{run}, we observe that $m'P^0 \leq s_m^0 < (m' + 1)P^0$, with $m \leq m' \leq n$. In other words, job $(0, m)$ was scheduled in a slot (interval of length P^0) that begins at time $m'P^0$. Then, job $(0, m)$ must have read the control state available in this slot, which allows us to construct a blocking implication that computes the correct control action as:

$$B_{uu\_b} := (\ e_n^0 > d_n^0 \wedge e_m^0 > d_m^0 \wedge e_m^0 \leq d_n^0 \wedge e_{m+1}^0 > d_n^0$$

$$\wedge\, m'P^0 \leq s_m^0 < (m' + 1)P^0\ ) \Rightarrow u_{n+1} = R - \sum_{j'=1}^{j} K_{j'}x_{j',m'} \qquad (12)$$

Here, the antecedent captures the conditions that: (i) jobs $(0, n)$ and $(0, m)$ missed their deadlines, (ii) job $(0, m)$ is closest one to be scheduled prior to the time instant d_n^0, and (iii) job $(0, m)$ was scheduled in the slot beginning at time $m'P^0$. The consequent constrains the control update to pick the control state $x_{j,m'}$ i.e. state at time $m'P^0$. This case is illustrated in Fig. 1, with jobs $k + 1$ and k missing their respective deadlines. Job k, however, is scheduled in the next slot post release ($m' = k + 1$), and terminates before the time instant $(k + 2)\delta$, leading to u_{k+2} matching the control update issued by job k, albeit reading the control state x_{k+1} instead of x_k.

Case 3: The last special case that no preceding job is found (all preceding jobs missed deadline) can be handled similarly by enforcing $u_{n+1} = u_0$.

3.5 Correctness of Refinement

Theorem 1. *Based on Eqs. 8–12, each refinement step removes only spurious runs and/or trajectories from the set of solutions of ϕ_{sys}.*

Proof (sketch). B_{ov} (Eq. 8) ensures that pairs of jobs do not overlap and does not obstruct any run of $\mathcal{T}$. B_{sv} (Eq. 9) prevents incorrect scheduling of pairs of jobs by blocking such spurious runs.

B_{wc} prevents processor idling in the presence of ready jobs, by "moving" the waiting job appropriately, thus blocking the spurious run. Note that the *prec* set (Sect. 3.3), by construction, *soundly over-approximates* the set of jobs that could precede the violating job *in all runs* of $\mathcal{T}$. Thus, the antecedent in B_{wc} (Eq. 10) is *guaranteed* to cover all possible spurious cases involving this job, *i.e.*, the refinement is *complete* with respect to work-conservation violation.

B_{uu} prevents unconstrained control updates by processing the trace σ_{run} to locate the closest preceding job and computes the control update issued by this job (if not already computed in σ_{traj}). The cases presented in Eqs. 11 and 12 guarantee that the *freshest* update is identified within σ_{traj} and matched to restore precision. Thus *in all cases*, the refinement implications block spurious behaviour or traces of ϕ_{sys} that *do not* constitute runs of $\mathcal{T}$ or $\mathcal{C}$. These scenarios are the only causes of spuriousness in ϕ_{sys}.

4   Tool Design

Figure 2 depicts our tool implementation of the abstraction (Sect. 2) and refinement (Sect. 3) using Python 3.8 and Z3 4.8.12. The tool accepts (i) control specification (A, B, K, X_0), analysis horizon h, (ii) safety and reachability sets of plant states, (iii) task specification, and scheduling policy. Jobs are spawned up to the analysis horizon and symbolic variables (Table 1) are introduced for each job. Formulas ϕ_{traj} and ϕ_{runs} are constructed and conjuncted along with the control property of interest. If Z3 reports unsatisfiability, the property holds.

If Z3 reports a witness, we parse it to extract assignments to the symbolic variables and reconstruct the task run and control trajectory. Internally, Z3

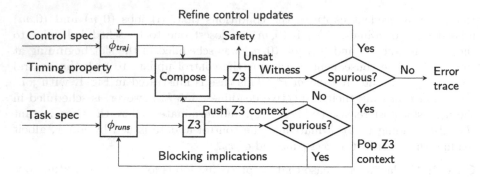

Fig. 2. Tool design

tracks the set of formulas on symbolic variables using a *context* stack. Refinement iterations *incrementally* add blocking clauses to the current context, leveraging the incremental analysis capability of Z3. The refinement loop is split into two phases, catering to the two sources of abstraction, ϕ_{traj} and ϕ_{runs}. During experiments, we observed that a majority of the refinements were required for pruning spurious task runs, as compared to spurious control trajectories. Hence, we specifically built a separate loop for quickly refining ϕ_{runs} with the advantage that the composition of ϕ_{traj} and ϕ_{runs}, which yields the larger formula ϕ_{sys} and consequently larger state space to be explored, is built and analyzed only after a valid task run is obtained, thus boosting Z3 performance.

Refinement loops interface using context pushing and popping API from Z3. Just before the composition step, the context is pushed *i.e.* saved on Z3 stack. Constraints from ϕ_{traj} are then added to the context, encoding the entire system ϕ_{sys}. Spurious control updates are processed according to Sect. 3.4. While refining ϕ_{sys}, if we obtain a spurious task run, it is likely that several iterations of refinements over ϕ_{runs} will be needed (as evidenced during experiments). At this point, the presence of constraints from ϕ_{traj} in the solver context is an unnecessary burden for the solver. Consequently, the saved context is popped out, flushing out ϕ_{traj} constraints and restoring ϕ_{runs} refined upto the last good point, thereby boosting the solver performance.

5   Case Study 1: DC Motor Control Model

Consider a DC motor speed model adapted from [11], specified by the model:

$$x_{k+1} = \begin{bmatrix} 0.9058 & 0.09617 & 0 \\ 0.01923 & 1.021 & 0 \\ 0 & 0 & 0 \end{bmatrix} x_k + \begin{bmatrix} -0.009742 \\ -0.2021 \\ 1 \end{bmatrix} u_k$$

$$u_k = \begin{bmatrix} -0.219719 & -0.942677 & 0.184469 \end{bmatrix} x_k$$

This discrete-time model has a period of 100ms. We assume a synthetic task set, consisting of 5 tasks, implementing the controller, described in Table 2. Task τ_0 is the controller task, thus $P^0 = 100$ ms. We considered the following properties:

Table 2. Synthetic task set for DC Motor controller

Id	Offset	Period	[BCET, WCET]	Jitter
τ_0	0	100	[15, 30]	2
τ_1	0	100	[15, 30]	2
τ_2	0	100	[15, 30]	2
τ_3	10	400	[15, 30]	2
τ_4	10	500	[20, 40]	2

Table 3. Task set for RC Network controller

Id	Offset	Period	[BCET, WCET]	Jitter
τ_0	0	100	[6, 13]	2
τ_1	0	50	[6, 16]	2
τ_2	0	100	[15, 30]	2
τ_3	2	250	[8, 16]	2
τ_4	6	100	[15, 30]	2
τ_5	2	500	[5, 15]	0

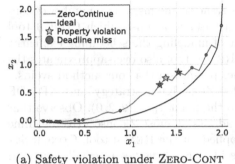

(a) Safety violation under ZERO-CONT

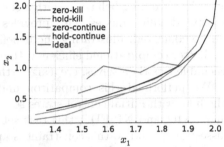

(b) Impact of deadline misses, NP-RM

Fig. 3. Analysis of DC Motor control system.

Property 1: Safe angular velocity of motor: $x_1^{ideal} - 0.3 \leq x_1 \leq x_1^{ideal} + 0.3$ *i.e.* the angular velocity must not deviate by more than 0.3 units from the corresponding ideal (*i.e* no deadline miss) control states, at each step of evolution.

Property 2: Safe current through armature: $x_2 \leq x_2^{ideal} + 0.5$ *i.e.* the current through armature must not rise by more than 0.5 units from the corresponding ideal current values, at each step of evolution.

We applied the tool to check these safety properties over the DC motor system. Analysis over 50 steps, under ZERO-CONTINUE strategy and NP-EDF schedule, revealed violation of the properties. Figure 3a shows the trajectory reported by the tool, with Property 1 (angular velocity staying within specified bounds) violated at steps 15 and 16. Property 2 (current through armature within specified bounds) was reported violated at steps 9, 11 and 12. The task set run corresponding to this trajectory had a total of 17 deadline misses of the control task (τ_0) spread over the 50 steps of evolution. The computation time was approximately 1.5 min, requiring 65 refinements. All experiments were executed on a laptop with Intel i5 processor, 16GB RAM and Ubuntu 20 OS.

Comparing Tool Precision. To illustrate improvement in precision in computing reach states using our tool (CONCH), we compared with a tool that computes

Table 4. Reach upper bounds, under ZERO-KILL

Var	Steps	Ideal	REACH	CONCH
x_1	10	1.2724	1.9051	1.61
x_2	10	0.2163	1.449	0.74
x_1	20	0.4681	1.5075	0.81
x_2	20	−0.0628	1.0539	0.28

Table 5. Tool performance for 60 steps, NP-EDF schedule

	B_{ov}	B_{sc}	B_{wc}	B_{uu}	R	Miss	Time
ZERO-KILL	819	501	2531	NA	189	6	466
HOLD-KILL	819	501	2531	NA	189	6	657
HOLD-CONT	565	212	202	20	56	18	274
ZERO-CONT	565	212	202	20	56	18	379

a sound over-approximation of the reachable set (REACH) [8]. Unlike our method, this tool only explicitly models the control system, and over-approximates the possible scheduling behaviors with a constraint on the maximum number of consecutive deadline misses. This provides a baseline against which CONCH tool can be compared, illustrating the benefit of modeling the scheduling explicitly. For better computational efficiency, the REACH tool also over-approximates the reachable sets themselves, creating further pessimism that our method avoids.

We performed this comparison under ZERO-KILL strategy and NP-EDF schedule, with initial control states set to the point $x_0 = (2, 2, 0)$. Observe that under KILL and NP-EDF, this task set admits at most 2 consecutive deadline misses for τ_0, and so this constraint is applied for the REACH tool. CONCH discovered the bounds by incrementing the ideal reach values in small steps and checking if the revised bound is violated, until it hit a safe value. Table 4 shows the **safe** reach upper bounds, for variables x_1, x_2, for 10 and 20 steps of evolution. Column "ideal" reports the value of states reached by the ideal trajectory (no deadline misses.) The safety bounds computed by REACH, with at most 2 consecutive deadline misses, is significantly over-approximated due to assuming a worst-case scheduling scenario of k-misses *every* $k + 1$ instances, which may not occur in practice, as illustrated by this task set.

Illustrating Deadline Miss Policies. Figure 3b illustrates the impact of the various deadline miss handling policies on control evolution, for this task set, under NP-RM. For KILL policy, the jobs that missed deadline were 0,5,6, and for CONTINUE policy, jobs 1,2 and 6 missed deadline. The graph zooms on the first 10 steps of control evolution, to illustrate the sets of control states (or alternately, segments of control evolution) that are more sensitive to deadline misses. Control behaviour under different strategies is impacted differently by similar sequences of deadline misses. We believe this analysis can help the control designer in uncovering finer insights into the interplay of scheduling policy, task parameters and strategies for deadline miss / control action update. Further, observe that for both NP-RM (Fig. 3b) and NP-EDF (Fig. 3a) policies, the maximum deviation from ideal behaviour generally occurs during the early steps of system evolution. This highlights the need to rigorously analyze small, transient segments of control evolution.

Tool Performance and Insights. Table 5 shows the scalability of the tool for 60 steps and the five tasks, for a custom reachability property, under NP-

EDF schedule. The B columns list the number of blocking implications mined across all iterations, column "R" lists refinements *i.e.* calls to the SMT solver Z3 [2], column "Miss" lists deadline misses witnessed in the property violation trace produced by the Z3. As seen from the table, tool performance is sensitive to the task set and deadline miss policy; this task set was crafted to admit a large number of runs arising from non-deterministic scheduling choices, jitter and execution budget, in an attempt to showcase the tool's capability.

6   Case Study 2: RC Network Control Model

Consider an RC network model, adapted from [7], specified as:

$$x_{k+1} = \begin{bmatrix} 0.5495 & 0.0724 & 0.1616 \\ 0.01448 & 0.9332 & 0.02665 \\ 0 & 0 & 0 \end{bmatrix} x_k + \begin{bmatrix} 0.2166 \\ 0.02569 \\ 1 \end{bmatrix} u_k$$

$$u_k = \begin{bmatrix} 0.0977 & 0.2504 & 0.0781 \end{bmatrix} x_k$$

This discrete-time model has a period of 100 ms. We assume that the controller is implemented by a task set inspired from the real-life PapaBench [9] task set for an unmanned aerial vehicle, adapted for our setting. The adapted task set used for our experiment is described in Table 3.

For the RC network control system, we consider the safety property that maximum voltage across both capacitors does not exceed the ideal voltage by 0.1 units: $x_1 \leq x_1^{ideal} + 0.1 \wedge x_2 \leq x_2^{ideal} + 0.1$. The scheduling policy is set to NP-EDF and the strategy chosen is ZERO-CONTINUE.

Application of our tool for this system reveals property violation, shown in Fig. 4. The control jobs that missed deadlines are 2, 6, 8, 10, 11, 12, 14, 15. Variable x_1 violates the safety property at steps 5 and 10 within the 20-step analysis horizon. Notice that continuous deadline misses (*e.g.* jobs 10, 11, 12) cause more deviation from the ideal behaviour than isolated incidents of deadline miss. Depending on the control application, the deviation might be unacceptable, and thus this requires a precise analysis of scheduling and its impact on control.

The REACH tool, under the above setting, reported an *upper bound* on the deviation experienced by x_1 as 0.2715, whereas our tool CONCH reported a *tighter* bound of 0.15, which took 745 refinements and 150 s, and this safe bound was arrived at by incrementing and checking in steps of 0.01 units.

For HOLD-CONTINUE strategy, the tool reported that x_1 did not violate the property *i.e.* the maximum voltage for capacitor 1 stays within the given safe bounds over the analysis horizon. Proving safety took 579 refinements and approximately 2.5 min.

For KILL strategy, no control job misses deadline (other task instances miss deadline and are killed, allowing the control task to be always successfully scheduled within the analysis horizon). This again demonstrates that the task specification in combination with the strategies for handling deadline miss and control action updates can have significantly differing impact on control behaviour.

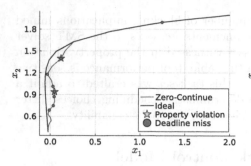
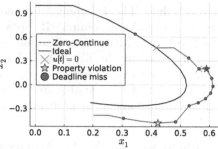

Fig. 4. Safety violating trajectory for RC Network, ZERO-CONT strategy

Fig. 5. Safety violation for F1Tenth car model

7 Case Study 3: F1Tenth Car Model

Our final model captures the motion of an F1Tenth [14] model car, adapted for our setting (linearized, x_1 dimension dropped, discretized at 20 ms), with controller adapted from [13], as:

$$x_{k+1} = \begin{bmatrix} 1 & 0.13 \\ 0 & 1 \end{bmatrix} x_k + \begin{bmatrix} 0.02559 \\ 0.3937 \end{bmatrix} u_k$$

$$u_k = \begin{bmatrix} 0.2935 & 0.4403 \end{bmatrix} x_{k-1}$$

The task set is adapted from the synthetic example presented in Table 2, where we drop task τ_4, periods of tasks $\tau_0 - \tau_2$ are set to 20 and their execution times are set to [4,6], period of τ_3 is set to 40 and execution time is set to [5,10]. The safety property of interest is that the steering angle should not deviate by more than 0.2 units from the ideal behaviour: $-0.2 \le x_2 - x_{ideal} \le 0.2$.

Under ZERO-CONTINUE strategy, CONCH reported property violation, as shown in Fig. 5. The task set run had a total of 12 deadline misses for the control task τ_0, but ZERO control update occurred only twice in this run (since under CONTINUE, these jobs were eventually scheduled). Observe that the control trajectory violated *both* the upper and lower safety threshold, at steps 8 and 16, respectively. Interestingly, under KILL strategy, the bound was not violated. Proving property safety took 193 refinements and nearly 53 s.

8 Conclusions and Future Work

Our approach for *exact* checking of control properties, by jointly encoding control evolution and task scheduling under common deadline miss handling policies, could successfully check both safety and reachability properties that might be impacted due to scheduling issues of controller tasks, within practically acceptable time limits. Additionally, our tool can provide useful insights to CPS designers to: (i) Precisely compute control behaviour at step-wise granularity of evolution, (ii) Explore the impact of design choices *e.g.* ZERO-CONT vs. HOLD-KILL, and (iii) Explore the impact of task parameters on control *e.g.* release jitter. We believe this can address a large variety of practical problems involving control and scheduling interaction, which may be otherwise hard to reproduce or debug. For future work, we plan to extend our encoding to model and analyze distributed CPS with three components: control, scheduling and network.

Acknowledgement. Hobbs and Chakraborty were funded by NSF grant 2038960.

References

1. Abate, A., et al.: Automated formal synthesis of digital controllers for state-space physical plants. In: Majumdar, R., Kunčak, V. (eds.) CAV 2017. LNCS, vol. 10426, pp. 462–482. Springer, Cham (2017). https://doi.org/10.1007/978-3-319-63387-9_23
2. Bjørner, N., Phan, A., Fleckenstein, L.: νz - an optimizing SMT solver. In: TACAS, pp. 194–199 (2015)
3. Dai, X., Burns, A.: Period adaptation of real-time control tasks with FP scheduling in cyber-physical systems. J. Syst. Arch. **103**, 101691 (2020)
4. Dai, X., Zhao, S., Jiang, Y., Jiao, X., Hu, X.S., Chang, W.: Fixed-priority scheduling and controller co-design for time-sensitive networks. In: CAV (2020)
5. Frehse, G., Hamann, A., Quinton, S., Woehrle, M.: Formal analysis of timing effects on closed-loop properties of control software. In: RTSS, pp. 53–62 (2014)
6. Frehse, G., et al.: SpaceEx: scalable verification of hybrid systems. In: Gopalakrishnan, G., Qadeer, S. (eds.) CAV 2011. LNCS, vol. 6806, pp. 379–395. Springer, Heidelberg (2011). https://doi.org/10.1007/978-3-642-22110-1_30
7. Gabel, R.A., Roberts, R.A.: Signals and Linear Systems, 2nd edn. Wiley, Hoboken (1980)
8. Hobbs, C., Ghosh, B., Xu, S., Duggirala, P.S., Chakraborty, S.: Safety analysis of embedded controllers under implementation platform timing uncertainties, IEEE TCAD (2022). (To appear)
9. Lunniss, W., Altmeyer, S., Davis, R.: Comparing FP and EDF accounting for cache related pre-emption delays. Leibniz Trans. Emb. Syst. **1**(1), 01:1–01:24 (2014)
10. Maggio, M., Hamann, A., Mayer-John, E., Ziegenbein, D.: Control system stability under consecutive deadline misses. In: ECRTS, vol. 165, pp. 21:1–21:24 (2020)
11. Messner, W., Tilbury, D.: Control Tutorials for MATLAB and Simulink: A Web-Based Approach. Addison-Wesley (1999)
12. Minaeva, A., Roy, D., Akesson, B., Hanzálek, Z., Chakraborty, S.: Control performance optimization for application integration. In: IEEE ToC (2021)
13. Murphy, K.N.: Analysis of robotic vehicle steering and controller delay (1994)
14. O'Kelly, M., Zheng, H., Karthik, D., Mangharam, R.: F1tenth: an evaluation environment for continuous control and reinforcement learning. In: NeurIPS (2019)
15. Pazzaglia, P., Pannocchi, L., Biondi, A., Natale, M.D.: Beyond the weakly hard model: cost of deadline misses. In: ECRTS, vol. 106, pp. 10:1–10:22 (2018)
16. Roy, D., Ghosh, S., Zhu, Q., Caccamo, M., Chakraborty, S.: GoodSpread: criticality-aware static scheduling of CPS with multi-QoS. In: RTSS, pp. 178–190 (2020)
17. Roy, D., Hobbs, C., Anderson, J.H., Caccamo, M., Chakraborty, S.: Timing debugging for cyber-physical systems. In: DATE, pp. 1893–1898 (2021)

18. Vreman, N., Cervin, A., Maggio, M.: Stability and performance analysis of control systems subject to deadline misses. In: ECRTS, vol. 196, pp. 15:1–15:23 (2021)
19. Vreman, N., Mandrioli, C., Anton, C.: Deadline-miss-adaptive controller implementation for real-time control systems. In: RTAS (2022)
20. Vreman, N., Mandrioli, C.: Evaluation of burst failure robustness of control systems in the fog. In: Workshop on Fog-IoT. OASIcs, Schloss Dagstuhl (2020)
21. Zhang, L., Lu, P., Kong, F., Chen, X., Sokolsky, O., Lee, I.: Real-time attack-recovery for CPS using linear-quadratic regulator. ACM TECS **20**(5s), 1–24 (2021)

Symbolic Runtime Verification for Monitoring Under Uncertainties and Assumptions

Hannes Kallwies[1]([✉]) [iD], Martin Leucker[1] [iD], and César Sánchez[2] [iD]

[1] University of Lübeck, Lübeck, Germany
{kallwies,leucker}@isp.uni-luebeck.de
[2] IMDEA Software Institute, Madrid, Spain
cesar.sanchez@imdea.org

Abstract. Runtime Verification deals with the question of whether a run of a system adheres to its specification. This paper studies runtime verification in the presence of partial knowledge about the observed run, particularly where input values may not be precise or may not be observed at all. We also allow declaring assumptions on the execution which permits to obtain more precise verdicts also under imprecise inputs. We encode the specification into a symbolic formula that the monitor solves iteratively, when more observations are given. We base our framework on stream runtime verification, which allows to express temporal correctness properties not only in the Boolean but also in richer logical theories. While in general our approach requires to consider larger and larger sets of formulas, we identify domains (including Booleans and Linear Algebra) for which pruning strategies exist, which allow to monitor with constant memory (i.e. independent of the length of the observation) while preserving the same inference power as the monitor that remembers all observations. We empirically exhibit the power of our technique using a prototype implementation under two important cases studies: software for testing car emissions and heart-rate monitoring.

1 Introduction

We study runtime verification (RV) for imprecise and erroneous inputs, and describe a solution—called *Symbolic Runtime Verification*—that can exploit assumptions about the input and the system under analysis. RV is a dynamic verification technique in which a given run of a system is checked against a specification, typically a correctness property (see [1,13,23]). In *online monitoring* a monitor—synthesized from the specification—attempts to produce a verdict incrementally from the input trace. Originally, variants of LTL [26] tailored to finite runs were employed to formulate properties [3]. However, since

This work was funded in part by the Madrid Regional Government under project "S2018/TCS-4339 (BLOQUES-CM)" and by a research grant from Nomadic Labs and the Tezos Foundation.

A. Bouajjani et al. (Eds.): ATVA 2022, LNCS 13505, pp. 117–134, 2022.
https://doi.org/10.1007/978-3-031-19992-9_8

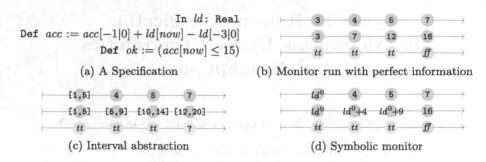

(a) A Specification

(b) Monitor run with perfect information

(c) Interval abstraction

(d) Symbolic monitor

Fig. 1. An example specification (a) and three monitors: (b) with perfect observability, (c) with an interval abstract domain, (d) a symbolic monitor developed in this paper. The symbolic monitor is enriched with the additional constraint that $1 \leq ld^0 \leq 5$.

RV requires to solve a variation of the word problem and not the harder model-checking problem, richer logics than LTL have been proposed that allow richer data and verdicts [10,14]. Lola [9] proposes *Stream Runtime Verification* (SRV) where monitors are described declaratively and compute output streams of verdicts from inputs streams (see also [12,21]). The development of this paper is based on Lola.

Example 1. Figure 1(a) shows a Lola specification with ld as input stream (the load of a CPU), acc as an output stream that represents the accumulated load, computed by adding the current value of ld and subtracting the third last value. Finally, ok checks whether acc is below 15. The expression $acc[-1|0]$ denotes the value of acc in the previous time point and 0 as default value if no previous time point exists.

Such a specification allows a direct evaluation strategy whenever values on the input streams arrive. If, for example, $ld = 3$ in the first instant, acc and ok evaluate to 3 and tt, respectively. Reading subsequently $4, 5, 7$ results in $7, 12, 16$ for acc and a violation is identified on stream ok. This is shown in Fig. 1(b).

A common obstacle in RV is that in practice sometimes input values are not available or not given precisely, due to errors in the underlying logging functionality or technical limitations of sensors. In Fig. 1(c) the first value on ld is not obtained (but we assume that the value of ld at instant 0 is between 1 and 5). One approach (followed in [22]) is to use interval arithmetic, which can be easily encoded as a domain in Lola. Even after reading precisely 4, 5 and 7, at time 4 the monitor cannot know for sure whether ok has been violated, as the interval $[12, 20]$ contains 15. If the unknown input on ld is denoted symbolically by ld^0 we still deduce that ok holds at time points 1 to 3. For time point 4, however, the symbolic representation $acc^4 = acc^3 + 7 - ld^0 = ld^0 + 9 + 7 - ld^0 = 16$ allows to infer that ok is clearly violated! This is shown in Fig. 1(d).   □

Example 1 illustrates our first insight: *Symbolic Runtime Verification* is more precise than monitoring using abstract domains.

Since an infinite symbolic unfolding of the specification and all assumptions is practically infeasible, our online monitor unfolds the specification as time increases. We show that our monitor is both *sound* and *perfect* in the sense that it only produces correct verdicts and these verdicts are as precise as possible with the information provided. However, even with an incremental unfolding of the specification the symbolic monitor can grow as more unknowns and their inter-dependencies are introduced. For example, in the run in Fig. 1(d) as more unknown ld values are received, more variables ld^i will be added, which makes the size of the symbolic formula depend on the trace length. We show that for certain logical theories, the current verdict may be still be computed even after *summarizing* the history into a compact symbolic representation, whose size is independent of the trace length. For other theories, preserving the full precision requires an amount of memory that can grow with the trace length. More precisely, we show that for the theories of Booleans and of Linear Algebra, bounded symbolic monitors exist while this is not the case for the combined theory, which is our second insight.

We empirically validate our symbolic RV approach— including constant memory monitoring on long traces—using two realistic case studies: the Legal Driving Cycle [5,19] and an ECG heartbeat analysis [25,27] (following the Lola encoding from [11]). When intervals are given for unknown values, our method provides precise answers more often than previous approaches based on interval domains [22]. Especially in the ECG example, these methods are unable to recover once the input is unknown for even a short time, but our symbolic monitors recover and provide again precise results, even when the input was unknown for a larger period.

Related Work. Monitoring LTL for traces with mutations (errors) is studied in [17] where properties are classified according to whether monitors can be built that are resilient against the mutation. However, [17] only considers Boolean verdicts and does not consider assumptions. The work in [22] uses abstract interpretation to soundly approximate the possible verdict values when inputs contain errors for the SRV language TeSSLa [7].

Calculating and approximating the values that programs compute is central to static analysis and program verification. Two traditional approaches are symbolic execution [18] and abstract interpretation [8] which frequently require over-approximations to handle loops. In monitoring, a step typically does not contain loops, but the set of input variables (unlike in program analysis) grows. Also, a main concern of RV is to investigate monitoring algorithms that are guaranteed to execute with constant resources. Works that incorporate assumptions when monitoring include [6,15,20] but uncertainty is not considered in these works, and verdicts are typically Boolean. A symbolic approach for monitoring but in the setting of timed data automata and without constant memory guarantee (thus perfect) is also presented in [28]. Monitoring under assumptions in form of a linear hybrid automaton, and sampling uncertainty for a different kind of specifications and Boolean verdicts is also studied in [29]. Note that bounded model checking [4] also considers bounded unfoldings, but it does not solve the problem of building monitors of constant memory for successive iterations.

In summary, our contributions are: (1) A Symbolic Runtime Verification algorithm that dynamically unfolds the specification, collects precise and imprecise input readings, and instantiates assumptions generating a conjunction of formulas. This representation can be used to deduce verdicts even under uncertainty, to precisely recover automatically for example under windows of uncertainty, and even to anticipate verdicts. (2) A pruning method for certain theories (Booleans and Linear Algebra) that guarantees bounded monitoring preserving the power to compute verdicts. (3) A prototype implementation and empirical evaluation on realistic case studies.

Missing proofs, further examples and figures can be found in an extended version of this paper [16].

2   Preliminaries

We use Lola [9] to express our monitors. Lola uses first-order sorted theories to build expressions. These theories are interpreted in the sense that every symbol is both a constructor to build expressions, and an evaluation function that produces values from the domain of results from values from the domains of the arguments. All sorts of all theories that we consider include the $=$ predicate.

A synchronous stream s over a non-empty data domain $\mathbb{D}$ is a function $s : \mathcal{S}_{\mathbb{D}} := \mathbb{T} \to \mathbb{D}$ assigning a value of $\mathbb{D}$ to every element of $\mathbb{T}$ (timestamp). We consider infinite streams ($\mathbb{T} = \mathbb{N}$) or finite streams with a maximal timestamp $t_{\max}$ ($\mathbb{T} = [0 \ldots t_{\max}]$). For readability we denote streams as sequences, so $s = \langle 1, 2, 4 \rangle$ stands for $s : \{0, 1, 2\} \to \mathbb{N}$ with $s(0) = 1, s(1) = 2, s(2) = 4$. A Lola specification describes a transformation from a set of input streams to a set of output streams.

Syntax. A Lola specification $\varphi = (I, O, E)$ consists of a set I of typed variables that denote the input streams, a set O of typed variables that denote the output steams, and E which assigns to every output stream variable $y \in O$ a defining expression E_y. The set of expressions over $I \cup O$ of type $\mathbb{D}$ is denoted by $E_{\mathbb{D}}$ and is recursively defined as: $E_{\mathbb{D}} = c \mid s[o|c] \mid f(E_{\mathbb{D}_1}, ..., E_{\mathbb{D}_n}) \mid ite(E_{\mathbb{B}}, E_{\mathbb{D}}, E_{\mathbb{D}})$, where c is a constant of type $\mathbb{D}$, $s \in I \cup O$ is a stream variable of type $\mathbb{D}$, $o \in \mathbb{Z}$ is an offset and f a total function $\mathbb{D}_1 \times \cdots \times \mathbb{D}_n \to \mathbb{D}$ (*ite* is a special function symbol to denote if-then-else). The intended meaning of the offset operator $s[o|c]$ is to represent the stream that has at time t the value of stream s at $t + o$, and value c used if $t + o \notin \mathbb{T}$. A particular case is when the offset is $o = 0$ in which case c is not needed, which we shorten by $s[now]$. Function symbols allow to build terms that represent complex expressions. The intended meaning of the defining equation E_y for output variable y is to declaratively define the values of stream y in terms of the values of other streams.

Semantics. The semantics of a Lola specification φ is a mapping from input to output streams. Given a tuple of concrete input streams $(\Sigma = (\sigma_1, \ldots, \sigma_n) \in \mathcal{S}_{\mathbb{D}_1} \times \cdots \times \mathcal{S}_{\mathbb{D}_n})$ corresponding to input stream identifier $s_1, \ldots, s_n$ and a specification φ the semantics of an expression $[\![\cdot]\!]_{\Sigma,\varphi} : E_{\mathbb{D}} \to \mathcal{S}_{\mathbb{D}}$ is iteratively defined as:

- $[\![c]\!]_{\Sigma,\varphi}(t) = c$

- $[\![s[o|c]]\!]_{\Sigma,\varphi}(t) = \begin{cases} \sigma_i(t+o) & \text{if } t+o \in \mathbb{T} \text{ and } s = s_i \in I \text{ (input stream)} \\ [\![e]\!]_{\Sigma,\varphi}(t+o) & \text{if } t+o \in \mathbb{T} \text{ and } E_s = e \text{ (output stream)} \\ c & \text{otherwise} \end{cases}$

- $[\![f(e_1, ..., e_n)]\!]_{\Sigma,\varphi}(t) = f([\![e_1]\!]_{\Sigma,\varphi}(t), \ldots, [\![e_n]\!]_{\Sigma,\varphi}(t))$

- $[\![ite(e_1, e_2, e_3)]\!]_{\Sigma,\varphi}(t) = \begin{cases} [\![e_2]\!]_{\Sigma,\varphi}(t) & \text{if } [\![e_1]\!]_{\Sigma,\varphi}(t) = tt \\ [\![e_3]\!]_{\Sigma,\varphi}(t) & \text{if } [\![e_1]\!]_{\Sigma,\varphi}(t) = ff \end{cases}$

The semantics of φ is a map $([\![\varphi]\!] : (\mathcal{S}_{\mathbb{D}_1} \times \cdots \times \mathcal{S}_{\mathbb{D}_n}) \to (\mathcal{S}_{\mathbb{D}'_1} \times \cdots \times \mathcal{S}_{\mathbb{D}'_m})$ defined as $[\![\varphi]\!](\sigma_1, ..., \sigma_n) = ([\![e'_1]\!]_{\Sigma,\varphi}, \ldots, [\![e'_m]\!]_{\Sigma,\varphi})$. The evaluation map $[\![\cdot]\!]_{\Sigma,\varphi}$ is well-defined if the recursive evaluation above has no cycles. This acyclicity can be easily checked statically (see [9]).

In online monitoring monitors receive the values incrementally. The *very efficiently monitorable* fragment of Lola consists of specifications where all offsets are negative or 0 (without transitive 0 cycles). It is well-known that the very efficiently monitorable specifications (under perfect information) can be monitored online in a trace length independent manner. In the rest of the paper we also assume that all Lola specifications come with -1 or 0 offsets. Every specification can be translated into such a normal form by introducing additional streams (flattening).

In this paper we investigate online monitoring under uncertainty and assumptions for three special fragments of Lola (and the constraints for uncertain input readings and assumptions), depending on the data theories used:

- **Propositional Logic** (Lola$_\mathbb{B}$): The data domain of all streams is the Boolean domain $\mathbb{D} = \mathbb{B} = \{tt, ff\}$ and available functions are $\wedge, \neg$.
- **Linear Algebra** (Lola$_{\mathcal{LA}}$): The data domain of all streams are real numbers $\mathbb{D} = \mathbb{R}$ and every stream definition has the form $c_0 + c_1 * s_0[o_1|d_1] + \cdots + c_n * s_n[o_n|d_n]$ where c_i, d_i are constants.
- **Mixed** (Lola$_{\mathbb{B}/\mathcal{LA}}$): The data domain is $\mathbb{B}$ or $\mathbb{R}$. Every stream definition is either contained in the Propositional Logic fragment extended by the functions $<, =$ for real variables or in the Linear Algebra fragment.

3   A Framework for Symbolic Runtime Verification

In this section we introduce a general framework for monitoring using symbolic computation, where the specification and the information collected by the monitor (including assumptions and precise and imprecise observations) are presented symbolically.

3.1 Symbolic Expressions

Consider a specification $\varphi = (I, O, E)$. We will use symbolic expressions to capture the relations between the different streams at different points in time. We introduce the *instant variables* x^t for a given stream variable $x \in I \cup O$ and instant $t \in \mathbb{T}$. The type of x^t is that of x. Considering Example 1, ld^3 represents the real value that corresponds to the input stream ld at instant 3 which is 7. The set of instant variables is $V = (I \cup O) \times \mathbb{T}$.

Definition 1 (Symbolic Expression). *Let φ be a specification and $\mathcal{A}$ a set of variables that contains all instant variables (that is $V \subseteq \mathcal{A}$), the set of symbolic expressions $\overline{\mathbb{D}}$ is the smallest set containing (1) all constants c and all symbols in $a \in \mathcal{A}$, (2) all expressions $f(t_1, \ldots, t_n)$ where f is a constructor symbol of type $\mathbb{D}_1 \times \cdots \times \mathbb{D}_n \to \mathbb{D}$ and t_i are elements of $\overline{\mathbb{D}}$ of type $\mathbb{D}_i$.*

We use $Expr_\varphi^{\mathbb{D}}(\mathcal{A})$ for the set of symbolic expressions of type $\mathbb{D}$ (and drop φ and $\mathcal{A}$ when it is clear from the context).

Example 2. Consider again Example 1. The symbolic expression $acc^3 + ld^4$, of type $\mathbb{R}$, represents the addition of the load at instant 4 and the accumulator at instant 3. Also, $acc^4 = acc^3 + ld^4$ is a predicate (that is, a $\mathbb{B}$ expression) that captures the value of acc at instant 4. The symbolic expression $ld^1 = 4$ corresponds to the reading of the value 4 for input stream ld at instant 1. Finally, $1 \leq ld^0 \wedge ld^0 \leq 5$ corresponds to the assumption at time 0 that ld has value between 1 and 5. □

3.2 Symbolic Monitor Semantics

We define the symbolic semantics of a Lola specification $\varphi = (I, O, E)$ as the expressions that result by instantiating the defining equations E.

Definition 2 (Symbolic Monitor Semantics). *The map $[\![\cdot]\!]_\varphi : E_{\mathbb{D}} \to \mathbb{T} \to Expr_\varphi^{\mathbb{D}}$ is defined as $[\![c]\!]_\varphi(t) = c$ for constants, and*

- $[\![f(e_1, \ldots, e_n)]\!]_\varphi(t) = f([\![e_1]\!]_\varphi(t), \ldots, [\![e_n]\!]_\varphi(t))$
- $[\![s[o|c]]\!]_\varphi(t) = s^{t+o}$ *if $t + o \in \mathbb{T}$, or $[\![s[o|c]]\!]_\varphi(t) = c$ otherwise.*

The symbolic semantics of a specification φ is the map $[\![\cdot]\!]_{sym} : \mathbb{T} \to 2^{Expr_\varphi^{\mathbb{B}}}$ defined as $[\![\varphi]\!]_{sym}^t = \{y^t = [\![E_y]\!]_\varphi(t) \mid \text{for every } y \in O\}$.

A slight modification of the symbolic semantics allows to obtain equations whose right hand sides only have input instant variables:

- $[\![s[o|c]]\!]_\varphi(t) = s^{t+o}$ if $t + o \in \mathbb{T}$ and $s \in I$
- $[\![s[o|c]]\!]_\varphi(t) = [\![E_s]\!](t + o)$ if $t + o \in \mathbb{T}$ and $s \in O$
- $[\![s[o|c]]\!]_\varphi(t) = c$ otherwise

We call this semantics the symbolic unrolled semantics, which corresponds to what would be obtained by performing equational reasoning (by equational substitution) in the symbolic semantics.

Example 3. Consider again the specification φ in Example 1. The first four elements of $[\![\varphi]\!]_{sym}$ are (after simplifications like $0 + x = x$ etc.):

0	1	2	3
$acc^0 = ld^0$	$acc^1 = acc^0 + ld^1$	$acc^2 = acc^1 + ld^2$	$acc^3 = acc^2 + ld^3 - ld^0$
$ok^0 = acc^0 \leq 15$	$ok^1 = acc^1 \leq 15$	$ok^2 = acc^2 \leq 15$	$ok^3 = acc^3 \leq 15$

Using the unrolled semantics the equations for ok would be, at time 0, $ok^0 = ld^0 \leq 15$, and at time 1, $ok^1 = ld^0 + ld^1 \leq 15$. In the unrolled semantics all equations contain only instant variables that represent inputs.   □

Recall that the denotational semantics of Lola specifications in Sect. 2 maps every tuple of input streams into a tuple of output streams, that is $[\![\varphi]\!] : \mathcal{S}_{\mathbb{D}_1} \times \cdots \times \mathcal{S}_{\mathbb{D}_n} \to \mathcal{S}_{\mathbb{D}'_1} \times \cdots \times \mathcal{S}_{\mathbb{D}'_m}$. The symbolic semantics also has a denotational meaning even without receiving the input stream, defined as follows.

Definition 3 (Denotational semantics). *Let $\varphi = (I, O, E)$ be a specification with $I = (x_1, \ldots, x_n)$ and $O = (y_1, \ldots, y_m)$. The denotational semantics of a set of equations $E \subseteq Expr^{\mathbb{B}}_\varphi$, $[\![E]\!]_{den} \subseteq \mathcal{S}_{\mathbb{D}_1} \times \cdots \times \mathcal{S}_{\mathbb{D}_n} \times \mathcal{S}_{\mathbb{D}'_1} \times \cdots \times \mathcal{S}_{\mathbb{D}'_m}$ is:*

$$[\![E]\!]_{den} = \{(\sigma_1, \ldots, \sigma_n, \sigma'_1, \ldots, \sigma'_m) \mid \text{ for every } e \in E$$
$$\{x^t_1 = \sigma_1(t), \ldots, x^t_n = \sigma_n(t), y^t_1 = \sigma'_1(t), \ldots, y^t_m = \sigma'_m(t)\} \models e\}$$

Using the previous definition, $[\![\bigcup_{i \leq t} [\![\varphi]\!]^i_{sym}]\!]_{den}$ corresponds to all the tuples of streams of inputs and outputs that satisfy the specification φ up to time t.

A Symbolic Encoding of Inputs, Constraints and Assumptions. Input readings can also be defined symbolically as follows. Given an instant t, an input stream variable x and a value v, the expression $x^t = v$ captures the precise reading of v at t on x. Imprecise readings can also be encoded easily. For example, if at instant 3 an input of value 7 for ld is received by a noisy sensor (consider a 1 unit of tolerance), then $6 \leq ld^3 \leq 8$ represents the imprecise reading.

Assumptions are relations between the variables that we assume to hold at all positions, which can be encoded as stream expressions of type $\mathbb{B}$. For example, the assumption that the load is always between 1 and 10 is $1 \leq ld[now] \leq 10$. Another example, $ld[-1|0] + 1 \geq ld[now]$ which encodes that ld cannot increase more than 1 per unit of time. We use A for the set of assumptions associated with a Lola specification φ (which are a set of stream expressions of type $\mathbb{B}$ over $I \cup O$).

3.3 A Symbolic Runtime Verification Algorithm

Based on the previous definitions we develop our symbolic RV algorithm shown in Algorithm 1. Line 3 instantiates the new equations and assumptions from the specification for time t. Line 4 incorporates the set of input

124   H. Kallwies et al.

readings ψ^t (perfect or imperfect). Line 5 performs evaluations and simplifications, which is dependent on the particular theory. In the case of past-specifications with perfect information this step boils down to substitution and evaluation. Line 6 produces the output of the monitor.

Alg. 1: Online Symbolic Monitor for φ

1 $t \leftarrow 0$ and $E \leftarrow \emptyset$;
2 **while** $t \in \mathbb{T}$ **do**
3 $\quad E \leftarrow E \cup \llbracket \varphi \rrbracket^t_{sym} \cup \llbracket A^t \rrbracket_\varphi$;
4 $\quad E \leftarrow E \cup \psi^t$;
5 $\quad$ Evaluate and Simplify;
6 $\quad$ Output;
7 $\quad$ Prune;
8 $\quad t \leftarrow t + 1$;

Again, this is application dependent. In the case of past specifications with perfect information the output value will be computed without delay and emitted in this step. In the case of $\mathbb{B}$ outputs with imperfect information, an SMT solver can be used to discard a verdict. For example, to determine the value of ok at time t, the verdict tt can be discarded if $\exists * . ok^t$ is UNSAT, and the verdict ff can be discarded if $\exists * . \neg ok^t$ is UNSAT. For richer domains specific reasoning can be used, like emitting lower and upper bounds or deducing the set of constraints. Finally, Line 7 eliminates constraints that will not be necessary for future deductions and performs variable renaming and summarization to restrict the memory usage of the monitor (see Sect. 4). For past specifications with perfect information, after step 5 every equation will be evaluated to $y^t = v$ and the pruning will remove from E all the values that will never be accessed again.

The symbolic RV algorithm generalizes the concrete monitoring algorithm by allowing to reason about uncertain values, while it still obtains the same results and performance under certainty. Concrete RV allows to monitor with constant amount of resources specifications with bounded future references when inputs are known with perfect certainty.

Symbolic RV, additionally, allows to handle uncertainties and assumptions, because the monitor stores constraints (equations) that include variables that capture the unknown information, for example the unknown input values. We characterize a symbolic monitor as a step function $M : 2^{Expr}_\varphi \to 2^{Expr}_\varphi$ that transforms expressions into expressions. At a given instant t the monitor collects readings $\psi^t \in Expr_\varphi$ about the input values and applies the step function to the previous information and the new information. Given a sequence of input readings $\psi^0, \psi^1 \ldots$ we use $M^0 = M(\psi^0)$ and $M^{i+1} = M(M^i \cup \psi^{i+1})$ for the sequence of monitor states reached by the repeated applications of M. We use $\Phi^t = \cup_{i \le t}(\llbracket \varphi \rrbracket^i_{sym} \cup \llbracket A^i \rrbracket_\varphi \cup \psi^i)$ for the formula that represents the unrolling of the specification and the current assumptions together with the knowledge about inputs collected up to t.

Definition 4 (Sound and Perfect monitoring). *Let φ be a specification, M a monitor for φ, $\psi^0, \psi^1 \ldots$ a sequence of input observations, and $M^0, M^1 \ldots$ the monitor states reached after repeatedly applying M. Consider an arbitrary predicate α involving only instant variables x^t at time t.*

- M is sound if whenever $M^t \models \alpha$ then $\Phi^t \models \alpha$ for all $t \in \mathbb{T}$.
- M is perfect if it is sound and if $\Phi^t \models \alpha$ then $M^t \models \alpha$ for all $t \in \mathbb{T}$.

Note that soundness and perfectness is defined in terms of the ability to infer predicates that only involve instant variables at time t, so the monitor is allowed to eliminate, rename or summarize the rest of the variables. It is trivial to extend this definition to expressions α that can use instant variables $x^{t'}$ with $(t - d) \leq t' \leq t$ for some constant d. If a monitor is perfect in this extended definition it will be able to answer questions for variables within the last d steps.

The version of the symbolic algorithm presented in Alg. 1 that never prunes (removing line 7) and computes at all steps Φ^t is a sound and perfect monitor. However, the memory that the monitor needs grows without bound if the number of uncertain items also grows without bound. In the next section we show that (1) trace length independent perfect monitoring under uncertainty is not possible in general, even for past only specifications and (2) we identify concrete theories, namely Booleans and Linear Algebra and show that these theories allow perfect monitoring with constant resources under unbounded uncertainty.

4 Symbolic Runtime Verification at Work

Example 4. Consider the Lola specification on the left, where the Real input stream ld indicates the current CPU load and the Boolean input stream usr_a indicates if the currently active user is user A. This specification checks whether the accumulated load of user A is at most 50% of the total accumulated load. Consider the inputs $ld = \langle ?, 10, 4, ?, ?, 1, 9, \dots \rangle$, $usr_a = \langle \mathit{ff}, \mathit{ff}, \mathit{ff}, \mathit{tt}, \mathit{tt}, \mathit{tt}, \mathit{ff}, \dots \rangle$ from 0 to 6. Also, assume that at every instant t, $0 \leq ld^t \leq 10$. At instant 6 our

$$acc := acc[-1|0] + ld[now]$$
$$acc_a := acc_a[-1|0] + ite(usr_a[now], ld[now], 0)$$
$$ok := acc_a[now] \leq 0.5 * acc[now]$$

monitoring algorithm would yield the symbolic constraints $(acc^6 = 24 + ld^0 + ld^3 + ld^4)$ and $(acc_a^6 = 1 + ld^3 + ld^4)$ for acc^6 and acc_a^6, and the additional one $(0 \leq ld^0 \leq 10 \wedge 0 \leq ld^3 \leq$ $10 \wedge 0 \leq ld^4 \leq 10)$. An existential query to an SMT solver allows to conclude that ok^6 is true since acc_a^6 is at most 21 but then acc^6 is 44. However, every unknown variable from the input will appear in one of the constraints stored and will remain there during the whole monitoring process. □

When symbolic computation is used in static analysis, it is not a common concern to deal with a growing number of unknowns as usually the number of inputs is fixed a-priori. In contrast, a goal in RV is to build online monitors that are trace-length independent, which means that the calculation time and memory consumption of a monitor stays below a constant bound and does not increase with the received number of inputs. In Example 4 above this issue can be tackled by rewriting the constraints as part of the monitor's pruning step using $n \leftarrow ld^0$, $m \leftarrow (ld^3 + ld^4)$ to obtain $(acc^t = 24 + n + m)$, $(acc_a^t = 1 + m)$ and $(0 \leq n \leq 10) \wedge (0 \leq m \leq 20)$. From the rewritten constraints it can still be deduced that $acc_a^6 \leq 0.5 * acc^6$. Note also that every instant variable in the specification only refers to previous instant variables. Thus for all $t \geq 7$, there is no direct reference to either ld^3 or ld^4. Variables ld^3 and ld^4 are, individually, no longer *relevant* for the verdict and it does not harm to denote $ld^3 + ld^4$ by a single variable m. We call this step of rewriting *pruning* (of non-relevant variables).

Let $\mathcal{C}^t \subseteq Expr_\varphi^{\mathbb{B}}$ be the set of constraints maintained by the monitor that encode its knowledge about inputs and assumptions for the given specification. In general, pruning is a transformation of a set of constraints $\mathcal{C}^t$ into a new set $\mathcal{C}'^t$ requiring less memory, but still describing the same relations between the instant variables:

Definition 5 (Pruning strategy). *Let $\mathcal{C} \subseteq Expr^{\mathbb{B}}$ be a set of constraints over variables $\mathcal{A}$ and $\mathcal{R} = \{r_1, \ldots, r_n\} \subseteq \mathcal{A}$ the subset of* relevant *variables. We use $|\mathcal{C}|$ for a measure on the size of $\mathcal{C}$. A pruning strategy $\mathcal{P} : 2^{Expr^{\mathbb{B}}} \to 2^{Expr^{\mathbb{B}}}$ is a transformation such that for all $\mathcal{C} \in Expr^{\mathbb{B}}$, $|\mathcal{P}(\mathcal{C})| \leq |\mathcal{C}|$. A Pruning strategy $\mathcal{P}$ is called*

- sound, *whenever for all $\mathcal{C} \subseteq Expr^{\mathbb{B}}$, $[\![\mathcal{C}]\!]_\mathcal{R} \subseteq [\![\mathcal{P}(\mathcal{C})]\!]_\mathcal{R}$,*
- perfect, *whenever for all $\mathcal{C} \subseteq Expr^{\mathbb{B}}$, $[\![\mathcal{C}]\!]_\mathcal{R} = [\![\mathcal{P}(\mathcal{C})]\!]_\mathcal{R}$,*

where $[\![\mathcal{C}]\!]_\mathcal{R} = \{(v_1, \ldots, v_n) | (r_1 = v_1 \wedge \cdots \wedge r_n = v_n) \models \mathcal{C}\}$ is the set of all value tuples for $\mathcal{R}$ that entail the constraint set $\mathcal{C}$. We say that the pruning strategy is constant *if for all $\mathcal{C} \subseteq Expr^{\mathbb{B}} : |\mathcal{P}(\mathcal{C})| \leq c$ for a constant $c \in \mathbb{N}$.*

A monitor that exclusively stores a set $\mathcal{C}^t$ for every $t \in \mathbb{T}$ is called a constant-memory monitor if there is a constant $c \in \mathbb{N}$ such that for all t, $|\mathcal{C}^t| \leq c$.

Previously we defined an online monitor M as a function that iteratively maps sets of constraints to sets of constraints. Clearly, the amount of information to maintain grows unlimited if we allow the monitor to receive constraints that contain information of an instant variable at time t at any other time t'. Consequently, we first restrict our attention to *atemporal monitors*, defined as those which receive proposition sets that only contain instant variables of the current instant of time. Atemporal monitors cannot handle assumptions like $ld[-1|0] \leq 1.1 * ld[now]$. At the end of this section we will extend our technique to monitors that may refer n instants to the past.

Theorem 1. *Given a specification φ and a constant pruning strategy $\mathcal{P}$ for $Expr_\varphi^{\mathbb{B}}$, there is an atemporal constant-memory monitor M_φ s.t.*

- M_φ *is sound if the pruning strategy is sound.*
- M_φ *is perfect if the pruning strategy is perfect.*

Yet we have not given a complexity measure for constraint sets. For our approach we use the number of variables and constants in the constraints, that is $|\mathcal{C}| = \sum_{\varphi \in \mathcal{C}} |\varphi|$ and $|c| = 1$, $|v| = 1$, $|f(e_1, \ldots, e_n)| = |e_1| + \cdots + |e_n|$, $|ite(e_1, e_2, e_3)| = |e_1| + |e_2| + |e_3|$ for a constant c and a variable v.

4.1   Application to Lola Fragments

We describe now perfect pruning strategies for $\text{Lola}_{\mathbb{B}}$ and $\text{Lola}_{\mathcal{LA}}$. For $\text{Lola}_{\mathbb{B}/\mathcal{LA}}$ we will show that no such perfect pruning strategy exists but present a sound and constant pruning strategy.

$\text{Lola}_{\mathbb{B}}$: First we consider the fragment $\text{Lola}_{\mathbb{B}}$ where all input and output streams, constants and functions are of type Boolean. Consequently, we assume constraints given to the monitor (input readings, assumptions) also only contain variables, constants and functions of type Boolean.

Example 5. Consider the following specification (where all inputs are uncertain, $\oplus$ denotes exclusive or) shown on the left. The unrolled semantics, shown on the right, indicates that *ok* is always true.

	0	1	2	3	...
$a := a[-1\|f\!f] \oplus x[now]$	x^0	$x^0 \oplus x^1$	$x^0 \oplus x^1 \oplus x^2$	$x^0 \oplus x^1 \oplus x^2 \oplus x^3$	...
$b := b[-1\|tt] \oplus x[now]$	$\neg x^0$	$\neg x^0 \oplus x^1$	$\neg x^0 \oplus x^1 \oplus x^2$	$\neg x^0 \oplus x^1 \oplus x^2 \oplus x^3$	...
$ok := a[now] \oplus b[now]$	tt	tt	tt	tt	...

However, the Boolean formulas maintained internally by the monitor are continuously increasing. Note that at time 1 the possible combinations of (a^1, b^1, ok^1) are $(f\!f, tt, tt)$ and $(tt, f\!f, tt)$, as shown below (left). By eliminating duplicates from this table we obtain another table with two columns which can be expressed by formulas over a single, fresh variable v^1 (as shown on the right). From this table we can directly infer the new formulas $a^1 = v^1$, $b^1 = \neg v^1$,

(x^0, x^1)	00	01	10	11
a^1	$f\!f$	tt	tt	$f\!f$
b^1	tt	$f\!f$	$f\!f$	tt
ok^1	tt	tt	tt	tt

v^1	0	1
a^1	$f\!f$	tt
b^1	tt	$f\!f$
ok^1	tt	tt

$ok^1 = tt$, which preserve the condensed information that a^1 and b^1 are opposites. We can use these new formulas for further calculation. At time 2, $a^2 = v^1 \oplus x^2$, $b^1 = \neg v^1 \oplus x^2$ which we rewrite as $a^2 = v^2$, $b^1 = \neg v^2$ again concluding $ok^1 = tt$. This illustrates how the pruning guarantees a constant-memory monitor. Note that this monitor will be able to infer at every step that *ok* is tt even without reading any input.   □

The strategy from the example above can be generalized to a pruning strategy. Let $\mathcal{R} = \{r_1, \ldots, r_m\}$ be the set of relevant variables (in our case the output variables s_i^t) and $\mathcal{V} = \{s_1, \ldots, s_n\} \cup \mathcal{R}$ all variables (in our case input variables and fresh variables from previous pruning applications). Let $\mathcal{C}$ be a set of constraints over $r_1, \ldots, r_m, s_1, \ldots, s_n$, which can be rewritten as a Boolean expression γ by conjoining all constraints.

The method generates a value table T which includes as columns all value combinations of $(v_1, \ldots, v_m)$ for $(r_1, \ldots, r_m)$ such that $(r_1 = v_1) \wedge \cdots \wedge (r_m = v_m) \models \gamma$. Then it builds a new constraint set $\mathcal{C}'$ with an expression $r_i = \psi_i(v_1, \ldots, v_k)$ for every $1 \leq i \leq m$ over k fresh variables, where the ψ_i are generated from the rows of the value table. The number of variables is $k = \lceil \log(c) \rceil$ with c being the number of columns in the table (i.e. combinations of r_i satisfying γ). This method is the $\text{Lola}_{\mathbb{B}}$ pruning strategy which is perfect. By Theorem 1 this allows to build a perfect atemporal constant-memory monitor for $\text{Lola}_{\mathbb{B}}$.

Lemma 1. *The Lola$_\mathbb{B}$ pruning strategy is perfect and constant.*

Lola$_{\mathcal{LA}}$: The same idea used for Lola$_\mathbb{B}$ can be adapted to Linear Algebra.

Example 6. Consider the specification on the left. The main idea is that acc_a

$$acc_a := acc_a[-1|0] + ld_a[now]$$
$$acc_b := acc_b[-1|0] + ld_b[now]$$
$$total := total[-1|0] + \tfrac{1}{2}(ld_a[now] +$$
$$ld_b[now])$$

accumulates the load of CPU A (as indicated by ld_a), and similarly acc_b accumulates the load of CPU B (as indicated by ld_b). Then, $total$ keeps the average of ld_a and ld_b. The unrolled semantics is

0	1	2	...
ld_a^0	$ld_a^0 + ld_a^1$	$ld_a^0 + ld_a^1 + ld_a^2$	...
ld_b^0	$ld_b^0 + ld_b^1$	$ld_b^0 + ld_b^1 + ld_b^2$	...
$\frac{1}{2}(ld_a^0 + ld_b^0)$	$\frac{1}{2}((ld_a^0 + ld_b^0) + (ld_a^1 + ld_b^1))$	$\frac{1}{2}((ld_a^0 + ld_b^0) + (ld_a^1 + ld_b^1) + (ld_a^2 + ld_b^2))$	...

Again, the formulas maintained during monitoring are increasing. The formulas at 0 cannot be simplified, but at 1, ld_a^0 and ld_a^1 have exactly the same influence on acc_a^1, acc_b^1 and $total$. To see this consider the calculation of $(acc_a^1, acc_b^1, total^1)$ as the matrix multiplication shown below on the left. The matrix in the middle just contains two linearly independent vectors. Hence the system of equations can be equally written as shown in the right, over two fresh variables u^1, v^1:

$$
\begin{pmatrix} acc_a^1 \\ acc_b^1 \\ total^1 \end{pmatrix} = \begin{pmatrix} 1 & 0 & 1 & 0 \\ 0 & 1 & 0 & 1 \\ \frac{1}{2} & \frac{1}{2} & \frac{1}{2} & \frac{1}{2} \end{pmatrix} * \begin{pmatrix} ld_a^0 \\ ld_b^0 \\ ld_a^1 \\ ld_b^1 \end{pmatrix}
\qquad
\begin{pmatrix} acc_a^1 \\ acc_b^1 \\ total^1 \end{pmatrix} = \begin{pmatrix} 1 & 0 \\ 0 & 1 \\ \frac{1}{2} & \frac{1}{2} \end{pmatrix} * \begin{pmatrix} u^1 \\ v^1 \end{pmatrix}
$$

The rewritten formulas then again follow directly from the matrix. Repeating the application at all times yields:

0	1	2	...
ld_a^0	$ld_a^0 + ld_a^1 \equiv u^1$	$u^1 + ld_a^2 \equiv u^2$	...
ld_b^0	$ld_b^0 + ld_b^1 \equiv v^1$	$v^1 + ld_b^2 \equiv v^2$	...
$\frac{ld_a^0 + ld_b^0}{2}$	$\frac{(ld_a^0 + ld_b^0) + (ld_a^1 + ld_b^1)}{2} \equiv \frac{u^1 + v^1}{2}$	$\frac{(u^1 + v^1) + (ld_a^2 + ld_b^2)}{2} \equiv \frac{u^2 + v^2}{2}$	...

which results in a constant monitor.   □

This pruning strategy can be generalized as well. Let $\mathcal{R} = \{r_1, \ldots, r_m\}$ be a set of relevant variables (in our case the output variables s_i^t) and $\mathcal{V} = \{s_1, \ldots, s_n\} \cup \mathcal{R}$ be the other variables (in our case input variables or fresh variables from previous pruning applications). Let $\mathcal{C}$ be a set of constraints maintained by our monitoring algorithm which has to be fulfilled over $r_1, \ldots, r_m, s_1, \ldots, s_n$, which contains equations of the form $c = \sum_{i=1}^{m} c_{r_i} * r_i + \sum_{i=1}^{n} c_{s_i} * s_i + c'$ where c, c', c_{s_i}, c_{r_i} are constants.

If the equation system is unsolvable (which can easily be checked) we return $\mathcal{C}' = \{0 = 1\}$, otherwise we can rewrite it as shown on the left. The matrix N of this equation system has m rows and n columns. Let r be the rank of this matrix which is limited by $\min\{m,n\}$. Consequently an $m \times r$ matrix N' with $r \leq m$ exists with the same span as N and the system can be rewritten (without loosing solutions to $(r_1,\ldots,r_m)$). From this rewritten equation system a new constraint set $\mathcal{C}'$ can be generated which

$$\begin{pmatrix} r_1 \\ \vdots \\ r_m \end{pmatrix} = \begin{pmatrix} c_{1,1} & \cdots & c_{1,n} \\ & \vdots & \\ c_{m,1} & \cdots & c_{m,n} \end{pmatrix} * \begin{pmatrix} s_1 \\ \vdots \\ s_n \end{pmatrix} + \begin{pmatrix} o_1 \\ \vdots \\ o_m \end{pmatrix}$$

contains the equations from the system. We call this method the $\text{Lola}_{\mathcal{LA}}$ pruning strategy, which is perfect and constant.

Lemma 2. *The $\text{Lola}_{\mathcal{LA}}$ pruning strategy is perfect and constant.*

$\text{Lola}_{\mathbb{B}/\mathcal{LA}}$. Consider the specification below (left) where i, a and b are input streams of type $\mathbb{R}$. Consider a trace where the values of stream i are unknown until time 2, but that we have the assumption $0 \leq i[now] \leq 1$. The unpruned symbolic expressions describing the values of x, y at time 2 would then be in matrix notation:

$$x := x[-1|0] + i[now]$$
$$y := 2 * y[-1|0] + i[now]$$
$$ok := (a[now] = x[now]) \wedge (b[now] = y[now])$$

$$\begin{pmatrix} x^2 \\ y^2 \end{pmatrix} = \begin{pmatrix} 1 & 1 & 1 \\ 4 & 2 & 1 \end{pmatrix} * \begin{pmatrix} i^0 \\ i^1 \\ i^2 \end{pmatrix}$$

Since the assumption forces all i^j to be between 0 and 1 the possible set of value combinations x and y can take at time 2 is described by a polygon with 6 edges depicted in Fig. 2. Describing this polygon requires 3 vectors. It is easy to see that each new unknown input generates a new vector, which is not multiple of another. Hence for n unknown inputs

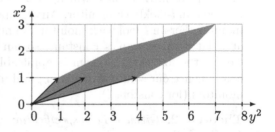

Fig. 2. Set of possible values of x^2 and y^2

on stream i the set of possible value combinations for (x^t, y^t) is described by a polygon with $2n$ edges for which a constraint set of size $\mathcal{O}(n)$ is required. This counterexample implies that for $\text{Lola}_{\mathbb{B}/\mathcal{LA}}$ there is no perfect pruning strategy. However, one can apply the following approximation: Given a constraint set $\mathcal{C}$ over $V = \{s_1,\ldots,s_n\} \cup \mathcal{R}$ with $\mathcal{R} = \{r_1,\ldots,r_m\}$ the set of relevant variables.

1. Split the set of relevant variables into $\mathcal{R}_\mathbb{B}$ containing those of type Boolean and $\mathcal{R}_\mathbb{R}$ containing those of type Real.
2. For $\mathcal{R}_\mathbb{B}$ do the rewriting as for $\text{Lola}_\mathbb{B}$ obtaining $\mathcal{C}'_\mathbb{B}$.
3. For $\mathcal{R}_\mathbb{R}$ do the rewriting as for $\text{Lola}_{\mathcal{LA}}$ over $\mathcal{C}^{\mathcal{LE}}$ with $\mathcal{C}^{\mathcal{LE}} \subseteq \mathcal{C}$ being the set of all linear equations in $\mathcal{C}$, obtaining $\mathcal{C}'_\mathbb{R}$.
4. For all fresh variables v_i with $1 \leq i \leq k$ in $\mathcal{C}'_\mathbb{R}$ calculate a minimum bound l_i and maximum bound g_i (may be over-approximating) over the constraints $\mathcal{C} \cup \mathcal{C}'_\mathbb{R}$ and build $\mathcal{C}''_\mathbb{R} = \mathcal{C}'_\mathbb{R} \cup \{l_i \leq v_i \leq g_i | 1 \leq i \leq k\}$.
5. Return $\mathcal{C}' = \mathcal{C}'_\mathbb{B} \cup \mathcal{C}''_\mathbb{R}$

We call this strategy the $Lola_{\mathbb{B}/\mathcal{LA}}$ pruning strategy, which allows to build an atemporal (imperfect but sound) constant-memory monitor.

Lemma 3. *The $Lola_{\mathbb{B}/\mathcal{LA}}$ pruning strategy is sound and constant.*

Note that with the $Lola_{\mathbb{B}/\mathcal{LA}}$ fragment we can also support if-then-else expressions. A definition $s = ite(c, t, e)$ can be rewritten to handle s as an input stream adding assumption $(c \wedge s = t) \vee (\neg c \wedge s = e)$. After applying this strategy the specification is within the $Lola_{\mathbb{B}/\mathcal{LA}}$ fragment and as a consequence the sound (but imperfect) pruning algorithm from there can be applied.

4.2 Temporal Assumptions

We study now how to handle temporal assumptions. Consider again Example 4, but instead of the assumption $0 \le ld[now] \le 10$ take $0.9 * ld[-1, 0] \le ld[now] \le 1.1 * ld[-1, 100]$. In this case it would not be possible to apply the presented pruning algorithms. In the pruning process at time 1 we would rewrite our formulas in a fashion that they do not contain ld^1 anymore, but at time 2 we would receive the constraint $0.9 * ld^1 \le ld^2 \le 1.1 * ld^1$ from the assumption.

Pruning strategies can be extended to consider variables which may be referenced by input constraints at a later time as relevant variables, hence they will not be pruned. A monitor which receives constraint sets over the last l instants is called an l-lookback monitor. An atemporal monitor is therefore a 0-lookback monitor. For an l-lookback monitor the number of variables that are referenced at a later timestamp is constant, so our pruning strategies remain constant. Hence, the following theorem is applicable to our pruning strategies and as a consequence our solutions for atemporal monitors can be adapted to l-lookback monitors (for constant l).

Theorem 2. *Given a Lola specification φ and a constant pruning strategy $\mathcal{P}$ for $Expr_\varphi^\mathbb{B}$ there is a constant-memory l-lookback monitor M_φ such that*

- *M_φ is sound if the pruning strategy is sound.*
- *M_φ is perfect if the pruning strategy is perfect.*

5   Implementation and Empirical Evaluation

We have developed a prototype implementation of the symbolic algorithm for past-only Lola in Scala, using Z3 [24] as solver. Our tool supports Reals and Booleans with their standard operations, ranges (e.g. $[3, 10.5]$) and ? for unknowns. Assumptions can be encoded using the keyword ASSUMPTION.[1] Our tool performs pruning (Sect. 4.1) at every instant, printing precise outputs when possible. If an output value is uncertain the formula and a range of possible values is printed.

---

[1] Note that for our symbolic approach assumptions can indeed be considered as a stream specification of type Boolean which has to be true at every time instant.

We evaluated two realistic case studies, a test drive data emission monitoring [19] and an electrocardiogram (ECG) peak detector [11]. All measurements were done on a 64-bit Linux machine with an Intel Core i7 and 8 GB RAM. We measured the processing time of single events in our evaluation, for inputs from 0% up to 20% of uncertain values, resulting in average of 25 ms per event (emissions case study) and 97 ms per event (ECG). In both cases the runtime per event did not depend on the length of the trace (as predicted theoretically). The long runtime is in general due to using Z3 naively to deduce bounds of unknown variables, other methods/specialized tools should be investigated in the future. The longer runtime per event in the second case study is explained because of a window of size 100 which is unrolled to 100 streams. We discuss the two case studies separately.

Case Study #1: Emission Monitoring. The first example is a specification that receives test drive data from a car (including speed, altitude, NOx emissions,...) from [19]. The Lola specification is within $Lola_{\mathcal{B}/\mathcal{LA}}$ (with *ite*), and checks several properties, including `trip_valid` which captures if the trip was a valid test ride. The specification contains around 50 stream definitions in total. We used two real trips as inputs, one where the allowed NOx emission was violated and one where the emission specification was satisfied.

We injected uncertainty into the two traces by randomly selecting $x\%$ of the events and modifying the value to an uncertainty interval of $\pm y\%$ around the correct value. The figure on the left shows the result of executing this experiment for all integer combinations of x and y

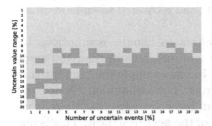

between 1 and 20, for one trace. The green space represents the cases for which the monitor computed the valid answer and the red space the cases where the monitor reported unknown. In both traces, even with 20% of incorrect samples within an interval of $\pm 7\%$ around the correct value the monitor was able to compute the correct answer. We also compared these results to the value-range approach, using interval arithmetic. However, the final verdicts do not differ here. Though the symbolic approach is able to calculate more precise intermediate results, these do not differ enough to obtain different final Boolean verdicts.

As expected, for fully unknown values and no assumptions, neither the symbolic nor the interval approaches could compute any certain verdict, because the input values could be arbitrarily large. However, in opposite to the interval approach, the symbolic approach allows adding assumptions (e.g. the speed or altitude does not differ much from the previous value). With this assumption, we received the valid result for `trip_valid` when up to 4% of inputs are fully uncertain. In other words, the capability of symbolic RV to encode physical dependencies as assumptions often allows our technique to compute correct verdicts in the presence of several unknown values.

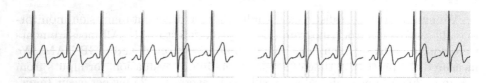

Fig. 3. ECG analysis. Left: symbolic approach, Right: value range approach. Green: certain heartbeats, Yellow: potential heartbeats, Red: bursts of unknown values. (Color figure online)

Case Study #2: Heart Rate Monitoring. Our second case study concerns the peak detection in electrocardiogram (ECG) signals [11]. The specification calculates a sliding average and stores the values of this convoluted stream in a window of size 100. Then it checks if the central value is higher than the 50 previous and the 50 next values to identifying a peak.

We evaluated the specification against a ECG trace with 2700 events corresponding to 14 heartbeats. We integrated uncertainty into the data in two different ways. First, we modified $x\%$ percent of the events to uncertainty intervals of $\pm y\%$. Even if 20% of the values were modified with an error of $\pm 20\%$, the symbolic approach returned the perfect result, while the interval approach degraded over time because of accumulated uncertainties (many peaks were incorrectly "detected", even under 5% of unknown values with a $\pm 20\%$ error—see front part of traces in Fig. 3). Second, we injected bursts of consecutive errors (? values) of different lengths into the input data. The interval domain approach lost track after the first burst and was unable to recover, while the symbolic approach returned some ? around the area with the bursts and recovered when new values were received (see Fig. 3).

We exploited the ability of symbolic monitors to handle assumptions by encoding that heartbeats must be apart from each other more than 160 steps (roughly 0.5 s), which increased the accuracy. In one example the monitor correctly detected a peak right after a burst of errors. The assumption allowed the monitor to infer values of certain variables from the knowledge that there is no heartbeat, which enabled in turn the detection of the next heartbeat. This is not possible if heartbeats that are not at least 160 steps apart are just filtered out.

6 Conclusion

We have introduced the concept of symbolic Runtime Verification to monitor in the presence of input uncertainties and assumptions on the system behavior. We showed theoretically and empirically that symbolic RV is more precise than monitoring with intervals, and have identified logical theories for which perfect symbolic RV can be implemented in constant memory. Future work includes: (1) to identify other logical theories and their combinations that guarantee perfect trace length independent monitoring; (2) to be able to anticipate verdicts ahead of time for rich data domains by unfolding the symbolic representation of the specification beyond, along the lines of [2,20,30] for Booleans;

Finally, we envision that symbolic Runtime Verification can become a general, foundational approach for monitoring that will allow to explain many existing monitoring approaches as instances of the general schema.

References

1. Bartocci, E., Falcone, Y. (eds.): Lectures on Runtime Verification - Introductory and Advanced Topics, LNCS, vol. 10457. Springer (2018). https://doi.org/10.1007/978-3-319-75632-5

2. Bauer, A., Leucker, M., Schallhart, C.: Monitoring of real-time properties. In: Arun-Kumar, S., Garg, N. (eds.) FSTTCS 2006. LNCS, vol. 4337, pp. 260–272. Springer, Heidelberg (2006). https://doi.org/10.1007/11944836_25

3. Bauer, A., Leucker, M., Schallhart, C.: Comparing LTL semantics for runtime verification. J. Logic Comput. **20**(3), 651–674 (2010)

4. Biere, A., Cimatti, A., Clarke, E.M., Strichman, O., Zhu, Y.: Bounded model checking. In: Highly Dependable Soft., chap. 3, pp. 118–149, No. 58 in Advances in Computers 2003. Academic Press (2003)

5. Biewer, S., Finkbeiner, B., Hermanns, H., Köhl, M.A., Schnitzer, Y., Schwenger, M.: RTLola on board: testing real driving emissions on your phone. In: TACAS 2021. LNCS, vol. 12652, pp. 365–372. Springer, Cham (2021). https://doi.org/10.1007/978-3-030-72013-1_20

6. Cimatti, A., Tian, C., Tonetta, S.: Assumption-based runtime verification of infinite-state systems. In: Feng, L., Fisman, D. (eds.) RV 2021. LNCS, vol. 12974, pp. 207–227. Springer, Cham (2021). https://doi.org/10.1007/978-3-030-88494-9_11

7. Convent, L., Hungerecker, S., Leucker, M., Scheffel, T., Schmitz, M., Thoma, D.: TeSSLa: temporal stream-based specification language. In: Massoni, T., Mousavi, M.R. (eds.) SBMF 2018. LNCS, vol. 11254, pp. 144–162. Springer, Cham (2018). https://doi.org/10.1007/978-3-030-03044-5_10

8. Cousot, P., Cousot, R.: Abstract interpretation: a unified lattice model for static analysis of programs by construction or approximation of fixpoints. In: POPL, pp. 238–252. ACM (1977)

9. D'Angelo, B., et al.: LOLA: runtime monitoring of synchronous systems. In: Proceeding of TIME 2005, pp. 166–174. IEEE Computer Society (2005)

10. Decker, N., Leucker, M., Thoma, D.: Monitoring mod. theories. STTT **18**(2), 205–225 (2016)

11. Gorostiaga, F., Sánchez, C.: Nested monitors: monitors as expressions to build monitors. In: Feng, L., Fisman, D. (eds.) RV 2021. LNCS, vol. 12974, pp. 164–183. Springer, Cham (2021). https://doi.org/10.1007/978-3-030-88494-9_9

12. Gorostiaga, F., Sánchez, C.: Stream runtime verification of real-time event streams with the Striver language. Int. J. Softw. Tools Technol. Transfer **23**(2), 157–183 (2021). https://doi.org/10.1007/s10009-021-00605-3

13. Havelund, K., Goldberg, A.: Verify your runs. In: Meyer, B., Woodcock, J. (eds.) VSTTE 2005. LNCS, vol. 4171, pp. 374–383. Springer, Heidelberg (2008). https://doi.org/10.1007/978-3-540-69149-5_40

14. Havelund, K., Peled, D.: An extension of first-order LTL with rules with application to runtime verification. Int. J. Softw. Tools Technol. Transfer **23**(4), 547–563 (2021). https://doi.org/10.1007/s10009-021-00626-y

15. Henzinger, T.A., Saraç, N.E.: Monitorability under assumptions. In: Deshmukh, J., Ničković, D. (eds.) RV 2020. LNCS, vol. 12399, pp. 3–18. Springer, Cham (2020). https://doi.org/10.1007/978-3-030-60508-7_1

16. Kallwies, H., Leucker, M., Sánchez, C.: Symbolic runtime verification for monitoring under uncertainties and assumptions. arXiv abs/2207.05678 (2022)

17. Kauffman, S., Havelund, K., Fischmeister, S.: What can we monitor over unreliable channels? STTT, 1–24 (2020). https://doi.org/10.1007/s10009-021-00625-z

18. King, J.C.: Symbolic execution and program testing. CACM **19**(7), 385–394 (1976)

19. Köhl, M.A., Hermanns, H., Biewer, S.: Efficient monitoring of real driving emissions. In: Colombo, C., Leucker, M. (eds.) RV 2018. LNCS, vol. 11237, pp. 299–315. Springer, Cham (2018). https://doi.org/10.1007/978-3-030-03769-7_17

20. Leucker, M.: Sliding between model checking and runtime verification. In: Qadeer, S., Tasiran, S. (eds.) RV 2012. LNCS, vol. 7687, pp. 82–87. Springer, Heidelberg (2013). https://doi.org/10.1007/978-3-642-35632-2_10

21. Leucker, M., Sánchez, C., Scheffel, T., Schmitz, M., Schramm, A.: Tessla: runtime verification of non-synchronized real-time streams. In: SAC 2018, pp. 1925–1933. ACM (2018)

22. Leucker, M., Sánchez, C., Scheffel, T., Schmitz, M., Thoma, D.: Runtime verification for timed event streams with partial information. In: Finkbeiner, B., Mariani, L. (eds.) RV 2019. LNCS, vol. 11757, pp. 273–291. Springer, Cham (2019). https://doi.org/10.1007/978-3-030-32079-9_16

23. Leucker, M., Schallhart, C.: A brief account of runtime verification. J. Log. Algebraic Meth. Program. **78**(5), 293–303 (2009)

24. de Moura, L., Bjørner, N.: Z3: an efficient SMT solver. In: Ramakrishnan, C.R., Rehof, J. (eds.) TACAS 2008. LNCS, vol. 4963, pp. 337–340. Springer, Heidelberg (2008). https://doi.org/10.1007/978-3-540-78800-3_24

25. Pan, J., Tompkins, W.J.: A real-time QRS detection algorithm. IEEE Trans. Biomed. Eng. BME **32**(3), 230–236 (1985)

26. Pnueli, A.: The temporal logic of programs. In: FOCS 1977, pp. 46–57. IEEE (1977)

27. Sznajder, M., Łukowska, M.: Python Online and Offline ECG QRS Detector based on the Pan-Tomkins algorithm (2017)

28. Waga, M., André, É., Hasuo, I.: Symbolic monitoring against specifications parametric in time and data. In: Dillig, I., Tasiran, S. (eds.) CAV 2019. LNCS, vol. 11561, pp. 520–539. Springer, Cham (2019). https://doi.org/10.1007/978-3-030-25540-4_30

29. Waga, M., André, É., Hasuo, I.: Model-bounded monitoring of hybrid systems. In: ICCPS, pp. 21–32. ACM (2021)

30. Zhang, X., Leucker, M., Dong, W.: Runtime verification with predictive semantics. In: Goodloe, A.E., Person, S. (eds.) NFM 2012. LNCS, vol. 7226, pp. 418–432. Springer, Heidelberg (2012). https://doi.org/10.1007/978-3-642-28891-3_37

SMT and Verification

Handling Polynomial and Transcendental Functions in SMT via Unconstrained Optimisation and Topological Degree Test

Alessandro Cimatti[1], Alberto Griggio[1], Enrico Lipparini[1,2($\boxtimes$)], and Roberto Sebastiani[3]

[1] Fondazione Bruno Kessler, Trento, Italy
{cimatti,griggio,elipparini}@fbk.eu
[2] DIBRIS, University of Genoa, Genoa, Italy
enrico.lipparini@edu.unige.it
[3] DISI, University of Trento, Trento, Italy
roberto.sebastiani@unitn.it

Abstract. We present a method for determining the satisfiability of quantifier-free first-order formulas modulo the theory of non-linear arithmetic over the reals augmented with transcendental functions. Our procedure is based on the fruitful combination of two main ingredients: unconstrained optimisation, to generate a set of candidate solutions, and a result from topology called the topological degree test to check whether a given bounded region contains at least a solution. We have implemented the procedure in a prototype tool called UGOTNL, and integrated it within the MATHSAT SMT solver. Our experimental evaluation over a wide range of benchmarks shows that it vastly improves the performance of the solver for satisfiable non-linear arithmetic formulas, significantly outperforming other available tools for problems with transcendental functions.

1 Introduction

When dealing with real arithmetic in SMT, a fundamental challenge is to go beyond the linear case ($\mathcal{LRA}$), by introducing nonlinear polynomials ($\mathcal{NRA}$), possibly augmented with transcendental functions like exponential and trigonometric ones ($\mathcal{NTA}$). In fact, the expressive power of $\mathcal{NTA}$ is required by many application domains (e.g. railways, aerospace, control software, and cyberphysical systems). Unfortunately, dealing with non-linearity is a very hard challenge. Going from SMT($\mathcal{LRA}$) to SMT($\mathcal{NRA}$) yields a complexity gap that results in a computational barrier in practice. Adding transcendental functions exacerbates the problem even further, because reasoning on $\mathcal{NTA}$ is undecidable [26]. Existing SMT solvers therefore have to resort to incomplete techniques in order to handle $\mathcal{NTA}$ constraints [7,16], which are however particularly ineffective at proving that a formula is satisfiable (i.e. that it has at least one model).

This work has been partly supported by project "AI@TN" funded by the Autonomous Province of Trento.

One of the main sources of complexity is the need to provide exact answers: when an SMT solver says "sat", the input problem must indeed be satisfiable, and not just "likely satisfiable" or "satisfiable with high probability". Removing this requirement makes it possible to use approximate techniques, such as numerical methods or procedures based on weaker notions of satisfiability such as δ-satisfiability [18], which are typically significantly more scalable in practice than exact methods.

In this paper, we present a technique for significantly improving the effectiveness of SMT($\mathcal{NTA}$) solvers in determining that a formula is satisfiable, by exploiting a fruitful combination of approximate and exact techniques. Our procedure uses numerical methods based on *unconstrained global optimisation* to quickly identify (small) boxes containing candidate solutions for a given set/conjunction of $\mathcal{NRA}$ and $\mathcal{NTA}$ constraints, which are then analysed with a procedure whose main ingredient is the *topological degree test* [14,24] – a result from topology that guarantees the existence of a solution for a set of equalities if certain conditions are met – to confirm whether a candidate box contains at least one solution. The procedure is then plugged into an SMT context, which allows us to handle problems containing arbitrary Boolean combinations of constraints.

The main contribution of this work is an effective combination of numeric and symbolic methods that allows to significantly enhance the capability of state-of-the-art SMT solvers to determine the satisfiability of formulas containing $\mathcal{NTA}$ constraints, as demonstrated by our extensive experimental evaluation. To this extent, although all the ingredients we use are known, our overall procedure is, to the best of our knowledge, novel. The synergy between numerical optimisation and the topological degree test is essential for the viability of our approach, as none of the two techniques in isolation is effective in practice. On one hand, being based on numerical methods, unconstrained global optimisation alone cannot detect exact solutions, but only approximate ones. On the other hand, the topological degree test alone is not immediately applicable to arbitrary sets of constraints, as it works only for problems in a specific form, in which (i) there are only equations, (ii) the number of equations is equal to the number of variables, (iii) all variables are bounded, and (as a more empirical requirement rather than theoretical limitation) (iv) the bounds on the variables are "sufficiently small" for the practical effectiveness of the test. The first limitation has been tackled in [15] by pairing the topological degree test with interval arithmetic to deal with inequalities. In this paper, we show how a further combination with numerical optimization can be exploited to obtain a practical and effective method that can be easily integrated in a modern SMT solver, thus overcoming the other three points.

In order to substantiate our claims, we have implemented our procedure in a prototype tool called UGOTNL, and we have integrated it within the MATHSAT SMT solver [8]. We have extensively evaluated our prototype on a wide range of $\mathcal{NRA}$ and $\mathcal{NTA}$ benchmarks, comparing it to the main state-of-the art tools. Our experimental evaluation shows that it vastly improves the performance of the MATHSAT solver for satisfiable $\mathcal{NRA}$ formulas, significantly outperforming the other tools on $\mathcal{NTA}$ problems.

Related Work. For $\mathcal{NRA}$, various techniques have been explored. Complete methods based on quantifier-elimination procedures such as Cylindric Algebraic Decomposition (CAD) [9] have been successfully implemented in several SMT-solvers (such as z3 [11], YICES [13], SMT-RAT [10]), proving their effectiveness especially when tightly integrated into the Boolean search through a model-constructing framework such as MCSAT [12,20]. However, their complexity is doubly-exponential in the worst case, and they cannot deal with transcendental functions.

For $\mathcal{NTA}$, there exist very few techniques able to prove satisfiability. Incremental linearization (IL) [7] starts from an abstract model and tries to check whether the formula is satisfiable under *all possible interpretations* (within a given bounded region) of the transcendental functions involved. This tactic works well when the transcendental functions are isolated in the formula, but it is quite ineffective when the transcendental component is more complex (expecially in the presence of equations). iSAT3 [16] implements a method based on a tight integration of Interval Constraint Propagation (ICP) [4] into the CDCL framework, and it is able to prove satisfiability if it finds a box in which every point is a solution.

Differently from these methods, our approach is not compelled to find more solutions than needed, and it is able to prove satisfiability even when the only models of the formula are isolated points. Interestingly, RASAT [27] combines ICP with the Generalized Intermediate Value Theorem (GIVT) [23], but does not support transcendental functions.

Other approaches, e.g. DREAL [19] and KSMT [5], rely on the notion of δ-satisfiability [18], which guarantees that there exists a perturbation (up to some $\delta > 0$ specified by the user) of the original formula that is satisfiable[1]. iSAT3 relies on a similar notion and, when not able to prove satisfiability nor to detect conflicts, returns a candidate solution. In comparison with these approaches, when we return "sat" we guarantee that the problem is actually satisfiable.

Content. The paper is organized as follows. In Sect. 2 we provide the necessary theoretical background; in Sect. 3 we describe how we use unconstrained optimisation to find candidate models; in Sect. 4 we describe a general procedure, restricted to conjunctions of $\mathcal{NTA}$ constraints, based on the topological degree test and interval arithmetic; in Sect. 5 we extend the previous procedure to general $\mathcal{NTA}$ formulas, following either an eager or a lazy approach; in Sect. 6 we present our experimental evaluation; in Sect. 7 we conclude.

2   Background

We work in the setting of SMT, with the quantifier-free theory of real arithmetic, either limited to polynomial constraints (denoted $\mathcal{NRA}$), or augmented with trigonometric and exponential transcendental functions (denoted $\mathcal{NTA}$). We

---

[1] Note that, according to this definition, a problem could be unsat and δ-sat at the same time.

assume the standard notions of interpretation, model, satisfiability, validity and logical consequence.

We use the following notation. We write logical variables with $x_1, x_2, \ldots$, and values in $\mathbb{R}$ with $x_1, x_2, \ldots$. If t is a generic (quantifier-free) term, we write $[t]$ for its interpretation in the standard model of arithmetic. If ϕ is a formula, we denote with $\text{Var}(\phi)$ the set of its (free) variables. We use f, g to denote logic symbols representing a polynomial or a transcendental function; when there is no ambiguity, we will use the same symbol also to denote the real function corresponding to its standard interpretation. We use boldface to denote vectors of values $\mathbf{x} \stackrel{\text{def}}{=} \{x_1, \ldots, x_m\} \in \mathbb{R}^m$, and intervals $I \stackrel{\text{def}}{=} \{x \in \mathbb{R} \mid a \leq x \leq b\}$ with $[a, b]$ (or simply $[a]$ when $a \equiv b$), where a and $b \in \mathbb{Q}$. Given a vector $\mathbf{x} \in \mathbb{R}^m$, we denote with $\|\mathbf{x}\|_2$ its Euclidean norm (i.e. $\sqrt{\sum_i x_i^2}$), and with $|\mathbf{x}|$ its maximum norm (i.e. $\max\{|x_1|, \cdots, |x_m|\}$). If ϕ is a formula with $\text{Var}(\phi) \equiv \{x_1, \ldots, x_m\}$, we denote with $M_\phi \stackrel{\text{def}}{=} \{\mathbf{x} \in \mathbb{R}^m \mid \mathbf{x} \text{ is a model of } \phi\}$ the set of its models.

We assume that the reader is familiar with the main theoretical and algorithmic concepts of SMT, as well as with its terminology. We recall that the lazy-SMT approach consists in building ad-hoc theory-specific procedures (called *theory solvers*, usually written just for conjunctions of literals, i.e. atomic formulas and their negations) and integrating them into a SAT-solver. The most used approach for lazy-SMT, called CDCL(T), is to modify the CDCL procedure [29] commonly used for SAT to work with formulas having a background theory T. We refer the reader to, e.g., [3] for more details on lazy SMT.

In the rest of this section, we introduce the necessary background techniques from the fields of unconstrained optimisation, interval arithmetic, and topology.

2.1   Unconstrained Global Optimisation

We say that $\mathbf{x}^*$ is a *local minimum* for $h : \mathbb{R}^m \to \mathbb{R}$, if there exists a neighborhood $S := \{\mathbf{x} \in \mathbb{R}^m : \|\mathbf{x}^* - \mathbf{x}\|_2 < \delta\}$ for some $\delta > 0$, such that $\forall \mathbf{x} \in S : h(\mathbf{x}^*) \leq h(\mathbf{x})$. We say that $\mathbf{x}^*$ is a *global minimum* for h if $\forall \mathbf{x} \in \mathbb{R}^m : h(\mathbf{x}^*) \leq h(\mathbf{x})$.

Unconstrained global optimisation is the problem of minimizing a function h on the entire space $\mathbb{R}^m$ of the real numbers. A common approach to tackle this problem is leveraging fast local optimisation techniques.

In this paper, we use a Monte Carlo Markov Chain method called Basin-hopping [28], based on the Metropolis-Hasting algorithm [21]. The idea of Basin-hopping is to do a random sampling of h to simulate a target distribution, and then alternate a local minimization phase with a stepping phase, used to decide, guided by the target distribution, how to *jump* from a local minimum to another. In particular, we use a slight modification of the algorithm that, given a maximum number of iterations, returns all the local minima found during the search.

2.2   Interval Arithmetic

Interval Arithmetic is a systematic approach to represent real numbers as intervals and to compute safe bounds that account for rounding errors. We define a *box* as a subset of $\mathbb{R}^m$ that is the Cartesian product of m intervals: $B = I_1 \times \cdots \times I_m \subset \mathbb{R}^m$. The width of an interval $I \stackrel{\text{def}}{=} [a_I, b_I]$ is defined as width$(I) \stackrel{\text{def}}{=} b_I - a_I$, and the width of a box is defined as width$(B) \stackrel{\text{def}}{=} \max_i(\text{width}(I_i))$. We can define several operations and relations between intervals, such as addition, multiplication, inclusion, and many more. For a more in-depth coverage of properties of and operations on intervals, we refer to [22].

We now give the definition of interval-computable functions, which plays an important role in our method. The intuition is that a function is interval-computable if it is possible to compute arbitrarily precise images for every interval domain. It has been proved that every function in $\mathcal{NTA}$ is interval computable (we refer to Sect. 5.4 of [22] for the proof)

Definition 1 (Function interval-computable). *A function* $f : \Omega \subseteq \mathbb{R}^m \to \mathbb{R}^n$ *is said to be* interval-computable *iff there exists an algorithm* $\mathcal{I}_f$ *that, for every box* $B' \subseteq \Omega$ *with rational vertices, computes a box* $\mathcal{I}_f(B')$ *with rational vertices, such that: (i)* $f(B') \subseteq \mathcal{I}_f(B')$*; and (ii)* $\forall \epsilon > 0 : \exists \delta > 0$ *such that for every* B' *having* width$(B') < \delta$*, then* width$(\mathcal{I}_f(B')) < \epsilon$*.*

Given a formula ϕ in m real variables and a box $B \stackrel{\text{def}}{=} I_1 \times \cdots \times I_m \subset \mathbb{R}^m$ (where $I_i \stackrel{\text{def}}{=} [a_i, b_i]$), we define the restriction of ϕ to the box B (and say $\phi_{|B}$ is a *bounded formula*) as

$$\phi_{|B} := \phi \wedge \bigwedge_{x_i \in \text{Var}(\phi)} (a_i \leq x_i \wedge x_i \leq b_i) \tag{1}$$

2.3 Robustness and Quasi-decidability

Intuitively, a formula is robust if its satisfiability status does not change under "small" perturbations[2]. Robustness is a desirable property in many real-world applications, as already observed in the literature (e.g. [18,25]). The related notion of quasi-decidability [15] is then a property that allows to circumvent general undecidability results for a class of formulas when focusing only on robust inputs.

Definition 2 (Quasi-decidability). *A class of problems is quasi-decidable if there exists an algorithm that always terminates on robust instances, and that always returns the right answer when terminating.*

2.4 Topological Degree Test

The topological degree of a continuous function $f : \mathbb{R}^n \to \mathbb{R}^n$ bounded over a box B is an integer $\deg(f, B)$ that can be defined in several different equivalent ways. Those definitions however require a consistent background, so for lack of space we refer to [24] for a detailed presentation. The property that we are interested in is the following, that we will call *topological degree test*:

---

[2] A formal definition of robustness can be found in Sect. 2 of [15].

Property 1. If $\deg(f, B) \neq 0$, then the equation $f = 0$ has a solution in B.

The topological degree has proven to be computable if $0 \notin f(\partial B)^3$ [1]. A practical tool for computing it is TOPDEG[4], implementing the algorithm described in [14].

3 Local Search Using Unconstrained Global Optimisation

In this section we explain how to exploit unconstrained global optimisation to help a generic SMT solver to find models for sets of constraints in $\mathcal{NRA}$ and $\mathcal{NTA}$. The general idea is that of mapping a formula ϕ over real variables $x_1, \ldots, x_m$ into a real-valued non-negative function $h : \mathbb{R}^m \mapsto \mathbb{R}^{\geq 0}$, such that $\mathbf{x}$ is a model of ϕ only if $h(\mathbf{x}) = 0$, and then use an unconstrained optimisation routine to determine global minima of h. An ad-hoc encoding for Boolean variables should be introduced. This technique, which we shall call *Logic-to-Optimisation*, has already been applied successfully in other theories, e.g. [17]. In general, there exist several approaches to perform logic-to-optimisation, that vary depending on which logical theory is considered, what the purpose of the translation is, and which properties of the cost function are desired.

We illustrate the specific translation that we use in our procedure. We assume w.l.o.g. that our input formula consists of conjunctions and disjunctions of Boolean variables $b_1, \ldots, b_k$, possibly negated, and constraints of the form $f \bowtie 0$, where $\bowtie \in \{<, \leq, =\}$, and f is a $\mathcal{NTA}$ term. We define an operator $\mathcal{L2O}$ that maps a formula to a non-negative real function from $\mathbb{R}^{m+k}$ to $\mathbb{R}^{\geq 0}$ as follows:

$$
\begin{aligned}
\mathcal{L2O}(f \bowtie 0), \ \bowtie \in \{\leq, =\} \ &\stackrel{\text{def}}{=} \ (\text{if } ([f](\mathbf{x}) \bowtie 0) \text{ then } 0 \text{ else } [f]^2(\mathbf{x})) \\
\mathcal{L2O}(f < 0) \ &\stackrel{\text{def}}{=} \ \mathcal{L2O}(f \leq 0) \\
\mathcal{L2O}(\neg(f \bowtie 0)), \ \bowtie \in \{<, \leq\} \ &\stackrel{\text{def}}{=} \ \mathcal{L2O}(-f \bowtie 0) \\
\mathcal{L2O}(\neg(f = 0)) \ &\stackrel{\text{def}}{=} \ (\text{if } ([f](\mathbf{x}) = 0) \text{ then } 1 \text{ else } 0) \\
\mathcal{L2O}(b) \ &\stackrel{\text{def}}{=} \ \mathcal{L2O}(-x_b \leq 0) \\
\mathcal{L2O}(\neg b) \ &\stackrel{\text{def}}{=} \ \mathcal{L2O}(x_b + 1 \leq 0) \\
\mathcal{L2O}(\phi_1 \wedge \phi_2) \ &\stackrel{\text{def}}{=} \ \mathcal{L2O}(\phi_1) + \mathcal{L2O}(\phi_2) \\
\mathcal{L2O}(\phi_1 \vee \phi_2) \ &\stackrel{\text{def}}{=} \ \mathcal{L2O}(\phi_1) * \mathcal{L2O}(\phi_2),
\end{aligned}
$$

where x_b is a fresh real variable.

Note that with this definition, our logic-to-optimisation transformation will produce an overapproximation, meaning that not all the points in which $\mathcal{L2O}(\phi)$ evaluates to 0 (the *zero set* of $\mathcal{L2O}(\phi)$, denoted Z_ϕ) are models of ϕ: specifically, this is due to the encoding used for strict inequalities and Boolean variables. What is important for our purposes, however, is the converse, i.e. the fact that Z_ϕ contains the set M_ϕ of all the models of ϕ. Moreover, since $\mathcal{L2O}(\phi)$ has non-negative values, if $Z_\phi \neq \emptyset$, then Z_ϕ contains all and only the global minima of the function. We can exploit these facts as follows.

---

[3] ∂B is the topological boundary of B, i.e. the set of points in the closure of B that are not in its interior.

[4] Available at https://www.cs.cas.cz/~ratschan/topdeg/topdeg.html.

Through the unconstrained global optimisation algorithm Basin-hopping mentioned in Sect. 2.1, we obtain a finite set of local minima $L_\phi \subseteq \{\mathbf{x} \in \mathbb{R}^m \mid \mathbf{x}$ is a local minimum of $\mathcal{L2O}(\phi)\}$. Implementation-wise, the output will consist of rational approximations of local minima. We denote this set by $\tilde{L}_\phi$. For each element $\tilde{\mathbf{x}} \in \tilde{L}_\phi$, we try to produce a model $\mathbf{x}$ for ϕ. We first propose two simple tactics that work only in the case that ϕ is in $\mathcal{NRA}$, and we will present a more elaborate procedure for $\mathcal{NTA}$ in the next section. Moreover, in the following we only consider formulas which are simply conjunctions of constraints, and that contain no Boolean variables. We shall deal with general formulas in Sect. 5.

Given $\tilde{\mathbf{x}} \stackrel{\text{def}}{=} \{\tilde{x}_1, \cdots, \tilde{x}_m\} \in \tilde{L}_\phi$, it is trivial to check whether $\tilde{\mathbf{x}}$ is a model for ϕ by substituting the variables with their values into the formula[5]. If $\tilde{\mathbf{x}}$ is not a model we can try to look in the surroundings of $\tilde{\mathbf{x}}$. An idea is to reduce ϕ to a linear under-approximation by forcing all the multiplications to be linear, similarly to what is done in [7] equation (3), in the context of the incremental linearization approach (we will refer to this techique as *check-crosses*). A third more general idea is restricting the problem to a bounded subformula $\phi_{|B}$, obtained by imposing that the variables range over a box $B \equiv I_1 \times \cdots \times I_m \subset \mathbb{R}^m$ (where $I_i \stackrel{\text{def}}{=} [a_i, b_i]$ and $\tilde{x}_i \in I_i$). A naive choice of B is the hyper-cube having $\tilde{\mathbf{x}}$ as its center (that is, $I_i \stackrel{\text{def}}{=} [\tilde{x}_i - c, \tilde{x}_i + c]$ for a given small $c \in \mathbb{Q}_{>0}$).

The reason to restrict to a box is that bounded problems are, in general, easier to solve, and, if the cost of $\tilde{\mathbf{x}}$ is zero or very close to zero, we can reasonably hope that a model lies in the box. However, restricting to bounded instances by itself does not help much in terms of classes of problems we are able to solve. In fact, if our SMT solver was unable to find irrational models before, it still is. Nonetheless, as we will see in the next section, the idea of finding a point $\tilde{\mathbf{x}}$ very close to being a model and then restrict the problem to a (possibly very tight) bounded instance, allows the adoption of a new procedure for $\mathcal{NTA}$.

4   Solving Bounded Instances with the Topological Degree Test and Interval Arithmetic

In this section we explain how, given a local minimum $\tilde{\mathbf{x}}$ obtained as in the previous section, we can prove the satisfiability of a bounded conjunction of constraints $\phi_{|B}$ in $\mathcal{NTA}$ through interval arithmetic and the computation of the topological degree.

First, in Sect. 4.1, we provide a practical quasi-decidability procedure for bounded formulas in m variables that contain n equations and k non-strict inequalities, and for which either $n = m$ or $n = 0$. We then generalize this in Sect. 4.2, by providing a method that, given a formula with the only condition that $n \leq m$ (and no conditions on the kind of inequalities), can generate subformulas for which the quasi-decidability procedure is applicable. Finally, in Sect. 4.3, we discuss how we can integrate these results within the Logic-to-Optimisation framework.

---

[5] We remind that we are assuming to be in $\mathcal{NRA}$ only here.

4.1   Quasi-decidability Procedure

Algorithm 1. QUASI-DEC
___

    Input: A formula $\phi_{|B}$ in m variables, n equations $f_1 = 0, \cdots, f_n = 0$, and k non-strict inequalities $g_i \leq 0, \cdots, g_k \leq 0$ s.t. $n = m$ or $n = 0$

    Output: <**False**> or <**True**, B_{sol}>   ▷ B_{sol} is a box containing a model

  1: **grid** ← $\{B\}$
  2: **conflict_indices** ← $\{0, \cdots, m\}$
  3: **while** True **do**
  4:    **for** $A \in$ **grid do**
  5:        **if** $(0 \notin \mathcal{I}_f(A)) \vee (\mathcal{I}_g(A) \cap (-\infty, 0]^k = \emptyset)$ **then**   ▷ $\mathcal{I}_f$ and $\mathcal{I}_g$ as in def. 1
  6:            **grid.remove**(A)
  7:    **if grid** = $\{\}$ **then return** <**False**>
  8:    **if** $n \neq 0$ **then**
  9:        **grid** ← Merge all the boxes in **grid** having a common face C s.t. $0 \in \mathcal{I}_f(C)$

10:        **grid**$_\partial$ ← $\{A \in$ **grid** | exists C a face of A s.t. $C \subseteq \partial B \wedge 0 \in \mathcal{I}_{f(C)}\}$
11:    **else**
12:        **grid**$_\partial$ ← $\{\}$
13:    **for** $A \in$ **grid** $\setminus$ **grid**$_\partial$ **do**
14:        **conflict_indices_A** ← $\{\}$
15:        **demerge**(A) := $\{E \mid E$ has been merged into A in line 9$\}$
16:        **for** $E \in$ **demerge**(A) **do**
17:            **for** $i \in \{0, \cdots, k\}$ **do**
18:                **if** $\mathcal{I}_{g_i}(E) \not\subseteq (-\infty, 0]$ **then**
19:                    **conflict_indices_A.add**($\{j \in \{0, \cdots, m\} \mid x_j$ appears in $g_i\}$)
20:        **if conflict_indices_A** = $\{\} \wedge (n = 0 \vee$ **TopDeg**$(f, A) \neq 0)$ **then**
21:            **return** <**True** , A >
22:        **conflict_indices.add(conflict_indices_A)**
23:    **refinement_index** ← Choose an index with the help of **conflict_indices**
24:    **grid** ← **refine**(**grid**, **refinement_index**) ▷ First, we demerge the grid; then, each sub-box is split in two sub-boxes along the axis **refinement_index**
25:    **conflict_indices** ← $\emptyset$

    The procedure that we introduce in Algorithm 1 is inspired by that proposed in [15], although some significant changes – discussed at the end of this subsection – have been made to ensure its applicability in practice. We stress that the condition $n = m \vee n = 0$ depends by the fact that the topological degree cannot be defined for $n \neq m$. Using symbolic rewriting tricks (e.g. adding redundant equalities, or rewriting an equality as the conjunction of two non-strict inequalities) to force a robust formula to satisfy the condition would not work, as it would make the formula *non-robust* and so the procedure – albeit applicable – would just not terminate. For the sake of brevity, we introduce the multi-valued functions $f := f_1 \times \cdots \times f_n$, and $g := g_1 \times \cdots \times g_k$.

The idea of the algorithm is to iteratively divide the starting box into smaller sub-boxes (the set of which is called a grid), removing at each step from the grid the sub-boxes for which either an equation or an inequality does not hold (lines 4–6), and using the topological degree test to prove if the system of equations admits a solution inside one of the sub-boxes (line 20), provided that the inequalities hold in that sub-box (lines 16-19). The algorithm terminates either returning **True** when a box respecting these last conditions has been found, or returning **False** if the grid is emptied (line 7).

In order to be computable in a box A, the topological degree requires that no zero lies in $f(\partial A)$. Because of that, we have to take some precautions, such as merging boxes having a common face in which a zero lies (line 9) and avoiding boxes having a face contained on the border of B and in which lies a zero (line 10). Regarding the last case we remark that, if the only solution of $\phi_{|B}$ lies in ∂B, then the formula is not robust (and the algorithm is allowed to never terminate).

Another sensitive point is to make sure that, given a robust formula, the algorithm always terminates. To this extent, it is essential that the following property is satisfied: "*for every $\epsilon > 0$, there is a finite number of iterations after which each sub-box A in the grid has* width$(A) < \epsilon$". In order to satisfy this property, a necessary and sufficient condition is that, for each $i \in \{0, \cdots, m\}$, the refinement index assumes infinitely many times the value i. One naive idea would be to assign the refinement index to $i + 1$ at each iteration. However, this is not practical. In fact, refining the grid without considering the reasons for which the algorithm does not terminate leads to an unmanageable growth in the size of the grid. Thus we use a greedy approach: at each step we take note of the indexes for which there is a conflict in the inequalities (line 19), and then we base our choice of the refinement index on that (line 24), preferring indices that appear in the conflicts (but making sure that eventually each index is chosen, even though with different frequency). This is a main difference compared to the algorithm from [15], where the grid is divided along all the indices at each step. This results in a double exponential growth in the number of sub-boxes to consider: after i steps, in the worst case the grid will contain $(2^i)^m$ sub-boxes. In our algorithm at each step we choose exactly one index along which to split the sub-boxes, choosing the index that most likely is causing the algorithm not to terminate. Avoiding splitting along indices that are not responsible for conflicts is essential to prevent an explosion in dimension which would make the algorithm impractical. Moreover, to the best of our knowledge, ours is the first implementation of this kind of procedures. In the next subsection, we will further modify the procedure to make it able to produce explanations for unsat cases.

4.2   From a Formula with $n \leq m$ to Quasi-dec

Let $\phi_{|B}$ be some bounded formula, with the only condition that $n \leq m$. We define $\hat{\phi}_{|B}$ as the formula obtained from $\phi_{|B}$ by replacing every constraint $e \stackrel{\text{def}}{=} (g > 0)$ with the constraint $\hat{e} \stackrel{\text{def}}{=} (g - \epsilon \geq 0)$, given a predefined constant $\epsilon > 0$. It is straightforward to prove that every model of $\hat{\phi}_{|B}$ is also a model of $\phi_{|B}$.

Algorithm 2. Solve a formula $\phi_{|B}$ with $n \leq m$

Input: A formula $\phi_{|B}$ in m variables, n equations, and k inequalities s.t. $n \leq m$
   A candidate point $\tilde{\mathbf{x}} \in \mathbb{R}^m$
Output: $<$True, $B_{sol}>$ or $<$Unknown$>$

1: $\hat{\phi}_{|B}$:= the formula obtained from $\phi_{|B}$ by replacing every $g > 0$ with $g - \epsilon \geq 0$
2: **if** $n = m \vee n = 0$ **then**
3:     res_quasidec $\leftarrow$ QUASI-DEC $(\hat{\phi}_{|B})$
4:     **if** res_quasidec $\equiv$ $<$True, B_{sol} $>$ **then return** $<$True, B_{sol} $>$
5:     **else return** $<$**Unknown**$>$
6: infeasible_var_subsets $\leftarrow \{\}$
7: **for** vars_subset $\in$ Combinations(Vars, $m - n$) **do**
8:     **if** vars_subset $\in$ infeasible_var_subsets **then**
9:         **continue**
10:     $\mu := \{var_i \mapsto \mathrm{x}_i \mid var_i \in$ vars_subset$\}$
11:     $<$sat, p$> \leftarrow$ QUASI-DEC $(\mu(\hat{\phi}_{|B}))$
12:     **if** $<$sat, p$> = <$True, B_{sol} $>$ **then**
13:         **return** $<$True, B_{sol} $>$
14:     **else if** $<$sat, p$> = <$False, $\mu(h)>$ **then**
15:         conflict_vars $:= \{var_i \in vars\_subset \mid var_i$ appears in $h\}$
16:         infeasible_var_subsets.add(conflict_vars)
17: **return** $<$**Unknown**$>$

If $n = m$ we can directly apply QUASI-DEC. If $n < m$, then we can try to assign $m - n$ variables to real values, and then apply QUASI-DEC to the formula obtained from the substitution. We start from a given point $\tilde{\mathbf{x}} \in \mathbb{R}^m$, and enumerate possible assignments to $m - n$ variables. In general, there are $\binom{m}{n} = \frac{m!}{n!(m-n)!}$ possible combinations to explore, but we can reduce their number via conflict-driven learning, as commonly done in SAT and SMT, by modifying the QUASI-DEC procedure (Algorithm 1), to make it return, before the while cycle in line 3, $<$**False**,$f_i >$ if $0 \notin \mathcal{I}_{f_i}(B)$, and $<$**False**, $g_j >$ if $\mathcal{I}_{g_j}(A) \cap (-\infty, 0] = \emptyset$. This modification helps the procedure by explaining why the problem is unsatisfiable, even though only for simple cases where no grid refinement is required. Given an explanation, we can extract the set E of variables involved, and use them to avoid the enumeration of assignments to supersets of E. In general, we could extend the idea of returning explanations for unsatisfiable instances to more complex situations. In this paper, we do not delve into this path, and leave further investigations for future work.

Overall, our approach to reduce to the QUASI-DEC procedure given a formula with the only restriction that $n \leq m$ is illustrated in Algorithm 2.

4.3   A General Procedure

We can now combine the results of the last two sections. First, we obtain several local minima $\tilde{\mathbf{x}}_1, \cdots, \tilde{\mathbf{x}}_k$ as in Sect. 3 . The two tactics described in the section (i.e., the simple check of $\tilde{\mathbf{x}}$, and the reduction to a linear underapproximation) are reasonably inexpensive for $\mathcal{NRA}$. Thus, if the problem is in $\mathcal{NRA}$, we first

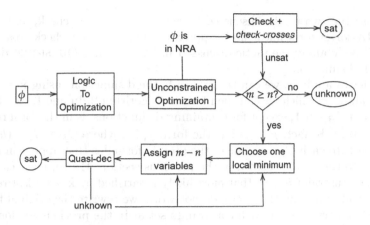

Fig. 1. Schema of the overall procedure.

apply these two tactics to each local minimum. If these two tactics fail, or the problem is in $\mathcal{NTA}$, we apply the algorithm described in Sect. 4.2 to each local minimum (starting from the minimum with the lowest cost). A sketch of this procedure is shown in Fig. 1.

Remark 1. Our general procedure is not a quasi-decidability procedure. However, relying on a quasi-decidability subprocedure is a crucial point of our method. By construction, the formulas that we feed to QUASI-DEC have the property that if they are unsatisfiable then they are also robust (Lemma 3 from [15])[6]. This means that QUASI-DEC always terminates on unsatisfiable subformulas, guaranteeing that we always progress towards a solution.

5   From Constraint Sets to Formulas

So far we have considered only sets of constraints. In this section, we present two different ways to solve a formula ϕ with arbitrary Boolean structure and that includes also Boolean variables. In the first way, we apply $\mathcal{L2O}$ *eagerly* to the formula, and then try to decide the disjunctions through the insight given by a local minimum, and then proceed to solve the constraints set as in Sect. 4. In the second way, we use the procedure of Sect. 4 as a theory solver inside a DPLL(T)-based lazy-SMT algorithm.

5.1   An Eager Approach

Let ϕ be a formula in CNF form. We can apply $\mathcal{L2O}$ to ϕ and obtain several local minima. Given a local minimum $\bar{\mathbf{x}}$, if there are no transcendental functions,

---

[6] This is not true for formulas containing strict inequalities, but we replaced strict inequalities in Algorithm 2 at line 1.

we can use the two tactics discussed in Sect. 3 (the simple check, and the call to an LRA-solver for a linear underapproximation of ϕ – i.e. check-crosses). We cannot directly apply the tactic discussed in Sect. 4, since QUASI-DEC does not work with disjunctions.

In order to apply it, we can try to decide the disjunctions using $\tilde{x}$, to obtain an implicant of ϕ which we can then feed to Algorithm 2. In line 1, we obtained a formula $\mu(\hat{\phi}|_B)$ that, except for containing disjunctions, is in the form required by QUASI-DEC. In fact, $\mu(\hat{\phi}|_B)$ has the form $\bigwedge C_j$, where $C_j \equiv \bigvee_{i \in I_j}(h_i \bowtie 0)$. If we substitute each C_j with one of the atomic formulas that appear in it, then we reduce to the case discussed in the previous section. Hence, for each C_j, we choose one constraint $h_i \bowtie 0$ that most likely is satisfied by $\tilde{x}$. As a last resort, if for each local minimum this tactic do not work, we rewrite the original formula into DNF and try to solve each constraints set as in the previous section.

5.2 A Lazy Approach

In the lazy approach, the method defined in Sect. 4 is used as a theory solver inside a DPLL(T) procedure. Since our method is able to prove only satisfiability, it needs to be paired with a method able to prove unsatisfiability. In our implementation, we pair it with incremental linearization [7], which is usually effective in proving unsatisfiability, and also good in finding linear models, but whose weak spot is finding irrational models.

Currently, our implementation is quite simple. Inside the DPLL(T) algorithm, we introduce a parameter n_calls_IncrLin that keeps track of the calls to incremental linearization, and that is reset whenever the DPLL(T) solver backtracks. After a given k number of calls to incremental linearization, we call our method. If it returns sat, we are done. Otherwise it returns unknown, and we proceed with incremental linearization.

6 Experimental Evaluation

Implementation We have implemented our method in a prototype written in Python, called UGOTNL (as in *Unconstrained Global Optimisation and Topological degree for Non-Linear*). We refer to the version based on the eager approach as UGOTNL_EAGER. For the lazy approach, we integrated UGOTNL as a theory solver inside the MATHSAT SMT solver [8]. We will refer to this version as MATHSAT+UGOTNL.

Setup. We have run our experiments[7] on a cluster equipped with 2.4 GHz Intel Xeon E5-2440 machines, using a time limit of 1000 s and a memory limit of 9 Gb. We compared our tools with z3 [11] and Yices [13] (CAD-based), raSAT [27] (that combines ICP and GIVT), CVC5 [6] (that combines IL with cylindrical algebraic

---

[7] Available at https://drive.google.com/file/d/1f6RmvojKw4om0L08g3hYMBl-wb6n vEpf/.

	Total	Sturm-MGC	ezsmt	Sturm-MBO	zankl	UltimateAut	Economics-M	meti-tarski	Heizmann	hycomp	kissing	LassoRanker
MathSAT	3193	0	32	0	32	31	85	2718	3	11	18	263
UGOTNL$_{\text{EAGER}}$	4388	0	0	1	52	32	68	4042	0	0	36	157
MathSAT+UGOTNL	4441	0	32	0	63	27	84	3948	3	13	35	236
RASAT	4285	0	0	0	45	0	0	4225	0	0	15	0
YICES	4946	0	32	0	58	39	91	4369	0	227	10	120
CVC5	5108	0	32	0	63	36	89	4342	2	226	18	300
Z3	5153	2	30	0	72	47	93	4391	6	280	35	198
DREAL	/(5021)	/(9)	/(0)	/(274)	/(153)	/(55)	/(126)	/(4079)	/(51)	/(45)	/(19)	/(210)

Fig. 2. Summary of results for SMT(NRA) sat cases. The results in parenthesis indicate "MAYBE SAT" answers.

	Total	dreal	bmc
MathSAT	94	37	57
UGOTNL$_{\text{EAGER}}$	304	255	49
MathSAT+UGOTNL	170	70	100
CVC5	94	40	54
ISAT3	/	/	/
DREAL	/ (578)	/ (423)	/ (155)

	Total	dreal	bmc
MathSAT	70	21	49
UGOTNL$_{\text{EAGER}}$	253	203	50
MathSAT+UGOTNL	140	35	105
CVC5	63	17	46
ISAT3	38 (828)	7 (599)	31 (229)
DREAL	/ (137)	/ (36)	/ (101)

Fig. 3. Summary of results for SMT(NTA) sat cases. On the left the original instances; on the right the bounded instances. The results in parenthesis indicate "MAYBE SAT" answers.

coverings [30]), iSAT3 [16] (based on ICP), and dReal [19] (that operates in the δ-sat framework [18]). Only the last three solvers can deal with $\mathcal{NTA}$.

We checked that, when terminating, our tools always return the correct result when the status of the benchmark is known, and never disagree with the other solvers; for $\mathcal{NRA}$, we checked with z3 that every box returned by our tools contains indeed a model.

Benchmarks. For $\mathcal{NRA}$, we consider all the SMT-LIB [2] benchmarks from the QF-NRA category. This is a class of 11523 benchmarks, among which 5142 are satisfiable, 5379 are unsatisfiable, and 1002 have unknown status. For $\mathcal{NTA}$, we considered the benchmarks from the dReal distribution [19], and other benchmarks deriving from discretization of Bounded Model Checking of hybrid automata. The problems in these classes come all with an unknown status. Since iSAT3 is not able to work with unbounded instances, in order to include it in the comparison, we generated for each benchmark a bounded version by adding constraints that force all the real variables in the problem to assume values in the $[-300, 300]$ interval.

Results (sat). First, we analyze the results for satisfiable instances, which are reported in Figs. 2 and 3. The tables show, for each solver, the number of successfully solved instances, both overall (1st column) and for each benchmark family (rest of the columns), with the best results highlighted in boldface.

	Total	Sturm-MGC	ezsmt	Sturm-MBO	zankl	UltimateAut	Economics-M	meti-tarski	Heizmann	hycomp	kissing	LassoRanker	hong
MathSAT	5280	0	2	285	34	7	11	2251	1	2259	0	412	20
MathSAT+ugotNL	5043	0	2	163	32	5	11	2239	0	2253	0	323	20
raSAT	4094	0	0	2	14	0	0	2018	0	1950	0	0	20
Yices	5449	0	2	285	32	12	39	2587	12	2201	0	259	20
cvc5	5645	0	2	285	31	10	35	2581	7	2206	0	468	20
z3	5281	5	2	153	27	12	19	2578	3	2225	0	248	9
dReal	3889	0	0	131	4	0	3	1784	0	1946	1	0	20

Fig. 4. Summary of results for SMT(NRA) unsat cases.

	Total	dreal	bmc		Total	dreal	bmc
MathSAT	533	85	448	MathSAT	524	88	436
MathSAT+ugotNL	522	85	437	MathSAT+ugotNL	521	88	433
cvc5	453	75	378	cvc5	465	85	380
iSAT3	/	/	/	iSAT3	449	63	386
dReal	468	184	284	dReal	446	156	290

Fig. 5. Summary of results for SMT(NTA) unsat cases. On the left the original instances; on the right the bounded instances.

For $\mathcal{NRA}$ (Fig. 2), we see that z3 is overall superior. Nevertheless, we see that both our new tools are very competitive, and perform significantly better than MathSAT. Moreover, since we are comparing new-born ideas implemented in a prototype with well-optimised CAD-based techniques that have a decade of progresses on their shoulders, we believe that these results are very encouraging.

Where our methods shine and go beyond the state of the art is when we consider problems with transcendental functions. In the results for $\mathcal{NTA}$ (Fig. 3) we see that both our tools outperform the others. For this, the synergy between numerical optimization and the procedure based on the topological degree test is essential, as neither of the two methods in isolation is effective: when disabling either of the two components, in fact, the performance is similar to that of the "stock" version of MathSAT (we omit the details due to lack of space). Moreover, there is a great complementarity between the two tools. For families in which the Boolean component is huge (such as bmc) we see that MathSAT+ugotNL is by far the best, whereas for benchmarks where the theory component is predominant (e.g. the dreal ones) the situation is reversed.

Results (unsat). Now we analyze the results for unsatisfiable cases (Figs. 4 and 5). Our methods are designed to finding models, so, for unsatisfiable instances, there are no advancements whatsoever. Nevertheless, we are interested in evaluating possible losses of the lazy version wrt. MathSAT due to the integration of our method. (The eager approach can never return unsat, so it does not compete.)

We see that for $\mathcal{NRA}$ there are some losses (expecially for very time-consuming benchmark families such as LassoRanker and MBO), that overall count for 4.5% of the benchmarks that MATHSAT is able to solve before the timeout. For $\mathcal{NTA}$, we observed that the losses are even less: respectively 2.1% and 0.6% for unbounded and bounded instances. We remark that these results do not imply that our new tool is unable to prove the unsatisfiability for those cases, rather that it is unable to prove it *within the same timeout*. In fact, since our theory solver always terminates for unsatisfiable instances (see Remark 1), we know that, if MATHSAT returns unsat for a problem, then eventually MATH-SAT+UGOTNL will return unsat as well.

We stress the fact that our implementation is currently still a research prototype, implemented in Python and integrated within MATHSAT in a quite inefficient manner, introducing a lot of overhead in the interaction with the DPLL(T) solver. We are confident that a more optimised and better integrated implementation can significantly reduce the overhead and improve the situation for unsatisfaible instances. Therefore, we believe that these results prove that our tool, albeit aimed specifically at proving satisfiability, works well even for unsatisfiable instances, and, in particular for $\mathcal{NTA}$ (which is our privileged theory of interest), there are no relevant downsides in pairing our sat-oriented theory solver with an unsat-oriented theory solver based on incremental linearization.

7   Conclusions and Future Work

In this paper we proposed a new procedure for proving satisfiability in $\mathcal{NTA}$, based on a fruitful synergy of numerical and symbolic methods. We implemented our ideas in a prototype called UGOTNL, and proposed two different approaches: an eager one and a lazy one (integrated inside MATHSAT). We tested the two methods on a wide variety of satisfiable benchmarks, and the results demonstrated that both our methods significantly outperform the state of the art for $\mathcal{NTA}$, while being competitive for $\mathcal{NRA}$. In the future, we plan to better integrate UGOTNL inside MATHSAT and to experiment with more thoughtful heuristics. Furthermore, we plan to investigate the potential of our ideas in several directions, including how to exploit the procedure also for proving unsatisfiability and whether similar techniques can be applied also to solve problems involving differential equations.

References

1. Aberth, O.: Computation of topological degree using interval arithmetic, and applications. Math. Comput. **62**(205), 171–178 (1994)
2. Barrett, C., Fontaine, P., Tinelli, C.: The Satisfiability Modulo Theories Library (SMT-LIB) (2016). www.SMT-LIB.org
3. Barrett, C., Sebastiani, R., Seshia, S.A., Tinelli, C.: Satisfiability Modulo Theories, chapter 26 (2009)
4. Benhamou, F., Granvilliers, L.: Chapter 16 - continuous and interval constraints. In: Handbook of Constraint Programming (2006)

5. Brauße, F., Korovin, K., Korovina, M.V., Müller, N.T.: The ksmt calculus is a δ-complete decision procedure for non-linear constraints. In: CADE (2021)
6. Barrett, C., et al.: CVC5 at the SMT Competition 2021 (2021)
7. Cimatti, A., Griggio, A., Irfan, A., Roveri, M., Sebastiani, R.: Incremental linearization for satisfiability and verification modulo nonlinear arithmetic and transcendental functions. ACM Trans. Comput. Logic 19(3), 1–52 (2018)
8. Cimatti, A., Griggio, A., Schaafsma, B.J., Sebastiani, R.: The MathSAT5 SMT solver. In: Piterman, N., Smolka, S.A. (eds.) TACAS 2013. LNCS, vol. 7795, pp. 93–107. Springer, Heidelberg (2013). https://doi.org/10.1007/978-3-642-36742-7_7
9. Collins, G.E.: Quantifier elimination for real closed fields by cylindrical algebraic decompostion. In: Brakhage, H. (ed.) GI-Fachtagung 1975. LNCS, vol. 33, pp. 134–183. Springer, Heidelberg (1975). https://doi.org/10.1007/3-540-07407-4_17
10. Corzilius, F., Kremer, G., Junges, S., Schupp, S., Ábrahám, E.: SMT-RAT: an open source C++ toolbox for strategic and parallel SMT solving. In: Heule, M., Weaver, S. (eds.) SAT 2015. LNCS, vol. 9340, pp. 360–368. Springer, Cham (2015). https://doi.org/10.1007/978-3-319-24318-4_26
11. de Moura, L., Bjørner, N.: Z3: an efficient SMT solver. In: Ramakrishnan, C.R., Rehof, J. (eds.) TACAS 2008. LNCS, vol. 4963, pp. 337–340. Springer, Heidelberg (2008). https://doi.org/10.1007/978-3-540-78800-3_24
12. de Moura, L., Jovanović, D.: A model-constructing satisfiability calculus. In: Giacobazzi, R., Berdine, J., Mastroeni, I. (eds.) VMCAI 2013. LNCS, vol. 7737, pp. 1–12. Springer, Heidelberg (2013). https://doi.org/10.1007/978-3-642-35873-9_1
13. Dutertre, B.: Yices 2.2. In: Biere, A., Bloem, R. (eds.) CAV 2014. LNCS, vol. 8559, pp. 737–744. Springer, Cham (2014). https://doi.org/10.1007/978-3-319-08867-9_49
14. Franek, P., Ratschan, S.: Effective topological degree computation based on interval arithmetic. Math. Comput. 84(293), 1265–1290 (2015)
15. Franek, P., Ratschan, S., Zgliczynski, P.: Quasi-decidability of a fragment of the first-order theory of real numbers. J. Autom. Reasoning 57(2), 157–185 (2015). https://doi.org/10.1007/s10817-015-9351-3
16. Fränzle, M., Herde, C., Teige, T., Ratschan, S., Schubert, T.: Efficient solving of large non-linear arithmetic constraint systems with complex boolean structure. JSAT (2007)
17. Fu, Z., Su, Z.: XSat: a fast floating-point satisfiability solver. In: Chaudhuri, S., Farzan, A. (eds.) CAV 2016. LNCS, vol. 9780, pp. 187–209. Springer, Cham (2016). https://doi.org/10.1007/978-3-319-41540-6_11
18. Gao, S., Avigad, J., Clarke, E.M.: δ-complete decision procedures for satisfiability over the reals. In: Gramlich, B., Miller, D., Sattler, U. (eds.) IJCAR 2012. LNCS (LNAI), vol. 7364, pp. 286–300. Springer, Heidelberg (2012). https://doi.org/10.1007/978-3-642-31365-3_23
19. Gao, S., Kong, S., Clarke, E.M.: dReal: an SMT solver for nonlinear theories over the reals. In: Bonacina, M.P. (ed.) CADE 2013. LNCS (LNAI), vol. 7898, pp. 208–214. Springer, Heidelberg (2013). https://doi.org/10.1007/978-3-642-38574-2_14
20. Jovanović, D., de Moura, L.: Solving non-linear arithmetic. ACM Commun. Comput. Algebra 46(3/4), 104–105 (2013)
21. Minh, D.D.L., Minh, D.L.P.: Understanding the hastings algorithm. Commun. Stat. Simul. Comput. 44(2), 332–349 (2015)
22. Moore, R., Kearfott, R., Cloud, M.: Introduction to Interval Analysis (2009)
23. Neumaier, A.: Interval Methods for Systems of Equations. Cambridge University Press (1991)

24. O'Regan, D., Je, C.Y., Chen, Y.: Topological Degree Theory and Applications. Taylor and Francis (2006)
25. Ratschan, S.: Safety verification of non-linear hybrid systems is quasi-decidable. Formal Meth. Syst. Des. **44**(1), 71–90 (2013). https://doi.org/10.1007/s10703-013-0196-2
26. Richardson, D.: Some undecidable problems involving elementary functions of a real variable. J. Symb. Log. **33**(4), 514–520 (1968)
27. Xuan, T.V., Khanh, T., Ogawa, M.: rasat: an smt solver for polynomial constraints. Formal Meth. Syst. Des. **51**, 12 (2017)
28. Wales, D.J., Doye, J.P.K.: Global optimization by basin-hopping and the lowest energy structures of lennard-jones clusters containing up to 110 atoms. J. Phys. Chem. A, (28) (1997)
29. Zhang, L., Madigan, C.F., Moskewicz, M.H., Malik, S.: Efficient conflict driven learning in a boolean satisfiability solver. In: ICCAD (2001)
30. Ábrahám, E., Davenport, J., England, M., Kremer, G.: Deciding the consistency of non-linear real arithmetic constraints with a conflict driven search using cylindrical algebraic coverings. J. Log. Algebraic Meth. Program. **119**, 100633 (2020)

Verification of SMT Systems
with Quantifiers

Alessandro Cimatti[ID], Alberto Griggio[ID], and Gianluca Redondi[✉][ID]

Fondazione Bruno Kessler, Trento, Italy
{cimatti, griggio, gredondi}@fbk.eu

Abstract. We consider the problem of invariant checking for transition systems using SMT and quantified variables ranging over finite but unbounded domains. We propose a general approach, obtained by combining two ingredients: exploration of a finite instance, to obtain candidate inductive invariants, and instantiation-based techniques to discharge quantified queries. A thorough experimental evaluation on a wide range of benchmarks demonstrates the generality and effectiveness of our approach. Our algorithm is the first capable of approaching in a uniform way such a large variety of models.

1 Introduction

Model checking algorithms based on efficient quantifier-free SAT and SMT reasoning have seen significant progress in the last few years. However, in many verification areas first-order quantifiers are needed, both in the symbolic description of the system and in the property to prove. This is the case, for example, of verification of parameterized systems.

Unfortunately, dealing with the combined case of transition systems with theories and first-order is far from trivial: SMT-based model checking algorithms can't be naturally extended. In this paper, we discuss the problem of model checking invariant properties in systems containing SMT theories and first-order quantifiers, with quantified variables ranging over finite but unbounded domains. For example, the (finite) size of the domain may depend on the number of processes in a protocol, or the number of components of the station in a railway interlocking system.

We present a simple yet general approach based on the interaction of two key ingredients. First, given a fixed cardinality for the domain, we compute a quantifier-free system (a *ground instance*) that can be model checked with existing techniques. We either get a counterexample, in which case the system is unsafe, or a proof for the property. Such a proof is lifted to a candidate invariant for the quantified system. This step is crucial, and is made effective by combining minimization and generalization techniques [15,17,26]. Second, we check

---

This work has been partly supported by project "AI@TN" funded by the Autonomous Province of Trento.

A. Bouajjani et al. (Eds.): ATVA 2022, LNCS 13505, pp. 154–170, 2022.
https://doi.org/10.1007/978-3-031-19992-9_10

the validity of the candidate invariant using quantified SMT reasoning. If the candidate invariant is valid, then the system is safe. Otherwise, further reasoning is required, e.g. by increasing the cardinality of the domain, and iterating the first step. Such a check can in principle be carried out by any off-the-shelf solver supporting SMT and quantifiers (e.g. Z3 [23]). However, a black-box approach to checking the validity of quantified invariants may cause the procedure to diverge in practice. Therefore, we adopt a more careful, resource-bounded approach to instantiation, that can be used to discharge quantified queries in a more controlled way.

The approach combines in a unique framework different aspects of the recent literature that have never been integrated. Compared to our approach, previous works on verification of parameterized systems with SMT [8,14] impose strong syntactic restrictions on the formulae used for defining systems, and allow only a very limited form of quantifier alternation. Other approaches based on modern SAT-based model checking algorithms such as [15,18,25] are more liberal, but they do not support theories.

The algorithm has been implemented and experimentally evaluated on various families of benchmarks, obtained from different sources, and making use of theories, quantifier alternations, or both. The experimental evaluation demonstrates that the algorithm is very general, being the only one able deal with all the benchmarks. As far as we know, our algorithm is the first capable of approaching in a uniform way such a large variety of systems. Furthermore, the experimental evaluation shows that, despite the relative simplicity of the implementation, the algorithm is quite efficient, and very effective, solving more instances than the competitor approaches in all the benchmarks classes.

2   Preliminaries

Our setting is standard first order logic. A theory T in the SMT sense is a pair $T = (\Sigma, C)$, where Σ is a first-order signature and C is a class of models over Σ. A theory T is closed under substructure if its class C of structures is such that whenever $M \in C$ and N is a substructure of M, then $N \in C$. We use the standard notions of Tarskian interpretation (assignment, model, satisfiability, validity, logical consequence). We refer to 0-arity predicates as Boolean variables, and to 0-arity uninterpreted functions as (theory) variables. A literal is an atom or its negation. A clause is a disjunction of literals. A ground term is a term which does not contain free variables. A formula is in conjunctive normal form (CNF) iff it is a conjunction of clauses. If $x_1, ..., x_n$ are variables and ϕ is a formula, we might write $\phi(x_1, ..., x_n)$ to indicate that all the variables occurring free in ϕ are in $x_1, ..., x_n$.

If ϕ is a formula, t is a term and v is a variable which occurs free in ϕ, we write $\phi[v/t]$ for the substitution of every occurrence of v with t. If $\underline{t}$ and $\underline{v}$ are vectors of the same length, we write $\phi[\underline{v}/\underline{t}]$ for the simultaneous substitution of each v_i with the corresponding term t_i.

Given a set of variables $\underline{v}$, we denote with $\underline{v}'$ the set $\{v' \,|v \in \underline{v}\}$. A symbolic transition system is a triple $(\underline{v}, I(\underline{v}), T(\underline{v}, \underline{v}'))$, where $\underline{v}$ is a set of variables, and

$I(\underline{v})$, $T(\underline{v}, \underline{v}')$ are first-order formulae over some signature. An assignment to the variables in $\underline{v}$ is a state. A state s is initial iff it is a model of $I(\underline{v})$, i.e. $s \models I(\underline{v})$. The states s, s' denote a transition iff $s \cup s' \models T(\underline{v}, \underline{v}')$, also written $T(s, s')$. A path is a sequence of states $s_0, s_1, \ldots$ such that s_0 is initial and $T(s_i, s'_{i+1})$ for all i. We denote paths with π, and with $\pi[j]$ the j-th element of π. A state s is reachable iff there exists a path π such that $\pi[i] = s$ for some i.

A formula $\phi(\underline{v})$ is an invariant of the transition system $C = (\underline{v}, I(\underline{v}), T(\underline{v}, \underline{v}'))$ iff it holds in all the reachable states. Following the standard model checking notation, we denote this with $C \models \phi(\underline{v})$.[1] A formula $\phi(\underline{v})$ is an inductive invariant for C iff $I(\underline{v}) \models \phi(\underline{v})$ and $\phi(\underline{v}) \wedge T(\underline{v}, \underline{v}') \models \phi(\underline{v}')$. Given a first-order formula ϕ over a signature Σ, containing arbitrary quantifiers, it is well known that it is possible to obtain a universal formula ϕ', called the *Skolemization* of ϕ, defined over a larger signature Σ', which is equisatisfiable to ϕ.

3 Verification of Quantified SMT Systems

3.1 Symbolic Formalism

The problem discussed in this paper is to prove or disprove that a given quantified formula is an invariant of a symbolic transition system. In this section, we describe the formalism that we use for defining systems and we present an overall picture of the algorithm we use to solve the problem.

We introduce a class of symbolic transition systems, which subsumes many formalisms presented in the literature [14,24]. We start by considering two theories; a theory $\mathcal{T_I} = (\Sigma_I, \mathcal{C}_I)$, called the *index* theory, which is closed under substructures. In practice, this is often the theory of an uninterpreted sort, whose class of models includes all possible finite (but unbounded) structures. In addition, we consider a theory of elements $\mathcal{T_E} = (\Sigma_E, \mathcal{C}_E)$, used to model the data of the system. Relevant examples consider as $\mathcal{T_E}$ the theory of an enumerated datatype, or linear arithmetic (integer or real). Then, with A_I^E we denote the theory whose signature is $\Sigma = \Sigma_I \cup \Sigma_E \cup \{[\_]\}$, and a model for it is given by a set of total functions from a model of $\mathcal{T_I}$ to a model of $\mathcal{T_E}$, where $[\_]$ is interpreted as the function application. In the following, we might refer to variables of sort A_I^E as *arrays*.

We restrict ourselves to one index theory and one element theory for the sake of simplicity, but typically applications include a multi-sorted setting, with several index theories and several element theories.

Definition 1. *In the following, we will considered a subclass of transition systems, defined by triples $S = (\underline{x}, \iota(\underline{x}), \tau(\underline{x}, \underline{x}'))$ where:*

- $\underline{x}$ *are arrays, i.e. variables of sort A_I^E interpreted as functions from a model of $\mathcal{T_I}$ to a model of $\mathcal{T_E}$. Note that this includes also 0-ary or constant functions, i.e. variables of sort $\mathcal{T_E}$.*

---

[1] Note that we use the symbol $\models$ with three different denotations: if ϕ, ψ are formulae, $\phi \models \psi$ denotes that ψ is a logical consequence of ϕ; if μ is an interpretation, and ψ is a formula, $\mu \models \psi$ denotes that μ is a model of ψ; if C is a transition system, $C \models \psi$ denotes that ψ is an invariant of C.

– $\iota(\underline{x}), \tau(\underline{x}, \underline{x}')$ *are first-order formulae over* Σ *possibly containing quantifiers over variables of sorts* T_I.

Example 1. (A simple train station). In this example, we describe an abstract simple train station, with an arbitrary number of tracks and routes; routes can be activated by locking the corresponding tracks. As index theories, we use two uninterpeted sorts: track and route. As element theory, we use two enumeratives, T_{E_1} with model {locked, free}, and T_{E_2} with model {active, inactive}. As state variables, we use an array $state\_t$: track $\rightarrow$ {locked, free}, and an array $state\_r$: route $\rightarrow$ {active, inactive}. Moreover, we define a relation symbol UsedBy : track $\times$ route $\rightarrow$ *Bool* to model the correspondences between tracks and routes. The initial formula of our model is:

$$\forall r : \text{route}.state\_r[r] = \text{inactive} \ \wedge \ \forall t : \text{track}.state\_t[t] = \text{free}.$$

The transition formula of the system is the disjunction of two formulae $\tau_1 \vee \tau_2$, corresponding to the activation or the deactivation of a route. The first disjunct is:

$$\exists r : \text{route}.(state\_r[r] = \text{inactive} \wedge \forall t : \text{track}.(\text{UsedBy}(t, r) \rightarrow state\_t[t] = \text{free})$$
$$\wedge\, state\_r'[r] = \text{active} \wedge \forall r1 : \text{route}.(r1 \neq r \rightarrow state\_r'[r1] = state\_r[r1])$$
$$\wedge\, \forall t1 : \text{track}.(\text{UsedBy}(t1, r) \rightarrow state\_t'[t1] = \text{locked})$$
$$\wedge\, \forall t1 : \text{track}.(\neg \text{UsedBy}(t1, r) \rightarrow state\_t'[t1] = state\_t[t1])).$$

The second disjunct is:

$$\exists r : \text{route}.(state\_r[r] = \text{active} \wedge state\_r'[r] = \text{inactive}$$
$$\wedge\, \forall r1 : \text{route}.(r1 \neq r \rightarrow state\_r'[r1] = state\_r[r1])$$
$$\wedge\, \forall t1 : \text{track}.(\text{UsedBy}(t1, r) \rightarrow state\_t'[t1] = \text{free})$$
$$\wedge\, \forall t1 : \text{track}.(\neg \text{UsedBy}(t1, r) \rightarrow state\_t'[t1] = state\_t[t1])).$$

The *Invariant Problem* we consider is the problem of proving (or disproving) that a given formula ϕ, possibly containing quantified variables of sort T_I, is an invariant for S. The problem is well-known to be undecidable, since it subsumes undecidable problems such as safety of parameterized systems [2].

Example 2. In the example before, we want to prove mutual exclusion of routes which are using a same track. To do this, we define a new relational symbol Incompatible : route $\times$ route $\rightarrow$ *Bool* and we introduce the following axiom:

$$\forall r1 : \text{route}, r2 : \text{route}.(\text{Incompatible}(r1, r2) \leftrightarrow$$
$$(r1 \neq r2 \wedge \exists t : \text{track}.\text{UsedBy}(t, r1) \wedge \text{UsedBy}(t, r2)))$$

Axioms are not defined in Definition 1, but they are common in the literature regarding symbolic transition systems. An axiom is a formula which is implicitly

considered in conjunction to both the initial and the transition formula. The
invariant we want to prove is the formula

$$\forall r1 : \text{route}, r2 : \text{route}.(\text{Incompatible}(r1, r2) \rightarrow$$
$$\neg(state\_r[r1] = \text{active} \wedge state\_r[r2] = \text{active}))$$

i.e. incompatible routes are never active together.   □

To solve the invariant problem affirmatively, we search for an inductive
strengthening, i.e. a first-order formula ψ such that $\psi \wedge \phi$ is an inductive invariant
for S.

Definition 2. *Let* $S = (\underline{x}, \iota(\underline{x}), \tau(\underline{x}, \underline{x}'))$ *a transition system, and* ϕ *a candidate
invariant. An invariant strengthening* ψ *is a first-order fomula such that the
following formulae are* A_I^E-*unsatisfiable:*

$$\iota(\underline{x}) \wedge \neg(\phi(\underline{x}) \wedge \psi(\underline{x})), \tau(\underline{x}, \underline{x}') \wedge \phi(\underline{x}) \wedge \psi(\underline{x}) \wedge \neg(\phi(\underline{x}') \wedge \psi(\underline{x}')). \tag{1}$$

Since a formula is valid iff its negation is unsatisfiable, it follows from the definition that $\psi \wedge \phi$ is an inductive invariant for S.

Our method will first automatically synthesize a *candidate* invariant strengthening ψ, and then try to discharge inductive queries with instantiation-based
methods to see if the guess was correct. In fact, after Skolemizing inductive
queries (1) to a universal form, our method will search for a set of ground terms
G such that the ground formula obtained by instantiating universal quantifiers
(in G) is unsatisfiable. We have, however, many open problems, which we can
summarize with the following questions: (i) How to find such candidate invariant
strengthenings? (ii) How to choose the set of ground terms G? (iii) If the query
is SAT, how to detect real counterexamples?

In the method we propose, we will try to address these problems with a
common approach, which is *ground* instance exploration. A ground instance
of the system is obtained by fixing the cardinality of models of T_I to a fixed
integer. In this way we can obtain (after removing quantifiers by instantiation)
a transition system defined by quantifier-free formulae, which can be analyzed
by standard SMT-based techniques.

We will describe our approach more thoroughly in the next sections. Here,
we give a high-level overview of our method, depicted also in Fig. 1.

3.2   Overview

As an input, we have a symbolic transition system S and a candidate invariant
ϕ. We set n, a counter for the size of the ground instance we explore, equal to
1. We perform the following steps:

– we consider a ground instance of cardinality n, and then use a model checker
  to get either a counterexample for the property (thus terminating the algorithm with UNSAFE result), or an inductive invariant in size n. More details
  about the computation of ground instances are given in Sect. 3.3.

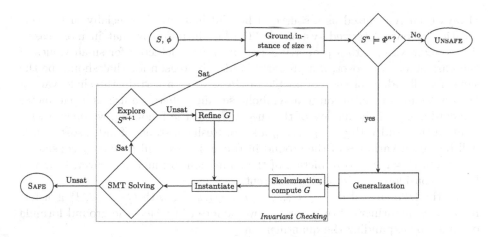

Fig. 1. An overview of the algorithm.

- From the invariant of size n, we synthesize a candidate invariant strenghtening ψ (Generalization).
- We consider the quantified queries (1), and try to prove their unsatisfiability (Invariant Checking box). In case of a success, the property is proved and we have found an inductive invariant. In case of a failure, we need a better candidate invariant: we restart the loop with a new exploration from size $n + 1$.

Since we are dealing with undecidable problems, there are many possible causes of non-termination of the algorithm: the main problems are the invariant checking box, which involves quantified reasoning, and the existence of a cut-off, i.e. an integer n such that the generalized formula obtained afted model checking a ground instance of size n is inductive also for all other instances. Note that the procedure of invariant checking could be implemented with the usage of any prover supporting SMT reasoning and quantifiers. However, especially for satisfiabile instances, such solvers can diverge easily. Thus, since many queries can be SAT, a naive usage of such tools will cause the procedure to get stuck in quantified reasoning with no progress obtained.

Therefore, we proposed a 'bounded' sub-procedure of Invariant Checking, explained in detail in Sect.3.5, in which instead of relying on an off-the-shelf SMT solver supporting quantifiers, we 'manually' apply standard instantiation-based techniques for quantified SMT reasoning [10], in which however we carefully manage the set of terms used to instantiate the quantifiers, in order to prevent divergence.

We now describe each step in more detail.

3.3 Ground Instances

We start by describing in detail the computation of a ground instance from the quantified system S. Traditionally, the exploration of ground instances has always been recognized as a source of helpful heuristics, especially in the verification of parameterized systems [9, 26]. The intuition is that in most cases, if a counterexample to a property exists, it can be detected for small values of the parameter. Moreover, if a property holds, the reason for that should be the same for all values of the parameter (at least after a certain threshold value). We try to use this intuition in a symbolic setting, where we use as a parameter the cardinality of the models of the theory T_I. In the following, we denote with n an integer, and with $\underline{c} = c_1, \ldots, c_n$ a set of fresh constants of index sort. These will be frozen variables of the ground instance, i.e. we will implicitly consider a constraint $\underline{c}' = \underline{c}$ as a conjunction of the transition formula; moreover, they will be also considered all implicitly different.

In the following, if $\phi = Q_1 i_1, \ldots, Q_m i_m . \phi'(\underline{i}, \underline{x}[\underline{i}])$, with $Q_j \in \{\forall, \exists\}$ is a formula with quantifiers of only sort T_I, we denote $\phi^n(\underline{c}, \underline{x}[\underline{c}])$ the ground formula obtained by expanding the quantifiers in $\underline{c}$.

Definition 3. *Given $S = (\underline{x}, \iota(\underline{x}), \tau(\underline{x}, \underline{x}'))$ a transition system and n an integer, the* ground instance *of S of size n, denoted with S^n, is obtained in the following way:*

- *for each function symbol a in Σ whose codomain type is T_I, consider the formula*

$$\forall i_1, \ldots, i_m \exists j . a(i_1, \ldots, i_m) = j,$$

  where m is the arity of a, and $i_1, \ldots, i_m, j$ are fresh variables of appropriate sort[2];
- *add the formulae generated in this way in conjuction to the initial formula ι and the transition formula τ;*
- *Instantiate all the quantifiers in the modified formulae with $\underline{c}$, thus obtaining a* **quantifier-free** *transition system*

$$S^n = \left(\underline{c} \cup \underline{x}, \iota^n(\underline{c}, \underline{x}[\underline{c}]), \tau^n(\underline{c}, \underline{x}[\underline{c}], \underline{x}'[\underline{c}])\right).$$

We observe that a state of S^n is given by: (i) an assignment of $\underline{c}$ to a finite model of cardinality n of T_I, and (ii) an interpretation of the state variables as functions from that model to a model of T_E. Note that even if the models of T_I have finte cardinality, the set of states of S^n can be infinite, since T_E could have an infinite model, e.g. if integer or real variables are in the system. Nevertheless, the system can be model checked efficiently by modern symbolic SMT techniques like [3].

Symmetric Presentation of Ground Instances. As already observed in previous works [4, 15, 20], transition systems obtained by instantiating quantified formulae have a certain degree of symmetry. We report here the notion that will be useful to our description.

---

[2] These are 'cardinality axioms', used to restrict the values of functions in appropriate models.

Definition 4. *If σ is a permutation of $1, ..., n$, and ϕ is a formula in which $c_1, ..., c_n$ occur free, we denote with $\sigma\phi$ the formula obtained by substituting every c_i with $c_{\sigma(i)}$.*

The following follows directly from the fact that ι^n and τ^n are obtained by instantiating a quantified formula with a set of fresh constants $\underline{c}$ [20]:

Lemma 1. *For every permutaion σ, we have that: (i) $\sigma\iota^n \equiv \iota^n$; (ii) $\sigma\tau^n \equiv \tau^n$.*

From this lemma and a simple induction proof, the following holds:

Proposition 2 (Invariance for permutation). *Let s be a state of S^n, reachable in k steps. Then $s \models \phi(\underline{c}, x[\underline{c}])$, if and only if, for every σ, there exists a state s' reachable in k steps such that $s' \models \sigma\phi(\underline{c}, x[\underline{c}])$*

This property will be exploited both for the verification of ground instances, and in the generalization process. In fact, from the last proposition we can simplify every invariant problem $S^n \models \bigwedge_\sigma \sigma\phi(\underline{c})$ – where σ ranges over all possible substitutions – to $S^n \models \phi(\underline{c})$. This simplification is of great help when checking properties which are the result of instantiating a formula with only universal quantifiers.

3.4   Generalizing Invariants from Instances

After computing S^n, let $\phi^n(\underline{c}, \underline{x}[\underline{c}])$ be the result of instantiating the quantifiers of the original candidate invariant ϕ in $\underline{c}$. Then, we suppose to have a model checker capable of proving or disproving that $S^n \models \phi^n(\underline{c}, \underline{x}[\underline{c}])$. If a counterexample is not found, we also suppose to have an formula $I^n(\underline{c}, \underline{x}[\underline{c}])$ which witnesses the proof, i.e. an inductive invariant. From this witness we generalize a candidate invariant for the unbounded case.

Definition 5 (Generalization). *Let S be a transition system and ϕ a candidate invariant. Let S^n be the ground instance of size n, and suppose $S^n \models \phi^n(\underline{c}, \underline{x}[\underline{c}])$. A generalization from size n is a (quantified) formula ψ such that ψ^n is an inductive invariant for ϕ^n.*

For generalization, we exploit the same technique that we used in [4], inspired by [26]. Suppose that I^n is in CNF. Then, $I^n = C_1 \wedge \cdots \wedge C_m$ is a conjunction of clauses. From every one of such clauses we will obtain a universally quantified formula. Let $AllDiff(\underline{i})$ be the formula which states that all variables in $\underline{i}$ are different from each other. For all $j \in \{1, ..., m\}$, let $\psi_j = \forall \underline{i}.AllDiff(\underline{i}) \rightarrow C_j[\underline{c}/\underline{i}]$. Let $\Psi = \bigwedge_{j=1}^m \psi_j$. It follows from Proposition (2) than such a Ψ is a generalization from size n.

It should be clear that our technique can infer invariant strenghtnenings with only universal quantifiers, but more generalizations are possible [11,15]. For example, if a clause of the inductive invariant is $l(c_1) \vee ... \vee l(c_n)$, a naive generalization of that clause would be $\exists x.l(x)$.

Example 3. Continuing our example, suppose to model check a ground instance with exactly two tracks (t_1, t_2) and two routes (r_1, r_2). Suppose that after succeeding in proving the property, a clause of the inductive invariant is the formula

$$\neg \mathsf{UsedBy}(t_1, r_1) \vee \neg state\_r[r_1] = \mathsf{active} \vee \neg state\_t[t_1] = \mathsf{free}$$

Our generalization is simply:

$$\forall t_1 : \mathsf{track}, r_1 : \mathsf{route}.(\neg \mathsf{UsedBy}(t_1, r_1) \vee \neg state\_r[r_1] = \mathsf{active} \vee \neg state\_t[t_1] = \mathsf{free}).$$

This is actually an inductive strengthening for the property we wanted to prove.

Minimizing Modulo Symmetries. Recall that our next step will be to try to prove that the generalized invariant from size n is inductive also for all other ground instances. Therefore, it is intuitive to try to weaken as much as possible the candidate strenghtening Ψ, to increase the chances that its inductiveness will be preserved in other instances. So, before generalization, we use the invariant minimization techniques described in [17] to weaken the inductive invariant I^n by removing unnecessary clauses. However, note that, with our generalization technique, two symmetric clauses produce the same quantified formula: if σ is a substitution of the $\underline{c}$'s, the formulae obtained by generalizing a clause $\mathcal{C}(\underline{c})$ or $\sigma\mathcal{C}(\underline{c})$ are logically equivalent. So, we apply the following strategy: given a clause $\mathcal{C}(\underline{c})$ in I^n, we add to the invariant all the 'symmetric' versions $\sigma\mathcal{C}$, where σ ranges over all possible substitutions of the $\underline{c}$'s. By Proposition (2), we can safely add those clause to I^n and it will remain inductive. Then, during the minimization process, a clause is removed from the invariant only if all its 'symmetric' versions are. In our experiments, minimizing invariants with this method has proved to be crucial for the effectiveness of our approach.

3.5   Invariant Checking

Having described how we synthesize candidate inductive invariants from a ground instance of size n, we now describe how we try to prove that our generalization is correct. Given a candidate inductive invariant, we perform Skolemization on the inductive query (1), obtaining a universal formula. Then, we look for a set of terms G such that the ground formula obtained by instantiating the universals with G is unsatisfiable. This is the standard approach used in SMT solvers for detecting unsatisfiability of quantied formulae [10,13]. The main difference is that instead of relying on heuristics to perform the instantiation lazily during the SMT search (e.g. [10,13]), we carefully control the quantifier instantiation procedure, and expand the quantifiers eagerly, so that we can use only quantifer-free SMT reasoning.

Let $\phi_S = \forall \underline{i}.\phi'_S(\underline{i}, \underline{x}[\underline{i}])$ be the result of the Skolemization process, where ϕ'_S is a quantifier-free formula over a signature Σ', obtained by expanding Σ with new Skolem symbols. Initially, we simply let G to be the set of 0-ary symbols of the index sort in the formula. Note that apart from constants in the original signature, new (Skolem) constants arise by eliminating existential quantifiers. Since we use only universal quantification the generalized invariant strengthening, Ψ is a conjunction of universal formulae, and we can commute the conjunction and the universal quantification to obtain a formula with only n universal quantified variables. Notice that, since the candidate inductive strengthening occurs also negated in the quantified formula, this will produce n new Skolem constants.

Finally, we can add to the inductive query an additional constraint. By induction on the structure of our algorithm, if Ψ is generalized from size n, we have proven already that the property ϕ holds in S for all the ground instances of size equal or less than n. Thus, we impose that in our universe G there are at least n different terms.

To sum up, let $\phi_S = \forall \underline{i}.\phi'_S(\underline{i}, \underline{x}[\underline{i}])$ be the universal formula obtained after Skolemization, and let m be the length of $\underline{i}$. Let n be the cardinality of the last visited ground instance. Let G be the set of constants of index sort in ϕ'_S (by the previous discussion, $|G| \geq n$). Let $c_1, \ldots, c_n$ be a set of fresh variables of index sort. We test with an SMT solver the satisfiability of the following formula

$$\bigwedge_{\underline{g} \in G^m} \phi'_S[\underline{i}/\underline{g}] \wedge \text{AllDiff}(\underline{c}) \wedge \bigwedge_{j=1}^{n} (\bigvee_{g \in G} c_j = g) \qquad (2)$$

We have that:

Proposition 3. *For any set of Σ_I-terms G, if (2) is unsatisfiable, then ψ is an inductive strengthening for ϕ.*

Refinement. If the former formula is SAT, there are two possibilities. Either we have a real counterexample to induction, and we need a better candidate, or our instantiation set G was too small to detect unsatisfiability. In general, if G covers all possible Σ_I-terms, then we can deduce that the counterexample is not spurious.

Definition 6. *Given an index theory T_I with signature Σ_I, we say that a set of Σ_I-terms G is saturated if, for all terms Σ_I-term t, there exists a $g \in G$ such that $T_I \models t = g$.*

So, if G is saturated, any model of (2) correspond to a counterexample to induction, and we need a better strenghtening. However, in case (2) is satisfiable, but G is not saturated, we use the following heuristic to decide whether we need a better candidate or a larger G. We consider the inductive query in S^{n+1}, using as a candidate inductive invariant $(\psi \wedge \phi)^{n+1}$. If the candidate invariant is still good (the query is UNSAT), we try to increase G to get the unsatisfiablity of the unbounded case. Our choice is to add to G terms of the form $f(\underline{x})$ where f is a function symbol of index type, and $\underline{x}$ are constants already in G. Note that if no function symbols are available, i.e. if Σ_I is a relational signature, then saturation of G follows already by considering 0-ary terms. Therefore, in case G is initially not saturated, the existence of at least one function symbol is guaranteed[3].

---

[3] In our implementation, the saturation of G is detected when no new function symbols are available.

If the query (2) is now UNSAT, we have succeeded. Otherwise, we continue to add terms to G, until either all function symbols have been used, or an UNSAT result is encountered. If the candidate invariant strengthening is not inductive for size $n + 1$ (the query is SAT), we search for a better candidate. To do so, before completely discharging the invariant generalized from size n, we can run an additional minimization procedure (see Sect. 3.4) in size S^{n+1}, to try to remove unnecessary clauses. If a new invariant is obtained, we repeat the instantiation procedure. Otherwise, we repeat the whole loop, starting by model checking the ground instance S^{n+1} and obtaining a new strenghtening from size $n + 1$.

3.6 Termination

In general, we do not have theoretical guarantees that our algorithm eventually terminates. In fact, there can be many causes of non termination: note that in case of infinite theories, the model checking of ground instances already can be non terminating. Moreover, in general universal formulae are not enough to strengthen an arbitrary invariant property [18], and existential quantification in the invariant strengthening might be needed.

However, we want to remark that even with our simple generalization technique we have obtained termination in many cases. An important remark is necessary to put more insight on the reasons of why our instantiation procedure is effective for the benchmarks we considered. In many systems descriptions, especially the ones arising from parameterized verification, the signature Σ_I is relational and all the formulae describing inductive queries contain only $\exists^*\forall^*$ quantifiers alternation. In this case, no function symbols are introduced during Skolemization: therefore, the set G of 0-ary terms already is saturated. Even in case of $\forall\exists$ alternation (but in a multi-sorted setting), saturation can be achieved after few refinement steps (as long as the Skolem functions introduced in the signature do not combine in cycles). More details about completeness of instantiation methods, especially for the verification of parameterized systems, can be found in [12,14]. Since we limit ourselves to terms of depth one, our method can fail to prove invariants requiring some more complex instantiations. Note that in that case it is always possible to change the choice and the refinement of the set G with more sophisticated methods [13,27]. Finally, we remark that, by limiting the possible refinements of G, our method has a notion of progress: given a transition system S and a candidate invariant ϕ, if there exists an n such that $S^n \not\models \phi^n$, and if all the model checking problems $S^{n'} \models \phi^{n'}$, with $n < n'$, terminate, then our algorithm eventually finds a counterexample.

4 Related Work

Verification of systems with quantifiers ranging over finite but unbounded domains has always received a lot of attention from the literature. A main area of application, for which our method is designed, is parameterized verification, where the parameters represent the cardinality of components of the system.

Many proposed methods for solving the problem are based on *cut-off* results. In our terms, a cut-off is an integer n such that the ground system S^n bisimulates the quantified system S. Cut-off values exist for large varieties of classes of systems, but such results strongly depend on the assumptions such as topology, data, etc. (see [2] for a survey). Nonetheless, we can see a posteriori that, when our algorithm terminates with a candidate invariant from size n, such a size is a candidate cut-off, since the proof of the property for that size holds also for all integers $n' > n$.

The method of invisible invariants [26] was to our knowledge the first which proposed the usage of finite instance exploration to produce universally quantified invariant strengthening. In that paper the invariant is generalized from the formula describing the set of reachable states of the finite instance. Systems considered in that work are, however, a subclass of ours.

Tools designed for the verification of systems with a combination of first-order quantifiers and SMT theories are MCMT [14] and Cubicle [8]. These tools use the framework of array-based transition systems, of which our formalism is an extension. They implement a fully symbolic backward reachability algorithm, where pre-images of states can be described by symbolic quantified formulae. Quantified queries are then discharged with an instantiation approach similar to ours. Nonetheless, many approximations can be introduced during the backward computation, which may cause spurious counterexamples [1]. Cubicle extends this algorithm by using finite instance exploration to speed up pre-image computation [9].

Ivy [12,24] is a tool for the verification of inductive invariants of parameterized systems. Again, the formalism for defining systems considered in Ivy can be seen as a subclass of ours: a translation can be obtained if we put T_E to be the theory of Booleans, and T_I is the theory of an uninterpreted sort. In Ivy, the quantified queries can always be embedded in EPR (Effective Propositional Logic), a decidable fragment of first-order logic where formulae have a $\exists^*\forall^*$ quantifier prefix, and do not contain function symbols. Therefore, the set of possible Σ_I-terms is always finite, and it is always possible to do complete instantiations. Inspired by Ivy, MYPYVY [19] is a tool which implements algorithms for the automatic discovery of inductive invariants. Among those we have **updr** [18], a version of the IC3 algorithm capable of inferring universally quantified invariants, **fol-ic3** [19], which extends IC3 by using separators to find invariants with quantifier alternation during the construction of frames, and **PdH**, a recent algorithm which combines the duality between states and predicates to discover invariants [25].

Various tools in the literature are designed to use finite instance exploration to guess invariants to lift to the unbounded case [11,16,21,22,28]. These tools either rely on cut-off results, or some external prover to discharge the quantified queries. Instead, we propose a tighter integration between finite instance exploration and quantified queries. Moreover, most of this approaches rely on enumerating possible models for finding inductive invariants; such an apprach cannot be extended naively to support theories. The tool IC3PO [15] proposes a generalization technique that can also infer formulae with quantifier alternation by detecting symmetries in a clausal proof. As a future work, we will try to combine their generalization technique with our method.

Abstraction methods are another major trend in verification of quantified systems. In our previous paper [4], we designed an CEGAR approach for the verification of array-based systems based on the Parameter Abstraction [20,21], which also used the ground instance exploration technique presented here. However, that approach imposed some syntactic restrictions on the definition of the systems, allowing only a single quantifier alternation with outermost existential quantification in transition formulae, and only universal quantification in the initial formula and in the candidate invariant. Our new approach, instead, is more general, and allows for arbitrary quantification in the definition of the transition system and properties to check.

5   Experimental Evaluation

To evaluate our approach, we have implemented our algorithm in the tool LAMBDA, which was initially developed in a previous work [4] for model checking parameterized systems. The tool accepts as input transition systems specified either in the language of MCMT [14], IC3PO, or in VMT format (a light-weight extension of SMT-LIB to model transition systems [6]).

For clarity, we use BI-LAMBDA (for bounded induction) to denote the algorithm described in this paper, while LAMBDA will denote the previously developed method. We used the SMT-based IC3 with implicit predicate abstraction of [3] as underlying verification engine for the finite instances, and MATHSAT5 [5] as the solver for ground checks. We also have implemented a version of the algorithm which uses Z3 [23] to discharge quantified queries, to compare the effectiveness of our instantiation-based procedure (this version will be referred to as BI-LAMBDA-Z3).

In case of successful termination, we generate either a counterexample trace (for violated properties) in a concrete instance of the quantified system, or a quantified inductive invariant that proves the property. In the latter case, we can also generate proof obligations that can be independently checked with an SMT solver supporting quantifiers.

For our evaluation, we have collected a total of 183 benchmarks, divided in five different groups:

Protocols consists of 42 instances taken from the MCMT or the CUBICLE distributions. Due to the very different format, we could not run IC3PO or the MYPYVY algorithms on them. This was not only a syntactic problem: many (but not all) benchmarks contain theory variables (like integers or reals), which are not supported in MYPYVY and IC3PO.

DynArch consists of 57 instances of verification problems of dynamic architectures, taken from [7]. These benchmarks make use of arithmetic constraints on index terms, which are not supported by CUBICLE, MYPYVY or IC3PO.

PdH consists of 20 benchmarks used in the experimental evaluation of [25], written in MYPYVY and IC3PO format. We could not run MCMT, CUBICLE or LAMBDA on them, for the different input language and for not supported features such as multi-sorted indexes.

Ic3po consists of 37 benchmarks from the experimental evaluation of [15], written in IC3PO format and in (old) MYPYVY format. For the same reasons as the previous set, we could not run MCMT, CUBICLE and LAMBDA on them. For compatibility issues, we could not run the **PdH** algorithm on them.

Trains consists of 17 instances derived by (a simplified version of) verification problems of railway interlocking. These benchmarks contains theory variables and synctactic requirements currently supported only by LAMBDA and BI-LAMBDA.

Trains-AE consists of 10 instances derived again by verification problems on railway interlocking logics; in these systems a forall-exists quantification alternation in a multi-sorted setting occurs, along with theory variables. Therefore, they are supported only by BI-LAMBDA.

We have run our experiments on a cluster of machines with a 2.90 GHz Intel Xeon Gold 6226R CPU running Ubuntu Linux 20.04.1, using a time limit of 1 h and a memory limit of 4 GB for each instance. For MCMT, we used standard settings. For CUBICLE, we used the `--brab` 2 option. For **fol-ic3** and **updr**, we used the implementation in the artifact given in [19]. For IC3PO, we used the option `--finv=2` to discharge unbounded checks with Z3. Without this option, IC3PO terminates when the tool finds a proof for size n which is still valid for size $n+1$; this was conjectured to be enough [15] to ensure that the proof was correct for all the instances, but, without unbounded checks, we have encountered errors of the tool in the PdH benchmarks. We also remark that in case of termination with UNSAFE result, our tool produces always concrete counterexamples in finite instances; on the other hand, counterexamples of MCMT, CUBICLE and **updr** can be spurious [1,18] (and in theory should be checked manually). The results of BI-LAMBDA-Z3 are obtained with a timeout of 120 s on every Z3 query, to avoid the prover being stuck in quantified reasoning as discussed in Sect.3.2 (without such timeout, we have obtained worse results, both in resource usage and number of instances solved). A summary of our experimental evaluation is presented in Table 1. A virtual machine with our implementation and all the benchmarks can be found at https://es-static.fbk.eu/people/gredondi/atva2022.html.

As we can see from the table, BI-LAMBDA is applicable on a large set of benchmarks and in every set it is competitive with other approaches. When comparing BI-LAMBDA with BI-LAMBDA-Z3, we see that our simple instantiation procedure is more effective than relying on the built-in support for quantifiers in Z3, allowing to solve 5 more instances (and in general reducing the execution time, though this is not reported in Table 1 for lack of space).

Table 1. Summary of experimental results. In every column, we have reported the number of solved instances or '-' for incompatibility.

	Tot	BI-LAMBDA	BI-LAMBDA-Z3	LAMBDA	MCMT	CUBICLE	updr	fol-ic3	PdH	IC3PO
Protocols	42	34	31	34	24	30	–	–	–	–
DynArch	57	50	50	48	49	–	–	–	–	–
Trains	17	16	16	17	–	–	–	–	–	–
Trains-AE	10	10	10	–	–	–	–	–	–	–
PdH	20	11	11	–	–	–	12	11	5	12
Ic3po	37	18	16	–	–	–	18	17	–	25
Tot	183	139	134	99	73	30	30	28	5	37

6   Conclusions and Future Work

In this paper we have presented a general approach for model checking systems with quantifiers and SMT variables; the novelty in the presented algorithm relies in the tight integration between finite instance exploration and instantiation-based techniques. However, our proposed method currently synthesizes only universal invariants, which in some cases are not enough to prove properties of quantified systems. In our future works, we will investigate how to combine our approach with techniques that infer invariants with quantifier alternations. Moreover, we will study how to combine our approach with more sophisticated instantiation techniques exploited in state-of-the-art provers.

References

1. Alberti, F., Ghilardi, S., Pagani, E., Ranise, S., Rossi, G.P.: Universal guards, relativization of quantifiers, and failure models in model checking modulo theories. J. Satisfiability, Boolean Model. Comput. **8**, 29–61 (2012)
2. Bloem, R., Jacobs, S., Khalimov, A.: Decidability of Parameterized Verification. Morgan & Claypool Publishers, San Rafael (2015)
3. Cimatti, A., Griggio, A., Mover, S., Tonetta, S.: Infinite-state invariant checking with IC3 and predicate abstraction. Formal Methods Syst. Des. **49**(3), 190–218 (2016). https://doi.org/10.1007/s10703-016-0257-4
4. Cimatti, A., Griggio, A., Redondi, G.: Universal invariant checking of parametric systems with quantifier-free SMT reasoning. In: CADE 28 (2021)
5. Cimatti, A., Griggio, A., Schaafsma, B.J., Sebastiani, R.: The MathSAT5 SMT solver. In: Piterman, N., Smolka, S.A. (eds.) TACAS 2013. LNCS, vol. 7795, pp. 93–107. Springer, Heidelberg (2013). https://doi.org/10.1007/978-3-642-36742-7_7
6. Cimatti, A., Griggio, A., Tonetta, S.: The VMT-LIB language and tools. CoRR abs/2109.12821 (2021)
7. Cimatti, A., Stojic, I., Tonetta, S.: Formal specification and verification of dynamic parametrized architectures. In: Havelund, K., Peleska, J., Roscoe, B., de Vink, E. (eds.) FM 2018. LNCS, vol. 10951, pp. 625–644. Springer, Cham (2018). https://doi.org/10.1007/978-3-319-95582-7_37

8. Conchon, S., Goel, A., Krstić, S., Mebsout, A., Zaïdi, F.: Cubicle: a parallel SMT-based model checker for parameterized systems. In: Madhusudan, P., Seshia, S.A. (eds.) CAV 2012. LNCS, vol. 7358, pp. 718–724. Springer, Heidelberg (2012). https://doi.org/10.1007/978-3-642-31424-7_55
9. Conchon, S., Goel, A., Krstic, S., Mebsout, A., Zaïdi, F.: Invariants for finite instances and beyond. In: Formal Methods in Computer-Aided Design, FMCAD (2013)
10. Detlefs, D., Nelson, G., Saxe, J.B.: Simplify: a theorem prover for program checking. J. ACM **52**(3), 365–473 (2005)
11. Dooley, M., Somenzi, F.: Proving parameterized systems safe by generalizing clausal proofs of small instances. In: Chaudhuri, S., Farzan, A. (eds.) CAV 2016. LNCS, vol. 9779, pp. 292–309. Springer, Cham (2016). https://doi.org/10.1007/978-3-319-41528-4_16
12. Feldman, Y.M.Y., Padon, O., Immerman, N., Sagiv, M., Shoham, S.: Bounded quantifier instantiation for checking inductive invariants. Log. Methods Comput. Sci. **15**, 18:1–18:47 (2019)
13. Ge, Y., Barrett, C., Tinelli, C.: Solving quantified verification conditions using satisfiability modulo theories. Ann. Math. Artif. Intell. **55**(1), 101–122 (2009)
14. Ghilardi, S., Ranise, S.: Backward reachability of array-based systems by SMT solving: Termination and invariant synthesis. Log. Methods Comput. Sci. **6**(4) (2010)
15. Goel, A., Sakallah, K.: On symmetry and quantification: a new approach to verify distributed protocols. In: Dutle, A., Moscato, M.M., Titolo, L., Muñoz, C.A., Perez, I. (eds.) NFM 2021. LNCS, vol. 12673, pp. 131–150. Springer, Cham (2021). https://doi.org/10.1007/978-3-030-76384-8_9
16. Hance, T., Heule, M., Martins, R., Parno, B.: Finding invariants of distributed systems: it's a small (enough) world after all. In: NSDI 2021, pp. 115–131. USENIX Association (2021)
17. Ivrii, A., Gurfinkel, A., Belov, A.: Small inductive safe invariants. In: Formal Methods in Computer-Aided Design, FMCAD 2014, Lausanne, Switzerland, 21–24 October 2014, pp. 115–122. IEEE (2014)
18. Karbyshev, A., Bjørner, N., Itzhaky, S., Rinetzky, N., Shoham, S.: Property-directed inference of universal invariants or proving their absence. In: Kroening, D., Pǎsǎreanu, C.S. (eds.) Computer Aided Verification (2015)
19. Koenig, J.R., Padon, O., Immerman, N., Aiken, A.: First-order quantified separators. In: PLDI (2020)
20. Krstic, S.: Parametrized system verification with guard strengthening and parameter abstraction (2005)
21. Li, Y., Duan, K., Jansen, D.N., Pang, J., Zhang, L., Lv, Y., Cai, S.: An automatic proving approach to parameterized verification. ACM Trans. Comput. Logic **19**(4), 1–25 (2018)
22. Ma, H., Goel, A., Jeannin, J.B., Kapritsos, M., Kasikci, B., Sakallah, K.A.: I4: incremental inference of inductive invariants for verification of distributed protocols. SOSP 2019 (2019)
23. de Moura, L., Bjørner, N.: Z3: an efficient SMT solver. In: Ramakrishnan, C.R., Rehof, J. (eds.) TACAS 2008. LNCS, vol. 4963, pp. 337–340. Springer, Heidelberg (2008). https://doi.org/10.1007/978-3-540-78800-3_24
24. Padon, O., McMillan, K.L., Panda, A., Sagiv, M., Shoham, S.: Ivy: safety verification by interactive generalization. SIGPLAN Not. **51**(6), 614–630 (2016)

25. Padon, O., Wilcox, J.R., Koenig, J.R., McMillan, K.L., Aiken, A.: Induction duality: primal-dual search for invariants. Proc. ACM Program. Lang. **6**(POPL), 1–29 (2022)
26. Pnueli, A., Ruah, S., Zuck, L.: Automatic deductive verification with invisible invariants. In: Margaria, T., Yi, W. (eds.) TACAS 2001. LNCS, vol. 2031, pp. 82–97. Springer, Heidelberg (2001). https://doi.org/10.1007/3-540-45319-9_7
27. Reynolds, A.: Quantifier instantiation beyond E-matching. In: Brain, M., Hadarean, L. (eds.) (CAV 2017) (2017)
28. Yao, J., Tao, R., Gu, R., Nieh, J., Jana, S., Ryan, G.: DistAI: data-driven automated invariant learning for distributed protocols. In: (OSDI 21) (2021)

Projected Model Counting: Beyond Independent Support

Jiong Yang[1](✉), Supratik Chakraborty[2], and Kuldeep S. Meel[1]

[1] School of Computing, National University of Singapore, Singapore, Singapore
jiong@comp.nus.edu.sg
[2] Indian Institute of Technology Bombay, Mumbai, India

Abstract. Given a system of constraints over a set X of variables, projected model counting asks us to count satisfying assignments of the constraint system projected on a subset $\mathcal{P}$ of X. A key idea used in modern projected counters is to first compute an *independent support*, say $\mathcal{I}$, that is often a small subset of $\mathcal{P}$, and to then count models projected on $\mathcal{I}$ instead of on $\mathcal{P}$. While this has been effective in scaling performance of counters, the question of whether we can benefit by projecting on variables beyond $\mathcal{P}$ has not been explored. In this paper, we study this question and show that contrary to intuition, it can be beneficial to project on variables even beyond $\mathcal{P}$. In several applications, a good upper bound of the projected model count often suffices. We show that in several such cases, we can identify a set of variables, called *upper bound support (UBS)*, that is not necessarily a subset of $\mathcal{P}$, and yet counting models projected on UBS guarantees an upper bound of the projected model count. Theoretically, a UBS can be exponentially smaller than the smallest independent support. Our experiments show that even otherwise, UBS-based projected counting can be faster than independent support-based projected counting, while yielding bounds of high quality. Based on extensive experiments, we find that UBS-based projected counting can solve many problem instances that are beyond the reach of a state-of-the-art independent support-based projected model counter.

1 Introduction

Given a Boolean formula φ over a set X of variables, and a subset $\mathcal{P}$ of X, the problem of projected model counting asks us to determine the number of satisfying assignments of φ projected on $\mathcal{P}$. Projected model counting is # NP-complete in general [33][1], and has several important applications ranging from verification of neural networks [4], hardware and software verification [32], reliability of power grids [11], probabilistic inference [25], and the like. This problem has therefore attracted significant attention from both theoreticians and practitioners over the

---

[1] A special case where $\mathcal{P} = X$ is known to be #P-complete [34].

The resulting tool is available open-source at https://github.com/meelgroup/arjun.

A. Bouajjani et al. (Eds.): ATVA 2022, LNCS 13505, pp. 171–187, 2022.
https://doi.org/10.1007/978-3-031-19992-9_11

years [7,9,18,27,28,30,34]. While an ideal projected model counter offers high scalability *and* strong quality guarantees for computed counts, these goals are often hard to achieve simultaneously in practice. A pragmatic approach in several applications is therefore to use counters that offer good scalability and good quality of counts in practice, even if worst-case quality guarantees are weaker than ideal. Unfortunately, designing such counters is not easy either, and this motivates our current work.

Over the past decade, hashing-based techniques have emerged as a promising approach to projected model counting, since they scale moderately in practice, while providing strong approximation guarantees [6,7,13,18,27]. For propositional model counting, the hash functions are implemented using random XOR clauses over variables in $\mathcal{P}$. Starting from a formula φ in conjunctive normal form (CNF), these techniques construct a CNF+XOR formula φ' consisting of a conjunction of CNF clauses from φ and random XOR clauses implementing the hash functions. If each variable in $\mathcal{P}$ is chosen with probability $1/2$ the expected size of a random XOR clause is $|\mathcal{P}|/2$. If the projection set is large, this can indeed result in large XOR clauses – a known source of poor performance of modern SAT solvers on CNF+XOR formulas [8,16]. Researchers have therefore explored the use of hash functions with *sparse* XOR clauses [1,12,16,19,23] with moderate success.

A practically effective idea to address the problem of large XOR clauses was introduced in [8], wherein the notion of an *independent support* $\mathcal{I}$ ($\subseteq \mathcal{P}$), was introduced. Specifically, it was shown in [8] that (a) random XOR clauses over $\mathcal{I}$ suffice to provide strong guarantees for computed bounds, and (b) for a large class of practical benchmarks, $|\mathcal{I}|$ is much smaller than $|\mathcal{P}|$. Hence, constructing random XOR clauses over $\mathcal{I}$ instead of over $\mathcal{P}$ reduces the expected size of a random XOR clause, thereby improving the runtime performance of hashing-based counters [19]. Subsequently, independent supports have also been found to be useful in the context of exact projected model counting [21,22,26].

The runtime performance improvements achieved by (projected) model counters over the past decade have significantly broadened the scope of their applications, which, in turn, has brought the focus sharply back on performance scalability. Importantly, for several crucial applications such as neural network verification [4], quantified information flow [5], software reliability [32], reliability of power grids [11], etc. we are primarily interested in good upper bound estimates of projected model counts. As aptly captured by Achlioptas and Theodoropoulos [1], while obtaining "lower bounds are easy" in the context of projected model counting, such is not the case for good upper bounds. Therefore, scaling up to large problem instances while obtaining good upper bound estimates remains an important challenge in this area.

The primary contribution of this paper is a new approach to selecting variables on which to project solutions, with the goal of improving scalability of hashing-based projected counters when good upper bounds of projected counts are of interest. Towards this end, we generalize the notion of an independent support $\mathcal{I}$. Specifically, we note that the restriction $\mathcal{I} \subseteq \mathcal{P}$ ensures a two-way implication: if two solutions agree on $\mathcal{I}$, then they also agree on $\mathcal{P}$, and vice-versa. Since we are interested in upper bounds, we relax this requirement to a one-sided implication, i.e., we wish to find a set $\mathcal{U} \subseteq X$ (not necessarily a subset of $\mathcal{P}$) such that if two solutions agree on $\mathcal{U}$, then they agree on $\mathcal{P}$, but not necessarily vice versa. We call such a set $\mathcal{U}$ an *Upper Bound Support*, or UBS for short. We show that using random XOR clauses over UBS in hashing-based projected counting yields provable upper bounds of the projected counts. We also show some important properties of UBS, including an exponential gap between the smallest UBS and the smallest independent support for a class of problems. Our study suggests a simple algorithm, called FINDUBS, to determine UBS, that can be fine-tuned heuristically.

To evaluate the effectiveness of our idea, we augment a state-of-the-art model counter, ApproxMC4, with UBS to obtain UBS+ApproxMC4. Through an extensive empirical evaluation on 2632 benchmark instances arising from diverse domains, we compare the performance of UBS+ApproxMC4 with IS+ApproxMC4, i.e. ApproxMC4 augmented with independent support computation. Our experiments show that UBS+ApproxMC4 is able to solve 208 more instances than IS+ApproxMC4. Furthermore, the geometric mean of the absolute value of log-ratio of counts returned by UBS+ApproxMC4 and IS+ApproxMC4 is 1.32, thereby validating the claim that using UBS can lead to empirically good upper bounds. In this context, it is worth remarking that a recent study [2] comparing different partition function[2] estimation techniques labeled a method with the absolute value of log-ratio of counts less than 5 as a *reliable method*.

The rest of the paper is organized as follows. We present notation and preliminaries in Sect. 2. To situate our contribution, we present a survey of related work in Sect. 3. We then present the primary technical contributions of our work, including the notion of UBS and an algorithmic procedure to determine UBS, in Sect. 4. We present our empirical evaluation in Sect. 5, and finally conclude in Sect. 6.

2   Notation and Preliminaries

Let $X = \{x_1, x_2 \ldots x_n\}$ be a set of propositional variables appearing in a propositional formula φ. The set X is called the *support* of φ, and denoted $\mathsf{Sup}(\varphi)$. A *literal* is either a propositional variable or its negation. The formula φ is said to be in Conjunctive Normal Form (CNF) if φ is a conjunction of *clauses*, where each *clause* is disjunction of literals. An *assignment* σ of X is a mapping $X \to \{0, 1\}$. If φ evaluates to 1 under assignment σ, we say that σ is a *model* or *satisfying assignment* of φ, and denote this by $\sigma \models \varphi$. For every $\mathcal{P} \subseteq X$, the *projection* of σ on $\mathcal{P}$, denoted $\sigma_{\downarrow \mathcal{P}}$, is a mapping $\mathcal{P} \to \{0, 1\}$ such that $\sigma_{\downarrow \mathcal{P}}(v) = \sigma(v)$ for all $v \in \mathcal{P}$. Conversely we say that an assignment $\hat{\sigma} : \mathcal{P} \to \{0, 1\}$ can be *extended* to

---

[2] The problem of partition function estimation is known to be #P-complete and reduces to model counting; the state of the art techniques for partition function estimates are based on model counting [10].

a model of φ if there exists a model σ of φ such that $\hat{\sigma} = \sigma_{\downarrow\mathcal{P}}$. The set of all models of φ is denoted $sol(\varphi)$, and the projection of this set on $\mathcal{P} \subseteq X$ is denoted $sol(\varphi)_{\downarrow\mathcal{P}}$. We call the set $\mathcal{P}$ a *projection set* in our subsequent discussion[3].

The problem of *projected model counting* is to compute $|sol(\varphi)_{\downarrow\mathcal{P}}|$ for a given CNF formula φ and projection set $\mathcal{P}$. An exact projected model counter is a deterministic algorithm that takes φ and $\mathcal{P}$ as inputs and returns $|sol(\varphi)_{\downarrow\mathcal{P}}|$ as output. A *probably approximately correct* (or PAC) projected model counter is a probabilistic algorithm that takes as additional inputs a tolerance $\varepsilon > 0$, and a confidence parameter $\delta \in (0, 1]$, and returns a count c such that $\Pr\left[\frac{|sol(\varphi)_{\downarrow\mathcal{P}}|}{(1+\varepsilon)} \leq c \leq (1 + \varepsilon) \cdot |sol(\varphi)_{\downarrow\mathcal{P}}|\right] \geq 1 - \delta$, where $\Pr[E]$ denotes the probability of event E.

Definition 1. *Given a formula φ and a projection set $\mathcal{P} \subseteq \mathsf{Sup}(\varphi)$, a subset of variables $\mathcal{I} \subseteq \mathcal{P}$ is called an* independent support *(IS) of $\mathcal{P}$ in φ if for every $\sigma_1, \sigma_2 \in sol(\varphi)$, we have $(\sigma_{1\downarrow\mathcal{I}} = \sigma_{2\downarrow\mathcal{I}}) \Rightarrow (\sigma_{1\downarrow\mathcal{P}} = \sigma_{2\downarrow\mathcal{P}})$.*

Since $(\sigma_{1\downarrow\mathcal{P}} = \sigma_{2\downarrow\mathcal{P}}) \Rightarrow (\sigma_{1\downarrow\mathcal{I}} = \sigma_{2\downarrow\mathcal{I}})$ holds trivially when $\mathcal{I} \subseteq \mathcal{P}$, it follows from Definition 1 that if $\mathcal{I}$ is an independent support of $\mathcal{P}$ in φ, then $(\sigma_{1\downarrow\mathcal{I}} = \sigma_{2\downarrow\mathcal{I}}) \Leftrightarrow (\sigma_{1\downarrow\mathcal{P}} = \sigma_{2\downarrow\mathcal{P}})$. Empirical studies have shown that the size of an independent support $\mathcal{I}$ is often significantly smaller than that of the original projection set $\mathcal{P}$ [8,19,21,26]. In fact, the overhead of finding a small independent support $\mathcal{I}$ is often more than compensated by the efficiency obtained by counting projections of satisfying assignments on $\mathcal{I}$, instead of on the original projection set $\mathcal{P}$.

3   Related Work

As mentioned in Sect. 1, state-of-the-art hashing-based projected model counters work by adding random XOR clauses over the projection set $\mathcal{P}$ to a given CNF formula φ before finding satisfying assignments of the CNF+XOR formula. There are several inter-related factors that affect the runtime performance of such counters, and isolating the effect of any one factor is difficult. Nevertheless, finding satisfying assignments of the CNF+XOR formula is among the most significant bottlenecks. Among other things, the average size (i.e. number of literals) in XOR clauses correlates positively with the time taken to solve CNF+XOR formulas using modern conflict-driven clause learning (CDCL) SAT solvers [19].

The idea of using random XOR clauses over an independent support $\mathcal{I}$ ($\subseteq \mathcal{P}$) that is potentially much smaller than $\mathcal{P}$ was introduced in [8]. This is particularly effective when a small subset of variables functionally determines the large majority of variables in a formula, as happens, for example, when Tseitin encoding is used to transform a non-CNF formula to an equisatisfiable CNF formula. State-of-the-art hashing-based model counters, viz. ApproxMC4 [27], therefore routinely use random XOR clauses over the independent support. While the naive way of choosing each variable in $\mathcal{I}$ with probability $1/2$ gives a random XOR clause with expected size $|\mathcal{I}|/2$, specialized hash functions can also be

---

[3] Projection set has also been referred to as sampling set in prior work [8,27].

defined such that the expected size of a random XOR clause is $p \cdot |\mathcal{I}|$, with $p < 1/2$ [1,12,23]. The works of [1,12] achieved this goal while guaranteeing a constant factor approximation of the reported count. The work of [23] achieved a similar reduction in the expected size of XOR clauses, while guaranteeing PAC-style bounds.

All earlier work focused on random XOR clauses chosen over subsets of the projection set $\mathcal{P}$. While this is a natural choice, we break free from this restriction and allow XOR clauses to be constructed over any subset of variables as long as the model count projected on the chosen subset bounds the model count projected on $\mathcal{P}$ from above. This allows us more flexibility in constructing CNF+XOR formulas, which as our experiments confirm, leads to improved overall performance of projected model counting in several cases. Since we guarantee upper bounds of the desired counts, our approach yields an *upper bounding projected model counter*. Nevertheless, as our experiments show, the bounds obtained using our approach are consistently very close to the projected counts reported using independent support. Therefore, in practice, our approach gives high quality bounds on projected model counts more efficiently than state-of-the-art hashing-based techniques that use independent supports.

It is worth mentioning that several *bounding model counters* have been reported earlier in the literature. These counters produce a count that is at least as large (or, as small, as the case may be) as the true model count of a given CNF formula with a specified confidence. Notable examples are SampleCount [17], BPCount [20], MBound and Hybrid-MBound [18] and MiniCount [20]. Owing to several technical reasons, however, these bounding counters scale poorly compared to state-of-the-art hashing-based counters like ApproxMC4 [27] in practice. Unlike earlier bounding counters, we first carefully identify a subset of variables (not restricted to be a subset of $\mathcal{P}$), and then use state-of-the-art hashing-based approximate projected counting using this subset as the new projection set. Therefore, our approach directly benefits from improvements in performance of hashing-based projected counting achieved over the years. Furthermore, by carefully controlling the chosen subset of variables, we can also control the quality of the bound. As an extreme case, if all variables are chosen from $\mathcal{P}$, then our approach produces counts with true PAC-style guarantees.

4   Technical Contribution

In this section, we generalize the notion of independent support, and give technical details of projected model counting using this generalization.

Definition 2. *Given a CNF formula φ and a projection set $\mathcal{P}$, let $\mathcal{S} \subseteq \mathsf{Sup}(\varphi)$ be such that for every $\sigma_1, \sigma_2 \in sol(\varphi)$, we have $(\sigma_{1\downarrow\mathcal{S}} = \sigma_{2\downarrow\mathcal{S}}) \bowtie (\sigma_{1\downarrow\mathcal{P}} = \sigma_{2\downarrow\mathcal{P}})$, where $\bowtie \ \in \{\Rightarrow, \Leftarrow, \Leftrightarrow\}$. Then $\mathcal{S}$ is called a*

1. generalized independent support (GIS) *of $\mathcal{P}$ in φ if $\bowtie$ is $\Leftrightarrow$*
2. upper bound support (UBS) *of $\mathcal{P}$ in φ if $\bowtie$ is $\Rightarrow$*
3. lower bound support (LBS) *of $\mathcal{P}$ in φ if $\bowtie$ is $\Leftarrow$*

Note that in the above definition, S need not be a subset of $\mathcal{P}$. In fact, if S is restricted to be a subset of $\mathcal{P}$, the definitions of GIS and UBS coincide with that of IS (Definition 1), while LBS becomes a trivial concept (every subset of $\mathcal{P}$ is indeed an LBS of $\mathcal{P}$ in φ). The following lemma now follows immediately.

Lemma 1. *Let* $\mathcal{G}, \mathcal{U}$ *and* $\mathcal{L}$ *be GIS, UBS and LBS, respectively, of* $\mathcal{P}$ *in* φ. *Then* $|sol(\varphi)_{\downarrow\mathcal{L}}| \leq |sol(\varphi)_{\downarrow\mathcal{P}}| = |sol(\varphi)_{\downarrow\mathcal{G}}| \leq |sol(\varphi)_{\downarrow\mathcal{U}}|$.

Let $\mathcal{UBS}, \mathcal{LBS}, \mathcal{GIS}$ and $\mathcal{IS}$ be the set of all UBS, LBS, GIS and IS respectively of a projection set $\mathcal{P}$ in φ. It is easy to see that $\mathcal{IS} \subseteq \mathcal{GIS} \subseteq \mathcal{UBS}$, and $\mathcal{GIS} \subseteq \mathcal{LBS}$. While each of the notions of GIS, UBS and LBS are of independent interest, this paper focuses primarily on UBS because we found this notion particularly useful in practical projected model counting. Additionally, as the above inclusion relations show, $\mathcal{UBS}$ and $\mathcal{LBS}$ are the largest classes among $\mathcal{UBS}, \mathcal{LBS}, \mathcal{GIS}$ and $\mathcal{IS}$; hence, finding an UBS is likely to be easier than finding a GIS. Furthermore, the notion of UBS continues to remain interesting (but not so for LBS) even when $\mathcal{I}$ is chosen to be a subset of $\mathcal{P}$.

We call a UBS $\mathcal{U}$ (resp. LBS $\mathcal{L}$, GIS $\mathcal{G}$ and IS $\mathcal{I}$) of $\mathcal{P}$ in φ *minimal* if there is no other UBS (resp. LBS, GIS and IS) of $\mathcal{P}$ in φ that is a strict subset of $\mathcal{U}$ (resp. of $\mathcal{L}$, $\mathcal{G}$ and $\mathcal{I}$).

Example 1. Consider a CNF formula $\varphi(x_1, x_2, x_3, x_4) \equiv (x_3 \vee x_4) \wedge (x_1 \vee x_4) \wedge (x_2 \vee x_3) \wedge (x_2 \vee x_4) \wedge (\neg x_1 \vee \neg x_2 \vee \neg x_4) \wedge (\neg x_3 \vee \neg x_4 \vee \neg x_2)$. There are four satisfying assignments of φ, given by $(x_1, x_2, x_3, x_4) \in \{(0,0,1,1), (0,1,0,1), (1,0,1,1), (1,1,1,0)\}$. If $\mathcal{P} = \{x_1, x_3, x_4\}$, it can be seen that the only minimal IS of $\mathcal{P}$ in φ is $\{x_1, x_3, x_4\}$, whereas $\{x_1, x_2\}$ is a minimal UBS and also GIS of $\mathcal{P}$ in φ. Any single variable subset of $\{x_1, x_2, x_3, x_4\}$ serves as a minimal LBS of $\mathcal{P}$ in φ.

In the remainder of this section, we first explore some interesting theoretical properties of GIS and UBS, and then proceed to develop a practical algorithm for computing a UBS from a given formula φ and projection set $\mathcal{P}$. Finally, we present an algorithm for computing bounds of projected model counts using the UBS thus computed.

4.1 Extremal Properties of GIS and UBS

We first show that by allowing variables on which to project to lie beyond the projection set $\mathcal{P}$, we can obtain an exponential reduction in the count of variables on which to project.

Theorem 1. *For every* $n > 1$, *there exists a propositional formula* φ_n *on* $(n-1) + \lceil \log_2 n \rceil$ *variables and a projection set* $\mathcal{P}_n$ *with* $|\mathcal{P}_n| = n - 1$ *such that*

- *The smallest GIS of* $\mathcal{P}_n$ *in* φ_n *is of size* $\lceil \log_2 n \rceil$.
- *The smallest UBS of* $\mathcal{P}_n$ *in* φ_n *is of size* $\lceil \log_2 n \rceil$.
- *The smallest IS of* $\mathcal{P}_n$ *in* φ_n *is* $\mathcal{P}_n$ *itself, and hence of size* $n - 1$.

Proof:

	x_1	x_2	$\cdots$	x_{n-1}	y_1	y_2	$\cdots$	$y_{\log_2 n}$
σ_0	0	0	$\cdots$	0	0	$\cdots$	0	0
σ_1	1	0	$\cdots$	0	0	$\cdots$	0	1
	$\vdots$	$\vdots$	$\vdots$	$\vdots$	$\vdots$	$\vdots$	$\vdots$	$\vdots$
σ_{n-1}	0	0	$\cdots$	1	1	$\cdots$	1	1

For notational convenience, we assume n to be a power of 2. Consider a formula φ_n on propositional variables $x_1, \ldots x_{n-1}$, $y_1, \ldots y_{\log_2 n}$ with n satisfying assignments, say $\sigma_0, \ldots \sigma_{n-1}$, as shown in the table below. Thus, for all $i \in \{1, \ldots n-1\}$, the values of $y_1 \ldots y_{\log_2 n}$ in σ_i encode i in binary (with y_1 being the most significant bit), the value of x_i is 1, and the values of all other x_j's are 0. For the special satisfying assignment σ_0, the values of all variables are 0.

Let $\mathcal{P}_n = \{x_1, \ldots x_{n-1}\}$. Clearly, $|sol(\varphi_n)| = |sol(\varphi_n)_{\downarrow\mathcal{P}_n}| = n$. Now consider the set of variables $\mathcal{G}_n = \{y_1, \ldots y_{\log_2 n}\}$. It is easy to verify that for every pair of satisfying assignments σ_i, σ_j of φ_n, $(\sigma_{i\downarrow\mathcal{G}_n} = \sigma_{j\downarrow\mathcal{G}_n}) \Leftrightarrow (\sigma_{i\downarrow\mathcal{P}_n} = \sigma_{j\downarrow\mathcal{P}_n})$. Therefore, $\mathcal{G}_n$ is a GIS, and hence also a UBS, of $\mathcal{P}_n$ in φ_n, and $|\mathcal{G}_n| = \log_2 n$. Indeed, specifying $y_1, \ldots y_{\log_2 n}$ completely specifies the value of all variables for every satisfying assignment of φ_n. Furthermore, since $|sol(\varphi_n)_{\downarrow\mathcal{P}_n}| = n$, every GIS and also UBS of $\mathcal{P}_n$ must be of size at least $\log_2 n$. Hence, $\mathcal{G}_n$ is a smallest-sized GIS, and also a smallest-sized UBS, of $\mathcal{P}_n$ in φ_n.

Let us now find how small an independent support (IS) of $\mathcal{P}_n$ in φ can be. Recall that $|sol(\varphi_n)_{\downarrow\mathcal{P}_n}| = n$. If possible, let there be an IS of $\mathcal{P}_n$, say $\mathcal{I}_n \subseteq \mathcal{P}_n$, where $|\mathcal{I}_n| < n-1$. Therefore, at least one variable in $\mathcal{P}_n$, say x_i, must be absent in $\mathcal{I}_n$. Now consider the satisfying assignments σ_i and σ_0. Clearly, both $\sigma_{i\downarrow\mathcal{I}_n}$ and $\sigma_{0\downarrow\mathcal{I}_n}$ are the all-0 vector of size $|\mathcal{I}_n|$. Therefore, $\sigma_{i\downarrow\mathcal{I}_n} = \sigma_{0\downarrow\mathcal{I}_n}$ although $\sigma_{i\downarrow\mathcal{P}_n} \neq \sigma_{0\downarrow\mathcal{P}_n}$. It follows that $\mathcal{I}_n$ cannot be an IS of $\mathcal{P}_n$ in φ_n. This implies that the smallest IS of $\mathcal{P}_n$ in φ_n is $\mathcal{P}_n$ itself, and has size $n-1$. $\quad\square$

Observe that the smallest GIS/UBS $\mathcal{G}_n$ above is disjoint from $\mathcal{P}_n$. Therefore, it can be beneficial to look outside the projection set when searching for a GIS or UBS. The next theorem shows that the opposite can also be true. The proof is deferred to the detailed technical report [35].

Theorem 2. *For every $n > 1$, there exist formulas φ_n and ψ_n on $(n-1) + \lceil\log_2 n\rceil$ variables and a projection set $\mathcal{Q}_n$ with $|\mathcal{Q}_n| = n - \lceil\log_2 n\rceil - 1$ such that the only GIS of $\mathcal{Q}_n$ in φ_n is $\mathcal{Q}_n$, and the smallest UBS of $\mathcal{Q}_n$ in ψ_n is also $\mathcal{Q}_n$.*

Theorems 1 and 2 indicate that the search for the smallest GIS or UBS is likely to be hard, since it has to potentially consider subsets of X ranging from those completely overlapping with $\mathcal{P}$ to those disjoint from $\mathcal{P}$. Below, we present an algorithm to compute a minimal (as opposed to smallest) UBS, for use in projected model counting.

4.2 Algorithm to Compute Projected Count Using UBS

We now describe an algorithm to compute a minimal UBS for a given CNF formula φ and projection set $\mathcal{P}$. We draw our motivation from Padoa's theorem [24], which provides a necessary and sufficient condition for a variable in the support of φ to be functionally determined by other variables in the support. Let $\mathsf{Sup}(\varphi) = X = \{x_1, x_2, \ldots x_t\}$; we also write $\varphi(X)$ to denote this. We create another set of *fresh* variables $X' = \{x'_1, x'_2, \ldots x'_t\}$. Let $\varphi(X \mapsto X')$ represent the formula where every $x_i \in X$ in φ is replaced by $x'_i \in X'$.

Lemma 2 (Padoa's Theorem [24]). *Let* $\psi(X, X', i)$ *be defined as* $\varphi(X) \wedge \varphi(X \mapsto X') \wedge \bigwedge_{\substack{j=1 \\ j \neq i}}^{t} (x_j \Leftrightarrow x'_j) \wedge x_i \wedge \neg x'_i$. *The variable* x_i *is defined by* $X \setminus \{x_i\}$ *in the formula* φ *iff* $\psi(X, X', i)$ *is unsatisfiable.*

Padoa's theorem has been effectively used in state-of-the-art hashing-based projected model counters such as ApproxMC4 [27] to determine small independent supports of given projection sets. In our setting, we need to modify the formulation since we seek to compute an upper bound support.

Given $\mathcal{P}$, we first partition $X = \mathsf{Sup}(\varphi)$ into sets J, D and Q as follows. The set J contains variables already determined to be in a minimal UBS of $\mathcal{P}$ in φ. The set D contains variables not necessarily in a minimal UBS of $\mathcal{P}$ in φ obtainable by adding elements from Q to J. Finally, Q contains all other variables in X.

Initially, J and D are empty sets, and $Q = X$. As the process of computation of a minimal UBS proceeds, we maintain the invariant that $J \cup Q$ is a UBS (not necessarily minimal) of $\mathcal{P}$ in φ. Notice that this is trivially true initially.

Let z be a variable in Q for which we wish to determine if it can be added to the partially computed minimal UBS J. In the following discussion, we use the notation $\varphi(J, Q \setminus \{z\}, D, z)$ to denote φ with its partition of variables, and with z specially identified in the partition Q. Recalling the definition of UBS from Sect. 2, we observe that if z is not part of a minimal UBS containing J, and if $J \cup Q$ is indeed a UBS of $\mathcal{P} \in \varphi$, then as long as values of variables other than z in $J \cup Q$ are kept unchanged, the projection of a satisfying assignment of φ on $\mathcal{P}$ must also stay unchanged. This suggests the following check to determine if z is not part of a minimal UBS containing J.

Define $\xi(J, Q \setminus \{z\}, D, z, D', z')$ as $\varphi(J, Q \setminus \{z\}, D, z) \wedge \varphi(J, Q \setminus \{z\}, D', z') \wedge \bigvee_{x_i \in \mathcal{P} \cap (D \cup \{z\})} (x_i \not\Leftrightarrow x'_i)$, where D' and z' represent fresh and renamed instances of variables in D and z, respectively. If ξ is unsatisfiable, we know that as long as the values of variables in $J \cup (Q \setminus \{z\})$ are kept unchanged, the projection of the satisfying assignment of φ on $\mathcal{P}$ cannot change. This allows us to move z from the set Q to the set D.

Theorem 3. *If* $\xi(J, Q \setminus \{z\}, D, z, D', z')$ *is unsatisfiable, then* $J \cup (Q \setminus \{z\})$ *is a UBS of* $\mathcal{P}$ *in* φ.

The proof of Theorem 3 is deferred to the extended version [35]. The above check suggests a simple algorithm for computing a minimal UBS. We present the pseudocode of our algorithm for computing UBS below.

After initializing J, Q and D, FINDUBS chooses a variable $z \in Q$ and checks if the formula ξ in Theorem 3 is unsatisfiable. If so, it adds z to D and removes it from Q. Otherwise, it adds z to J. The algorithm terminates when Q becomes empty. On termination, J gives a minimal UBS of $\mathcal{P}$ in φ. The strategy for choosing the next z from Q, implemented by sub-routine ChooseNextVar,

---

Algorithm 1. FINDUBS($\varphi, \mathcal{P}$)

1: $J \leftarrow \emptyset; Q \leftarrow \mathsf{Sup}(\varphi); D \leftarrow \emptyset;$
2: **repeat**
3:      $z \leftarrow \mathsf{ChooseNextVar}(Q);$
4:      $\xi \leftarrow \left(\begin{array}{c} \varphi(J, Q \setminus z, D, z) \ \wedge \ \varphi(J, Q \setminus z, D', z') \ \wedge \\ \bigvee_{x_i \in \mathcal{P} \cap (D \cup \{z\})} \neg(x_i \Leftrightarrow x_i') \end{array} \right);$
5:      **if** ξ is UNSAT **then**
6:          $D \leftarrow D \cup \{z\};$
7:      **else**
8:          $J \leftarrow J \cup \{z\};$
9:      $Q \leftarrow Q \setminus \{z\};$
10: **until** Q is $\emptyset;$
11: **return** $J;$

---

clearly affects the quality of UBS obtained from this algorithm. We require that ChooseNextVar(Q) return a variable from Q as long as $Q \neq \emptyset$. Choosing z from outside $\mathcal{P}$ gives a UBS that is the same as an IS of $\mathcal{P}$ in φ. In our experiments, we therefore bias the choice of z to favour those in $\mathcal{P}$.

In our prototype implementation, ChooseNextVar chooses variables from within $\mathcal{P}$ before variables outside $\mathcal{P}$. Note that this policy heuristically prioritizes removal of variables in $\mathcal{P}$ from the set J. To see why this is so, suppose $x_1 \leftrightarrow x_2$ is entailed by φ, and $x_1 \in \mathcal{P}$ while $x_2 \notin \mathcal{P}$. Suppose neither x_1 nor x_2 have been chosen so far. If we first choose x_1 as z, the formula ξ in line 4 of Algorithm 1 will be UNSAT, and x_1 will be moved to D and finally x_2 will be added to J (and hence to UBS). However, if we first choose x_2 as z, x_2 will be moved to D while x_1 will subsequently get added to J, and hence to UBS. We hope to leave x_2 (outside $\mathcal{P}$) in UBS and thereby first choose x_1 (within $\mathcal{P}$).

We further use an incidence-based heuristic to prioritize variables within $\mathcal{P}$, or outside $\mathcal{P}$ (after all variables in $\mathcal{P}$ have been considered). The incidence for each variable is defined as the number of clauses containing the variable or its negation in the given CNF. ChooseNextVar always returns the variable with the smallest incidence (within $\mathcal{P}$, or outside $\mathcal{P}$, as the case may be) that has not been considered so far. This is based on our observation that these variables often do not belong to upper bound support in practice.

We now state some key properties of Algorithm FINDUBS. All proofs are deferred to the extended version [35].

Lemma 3. *There exists a minimal UBS $\mathcal{U}^*$ of $\mathcal{P}$ in φ such that $J \subseteq \mathcal{U}^* \subseteq J \cup Q$, where J and Q refer to the respective sets at the loop head (line 2) of Algorithm 1.*

Theorem 4. *Algorithm 1, when invoked on φ and $\mathcal{P}$, terminates and computes a minimal UBS of $\mathcal{P}$ in φ.*

The overall algorithm for computing an upper bound of the projected model count of a CNF formula using UBS is shown in Algorithm 2. This algorithm takes a timeout parameter τ_{pre} to limit the time taken for computing a UBS $\mathcal{U}$ using algorithm FINDUBS. If FINDUBS times out, it uses the projection set $\mathcal{P}$ itself for $\mathcal{U}$. It also invokes a PAC-style projected model counter ComputeCount to estimate the count of φ projected on $\mathcal{U}$.

Algorithm 2. UBCount($\varphi, \mathcal{P}, \varepsilon, \delta, \tau_{\mathrm{pre}}$)

1: $\mathcal{U} \leftarrow$ FINDUBS($\varphi, \mathcal{P}$) with timeout τ_{pre};
2: **if** call to FINDUBS times out **then**
3:     $\mathcal{U} \leftarrow \mathcal{P}$;
4: **return** ComputeCount($\varphi, \mathcal{U}, \varepsilon, \delta$)

Theorem 5. *Given a CNF formula φ, a projection set $\mathcal{P}$, timeout parameter $\tau_{\mathrm{pre}} > 0$, parameters $\varepsilon\ (> 0)$ and $\delta\ (0 < \delta \leq 1)$, and given access to a (ε, δ)-PAC projected counter ComputeCount, suppose Algorithm UBCount returns a count c. Then for every choice of sub-routine ChooseNextVar in Algorithm FINDUBS, we have $\Pr\left[|sol(\varphi)_{\downarrow\mathcal{P}}| \leq (1 + \varepsilon) \cdot c\right] \geq 1 - \delta$.*

Theorem 5 provides the weakest worst-case guarantee for Algorithm UBCount, over all possible choices of sub-routine ChooseNextVar. In practice, the specifics of ChooseNextVar can be factored in to strengthen the guarantee, including PAC-style guarantees in the extreme case if ChooseNextVar always chooses variables from the projection set $\mathcal{P}$. A more detailed analysis of UBCount, taking into account the specifics of ChooseNextVar, is beyond the scope of this paper. Note, however, that despite the apparent weakness of worst-case guarantees, Algorithm UBCount consistently computes high quality bounds for projected counts in practice, as detailed in the next section.

5 Experimental Evaluation

To evaluate the practical performance of UBCount, we implemented a prototype in C++. Our prototype implementation[4] builds on Arjun [29], a state of the art independent support computation tool, which is shown to significantly improve over prior state of the art approaches for computation of independent support [21, 22]. For projected model counting, we employ the version of ApproxMC4 that was used as a winning entry to the model counting competition 2020 [14][5]. Since all prior applications and benchmarking for approximation techniques have been presented with $\varepsilon = 0.8$ in the literature, we continue to use the same value of ε in this work. Note, however, that UBS can be used with any backend tool that computes projected model counts, and the benefits of UBS are orthogonal to those of choosing the backend projected model counter.

We use UBS+ApproxMC4 to denote the case when ApproxMC4 is invoked with the computed UBS as the projection set, while we use IS+ApproxMC4 to refer to the version of ApproxMC4 invoked with IS as the projection set.

Benchmarks. Our benchmark suite consists of 2632 instances, which are categorized into four categories: BNN, Circuit, QBF-exist and QBF-circuit. The

---

[4] The tool is available open-source at https://github.com/meelgroup/arjun.
[5] The ApproxMC4-based entry achieved 3rd place in the 2021 competition, with the tolerance for error (ε) set to 0.01. As mentioned during the competitive event presentation at the SAT 2021 conference, had ε been set to 0.05, the ApproxMC4-based entry would have indeed won the competition.

'BNN' benchmarks arc adapted from [4]. Each instance contains CNF encoding of a binarized neural network (BNN) and constraints from properties of interest such as robustness, cardinality, and parity. The projection set $\mathcal{P}$ is set to variables from a chosen layer in the BNN. The class 'Circuit' refers to instances from [8], which encode circuits arising from ISCAS85/ISCAS89 benchmarks conjuncted with random parity constraints imposed on output variables. The projection set, as set by authors in [8], corresponds to output variables. The 'QBF' benchmarks are based on instances from the Prenex-2QBF track of QBFEval-17[6], QBFEval-18[7], and disjunctive decomposition [3], arithmetic [31] and factorization [3] benchmarks for Boolean functional synthesis. Each 'QBF-exist' benchmark is a CNF formula transformed from a QBF instance. We remove quantifiers for the (2-)QBF instances and set the projection set to the variables originally existentially quantified. The class 'QBF-circuit' refers to circuits synthesized using the state-of-the-art functional synthesis tool, Manthan [15]. The projection set here is set to output variables.

Our choice of benchmark categories is motivated by the observation that UBS-based approximate model counting is likely to perform well when the variables in a problem instance admit partitioning into a sequence of "layers", with variables in each layer functionally determined by those in preceding layers. Note that this may not hold for arbitrary model counting benchmarks. We defer additional discussion on this to [35] for lack of space.

Experiments were conducted on a high-performance computer cluster, each node consisting of 2xE5-2690v3 CPUs with 2×12 real cores and 96 GB of RAM. For each benchmark, the projected model counter with each preprocessing technique runs on a single core. We set the time limit to 5000 s for each of preprocessing and counting, and the memory limit to 4 GB. The maximal number of conflicts in SAT solver calls during pre-processing is set to 100k. To compare runtime performance, we use PAR-2 scores, which is the de-facto standard in the SAT community. Each benchmark contributes a score that is the time in seconds taken by the corresponding tool to successfully complete execution or in case of a timeout or memory out, twice the timeout in seconds. We then calculate the average score for all benchmarks, obtaining the PAR-2 score.

We seek to answer the following research questions:

RQ 1 Does the usage of UBS enable ApproxMC4 to solve more benchmarks in comparison to the usage of IS ?

RQ 2 How does the quality of counts computed by UBS+ApproxMC4 vary in comparison to IS+ApproxMC4?

RQ 3 How does the runtime behavior of UBS+ApproxMC4 compare with that of IS+ApproxMC4?

Summary. In summary, UBS+ApproxMC4 solves 208 more instances than IS+ApproxMC4. Furthermore, while computation of UBS takes 777 more

---

[6] http://www.qbflib.org/qbfeval17.php.
[7] http://www.qbflib.org/qbfeval18.php.

seconds, the PAR-2 score of UBS+ApproxMC4 is 817 s less than that of IS+ApproxMC4. Finally, for all the instances where both UBS+ApproxMC4 and IS+ApproxMC4 terminated, the geometric mean of log-ratio of counts returned by IS+ApproxMC4 and UBS+ApproxMC4 is 1.32, indicating that UBS+ApproxMC4 provides good upper bound estimates. Therefore, UBS+ApproxMC4 can be used instead of IS+ApproxMC4 for applications that really care about upper bounds of projected counts.

In this context, it is worth highlighting that since there has been considerable effort in recent years in optimizing computation of IS, one would expect that further engineering efforts would lead to even more runtime savings for UBS.

Number of Solved Benchmarks. Table 1 compares the number of benchmarks solved by IS+ApproxMC4 and UBS+ApproxMC4. Observe that the usage of UBS enables ApproxMC4 to solve 435, 291, and 145 instances on Circuit, QBF-exist, and QBF-circuit benchmark sets respectively while the usage of IS+ApproxMC4 solved 407, 156 and 100 instances. In particular, UBS+ApproxMC4 solved almost twice as many instances on QBF-exist benchmarks.

Table 1. The number of solved benchmarks.

Benchmarks	Total	VBS	IS+ApproxMC4	UBS+ApproxMC4
BNN	1224	868	823	823
Circuit	522	455	407	**435**
QBF-exist	607	314	156	**291**
QBF-circuit	279	152	100	**145**

The practical adoption of tools for NP-hard problems often relies on portfolio solvers. Therefore, from the perspective of practice, one is often interested in evaluating the impact of a new technique to the portfolio of existing state of the art. To this end, we often focus on Virtual Best Solver (VBS), which can be viewed as an ideal portfolio. An instance is considered to be solved by VBS if is solved by at least one solver in the portfolio. Observe that in our experiments on BNN benchmarks, while UBS+ApproxMC4 and IS+ApproxMC4 solved the same number (not same set) of instances, VBS solves 45 more instances since there were instances solved by one solver and not the other.

Time Analysis. To analyze the runtime behavior, we separate the preprocessing time (computation of UBS and IS) and the time taken by ApproxMC4. Table 2 reports the mean of preprocessing time over benchmarks and the PAR-2 score for counting time. The usage of UBS reduces the PAR-2 score for counting from 3680, 2206, 7493, and 6479 to 3607, 1766, 5238, and 4829 respectively on the four benchmark sets. Remarkably, UBS reduces PAR-2 score by over 2000 s on QBF-exist benchmarks and over by 1000 s on QBF-circuit – a significant improvement!

Table 2. The mean of preprocessing time and PAR-2 score of counting time

	Preprocessing time		PAR-2 score of counting time	
Benchmarks	IS (s)	UBS (s)	IS (s)	UBS (s)
BNN	2518	2533	3680	**3607**
Circuit	229	680	2206	**1766**
QBF-exist	70	2155	7493	**5238**
QBF-circuit	653	2541	6479	**4829**

Observe that the mean pre-processing time taken by UBS is higher than that of IS across all four benchmark classes. Such an observation may lead one to wonder whether savings due to UBS are indeed useful; in particular, one may wonder what would happen if the total time of IS+ApproxMC4 is set to 10,000 s so that the time remaining after IS computation can be used by ApproxMC4. We observe that even in such a case, IS+ApproxMC4 is able to solve only four more instances than Table 1. To further emphasize, UBS+ApproxMC4 where ApproxMC4 is allowed a timeout of 5000 s can still solve more instance than IS+ApproxMC4 where ApproxMC4 is allowed a timeout of $10,000 - t_{IS}$ where t_{IS} is time taken to compute IS with a timeout of 5000 s.

Table 3. Performance comparison of UBS vs. IS. The runtime is reported in seconds and "−' in a column reports timeout after 5000 s.

Benchmarks	$\|X\|$	$\|\mathcal{P}\|$	IS+ApproxMC4			UBS+ApproxMC4		
			|IS|	Time (s)	Count	|UBS|	Time (s)	Count
amba2c7n.sat	1380	1345	313	0.24+2853	$50 * 2^{65}$	73	17+1	$63 * 2^{67}$
bobtuint31neg	1634	1205	678	0.37+5000	−	417	148+16	$64 * 2^{411}$
ly2-25-bnn_32-bit-5-id-11	131	32	32	1313+3416	$94 * 2^9$	59	2113+1034	$63 * 2^{10}$
ly3-25-bnn_32-bit-5-id-10	131	32	32	1389+5000	−	61	2319+841	$60 * 2^9$
floor128	891	879	254	0.07+5000	−	256	9+6	$64 * 2^{250}$
s15850_10_10.cnf	10985	684	605	0.50+5000	−	600	41+2070	$50 * 2^{566}$
arbiter_10_5	23533	129	118	0.71+4	$64 * 2^{112}$	302	7+5000	−
cdiv_10_5	101705	128	60	102+50	$72 * 2^{50}$	−	5000+5000	−
rankfunc59_signed_64	5140	4505	1735	3+274	$43 * 2^{1727}$	−	5000+5000	−

Detailed Runtime Analysis. Table 3 presents the results over a subset of benchmarks. Column 1 of the table gives the benchmark name, while columns 2 and 3 list the size of support X and the size of projection set $\mathcal{P}$, respectively. Columns 4–6 list the size of computed IS, runtime of IS+ApproxMC4, and model count over IS while columns 7–9 correspond to UBS. Note that the time is represented in the form $t_p + t_c$ where t_p refers to the time taken by IS (resp. UBS) and t_c refers to the time taken by ApproxMC4. We use '−' in column 6 (resp. column 9) for the cases where IS+ApproxMC4 (resp. UBS+ApproxMC4) times out.

The benchmark set was chosen to showcase different behaviors of interest: First, we observe that the smaller size of UBS for amba2c7n.sat helps UBS+ApproxMC4 while IS+ApproxMC4 times out. It is, however, worth emphasizing that the size of UBS and IS is not the only factor. To this end, observe that for the two benchmarks arising from BNN, represented in the third and fourth row, even though the size of UBS is large, the runtime of ApproxMC4 is still improved. Furthermore, in comparison to IS (which is heavily optimized in Arjun [29], our implementation for UBS did not explore engineering optimizations, which explains why UBS computation times out in the presence of the large size of support. Therefore, an important direction of future research is to further optimize the computation of UBS to fully unlock the potential of UBS.

Quality of Upper Bounds. To evaluate the quality of computed upper bounds, we compare the counts computed by UBS+ApproxMC4 with those of IS+ApproxMC4 for 1376 instances where both IS+ApproxMC4 and UBS+ApproxMC4 terminated. Suppose C_{IS} and C_{UBS} denote the model count using IS and UBS respectively. The error is computed as Error $= \log_2 C_{UBS} - \log_2 C_{IS}$, using common comparing convention for model counters. Figure 1 shows the Error distribution over our benchmarks. A point (x, y) represents Error $\leq y$ on the first x benchmarks. For example, the point $(1000, 2.2)$ means that Error ≤ 2.2 on 1000 benchmarks. Overall, the geometric mean of Error is 1.32. Furthermore, for more than 67% benchmarks, Error is less than 1, and for 81% benchmarks, Error is less than 5. Only 11% benchmarks have Error larger than 10. We intend to investigate heuristics for ChooseNextVar to reduce Error in these extremal cases as part of future work. To put the significance of Error in context, we refer to the recent survey [2] comparing several partition function estimation techniques, wherein a method with Error less than 5 is considered a *reliable method*. It is known that partition function estimation reduces to model counting, and the best performing technique identified in that study relies on model counting.

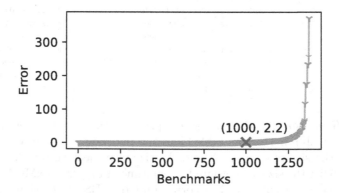

Fig. 1. Error of upper bound.

6   Conclusion

In this work, we introduced the notion of Upper Bound Support (UBS), which generalizes the well-known notion of independent support. We then observed that the usage of UBS for generation of XOR constraints allows the computation of upper bound of projected model counts. Our empirical analysis demonstrates that UBS+ApproxMC leads to significant runtime improvement in terms of the number of instances solved as well as the PAR-2 score. Since identification of the importance of IS in the context of counting led to follow-up work focused on efficient computation of IS, we hope our work will excite the community to work on efficient computation of UBS.

References

1. Achlioptas, D., Theodoropoulos, P.: Probabilistic model counting with short XORs. In: Gaspers, S., Walsh, T. (eds.) SAT 2017. LNCS, vol. 10491, pp. 3–19. Springer, Cham (2017). https://doi.org/10.1007/978-3-319-66263-3_1
2. Agrawal, D., Pote, Y., Meel, K.S.: Partition function estimation: a quantitative study. In: Proceedings of IJCAI (2021)
3. Akshay, S., Chakraborty, S., John, A.K., Shah, S.: Towards parallel Boolean functional synthesis. In: Legay, A., Margaria, T. (eds.) TACAS 2017. LNCS, vol. 10205, pp. 337–353. Springer, Heidelberg (2017). https://doi.org/10.1007/978-3-662-54577-5_19
4. Baluta, T., Shen, S., Shine, S., Meel, K.S., Saxena, P.: Quantitative verification of neural networks and its security applications. In: Proceedings of CCS (2019)
5. Biondi, F., Enescu, M.A., Heuser, A., Legay, A., Meel, K.S., Quilbeuf, J.: Scalable approximation of quantitative information flow in programs. In: Dillig, I., Palsberg, J. (eds.) VMCAI 2018. LNCS, vol. 10747, pp. 71–93. Springer, Cham (2018). https://doi.org/10.1007/978-3-319-73721-8_4
6. Chakraborty, S., Meel, K.S., Vardi, M.Y: A scalable and nearly uniform generator of SAT witnesses. In: Sharygina, N., Veith, H. (eds.) CAV 2013. LNCS, vol. 8044, pp. 608–623. Springer, Heidelberg (2013). https://doi.org/10.1007/978-3-642-39799-8_40
7. Chakraborty, S., Meel, K.S., Vardi, M.Y.: A scalable approximate model counter. In: Schulte, C. (ed.) CP 2013. LNCS, vol. 8124, pp. 200–216. Springer, Heidelberg (2013). https://doi.org/10.1007/978-3-642-40627-0_18
8. Chakraborty, S., Meel, K.S., Vardi, M.Y.: Balancing scalability and uniformity in SAT-witness generator. In: Proceedings of DAC, pp. 60:1–60:6 (2014)
9. Chakraborty, S., Meel, K.S., Vardi, M.Y.: Algorithmic improvements in approximate counting for probabilistic inference: from linear to logarithmic SAT calls. In: Proceedings of IJCAI (2016)
10. Chavira, M., Darwiche, A.: Compiling Bayesian networks with local structure. In: IJCAI, vol. 5, pp. 1306–1312 (2005)
11. Duenas-Osorio, L., Meel, K.S., Paredes, R., Vardi, M.Y.: Counting-based reliability estimation for power-transmission grids. In: Proceedings of AAAI (2017)
12. Ermon, S., Gomes, C., Sabharwal, A., Selman, B.: Low-density parity constraints for hashing-based discrete integration. In: Proceedings of ICML (2014)

13. Ermon, S., Gomes, C.P., Sabharwal, A., Selman, B.: Taming the curse of dimensionality: discrete integration by hashing and optimization. In: Proceedings of ICML (2013)
14. Fichte, J.K., Hecher, M., Hamiti, F.: The model counting competition 2020. arXiv preprint arXiv:2012.01323 (2020)
15. Golia, P., Roy, S., Meel, K.S.: Manthan: a data-driven approach for Boolean function synthesis. In: Lahiri, S.K., Wang, C. (eds.) CAV 2020. LNCS, vol. 12225, pp. 611–633. Springer, Cham (2020). https://doi.org/10.1007/978-3-030-53291-8_31
16. Gomes, C.P., Hoffmann, J., Sabharwal, A., Selman, B.: Short XORs for model counting: from theory to practice. In: Marques-Silva, J., Sakallah, K.A. (eds.) SAT 2007. LNCS, vol. 4501, pp. 100–106. Springer, Heidelberg (2007). https://doi.org/10.1007/978-3-540-72788-0_13
17. Gomes, C., Hoffmann, J., Sabharwal, A., Selman, B.: From sampling to model counting, pp. 2293–2299 (2007)
18. Gomes, C.P., Sabharwal, A., Selman, B.: Model counting: a new strategy for obtaining good bounds. In: Proceedings of AAAI (2006)
19. Ivrii, A., Malik, S., Meel, K.S., Vardi, M.Y.: On computing minimal independent support and its applications to sampling and counting. Constraints 21(1) (2016)
20. Kroc, L., Sabharwal, A., Selman, B.: Leveraging belief propagation, backtrack search, and statistics for model counting. In: Perron, L., Trick, M.A. (eds.) CPAIOR 2008. LNCS, vol. 5015, pp. 127–141. Springer, Heidelberg (2008). https://doi.org/10.1007/978-3-540-68155-7_12
21. Lagniez, J.M., Lonca, E., Marquis, P.: Improving model counting by leveraging definability. In: IJCAI, pp. 751–757 (2016)
22. Lagniez, J.M., Lonca, E., Marquis, P.: Definability for model counting. Artif. Intell. 281, 103229 (2020)
23. Meel, K.S., Akshay, S.: Sparse hashing for scalable approximate model counting: theory and practice. In: Proceedings of LICS (2020)
24. Padoa, A.: Essai d'une théorie algébrique des nombres entiers, précédé d'une introduction logique á une théorie déductive quelconque. Bibliothèque du Congrès International de Philosophie 3, 309 (1901)
25. Sang, T., Bearne, P., Kautz, H.: Performing Bayesian inference by weighted model counting. In: Proceedings of AAAI, AAAI 2005, vol. 1, pp. 475–481 (2005)
26. Sharma, S., Roy, S., Soos, M., Meel, K.S.: GANAK: a scalable probabilistic exact model counter. In: IJCAI, vol. 19, pp. 1169–1176 (2019)
27. Soos, M., Gocht, S., Meel, K.S.: Tinted, detached, and lazy CNF-XOR solving and its applications to counting and sampling. In: Lahiri, S.K., Wang, C. (eds.) CAV 2020. LNCS, vol. 12224, pp. 463–484. Springer, Cham (2020). https://doi.org/10.1007/978-3-030-53288-8_22
28. Soos, M., Meel, K.S.: Bird: engineering an efficient CNF-XOR sat solver and its applications to approximate model counting. In: Proceedings of AAAI (2019)
29. Soos, M., Meel, K.S.: Arjun: an efficient independent support computation technique and its applications to counting and sampling. arXiv preprint arXiv:2110.09026 (2021)
30. Stockmeyer, L.: The complexity of approximate counting. In: Proceedings of STOC (1983)
31. Tabajara, L.M., Vardi, M.Y.: Factored Boolean functional synthesis. In: Proceedings of FMCAD, FMCAD 2017, pp. 124–131 (2017)
32. Teuber, S., Weigl, A.: Quantifying software reliability via model-counting. In: Abate, A., Marin, A. (eds.) QEST 2021. LNCS, vol. 12846, pp. 59–79. Springer, Cham (2021). https://doi.org/10.1007/978-3-030-85172-9_4

33. Valiant, L.G.: The complexity of computing the permanent. Theor. Comput. Sci. 8(2), 189–201 (1979)
34. Valiant, L.G.: The complexity of enumeration and reliability problems. SIAM J. Comput. 8(3), 410–421 (1979)
35. Yang, J., Chakraborty, S., Meel, K.S.: Projected model counting: beyond independent support. arXiv preprint arXiv:2110.09171 (2022)

Automata and Applications

Minimization of Automata for Liveness Languages

Bader Abu Radi$^{(\boxtimes)}$ [iD] and Orna Kupferman [iD]

School of Computer Science and Engineering, Hebrew University, Jerusalem, Israel
bader.aburadi@gmail.com, orna@cs.huji.ac.il

Abstract. While the *minimization problem* for deterministic Büchi
word automata is known to be NP-complete, several fundamental problems around it are still open. This includes the complexity of minimzation
for *transition-based* automata, where acceptance is defined with respect
to the set of transitions that a run traverses infinitely often, and minimization for *good-for-games* (GFG) automata, where nondeterminism is
allowed, yet has to be resolved in a way that only depends on the past. Of
special interest in formal verification are *liveness* properties, which state
that something "good" eventually happens. Liveness languages constitute a strict fragment of ω-regular languages, which suggests that minimization of automata recognizing liveness languages may be easier, as
is the case for languages recognizable by weak automata, in particular
safety languages. We define three classes of liveness, and study the minimization problem for automata recognizing languages in the classes. Our
results refer to the basic minimization problem as well as to its extension to transition-based and GFG automata. In some cases, we provide
bounds, and in others we provide connections between the different settings. Thus, our results are of practical interest and also improve our
understanding of the (still very mysterious) minimization problem.

Keywords: Automata on infinite words · Minimization · Complexity ·
Good-for-games automata · Büchi · Liveness

1 Introduction

A prime application of *automata theory* is specification, verification, and synthesis of reactive systems. Since we care about the on-going behavior of nonterminating systems, the automata run on infinite words. Acceptance in such
automata is determined according to the set of states that are visited infinitely
often along the run. In *Büchi* automata (NBWs and DBWs, for nondeterministic
and deterministic Büchi word automata, respectively), the acceptance condition
is a subset α of states, and a run is accepting iff it visits α infinitely often. Dually,
in *co-Büchi* automata (NCWs and DCWs), a run is accepting iff it visits α only
finitely often.

Supported by The Neubauer Foundation of Ph.D Fellowship.

A classical problem in automata theory is *minimization*: the generation of an equivalent automaton with a minimal number of states. For NBWs and NCWs, minimization is PSPACE-complete, as it is for nondeterministic automata on finite words [9]. For DBWs and DCWs, minimization is NP-complete [20]. Thus, the transition to infinite words makes the problem harder. Indeed, for deterministic automata on finite words (DFWs), a minimization algorithm, based on the Myhill-Nerode right congruence [17,18], generates in polynomial time a canonical minimal deterministic automaton.

While [20] solves the question of the complexity of DBW and DCW minimization, several fundamental questions around the problem are still open. This includes the complexity of minimzation for *transition-based* automata and *good-for-games* (GFG) automata.

In transition-based automata, acceptance is defined with respect to the set of transitions that a run traverses infinitely often. In particular, in Büchi automata (tNBWs and tDBWs), the acceptance condition is a subset α of transitions, and a run is required to traverse transitions in α infinitely often, and dually for co-Büchi. Beyond the theoretical interest, there is recently growing use of transition-based automata in practical applications, with evidences they offer a simpler translation of LTL formulas to automata and enable simpler constructions and decision procedures [14].

In GFG automata, nondeterminism is allowed, yet has to be resolved in a way that only depends on the past. Consequently, GFG automata can be used instead of deterministic automata in games whose winning condition is specified by an ω-regular language [5,7,12]. Such games are extensively used in the solution of the *synthesis* problem from LTL or ω-regular specifications. Formally, a nondeterministic automaton $\mathcal{A}$ over an alphabet Σ is GFG if there is a strategy g that maps each finite word $u \in \Sigma^*$ to the transition to be taken after u is read; and following g results in accepting all the words in the language of $\mathcal{A}$. Note that a state q of $\mathcal{A}$ may be reachable via different words, and g may suggest different transitions from q after different words are read. Still, g depends only on the past, namely on the word read so far. Obviously, there exist GFG automata: deterministic ones, or nondeterministic ones that are *determinizable by pruning* (DBP); that is, ones that just add transitions on top of a deterministic automaton. Surprisingly, however, GFG-NBWs need not be DBP [3]. Moreover, the best known determinization construction for GFG-NBWs is quadratic, whereas determinization of GFG-NCWs has a tight exponential bound [10]. Thus, GFG automata on infinite words are more succinct (possibly even exponentially) than deterministic ones. In recent years, we see growing research on GFG automata, their theoretical properties, and applications [2,6,10].

Proving NP-hardness for DBW minimization, Schewe used a reduction from the vertex-cover problem [20]. Essentially[1], given an undirected graph

---

[1] The reduction in [20] is more complicated and involves an additional letter. One of our contributions here is to show that the vertex-cover problem is NP-hard already for a class of graphs for which these complications are not required. Consequently, it is possible to simplify the reduction, and the description above is of the simplified version.

$G = \langle V, E \rangle$, we seek a minimal DBW for the language S_G of words of the form $v_{i_1}^+ \cdot v_{i_2}^+ \cdot v_{i_3}^! \cdots \in V^\omega$, where for all $j \geq 1$, we have that $\{v_{i_j}, v_{i_{j+1}}\} \in E$. We can recognize S_G by an automaton obtained from G by replacing an edge $\{u_1, u_2\}$ by transitions from u_1 to u_2 and from u_2 to u_1, adding self loops to all vertices, labelling each transition by its destination, and requiring a run to traverse infinitely many transitions induced by edges of G. Indeed, such runs correspond to words that traverse an infinite path in G, possibly looping at vertices, but not getting trapped in a self loop, as required by S_G. When, however, the acceptance condition is defined by a set of states, rather than transitions, we need to duplicate some states, and a minimal duplication corresponds to a minimal vertex cover. Consequently, finding a minimal DBW for S_G (or a minimal DCW for its complement) corresponds to finding a minimal vertex cover in G. Clearly, as a tDBW for S_G has the same structure as G, the reduction does not apply to tDBWs or tDCWs. On the other hand, it can be extended to GFG-NBWs and GFG-NCWs [21]. Interestingly, though, for GFG-tNCWs, minimization can be done in PTIME [1]. Thus, the complexity of minimization of tDBWs and tDCWs is still open, and so is the complexity for GFG-tNBWs.

Recall that for languages of finite words, a minimal DFW can be obtained in PTIME by merging of equivalent states. A similar algorithm is valid for determinisitic *weak* automata on infinite words: DBWs in which each strongly connected component is either contained in α or is disjoint from α [15,16]. In particular, *safety properties*, which assert that the system stays within some allowed region, can be recognized by DBWs in which all states are in α, which are a special case of weak automata. This raises the question of finding other natural fragments of ω-regular languages for which minimization could be solved in PTIME.

Of special interest in formal verification are *liveness* properties, which assert that something "good" eventually happens. For example, a process eventually enters its critical section or a grant is given infinitely often. We distinguish between three classes of liveness. Specifically, a language $L \subseteq \Sigma^\omega$ is LIVE1 if it has no "bad prefixes", thus every finite word in Σ^* can be extended to a word in L. Then, L is LIVE2 if $L = \Sigma^* \cdot L$, thus, every finite word in Σ^* can be extended by a word in L to a word in L, or, equivalently, every infinite word that has a suffix in L is also in L. Finally, L is LIVE3 if $L = \infty R$, for some language $R \subseteq \Sigma^*$ of finite words, thus L consists of words with infinitely many disjoint infixes in R. It is not hard to see that the classes are strictly ordered, in the sense that every LIVE3 language is LIVE2, every LIVE2 language is LIVE1, yet implication in the other direction does not hold. Also, the language S_G used for proving NP-hardness in [20] is not a liveness language. Indeed, finite sequences of vertices that do not correspond to a path in G are bad prefixes for S_G.

We study the minimization problem for automata recognizing languages in the three classes. We also consider the dual setting, where we minimize co-Büchi automata for languages that complement liveness languages. Note that while for deterministic automata, dualization of the acceptance condition complements the automaton, thus DBW and tDBW minimization coincides with DCW and tDCW minimization, this is not the case for GFG automata, where complementation should involve also a dualization of the nondeterministic branching mode (see [4] for a study of alternating GFG automata). In particular, as noted above, while minimization of GFG-tNCWs is in PTIME [1], the complexity for GFG-tNBWs is still open.

We first show that Schewe's reduction can be modified so that the vertex-cover problem is reduced to minimization of automata for LIVE1 languages. The main contribution in this part is a characterization of *nice* graphs: graphs for which the vertex-cover problem stays NP-hard yet they enjoy properties that enable us to significantly simplify the languages needed for the reduction. Then, given a nice graph G, we define a LIVE1 language L_G such that finding a minimal vertex-cover for G can be reduced to minimizing a DBW or a GFG-NBW for L_G, or to minimizing a DCW or a GFG-NCW for the complement of L_G. Essentially, while the language S_G does not allow prefixes that do not correspond to paths in G, the language L_G handles attempts to proceed to a vertex that is not connected by an edge the same way S_G handles self loops.

We continue to LIVE2 languages and describe a general scheme for transforming a language L to a LIVE2 language $L^{\#}$ such that minimization of automata for L can be reduced to minimization of automata for $L^{\#}$. Thus, minimization stays NP-hard for LIVE2 languages. Our scheme applies to deterministic and GFG automata, Büchi and co-Büchi, with either state-based or transition-based acceptance. Consequently, while the problem of minimizing tDBWs and GFG-tNBWs is still open, our results imply that its complexity for general ω-regular languages coincides with its complexity for LIVE2 languages. Thus, efforts to find a PTIME algorithm can focus on the LIVE2 fragment.

Finally, we show that the transition from LIVE2 to LIVE3 languages is significant: while minimization of GFG-NCWs that recognize the complement of LIVE2 languages is NP-hard, minimization of GFG-NCWs that recognize the complement of LIVE3 languages can be done in PTIME. We find this result interesting, as we also show that LIVE3 languages maintain the combinatorial richness of GFG automata over deterministic ones. In particular, the exponential succinctness of GFG-NCWs over DCWs [10] applies also for languages whose complements are LIVE3, and the fact that GFG-NBWs need not be DBP [3] is exhibited also for LIVE3 languages. Also, for other classes of automata, the complexity of minimization of LIVE3 languages remains open.

Due to the lack of space, some proofs are omitted and can be found in the full version, in the authors' URLs.

2   Preliminaries

For a finite nonempty alphabet Σ, an infinite *word* $w = \sigma_1 \cdot \sigma_2 \cdots \in \Sigma^\omega$ is an infinite sequence of letters from Σ. A *language* $L \subseteq \Sigma^\omega$ is a set of words. We denote the empty word by ϵ, and the set of finite words over Σ by Σ^*. For an index $i \geq 0$, we use $w[1, i]$ to denote the (possibly empty) prefix $\sigma_1 \cdot \sigma_2 \cdots \sigma_i$ of w. For $1 \leq i \leq j$, we use $w[i, j]$ to denote the infix $\sigma_i \cdot \sigma_{i+1} \cdots \sigma_j$ of w, and use $w[i, \infty]$ to denote the infinite suffix $\sigma_i \cdot \sigma_{i+1} \cdots$ of w. For a set A, we denote its complement by $\overline{A}$. In particular, if $R \subseteq \Sigma^*$ is a language over finite words and $L \subseteq \Sigma^\omega$ is language over infinite words, then $\overline{R} = \Sigma^* \backslash R$ and $\overline{L} = \Sigma^\omega \backslash L$.

2.1 Automata

A *nondeterministic automaton* on infinite words is a tuple $\mathcal{A} = \langle \Sigma, Q, q_0, \delta, \alpha \rangle$, where Σ is an alphabet, Q is a finite set of *states*, $q_0 \in Q$ is an *initial state*, $\delta : Q \times \Sigma \to 2^Q \backslash \emptyset$ is a *transition function*, and α is an *acceptance condition*, to be defined below. For states q and s and a letter $\sigma \in \Sigma$, we say that s is a σ-successor of q if $s \in \delta(q, \sigma)$. If $|\delta(q, \sigma)| = 1$ for every state $q \in Q$ and letter $\sigma \in \Sigma$, then $\mathcal{A}$ is *deterministic*. The transition function δ can be viewed as a transition relation $\Delta \subseteq Q \times \Sigma \times Q$, where for every two states $q, s \in Q$ and letter $\sigma \in \Sigma$, we have that $\langle q, \sigma, s \rangle \in \Delta$ iff $s \in \delta(q, \sigma)$. We define the *size* of $\mathcal{A}$, denoted $|\mathcal{A}|$, as its number of states, thus, $|\mathcal{A}| = |Q|$.

Given an input word $w = \sigma_1 \cdot \sigma_2 \cdots$, a *run* of $\mathcal{A}$ on w is an infinite sequence of states $r = r_0, r_1, r_2, \ldots \in Q^\omega$, such that $r_0 = q_0$, and for all $i \geq 0$, we have $r_{i+1} \in \delta(r_i, \sigma_{i+1})$, i.e., the run starts in the initial state and proceeds according to the transition function. We sometimes view the run $r = r_0, r_1, r_2, \ldots$ on $w = \sigma_1 \cdot \sigma_2 \cdots$ as an infinite sequence of successive transitions $\langle r_0, \sigma_1, r_1 \rangle, \langle r_1, \sigma_2, r_2 \rangle, \ldots \in \Delta^\omega$. We sometimes consider finite runs on finite words. In particular, we sometimes extend δ to sets of states and finite words. Then, $\delta : 2^Q \times \Sigma^* \to 2^Q$ is such that for every $S \in 2^Q$, finite word $u \in \Sigma^*$, and letter $\sigma \in \Sigma$, we have that $\delta(S, \epsilon) = S$, $\delta(S, \sigma) = \bigcup_{s \in S} \delta(s, \sigma)$, and $\delta(S, u \cdot \sigma) = \delta(\delta(S, u), \sigma)$. Thus, $\delta(S, u)$ is the set of states that $\mathcal{A}$ may reach when it reads u from some state in S.

The acceptance condition α determines which runs are "good". We consider *state-based* and *transition-based* automata. Let us start with *state-based* automata. Here, $\alpha \subseteq Q$, and we use the terms α-*states* and $\overline{\alpha}$-*states* to refer to states in α and in $Q \backslash \alpha$, respectively. For a run $r \in Q^\omega$, let $inf(r) \subseteq Q$ be the set of states that r visits infinitely often. Thus, $inf(r) = \{q : q = r_i \text{ for infinitely many } i\text{'s}\}$. In *Büchi* automata, r is *accepting* iff $inf(r) \cap \alpha \neq \emptyset$, thus if r visits states in α infinitely often. In *co-Büchi* automata, r is *accepting* iff $inf(r) \cap \alpha = \emptyset$, thus if r visits states in α only finitely often.

We proceed to *transition-based* automata. There, $\alpha \subseteq \Delta$ and acceptance depends on the set of transitions that are traversed infinitely often during the run. We use the terms α-*transitions* and $\overline{\alpha}$-*transitions* to refer to transitions in α and in $\Delta \backslash \alpha$, respectively. For a run $r \in \Delta^\omega$, we define $inf(r) = \{\langle q, \sigma, s \rangle \in \Delta : q = r_i, \sigma = \sigma_{i+1}, \text{ and } s = r_{i+1} \text{ for infinitely many } i\text{'s}\}$. As expected, in transition-based Büchi automata, r is accepting iff $inf(r) \cap \alpha \neq \emptyset$, and in transition-based co-Büchi automata, r is accepting iff $inf(r) \cap \alpha = \emptyset$. A run that is not accepting is *rejecting*. A word w is accepted by an automaton $\mathcal{A}$ if there is an accepting run of $\mathcal{A}$ on w. The language of $\mathcal{A}$, denoted $L(\mathcal{A})$, is the set of words that $\mathcal{A}$ accepts.

Consider an automaton $\mathcal{A} = \langle \Sigma, Q, q_0, \delta, \alpha \rangle$. For a state $q \in Q$ of $\mathcal{A}$, we define $\mathcal{A}^q = \langle \Sigma, Q, q, \delta, \alpha \rangle$, i.e., $\mathcal{A}^q$ is the automaton obtained from $\mathcal{A}$ by setting the initial state to be q. We say that two states $q, s \in Q$ are *equivalent*, denoted

$q \sim_{\mathcal{A}} s$, if $L(\mathcal{A}^q) = L(\mathcal{A}^s)$. We say that q *is reachable* if there is a word $x \in \Sigma^*$ with $q \in \delta(q_0, x)$, and say that q *is reachable from* s if q is reachable in $\mathcal{A}^s$.

An automaton $\mathcal{A}$ is *good for games* (*GFG*, for short) if its nondeterminism can be resolved based on the past, thus on the prefix of the input word read so far. Formally, $\mathcal{A}$ is *GFG* if there exists a *strategy* $f : \Sigma^* \to Q$ such that the following hold:

1. The strategy f is consistent with the transition function. That is, $f(\epsilon) = q_0$, and for every finite word $u \in \Sigma^*$ and letter $\sigma \in \Sigma$, we have that $f(u \cdot \sigma) \in \delta(f(u), \sigma)$.
2. Following f causes $\mathcal{A}$ to accept all the words in its language. That is, for every infinite word $w = \sigma_1 \cdot \sigma_2 \cdots \in \Sigma^\omega$, if $w \in L(\mathcal{A})$, then the run $f(w[1,0]), f(w[1,1]), f(w[1,2]), \ldots$, which we denote by $f(w)$, is an accepting run of $\mathcal{A}$ on w.

We say that the strategy f *witnesses* $\mathcal{A}$'s GFGness. For an automaton $\mathcal{A}$, we say that a state q of $\mathcal{A}$ is *GFG*, if $\mathcal{A}^q$ is GFG. Note that every deterministic automaton is GFG.

We use three-letter acronyms in $\{\mathrm{D}, \mathrm{N}\} \times \{\mathrm{B}, \mathrm{C}\} \times \{\mathrm{W}\}$ to denote the different automata classes. The first letter stands for the branching mode of the automaton (deterministic or nondeterministic); the second for the acceptance condition type (Büchi or co-Büchi); and the third indicates that we consider automata on words. For transition-based automata, we start the acronyms with the letter "t", and for GFG automata, we write "GFG-" before the acronyms. For example, a GFG-NBW is a state-based GFG Büchi automaton, and a tDCW is a transition-based deterministic co-Büchi automaton.

For a class γ of automata, e.g., $\gamma = $ GFG-NCW or $\gamma = $ tDBW, we say that a language $L \subseteq \Sigma^\omega$ is γ-*recognizable* iff there is an automaton in the class γ that recognizes L. It is known [12,19] that GFG automata are as expressive as deterministic automata of the same acceptance condition, e.g., L is GFG-tNBW recognizable iff L is DBW recognizable.

For a class γ of automata, we say that a γ automaton $\mathcal{A}$ is *minimal* if for every equivalent γ automaton $\mathcal{B}$, namely one with $L(\mathcal{A}) = L(\mathcal{B})$, it holds that $|\mathcal{A}| \leq |\mathcal{B}|$.

2.2   Liveness Languages

For a language $R \subseteq \Sigma^*$ of finite words, we use ∞R to denote the language of infinite words that contain infinitely many disjoint infixes in R. Thus, $w \in \infty R$ iff there are infinitely many indices $i_1 \leq i_1' < i_2 \leq i_2' < \cdots$ such that $w[i_j, i_j'] \in R$, for all $j \geq 1$. Dually, $\neg \infty R$ is the language of infinite words that eventually contain only infixes in $\overline{R}$. Thus, there is an index i such that for all $j' \geq j \geq 0$ we have that $w[i+j, i+j'] \in \overline{R}$. Note that $\overline{\infty R} = \neg \infty R$.

Consider a language $L \subseteq \Sigma^\omega$. We say that a finite word $x \in \Sigma^*$ is a *bad prefix* for L if for all infinite words $y \in \Sigma^\omega$, we have that $x \cdot y \notin L$. Thus, there is no way to extend x to a word in L. Dually, x is a *good prefix* for L if all its extensions to an infinite word result in a word in L, thus $x \cdot y \in L$ for all $y \in \Sigma^\omega$.

We consider three levels of liveness. Consider a nonempty language $L \subseteq \Sigma^\omega$.

1. L is a LIVE1 language if it has no bad prefixes. Formally, for every finite word $x \in \Sigma^*$, there is an infinite word $y \in \Sigma^\omega$ such that $x \cdot y \in L$.
2. L is a LIVE2 language if $L = \Sigma^* \cdot L$. Formally, for every finite word $x \in \Sigma^*$, and infinite word $y \in L$, it holds that $x \cdot y \in L$. Equivalently, every word that has a suffix in L, is in L.
3. L is a LIVE3 language if $L = \infty R$, for some $R \subseteq \Sigma^*$. Thus, L consists of words with infinitely many disjoint infixes in R.

It is not hard to see that LIVE3 $\subseteq$ LIVE2 $\subseteq$ LIVE1. The other direction is not valid. For example, taking $\Sigma = \{a, b\}$, the language $L_1 = a \cdot \Sigma^\omega + \Sigma^* \cdot a \cdot a \cdot \Sigma^\omega$, of words that start with a or contain the infix $a \cdot a$, is LIVE1 and not LIVE2. Indeed, the word $b \cdot a \cdot b^\omega$ is in $(\Sigma^* \cdot L_1) \backslash L_1$. Then, $L_2 = \Sigma^* \cdot a \cdot a \cdot \Sigma^\omega$ is LIVE2 and not LIVE3.

Note that liveness languages need not be DBW-recognizable. For example, the LIVE1 and LIVE2 language $\Sigma^* \cdot b^\omega$ is not DBW-recognizable [13]. As for LIVE3 languages, if R is regular, then ∞R is DBW-recognizable [11].

We also consider languages that complement a liveness language, and say that a language L is a DOOM1 language if $\overline{L}$ is a LIVE1 language, and similarly for DOOM2 and DOOM3 languages.

2.3   Graphs, Nice Graphs, and the Vertex-Cover Problem

We consider undirected graphs $G = \langle V, E \rangle$, with a finite nonempty set V of vertices and a symmetric set $E \subseteq V \times V$ of edges. For simplicity, we assume that G has no loops or parallel edges. For a vertex $u \in V$, let $\eta(u)$ denote the set of u's *neighbors* in G; that is, $\eta(u) = \{v \in V : E(u, v)\}$. Then, $\overline{\eta(u)} = V \backslash \eta(u) = \{v \in V : \neg E(u, v)\}$. Note that since G has no self loops, then $u \in \overline{\eta(u)}$ for all vertices $u \in V$. For a vertex $u \in V$ and an edge $e = \langle x, y \rangle \in E$, we say that e is a *neighbor* of u if it at least one of its endpoints is a neighbor of u, thus $E(u, x)$ or $E(u, y)$.

For two vertices $u, v \in V$, we say that u and v are *separable* if there is an edge that is a neighbor of u but is not a neighbor of v, as well as an edge that is a neighbor of v but is not a neighbor of u. We say that G is *separable* if every two vertices $u, v \in V$ are separable. Then, G is *nice* if it is connected, separable, and for every vertex $u \in V$, there is a vertex v such that $v \neq u$ and $v \in \overline{\eta(u)}$. In particular, every nice graph has at least two vertices.

A set $C \subseteq V$ is a *vertex-cover* of G if each edge in G has at least one endpoint in C; that is, if $E(u, v)$, then $u \in C$ or $v \in C$. In the vertex-cover problem, we are given a graph G and an integer $k \geq 1$, and we have to decide whether G has a vertex-cover of size at most k.

In the rest of this section we prove that the vertex-cover problem is NP-hard already for nice graphs. For this, we analyze the reduction from 3SAT to the vertex-cover problem and argue that we can modify each 3CNF formula φ to an equivalent 3CNF formula φ' such that the graph that the reduction produces from φ' is nice.

Consider a 3CNF Boolean formula φ over the set of variables $X = \{x_1, \ldots, x_n\}$. Let $C = \{c_1, c_2, \ldots, c_m\}$ be the set of clauses in φ, with $c_j = (l_1^j \vee l_2^j \vee l_3^j)$. The standard reduction from satisfiability of 3CNF formulas to the vertex-cover problem generates, given φ, an undirected graph $G_\varphi = \langle V, E \rangle$ that consists of two types of "gadgets". For every variable $x_i \in X$, we have a variable-gadget consisting of two vertices x_i and $\overline{x_i}$, connected by an edge. Then, for each clause $c_j = (l_1 \vee l_2 \vee l_3)$, we have a clause-gadget, which is a triangle with three vertices, $c_{l_1}^j, c_{l_2}^j$, and $c_{l_3}^j$. Each vertex $c_{l_i}^j$ in the clause-gadget is connected by an edge to the literal l_i in its variable-gadget. It is not hard to see that the formula φ is satisfiable iff G_φ has a vertex-cover of size at most $n + 2m$. Indeed, each assignment induces a choice of one vertex from each variable-gadget, this choice covers the edges in the variable gadgets. In addition, we need two vertices to cover the edges in the triangles in the clause gadgets and we can choose these vertices in a way that also covers the edges between the vertex and clause gadgets iff the assignment is satisfying.

Theorem 1. *The vertex-cover problem for nice graphs is NP-hard.*

Proof. Consider a 3CNF formula φ with m clauses over the variables $\{x_1, \ldots, x_n\}$. We assume that every clause in φ includes literals referring to three different variables. Note that otherwise, we can add variables and rewrite φ so that it satisfies this property. We define $\varphi' = \varphi \wedge \bigwedge_{1 \leq i \leq n} (x_i \vee z_1 \vee \neg z_2) \wedge (\neg x_i \vee \neg z_1 \vee z_2) \wedge (x_i \vee \neg z_1 \vee z_2) \wedge (\neg x_i \vee z_1 \vee \neg z_2)$, where z_1 and z_2 are two new variables. It is not hard to see that φ is satisfiable iff φ' is satisfiable. Indeed, a satisfying assignment for φ can be extended to a satisfying assignment for φ' by assigning True to z_1 and z_2. Conversely, as φ' implies φ, then a satisfying assignment for φ' also satisfies φ. Thus, φ is satisfiable iff the graph $G_{\varphi'}$ contains a vertex-cover of size at most $(n+2) + 2(m + 4n)$. In the full version, we prove that $G_{\varphi'}$ is nice. $\qquad\square$

3   Live1 Languages

In this section we study the minimization problem for deterministic and GFG automata recognizing Live1 and Doom1 languages. For a graph $G = \langle V, E \rangle$, we define the ω-regular language L_G over the alphabet V as the set of infinite words of the form

$$v_0 \cdot (\overline{\eta(v_0)})^* \cdot v_1 \cdot (\overline{\eta(v_1)})^* \cdot v_2 \cdot (\overline{\eta(v_2)})^* \cdots ,$$

where for all $i \geq 0$, it holds that $v_{i+1} \in \eta(v_i)$. Thus, a word $w \in L_G$ corresponds to an infinite path $v_0, v_1, v_2, \ldots$ in G, where each vertex v_i in the path contributes to w an infix in $v_i \cdot (\overline{\eta(v_i)})^*$, which is followed by the infix induced by v_{i+1}.

Note that every finite nonempty word $x = u_0 \cdot u_1 \cdot u_2 \cdots \in V^+$ induces a unique finite path in G: the path starts in u_0, and whenever it is in vertex v and the next letter is u_i, the path stays in v if $u_i \notin \eta(v)$ and proceeds to u_i if $u_i \in \eta(v)$. We say that the word x *leads to* vertex v if the path induced by x leads to v. In other words, x leads to v if $x \in v_0 \cdot (\overline{\eta(v_0)})^* \cdot v_1 \cdot (\overline{\eta(v_1)})^* \cdot v_2 \cdot (\overline{\eta(v_2)})^* \cdots v_k \cdot (\overline{\eta(v_k)})^*$, where $v_k = v$ and for all $0 \leq i \leq k - 1$, it holds that $v_{i+1} \in \eta(v_i)$.

Example 1. Consider the graph G appearing in Fig. 1. A nonempty word of the form $(v_2 \cdot v_1)^*$ leads to v_1 and a word of the form $(v_2 \cdot v_1)^* \cdot v_2$ leads to v_2. Accordingly, the word $(v_2 \cdot v_1)^\omega$ is in L_G. All the words of the form $v_4 \cdot (v_2 \cdot v_1)^*$ or $v_4 \cdot (v_2 \cdot v_1)^* \cdot v_2$ lead to v_4, and so the word $v_4 \cdot (v_2 \cdot v_1)^\omega$ is not in L_G.

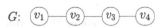

G: v_1 — v_2 — v_3 — v_4

Fig. 1. The graph G.

Lemma 1. *For every nice graph $G = \langle V, E \rangle$, the language L_G is LIVE1.*

Proof. Consider a finite word $x \in V^+$, and assume that x leads to vertex v. Since G is nice, in particular connected and has at least two vertices, we get that there is a vertex $u \in \eta(v)$. Then, the word $x \cdot (u \cdot v)^\omega$ is in L_G.   □

Note that L_G also has no good prefixes. Indeed, for every finite word x, the word $x \cdot u^\omega$ is not in L_G, for every vertex $u \in V$.

3.1 Minimizing Automata for LIVE1 and DOOM1 Languages

In this section we show that minimizing a GFG-NBW or a DBW that recognizes L_G, for a nice graph G, is NP-hard, and so is minimizing a GFG-NCW or a DCW that recognizes $\overline{L_G}$. We conclude that the minimization problem is NP-hard already for LIVE1 and DOOM1 languages.

We start by defining a DBW that recognizes L_G. Consider a nice graph $G = \langle V, E \rangle$. As has been the case with Schewe's language S_G, it is easy to define a tDBW for L_G from G by replacing each edge $\langle u_1, u_2 \rangle$ by a u_2-transition from u_1 to u_2, adding to each state v a self-loop labeled by all the letters in $\overline{\eta(v)}$, and requiring a run to traverse infinitely many transitions induced by edges of G. When considering DBWs, we define, for a subset of vertices $S \subseteq V$, the DBW $\mathcal{A}_{G,S} = \langle V, \{q_0\} \cup (V \times \{0\}) \cup (S \times \{1\}), q_0, \delta, \alpha \rangle$, where $\alpha = S \times \{1\}$, and δ is defined as follows (see Example 2): First, for all $u \in V$, we have $\delta(q_0, u) = \langle u, 0 \rangle$. Then, for all $u \in V$ and $v \in \overline{\eta(u)}$, we have $\delta(\langle u, 0 \rangle, v) = \langle u, 0 \rangle$. In addition, if $u \in S$, then $\delta(\langle u, 1 \rangle, v) = \langle u, 0 \rangle$. Finally, for all $u \in V$ and $v \in \eta(u)$, if $v \in S$, then $\delta(\langle u, 0 \rangle, v) = \langle v, 1 \rangle$, and if $v \notin S$, then $\delta(\langle u, 0 \rangle, v) = \langle v, 0 \rangle$. In addition, if $u \in S$, then $\delta(\langle u, 1 \rangle, v) = \delta(\langle u, 0 \rangle, v)$.

Thus, for every vertex $v \notin S$, the DBW $\mathcal{A}_{G,S}$ includes a "0-state" $\langle v, 0 \rangle$, and for every vertex $v \in S$, it includes both a "0-state" $\langle v, 0 \rangle$ and a "1-state" $\langle v, 1 \rangle$. The 0-state $\langle v, 0 \rangle$ has a self-loop labeled by letters in $\overline{\eta(v)}$. Reading a letter $u \in \eta(v)$ from $\langle v, 0 \rangle$ or from $\langle v, 1 \rangle$, the DBW moves to $\langle u, 0 \rangle$ if $u \notin S$ and moves to $\langle u, 1 \rangle$ if $u \in S$. The 1-state $\langle v, 1 \rangle$ does not have a self loop, and rather it moves to $\langle v, 0 \rangle$ with letters in $\overline{\eta(v)}$. As $\alpha = S \times \{1\}$, the run of $\mathcal{A}_{G,S}$ is accepting iff the path induced by the input word traverses infinitely many edges with endpoints in S. Hence, $\mathcal{A}_{G,S}$ captures infinitely many traversals of edges of G iff the set S is a vertex-cover of G. Formally, we have the following (see proof in the full version).

Lemma 2. $L(\mathcal{A}_{G,S}) \subseteq L_G$, and $L_G \subseteq L(\mathcal{A}_{G,S})$ iff S is a vertex-cover of G.

Example 2. Consider the graph $G = \langle\{v_1, v_2, v_3\}, E\rangle$, appearing in Fig. 2. Note that G is not nice, yet L_G is LIVE1. For the set $S = \{v_1, v_3\}$, the DBW $\mathcal{A}_{G,S}$ appears in Fig. 3.

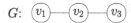

G:

Fig. 2. The graph G.

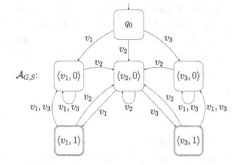

Fig. 3. The DBW $\mathcal{A}_{G,S}$.

While $\mathcal{A}_{G,S}$, for a minimal vertex cover S, is a natural candidate for a minimal DBW that recognizes L_G, a general result about minimization should consider arbitrary DBWs and GFG-NBWs for the language. We continue and specify properties of such automata. Consider a nice graph $G = \langle V, E\rangle$. Let $\mathcal{A} = \langle V, Q, q_0, \delta, \alpha\rangle$ be a GFG-NBW that recognizes the language L_G. For a vertex $v \in V$ and a state $q \in Q$, we say that q is a v-state if q is reachable from q_0 upon reading a finite nonempty word that leads to v. In particular, all the v-successors of q_0 are v-states.

Proposition 1. *For every GFG-NBW $\mathcal{A} = \langle V, Q, q_0, \delta, \alpha\rangle$ that recognizes the language L_G, the following hold: (1) For every vertex $v \in V$, all the v-states are equivalent. (2) For every two vertices $u \neq v \in V$, the u-states are not equivalent to the v-states. (3) The initial state q_0 is not a v-state, for all vertices $v \in V$. (4) $|\{q \in Q\backslash\alpha : q$ is av-state for some vertex $v \in V\}| \geq |V|$; that is, the number of v-states not in α is at least $|V|$. (5) For every edge $\langle u, v\rangle \in E$, there is a v-state or a u-state in α.*

Using the properties in Proposition 1 (see proof in the full version), we can argue that a nice graph G has a vertex cover of size at most $k \geq 1$ iff the DBW $\mathcal{A}_{G,V}$, which recognizes L_G, has an equivalent GFG-NBW or DBW with at most $|V| + k + 1$ states. Hence, we can conclude with the following (see proof in the full version).

Theorem 2. *The minimization problem is NP-hard already for DBWs and GFG-NBWs that recognize LIVE1 languages.*

We continue to DCWs and GFG-NCWs that recognize DOOM1 languages. For DCWs, NP-hardness for minimization follows immediately from Theorem 2. For GFG-NCWs, we have to carefully examine the proof of Proposition 1 and see that it stays valid in the dual setting. In the full version we describe the proposition and its proof for the co-Büchi case, as well as its use in proving the following, namely the co-Büchi counterpart of Theorem 2.

Theorem 3. *The minimization problem is NP-hard already for DCWs and GFG-NCWs that recognize* DOOM1 *languages.*

4   LIVE2 **Languages**

In this section, we study minimization for LIVE2 and DOOM2 languages. Note that the language L_G used in Sect. 3 is not LIVE2. To see this, consider the graph G from Example 1. Note that the word $w = v_4 \cdot (v_2 \cdot v_1)^\omega \in V^* \cdot L_G$ has the suffix $(v_2 \cdot v_1)^\omega \in L_G$, yet $w \notin L_G$. In fact, for every nice graph G, we have that L_G is not LIVE2. Indeed, every nice graph G has at least two vertices u and v. Then, as u and v are separable, there is an edge $\langle u_1, u_2 \rangle \in E$ that is a neighbor of u but not a neighbor of v. The word $w = v \cdot (u_1 \cdot u_2)^\omega \in V^* \cdot L_G$ has the suffix $(u_1 \cdot u_2)^\omega \in L_G$, yet $w \notin L_G$.

4.1   **Minimizing DBWs and GFG-NBWs for** LIVE2 **Languages**

In this section, we show that minimizing DBWs and GFG-NBWs that recognize LIVE2 languages is NP-hard.

The idea behind our proof is as follows. We define an operation on ω-regular languages, such that for every language $L \subseteq \Sigma^\omega$, and letter $\# \notin \Sigma$, the operation constructs a language $L^\# \subseteq (\Sigma \cup \{\#\})^\omega$ that is LIVE2. Then, we define two operations on automata. The first is applied to a DBW $\mathcal{A}$ over the alphabet Σ and it constructs a DBW $\mathcal{A}^\#$ over the alphabet $\Sigma \cup \{\#\}$, such that $L(\mathcal{A}^\#) = L(\mathcal{A})^\#$. The second operation is applied to a GFG-NBW $\mathcal{A}^\#$ over the alphabet $\Sigma \cup \{\#\}$, it constructs a GFG-NBW $\mathcal{A}$ over the alphabet Σ, and if $L(\mathcal{A}^\#) = L^\#$ for some language $L \subseteq \Sigma^\omega$, then $L(\mathcal{A}) = L$. Moreover, the construction preserves determinization. The blow-up in both constructions is such that when we take L to be the language L_G from Sect. 3.1, we can replace the reduction there by a reduction that seeks minimal automata for the language $L_G^\#$.

We first describe the operation on ω-regular languages. For $L \subseteq \Sigma^\omega$, let

$$L^\# = ((\Sigma \cup \{\#\})^* \cdot \# \cdot L) \cup (\infty \#).$$

Thus, $L^\#$ is defined over the alphabet $\Sigma \cup \{\#\}$, and it consists of all infinite words that either have a suffix of the form $\# \cdot L$ or contain infinitely many $\#$'s. It is not hard to see that $L^\# = (\Sigma \cup \{\#\})^* \cdot L^\#$, thus $L^\#$ is LIVE2.

We continue with the operations on automata.

Theorem 4. *Given a DBW $\mathcal{A}$ over Σ such that the initial state of $\mathcal{A}$ has no incoming transitions, we can construct a DBW $\mathcal{A}^\#$ over $\Sigma \cup \{\#\}$ such that the following hold: (1) $L(\mathcal{A}^\#) = L(\mathcal{A})^\#$. (2) If $L(\mathcal{A})$ is LIVE1, then $|\mathcal{A}^\#| = |\mathcal{A}| + 1$. Otherwise, $|\mathcal{A}^\#| = |\mathcal{A}|$.*

Proof. Let $\mathcal{A} = \langle \Sigma, Q, q_0, \delta, \alpha \rangle$. If $L(\mathcal{A})$ is LIVE1, then we define $\mathcal{A}^{\#} = \langle \Sigma \cup \{\#\}, Q \cup \{q_{\#}^0\}, q_{\#}^0, \delta_{\#}, \alpha_{\#} \rangle$, for $q_{\#}^0 \notin Q$, and a transition function $\delta_{\#}$ defined as follows (see an example in the full version). For every $s \in Q$ and $\sigma \in \Sigma$, we have $\delta_{\#}(s, \sigma) = \delta(s, \sigma)$ and $\delta_{\#}(s, \#) = q_0$. Then, for the state $q_{\#}^0$, we have that $\delta(q_{\#}^0, \sigma) = q_{\#}^0$ for all $\sigma \in \Sigma$, and $\delta(q_{\#}^0, \#) = q_0$. Thus, $\mathcal{A}^{\#}$ is obtained from $\mathcal{A}$ by adding a new state $q_{\#}^0$ that has a Σ-labeled self-loop that goes with $\#$ to the state q_0, to which we move upon reading $\#$ from all states. In addition, $\alpha_{\#} = \alpha \cup \{q_0\}$.

If $L(\mathcal{A})$ is not LIVE1, then $L(\mathcal{A})$ has at least one bad prefix, and so $\mathcal{A}$ must contain a state q with $L(\mathcal{A}^q) = \emptyset$. We assume w.l.o.g that q is a rejecting sink in $\mathcal{A}$, and define $\mathcal{A}^{\#}$ as above, except that instead of defining the state $q_{\#}^0$ as a new state, we define $q_{\#}^0 = q$. Note that also in this case, the initial state $q_{\#}^0$ has a Σ-labeled self-loop and a $\#$-transition to q_0.

In the full version, we prove that $\mathcal{A}^{\#}$ satisfies the two properties. $\qquad\square$

We continue to the reverse operation, where we start with a GFG-NBW.

Theorem 5. *Given a GFG-NBW $\mathcal{A}^{\#}$ over $\Sigma \cup \{\#\}$ such that $L(\mathcal{A}^{\#}) = L^{\#}$ for some $L \subseteq \Sigma^{\omega}$, we can construct a GFG-NBW $\mathcal{A}$ over Σ, such that the following hold: (1) $\mathcal{A}$ recognizes L. (2) If $\mathcal{A}^{\#}$ is determinstic, then so is $\mathcal{A}$. (3) If L is LIVE1, then $|\mathcal{A}| \leq |\mathcal{A}^{\#}| - 1$. Otherwise, $|\mathcal{A}| \leq |\mathcal{A}^{\#}|$.*

Proof. Let $\mathcal{A}^{\#} = \langle \Sigma \cup \{\#\}, Q, q_0, \delta, \alpha \rangle$, and let $f : (\Sigma \cup \{\#\})^* \to Q$ be a strategy witnessing the GFGness of $\mathcal{A}^{\#}$. We obtain $\mathcal{A}$ from $\mathcal{A}^{\#}$ by removing all $\#$-transitions and choosing $q_{\#} = f(\#)$ to be its initial state. Clearly, $\mathcal{A}$ is over Σ and determinization of $\mathcal{A}^{\#}$ is preserved in $\mathcal{A}$. In the full version, we prove that $\mathcal{A}$ is GFG and recognizes L. Moreover, if L is LIVE1, then we can remove a state from $\mathcal{A}$ and get an equivalent automaton, resulting in an automaton with at most $|\mathcal{A}^{\#}| - 1$ states. Essentially, the strategy $g : \Sigma^* \to Q$ that witnesses the GFGness of $\mathcal{A}$ is such that for all $x \in \Sigma^*$, we have $g(x) = f(\# \cdot x)$. $\qquad\square$

We can now use the operations in order to extend the reduction from Sect. 3.1 to LIVE2 languages. Essentially (see proof in the full version), we show that a nice graph $G = \langle V, E \rangle$ has a vertex cover of size at most $k \geq 1$ iff the DBW $\mathcal{A}_{G,V}^{\#}$, namely the DBW obtained by applying the construction from Theorem 4 on the DBW $\mathcal{A}_{G,V}$ from Sect. 3.1, has an equivalent GFG-NBW or DBW with at most $|V| + k + 2$ states.

Theorem 6. *The minimization problem is NP-hard for DBWs and GFG-NBWs that recognize LIVE2 languages.*

4.2   Minimizing DCWs and GFG-NCWs for DOOM2 Languages

We continue to co-Büchi automata for DOOM2 languages. As has been the case with LIVE1 languages, Theorem 6 implies that the minimization problem for DCWs that recognize DOOM2 languages is NP-hard, yet does not imply hardness of minimizing GFG-NCWs that recognize DOOM2 languages. Also, while

Theorem 4 considers DBWs and can be dualized, Theorem 5 considers GFG-NBWs, and thus its dualization requires a proof (see the full version):

Theorem 7. *Given a GFG-NCW $\mathcal{A}^{\#}$ over $\Sigma \cup \{\#\}$ such that $L(\mathcal{A}^{\#}) = \overline{L^{\#}}$ for some $L \subseteq \Sigma^{\omega}$, we can construct a GFG-NCW $\mathcal{A}$ over Σ such that the following hold: (1) $\mathcal{A}$ recognizes $\overline{L}$. (2) If $\mathcal{A}^{\#}$ is determinstic, then so is $\mathcal{A}$. (3) If $\overline{L}$ is* DOOM1, *then $|\mathcal{A}| \leq |\mathcal{A}^{\#}| - 1$. Otherwise, $|\mathcal{A}| \leq |\mathcal{A}^{\#}|$.*

We can now use a reduction similar to the one in Theorem 6 and prove that a nice graph G has a vertex-cover of size at most $k \geq 1$ iff the DCW $\widetilde{\mathcal{A}}^{\#}_{G,V}$, which dualizes $\mathcal{A}^{\#}_{G,V}$, has an equivalent GFG-NCW of size at most $|V| + k + 2$. See proof in the full version.

Theorem 8. *The minimization problem is NP-hard for DCWs and GFG-NCWs that recognize* DOOM2 *languages.*

4.3 Minimizing Automata with Transition-Based Acceptance for LIVE2 Languages

In this section, we show that minimizing GFG-tNBWs or tDBWs recognizing LIVE2 languages is not easier than minimizing GFG-tNBWs or tDBWs, respectively, recognizing general languages. Thus, while the complexity of minimization of tDBWs and GFG-tNBWs is still open, it is sufficient to restrict attention to transition-based Büchi automata recognizing LIVE2 languages.

The idea of our proof is to modify the constructions used in Sect. 4.1 to GFG-tNBWs. Note that while Theorem 5 already considers GFG-NBWs, and thus the extension only has to adjust the type of acceptance, which is easy, Theorem 4 considers deterministic automata, and so the extension is more involved. In particular, one has to show how a function that witnesses the GFGness of $\mathcal{A}$ induces a strategy that witnesses the GFGness of $\mathcal{A}^{\#}$. Formally, we have the following (see proof in the full version).

Theorem 9. *Given a GFG-tNBW $\mathcal{A}$ over Σ, we can construct a GFG-tNBW $\mathcal{A}^{\#}$ over $\Sigma \cup \{\#\}$ such that the following hold: (1) $L(\mathcal{A}^{\#}) = L(\mathcal{A})^{\#}$. (2) If $\mathcal{A}$ is determinsitic, then so is $\mathcal{A}^{\#}$. (3) If $L(\mathcal{A})$ is* LIVE1, *then $|\mathcal{A}^{\#}| = |\mathcal{A}| + 1$. Otherwise, $|\mathcal{A}^{\#}| = |\mathcal{A}|$.*

We can now reduce minimization of a general GFG-tNBW to minimization of a GFG-tNBW for a LIVE2 language as follows. Given a GFG-tNBW $\mathcal{A}$ and an integer $k \geq 1$, our reduction returns the GFG-tNBW $\mathcal{A}^{\#}$ and the integer k' such that $k' = k + 1$ if $L(\mathcal{A})$ is LIVE1, and $k' = k$ otherwise (note that the latter condition can be checked in polynomial time). In the full version we prove that $\mathcal{A}$ has an equivalent GFG-tNBW of size at most k iff $\mathcal{A}^{\#}$ has an equivalent GFG-tNBW of size at most k', and similarly for tDBWs. Hence, we can conclude with the following.

Theorem 10. *Minimizing GFG-tNBWs or tDBWs recognizing* LIVE2 *languages is not easier than minimizing general GFG-tNBWs or tDBWs, respectively.*

We continue to tDCWs and show that the reduction from Theorem 10 implies that minimizing tDCWs recognizing DOOM2 languages is not easier than minimizing tDCWs recognizing general languages. Hence, we can conclude with the following (see proof in the full version):

Theorem 11. *Minimizing tDCWs recognizing* DOOM2 *languages is not easier than minimizing general tDCWs.*

5   LIVE3 Languages

Recall that minimization of GFG-NCWs is NP-hard [21]. Moreover, by Theorem 8, NP-hardness applies already to DOOM2 languages. Our main result in this section is that the transition from LIVE2 to LIVE3 languages is significant: minimization of GFG-NCWs that recognize DOOM3 languages can be done in PTIME. We first argue that our result is surprising, in the sense that LIVE3 and DOOM3 languages maintain the combinatorial richness of GFG automata. Specifically, recall that GFG-NBWs and GFG-NCWs may not be determinizable by pruning (DBP), and GFG-NCWs may be exponentially more succinct than DCWs [3,8,10]. We show that these advantages of GFG automata are valid already for LIVE3 and DOOM3 languages. For the co-Büchi case, the languages used in [8,10] are already DOOM3. For the Büchi case, our example is new.

Theorem 12. *There are GFG-NBWs and GFG-NCWs for* LIVE3 *and* DOOM3 *languages that are not DBP. Moreover, GFG-NCWs for* DOOM3 *languages may be exponentially more succinct than DCWs.*

Proof. It was shown [8,10] that GFG-NCWs may be exponentially more succinct than DCWs. It is not hard to see that the languages used there are DOOM3. The latter implies also that GFG-NCWs recognizing DOOM3 languages need not be DBP. Also, while the results there are for automata with transition-based acceptance, they apply also in the state-based setting. Indeed, transforming an NCW to an equivalent tNCW involves no blow-up, and transforming a tNCW to an NCW at most doubles the state-space. Both transformation preserve determinism, GFGness, and DBPness.

For LIVE3 languages and GFG-tNBWs, consider the tNBW $\mathcal{A} = \langle \Sigma, Q, q_0, \delta, \alpha \rangle$ appearing in Fig. 4 (in the figure, dashed transitions are α-transitions). Let $R_x = a^+ \cdot x \cdot (x + y)^*$, $R_y = a^+ \cdot y \cdot (x+y)^*$, and $R = (R_x \cdot R_x + R_y \cdot R_y)$. In the full version, we prove that $\mathcal{A}$ recognizes the LIVE3 language ∞R, is GFG, yet not DBP. In addition, we show that by duplicating the state space of a GFG-tNBW $\mathcal{A}$ we can obtain an equivalent GFG-NBW $\mathcal{A}'$ such that $\mathcal{A}$ is DBP iff $\mathcal{A}'$ is DBP. Thus, the example applies also to GFG-NBWs.   □

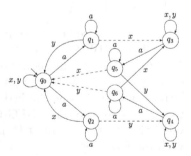

Fig. 4. The GFG-tNBW $\mathcal{A}$ for ∞R.

We continue and show that minimizing GFG-NCWs that recognize DOOM3 languages can in done in PTIME. The main idea behind the minimization process is a construction that given a GFG-tNCW for a DOOM3 language L, returns a GFG-NCW for L with one additional state, along with an observation that for every (non-trivial) DOOM3 language L, a minimal GFG-NCW for L must be strictly bigger than a minimal GFG-tNCW for L. Thus, it is possible to use minimization of GFG-tNCWs, which can be done in PTIME [1].

Theorem 13. *The minimization problem for GFG-NCWs recognizing* DOOM3 *languages can be solved in PTIME.*

Proof. Consider a GFG-NCW $\mathcal{A} = \langle \Sigma, Q, q_0, \delta, \alpha \rangle$ that recognizes a language of the form $\neg\infty R$, for some $R \subseteq \Sigma^*$, and consider the NCW $\mathcal{B}$ that is obtained from $\mathcal{A}$ as follows (see Example 3).

1. Let $\mathcal{U} = \langle \Sigma, Q_\mathcal{U}, q_\mathcal{U}^0, \Delta_\mathcal{U}, \alpha_\mathcal{U} \rangle$ be the GFG-tNCW obtained by applying the minimization algorithm of [1] on the GFG-tNCW obtained from $\mathcal{A}$ by defining all the transitions that leave an α-state as α-transitions.
2. If $L(\mathcal{A})$ is trivial, then $\mathcal{B}$ can be defined as a one state DCW that is equivalent to $\mathcal{A}$. Otherwise, $\mathcal{B} = \langle \Sigma, Q_\mathcal{U} \cup \{s\}, q_\mathcal{U}^0, \Delta_\mathcal{B}, \alpha_\mathcal{B} \rangle$, where $\alpha_\mathcal{B} = \{s\}$ and $\Delta_\mathcal{B} = (\Delta_\mathcal{U} \backslash \alpha_\mathcal{U}) \cup \{\langle q, \sigma, s \rangle : \text{ there exists } q' \in Q_\mathcal{U} \text{ such that } \langle q, \sigma, q' \rangle \in \alpha_\mathcal{U}\} \cup (\{s\} \times \Sigma \times Q_\mathcal{U})$. Thus, $\mathcal{B}$ is obtained from $\mathcal{U}$ by adding the new state s, which is the only state in $\alpha_\mathcal{B}$, redirecting all the $\alpha_\mathcal{U}$-transitions of $\mathcal{U}$ to s, and adding σ-transitions from s to all the states of $\mathcal{U}$, for all $\sigma \in \Sigma$.

In the full version we show that after applying a simple preprocessing step, we can modify $\mathcal{A}$ so that it satisfies some simple syntactic and semantic properties. Then, we prove that $\mathcal{B}$ is a GFG-NCW for $L(\mathcal{A})$. Finally, a minimal GFG-tNCW $\mathcal{U}$ recognizing a non-trivial DOOM3 language, cannot have states such that all cycles through them traverse transitions in $\alpha_\mathcal{U}$. We show that this implies that a minimal equivalent GFG-NCW must be strictly bigger than a minimal GFG-tNCW, which implies the minimality of $\mathcal{B}$.   □

Example 3. Consider the tNCW $\mathcal{U}$ below. The dashed transitions are α-transitions. The tNCW $\mathcal{U}$ recognizes the DOOM3 language $L = \neg\infty(a \cdot (a+b)^* \cdot b)$, consisting of words with finitely many a's or finitely many b's. It is not hard to see that by pruning out the α-self-loops, we get an equivalent tDCW, thus $\mathcal{U}$ is DBP, in particular GFG. In addition, as there is no GFG-tNCW recognizing L with a single state, then $\mathcal{U}$ is a minimal GFG-tNCW. The GFG-NCW $\mathcal{B}$ is obtained form $\mathcal{U}$ by adding a new state s, directing the α-transitions to s, and nondeterministically branching from s to all states, with all letters.

References

1. Abu Radi, B., Kupferman, O.: Minimizing GFG transition-based automata. In: Proceedings of 46th International Colloquium on Automata, Languages, and Programming. LIPIcs, vol. 132, pp. 100:1–100:16. Schloss Dagstuhl - Leibniz-Zentrum fuer Informatik (2019)
2. Abu Radi, B., Kupferman, O., Leshkowitz, O.: A hierarchy of nondeterminism. In: 46th International Symposium on Mathematical Foundations of Computer Science. LIPIcs, vol. 202, pp. 85:1–85:21 (2021)
3. Boker, U., Kuperberg, D., Kupferman, O., Skrzypczak, M.: Nondeterminism in the presence of a diverse or unknown future. In: Fomin, F.V., Freivalds, R., Kwiatkowska, M., Peleg, D. (eds.) ICALP 2013. LNCS, vol. 7966, pp. 89–100. Springer, Heidelberg (2013). https://doi.org/10.1007/978-3-642-39212-2_11
4. Boker, U., Lehtinen, K.: Good for games automata: from nondeterminism to alternation. In: Proceedings of 30th International Conference on Concurrency Theory. LIPIcs, vol. 140, pp. 19:1–19:16. Schloss Dagstuhl - Leibniz-Zentrum für Informatik (2019)
5. Colcombet, T.: The theory of stabilisation monoids and regular cost functions. In: Albers, S., Marchetti-Spaccamela, A., Matias, Y., Nikoletseas, S., Thomas, W. (eds.) ICALP 2009. LNCS, vol. 5556, pp. 139–150. Springer, Heidelberg (2009). https://doi.org/10.1007/978-3-642-02930-1_12
6. Faran, R., Kupferman, O.: On (I/O)-aware good-for-games automata. In: Hung, D.V., Sokolsky, O. (eds.) ATVA 2020. LNCS, vol. 12302, pp. 161–178. Springer, Cham (2020). https://doi.org/10.1007/978-3-030-59152-6_9
7. Henzinger, T.A., Piterman, N.: Solving games without determinization. In: Ésik, Z. (ed.) CSL 2006. LNCS, vol. 4207, pp. 395–410. Springer, Heidelberg (2006). https://doi.org/10.1007/11874683_26
8. Iosti, S., Kuperberg, D.: Eventually safe languages. In: Hofman, P., Skrzypczak, M. (eds.) DLT 2019. LNCS, vol. 11647, pp. 192–205. Springer, Cham (2019). https://doi.org/10.1007/978-3-030-24886-4_14
9. Jiang, T., Ravikumar, B.: Minimal NFA problems are hard. SIAM J. Comput. **22**(6), 1117–1141 (1993)
10. Kuperberg, D., Skrzypczak, M.: On determinisation of good-for-games automata. In: Halldórsson, M.M., Iwama, K., Kobayashi, N., Speckmann, B. (eds.) ICALP 2015. LNCS, vol. 9135, pp. 299–310. Springer, Heidelberg (2015). https://doi.org/10.1007/978-3-662-47666-6_24
11. Kupferman, O., Leshkowitz, O.: On repetition languages. In: 45th International Symposium on Mathematical Foundations of Computer Science. Leibniz International Proceedings in Informatics (LIPIcs) (2020)
12. Kupferman, O., Safra, S., Vardi, M.: Relating word and tree automata. Ann. Pure Appl. Logic **138**(1–3), 126–146 (2006)
13. Landweber, L.: Decision problems for ω-automata. Math. Syst. Theory **3**, 376–384 (1969)
14. Li, W., Kan, S., Huang, Z.: A better translation from LTL to transition-based generalized Büchi automata. IEEE Access **5**, 27081–27090 (2017)
15. Löding, C.: Efficient minimization of deterministic weak ω-automata. Inf. Process. Lett. **79**(3), 105–109 (2001)
16. Muller, D., Saoudi, A., Schupp, P.E.: Weak alternating automata give a simple explanation of why most temporal and dynamic logics are decidable in exponential time. In: Proceedings of 3rd IEEE Symposium on Logic in Computer Science, pp. 422–427 (1988)

17. Myhill, J.: Finite automata and the representation of events. Technical report WADD TR-57-624, pp. 112–137. Wright Patterson AFB, Ohio (1957)
18. Nerode, A.: Linear automaton transformations. Proc. Am. Math. Soc. **9**(4), 541–544 (1958)
19. Niwiński, D., Walukiewicz, I.: Relating hierarchies of word and tree automata. In: Morvan, M., Meinel, C., Krob, D. (eds.) STACS 1998. LNCS, vol. 1373, pp. 320–331. Springer, Heidelberg (1998). https://doi.org/10.1007/BFb0028571
20. Schewe, S.: Beyond Hyper-Minimisation–Minimising DBAs and DPAs is NP-complete. In: Proceedings of 30th Conference on Foundations of Software Technology and Theoretical Computer Science. Leibniz International Proceedings in Informatics (LIPIcs), vol. 8, pp. 400–411 (2010)
21. Schewe, S.: Minimising good-for-games automata is NP-complete. In: Proceedings of 40th Conference on Foundations of Software Technology and Theoretical Computer Science. LIPIcs, vol. 182, pp. 56:1–56:13. Schloss Dagstuhl - Leibniz-Zentrum für Informatik (2020)

Temporal Causality in Reactive Systems

Norine Coenen[1], Bernd Finkbeiner[1], Hadar Frenkel[1],
Christopher Hahn[2], Niklas Metzger[1], and Julian Siber[1]($\boxtimes$)

[1] CISPA Helmholtz Center for Information Security, Saarbrücken, Germany
{norine.coenen,finkbeiner,hadar.frenkel,niklas.metzger,
julian.siber}@cispa.de
[2] Stanford University, Stanford, USA
hahn@cs.stanford.edu

Abstract. Counterfactual reasoning is an approach to infer what causes an observed effect by analyzing the hypothetical scenarios where a suspected cause is not present. The seminal works of Halpern and Pearl have provided a workable definition of counterfactual causality for finite settings. In this paper, we propose an approach to check causality that is tailored to reactive systems, i.e., systems that interact with their environment over a possibly infinite duration. We define causes and effects as trace properties which characterize the input and observed output behavior, respectively. We then instantiate our definitions for ω-regular properties and give automata-based constructions for our approach. Checking that an ω-regular property qualifies as a cause can then be encoded as a hyperproperty model-checking problem.

1 Introduction

Causality plays an increasingly important role in computer science, e.g., to explain the behavior of a system [3,4,7,9], to establish accountability in multi-agent systems [10], or to solve challenging algorithmic problems [2,21]. These approaches commonly draw upon the rich philosophical literature that has laid the foundation for *counterfactual reasoning* [19,23], a method of establishing causal relationships between events. According to this line of reasoning, a cause is an event such that, if it had not happened, the effect would not have happened either. A rigorous formalization of counterfactual causality has been proposed by Halpern and Pearl [16]. This formalization is first and foremost concerned with models that can be described by a finite set of variables. When naively applying it to reactive systems that interact with their environment continuously, however, the analysis may infer that an infinite number of events (variable valuation at time step) are causes for an observed effect, falling short of providing the intended comprehensible explanation [17].

In this paper, we therefore propose an approach to causal analysis in reactive systems that provides a symbolic description of causes. We define counterfactual

This work was funded by DFG grant 389792660 as part of TRR 248 – CPEC and by the German Israeli Foundation (GIF) Grant No. I-1513-407./2019.

A. Bouajjani et al. (Eds.): ATVA 2022, LNCS 13505, pp. 208–224, 2022.
https://doi.org/10.1007/978-3-031-19992-9_13

causality on the basis of trace properties (Sect. 4), i.e., causes are properties of
a given input sequence, and effects are properties of the corresponding output
sequence, and apply this definition to ω-regular properties to obtain concrete
automata-based constructions (Sect. 5). As one of our building blocks, we adapt
counterfactual automata [9] so they generate all relevant counterfactual traces in
our setting. Our definitions are sufficiently general to be instantiated by a variety
of temporal logics, such as LTL [25] or QPTL [27]. This general approach allows
us to leverage the significant previous work on temporal logics and for the usual
trade-off between expressiveness and decidability.

Our notion of causality is an *actual* kind of causality in the spirit of Halpern
and Pearl [16]. This means we provide a precise description of the temporal
behavior responsible for the effect on a given, *actual trace* of the reactive system.
This actual trace can, for example, be provided as a counterexample by a model
checker, where the effect then is the violation of the specification. We define
what it means to *intervene* on the cause property of an actual trace, i.e., how to
modify the trace such that the property is not satisfied anymore, but the resulting
counterfactual trace is still sufficiently close to the actual trace to comply with
the closest possible worlds principle [23]. We then further allow for *contingencies*
as introduced by Halpern and Pearl [16], to isolate the exact causal behavior in
case of preemption of other potential causes.

Previous approaches to provide symbolic descriptions of counterfactual
causes use an event-based logic [6,22], which allows reasoning about the order
of events, but cannot, e.g., specify at which time step a causal input occurs. In
contrast, our framework is only limited by the expressiveness of the logic used to
describe the causal trace properties. We study a decidable instantiation of our
definitions with Quantified Propositional Temporal Logic (QPTL), an extension
of LTL with quantified atomic propositions. Causes can be identified as a temporal property (see Sect. 3 for an example). Moreover, the event-based approaches
are restricted to finitely observable effects [22] or define a system-level causality
that does not consider the causal dependencies on a given, actual trace [6]. In
comparison, our approach allows for a significantly more precise description of
the temporal causal behavior on an observed system trace.

As an intriguing theoretical result, we show that when a candidate cause for
an effect is given as a trace property, checking whether it is indeed the actual
cause on a trace of a system cannot be stated as a trace property, which formalizes previous observations on counterfactual causality [10]. The result motivates
us to consider causality as a hyperproperty [8] in our approach. In particular, we
show that verifying ω-regular causality on lasso-shaped traces is decidable via
HyperQPTL model checking.

2   Preliminaries

Systems and Traces. We model a reactive system as a (nondeterministic)
Moore machine [24] $\mathcal{T} = (S, s_0, AP, \delta, l)$ where S is a finite set of states, $s_0 \in S$
is the initial state, $AP = I \uplus O$ is the set of atomic propositions consisting of

inputs I and outputs O, $\delta : S \times 2^I \to 2^S$ is the transition function determining a set of successor states for a given state and input, and $l : S \to 2^O$ is the labeling function mapping each state to a set of outputs. A path $s = s_0 s_1 \ldots \in S^\omega$ of $\mathcal{T}$ is an infinite sequence with $s_{i+1} \in \delta(s_i, I_i)$ for all $i \in \mathbb{N}$ and for some $I_i \subseteq I$, we assume there exists such $s' \in \delta(s, Y)$ for all $s \in S$ and $Y \subseteq I$. The corresponding trace is $\pi = \pi_0 \pi_1 \pi_2 \ldots \in (2^{AP})^\omega$, such that $\pi_i = I_i \cup l(s_i)$ for the I_i used by δ. With $traces(\mathcal{T})$, we denote the set of all traces of $\mathcal{T}$. For two subsets of atomic propositions $V, W \subseteq AP$, let $V|_W = V \cap W$ and $\pi|_W = \pi_0|_W \, \pi_1|_W \ldots$ for some trace π. We say a trace π is *lasso-shaped*, if there exist $i, j = i + 1, k \in \mathbb{N}$ such that $\pi = \pi_0 \ldots \pi_i \cdot (\pi_j \ldots \pi_k)^\omega$. For some subset $A \subseteq AP$, we call a set of traces $\mathsf{P} \subset (2^A)^\omega$ a *trace property*. A trace π satisfies P, denoted by $\pi \vDash \mathsf{P}$ iff $\pi|_A \in \mathsf{P}$.

QPTL and HyperQPTL. HyperQPTL [26] is a temporal logic that can express ω-regular hyperproperties. HyperQPTL is derived from linear-time temporal logic (LTL) [25] by adding explicit quantification over atomic propositions (leading to quantified propositional temporal logic (QPTL) [27]) and explicit quantification over trace variables (for relating multiple traces):

$$\varphi ::= \forall \pi. \, \varphi \mid \exists \pi. \, \varphi \mid \forall q. \, \varphi \mid \exists q. \, \varphi \mid \psi$$
$$\psi ::= a_\pi \mid q \mid \neg \psi \mid \psi \wedge \psi \mid \bigcirc \psi \mid \psi \mathcal{U} \psi$$

for a trace variable $\pi \in \mathcal{V}$, fresh atomic proposition $q \notin AP$, and atomic proposition $a \in AP$. We also consider the usual derived Boolean ($\vee$, $\to$, $\leftrightarrow$) and temporal operators ($\varphi \mathcal{R} \psi \equiv \neg(\neg\varphi \mathcal{U} \neg\psi)$, $\Diamond \varphi \equiv true \, \mathcal{U} \, \varphi$, $\Box \varphi \equiv false \, \mathcal{R} \, \varphi$). The semantics of HyperQPTL is defined with respect to a time point i, a set of traces Tr and a trace assignment $\Pi : \mathcal{V} \to Tr$ that maps trace variables to traces. To update the trace assignment so that it maps trace variable π to trace t, we write $\Pi[\pi \mapsto t]$. HyperQPTL introduces an auxiliary trace variable π_q for every quantified atomic proposition q. The semantics is as follows:

$$
\begin{array}{lll}
\Pi, i \vDash_{Tr} a_\pi & \text{iff} & a \in \Pi(\pi)[i] \\
\Pi, i \vDash_{Tr} q & \text{iff} & q \in \Pi(\pi_q)[i] \\
\Pi, i \vDash_{Tr} \neg\varphi & \text{iff} & \Pi, i \nvDash_{Tr} \varphi \\
\Pi, i \vDash_{Tr} \varphi \wedge \psi & \text{iff} & \Pi, i \vDash_{Tr} \varphi \text{ and } \Pi, i \vDash_{Tr} \psi \\
\Pi, i \vDash_{Tr} \bigcirc\varphi & \text{iff} & \Pi, i + 1 \vDash_{Tr} \varphi \\
\Pi, i \vDash_{Tr} \varphi \mathcal{U} \psi & \text{iff} & \exists j \geq i. \, \Pi, j \vDash_{Tr} \psi \wedge \forall i \leq k < j. \, \Pi, k \vDash_{Tr} \varphi \\
\Pi, i \vDash_{Tr} \forall\pi. \varphi & \text{iff} & \text{for all } t \in Tr \text{ it holds that } \Pi[\pi \mapsto t], i \vDash_{Tr} \varphi \\
\Pi, i \vDash_{Tr} \exists\pi. \varphi & \text{iff} & \text{there is some } t \in Tr \text{ such that } \Pi[\pi \mapsto t], i \vDash_{Tr} \varphi \\
\Pi, i \vDash_{Tr} \forall q. \varphi & \text{iff} & \text{for all } t \in (2^{\{q\}})^\omega \text{ it holds that } \Pi[\pi_q \mapsto t], i \vDash_{Tr} \varphi \\
\Pi, i \vDash_{Tr} \exists q. \varphi & \text{iff} & \text{there is some } t \in (2^{\{q\}})^\omega \text{ it holds that } \Pi[\pi_q \mapsto t], i \vDash_{Tr} \varphi.
\end{array}
$$

The semantics of a QPTL formula φ can be derived from HyperQPTL formula $\forall \pi. \, \varphi_\pi$, where φ_π is obtained by indexing all atomic propositions in φ with π.

Actual Causality. We shortly outline actual causality originally proposed by Halpern and Pearl [16], in the version modified by Halpern [15]. A *causal model*

$\mathcal{M} = (\mathcal{S}, \mathcal{F})$ is defined by a *signature* $\mathcal{S}$ and set of *structural equations* $\mathcal{F}$. A signature $\mathcal{S}$ is a tuple $(\mathcal{E}, \mathcal{V}, \mathcal{R})$, where $\mathcal{E}$ is a set of *exogenous* variables, $\mathcal{V}$ is a set of *endogenous* variables, and $\mathcal{R}$ defines the *range* of possible values $\mathcal{R}(Y)$ for all variables $Y \in \mathcal{E} \cup \mathcal{V}$. For some context $\vec{u}$, the value of an exogenous variable is determined by factors outside of the model, while the value of some endogenous variable X is defined by the associated structural equation $f_X \in \mathcal{F}$.

Definition 1. $\vec{X} = \vec{x}$ *is an* actual cause *of φ in* $(\mathcal{M}, \vec{u})$, *if the following holds.*

AC1: $(\mathcal{M}, \vec{u}) \vDash \vec{X} = \vec{x}$ *and* $(\mathcal{M}, \vec{u}) \vDash \varphi$, *i.e., both cause and effect are true in the actual world, and*
AC2: There is a set $\vec{W}$ of variables in $\mathcal{V}$ and a setting $\vec{x}'$ of the variables in $\vec{X}$ such that if $(\mathcal{M}, \vec{u}) \vDash \vec{W} = \vec{w}$, *then* $(\mathcal{M}, \vec{u}) \vDash [\vec{X} \leftarrow \vec{x}', \vec{W} \leftarrow \vec{w}] \neg \varphi$, *and*
AC3: $\vec{X}$ is minimal, i.e. no subset of $\vec{X}$ satisfies AC1 and AC2.

Intuitively, AC2 means that after *intervening* on the actual world such that the cause $\vec{X} = \vec{x}$ is not satisfied, the effect is not satisfied either. AC2 allows further modification through the notion of *contingencies*. The contingency $\vec{W}$ can, in the hypothetical world, be reset to the original value it takes in the actual world, even when the intervention on $\vec{X}$ may have altered it.

3   Motivating Example

As an illustration of our approach, we consider the problem of identifying a spurious arbiter. The purpose of an arbiter is to organize mutually exclusive access to a shared resource by eventually answering a request of this resource with a grant. This may be achieved by simply giving grants in a round-robin strategy, regardless of incoming requests. Such spurious and inefficient behavior is unwanted in practice but may result from a sub-optimal specification as input to a reactive synthesis procedure. Our causality-checking approach can identify it by checking whether, e.g., a request r_1 is a cause for a grant g_1 by checking whether the temporal property $\Diamond r_1$ *causes* the observed behavior described by the temporal property $\Diamond g_1$ on a given trace π.

The causal analysis utilizes counterfactual reasoning: if on the traces π' of the system that are similar to π, but where the cause-property $\Diamond r_1$ is not satisfied, the effect-property $\Diamond g_1$ also does not occur, we can infer a causal relationship between the two properties on input and output sequence. As an example, consider the following trace of the system depicted on the left in Fig. 1: $\pi_1 = (\{r_1, g_1\}\{r_0, g_0\})^\omega$. Counterfactual reasoning now requires us to consider similar traces where no r_1 occurs, i.e., the negation of the cause property, which is $\Box \neg r_1$, holds. In particular, since we consider sequences that are still sufficiently similar to π, we require that the sequence does not change the occurrences of r_0. Consequently, the counterfactual trace we are interested in is given by $\pi_1' = (\{g_1\}\{r_0, g_0\})^\omega$.

As we can see, the effect still occurs on π_1', therefore $\Diamond r_1$ is *not* a cause for $\Diamond g_1$ on π_1 in the spurious arbiter. In contrast, consider the arbiter depicted

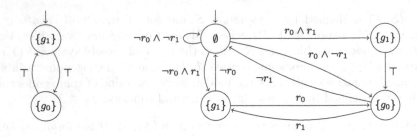

Fig. 1. The models of a spurious (left) and non-spurious arbiter (right). Here, edges are labeled with symbolic constraints, e.g., $\neg r_1$ for all sets without r_1.

on the right in Fig. 1, which works as expected, i.e., only gives out grants upon receiving a request. Let us check whether the causal relationship between the properties from above holds on the trace $\pi_2 = \{r_1\} \cdot (\{r_0, g_1\}\{r_1, g_0\})^\omega$. Here, applying the same counterfactual reasoning technique from before actually yields the following trace, which does not satisfy the effect property: $\pi_2' = \{\} \cdot (\{r_0\}\{g_0\})^\omega$. Hence, we can infer that $\Diamond r_1$ is a cause for $\Diamond g_1$ on π_2.

Even in correct systems, our causal analysis allows further insight into which exact behavior is responsible for a certain observed effect. In particular, *contingencies* allow to isolate a cause in the presence of multiple potential causes on the trace that were preempted. To illustrate, consider again the right arbiter from Fig. 1 and the following trace: $\pi_3 = \{r_1\}\{r_1, g_1\} \cdot \{\}^\omega$. We may now ask whether it is the first or the second r_1 that causes the effect $\Diamond g_1$ on π_3. When considering only the naive counterfactual trace $\pi_3' = \{\}\{r_1\}\{g_1\} \cdot \{\}^\omega$ during analysis of formula r_1 a problem occurs. In π_3', the second request takes effect even though it had no effect in π_3. Contingencies now allow us to reset certain parts of the counterfactual trace back to the actual trace. In particular, we are allowed to change the state and outputs at the third position to their value in π_3, which yields the following counterfactual trace under the contingency: $\pi_3'' = \{\}\{r_1\} \cdot \{\}^\omega$. Since π_3'' does not satisfy the effect, the analysis establishes a causal relationship between the property r_1 of the input sequence and the property $\Diamond g_1$ of the output sequence. Note that considering the alternative, intuitively more precise effect-property $\bigcirc g_1$ leads to the same result without the need for contingencies. Hence, contingencies allow us to precisely infer the causal behavior even if the effect is described in a more general manner.

4   Property Causality

In this section we lift the definitions of Halpern and Pearl to the setting of causes and effects given as general trace properties. We define when some temporal behavior on the input sequence of a reactive system is considered a cause for some temporal behavior observed on the output sequence. We assume a cause

$C \subseteq (2^I)^\omega$ to be a trace property reasoning only over the input variables of the system and an effect $E \subseteq (2^O)^\omega$ to be a trace property ranging over the output variables. We call such properties *cause property* and *effect property*, respectively. In an abuse of notation, we will sometimes use QPTL formulas for C and E in this section when we interpret their language as a trace property.

In order to lift Definition 1 to the setting of both infinite traces and infinite sets of traces for cause and effect, we need to be able to reason about *interventions* (Sect. 4.1), i.e., how to modify the actual trace such that the cause property does not hold anymore; and *contingencies* (Sect. 4.2), that allow to infer the exact causal behavior when it preempts other potential causes. We then can introduce our full definition for temporal causality in Sect. 4.3.

4.1   Interventions

Recall that at the core of counterfactual reasoning lies the idea that if the cause had not appeared on the given trace, then the effect would not have happened either. Hence, as a first step we need to define how the counterfactual traces, i.e., the traces that are just like our given trace, but where the cause-property C is not satisfied, look like. We follow the classic theory of closest possible worlds introduced by Lewis [23] to characterize a set of counterfactual traces that lie just outside of C. For that, we are interested in defining the minimal sets that modify the given trace such that some cause-property C is not satisfied anymore. We call such a set an *intervention*. Following Halpern and Pearl definition, a set is minimal if none of its subsets alone suffice to change the evaluation of C on π. However, for the case of general trace properties as cause and effect, this notion would not allow us to find any minimal interventions.

Example 2. Consider again the non-spurious arbiter from Fig. 1 (right), the cause $C = \square \lozenge r_1$ and the effect $E = \square \lozenge g_1$, and the trace $\pi = \{r_1\} \cdot \{r_1, g_1\}^\omega$. Traces that falsify the effect are traces with only finitely many occurrences of r_1. However, if we follow the subset definition for minimal interventions (see Definition 1), and values of atomic propositions at time point as the respective variables, we get that each trace of the form $\{r_1\}\{r_1, g_1\}^k\{g_1\} \cdot \{\}^\omega$ has a trace with less changes with respect to π, that also falsify the effect, e.g., $\{r_1\}\{r_1, g_1\}^{k+1}\{g_1\} \cdot \{\}^\omega$. Therefore, if we look for minimal interventions using this naive reasoning, we will never find counterfactual traces.

As a solution, we link the satisfaction of the cause property to a distance measure that partially orders counterfactual traces with respect to π. Because this concept is applicable beyond the models and logics considered in this paper, we give a general definition that can be applied to other domains as well.

Formally, we require the existence of a distance measure $<_\pi^C$ that conforms with the underlying logic to detect minimal intervention traces. Such traces σ are the closest to π according to $<_\pi^C$ that do not satisfy C, i.e., there is no $\rho \notin C$ such that $\rho <_\pi^C \sigma$. Generally, multiple traces might satisfy this criterion, so we define a set of minimal interventions.

Definition 3 (Intervention Set). *Let* C *be a cause property, let* $\pi \models$ C *be a trace, and let* $<_\pi^C$ *be a distance measure that partially orders traces with respect to* π. *The set* V_π^C *of interventions on* C *with respect to* π *contains exactly all minimal interventions with respect to* π *according to* $<_C^\pi$. *That is*

$$V_\pi^C = \{\sigma \not\models C \mid \forall \rho \not\models C.\ \rho \not<_\pi^C \sigma\}.$$

4.2 Contingencies

Next, we discuss the treatment of *contingencies* in reactive systems. The motivation behind contingencies is to isolate the truly causal behavior when there is preemption of other potential causes on the actual trace. Contingencies allow certain variables in the counterfactual trace to be reset to their value in the actual trace, in this way mimicking the fact that the second potential cause was preempted in the actual trace. To fully account for this preemption, it is not sufficient that only the output value at a single position is changed to the value in the actual trace: the future dynamics have to respect the contingency by additionally *changing the state* the trace is in when a contingency is evoked.

For a given counterfactual trace, we inductively define the resulting contingencies. Here, we assume a transition relation for the system that is not necessarily memoryless, as we consider general trace logics for now. However, we do assume that transitions only depend on the history of the trace and not on its future. This corresponds to the non-recursive models assumed by Halpern and Pearl. We thus extend the definition of transition function for Moore machines, given in Sect. 2, to a transition function that relies on the whole sequence of inputs and outputs observed so far.

Definition 4 (Contingency Set). *Let* $\delta^* : (2^I \times 2^O)^* \times 2^I \to 2^O$ *be a function that returns the possible next outputs* (2^O) *according to the history of the trace and the current input* (2^I), *modeling the behavior of the system. Given an intervention trace* σ *and an original trace* π, *we define the* contingency set C_π^σ *where* $\pi' = \pi_0'\pi_1' \ldots \in (2^I \times 2^O)^\omega$ *is in* C_π^σ *if the following two conditions hold:*

1. $\forall j \in \mathbb{N}:\ \pi_j' \cap 2^I = \sigma_j \cap 2^I$; *That is,* π' *has the same input sequence as* σ.
2. $\forall j \in \mathbb{N}:\ (o \in \pi_j' \leftrightarrow o \in \delta^*(\pi_0' \cdots \pi_{j-1}' \cdot (\pi_j' \cap 2^I))) \vee (o \in \pi_j)$; *That is, the output sequence of* π' *is determined according to the behavior of the system, together with "jumps" to the original trace* π. *Note that since the input sequence of* σ *and* π' *is the same, it holds that until the first jump to* π, *the output sequence of* σ *and* π' *is also the same.*

Since a contingency only allows to reset outputs to their value in the actual trace, the set of traces under a contingency is defined relative to the actual trace π. The trace under the counterfactual input sequence σ, without modifications, is always part of the contingency set. Starting from this trace, contingencies can be enforced at infinitely many positions.

4.3 Actual Causality for Trace Properties

Minimality of the cause is defined simply based on strict set inclusion, and provides the last condition for our following definition of property-based causality.

Definition 5 (Property Causality). *Let* $\mathcal{T}$ *be a system,* $\pi \in traces(\mathcal{T})$ *a trace,* $\mathsf{C} \subseteq (2^I)^\omega$ *a cause property, and* $\mathsf{E} \subseteq (2^O)^\omega$ *an effect property. We say that* C *is a cause of* E *on* π *in* $\mathcal{T}$ *if the following three conditions hold:*

PC1: $\pi \vDash \mathsf{C}$ *and* $\pi \vDash \mathsf{E}$, *i.e., cause property and effect property are satisfied by the actual trace.*

PC2: *For every counterfactual input sequence* $\sigma \in V_\pi^{\mathsf{C}}$, *there is some contingency* $\pi' \in C_\pi^\sigma$ *s.t.* $\pi' \nvDash \mathsf{E}$, *i.e., the counterfactual trace under contingency does not satisfy the effect property.*

PC3: *There is no* C' *s.t.* $\mathsf{C}' \subset \mathsf{C}$ *and* C' *satisfies PC1 and PC2.*

As a consequence of our treatment of minimality, there is always a maximal cause-property $\mathsf{C}_{max} = (2^I)^\omega$ that trivially satisfies PC1 and PC2. On the other hand, the minimal relevant cause property for a given trace π is $\mathsf{C}_{min} = \{\pi|_I\}$, i.e., the input sequence of the trace itself. This is because the empty set will never qualify for PC1. However, this does not imply that there is a well-defined minimal cause in all cases, because if the considered properties are expressive enough, it may be possible to find a subset that satisfies PC1 and PC2 for any candidate cause property, thus falsifying PC3.

It has been conjectured before that finding causes cannot be stated as a trace property [10]. This hypothesis has intuitive appeal because most notions of causality relate the actual world with counterfactual worlds based on certain similarity metrics. For our proposed notion of trace-based causality, we answer this intriguing question affirmatively in the following theorem and show that even deciding whether a cause candidate is an actual cause cannot be stated as a trace property.

Theorem 6. *Given a cause-property* C, *an effect-property* E, *and some trace* π, *there is no trace-property* P *such that for all systems* $\mathcal{T}$ *with* $\pi \in traces(\mathcal{T})$ *it holds that* $\mathcal{T} \vDash \mathsf{P}$ *iff* C *is a cause for* E *on* π *in* $\mathcal{T}$.

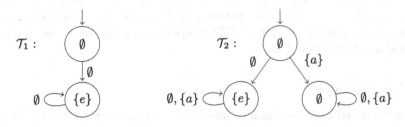

Fig. 2. The systems $\mathcal{T}_1$ and $\mathcal{T}_2$ used in the proof of Theorem 6.

Proof. By contradiction. Assume there is such a trace-property P for the cause-property $C = \neg a$, the effect-property $E = \Diamond e$, and the trace $\pi = \{\}\{e\}^\omega$. Now, consider the two systems depicted in Fig. 2: $\mathcal{T}_1$ with $I_1 = \{\}$ and $\mathcal{T}_2$ with $I_2 = \{a\}$, and $O_1 = O_2 = \{e\}$. We have that C is a cause for E on π in $\mathcal{T}_2$, because we can avoid E in this system with the counterfactual input sequence $\sigma = \{a\}\{\}^\omega \in V_\pi^C$. Note that contingencies do not matter in both systems because they can only set the trace to a state which immediately satisfies E. In $\mathcal{T}_1$, however, E cannot be avoided at all, hence C is not a cause for E in $\mathcal{T}_1$. However, since $traces(\mathcal{T}_1) \subset traces(\mathcal{T}_2)$, we have that $\mathcal{T}_2 \vDash P$ implies $\mathcal{T}_1 \vDash P$. It follows that C has to be a cause in $\mathcal{T}_1$, which contradicts the assumption.   □

In this section, we have presented a general framework that establishes causal relationships between temporal properties given as sets of traces, on a given actual trace. The key idea is to link satisfaction of the property to a distance measure over potential counterfactual traces to obtain meaningful interventions, and to allow for contingencies based on relaxing the dynamics of the model such that it can jump back to states of the actual trace. The proposed concept can conceivably be applied to a variety of models and corresponding logics with a linear-time semantics. However, to allow algorithmic reasoning about the proposed property causality, it is of course necessary to fix a finite representation of the infinite traces and infinite sets, as we do in the following section.

5   Checking ω-Regular Causality

In this section we provide a decision procedure that allows us to check ω-regular causes with respect to ω-regular effects, i.e., verify whether a given candidate cause property is indeed a cause for an observed effect property on an actual trace. We use causes and effects given in the logic QPTL (see Sect. 2), which is equivalent to the class of ω-regular properties. Note that Linear Temporal Logic (LTL), which is one of the standard specification languages for specifying temporal properties in reactive systems, is subsumed by QPTL. We further assume that our actual trace π is given in a finite, lasso-shaped representation (as defined in Sect. 2). This is a common assumption when verifying LTL properties, since if there exists a violation, in particular there exists also a lasso-shaped violation. Model-checking tools (e.g. [18]) usually return such a structured trace. Due to space constraints, we omit language-theoretic definitions in this section and provide definitions directly as HyperQPTL properties, as this allows us to directly reason about their decidability.

5.1   Interventions

We now formalize our discussion of interventions from Sect. 4.1 for QPTL. Our distance measure closely mirrors the original minimality criterion of Halpern and Pearl over sets of variables (see Definition 1), i.e., a trace ρ is closer to the actual trace π than some other trace σ if the events differing between π and ρ are a strict subset of the events differing between π and σ. We can formalize this with the following HyperQPTL property.

$$\psi_{min}(\pi, \rho, \sigma) = \left(\Box \bigwedge_{a \in I} \left((a_\rho \not\leftrightarrow a_\pi) \rightarrow (a_\sigma \not\leftrightarrow a_\pi) \right) \right) \wedge \left(\Diamond \bigvee_{a \in I} (a_\rho \not\leftrightarrow a_\sigma) \right)$$

However, to avoid the issue discussed in Example 2, we only order counterfactual traces that share the same *rejection structure* with respect to the cause-property C, i.e., if they satisfy the right-hand subformulas of every $\mathcal{U}$ (and the derived temporal operators $\Diamond$ and $\Box$) appearing in $\neg$C at the same positions.[1] To formalize this requirement as a HyperQPTL property, let $\varphi_{\neg C}^{\mathcal{U}_1}(\pi), \ldots, \varphi_{\neg C}^{\mathcal{U}_n}(\pi)$ be these subformulas appearing in $\neg$C, with their atomic propositions indexed by the parameterized π. The two traces σ and ρ have the same rejection structure with respect to C if they satisfy the following HyperQPTL property $\psi_{struct}^{C}(\rho, \sigma)$.

$$\psi_{struct}^{C}(\rho, \sigma) = \bigwedge_{i \in [1,n]} \Box \left(\varphi_{\neg C}^{\mathcal{U}_i}(\rho) \leftrightarrow \varphi_{\neg C}^{\mathcal{U}_i}(\sigma) \right)$$

Finally, we obtain an instantiation of the partial order $<_\pi^C$ for QPTL such that for two traces σ, ρ: $\rho <_\pi^C \sigma$ iff $\psi_{min}(\pi, \rho, \sigma) \wedge \psi_{struct}^{C}(\rho, \sigma)$ holds. Note that since we only compare traces with the same rejection structure, we can always find minimal interventions, except if the cause property is a tautology.

Example 7. To illustrate how the above solves the problem raised in Example 2, consider the traces $\sigma = \{r_0, r_1\}^k \cdot \{r_0\}^\omega$ and $\rho = \{r_0, r_1\}^{k+1} \cdot \{r_0\}^\omega$, both in relation to $\pi = \{r_0, r_1\}^\omega$ and the cause-property $C = \Box \Diamond r_1$. While we still have that $\psi_{min}(\pi, \rho, \sigma)$ holds, we have that $\psi_{struct}^{C}(\rho, \sigma)$ does not hold because σ and ρ satisfy $\Box \neg r_1$ at different positions. Hence, σ, ρ are not ordered by $<_\pi^C$ so both are in V_π^C. However, minimality still plays a key role such that we cannot manipulate r_0 in any valid intervention. Consider $\sigma' = \{r_1\}^k \cdot \{\}^\omega$. We have that $\psi_{struct}^{C}(\sigma', \sigma)$ holds since both traces have the same rejection structure with respect to $\neg$C. However, the changes in σ imply changes in σ', but not in the other direction. Hence, $\psi_{min}(\pi, \sigma, \sigma')$ and $\sigma <_\pi^C \sigma'$, so only σ is in V_π^C.

5.2 Contingencies

We formalize the behavior of contingencies for ω-regular properties using a generalization of counterfactual automata as introduced by Coenen et al. [9]. In the original definition, they are restricted to systems whose states are uniquely labeled and which have a state for every output combination. We avoid this restriction by leveraging Halpern and Pearl's thoughts on models in which there exists no unique solution to the structural equations [16]. In these cases, they

---

[1] This is related to the notion of acceptance for words in nondeterministic Büchi automata [5], which recognize the class of ω-regular languages.

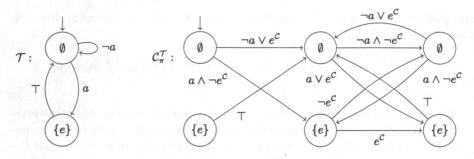

Fig. 3. System $\mathcal{T}$ and the counterfactual automaton $\mathcal{C}_\pi^\mathcal{T}$ for $\pi = \{\} \cdot (\{a\}\{a, e\})^\omega$.

propose to use existential quantification over the solutions. In the same manner, we allow changing the underlying state of the trace to any state that is labeled with the right outputs. Since this means there might be several successor states for a given input and contingency combination, we formalize the counterfactual automaton as a nondeterministic Moore machine.

Definition 8 (Counterfactual Automaton [9] for General Systems). *Let* $\mathcal{T} = (S, s_0, AP, \delta, l)$ *be a system and* $\pi = \pi_0 \ldots \pi_i \cdot (\pi_j \ldots \pi_k)^\omega \in \text{traces}(\mathcal{T})$ *be a lasso-shaped trace. The* counterfactual automaton *for* π *and* $\mathcal{T}$ *is a Moore machine* $\mathcal{C}_\pi^\mathcal{T} = (S^\mathcal{C}, s_0^\mathcal{C}, I^\mathcal{C} \cup O, \delta^\mathcal{C}, l^\mathcal{C})$, *such that:*

- $S^\mathcal{C} = S \times \{0 \ldots k\}$, *we have k copies of the original system;*
- $s_0^\mathcal{C} = (s_0, 0)$, *paths start in the initial state of the first copy;*
- $I^\mathcal{C} = I \cup \{o^\mathcal{C} \mid o \in O\}$, *additional inputs for setting an output as contingency;*
- $(s', n') \in \delta^\mathcal{C}((s, n), Y)$ *iff the following holds:*
  1. *if $n = k$ then $n' = j$ else $n' = n + 1$, and*
  2. *there is some $s'' \in \delta(s, Y|_I)$ such that for all $o^\mathcal{C} \in Y: o \in l(s') \leftrightarrow o \in \pi_n$ and for all $o^\mathcal{C} \notin Y: o \in l(s') \leftrightarrow o \in l(s'')$;*
- $l^\mathcal{C}((s, k)) = l(s)$, *the labeling function is based on the original states.*

The counterfactual automaton simulates arbitrary traces of the original system $\mathcal{T}$, which additionally can at every position choose to invoke a contingency through the additional inputs in $I^\mathcal{C}$ (see Condition 2), i.e., change the subsequent path to a state whose label is as of the next state determined by the original transition relation δ, but with all $o \in O$ that have their corresponding input $o^\mathcal{C} \in I^\mathcal{C}$ enabled set to their value as in π. Since π is of a finite, lasso-shaped form of length $k + 1$, we can construct this behavior based on $k + 1$ copies of the original system and enforce that a path proceeds from one copy to the next in every step (see Condition 1). In this way, the traces of the counterfactual automaton describe the set of all possible counterfactual traces under arbitrary contingencies. The idea is to then pick the subset of traces whose input behavior corresponds to interventions as defined in the previous section.

Example 9. To illustrate the idea of counterfactual automata, consider system $\mathcal{T}$ depicted in Fig. 3 and the trace $\pi = \{\} \cdot (\{a\}\{a, e\})^\omega$. Since the trace has three positions, the counterfactual automaton $\mathcal{C}_\pi^{\mathcal{T}}$ consists of three copies of the original system. It has a single additional input $e^{\mathcal{C}}$. Every step in $\mathcal{C}_\pi^{\mathcal{T}}$ moves through the copies according to π's lasso structure, e.g., the copies of the prefix are only visited once on every path. If a trace does not set a contingency, it directly corresponds to a trace in $\mathcal{T}$, e.g., the trace $\pi' = \{\}^\omega$ is also a trace of $\mathcal{C}_\pi^{\mathcal{T}}$. However, setting contingencies allows to build traces in $\mathcal{C}_\pi^{\mathcal{T}}$ that do not have a corresponding trace in $\mathcal{T}$, e.g., $\pi'' = \{\} \cdot (\{e^{\mathcal{C}}\}\{e\})^\omega \notin traces(\mathcal{T})$.

Note that there might be several states that satisfy Condition 2 in Definition 8. This means that the precision of our causal analysis depends on how much state information the system exposes via its outputs: If every state is uniquely labeled, then a contingency can only set the trace to the state as in the actual trace and there is no ambiguity. Any system can be made amenable to this with auxiliary output variables for the state space.

5.3   Minimality

Our approach to check the minimality of a given ω-regular cause property is based on the observation that it suffices to find exactly one trace in C that can be characterized by an ω-regular language R, which can be removed from C to obtain a smaller ω-regular cause-property C'. This observation is formalized in the following lemma.

Lemma 10. *Let π be a trace and C a cause property that satisfies PC1 and PC2 for some effect-property E. Then, C satisfies PC3 if and only if $\forall \sigma \in C, \forall \pi' \in C_\pi^\sigma.\ \pi' \models E$ and $\forall \sigma \in C, \forall \sigma' \in V_\pi^C.\ \sigma' \not<_\pi^C \sigma$.*

Proof. "$\Longrightarrow$": By contraposition. Let us distinguish two cases based on which of the conjuncts is false. We show that in both cases we can remove some ω-regular property R from C such that PC1 and PC2 still hold.

For the first case, assume there exist some $\sigma \subset C$ and $\pi' \in C_\pi^\sigma$ such that $\pi' \not\models E$. Since the quantified formula can be expressed as a HyperQPTL property of $\mathcal{C}_\pi^{\mathcal{T}}$, which encodes C_π^σ, we know that in particular there exists a witness σ that can be characterized by an ω-regular property $R = \{\sigma\}$. We have $\sigma \neq \pi|_I$ because $C_\pi^\pi = \{\pi\}$ and $\pi \models E$. Hence $C' = C\backslash R$, which is again an ω-regular property, satisfies PC1, as $\pi \in C'$. For PC2, consider the set $V' = \{\sigma' \in V_\pi^C \mid \sigma <_\pi^C \sigma'\}$ of intervention traces that follow the same structure as σ (and are less minimal). If V' is not empty, we have $V_\pi^{C'} = (V_\pi^C \backslash V') \cup \{\sigma\}$, as σ is now a more minimal intervention than traces in V'. If V' is empty, we have $V_\pi^C = V_\pi^{C'}$. In both cases, PC2 is still satisfied (as π' serves as a contingency for σ in the former case) which concludes this case.

For the second case, assume there exist some $\sigma \in C$ and $\sigma' \in V_\pi^C$ such that $\sigma' <_\pi^C \sigma$ holds. With the same reasoning as before, it follows that $C' = C\backslash R$ with $R = \{\sigma\}$ is an ω-regular property. Note that $V_\pi^C = V_\pi^{C'}$, because the set V' above has to be empty, as there is an intervention trace that is more minimal than σ. Hence PC2 holds for C'. Also, $\pi|_I$ is by definition most minimal, hence $\sigma \neq \pi|_I$ and PC1 holds for C'.

In both cases we have found a smaller ω-regular property $C' \subset C$.
"$\Longleftarrow$": By contraposition. Assume that there is some $C' \subset C$ that satisfies PC1 and PC2, and let $\sigma \in C \backslash C'$. We distinguish between two cases, and show that in any case one of the conjuncts is false.

First, assume $V_\pi^C = V_\pi^{C'}$. Therefore, as $\sigma \in C$, we have $\sigma \notin V_\pi^C$ and thus $\sigma \notin V_\pi^{C'}$. Now, consider all traces σ' such that $\sigma' <_\pi^C \sigma$. There exists at least one such σ' with $\sigma' \notin C'$, otherwise $\sigma \in V_\pi^{C'}$ as a minimal intervention trace for C'. Let σ' be such a minimal trace, according to $<_\pi^C$. Now, if σ' was in $C \backslash C'$, then $\sigma' \notin V_\pi^C$, but we would have $\sigma' \in V_\pi^{C'}$ as a minimal intervention, again a contradiction. Therefore, $\sigma' \notin C$, and since σ' is minimal, we have $\sigma' \in V_\pi^C$. Hence, we have found a σ for which there exists a $\sigma' \in V_\pi^C$ such that $\sigma' <_\pi^C \sigma$, thus the second conjunct is falsified.

For the second case, assume $V_\pi^C \neq V_\pi^{C'}$. First, consider the case where there is a trace $\sigma' \in V_\pi^{C'}$ with $\sigma' \notin V_\pi^C$. All traces $\sigma'' <_\pi^C \sigma'$ are in C', and so they are also in C as $C' \subset C$. Then, $\sigma' \in C$, as otherwise, as a minimal intervention for C', it would have also been a minimal intervention for C, and thus in V_π^C. Then, since C' is a cause, there exists some contingency π' for σ', $\pi' \in C_\pi^{\sigma'}$ such that $\pi' \nvDash E$, which concludes this case. For the other case, consider $\sigma' \in V_\pi^C$ with $\sigma' \notin V_\pi^{C'}$. From $\sigma' \in V_\pi^C$ we have $\sigma' \notin C$ and thus $\sigma' \notin C'$. Since $\sigma' \notin V_\pi^{C'}$, there exists a more minimal trace σ'' such that $\sigma'' \in C$ but $\sigma'' \notin C'$. Pick σ'' as the most minimal, hence we have $\sigma'' \in V_\pi^{C'}$. Since C' is a cause, there exists some $\pi'' \in C_\pi^{\sigma''}$ such that $\pi'' \nvDash E$, which concludes this case. In both cases, we have found a trace in C that has a contingency that avoids the effect, which falsifies the first conjunct. □

5.4   Deciding ω-Regular Causality

Putting everything together, we obtain that checking whether some C is a cause for some E on a trace π in system $\mathcal{T}$ can be realized by checking whether the counterfactual automaton $\mathcal{C}_\pi^\mathcal{T}$ satisfies a HyperQPTL property, as outlined in the proof of the following theorem.

Theorem 11. *The problem of verifying an ω-regular cause to an ω-regular effect on a lasso-shaped trace is decidable as a HyperQPTL model-checking problem.*

Proof. Assume φ_C and φ_E are QPTL formulas characterizing the cause and effect properties, respectively, and let π be a lasso-shaped trace. We encode the conditions PC1, PC2 and PC3 directly as a HyperQPTL formula $PC_E^C(\pi)$, utilizing the insight from Lemma 10. The formula is parameterized by π for brevity, however this can be translated to a proper HyperQPTL formula with an additional universal quantifier and a QPTL formula enforcing equality with π. This is possible because π has a lasso shape and can be characterized in QPTL.

In (1), we encode PC1: Both C and E have to be satisfied by the actual trace π. In (2), we enforce that σ is a valid intervention trace with respect to π: All other traces σ' either satisfy C or are not more minimal with respect to π. We then enforce PC2 and PC3. In (4) we state that all traces π' in $\mathcal{C}_\pi^\mathcal{T}$ that satisfy

C have to satisfy the effect, and in (3) we enforce that σ is not more minimal than any trace σ'' in C. Together this ensures PC3 due to Lemma 10. The left part of (4) states that there must be a trace π'' under contingency in $\mathcal{C}_\pi^\mathcal{T}$ that violates E with the same input sequence as σ, which corresponds to PC2.

$$PC_E^C(\pi) = \forall\sigma\forall\sigma'\forall\sigma''\forall\pi'\exists\pi''.\ \varphi_C(\pi) \wedge \varphi_E(\pi) \wedge \tag{1}$$

$$\left(\neg\varphi_C(\sigma) \wedge \left(\varphi_C(\sigma') \vee \neg(\psi_{struct}^C(\sigma,\sigma') \wedge \psi_{min}(\pi,\sigma',\sigma))\right)\right) \rightarrow \tag{2}$$

$$\left((\varphi_C(\sigma'') \rightarrow \neg(\psi_{struct}^C(\sigma'',\sigma) \wedge \psi_{min}(\pi,\sigma,\sigma''))\right) \wedge \tag{3}$$

$$\neg\varphi_E(\pi'') \wedge \bigwedge_{a\in I}\Box(a_{\pi''} \leftrightarrow a_\sigma))\right) \wedge (\varphi_C(\pi') \rightarrow \varphi_E(\pi')) \tag{4}$$

We then model check the formula PC_E^C against the counterfactual automaton $\mathcal{C}_\pi^\mathcal{T}$. Since model checking HyperQPTL is decidable [26], the theorem follows. $\square$

We conclude by demonstrating the usefulness of an expressive logic such as QPTL for describing causes symbolically, as a similar expression of parity as in the example below would not be possible with previous event-based logics [22].

Example 12. Consider the system $\mathcal{T}$ depicted in Fig. 3, the actual trace $\pi = \{\} \cdot (\{a\}\{a,e\})^\omega$, and the effect $E = \Diamond e$. Disregarding contingencies, the effect can only be avoided by never setting input a at all, i.e., with cause candidate $C_1 = \Diamond a$ and the resulting set of counterfactual traces $V_\pi^{C_1} = \{\emptyset^\omega\}$. However, note that the input a at every even position in the trace has no influence on the effect: the system does not discern between the two input sequences $\{\} \cdot (\{a\}\{a\})^\omega$ and $\{\} \cdot (\{a\}\{\})^\omega$. However, that does not mean that the second a is not a potential cause: in the input sequence $\sigma = \{\} \cdot (\{\}\{a\})^\omega$ it is the input that repeatedly moves the trace to state labeled with e. In such situations as on the actual trace π, we say that the second a was *preempted* by the first. Reasoning about contingencies now allows us to find a more accurate cause for E on π. Consider the cause-property $C_2 = \exists q.\neg q \wedge \Box(\bigcirc q \leftrightarrow \neg q) \wedge \Diamond(q \rightarrow a)$, i.e., eventually a holds at an odd position, we have $V_\pi^{C_2} = \{\sigma\}$. Following the above discussion we have that the trace corresponding to the inputs of σ still satisfies the effect property. However, in the counterfactual automaton we find a trace that agrees with the inputs of σ but avoids the effect: $\pi' = \{\} \cdot (\{\}\{a,e^C\})^\omega \in traces(\mathcal{C}_\pi^\mathcal{T})$. We have $\pi' \not\in E$. For a short argument why C_2 is also minimal and therefore the cause for E, consider what happens if we require a to appear at multiple (or all) odd positions with $C_3 = \exists q.\neg q \wedge \Box(\bigcirc q \leftrightarrow \neg q) \wedge \Box(q \rightarrow a)$. Now, valid counterfactuals that negate C_3 can be built by simply removing a at some, but not all odd positions, e.g., $\sigma' = \{\}\{a\} \cdot \{\}^\omega \in V_\pi^{C_3}$. For these sequences, we cannot find a trace in the counterfactual automaton that avoids the effect of the remaining a's at odd positions.

6   Related Work

The increasing number of applications of causality to the formal analysis and explanation of systems has been surveyed comprehensively by Baier et al. [3]. There are several works that define causality formally for computing systems. Gössler and Métayer consider component-based systems and define causality on the component level [12], which differs from our actual causality on the property level. A general framework for counterfactual reasoning in multi-component systems based on counterfactual builders has also been proposed [13], which in particular highlights certain desirable properties of causal analyses. Groce et al. use distance metrics to define the closest trace not producing the effect and define the cause as the difference between the traces [14], which has similarities to our definition of minimal interventions.

Related to our approach, Leitner-Fischer and Leue's causality definitions offer a symbolic description of counterfactual causes in *Event Order Logic* [22]. As effects, they originally considered only violations of safety properties, but their approach has been extended to LTL-definable effects [6]. In both works, the goal of the symbolic causes is to give a high-level description of the orderings of events that lead to a violation in the system, but less to give a precise characterization of the causal input behavior on an observed, actual trace.

Coenen et al. [9] have considered the problem of identifying the actual cause of a counterexample violating a hyperproperty. In their setting, the effect is a hyperproperty while the cause is a concrete set of events appearing in a counterexample. In this work, we consider symbolic causes given as trace properties, and we adapt the counterfactual automata from this aforementioned work [9].

It has been noted before that probabilistic causality can be expressed as a hyperproperty [1,11]. The considered version of probabilistic causation is founded on the probability raising principle. However, this type of probabilistic causation can also be expressed in branching-time temporal logics, as shown by Kleinberg and Mishra [20]. For probabilistic systems, there has recently been proposed a notion of causality that combines probability raising with the counterfactuality principle [28]. To the best of our knowledge, the observation that counterfactual causality is not a trace property [10] has not been formalized and proven before.

7   Conclusion

Inspired by Halpern and Pearl's definition of actual causality, we define causality for reactive systems that gives symbolic descriptions of causal temporal behavior as trace properties. We define interventions and contingencies to enable counterfactual reasoning in this infinite setting. The key idea of our work is to link satisfaction of a property with a distance measure over traces, to define the closest counterfactual traces that do not satisfy the cause. We show that checking causality for trace properties cannot itself be expressed as a trace property but as a hyperproperty. Our definitions can be instantiated with explicit logics to express cause and effect properties. We present a decidable instantiation with QPTL along with the corresponding automata-based constructions to verify actual causes based on HyperQPTL model checking, covering the whole practically relevant class of ω-regular properties. Future work includes examining ways of leveraging the existing research on hyperproperties when analyzing causal relationships, and applying our conceptual framework to other domains.

References

1. Ábrahám, E., Bonakdarpour, B.: HyperPCTL: a temporal logic for probabilistic hyperproperties. In: McIver, A., Horvath, A. (eds.) QEST 2018. LNCS, vol. 11024, pp. 20–35. Springer, Cham (2018). https://doi.org/10.1007/978-3-319-99154-2_2
2. Baier, C., Coenen, N., Finkbeiner, B., Funke, F., Jantsch, S., Siber, J.: Causality-based game solving. In: Silva, A., Leino, K.R.M. (eds.) CAV 2021. LNCS, vol. 12759, pp. 894–917. Springer, Cham (2021). https://doi.org/10.1007/978-3-030-81685-8_42
3. Baier, C., et al.: From verification to causality-based explications. In: ICALP 2021 (2021)
4. Beer, I., Ben-David, S., Chockler, H., Orni, A., Trefler, R.: Explaining counterexamples using causality. Formal Methods Syst. Design 40, 20–40 (2012)
5. Buechi, J.R.: On a decision method in restricted second-order arithmetic. In: International Congress on Logic, Methodology, and Philosophy of Science (1962)
6. Caltais, G., Guetlein, S.L., Leue, S.: Causality for general LTL-definable properties. In: CREST@ETAPS 2018 (2018)
7. Chockler, H., Halpern, J.Y., Kupferman, O.: What causes a system to satisfy a specification? ACM Trans. Comput. Log. 9, 1–26 (2008)
8. Clarkson, M.R., Schneider, F.B.: Hyperproperties. J. Comput. Secur. 18, 1157–1210 (2010)
9. Coenen, N., et al.: Explaining hyperproperty violations. In: Shoham, S., Vizel, Y. (eds.) CAV 2022. LNCS, vol. 13371, pp. 407–429. Springer, Cham (2022). https://doi.org/10.1007/978-3-031-13185-1_20
10. Datta, A., Garg, D., Kaynar, D.K., Sharma, D., Sinha, A.: Program actions as actual causes: a building block for accountability. In: CSF 2015 (2015)
11. Dimitrova, R., Finkbeiner, B., Torfah, H.: Probabilistic hyperproperties of Markov decision processes. In: Hung, D.V., Sokolsky, O. (eds.) ATVA 2020. LNCS, vol. 12302, pp. 484–500. Springer, Cham (2020). https://doi.org/10.1007/978-3-030-59152-6_27
12. Gössler, G., Le Métayer, D.: A general trace-based framework of logical causality. In: Fiadeiro, J.L., Liu, Z., Xue, J. (eds.) FACS 2013. LNCS, vol. 8348, pp. 157–173. Springer, Cham (2014). https://doi.org/10.1007/978-3-319-07602-7_11
13. Gössler, G., Stefani, J.: Causality analysis and fault ascription in component-based systems. Theor. Comput. Sci. 837, 158–180 (2020)
14. Groce, A., Chaki, S., Kroening, D., Strichman, O.: Error explanation with distance metrics. Int. J. Softw. Tools Technol. Transf. 8, 229–247 (2006)
15. Halpern, J.Y.: A modification of the Halpern-Pearl definition of causality. In: IJCAI 2015 (2015)
16. Halpern, J.Y., Pearl, J.: Causes and explanations: a structural-model approach. Part I: causes. Br. J. Philos. Sci. 56, 843–887 (2005)

17. Halpern, J.Y., Pearl, J.: Causes and explanations: a structural-model approach. Part II: explanations. Br. J. Philos. Sci. **56**, 889–911 (2005)
18. Holzmann, G.J.: The model checker SPIN. IEEE Trans. Softw. Eng. **23**, 279–295 (1997)
19. Hume, D.: An Enquiry Concerning Human Understanding. London (1748)
20. Kleinberg, S., Mishra, B.: The temporal logic of causal structures. In: UAI 2009 (2009)
21. Kupriyanov, A., Finkbeiner, B.: Causal termination of multi-threaded programs. In: Biere, A., Bloem, R. (eds.) CAV 2014. LNCS, vol. 8559, pp. 814–830. Springer, Cham (2014). https://doi.org/10.1007/978-3-319-08867-9_54
22. Leitner-Fischer, F., Leue, S.: Causality checking for complex system models. In: Giacobazzi, R., Berdine, J., Mastroeni, I. (eds.) VMCAI 2013. LNCS, vol. 7737, pp. 248–267. Springer, Heidelberg (2013). https://doi.org/10.1007/978-3-642-35873-9_16
23. Lewis, D.K.: Counterfactuals. Blackwell, Cambridge (1973)
24. Moore, E.F.: Gedanken-experiments on sequential machines. Aut. stud. **34**, 129–153 (1956)
25. Pnueli, A.: The temporal logic of programs. In: FOCS 1977 (1977)
26. Rabe, M.N.: A temporal logic approach to information-flow control. Ph.D. thesis, Saarland University (2016)
27. Sistla, A.P.: Theoretical issues in the design and verification of distributed systems. Ph.D. thesis (1983)
28. Ziemek, R., Piribauer, J., Funke, F., Jantsch, S., Baier, C.: Probabilistic causes in Markov chains. Innov. Syst. Softw. Eng. **18**, 347–367 (2022)

PDAAAL: A Library for Reachability Analysis of Weighted Pushdown Systems

Peter G. Jensen[1], Stefan Schmid[2,3], Morten K. Schou[1], and Jiří Srba[1(✉)]

[1] Department of Computer Science, Aalborg University, Aalborg, Denmark
srba@cs.aau.dk
[2] TU Berlin, Berlin, Germany
[3] University of Vienna, Vienna, Austria

Abstract. We present PDAAAL, an open source C++ library and tool for weighted reachability analysis of pushdown systems, including generation of both shortest and longest witness traces. We consider totally ordered weight domains which have important applications, e.g. in network verification, and achieve a speedup of two orders of magnitude compared to the state-of-the-art tool WALi. Our tool further extends the state of the art by supporting the generation of the longest trace in case it exists, or reporting that no finite longest trace can be generated. PDAAAL is provided both as a stand-alone tool accepting JSON files and as a C++ library. This allows for integration in software pipelines as well as in verification tools like AalWiNes.

1 Introduction

Pushdown automata are a fundamental model in computer science and they are often used as an underlying formalism for data-flow analysis of recursive programs [1,3,14,17], parsing of XML streams [11], modelling of network protocols [5,13] and others [9,12]. The verification questions on different types of models can be reduced to reachability analysis for pushdown systems.

In order to support quantitative extensions of such systems, we need to study weighted extensions of pushdown automata. In general, these weights are defined over an idempotent semiring and we need to consider meet-over-all-paths values for reaching certaing pushdown configurations. There is a rich literature of theory showing the application of weighted pushdown automata [9,10,12,14] to various application domains and several tools for the reachability analysis of pushdown systems exist, including the tools Moped [16] used for the analysis of Java programs (in the jMoped framework [17]), WPDS++ [7] for program analysis as well as its more recent successor WALi [8] employed in tools like ICRA [9] performing interprocedureal compositional recurrence analysis and the static analysis tool Phasar [14] for C/C++ programs.

We present an open source C++ library and stand-alone tool PDAAAL for efficient reachability analysis of pushdown automata over the weight domain of totally ordered idempotent semirings. The study of such totally ordered semirings is fundamental and has important applications, e.g., in the context of the

A. Bouajjani et al. (Eds.): ATVA 2022, LNCS 13505, pp. 225–230, 2022.
https://doi.org/10.1007/978-3-031-19992-9_14

verification of communication networks [5,13]. PDAAAL implements the classical *pre** and *post** saturation algorithms for unweighted pushdown systems, including the new *dual** algorithms [6] and extends these algorithms for weighted reachability analysis, computing the weights of not only the shortest traces but also the longest traces, while returning such trace witnesses in case they exist. The study of longest traces is practically relevant, as it allows, for example, to perform a worst-case analysis of the routing paths in a communication network, e.g., in terms of delay or size of packet headers [5]. It is, however, also challenging to analyze, as the longest trace may be unbounded and hence impossible to compute directly. To the best of our knowledge, PDAAAL is the first tool providing the exact computation of the longest traces as the debugging information.

We introduce the formalism of weighted pushdown systems (Sect. 2), present the implemented algorithms and tool usage (Sect. 3) and compare the performance of PDAAAL with the state-of-the-art tool WALi for weighted reachability analysis (Sect. 4) where we observe up to two orders of magnitude faster performance. Finally, we elaborate on a specific use case in network verification (Sect. 5) related to MPLS networks [5].

2 Weighted Pushdown Systems and Reachability

PDAAAL can accept weights from the domain of totally ordered idempotent semirings $S = (D, \sqcap, \oplus, \top, \bot)$. An example of a weight domain for computing the shortest paths is $S_1 = (\mathbb{N} \cup \{\infty\}, \min, +, \infty, 0)$ where weights are natural numbers including infinity, the weights are additive along a single path and minimum is the meet-over-all-path operation. A domain for the computation of the longest path is $S_2 = (\mathbb{Z} \cup \{-\infty\}, \max, +, -\infty, 0)$.

Definition 1. *A Weighted Pushdown System (WPDS) over a weight semiring $S = (D, \sqcap, \oplus, \top, \bot)$ is a tuple (P, Γ, Δ) where P is a finite set of control locations, Γ is a finite stack alphabet, and the set of rules Δ is a finite subset of $(P \times \Gamma) \times D \times (P \times \Gamma^*)$, written $\langle p, \gamma \rangle \xrightarrow{d} \langle p', w \rangle$, if $((p, \gamma), d, (p', w)) \in \Delta$.*

A *configuration* in a pushdown system is a pair $\langle p, w \rangle$ where $p \in P$ is the current control location and $w \in \Gamma^*$ is the stack content (head of the stack on the left). A WPDS induces a labelled transition system $T = (P \times \Gamma^*, D, \Rightarrow)$, where for all $w' \in \Gamma^*$ $\langle p, \gamma w' \rangle \xrightarrow{d} \langle p', ww' \rangle$, provided that there is a pushdown rule $\langle p, \gamma \rangle \xrightarrow{d} \langle p', w \rangle$. We write $c_0 \xrightarrow{d}^\oplus c_n$ if there is a path in the labelled transition system $c_0 \xrightarrow{d_1} \ldots \xrightarrow{d_n} c_n$ such that $d = d_1 \oplus \ldots \oplus d_n$. The *distance* between two configurations c and c' is given by $\delta(c, c') = \sqcap\{d \mid c \xrightarrow{d}^\oplus c'\}$. If S is a bounded idempotent semiring (i.e. has no infinite descending chains), the distance is well defined. If S is unbounded, the supremum may not be in the domain D; for example in the semiring S_2, the distance is ∞ if there is a positive-weight loop.

The problem solved by PDAAAL is: given a WPDS (P, Γ, Δ) and two regular sets of configurations $C, C' \subseteq P \times \Gamma^*$, compute the distance $\sqcap\{\delta(c, c') \mid c \in C, c' \in C'\}$ and return a witness trace (if any) with this distance.

3   Implemented Algorithms and PDAAAL Architecture

It is well known that the sets of all predecessors $pre^*(C)$ and successors $post^*(C)$ of a regular set of pushdown configurations C are also regular [2]. The classical pre^* and $post^*$ saturation algorithms [1,4,15] solve reachability for pushdown systems without weights. Schwoon [15] describes how to find a shortest witness trace for totally ordered weight domains by using a priority queue to select the next step of the saturation. This is later generalized to bounded idempotent semirings [12], and implemented in the tool WALi [8]. Here the saturation algorithms use a workset where transitions may be added multiple times, hence possibly loosing some efficiency compared to the priority queue that exploits the total ordering. Extensions to unbounded semirings are considered in [10] by detecting that exceeding a given number of iterations of the saturation algorithm causes nontermination of the procedure. PDAAAL implements the ideas from [10] to pre^*, $post^*$ as well as $dual^*$ (combination of the first two approches) for unbounded but totally ordered weight domains.

To achieve a high performance, we employ numerous algorithmic optimizations. We extend the early termination and bidirectional-search ($dual^*$) technique from unweighted pushdowns [6] to shortest trace queries for weighted systems. The main challenge here is that the on-the-fly construction of the product automata must keep track of the weight of the best path to any state, and the saturation only terminates if the best weight of an accepting path is no higher than the current weight in the priority queue in the saturation. For longest trace queries the $dual^*$ approach simply interleaves the saturation of pre^* and $post^*$ and returns when either of them terminates. We also efficiently handle rules that apply to any top-of-stack label, using of a wildcard flag in the precondition, and adapting the pre^* and $post^*$ algorithms to efficiently handle wildcards.

PDAAAL is designed to be included as a library in other C++ projects, but it also functions as a stand-alone tool with JSON parsers for pushdown systems and $\mathcal{P}$-automata (nondeterministic automata used to represent regular sets of pushdown configurations). The tool has predefined weight domains for integers and natural numbers as well as vectors of these. In all cases, the weight semiring can either minimize or maximize the weight, depending on whether a shortest or longest trace is required. Other weight domains can be defined by the user, when PDAAAL is used as a C++ library.

As an example, a $\mathcal{P}$-automaton for the following set of pushdown configurations $\{\langle p_0, BA \rangle, \langle p_0, A \rangle, \langle p_1, A \rangle\}$ can be defined either in JSON format, or by using regular expressions for the stack, symbols '<' and '>' to denote configurations, and the symbol '|' to union multiple configuration sets: < [p0] , [B]? [A] > | < [p1], [A] >.

To run PDAAAL from the command line, an input file must be provided along with the algorithm to use: -e 1 ($post^*$), -e 2 (pre^*), or -e 3 ($dual^*$) and the trace type -t 0 (no trace), -t 1 (any trace), -t 2 (shortest trace), or -t 3 (longest trace). For instance to run the $post^*$ shortest trace algorithm: pdaaal --input example.json -e 1 -t 2.

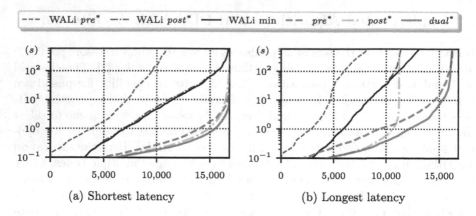

(a) Shortest latency   (b) Longest latency

Fig. 1. Performance plots of WALi (*pre**, *post** and minimum of both) in thin lines, compared to PDAAAL (*pre**, *post** and *dual**) in thick lines; all instances on x-axis are independently sorted by the increasing verification time that is plotted on y-axis (log-scale) in seconds.

4   Comparison with State-of-the-Art

The first library for weighted pushdown systems, called WPDS [15], was provided by Schwoon and used in Moped version 2. Later, WPDS++ [7] was developed by Reps et al. and included further performance optimizations. The state-of-the-art tool WALi [8] was developed as a successor of WPDS++ and it is used as a backend in recent static analyzers ICRA [9] and Phasar [14].

We compare PDAAAL to WALi by running the shortest and longest trace queries on weighted pushdown systems produced by AalWiNes [5] on a large benchmark of real communication networks from ISP providers. All together, we run 16,800 reachability queries on pushdown systems of varying sizes. WALi does not support a generation of the longest traces, unless a bound on the weight of the longest trace is known a priori. In order to enable this, we set the bound to the highest possible value of 32bit integer. On contrary, the implementation in PDAAAL is able to effectively compute a bound on the number of iterations, and hence it guarantees the termination even for unbounded longest traces.

Figure 1 shows the results comparing WALi and PDAAAL. We consider both the computation of shortest traces and longest traces where the weight domain represents the latency (which is additive along a pushdown trace). PDAAAL supports both *pre**, *post** and *dual** (interleaving of *pre** and *post**), while WALi does not support *dual**. We instead present the minimum of the verification time of *pre** and *post**, which shows an improvement on the largest instances for the longest latency. For the shortest trace experiment, all variants of PDAAAL saturation algorithms outperform WALi by several orders of magnitude. For the longest traces, this is also the case for our *dual** algorithm, even though the *post** algorithm times out about at the same instance as WALi. We can also observe that our *pre** implementation is in general performing as good (or even better) than our *post**, while this is not the case for WALi.

PDAAAL is available on https://github.com/DEIS-Tools/PDAAAL together with specifications of input/output formats and how to run the tool. A reproducibility package is available at https://doi.org/10.5281/zenodo.6833493.

5 Applications

Pushdown automata find broad and practical applications in many domains where verification tasks are often reduced to a pushdown reachability analysis. As an example, PDAAAL can be used to model MPLS networks, a popular and widely-used type of communication network used by most Internet Service Providers for efficient traffic engineering [5]. MPLS networks interconnect a set of routers which forward packets, where packets contain stacks of labels which can be pushed and popped, and the forwarding is based on the top-of-stack label. Such networks can hence be modelled as pushdown systems.

PDAAAL can be used in combination with AalWiNes [5] as part of a what-if analysis tool (behaviour under link failures) to ensure a dependable service and policy-compliant routing. In particular, PDAAAL's support for longest traces is attractive to perform a worst-case analysis of the network's routing behavior. For example, PDAAAL can be used to compute the longest possible routes that may occur under one or multiple link failures, both in terms of the number of hops (which is directly related to the amount of bandwidth resources consumed in the network) as well as in terms of the overall delay (an important metric for latency-critical applications). Furthermore, PDAAAL can also be used to verify further quantitative metrics of interest. An online demo is available at http://demo.aalwines.cs.aau.dk.

Similar applications for the longest trace analysis also arise in other domains, allowing to perform worst-case time analyses of possible control flows in recursive programs or the execution of parsers of XML streams, shedding light on the possible overheads of such operations.

6 Conclusion

We presented PDAAAL, a tool for reachability analysis of weighted pushdown automata over possibly unbounded weight domains. Our tool can be used also as a library, and it is integrated into a recent network analysis tool AalWiNes that relies on pushdown systems produced from widely used MPLS networks. Apart from being two orders of magnitude faster than the state-of-the-art competitor, it supports the detection of the existence of longest traces which finds practical applications in e.g., the analysis of network protocols. Our tool uses unbounded but totally ordered weight domains but despite of this limitation, it finds numerous applications and can in the case of totally ordered domains replace the backend weighted engines like Moped, WPDS++ and WALi with a generic, modern and efficient library.

References

1. Bouajjani, A., Esparza, J., Maler, O.: Reachability analysis of pushdown automata: application to model-checking. In: Mazurkiewicz, A., Winkowski, J. (eds.) CONCUR 1997. LNCS, vol. 1243, pp. 135–150. Springer, Heidelberg (1997). https://doi.org/10.1007/3-540-63141-0_10
2. Büchi, J.R.: Regular canonical systems. Arch. für mathematische Logik Grundlagenforschung 6(3–4), 91–111 (1964)
3. Esparza, J., Knoop, J.: An automata-theoretic approach to interprocedural dataflow analysis. In: Thomas, W. (ed.) FoSSaCS 1999. LNCS, vol. 1578, pp. 14–30. Springer, Heidelberg (1999). https://doi.org/10.1007/3-540-49019-1_2
4. Finkel, A., Willems, B., Wolper, P.: A direct symbolic approach to model checking pushdown systems. In: INFINITY 1997. ENTCS, vol. 9, pp. 27–37. Elsevier (1997)
5. Jensen, P.G., Kristiansen, D., Schmid, S., Schou, M.K., Schrenk, B.C., Srba, J.: AalWiNes: a fast and quantitative what-if analysis tool for MPLS networks. In: CoNEXT 2020, p. 474–481. ACM (2020)
6. Jensen, P.G., Schmid, S., Schou, M.K., Srba, J., Vanerio, J., Duijn, I.: Faster pushdown reachability analysis with applications in network verification. In: Hou, Z., Ganesh, V. (eds.) ATVA 2021. LNCS, vol. 12971, pp. 170–186. Springer, Cham (2021). https://doi.org/10.1007/978-3-030-88885-5_12
7. Kidd, N., Reps, T., Melski, D., Lal, A.: WPDS++: a C++ library for weighted pushdown systems. University of Wisconsin (2004)
8. Kidd, N., Lal, A., Reps, T.: WALi: the weighted automaton library (2007). https://research.cs.wisc.edu/wpis/wpds/wali/
9. Kincaid, Z., Breck, J., Boroujeni, A.F., Reps, T.: Compositional recurrence analysis revisited. In: Conference on Programming Language Design and Implementation, pp. 248–262. PLDI (2017)
10. Kühnrich, M., Schwoon, S., Srba, J., Kiefer, S.: Interprocedural dataflow analysis over weight domains with infinite descending chains. In: de Alfaro, L. (ed.) FoSSaCS 2009. LNCS, vol. 5504, pp. 440–455. Springer, Heidelberg (2009). https://doi.org/10.1007/978-3-642-00596-1_31
11. Kumar, V., Madhusudan, P., Viswanathan, M.: Visibly pushdown automata for streaming XML. In: WWW 2007, pp. 1053–1062. ACM (2007)
12. Reps, T., Schwoon, S., Jha, S., Melski, D.: Weighted pushdown systems and their application to interprocedural dataflow analysis. Sci. Comput. Program. 58(1–2), 206–263 (2005)
13. Schmid, S., Srba, J.: Polynomial-time what-if analysis for prefix-manipulating MPLS networks. In: IEEE INFOCOM 2018, pp. 1799–1807. IEEE (2018)
14. Schubert, P.D., Hermann, B., Bodden, E.: PhASAR: an inter-procedural static analysis framework for C/C++. In: Vojnar, T., Zhang, L. (eds.) TACAS 2019. LNCS, vol. 11428, pp. 393–410. Springer, Cham (2019). https://doi.org/10.1007/978-3-030-17465-1_22
15. Schwoon, S.: Model-checking pushdown systems. Ph.D. thesis, Technische Universität München (2002)
16. Schwoon, S.: Moped (2002). https://www2.informatik.uni-stuttgart.de/fmi/szs/tools/moped/
17. Suwimonteerabuth, D., Schwoon, S., Esparza, J.: jMoped: a Java bytecode checker based on moped. In: Halbwachs, N., Zuck, L.D. (eds.) TACAS 2005. LNCS, vol. 3440, pp. 541–545. Springer, Heidelberg (2005). https://doi.org/10.1007/978-3-540-31980-1_35

Active Learning

Learning Deterministic One-Clock Timed Automata via Mutation Testing

Xiaochen Tang[1], Wei Shen[1], Miaomiao Zhang[1]($\boxtimes$), Jie An[2],
Bohua Zhan[3,4], and Naijun Zhan[3,4]

[1] School of Software Engineering, Tongji University, Shanghai, China
{xiaochen9697,weishen,miaomiao}@tongji.edu.cn
[2] Max Planck Institute for Software Systems (MPI-SWS), Kaiserslautern, Germany
[3] State Key Laboratory of Computer Science, Institute of Software,
CAS, Beijing, China
[4] University of Chinese Academy of Sciences, Beijing, China

Abstract. In active learning, an equivalence oracle is supposed to answer whether a hypothesis model is equivalent to the system under learning. Its implementation in real applications is considered a major bottleneck for active automata learning. The problem is especially difficult in the context of learning timed automata due to the infinitely large state space involved. In this paper, following the framework of combining mutation analysis and random testing, we propose an implementation of equivalence oracle in the context of learning deterministic one-clock timed automata (DOTAs). This includes two learning-friendly mutation operators, a heuristic test-case generation method, and a score-based test-case selection method. We implemented a prototype applying our approach by extending an existing tool on active learning of DOTAs and conducted extensive experiments. The results indicate that our method improves upon existing methods on the rate of learning correct models, the number of test cases required, and accumulated delay time in test cases.

Keywords: Active learning · Timed automata · Model-based mutation testing

1 Introduction

Active (model) learning [28] has emerged as a highly effective technique for learning the model of a system under learning (SUL). Most of active learning methods follow the L^* framework proposed by Angluin [12]. The learning process to achieve a hypothesis of the SUL can be viewed as an interaction between a *learner* and a *teacher*, where the learner asks *membership queries* (MQs) and *equivalence queries* (EQs) to a teacher who holds oracles to answer these queries. The former corresponds to a single test of the SUL to check whether a sequence of actions

This work has been partially funded by NSFC under grant No. 61972284, 62032019, 62032024, 62192732, 62192730, and 61625206, by DFG project 389792660-TRR 248.

can be executed. EQs check whether a learned hypothesis represents the SUL. The teacher either answers affirmatively or generates a counterexample showing the difference between the SUL and the hypothesis. Compared to active learning of deterministic finite state automata (DFAs) [12], learning timed automata [7] is much more complex since it involves an infinite set of timed actions and clock reset information while the alphabets of DFAs is finite. Among the existing works [8–10, 16, 17, 29] on active learning of the different timed models, An et al. proposed an active learning method for deterministic one-clock timed automata (DOTAs) in [8]. Inherited from L^*, this method also assumes an ideal setting where the EQs can be answered exactly by an oracle. However, exact equivalence oracles are usually unrealistic in most practical situations, which is a well-known problem that learning methods based on L^* in practice face and can be considered as "the true bottleneck of automata learning" [13].

To address the issues mentioned above, various attempts have been carried out. For real applications, one of the most widely studied approach for EQs is *conformance testing* [1, 13–15, 22, 25]. However, the size of the constructed test suite is usually exponential in the number of states of the SUL, which makes it inefficient in many industrial scenarios. Another limitation is that most of the existing methods for timed systems do not consider the accumulated delay time of test suites. Therefore, a new target for conformance testing is to find counterexamples fast, rather than trying to prove equivalence [19]. Model-based testing [27], a popular technique for automated test-case generation, can be used as an approach for conformance testing. Commonly relying on some coverage criterion, it produces new test cases until that criterion is satisfied. Model-based mutation testing [2, 3, 23] uses *faults* as such a criterion: the original model is modified by different fault injections, called *mutation operators*, which results in a set of faulty models called *mutants*. In [6], Aichernig et al. combined random testing and mutation analysis [11] to learn Mealy machines and show their effectiveness. Here random testing is used to achieve high variability of tests, while mutation analysis is used to ensure appropriate coverage.

In this paper, we propose a conformance testing approach combining random testing and mutation-based testing to replace exact EQs in the active learning of DOTAs. Even though many existing studies proposed mutation operators for timed automata, which generate mutants covering specific faults [4, 26, 31], there are many redundancies among these mutation operators, and the mutants generated by these operators are possibly non-deterministic. These make the existing mutation operators not well-suited to the context of active automata learning. Thus, we design two mutation operators to address DOTAs learning. The approach we presented aims at finding counterexamples quickly, and reducing the total amount of time of executing test cases, in addition to the reduction of tests as in [6]. Moreover, to design the test suits, we take previous counterexamples into consideration and the modifications between two successive hypotheses in the learning procedure for DOTAs. Our contributions are summarized as follows.

– A heuristic algorithm for random test-case generation. We take counterexamples into consideration and apply three heuristics to random testing, aiming at generating more useful test cases.

- Two learning-friendly mutation operators. In contrast to generating only first-order mutants [4,26,31], which usually contain one fault, we take into account the deterministic behaviours of the model and the modifications between two successive hypotheses obtained in the learning process, so that more faults are considered in the construction of mutants.
- A mutation and score-based selection of test cases. In addition to mutation coverage, we also take the length and accumulated delay time of the test cases into consideration to achieve faster testing.
- An implementation of our method. To investigate the effectiveness and efficiency of our method, we extend the prototype tool for DOTAs learning [8] and compare our method with various existing methods.

The rest of the paper is organized as follows. In Sect. 2, we review the learning algorithm for DOTAs in [8] and the model-based mutation testing framework. In Sect. 3, we describe the mutation-based testing in the context of active learning of DOTAs in detail. In Sect. 4, we introduce two mutation operators used in the mutation-based testing framework. The experimental results are reported in Sect. 5. Finally, Sect. 6 concludes this paper.

2   Preliminaries

2.1   Deterministic One-Clock Timed Automata

In this paper, we consider a subclass of timed automata [7] that are deterministic and contain only a single clock, called *Deterministic One-Clock Timed Automata* (DOTAs). Let $\mathbb{N}$ be the natural numbers and $\mathbb{R}_{\geq 0}$ be the non-negative real numbers. We use $\top$ to stand for true and $\bot$ for false. Let $\mathbb{B} = \{\top, \bot\}$. Let c be the clock variable, denote by Φ_c the set of clock constraints of the form $\phi:: = \top \mid c \bowtie m \mid \phi \wedge \phi$, where $m \in \mathbb{N}$ and $\bowtie \in \{=, <, >, \leq, \geq\}$.

Definition 1 (One-clock timed automata). *A one-clock timed automaton (OTA) is a 6-tuple $\mathcal{A} = (\Sigma, Q, q_0, F, c, \Delta)$, where Σ is a finite set of actions, Q is a finite set of locations, q_0 is the initial location, $F \subseteq Q$ is a set of final locations, c is the unique clock and $\Delta \subseteq Q \times \Sigma \times \Phi_c \times \mathbb{B} \times Q$ is a finite set of transitions.*

A transition $\delta \in \Delta$ is a 5-tuple (q, σ, ϕ, b, q'), where $q, q' \in Q$ are the source and target locations respectively, $\sigma \in \Sigma$ is an action, $\phi \in \Phi_c$ is a clock constraint, and b is the reset indicator. Such δ allows a jump from q to q' by performing an action σ if the current clock valuation ν satisfies the constraint ϕ. We also call ϕ as a *guard*. Meanwhile, clock c is reset to zero if $b = \top$ and remains unchanged otherwise. A *clock valuation* is a function $\nu : c \mapsto \mathbb{R}_{\geq 0}$ that assigns a non-negative real number to the clock. For $t \in \mathbb{R}_{\geq 0}$, let $\nu + t$ be the clock valuation with $(\nu + t)(c) = \nu(c) + t$. A *state* is a pair (q, ν), where $q \in Q$ and ν is a clock valuation. A *timed action* is a pair (σ, t) that indicates the action σ is applied after t time units since the occurrence of the previous action. A *timed trace* is a sequence $\omega = (\sigma_1, t_1)(\sigma_2, t_2) \ldots (\sigma_n, t_n)$ of timed actions $(\sigma_i, t_i) \in \Sigma \times \mathbb{R}_{\geq 0}$. A finite *run* ρ of $\mathcal{A}$ over a timed trace $\omega = (\sigma_1, t_1)(\sigma_2, t_2) \ldots (\sigma_n, t_n)$ is a sequence of timed states and timed actions $\rho = (q_0, \nu_0) \xrightarrow{\sigma_1, t_1} (q_1, \nu_1) \xrightarrow{\sigma_2, t_2} \cdots \xrightarrow{\sigma_n, t_n} (q_n, \nu_n)$ where $\nu_0 = 0$, and for all $1 \leq i \leq n$ there exists a transitions $(q_{i-1}, \sigma_i, \phi_i, b_i, q_i) \in \Delta$ such that $\nu_{i-1} + t_i$ satisfies ϕ_i, and $\nu_i(c) = 0$ if $b_i = \top$, $\nu_i(c) = \nu_{i-1}(c) + t_i$ otherwise. Since time values t_i represents *delay* times, we call such a timed trace a *delay-timed word*. The delay-timed word is observed outside from the view of the global clock. On the other hand, the behavior can also be observed inside from the view of the local clock. This results in a *logical-timed word* of the form $\gamma = (\sigma_1, \mu_1)(\sigma_2, \mu_2) \cdots (\sigma_n, \mu_n)$ with $\mu_i = t_i$ if $i = 1$ or $b_{i-1} = \top$, otherwise $\mu_i = \mu_{i-1} + t_i$. The time spent in a timed trace ω, denoted $time(\omega)$ is the sum of all delays in ω, for example, $time(\epsilon) = 0$ and $time((a, 1.0)(b, 1.5)) = 2.5$.

Definition 2 (Deterministic OTA). *An OTA is a deterministic one-clock timed automaton (DOTA) if there is at most one run for a given timed word.*

A DOTA $\mathcal{A}$ is *complete* if for any location q and action σ, the constraints form a partition of $\mathbb{R}_{\geq 0}$. Any incomplete DOTA $\mathcal{A}$ can be transformed into a complete DOTA accepting the same timed language by adding a non-accepting *sink* location q_{sink}, and adding transitions to the sink location for each unavailable action [8]. We therefore assume that we are working with complete DOTAs.

2.2 Active Learning Algorithm for DOTAs

In this section, we provide a brief description of the active learning algorithm [8] for a black-box SUL which can be represented by a DOTA $\mathcal{A}$. The existing work distinguishes two learning scenarios: learning from a *normal teacher* or a *smart teacher*. As the work in this paper concerns EQs only, it applies to both normal teacher and smart teacher scenarios. For the experiments, we mainly consider the case of smart teachers. In practical applications, this corresponds to executing the test case, where information about clock-resets is known by code instrumentation or watchdogs (refer to the concept of testable systems in [15,18]). The learner maintains an *observation table* to collect the answers of MQs. The table will be transformed to a DOTA $\mathcal{H}$ as a hypothesis if it satisfies several preparedness conditions. The learner then performs an EQ by submitting $\mathcal{H}$ to the teacher. In theory, we assume that the teacher holds an equivalence oracle to answer EQs, returning whether the timed languages of $\mathcal{H}$ and $\mathcal{A}$ are equivalent. If the answer is no, the teacher also returns a logical-timed word with reset information as a counterexample. The learner then performs more MQs guided by the counterexample. The learning loop terminates when an EQ returns a positive answer. We refer to [8] for more details.

However, since such equivalence oracles may not exist in practical situations, the equivalence oracle is often achieved through conformance testing, i.e., asking a lot of MQs to answer a single EQ. If, for every MQ, the output produced by the SUL is consistent with hypothesis $\mathcal{H}$, the answer to the EQ is "Yes". Otherwise, the answer "No" is provided, together with a counterexample that indicates a difference between $\mathcal{H}$ and the SUL. In this paper, we address the implementation of equivalence oracle through a combination of random testing and mutation analysis.

2.3 Model-Based Mutation Testing

Model-based mutation testing [2,3,23] is a promising technique combining the central ideas of mutation testing [21] and model-based testing [27]. By making some adaptions, it can be regarded as an equivalence oracle in the context of active learning. The process starts with the current hypothesis $\mathcal{H}$. A set of mutants from $\mathcal{H}$ are generated by mutation operators. Once all mutants are created, the actual test suite generation starts. The original $\mathcal{H}$ is compared to each mutant via an equivalence check (this can be done exactly since models for both $\mathcal{H}$ and the mutant are available). If a mutant $\mathcal{M}$ is not equivalent to $\mathcal{H}$, the checking procedure returns a trace that serves as a witness, and this trace can be converted into a test case.

The equivalence checks in the above process can be computationally expensive. Therefore, the work in [6] considers a new model-based mutation testing framework combined with random testing for learning Mealy machines, and the experiments have demonstrated that a combination of random exploration and mutation-based test-case generation is beneficial. Briefly, the framework includes the following steps to generate test suites for conformance testing. First, it utilizes random testing to generate a large set of test cases $\mathbf{T}$. Then it analyzes the mutation coverage of each test case in $\mathbf{T}$, i.e., it executes each test case and determines which of the mutants produces outputs different from $\mathcal{H}$. Finally, the test suite is created by selecting a subset of $\mathbf{T}$ based on the computed mutation coverage. After that, the conformance testing between $\mathcal{H}$ and the SUL can be conducted by executing test cases of the test suite on both respectively. The test case producing different outputs between $\mathcal{H}$ and the SUL is a counterexample to the equivalence, which is utilized to further refine the current hypothesis $\mathcal{H}$.

3   Mutation-Based Testing for DOTAs

In this section, we introduce our mutation-based testing process for solving the EQs in learning DOTAs. We first describe the whole process and then present the heuristic method to generate test cases and the mutation-based selection of the test suite. The details on the mutation operators and mutation generation are described in Sect. 4.

3.1   The Process Overview

Following the idea in [6], we use a combination of random testing, to achieve high variability of tests, and mutation analysis, to address coverage appropriately. However, given the particular characteristics of DOTAs learning, that is, counterexample processing will generate two kinds of modifications between two

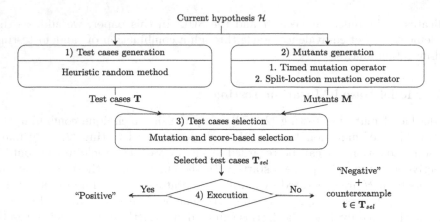

Fig. 1. The overview of mutation-testing-based equivalence checking for learning DOTAs.

successive hypotheses, we have to design new mutation operators and adapt the framework accordingly. The whole process is depicted in Fig. 1. The input for this process is a hypothesis $\mathcal{H}$, a learned intermediate DOTA, while the output is the answer of an EQ.

1. From the model $\mathcal{H}$, we first develop a heuristic test-case generation algorithm to obtain a large set of test cases $\mathbf{T}$ (see Sect. 3.2).
2. Independently, we generate a set of mutants $\mathbf{M}$ from $\mathcal{H}$ based on the timed mutation operator (see Sect. 4.1) and the split-location mutation operator (see Sect. 4.2).
3. Using a score-based test-case selection method, together with mutation analysis, a subset $\mathbf{T}_{sel}$ of $\mathbf{T}$ is selected (see Sect. 3.3). The purpose is to select a subset of test cases from $\mathbf{T}$ that are likely to distinguish between the original hypothesis $\mathcal{H}$ and the mutants as the test suite to execute, i.e. to select the test cases that cover the mutants.
4. Finally, we execute all test cases in $\mathbf{T}_{sel}$ on the hypothesis $\mathcal{H}$ and the SUL respectively. A test case is a counterexample if producing different outputs on the SUL and $\mathcal{H}$. If such a counterexample is found, it is returned to the learning algorithm. Otherwise, the EQ returns a positive answer.

Different from [6] using only one mutation operator for generating mutants, we hereby use two mutation operators to cover the different possibilities of mutations for timed automata. This produces a set of mutants helpful for generating a more complete test suite that is able to find potential differences between $\mathcal{H}$ and the SUL. Our experiments have shown that both mutation operators are necessary for improving the rate of learning the correct model of the SUL. In addition, to avoid interleaving complexity, instead of simultaneously using two mutation operators to generate test cases, we divide the process into two phases using two operators respectively. In our case, we choose to first use the timed

Algorithm 1. Heuristic test-case generation

Input: hypothesis $\mathcal{H} = (\Sigma, Q, q_0, F, c, \Delta)$;
the previous counterexample ctx;
the maximal length len of "xy"
part of a test case; three probabi-
lity values p_{start}, p_{valid} and p_{stop}.

Output: a test case **t**.

1: $\mathbf{t} \leftarrow \epsilon$;
2: $q_c \leftarrow q_0$; $\nu \leftarrow 0$;
3: $Q_{visited} \leftarrow \emptyset$;
4: **if** $\mathbf{prob}(p_{start})$ **then** $\mathbf{t} \leftarrow ctx$;
5:    **for** $i \leftarrow 0$ to $|ctx| - 1$ **do**
6:      $q_c, \nu \leftarrow execute((q_c, \nu), ctx[i])$;
7:      $Q_{visited} \leftarrow Q_{visited} \cup \{q_c\}$;
8: **while** $|\mathbf{t}| < len$ **do**
9:    **if** $\mathbf{prob}(p_{valid})$ **then**
10:      $\Delta' \leftarrow \{\delta | \delta = (q, \sigma, \phi, b, q') \in \Delta \wedge q = q_c \wedge q' \neq q_{sink}\}$;
11:    **else**

12:      $\Delta' \leftarrow \{\delta | \delta = (q, \sigma, \phi, b, q') \in \Delta \wedge q = q_c \wedge q' = q_{sink}\}$;
13:    **if** $\Delta' \neq \emptyset$ **then**
14:      $(q, \sigma, \phi, b, q') \leftarrow getRandom(\Delta')$;
15:      $t \leftarrow getRandomDelay(\nu, \phi)$;
16:      **if** $t \neq None$ **then**
17:        $\mathbf{t} \leftarrow \mathbf{t} \cdot (\sigma, t)$;
18:        $q_c, \nu \leftarrow execute((q_c, \nu), (\sigma, t))$;
19:        $Q_{visited} \leftarrow Q_{visited} \cup \{q_c\}$;
20:    **if** $\mathbf{prob}(p_{stop})$ **then**
21:      **break**;
22: **if** $Q \backslash Q_{visited} \neq \emptyset$ **then**
23:    $q_t \leftarrow getRandomLocation(Q \backslash Q_{visited})$;
24:    $\omega \leftarrow findTimedTrace((q_c, \nu), q_t)$;
25:    **if** $\omega \neq \epsilon$ **then**
26:      $\mathbf{t} \leftarrow \mathbf{t} \cdot \omega$;
27: **return t**;

mutation operator only, and if no counterexample is found, then use the split-location mutation operator and repeat Step 2 to Step 4.

3.2 Heuristic Test-Case Generation

Random testing is a widely-used method and has been integrated in the learning library LearnLib [20] as an EQ method for untimed models. In this section, we apply three heuristics to generate test cases randomly, aiming at generating more useful test cases. Algorithm 1 presents the generation process, containing three main steps corresponding to the heuristics. The inputs include the current hypothesis $\mathcal{H}$ and several relevant parameters, and the output is a test case $\mathbf{t} \in (\Sigma \times \mathbb{R}_{\geq 0})^*$ of the form xyz, where x is the prefix, y a random sequence of timed actions, and z the suffix. Function $\mathbf{prob}(p)$ returns true with probability p and false with probability $1 - p$. The generation process is performed many times to generate a large-size (can be parameterized by the user) test set $\mathbf{T}$, whose size is related to the number of actions and transitions, and the timing parameters of $\mathcal{H}$ (see Sect. 5).

1. Firstly, according to our observation that a counterexample is often prefixed with its previous counterexample, we reuse the previous counterexample ctx as the prefix x with probability p_{start} (Line 4 to Line 7).
2. Then, consider for many reactive systems, from the current timed state, randomly selecting an action is likely to transit to a sink location, since not all timed actions can be executed or make sense at the current state. Therefore, we prefer to explore non-sink locations with probability p_{valid} when using random walking method to find timed actions (σ, t). Such timed actions form the segment y extending the test case (Line 8 to Line 21). The parameter len

---

Algorithm 2. Mutation and score-based test-case selection

Input: $\mathbf{M}$; $\mathbf{T}_{\mathcal{M}}$ for all $\mathcal{M} \in \mathbf{M}$;
    V_t for all $\mathbf{t} \in \mathbf{T}$.
Output: a subset of test cases $\mathbf{T}_{sel}$.
1: $\mathbf{T}_{sel} \leftarrow \emptyset$;
2: **while** $\mathbf{M} \neq \emptyset$ **do**
3:    $\mathcal{M}_{opt} \leftarrow argmin_{\mathcal{M} \in \mathbf{M}} |\mathbf{T}_{\mathcal{M}}|$;

4:    **if** $\mathbf{T}_{\mathcal{M}_{opt}} \neq \emptyset$ and $\mathbf{T}_{\mathcal{M}_{opt}} \cap \mathbf{T}_{sel}$
      $= \emptyset$ **then**
5:      $\mathbf{t}_{opt} \leftarrow argmax_{\mathbf{t} \in \mathbf{T}_{\mathcal{M}_{opt}}} V_t$;
6:      $\mathbf{T}_{sel} \leftarrow \mathbf{T}_{sel} \cup \{\mathbf{t}_{opt}\}$;
7:    $\mathbf{M} \leftarrow \mathbf{M} \backslash \{\mathcal{M}_{opt}\}$;
8: **return** $\mathbf{T}_{sel}$;

---

limits the maximal length of the "xy" part. The exploring process stops with probability p_{stop} at the end of each round.

3. Finally, we add the path from the current location to a non-visited location as suffix z to increase the coverage of each test case (Line 22 to Line 26).

3.3 Mutation and Score-Based Test-Case Selection

In order to improve the mutation coverage of test cases, we define a special output function in response to a given delay-timed word. Let $\mathcal{D} = \{+, -\}$ be the output domain, indicating whether the trace is accepted $(+)$ or not $(-)$.

Definition 3 (Output function). *Given a test case (delay-timed word) $\mathbf{t} = (\sigma_1, t_1) (\sigma_2, t_2) \cdots (\sigma_n, t_n)$ and a (complete) DOTA $\mathcal{A} = (\Sigma, Q, q_0, F, c, \Delta)$, corresponding a run $\rho = (q_0, \nu_0) \xrightarrow{\sigma_1, t_1} (q_1, \nu_1) \xrightarrow{\sigma_2, t_2} \cdots \xrightarrow{\sigma_n, t_n} (q_n, \nu_n)$ in $\mathcal{A}$, the output function for the test case is defined as $out_{\mathcal{A}}(\mathbf{t}) = o_1 o_2 \cdots o_n$, where $o_i = +$ if $q_i \subseteq F$ and $o_i = -$ otherwise.*

Given two models $\mathcal{A}_1$ and $\mathcal{A}_2$, we say $\mathbf{t}$ *passes* if $out_{\mathcal{A}_1}(\mathbf{t}) = out_{\mathcal{A}_2}(\mathbf{t})$, otherwise, it *fails* and serves as a counterexample to the equivalence.

After the heuristic test-case generation described previously, we have obtained a large-size test set $\mathbf{T}$. However, it may contain just a small number of test cases that can be counterexamples due to the randomness. Therefore, we further need to select a subset $\mathbf{T}_{sel}$ from $\mathbf{T}$ consisting of test cases that are more likely to be counterexamples. Normally, the selection is based purely on a kind of coverage, e.g. location or transition coverage. However, unlike testing for Mealy machines [6,14] or other finite labeled transition systems, for timed systems, we should also consider the time elapsed in two consecutive input actions. Therefore, the main objective in addition to the number of test cases is to reduce the accumulated delay time of all test cases used in conformance testing, provided that the maximum mutant coverage is achieved. Our selection process is based on a set of mutants of the hypothesis $\mathcal{H}$. We leave the details of mutation generation in Sect. 4 and suppose that a set of mutants $\mathbf{M}$ has been generated.

Algorithm 2 presents the mutation and score-based selection method, which considers several factors of the test cases. At beginning, we need to prepare the inputs. First, we associate each test case $\mathbf{t} \in \mathbf{T}$ with a set of mutants $\mathbf{M}_t$ covered by $\mathbf{t}$, i.e. $\mathbf{M}_t = \{\mathcal{M} \in \mathbf{M} \mid out_{\mathcal{H}}(\mathbf{t}) \neq out_{\mathcal{M}}(\mathbf{t})\}$, and associate each mutant $\mathcal{M} \in \mathbf{M}$ with a set of test cases $\mathbf{T}_{\mathcal{M}} \in \mathbf{T}$ that can cover $\mathcal{M}$, i.e. $\mathbf{T}_{\mathcal{M}} = \{\mathbf{t} \in \mathbf{T} \mid out_{\mathcal{H}}(\mathbf{t}) \neq out_{\mathcal{M}}(\mathbf{t})\}$. Then, we use the following four attributes to decide whether a test case $\mathbf{t}$ is selected: (1) $time(\mathbf{t})$ is the total delay time of $\mathbf{t}$, (2) $|\mathbf{t}|$ is the length of $\mathbf{t}$, (3) $|\mathbf{M}_{\mathbf{t}}|$ is the mutation coverage of $\mathbf{t}$, and (4) $|\mathbf{C}_{\mathbf{t}}|$ is the transition coverage of $\mathbf{t}$. After normalization for the attributes, we acquire the score $V_{\mathbf{t}} = a \cdot (1 - time(\mathbf{t})') + b \cdot (1 - |\mathbf{t}|') + c \cdot |\mathbf{M}_{\mathbf{t}}|' + d \cdot |\mathbf{C}_{\mathbf{t}}|'$, where a, b, c, d are the weights. Upon obtaining $\mathbf{T}_{\mathcal{M}}$ for each mutant $\mathcal{M}$ and $V_{\mathbf{t}}$ for each test case $\mathbf{t}$, the algorithm follows the basic idea that the higher the score value, the more likely the test case will be selected. So, at each round, first select the mutant $\mathcal{M}$ covered by the least number of test cases (Line 3). If the currently selected test cases $\mathbf{T}_{sel}$ cannot cover it, the test case $\mathbf{t}$ with the largest score $\mathbf{V}_{\mathbf{t}}$ is chosen from $\mathbf{T}_{\mathcal{M}_{opt}}$ and added to $\mathbf{T}_{sel}$ (Line 4 to Line 6). Then remove $\mathcal{M}$ from $\mathbf{M}$. The steps repeat until all mutants covered by at least one test case are considered, i.e. the selected test cases have been able to achieve the maximum possible coverage of the mutant set. Mutants that cannot be covered by any test case are removed by constraint $\mathbf{T}_{\mathcal{M}_{opt}} \neq \emptyset$ in Line 4.

4   Learning-Friendly Mutation Operators for DOTAs

In order to provide the mutants of hypothesis $\mathcal{H}$ for the processes in Sect. 3, we need to design suitable mutation operators for DOTAs. Considering the learning method in [8], we find that counterexample handling will lead to generating two kinds of modifications between the successive hypotheses $\mathcal{H}$ and $\mathcal{H}'$. Similar to the terms used in [24], the first is called *expansive modification*, which means that $\mathcal{H}'$ has more locations and/or transitions than $\mathcal{H}$. While the second is called *non-expansive modification*, which implies that only the timed constraints and/or the reset indicators of some transitions differ between $\mathcal{H}$ and $\mathcal{H}'$. Inspired by the observations, we design two *mutation operators*. The first one is *timed mutation operator* given in Sect. 4.1, which includes a series of mutation operations specific to DOTAs learning, corresponding to the transition changes of the expansive and non-expansive modification. The second, *split-loaction mutation operator* given in Sect. 4.2, is closely related to [6], corresponding to the location change of the *expansive modification*. In terms of the two designed operators, all the mutants generated from $\mathcal{H}$ are still deterministic automata.

4.1   Timed Mutation Operator

Given the current hypothesis $\mathcal{H}$, the timed mutation operator is conducted on every transition in turn to generate mutants. Consider a transition $\delta = (q, \sigma, \phi, b, q')$, the basic idea is as follows. For the timed interval ϕ, we will first slice it into sub-intervals as a partition (see Definition 4), resulting in several new transitions. Then we conduct two operations (see Definition 5) on each new transition to generate mutants. One operation is to change the target location of one transition, which helps us to modify the timed interval ϕ. The other operation is to change the reset indicator of one transition. Actually, we can also apply the two operations to some transitions at the same time.

Algorithm 3. Mutants generation via the timed mutation operator

Input: a DOTA $\mathcal{H} = (\Sigma, Q, q_0, F, c, \Delta)$;   4:   **for each** $\delta_s \in \Delta_s$ **do**
     the greatest integer constant B;   5: $\Delta_m \leftarrow rt(\delta_s) \cup fl(\delta_s) \cup$
     a slicing step w. $fl \circ rt(\delta_s)$;
OUTPUT: a set of mutants **M**.   6:   **for each** $\delta_m \in \Delta_m$ **do**
1: $\mathbf{M} \leftarrow \emptyset$ 7: $\mathcal{M} \leftarrow (\Sigma, Q, q_0, F, c, \Delta\backslash\{\delta\};$
2: **for each** $\delta = (q, \sigma, \phi, b, q') \in \Delta$ **do** $\cup \Delta_s\backslash\{\delta_s\} \cup \{\delta_m\});$
3:     $\Delta_s \leftarrow \{(q, \sigma, \phi_s, b, q') \mid \phi_s \in$ 8: $\mathbf{M} \leftarrow \mathbf{M} \cup \{\mathcal{M}\};$
          $S_g(\phi, B, w)\};$ 9: **return M**;

Definition 4 (Slicing timed interval). *Let B be the greatest integer constant appearing in the DOTA to be learned (can also be set by the user), and $w \in \mathbb{N}_{>0}$ be the slicing step. Given a timed interval $\langle \alpha, \beta \rangle$, where $\langle \in \{(, [\} \text{ and } \rangle \in \{),]\}$, the slicing can generate a partition of $\langle \alpha, \beta \rangle$ as follows:*

- *If $\beta > B$ (including $\beta = \infty$), $S_g(\langle \alpha, \beta \rangle, B, w)$*
  $= \{\langle \alpha, \alpha + w) \mid \alpha + w \leq B\} \cup \{[\alpha + w * i, \alpha + w * i] \mid \alpha + w * i \leq B, i \in \mathbb{N}_{>0}\}$
  $\cup \{(\alpha + w * i, \alpha + w * (i + 1)) \mid \alpha + w * (i + 1) \leq B, i \in \mathbb{N}_{>0}\}$
  $\cup \{(\alpha + w * i, \beta\rangle \mid \alpha + w * i \leq B \wedge \alpha + w * (i + 1) > B, i \in \mathbb{N}_{>0}\}$
- *If $\beta \leq B$, $S_g(\langle \alpha, \beta \rangle, B, w)$*
  $= \{\langle \alpha, \alpha + w) \mid \alpha + w < \beta\} \cup \{[\alpha + w * i, \alpha + w * i] \mid \alpha + w * i < \beta, i \in \mathbb{N}_{>0}\}$
  $\cup \{(\alpha + w * i, \alpha + w * (i + 1)) \mid \alpha + w * (i + 1) < \beta, i \in \mathbb{N}_{>0}\}$
  $\cup \{(\alpha + w * i, \beta\rangle \mid \alpha + w * i < \beta \wedge \alpha + w * (i + 1) \geq \beta, i \in \mathbb{N}_{>0}\}$

Therefore, for a transition $\delta = (q, \sigma, \phi, b, q')$ in $\mathcal{H}$, ϕ is sliced into several timed intervals $S_g(\phi, B, w)$. This implies that instead of δ, a new transition set $\Delta_s = \{(q, \sigma, \phi_s, b, q') \mid \phi_s \in S_g(\phi, B, w)\}$ with $|\Delta_s| = |S_g(\phi, B, w)|$ is generated. Obviously, if the slicing step $w = 1$, the intervals in S_g are *regions* [7].

Definition 5 (Timed mutation operations). *Given a sliced transition $\delta_s = (q, \sigma, \phi_s, b, q') \in \Delta_s$, the timed mutation operator includes the following two operations: (1) Re-target: $rt(\delta_s) = \{(q, \sigma, \phi_s, b, q'') \mid q'' \in Q\backslash q'\}$; (2) Flop-reset: $fl(\delta_s) = \{(q, \sigma, \phi_s, b', q') \mid b' \in \mathbb{B}\backslash b\}$.*

Algorithm 3 presents the procedure generating mutants from $\mathcal{H}$ using the timed mutation operator. First, for each transition δ, we build the sliced transition set Δ_s (Line 3). Second, for each sliced transition $\delta_s \in \Delta_s$, we conduct the mutation operations rt and fl separately and both on it, and thus get a mutated transition set Δ_m (Line 5). Then, for each mutated transition $\delta_m \in \Delta_m$, we can build a mutant by removing δ, δ_s, and adding the new mutated transition δ_m to the transition set (Line 7). Therefore, every mutant is obtained from $\mathcal{H}$ via the options of changing the timed constraints, or flopping the reset indicator, or adding new transitions, or a combination of the above three, so that the mutant gets closer to the successor hypothesis $\mathcal{H}'$. To simplify a mutant, we merge two transitions if they have the same source location, target location, action, and reset indicator respectively. For example, given two transitions $(q, \sigma, [2, 4], b, q')$ and $(q, \sigma, (4, 5], b, q')$, the merged transition is $(q, \sigma, [2, 5], b, q')$.

4.2 Split-Location Mutation Operator

The *split-location mutation operator* mainly involves modification on locations while not the timed information on transitions, which was first introduced in [6] for the learning of Mealy machines. To deal with DOTAs, we make some modifications for the operator that includes the execution of the following steps: (1) making abstraction from a DOTA to a DFA by labeling every transition with a different abstract action u, (2) mutating the DFA using split-location operator referring to [6], and (3) transforming the mutated DFA back to a DOTA as a mutant of the original DOTA. In order to instantiate the split-location mutation operator in our implementation and experiments, we also need two parameters: n_{acc} is an upper bound on the number of access sequences leading to a split location and k is the length of a distinguishing sequence.

5 Implementation and Experiments

To further investigate the efficiency of the proposed method, we extend the existing DOTAs learning prototype tool in [8] with the proposed EQ implementation and evaluate it on a set of DOTAs. The experiments are meant to check whether the proposed technique is an effective implementation of equivalence oracle to find counterexamples for incorrect hypotheses under the DOTAs learning setting. The prototype tool and experiments are available on the tool page https:// github.com/Anna9697/mut_learn_DOTAs.

5.1 Case Studies

First, we evaluated the DOTAs learning with mutation-based testing on 18 randomly generated DOTAs. We divided them into 6 groups depending on the number of locations ($|Q|$), the number of untimed actions ($|\Sigma|$), and the maximum constant appearing in the models (B). In addition, there are also three manually created examples from the real world: a lamp touch control model (Lamp) from [5], a coffee vending machine model (Coffee) from [30], and the model of TCP protocol (TCP) from [8].

For each case, we executed 15 times to acquire the average number of tests ($\#tests$) and actions ($\#actions$), the average accumulated delay time in tests (t_{delay}), and the number of correct models learned (n_{exact}). We used the same exact equivalence oracle in [8] to judge whether the learned automata were completely correct or not. The related parameters to run the experiments are as follows. To generate test cases via Algorithm 1, we set parameters $p_{start} = 0.4$, $p_{valid} = 0.8$, $p_{stop} = 0.05$ and $len = 2 \cdot |Q|$, where $|Q|$ is the number of locations of models in each group, and sampled delay-time value at a granularity of 0.5 with the upper bound $1.5 \cdot B$. We obtain a test suite $\mathbf{T}$ with size $|\mathbf{T}| = 30 \cdot |Q_{\mathcal{H}}| \cdot |\Sigma_{\mathcal{H}}| \cdot B$ by repeatedly calling Algorithm 1, where $|Q_{\mathcal{H}}|$ and $|\Sigma_{\mathcal{H}}|$ are the number of locations and actions of the current hypothesis $\mathcal{H}$ respectively. In the mutation generation, for the timed mutation operator, we set the slicing step w to the minimal *duration* of the constraints of the models[1]. While for split-location mutation

---

[1] Set $w = 1$ if no additional information is known.

Table 1. Experimental results of case studies.

Case ID	Mutation_new				Mutants_checking				Heuristic_random_testing			
	#tests	#actions	t_{delay}	n_{exact}	#tests	#actions	t_{delay}	n_{exact}	#tests	#actions	t_{delay}	n_{exact}
6_2_10-1	443.1	2592.1	9012.3	15	2640.2	9295.9	28774.7	15	3372.0	14405.0	46005.1	15
6_2_10-2	559.9	3254.1	15934.2	15	3004.6	9141.6	36273.7	15	4204.3	20711.0	97402.2	15
6_2_10-3	967.1	6218.8	21540.9	15	9389.0	32769.5	94801.4	15	5640.5	34557.3	132976.6	12
6_2_20-1	1085.8	7475.5	41588.0	15	11616.6	42426.0	171239.0	15	6957.6	36032.3	206737.9	15
6_2_20-2	614.4	3669.9	21300.3	15	3572.5	13607.7	58794.7	15	6885.5	33562.3	181704.7	15
6_2_20-3	1428.3	8817.3	59688.2	15	12931.5	40198.2	233110.7	15	9529.8	53712.3	387141.1	15
6_2_30-1	859.6	6626.6	54486.0	15	4244.8	13544.9	100506.4	15	9238.7	61385.1	729274.2	15
6_2_30-2	2381.5	18481.1	181969.8	15	43635.6	155341.7	1236780.6	15	17205.5	112464.1	1346503.8	15
6_2_30-3	1321.1	7378.7	68047.2	15	9877.7	27839.6	259687.3	15	9600.3	41289.2	419800.6	15
6_4_10-1	1003.0	7129.3	24928.0	15	7582.0	19563.7	57116.9	15	6430.1	27362.5	90757.6	15
6_4_10-2	797.5	5618.1	15934.7	15	8857.2	24367.8	65501.0	15	6042.5	30837.7	103849.5	15
6_4_10-3	805.9	5299.8	18883.0	15	9668.0	27604.1	60054.4	15	6605.8	33476.7	124421.4	15
6_6_10-1	1052.0	5822.4	19984.1	15	13569.4	31987.9	70455.2	15	9058.4	40925.5	125318.0	15
6_6_10-2	956.8	5965.6	29055.3	15	16273.2	39944.4	151809.1	15	11260.3	50044.5	193209.0	15
6_6_10-3	1243.9	7204.4	25286.5	15	11422.4	25626.3	68280.0	15	9161.1	43958.1	166033.1	15
10_2_10-1	883.7	8550.7	24911.4	15	13000.7	61353.5	105297.1	15	5168.2	39441.7	128707.0	15
10_2_10-2	1512.5	12905.2	38655.8	15	5826.2	26173.5	50920.1	15	7016.8	50663.2	177461.2	15
10_2_10-3	1398.5	12173.1	49605.8	15	22901.7	96580.9	265156.0	15	8166.5	63442.1	253596.7	15
5_5_10-Lamp	568.3	3396.8	18240.8	15	3076.3	8113.6	31719.7	15	11776.9	51956.6	287967.0	15
4_7_10-Coffee	766.3	3585.8	12264.1	15	6329.7	13279.9	33141.1	15	7374.7	35100.8	126433.5	15
11_10_10-TCP	4525.6	26779.9	87720.3	15	160482.1	480235.5	841312.0	15	36427.1	206505.9	483336.1	15

operator, we set $n_{acc} = 8$ and $k = 1$. In the mutation-based selection of test cases, we set the weights with a = 0.4, b = 0.4, c = 0.6, and d = 0.2 to calculate the scores.

We refer to our mutation-based testing for DOTAs learning as **Mutation_new**. We also set two baseline methods, **Mutants_checking** and **Heuristic_random_testing**. In the former, we first generate mutants using the method in Sect. 4 and then generate test cases by equivalence checking between the current hypothesis and each mutant as introduced in [23]. Hence, a test case is a timed word showing the violation of equivalence. In the latter, we directly use the test cases **T** generated by repeating Algorithm 1 without any mutation or selection. We compare our technique with the two baseline methods. To ensure the comparability of the different techniques, the parameter settings are the same as those mentioned previously.

The experimental results of the three methods are given in Table 1. It shows that the three methods can learn the correct model in all cases except for one failure for **Heuristic_random_testing** on model 6_2_10-3. Our method takes the least number of test cases, actions, and accumulated delay time on all cases, beating the two baseline methods by about an order of magnitude. Among the baseline methods, **Mutants_checking** costs less on average than **Heuristic_random_testing**, but the comparison is highly variable across cases. In order to evaluate the quality of the incorrect learned model for 6_2_10-3, we randomly generated extra 50000 test cases to test the learned model. The passing rate is 99.27%. Additionally, we analyze why **Heuristic_random_testing** failed once but **Mutation_new** did not. As we know, for an EQ, T_{sel} is a subset of **T**.

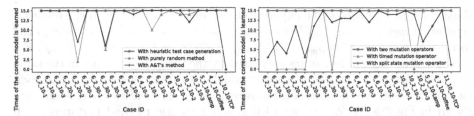

(a) The comparison on the number of times the correct models learned using different test-case generation methods.

(b) The comparison on the number of times the correct models learned using two mutation operators separately and both.

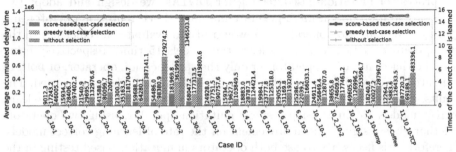

(c) The comparisons on average accumulated delay time in test cases and the number of times the correct models learned using different test-case selection methods.

Fig. 2. Experimental results of the evaluation of improvements.

The found counterexamples for an EQ may be different using two methods, thus leading to different hypotheses which will affect the learning process further.

5.2 Evaluation of Improvements

We continue to use the cases in Table 1 to evaluate the improvements of the three main contributions in the context of learning: heuristic test-case generation method, two special mutation operators, and score-based test-case selection. The following three experiments are conducted:

E1. Comparison of the heuristic test-case generation and the baseline.
E2. Comparison of the algorithm with and without the two mutation operators.
E3. Comparison of the mutation and score-based test-case selection, the greedy test-case selection, and without selection.

E1. Evaluation of the Heuristic Test-Case Generation. The quality of the test cases **T** obtained using heuristic test-case generation is critical, as the test cases we execute on the system are selected from **T**. In order to evaluate our heuristic test-case generation method, we compare it with a purely random method (randomly select actions and delay times to form timed traces) and the A&T's method (another random testing approach discussed in [6]). In other words, in the whole testing process, the experiments conducted only differ in the test-case generation method. For A&T's method, we set values to the parameters in the method as $p_{retry} = 0.9$, $p_{stop} = 0.05$, $l_{infix} = |Q|/2$, and $maxSteps = 2 \cdot |Q|$. For each case, the original test suites generated by the three methods are of the same size. Still, for each case, we learn the models 15 times respectively using each method and observe the times of the correct models are learned. The results are shown in Fig. 2(a). It can be found that our heuristic method performs much better than the other two methods on learning out correct models.

E2. Evaluation of the Two Mutation Operators. As described in Sect. 3.1, during the process of mutation-based testing for DOTAs, we design and adopt two kinds of mutation operators to generate mutants: timed mutation operator and split-location mutation operator. We would like to evaluate the efficiency of the two operators. For each case, we learn the models 15 times respectively using only the timed mutation operator, or only the split-location operator, or both to generate mutants, and observe the times of the correct models are learned. The results, given in Fig. 2(b), shows that although for some cases we are able to learn correct models 15 times using a single mutation operator, using two operators together gives a significant improvement on the rate of learning correct models. Therefore, it is necessary to use both operators in mutation-based testing in the context of DOTAs learning.

E3. Evaluation of the Mutation and Score-Based Test-Case Selection. Our mutation-score-based test-case selection algorithm considers various attributes and guarantees mutation coverage at the same time. We compared the method with a greedy test-case selection method [6] which only guarantees that the test suite selected provides maximum coverage of the mutants. The experiments are conducted differently only in the selection of test cases. Running all cases without any test-case selection procedure is as the baseline. We run each experiment for 15 times on each case and the results are shown in Fig. 2(c). Considering the number of times the correct model is learned, both selection methods performed better than the baseline (this is because the found counterexamples for an EQ are different by different methods, which lead to different hypotheses and will affect the learning process further). On most cases, our selection approach has the least accumulated delay time except for case 6_6_10-3 and case 11_10_10-TCP. However, for these two cases, we can still achieve better results than the greedy test-case selection method by adjusting parameters.

6   Conclusion

We presented a conformance testing approach combining random testing and model-based mutation testing, which can be used for EQs in the active learning of DOTAs. The experimental results show the effectiveness and efficiency of our two learning-friendly mutation operators and several heuristics in the generation and selection of test cases. Since the performance depends on the instantiation of parameters and we set parameters according to our experience, one possible future work is to determine automatic methods for setting or online adaption of parameters according to the learning scenarios.

References

1. Aarts, F., Kuppens, H., Tretmans, J., Vaandrager, F., Verwer, S.: Improving active Mealy machine learning for protocol conformance testing. Mach. Learn. **96**, 189–224 (2013). https://doi.org/10.1007/s10994-013-5405-0
2. Aichernig, B.K., et al.: Model-based mutation testing of an industrial measurement device. In: Seidl, M., Tillmann, N. (eds.) TAP 2014. LNCS, vol. 8570, pp. 1–19. Springer, Cham (2014). https://doi.org/10.1007/978-3-319-09099-3_1
3. Aichernig, B.K., Brandl, H., Jöbstl, E., Krenn, W., Schlick, R., Tiran, S.: Killing strategies for model-based mutation testing. Softw. Test. Verification Reliab. **25**(8), 716–748 (2015). https://doi.org/10.1002/stvr.1522
4. Aichernig, B.K., Lorber, F., Ničković, D.: Time for mutants—model-based mutation testing with timed automata. In: Veanes, M., Viganò, L. (eds.) TAP 2013. LNCS, vol. 7942, pp. 20–38. Springer, Heidelberg (2013). https://doi.org/10.1007/978-3-642-38916-0_2
5. Aichernig, B.K., Pferscher, A., Tappler, M.: From passive to active: learning timed automata efficiently. In: Lee, R., Jha, S., Mavridou, A., Giannakopoulou, D. (eds.) NFM 2020. LNCS, vol. 12229, pp. 1–19. Springer, Cham (2020). https://doi.org/10.1007/978-3-030-55754-6_1
6. Aichernig, B.K., Tappler, M.: Efficient active automata learning via mutation testing. J. Autom. Reason. **63**(4), 1103–1134 (2018). https://doi.org/10.1007/s10817-018-9486-0
7. Alur, R., Dill, D.L.: A theory of timed automata. Theoret. Comput. Sci. **126**(2), 183–235 (1994). https://doi.org/10.1016/0304-3975(94)90010-8
8. An, J., Chen, M., Zhan, B., Zhan, N., Zhang, M.: Learning one-clock timed automata. In: TACAS 2020. LNCS, vol. 12078, pp. 444–462. Springer, Cham (2020). https://doi.org/10.1007/978-3-030-45190-5_25
9. An, J., Wang, L., Zhan, B., Zhan, N., Zhang, M.: Learning real-time automata. Sci. China Inf. Sci. **64**(9), 1–17 (2021) https://doi.org/10.1007/s11432-019-2767-4
10. An, J., Zhan, B., Zhan, N., Zhang, M.: Learning nondeterministic real-time automata. ACM Trans. Embed. Comput. Syst. **20**(5s), 1–26 (2021). https://doi.org/10.1145/3477030
11. Andrews, J.H., Briand, L.C., Labiche, Y., Namin, A.S.: Using mutation analysis for assessing and comparing testing coverage criteria. IEEE Trans. Software Eng. **32**(8), 608–624 (2006). https://doi.org/10.1109/TSE.2006.83
12. Angluin, D.: Learning regular sets from queries and counterexamples. Inf. Comput. **75**(2), 87–106 (1987). https://doi.org/10.1016/0890-5401(87)90052-6
13. Berg, T., Grinchtein, O., Jonsson, B., Leucker, M., Raffelt, H., Steffen, B.: On the correspondence between conformance testing and regular inference. In: Cerioli, M. (ed.) FASE 2005. LNCS, vol. 3442, pp. 175–189. Springer, Heidelberg (2005). https://doi.org/10.1007/978-3-540-31984-9_14
14. Chow, T.: Testing software design modeled by finite-state machines. IEEE Trans. Software Eng. **3**, 178–187 (1978). https://doi.org/10.1109/TSE.1978.231496
15. En-Nouaary, A., Dssouli, R., Khendek, F.: Timed Wp-method: Testing real-time systems. IEEE Trans. Software Eng. **28**(11), 1023–1038 (2002). https://doi.org/10.1109/TSE.2002.1049402

16. Grinchtein, O., Jonsson, B., Leucker, M.: Learning of event-recording automata. Theoret. Comput. Sci. **411**(47), 4029–4054 (2010). https://doi.org/10.1016/j.tcs.2010.07.008

17. Henry, L., Jéron, T., Markey, N.: Active learning of timed automata with unobservable resets. In: Bertrand, N., Jansen, N. (eds.) FORMATS 2020. LNCS, vol. 12288, pp. 144–160. Springer, Cham (2020). https://doi.org/10.1007/978-3-030-57628-8_9

18. Howar, F., Jonsson, B., Vaandrager, F.: Combining black-box and white-box techniques for learning register automata. In: Steffen, B., Woeginger, G. (eds.) Computing and Software Science. LNCS, vol. 10000, pp. 563–588. Springer, Cham (2019). https://doi.org/10.1007/978-3-319-91908-9_26

19. Howar, F., Steffen, B., Merten, M.: From ZULU to RERS. In: Margaria, T., Steffen, B. (eds.) ISoLA 2010. LNCS, vol. 6415, pp. 687–704. Springer, Heidelberg (2010). https://doi.org/10.1007/978-3-642-16558-0_55

20. Isberner, M., Howar, F., Steffen, B.: The open-source learnlib. In: Kroening, D., Pǎsǎreanu, C.S. (eds.) CAV 2015. LNCS, vol. 9206, pp. 487–495. Springer, Cham (2015). https://doi.org/10.1007/978-3-319-21690-4_32

21. Jia, Y., Harman, M.: An analysis and survey of the development of mutation testing. IEEE Trans. Software Eng. **37**(5), 649–678 (2011). https://doi.org/10.1109/TSE.2010.62

22. Krichen, M., Tripakis, S.: Conformance testing for real-time systems. Formal Methods Syst. Des. **34**(3), 238–304 (2009). https://doi.org/10.1007/s10703-009-0065-1

23. Larsen, K.G., Lorber, F., Nielsen, B., Nyman, U.: Mutation-based test-case generation with Ecdar. In: ICST Workshops 2017, pp. 319–328. IEEE (2017). https://doi.org/10.1109/ICSTW.2017.60

24. Maler, O., Mens, I.-E.: Learning regular languages over large alphabets. In: Ábrahám, E., Havelund, K. (eds.) TACAS 2014. LNCS, vol. 8413, pp. 485–499. Springer, Heidelberg (2014). https://doi.org/10.1007/978-3-642-54862-8_41

25. Peled, D.A., Vardi, M.Y., Yannakakis, M.: Black box checking. J. Autom. Lang. Comb. **7**(2), 225–246 (2002). https://doi.org/10.25596/jalc-2002-225

26. Trab, M.S.A., Counsell, S., Hierons, R.M.: Specification mutation analysis for validating timed testing approaches based on timed automata. In: COMPSAC 2012, pp. 660–669. IEEE Computer Society (2012). https://doi.org/10.1109/COMPSAC.2012.93

27. Utting, M., Pretschner, A., Legeard, B.: A taxonomy of model-based testing approaches. Softw. Test. Verification Reliab. **22**(5), 297–312 (2012). https://doi.org/10.1002/stvr.456

28. Vaandrager, F.: Model learning. Commun. ACM **60**(2), 86–95 (2017). https://doi.org/10.1145/2967606

29. Vaandrager, F., Bloem, R., Ebrahimi, M.: Learning mealy machines with one timer. In: Leporati, A., Martín-Vide, C., Shapira, D., Zandron, C. (eds.) LATA 2021. LNCS, vol. 12638, pp. 157–170. Springer, Cham (2021). https://doi.org/10.1007/978-3-030-68195-1_13

30. Van Beek, D., Man, K., Reniers, M., Rooda, J., Schiffelers, R.: Syntax and semantics of timed Chi. J. Symb. Comput. JSC (2005)

31. Vega, J.J.O., Perrouin, G., Amrani, M., Schobbens, P.: Model-based mutation operators for timed systems: a taxonomy and research agenda. In: QRS 2018, pp. 325–332. IEEE (2018). https://doi.org/10.1109/QRS.2018.00045

Active Learning of One-Clock Timed Automata Using Constraint Solving

Runqing Xu[1,2]($\boxtimes$) (ID), Jie An[3]($\boxtimes$) (ID), and Bohua Zhan[1,2]($\boxtimes$) (ID)

[1] State Key Laboratory of Computer Science, Institute of Software, CAS, Beijing, China
{xurq,bzhan}@ios.ac.cn
[2] University of Chinese Academy of Sciences, Beijing, China
[3] Max Planck Institute for Software Systems, Kaiserslautern, Germany
jiean@mpi-sws.org

Abstract. Active automata learning in the framework of Angluin's L^* algorithm has been applied to learning many kinds of automata models. In applications to timed models such as timed automata, the main challenge is to determine guards on the clock value in transitions as well as which transitions reset the clock. In this paper, we introduce a new algorithm for active learning of deterministic one-clock timed automata and timed Mealy machines. The algorithm uses observation tables that do not commit to specific choices of reset, but instead rely on constraint solving to determine reset choices that satisfy readiness conditions. We evaluate our algorithm on randomly-generated examples as well as practical case studies, showing that it is applicable to larger models, and competitive with existing work for learning other forms of timed models.

Keywords: Active learning · Timed automata · Constraint solving

1 Introduction

Within Angluin's L^* framework [7], active learning is a type of model inference to learn an unknown language by making queries to a teacher. There are two kinds of queries: membership queries and equivalence queries. For a membership query, the teacher answers whether the queried word is in the target language. Usually, the learner collects query results in an *observation table*. When the observation table satisfies some readiness conditions, it can be transformed to a candidate automaton for an equivalence query. The teacher answers whether the candidate automaton recognizes the target language, and returns a counterexample if the answer is negative. In recent decades, the core algorithm has seen many technical improvements, has been extended to learn different kinds of models, and has been applied to many realistic settings. We refer to [17,20] for surveys.

For timed systems, timing constraints play a key role in the correctness of the system. In general, automata learning of timed systems require learning a timed model from either passive or active observations of the system, consisting of a collection of

This work has been partially funded by NSFC under grant No. 62032024, and by DFG project 389792660-TRR 248.

time-event sequences. The learned model should describe these timing behaviors correctly. Timed automata [2], extending DFAs with clock variables, is a popular formal model of timed systems. However, there are several obstacles to active learning of timed automata. Since the transitions of timed automata contain both timing constraints that test the values of clocks, and resets that update the clocks, we need to determine (1) the number of clocks, (2) the reset information, and (3) the timing constraints, none of which are directly observable from time-event sequences. Hence, existing work consider timed automata with different restrictions. Among them, An et al. introduced an active learning algorithm for deterministic one-clock timed automata (DOTAs) [4]. They first suppose that the teacher can return reset information in the queries, then the assumption is dropped by allowing the algorithm to search through possible combinations of reset information. However, this search process results in an exponential blow up, limiting the scalability of the algorithm in practical applications. Vaandrager et al. [21] considered a different class of timed models called Mealy machines with one timer, and proposed a learning algorithm with polynomial complexity.

In this paper, we present a new active learning algorithm for deterministic one-clock timed automata[1]. The main innovation of the algorithm is to maintain all available observations in a single observation table, without committing to a particular choice of resets. The readiness conditions of the observation table, such as closedness, consistency, etc., are encoded as formulas in terms of variables for reset information and location assignments. These constraints are then solved using SMT solvers to determine feasible assignments of resets and locations that make the observation table ready, and from which a candidate automaton can be constructed. The learning algorithm is guaranteed to terminate and return a correct automaton. While the theoretical worst-case complexity of the algorithm is still exponential, by leveraging the efficiency of SMT solvers, it is much more efficient than the algorithm in [4] in practice. In order to apply the algorithm to learning real-time reactive systems, we extend it to timed Mealy machines, which can be considered as an extension of Mealy machines with one clock, or extension of deterministic one-clock timed automata to include inputs and outputs.

The algorithm is implemented and evaluated on a number of randomly generated models and four models from practical applications. The experimental results show that our algorithm is scalable to much larger models compared to [4]. Additionally, our method successfully learns all four models from practical applications, with costs that is competitive against algorithms designed for other forms of models.

The organization of the paper is as follows. We give some background material in Sect. 2. The algorithm for learning DOTAs is described in Sect. 3, and its extension to timed Mealy machines in Sect. 4. We describe the implementation and experiments in Sect. 5, and finally conclude in Sect. 6.

Related Work. Active learning of timed systems has been studied on many kinds of models with different restrictions. In [10, 11], Grinchtein et al. proposed learning algorithms for event-recording automata (ERAs) [3], a kind of timed automata associating every action a with a clock x_a that records the length of time since the last occurrence of a. Henry et al. considered in [12] reset-free ERAs, where some transitions may reset

---

[1] The full version is available at https://arxiv.org/abs/2208.00412.

no clocks. An et al. introduced a learning algorithm for deterministic one-clock timed automata (DOTAs) in [4], but due to the brute-force search over choice of resets, the algorithm is limited to timed automata with a small number of locations. For real-time automata (RTA) [8], efficient learning algorithms have been designed in both the deterministic [5] and nondeterministic case [6]. Recently, Vaandrager et al. introduced a new kind of timed models named Mealy machine with one timer (MM1T), and proposed an efficient active learning algorithm for such models [21]. It extends Mealy machine with a single timer which can be set to an integer value at transitions.

Passive learning has also been investigated for learning timed automata based on different methods [1,18,22–24]. Constraint solving has been used extensively in passive learning. For example, Smetsers et al. used this technique in passive learning of DFAs, Mealy machines and register automata [16], by encoding the existence of an automaton with n locations consistent with a set of observations in a logical formula. Recent work [19] also applied constraint solving to passive learning of timed automata. Compared to these works, we remain in the active learning setting, encoding constraints for the readiness of observation tables rather than consistency with a set of observations. Our work demonstrates that constraint solving can be fruitfully applied in active learning, determining not only location assignments but also other hidden parts of the model such as clock-reset information.

2 Preliminaries

In this section, we introduce several concepts of one-clock timed automata. Let $\mathbb{R}_{\geq 0}$ and $\mathbb{N}$ be the set of non-negative reals and natural numbers, respectively. The set of boolean values is denoted as $\mathbb{B} = \{\top, \bot\}$, where $\top$ stands for *true* and $\bot$ for *false*.

Let c be the single clock variable, denote by Φ_c the set of clock constraints of the form $\phi ::= \top \mid c \bowtie m \mid \phi \wedge \phi$, where $m \in \mathbb{N}$ and $\bowtie \in \{=, <, >, \leq, \geq\}$. Since there is only one clock, a clock constraint can be represented as an integer-bounded interval whose endpoints are in $\mathbb{N} \cup \{\infty\}$. For example, $c \leq 5 \wedge c > 4$ is represented as $(4, 5]$, $c = 6$ as $[6, 6]$, and $\top$ as $[0, \infty)$. We will use inequality and interval representations interchangeably in this paper. Let the finite set of actions Σ be fixed.

Definition 1 (One-clock timed automata [4]). *A one-clock timed automaton (OTA) $\mathcal{A}$ is a 6-tuple $(\Sigma, Q, q_0, F, c, \Delta)$, where Σ is a finite set of actions, called the* alphabet; *Q is a finite set of locations; $q_0 \in Q$ is the initial location; $F \subseteq Q$ is a set of accepting locations; c is the unique clock; and $\Delta \subseteq Q \times \Sigma \times \Phi_c \times \mathbb{B} \times Q$ is a finite set of transitions.*

A transition $\delta = (q, \sigma, \phi, b, q')$ allows a jump from the *source location* q to the *target location* q' by performing the action $\sigma \in \Sigma$ if the *guard* $\phi \in \Phi_c$ is satisfied. Meanwhile, clock c is reset to zero if $b = \top$, and remains unchanged otherwise. *Clock valuation* is a function $\nu : c \to \mathbb{R}_{\geq 0}$ that assigns a non-negative real number to the clock. A *state* of $\mathcal{A}$ is a pair (q, ν), where $q \in Q$ and ν is a clock valuation.

Given an OTA $\mathcal{A}$, with κ being the maximum constant appearing in the guards, then the clock valuations can be divided into *regions*, where each region is of the form $[n, n]$ for $n \leq \kappa$, or $(n, n+1)$ for $n < \kappa$, or (κ, ∞). This gives a partition of $\mathbb{R}_{\geq 0}$. For clock valuation ν, we denote by $[\![\nu]\!]$ the region containing it. Regions are commonly used in algorithms for analyzing timed automata, making the state space essentially finite.

Given a *timed word* $\omega = (\sigma_1, t_1)(\sigma_2, t_2) \cdots (\sigma_n, t_n) \in (\Sigma \times \mathbb{R}_{\geq 0})^*$, where t_i represents the delay time between two actions σ_{i-1} and σ_i, there is a *run* of $\mathcal{A}$ such that $\rho = (q_0, \nu_0) \xrightarrow{t_1, \sigma_1} (q_1, \nu_1) \xrightarrow{t_2, \sigma_2} \cdots \xrightarrow{t_n, \sigma_n} (q_n, \nu_n)$, where $\nu_0(c) = 0$, only if (1) $(q_{i-1}, \sigma_i, \phi_i, b_i, q_i) \in \Delta$, (2) $\nu_{i-1}(c) + t_i$ satisfies ϕ_i, (3) $\nu_i(c) = \nu_{i-1}(c) + t_i$ if $b_i = \perp$ and $\nu_i(c) = 0$ otherwise, for all $1 \leq i \leq n$. Let $|\omega|$ denote its *length*. When the timed automaton $\mathcal{A}$ is known, each timed word ω can be extended by including the reset information b_i, indicating whether there is a reset after taking the transition for (σ_i, t_i). We denote the corresponding *reset timed word* as $\omega_r = (\sigma_1, t_1, b_1)(\sigma_2, t_2, b_2) \cdots (\sigma_n, t_n, b_n)$. If $q_n \in F$, then ω is an accepting timed word of $\mathcal{A}$. The *(recognized) timed language* $L(\mathcal{A})$ is the set of accepting timed words of $\mathcal{A}$.

An OTA is a *deterministic one-clock timed automaton* (DOTA) if there is at most one run for any timed word (equivalently, if the guards of transitions from any location under the same action do not intersect each other). Two DOTAs are equivalent if they recognize the same timed language. A DOTA is *complete* if for any $q \in Q$ and action $\sigma \in \Sigma$, the corresponding guards form a partition of $\mathbb{R}_{\geq 0}$. This means any given timed word has exactly one run. Any DOTA $\mathcal{A}$ can be transformed into a complete DOTA (COTA) accepting the same timed language by introducing a non-accepting "sink" location and

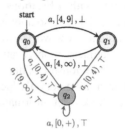

Fig. 1. An example of complete DOTA

letting all invalid or non-described behaviors go to the sink. We therefore assume that we are working with complete DOTAs. Figure 1 shows a DOTA $\mathcal{A}$, with q_2 added as the sink location to make it complete.

The classic method of active learning is L^* algorithm [7] which can be regarded as an interaction between a learner and a teacher, where the teacher can answer membership and equivalence queries. In a membership query, the learner can ask if a word belongs to the target language, or if a constructed automaton accepts that language as an equivalence query. The teacher can answer "yes" or "no" for the queries and return counterexamples for the equivalence queries. The learner collects query results and counterexamples in the observation table consisting of three sets of words: a prefix-closed set S, a set R and a suffix-closed set E. Each word in S corresponds to a unique location. Words in R can be considered the "boundary" of S, and E contains suffixes to distinguish different words in $S \cup R$.

An et al. [4] described an active learning algorithm for DOTAs. Inherited from L^*, in a membership query, the teacher is given a timed word. We use $\mathsf{MQ} : (\Sigma \times \mathbb{R}_{\geq 0})^* \to \{+, -\}$ to denote the function mapping timed words to $+$ if it is accepted, and $-$ otherwise. In an equivalence query, the teacher receives a hypothesis DOTA $\mathcal{H}$, and return a counterexample in the negative case in addition. In that work, a "smart" teacher is first assumed, who also returns the reset information for any timed word given as membership query. With this reset information, an observation table can be maintained where each row in $S \cup R$ and each column in E is a *logical timed word*, which contains the clock valuation after each transition rather than the delay times. When the observation table satisfies readiness conditions, a candidate automaton is constructed in a manner similar to the learning of symbolic automata [9]. Next, in the "normal" teacher setting, where the teacher does not return reset information, the algorithm searches over all possible choices of resets for timed words in $S \cup R$, constructing one observation table for each. Due to the large time and memory requirements, the algorithm has limited scalability (up to six locations for the randomly constructed examples in the paper).

3 Learning Algorithm

In this section, we describe a new algorithm for active learning of DOTAs by incorporating constraint solving using SMT solvers. The main idea of the algorithm is to maintain a single observation table that collects all results from previous membership queries, rather than one observation table for each possible choice of resets. Instead, the reset information is encoded as boolean variables with unknown values. At any time, the observation table may be ready for some choice of resets, but not for others. We encode the readiness conditions for the observation table as a formula on the variables for reset information, as well as for the location assignments of rows in the table. An SMT solver is then used to solve these constraints, returning a choice of resets that make the table ready, as well as a candidate automaton that can be sent for equivalence query.

Several difficulties must be addressed in order to realize this idea. In particular, whether two rows in the observation table are distinguishable is no longer clear-cut, but may depend on the choice of resets. This also means the partition of rows into S and R in the traditional L^* algorithm need to be extended, by adding a category S_+ of rows that are distinguishable from rows in S only for some choice of resets, that are needed for building candidate automaton.

In the remainder of this section, we first discuss comparison of timed words without being certain of clock-reset information, then extensions made to the observation table, method of encoding readiness constraints, and finally the main algorithm together with termination and complexity analysis.

3.1 Alignment and Comparison of Timed Words

In the L^* framework, one key step is to determine if two words w_1 and w_2 belong to different equivalence classes of the target regular language, i.e., arrive at different locations of the underlying target DFA A. It is achieved by membership queries via testing words w_1 and w_2 after appending some suffix e. If $w_1 \cdot e$ is an accepting word and $w_2 \cdot e$ is not (or vice versa), then w_1 and w_2 must arrive at different locations.

In our case, suppose $\mathcal{A}$ is the target DOTA to be learned. Given two timed words ω_1 and ω_2, we wish to determine whether they arrive at different locations of $\mathcal{A}$. However, since the reset information is not observable when running timed words ω_1 and ω_2, the values of the clock at the end is unknown. If the values of the clock are not the same, the result of running $\omega_1 \cdot e$ and $\omega_2 \cdot e$ may be different even if ω_1 and ω_2 arrive at the same location. In order to effectively test using the suffix e, we need to suppose that the last time when the clock resets in ω_1 and ω_2 are known, and then align the values of the clock before executing the suffix e. We state these concepts more formally in the following definitions.

Definition 2 (Last reset of a timed word). *Given a timed word* $\omega = (\sigma_1, t_1)(\sigma_2, t_2)$
$\cdots (\sigma_n, t_n)$, *and DOTA* $\mathcal{A}$. *Let* $\omega_r = (\sigma_1, t_1, b_1)(\sigma_2, t_2, b_2) \cdots (\sigma_n, t_n, b_n)$ *be the reset
timed word that results from running* ω *on* $\mathcal{A}$. *The* last reset $k_{\mathcal{A}}(\omega)$ *is defined to be 0 if*
$b_i = \perp$ *for all* $1 \leq i \leq n$, *and* $k_{\mathcal{A}}(\omega) = i$ *if* $b_i = \top$ *and* $b_j = \perp$ *for all* $j > i$.

Suppose the last reset $k_{\mathcal{A}}(\omega)$ is known for a timed word ω, then we can compute
the value of clock after executing ω on $\mathcal{A}$. Let $\nu_c(\omega, i)$ be the value of clock after
executing ω if the last reset equals i. This is computed as the sum of t_{i+1} to t_n, where
n is the length of ω (if $i = n$, for the case where the last reset occurs after (σ_n, t_n),
then $\nu_c(\omega, i) = 0$). Hence, given two timed words ω_1 and ω_2 with known values of last
resets i_1, i_2, it is possible to *align* the two timed words for testing a suffix e.

Definition 3 (Alignment for testing on a suffix). *Consider two timed words* ω_1, ω_2,
and suppose their last resets are i_1, i_2 *respectively. Let* $e = (\sigma_1, t_1)(\sigma_2, t_2) \cdots (\sigma_m, t_m)$
be a nonempty suffix. Let $\nu_1 = \nu_c(\omega_1, i_1)$ *and* $\nu_2 = \nu_c(\omega_2, i_2)$. *Then form the suffixes*
e_1, e_2 *depending on the following cases:*

- *If* $\nu_1 > \nu_2$, *then let* $e_1 = e$ *and* $e_2 = (\sigma_1, t_1 + (\nu_1 - \nu_2)) \cdot (\sigma_2, t_2) \cdots (\sigma_m, t_m)$.
- *If* $\nu_1 < \nu_2$, *then let* $e_1 = (\sigma_1, t_1 + (\nu_2 - \nu_1)) \cdot (\sigma_2, t_2) \cdots (\sigma_m, t_m)$ *and* $e_2 = e$.
- *If* $\nu_1 = \nu_2$, *then let* $e_1 = e_2 = e$.

Define a test $T(\omega_1, \omega_2, i_1, i_2, e)$ *between* ω_1 *and* ω_2 *with suffix* e *and last resets* i_1, i_2
as follows. If e *is nonempty, then the test compares results for two membership queries*
$\omega_1 \cdot e_1$ *and* $\omega_2 \cdot e_2$. *The test succeeds, i.e.* $T(\omega_1, \omega_2, i_1, i_2, e) = \top$, *if* $MQ(\omega_1 \cdot e_1) =$
$MQ(\omega_2 \cdot e_2)$. *Otherwise* $T(\omega_1, \omega_2, i_1, i_2, e) = \perp$. *If* e *is empty, the test simply compares
the results for membership queries* ω_1 *and* ω_2.

It is clear that with the definition of e_1 and e_2, the value of clock when executing
the first timed action of e_1 and e_2 during the tests must be the same. Hence, if ω_1 and
ω_2 arrive at the same location, then the behavior on e_1 and e_2 must be the same as well.
Hence, we obtain the following lemma.

Lemma 1 (Distinguishable timed words). *If the test* T *between* ω_1 *and* ω_2 *with suffix
e and last resets* i_1, i_2 *fails, then for any DOTA* $\mathcal{A}$ *such that* $i_1 = k_{\mathcal{A}}(\omega_1)$ *and* $i_2 =$
$k_{\mathcal{A}}(\omega_2)$, *the timed words* ω_1 *and* ω_2 *must arrive at different locations in* $\mathcal{A}$.

Example 1. Consider two timed words $\omega_1 = (a, 4)$ and $\omega_2 = \epsilon$. They are both accepted
by $\mathcal{A}$ in Fig. 1. Consider suffix $e = (a, 5.5)$. If the last resets are $i_1 = 0$ and $i_2 = 0$
(the correct reset for $\mathcal{A}$), then $e_1 = (a, 5.5)$ and $e_2 = (a, 9.5)$, and $MQ(\omega_1 \cdot e_1) =$
$+$, $MQ(\omega_2 \cdot e_2) = -$, so they can be distinguished, and indeed ω_1 and ω_2 arrive at
different locations as required by Lemma 1. If the last resets are $i_1 = 1$ and $i_2 = 0$,
then $e_1 = e_2 = (a, 5.5)$, and $MQ(\omega_1 \cdot e_1) = MQ(\omega_2 \cdot e_2) = +$, so they cannot be
distinguished. Hence, when we do not know the true reset information, whether ω_1 and
ω_2 are distinguishable by $e = (a, 5.5)$ depends on the choice of resets.   ◁

Since $\mathcal{A}$ is unknown during learning, we need to iterate over all possible combinations of last resets. For two timed words ω_1 and ω_2, we define the set of valid combinations of last resets as follows.

Definition 4 (Valid combinations of last resets). *Consider two timed words* ω_1, ω_2 *and suppose the length of the longest common prefix of* ω_1 *and* ω_2 *is* m. *Then the set* $C(\omega_1, \omega_2)$ *of valid combinations of last resets is*

$$C(\omega_1, \omega_2) = \{(i_1, i_2) \mid 0 \leq i_1 \leq |\omega_1| \wedge 0 \leq i_2 \leq |\omega_2| \wedge (i_1 \leq m \wedge i_2 \leq m \Rightarrow i_1 = i_2)\}.$$

Example 2. Suppose $\omega_1 = (a, 4)$ and $\omega_2 = (a, 4)(a, 5.5)$, then $m = 1$, and the set of valid combinations are $C(\omega_1, \omega_2) = \{(0, 0), (0, 2), (1, 1), (1, 2)\}$. In particular $(0, 1)$ or $(1, 0)$ are not allowed, since they give contradicting reset choices for the transition taken by $(a, 4)$. ◁

3.2 Timed Observation Table

Definition 5 (Observation table). *An observation table* $\mathcal{O} = (S, S_+, R, E, f, N)$ *is a 6-tuple, satisfying the following conditions:*

- S, S_+, R *are disjoint finite sets of timed words called* prefixes. $S \cup S_+ \cup R$ *is prefix-closed and* $\epsilon \in S$. *If* $\omega \in S \cup S_+$ *and* $\sigma \in \Sigma$, *then* $\omega \cdot (\sigma, 0) \in S \cup S_+ \cup R$.
- E *is a finite set of timed words called* suffixes, *with* $\epsilon \in E$.
- f *is a function mapping pairs* $\omega_1, \omega_2 \in S \cup S_+ \cup R$ *and* $(i_1, i_2) \in C(\omega_1, \omega_2)$ *to* $\mathbb{B}$, *indicating whether* ω_1 *and* ω_2 *are currently distinguished under last resets* i_1, i_2.
- N *is the current limit on the number of locations in the candidate automaton.*

The value $f(\omega_1, \omega_2, i_1, i_2)$ is computed as follows. For each suffix $e \in E$, test the pair ω_1, ω_2 under last resets i_1, i_2 and suffix e as in Definition 3. If $T(\omega_1, \omega_2, i_1, i_2, e) = \top$ for all $e \in E$, then $f(\omega_1, \omega_2, i_1, i_2) = \top$, otherwise $f(\omega_1, \omega_2, i_1, i_2) = \bot$.

Definition 6 (Certainly distinct rows). *Given an observation table* $\mathcal{O}$, *two rows* ω_1, ω_2 *are* certainly distinct *if* $f(\omega_1, \omega_2, i_1, i_2) = \bot$ *for all* $i_1, i_2 \in C(\omega_1, \omega_2)$.

We first explain the different components of $\mathcal{O}$ in an intuitive way. The set S contains timed words that are certainly distinct from each other. The set S_+ are additional rows in the observation table that are distinct from rows in S under some choice of resets, that are required to be in the interior for some candidate automata. The set R is the boundary of the observation table as usual for L^* algorithms. The condition that $\omega \cdot (\sigma, 0) \in S \cup S_+ \cup R$ is analogous to the condition that $\omega \cdot \sigma \in S \cup R$ in the DFA case. It enforces that information is available to construct the transitions in the candidate automaton for each location and action $\sigma \in \Sigma$.

$\mathcal{O}$		ϵ	$(a,0)$	$(a,4)\,(a,5.5)$	$(a,0)\,(a,0)$	$(a,4)$	$(a,9.5)$	E
				$S \cup S_+ \cup R$				
S $\quad \epsilon$	b_0	$\top$	$\bot$	$\neg b_5$	$\bot$	b_3	$\bot$	ϵ
$\quad (a,0)$	b_1	$\bot$	$\top$	$\bot$	$\top$	$\bot$	$\top$	
R $\;(a,4)\,(a,5.5)$	b_5	$\neg b_5$	$\bot$	$\top$	$\bot$	$\bot$	$\bot$	$(a,5.5)$
$\quad (a,0)\,(a,0)$	b_2	$\bot$	$\top$	$\bot$	$\top$	$\bot$	$\top$	
$\quad (a,4)$	b_3	b_3	$\bot$	$\bot$	$\bot$	$\top$	$\bot$	
$\quad (a,9.5)$	b_4	$\bot$	$\top$	$\bot$	$\top$	$\bot$	$\top$	

Fig. 2. Left: an instance of observation table $\mathcal{O}$ during learning of $\mathcal{A}$ in Fig. 1; **Right:** candidate DOTA constructed from the table after moving $(a, 4)(a, 5.5)$ to S_+.

Example 3. Figure 2 shows an instance of the observation table. The rows of the table are timed words in S, S_+ and R (here S_+ is empty). The columns of the table are indexed by the same timed words. Each cell in the table summarizes when two timed words are distinguished (the function f), using formulas in terms of reset variables $\mathbb{b}$ introduced in Sect. 3.3. The table also shows the list of suffixes E. For example, for timed words $(a, 4)$ and ϵ, we need to compare them on suffix $(a, 5.5)$ after alignment. According to the analysis in Example 1, we have $f((a, 4), \epsilon, 0, 0) = \bot$ and $f((a, 4), \epsilon, 1, 0) = \top$. This is summarized as the expression $\mathbb{b}_3$.   ◁

The main difference between the observation table defined here and the usual ones for L^* algorithms is that we do not record a particular query result for each prefix in $S \cup S_+ \cup R$ and suffix E, as these results cannot be used effectively without knowing reset information. In contrast, we maintain which pairs of rows can be distinguished for each possible choice of reset information. This can be contrasted with the approach in [4]. Rather than maintaining a copy of the observation table for each combination of reset information, our method records all information obtained so far in a single table, with reset information determined by constraint solving.

3.3 Encoding of Readiness Constraints

To obtain a hypothesis DOTA $\mathcal{H}$ from observation table $\mathcal{O}$, we should provide an assignment for the location and reset information of each timed word in $S \cup S_+ \cup R$, which ensure readiness conditions for the table, such as closedness and consistency. The main idea is to encode such readiness conditions as formulas in terms of location and reset assignments, and then use SMT solvers to find feasible solutions to these constraints or prove that they are not satisfiable. The constraints are stated in terms of two variables for each row $\omega \in S \cup S_+ \cup R$: an *ending reset variable* $\mathbb{b}_\omega$ and a *location variable* $\mathbb{q}_\omega$.

Definition 7 (Ending reset variable and location variable). *Given a timed word* $\omega = (\sigma_1, t_1) \ldots (\sigma_n, t_n) \in S \cup S_+ \cup R$, *define the* ending reset variable $\mathbb{b}_\omega \in \{\top, \bot\}$ *to denote whether clock resets after running the final timed action* (σ_n, t_n) *(for the empty timed word ϵ, we declare* $\mathbb{b}_\epsilon = \top$*). Define the* location variable $\mathbb{q}_\omega \in \{1, \ldots, N\}$ *to represent the location after running ω in the candidate automaton.*

Since the set of timed words $S \cup S_+ \cup R$ is prefix-closed, the ending reset variables $\{\mathbb{b}_\omega\}_{\omega \in S \cup S_+ \cup R}$ in fact determine whether the clock resets after each timed action for each row in $S \cup S_+ \cup R$. In particular, we can encode the last reset for ω in terms of the ending reset variables.

Definition 8 (Encoding of last reset). *Given* $\omega = (\sigma_1, t_1) \ldots (\sigma_n, t_n) \in S \cup S_+ \cup R$. *Let $\omega|_i$ for $0 \leq i \leq n$ be the prefix of ω with length i. Since $S \cup S_+ \cup R$ is prefix-closed, we have each $\omega|_i \in S \cup S_+ \cup R$ as well. Let $lr(\omega, i)$, encoding the condition that the last reset of ω equals i, be defined as follows.*

$$lr(\omega, i) \triangleq \mathbb{b}_{\omega|_i} \wedge \bigwedge_{i < j \leq n} \neg \mathbb{b}_{\omega|_j}.$$

For each pair of rows $\omega_1, \omega_2 \in S \cup S_+ \cup R$ *and each pair of last resets* $(i,j) \in \mathcal{C}(\omega_1, \omega_2)$, *the condition that the last resets of* ω_1, ω_2 *equal* i, j *respectively is encoded as follows.*

$$LR(\omega_1, \omega_2, i, j) \triangleq lr(\omega_1, i) \wedge lr(\omega_2, j).$$

Based on the encoding of last reset, the readiness constraints for the observation table can be encoded in terms of the above variables as follows.

Constraint 1 (Distinctness of rows). Given timed words $\omega_1, \omega_2 \in S \cup S_+ \cup R$, and last resets $i, j \in \mathcal{C}(\omega_1, \omega_2)$, suppose $f(\omega_1, \omega_2, i, j) = \bot$ (meaning ω_1 and ω_2 can be distinguished under last resets i, j in the observation table), then we have the following constraint, indicating ω_1 and ω_2 cannot be assigned to the same location.

$$C_1(\omega_1, \omega_2, i, j) \triangleq LR(\omega_1, \omega_2, i, j) \Rightarrow q_{\omega_1} \neq q_{\omega_2}.$$

Define the constraint C_1 to be the conjunction of all $C_1(\omega_1, \omega_2, i, j)$, for all pairs of rows and valid last resets that can be distinguished.

$$C_1 \triangleq \bigwedge_{\substack{\omega_1, \omega_2 \in S \cup S_+ \cup R, \\ (i,j) \in \mathcal{C}(\omega_1, \omega_2), \\ f(\omega_1, \omega_2, i, j) = \bot}} C_1(\omega_1, \omega_2, i, j).$$

Constraint 2 (Consistency). Given timed words $\omega_1, \omega_2 \in S \cup S_+ \cup R$ and last resets $i, j \in \mathcal{C}(\omega_1, \omega_2)$. Suppose $\omega_1' = \omega_1 \cdot (\sigma, t_1)$ and $\omega_2' = \omega_2 \cdot (\sigma, t_2)$ also appear in $S \cup S_+ \cup R$, for some $\sigma \in \Sigma$ and $t_1, t_2 \in \mathbb{R}_{\geq 0}$. Suppose that under the last resets i, j, the value of clock after executing last timed action of ω_1', but before possible resets, is in the same region as that for ω_2', then if ω_1 and ω_2 also go to the same location, the transition to be carried out for the last timed action of ω_1' and ω_2' must be the same. Hence both ending reset and location for ω_1' and ω_2' must be the same. This is encoded as constraints as follows.

$$C_2(\omega_1, \omega_2, i, j, \sigma, t_1, t_2) \triangleq q_{\omega_1} = q_{\omega_2} \wedge LR(\omega_1, \omega_2, i, j) \Rightarrow b_{\omega_1'} = b_{\omega_2'} \wedge q_{\omega_1'} = q_{\omega_2'}.$$

It is added as a constraint only if $\llbracket \nu_c(\omega_1, i) + t_1 \rrbracket = \llbracket \nu_c(\omega_2, j) + t_2 \rrbracket$, and if $f(\omega_1, \omega_2, i, j) = \top$. We define constraint C_2 to be the conjunction of all such constraints.

$$C_2 \triangleq \bigwedge_{\substack{\omega_1, \omega_2 \in S \cup S_+ \cup R, \\ \omega_1 \cdot (\sigma, t_1), \omega_2 \cdot (\sigma, t_2) \in S \cup S_+ \cup R, \\ (i,j) \in \mathcal{C}(\omega_1, \omega_2), f(\omega_1, \omega_2, i, j) = \top, \\ \llbracket \nu_c(\omega_1, i) + t_1 \rrbracket = \llbracket \nu_c(\omega_2, j) + t_2 \rrbracket}} C_2(\omega_1, \omega_2, i, j, \sigma, t_1, t_2).$$

Constraint 3 (Closedness). The closedness condition for usual L^* algorithms states that each row in R must be represented by a row in S. In our case, we require that each row in R is represented by a row in $S \cup S_+$. This translates to the constraint that each location in the candidate automaton must be represented by a row in $S \cup S_+$, encoded as follows (recall N is the current limit on the number of locations).

$$C_3 \triangleq \bigwedge_{1 \leq i \leq N} \bigvee_{\omega \in S \cup S_+} q_\omega = i \wedge C_3' \text{ where } C_3' \triangleq \bigwedge_{\omega \in S \cup S_+ \cup R} 1 \leq q_\omega \leq N.$$

During the algorithm, we also make constraint solving queries where the closedness condition is not enforced. Then only the second part C_3' is used.

Constraint 4 (Special assignments). In order to speed-up constraint solving, we directly make assignments to the location variables of rows in S. Order the rows of S as $S = \{\omega_1, \omega_2, \ldots, \omega_{|S|}\}$, then the special assignments are encoded as follows.

$$C_4 \triangleq \bigwedge_{1 \leq i \leq |S|} q_{\omega_i} = i.$$

In the main learning algorithm, we will use SMT solvers to attempt to find solutions to these constraints. The algorithm will first attempt to find a solution using C_3 together with C_1, C_2 and C_4. If a solution is found, it proceeds to hypothesis construction as described in Sect. 3.4. Otherwise, it attempts to find a solution using C_3' or by increasing N. The details are described in Sect. 3.5.

3.4 Hypothesis Construction

Once the SMT solver gives a model satisfying constraints in Sect. 3.3, we can build a hypothesis DOTA $\mathcal{H} = (\Sigma, Q_{\mathcal{H}}, q_0^{\mathcal{H}}, F_{\mathcal{H}}, c, \Delta_{\mathcal{H}})$ from observation table $\mathcal{O} = (S, S_+, R, E, f, N)$ and assignments $\overline{b_\omega}$ and $\overline{q_\omega}$ to ending reset variable and location variables in the model. We define location set $Q_{\mathcal{H}} = \{\overline{q_\omega} \mid \omega \in S \cup S_+\}$, initial location $q_0^{\mathcal{H}} = \overline{q_\epsilon}$, and accepting locations $F_{\mathcal{H}} = \{\overline{q_\omega} \mid \mathsf{MQ}(\omega) = + \wedge \omega \in S \cup S_+\}$. Next, we describe how to construct the transitions $\Delta_{\mathcal{H}}$.

Given two rows $\omega_1, \omega_2 \in S \cup S_+ \cup R$ such that $\omega_2 = \omega_1 \cdot (\sigma, t)$, we can construct an auxiliary transition $\delta' = (\overline{q_{\omega_1}}, \sigma, \psi, \overline{b_{\omega_2}}, \overline{q_{\omega_2}})$ with $\psi = \nu(\omega_1) + t$ where $\nu(\omega_1)$ is the value of clock after executing ω_1. Since the table is prefix-closed, the reset information for every timed action in ω_1 has been determined. Therefore, we can determine $\nu(\omega_1)$. We collect all such auxiliary transitions as the set Δ'.

For any $q \in Q_{\mathcal{H}}$ and $\sigma \in \Sigma$, let $\Psi_{q,\sigma} = \{\psi \mid (q, \sigma, \psi, b, q') \in \Delta'\}$ be the list of clock values on auxiliary transitions from q and with action σ. We sort $\Psi_{q,\sigma}$ and apply the partition function $P(\cdot)$ to obtain m intervals, written as $g_1, \cdots, g_m$, satisfying $\psi_i \in g_i$ for any $1 \leq i \leq m$, where $m = |\Psi_{q,\sigma}|$; consequently, for every $(q, \sigma, \psi_i, b, q') \in \Delta'$, a transition $\delta_i = (q, \sigma, g_i, b, q')$ is added to $\Delta_{\mathcal{H}}$. This determines the transitions between locations in $\mathcal{H}$ and hence finishes the construction. The partition function $P(\cdot)$ is taken from [4], and also similar to that used for learning symbolic automata [9]. Note the condition $\omega \cdot (\sigma, 0) \in S \cup S_+ \cup R$ in Definition 5 enforces $\mu_0 = 0$ below.

Definition 9 (Partition function). *Given a list of clock valuations* $\ell = \mu_0, \mu_1, \cdots, \mu_n$ *with* $0 = \mu_0 < \mu_1 \cdots < \mu_n$, *and* $\lfloor \mu_i \rfloor \neq \lfloor \mu_j \rfloor$ *if* $\mu_i, \mu_j \in \mathbb{R}_{\geq 0} \backslash \mathbb{N}$ *and* $i \neq j$ *for all* $1 \leq i, j \leq n$, *let* $\mu_{n+1} = \infty$, *then a partition function* $P(\cdot)$ *mapping* ℓ *to a set of intervals* $\{g_0, g_1, \ldots, g_n\}$, *which is a partition of* $\mathbb{R}_{\geq 0}$, *is defined as*

$$g_i = \begin{cases} [\mu_i, \mu_{i+1}), & \text{if } \mu_i \in \mathbb{N} \wedge \mu_{i+1} \in \mathbb{N}; \\ (\lfloor \mu_i \rfloor, \mu_{i+1}), & \text{if } \mu_i \in \mathbb{R}_{\geq 0} \backslash \mathbb{N} \wedge \mu_{i+1} \in \mathbb{N}; \\ [\mu_i, \lfloor \mu_{i+1} \rfloor], & \text{if } \mu_i \in \mathbb{N} \wedge \mu_{i+1} \in \mathbb{R}_{\geq 0} \backslash \mathbb{N}; \\ (\lfloor \mu_i \rfloor, \lfloor \mu_{i+1} \rfloor], & \text{if } \mu_i \in \mathbb{R}_{\geq 0} \backslash \mathbb{N} \wedge \mu_{i+1} \in \mathbb{R}_{\geq 0} \backslash \mathbb{N}. \end{cases}$$

Algorithm 1: Learning DOTA using constraint solving

---

input : an observation table $\mathcal{O} = (S, S_+, R, E, f, N)$, the alphabet Σ.
output: an automata $\mathcal{H}$ recognizing the target language L.

1 $S \leftarrow \{\epsilon\}, S_+ \leftarrow \emptyset, R \leftarrow \{(\sigma, 0) \mid \sigma \in \Sigma\}, E \leftarrow \{\epsilon\}, N \leftarrow 1$;   // initialization
2 **while** $\top$ **do**
3     $\mathcal{O} \leftarrow$ move_to_S($\mathcal{O}$);
4     $flag, M \leftarrow$ SMT($C_1 \wedge C_2 \wedge C_3 \wedge C_4$);   // solve constraints to get model M
5   **if** $flag = \top$ **then**
6        $\mathcal{H} \leftarrow$ build_hypothesis($\mathcal{O}, M$);   // build $\mathcal{H}$ from table $\mathcal{O}$ and model M
7        $equivalent, ctx \leftarrow$ equivalence_query($\mathcal{H}$);
8   **if** $equivalent = \top$ **then**
9   **return** $\mathcal{H}$;   // success
10   **else**
11          $\mathcal{O} \leftarrow$ ctx_processing($\mathcal{O}, ctx$);   // counterexample processing
12   **else**
13       $flag, M' \leftarrow$ SMT($C_1 \wedge C_2 \wedge C_3' \wedge C_4$);   // solve relaxed constraints
14   **if** $flag = \top$ **then**
15          $\mathcal{O} \leftarrow$ move_to_S$_+$($\mathcal{O}, M'$);   // modify table $\mathcal{O}$ guided by solution M'
16   **else**
17          $N \leftarrow N + 1$;   // try for larger number of locations

---

Since the table $\mathcal{O}$ with the feasible assignments satisfies the readiness constraints, the constructed hypothesis is a deterministic one-clock timed automaton, and agrees with accepting information for rows in $S \cup S_+ \cup R$. This is stated as the following theorem.

Theorem 1. *Given observation table $\mathcal{O} = (S, S_+, R, E, f, N)$ and feasible assignments to $\overline{\mathbb{b}_\omega}$ and $\overline{q_\omega}$, the hypothesis $\mathcal{H} = (\Sigma, Q, q_0, F, c, \Delta)$ is deterministic. For each row $\omega \in S \cup S_+ \cup R$, $\mathcal{H}$ accepts the timed word ω iff $\mathsf{MQ}(\omega) = +$. Finally, for any two rows $\omega_1, \omega_2 \in S \cup S_+ \cup R$, if the value of f on ω_1, ω_2 and the setting of reset variables $\overline{\mathbb{b}}$ is $\bot$, then $\overline{q_{\omega_1}} \neq \overline{q_{\omega_2}}$, and the two rows reach distinct locations in $\mathcal{H}$.*

After the hypothesis $\mathcal{H}$ is built, it is sent for an equivalence query. If the teacher returns a counterexample ctx, the learner adds all prefixes of ctx to R during counterexample processing.

3.5 Main Algorithm and Correctness

The overall procedure of the algorithm is given in Algorithm 1. The observation table $\mathcal{O} = (S, S_+, R, E, f, N)$ is initialized with $S = \{\epsilon\}$, $S_+ = \emptyset$, $R = \{(\sigma, 0) \mid \sigma \in \Sigma\}$, $E = \{\epsilon\}$, and $N = 1$. The function move_to_S tests each row in R to see if it is certainly distinct (according to Definition 6) from each row in S. If so the certainly distinct row is moved to S. For each row ω moved to S, $\omega \cdot (\sigma, 0)$ is added to R for every $\sigma \in \Sigma$ (Line 3). After that, the formula $C_1 \wedge C_2 \wedge C_3 \wedge C_4$ is built and sent to an SMT solver (Line 4). If a solution M is found for the ending reset and location variables, then a hypothesis $\mathcal{H}$ is constructed from the table $\mathcal{O}$ and the solution M (Line 6), and an equivalence query is performed to determine whether the hypothesis $\mathcal{H}$ is correct. If the answer is positive, the algorithm returns with automaton $\mathcal{H}$ (Line 9). Otherwise, the learner updates the table $\mathcal{O}$ by adding all prefixes of the returned counterexample ctx to R (Line 11), and begins a new iteration starting from finding certainly distinct rows (Line 3) and updating constraints. Note that new suffixes may be added to E during the computation of constraint C_2. If two timed words $\omega_1 \cdot (\sigma, t_1)$ and $\omega_2 \cdot (\sigma, t_2)$ end in the same region under some choice of resets, ω_1 and ω_2 are currently indistinguishable under this choice, but $\omega_1 \cdot (\sigma, t_1)$ and $\omega_2 \cdot (\sigma, t_2)$ can be distinguished with suffix $e \in E$, then the timed word $(\sigma, \min(t_1, t_2)) \cdot e$ is added to E. This allows us to distinguish ω_1 and ω_2 directly using $(\sigma, \min(t_1, t_2)) \cdot e \in E$. After new suffixes are added to E, the entire observation table need to be updated, with possible new distinguishable pairs and new rows added to S.

If there is no solution to $C_1 \wedge C_2 \wedge C_3 \wedge C_4$, then the learner first relaxes C_3 to C_3' (Line 13). It is now permitted that some rows in R are assigned to a location different from any row in $S \cup S_+$. If there is a solution for the relaxed condition, it indicates that some row in R may represent a new location, even though it is not certainly distinct from all rows in S. The function move_to_S_+ moves such rows from R to S_+, and add $\omega \cdot (\sigma, 0)$ to R for each $\sigma \in \Sigma$ and each ω moved to S_+ (Line 15). If there is no solution even for the relaxed constraints, the learner increases N by 1 (Line 17), attempting to find a model with larger size.

Example 4. In the observation table in Fig. 2, each cell at row ω_1 and column ω_2 records at which choice of resets ω_1 and ω_2 *cannot* be distinguished, as an expression in terms of $\mathbb{b}_\omega$'s. For example, the expression $\top$ means ω_1 and ω_2 cannot be distinguished for all choice of resets, while $\perp$ means ω_1 and ω_2 are certainly distinct.

Constraint 3 (Closedness) requires that each row in R is represented by some row in $S \cup S_+$. Although $\omega_3 = (a, 4)$ or $\omega_5 = (a, 4)(a, 5.5)$ can be represented by ϵ by setting $\mathbb{b}_3 = \top$ or $\mathbb{b}_5 = \perp$, they are known to be certainly distinct from each other (indicated by the red $\perp$ in the table), so they cannot be both represented by ϵ. This means $C_1 \wedge C_2 \wedge C_3 \wedge C_4$ is not satisfiable, so we relax the constraint to $C_1 \wedge C_2 \wedge C_3' \wedge C_4$. This is solvable by setting $\mathbb{b}_3 = \top$, and let ω_5 represent an additional location. Then ω_5 is moved to S_+, and the candidate DOTA at the right of Fig. 2 can be constructed from the updated observation table.   ◁

Analysis of the Algorithm. The algorithm is sound since it returns an automaton only if it passes equivalence queries. The termination of the algorithm can be explained through a comparison with a brute-force search version of the algorithm similar to the normal teacher case in [4]. The brute-force search constructs a binary tree of observation tables, with each branching corresponds to a choice of reset for some row in $S \cup R$ (here S_+ is not needed since reset information is now certain). Our algorithm simulates a breadth-first search on the tree based on the number of locations. Rows in S_+ can be viewed as rows that are added to S in some (but not all) branches of the search tree. A simple estimate for the number of rows in $S \cup S_+$, and hence in R gives an exponential worst-case bound in terms of N. However, in practice it usually increases slowly as shown in our experiments.

Theorem 2 (Correctness and termination). *Algorithm 1 always terminates and returns a correct DOTA recognizing the underlying target timed language.*

4   Extension to Deterministic Timed Mealy Machines

For practical applications on real-time reactive systems with input/output behavior, we consider a timed version of Mealy machines. Inspired by Mealy machine with one timer (MM1T) [21], we divide the actions in Σ into *input* and *output* actions. The special *empty action* ϵ represents the invisible action or nothing happening. We assume that there is a pair of input and output actions on each transition. Hence, the model can also be viewed as a Mealy machine with one clock.

Definition 10 (Timed Mealy Machines). *A timed Mealy machine (TMM) is a 6-tuple* $\mathcal{M} = (Q, I, O, q_0, c, \Delta)$, *where* Q *is a finite set of locations;* I *is a finite set of inputs, containing the special empty action* ϵ; O *is a finite set of outputs, containing the special empty action* ϵ; q_0 *is the unique initial location;* c *is the single clock; and* $\Delta \subseteq Q \times I \times O \times \Phi_c \times \mathbb{B} \times Q$ *is a finite set of transitions.*

A transition $\delta = (q, i, o, \phi, b, q')$ allows a jump from q to q' and generates an output o when provided input $i \in I$ and if $\phi \in \Phi_c$ is satisfied. Meanwhile, clock c is reset to zero if $b = \top$, and remains unchanged otherwise. Given a timed word over inputs $\omega = (i_1, t_1)(i_2, t_2) \cdots (i_n, t_n) \in (I \times \mathbb{R}_{\geq 0})^*$, a *deterministic timed Mealy machine* (DTMM) $\mathcal{M}$ returns at most one output sequence $\mathcal{M}(\omega) = o_1 o_2 \cdots o_n$. Given two DTMMs $\mathcal{M}_1$ and $\mathcal{M}_2$, for any timed word ω over inputs I, if the output sequences of two DTMMs are equal, i.e., $\mathcal{M}_1(\omega) = \mathcal{M}_2(\omega)$, then the two DTMMs are equivalent, denoted as $\mathcal{M}_1 \approx \mathcal{M}_2$. We modify the learning algorithm to take into account of inputs and outputs. By the same argument as for DOTAs, we can show correctness and termination of the learning algorithm for DTMMs.

Theorem 3 (Correctness and termination for learning DTMMs). *The learning algorithm for DTMMs always terminates and returns a correct DTMM.*

5   Implementation and Experiments

To investigate the efficiency and scalability of our methods, we implemented a prototype in Python named SL for both DOTAs and DTMMs based on the tool provided in [4]. We use Z3 [14] as the constraint solving engine. We describe some detailed aspects of the implementation below. The implementation and models used for experiments are available at https://github.com/Leslieaj/DOTALearningSMT.

Incremental solving Our implementation takes advantage of incremental SMT solving functionality in Z3. This allows Z3 to reuse information from previous calls to accelerate the solving process. For each query, we push a backtracking point after adding all new constraints in $C_1 \wedge C_2 \wedge C_4$, then insert the constraints C_3 or C_3' depending on the stage of the algorithm. After the query finished, we pop to the previous backtracking point, hence removing C_3 or C_3' before the next query.

Sink location We use a sink location to denote timed behaviors that are invalid or non-described, and it is sometimes possible for membership queries to return whether a timed word reached a sink location. Our implementation takes advantage of this information when it is available. This results in a significant acceleration of the learning process. The technique has been introduced in the previous work [4].

Table 1. Experimental results on DOTAs.

Group	$|\Delta|$	Method	#Membership			#Equivalence			$|Q_{\mathcal{H}}|$	#Learnt	$t(s)$
			N_{min}	N_{mean}	N_{max}	N_{min}	N_{mean}	N_{max}			
6_2_10	11.9	DOTAL	73	348.3	708	10	16.7	30	5.6	7/10	39.88
		SL	104	1894.8	3929	11	20.8	35	5.6	10/10	0.78
4_4_20	16.3	DOTAL	231	317.0	564	27	30.8	40	4.0	6/10	100.22
		SL	1740	3497.7	5329	24	32.8	42	4.0	10/10	1.42
7_4_20	26.0	SL	6092	9393.3	15216	44	51.5	69	7.0	10/10	2.90
10_4_20	39.1	SL	8579	16322.3	23726	59	76.5	93	10.0	10/10	5.89
12_4_20	47.6	SL	13780	20345.5	29011	70	88.0	102	12.0	10/10	10.05
14_4_20	58.4	SL	18915	28569.0	40693	92	110.6	126	14.0	10/10	14.69
AKM (17_12_5)	40.0	SL	3453	3453.0	3453	49	49.0	49	12	1/1	7.19
TCP (22_13_2)	22.0	SL	4713	4713.0	4713	32	32.0	32	20	1/1	19.04
CAS (14_10_27)	23.0	SL	4769	4769.0	4769	18	18.0	18	14	1/1	126.30
PC (26_17_10)	42.0	SL	10854	10854.0	10854	28	28.0	28	25	1/1	109.01

Group: each group has ID of the form $|Q|\_|\Sigma|\_\kappa$, where $|Q|$ is the number of locations, $|\Sigma|$ is the size of the alphabet, and κ is the maximum constant appearing in the clock constraints. $|\Delta|$: average number of transitions of a DOTA in the corresponding group. **Method:** DOTAL and SL represent the method in [4] and our method respectively. **#Membership** & **#Equivalence:** number of membership and equivalence queries, respectively. N_{min}: minimal, N_{mean}: mean, N_{max}: maximum. $|Q_{\mathcal{H}}|$: average number of locations of the learned automata for each group. **#Learnt:** the number of the learnt DOTAs (learnt/total). t: average wall-clock time in seconds.

Equivalence query Equivalence between timed automata with one clock is decidable. We implemented an equivalence query oracle based on [15], but simplified for the deterministic case. In actual applications when the target automaton is unknown, this can be usually replaced by techniques based on conformance testing.

We evaluated our prototype tool on two benchmarks that are previously used in [4] and [21]. They respectively contain hundreds of randomly generated DOTAs and several models from practical applications which are in the form of DOTAs and MM1Ts. The models from practical applications consist of the abstract automata of an Authentication and Key Management service of the WiFi (AKM), the functional specification of TCP protocol, a car alarm system (CAS), and a particle counter (PC). All experiments have been carried out on an Intel Core i7-9750H @ 2.6 GHz processor with 16 GB RAM running Ubuntu 20.04 Linux system.

5.1 Experiments on DOTAs

We first compared the performance of our learning algorithm SL with the algorithm DOTAL of [4] in the normal teacher setting (see Sect. 2). In [4], the generated random DOTAs are up to 14 locations, but the algorithm only managed to learn automata with up to 6 locations. The examples are divided into different groups depending on the number of locations, number of actions, and maximum clock value in guards. Each group contains ten automata. Moreover, we tested translations of practical models to DOTA provided in [21]. The experimental results are shown in Table 1.

The algorithm DOTAL fails in all of the larger examples due to time and memory limits. Hence, we omit them in the table. In the two groups of smaller examples

Table 2. Experimental results on DTMMs and MM1Ts.

Case	DTMM			SL			MM1T			MM1T-L_M^* [21]		
	$\|Q\|$	$\|I\|$	$\|\Delta\|$	#M	#E	$t(s)$	$\|Q\|$	$\|I\|$	$\|\Delta\|$	#R	#I	$t(s)$
AKM	5	5	28	691	34	2.6	4	5	24	5361	29693	5070.4
TCP	11	8	19	751	10	1.9	11	8	19	401	1868	65.7
CAS	8	4	17	1654	21	17.1	8	4	17	494	2528	79.5
AKM	8	8	24	1194	27	6.8	8	8	24	392	1864	85.1

6_2_10 and 4_4_20, the algorithm DOTAL can learn some of the cases. In the comparison between number of membership and equivalence queries, we see that SL takes about the same number of equivalence queries, and several times more membership queries. This is likely due to the fact that we exhaustively test all pairs of rows in the table under all reset conditions. However, the algorithm SL is scalable to much larger examples than DOTAL. SL also successfully learns the DOTA models of four practical applications which are all bigger than the randomly generated DOTAs, and far above the ability of the DOTAL algorithm. This shows the potential of SL in real applications.

5.2   Experiments on TMMs

We also evaluated our learning algorithm for timed Mealy machines. We first transformed the four MM1T models to DTMMs. As shown in Table 2, for each practical application, its DTMM model is more succinct than the corresponding DOTA model in Table 1. The size of the DTMM model is also comparable to the size of the MM1T model (the two are equal except the AKM case).

We then run our learning algorithm SL on these models. Compared to learning the corresponding DOTA, learning DTMM takes fewer membership and equivalence queries, except for taking more equivalence queries in the case CAS. Hence, we find DTMMs to be more suitable for learning timed reactive systems than DOTAs. We also run the experiment on MM1T using the algorithm MM1T-L_M^*. As reported in [21], the performance is evaluated according to the total number of resets to the system under learning (SUL) #R and the total number of the performed input actions #I. As these are not directly comparable to number of membership and equivalence queries, we list the results side-by-side in the table. Note also that their implementation is based on LearnLib [13] and uses a *random word* equivalence oracle with 1000 tests, while we conduct an exact equivalence checking. The computation time is listed to show that our method can learn the examples efficiently, but the computation times are not directly comparable across methods with different ways to conduct equivalence queries. We also note that [21] showed experimentally that the algorithm MM1T-L_M^* compares favorably against heuristic learning methods based on genetic programming [1, 18].

6   Conclusion

In this paper, we proposed a new algorithm for active learning of deterministic one-clock timed automata and timed Mealy machines, using constraint solving based on

SMT solving to determine resets and location assignments. This takes advantage of the ability of SMT to solve large constraint systems efficiently, allowing the algorithm to scale up to much larger timed automata models.

In future work, we wish to consider extension of the algorithm to learning timed automata with multiple clocks as well as the non-determinstic case. We wish to also consider incorporating ideas from algorithms such as TTT in order to improve efficiency, in particular reducing the number of membership queries.

References

1. Aichernig, B.K., Pferscher, A., Tappler, M.: From passive to active: learning timed automata efficiently. In: Lee, R., Jha, S., Mavridou, A., Giannakopoulou, D. (eds.) NFM 2020. LNCS, vol. 12229, pp. 1–19. Springer, Cham (2020). https://doi.org/10.1007/978-3-030-55754-6_1
2. Alur, R., Dill, D.L.: A theory of timed automata. Theor. Comput. Sci. **126**(2), 183–235 (1994)
3. Alur, R., Fix, L., Henzinger, T.A.: Event-clock automata: a determinizable class of timed automata. Theor. Comput. Sci. **211**(1–2), 253–273 (1999)
4. An, J., Chen, M., Zhan, B., Zhan, N., Zhang, M.: Learning one-clock timed automata. In: TACAS 2020. LNCS, vol. 12078, pp. 444–462. Springer, Cham (2020). https://doi.org/10.1007/978-3-030-45190-5_25
5. An, J., Wang, L., Zhan, B., Zhan, N., Zhang, M.: Learning real-time automata. Sci. China Inf. Sci. **64**(9), 1–17 (2021). https://doi.org/10.1007/s11432-019-2767-4
6. An, J., Zhan, B., Zhan, N., Zhang, M.: Learning nondeterministic real-time automata. ACM Trans. Embed. Comput. Syst. **20**(5s), 1–26 (2021)
7. Angluin, D.: Learning regular sets from queries and counterexamples. Inf. Comput. **75**(2), 87–106 (1987)
8. Dima, C.: Real-time automata. J. Automata Lang. Comb **6**(1), 3–23 (2001)
9. Drews, S., D'Antoni, L.: Learning symbolic automata. In: Legay, A., Margaria, T. (eds.) TACAS 2017. LNCS, vol. 10205, pp. 173–189. Springer, Heidelberg (2017). https://doi.org/10.1007/978-3-662-54577-5_10
10. Grinchtein, O., Jonsson, B., Leucker, M.: Learning of event-recording automata. Theor. Comput. Sci. **411**(47), 4029–4054 (2010)
11. Grinchtein, O., Jonsson, B., Pettersson, P.: Inference of event-recording automata using timed decision trees. In: Baier, C., Hermanns, H. (eds.) CONCUR 2006. LNCS, vol. 4137, pp. 435–449. Springer, Heidelberg (2006). https://doi.org/10.1007/11817949_29
12. Henry, L., Jéron, T., Markey, N.: Active learning of timed automata with unobservable resets. In: Bertrand, N., Jansen, N. (eds.) FORMATS 2020. LNCS, vol. 12288, pp. 144–160. Springer, Cham (2020). https://doi.org/10.1007/978-3-030-57628-8_9
13. Isberner, M., Howar, F., Steffen, B.: The open-source LearnLib - a framework for active automata learning. In: Kroening, D., Păsăreanu, C.S. (eds.) CAV 2015. LNCS, vol. 9206, pp. 487–495. Springer, Cham (2015). https://doi.org/10.1007/978-3-319-21690-4_32
14. de Moura, L., Bjørner, N.: Z3: an efficient SMT solver. In: Ramakrishnan, C.R., Rehof, J. (eds.) TACAS 2008. LNCS, vol. 4963, pp. 337–340. Springer, Heidelberg (2008). https://doi.org/10.1007/978-3-540-78800-3_24
15. Ouaknine, J., Worrell, J.: On the language inclusion problem for timed automata: closing a decidability gap. In: LICS 2004, pp. 54–63 (2004)
16. Smetsers, R., Fiterău-Broştean, P., Vaandrager, F.: Model learning as a satisfiability modulo theories problem. In: Klein, S.T., Martín-Vide, C., Shapira, D. (eds.) LATA 2018. LNCS, vol. 10792, pp. 182–194. Springer, Cham (2018). https://doi.org/10.1007/978-3-319-77313-1_14

17. Steffen, B., Howar, F., Merten, M.: Introduction to active automata learning from a practical perspective. In: Bernardo, M., Issarny, V. (eds.) SFM 2011. LNCS, vol. 6659, pp. 256–296. Springer, Heidelberg (2011). https://doi.org/10.1007/978-3-642-21455-4_8
18. Tappler, M., Aichernig, B.K., Larsen, K.G., Lorber, F.: Time to learn – learning timed automata from tests. In: André, É., Stoelinga, M. (eds.) FORMATS 2019. LNCS, vol. 11750, pp. 216–235. Springer, Cham (2019). https://doi.org/10.1007/978-3-030-29662-9_13
19. Tappler, M., Aichernig, B.K., Lorber, F.: Timed automata learning via SMT solving. In: Deshmukh, J.V., Havelund, K., Perez, I. (eds.) NASA Formal Methods. LNCS, vol. 13260, pp. 489–507. Springer, Cham (2022). https://doi.org/10.1007/978-3-031-06773-0_26
20. Vaandrager, F.W.: Model learning. Commun. ACM **60**(2), 86–95 (2017)
21. Vaandrager, F., Bloem, R., Ebrahimi, M.: Learning mealy machines with one timer. In: Leporati, A., Martín-Vide, C., Shapira, D., Zandron, C. (eds.) LATA 2021. LNCS, vol. 12638, pp. 157–170. Springer, Cham (2021). https://doi.org/10.1007/978-3-030-68195-1_13
22. Verwer, S., de Weerdt, M., Witteveen, C.: One-clock deterministic timed automata are efficiently identifiable in the limit. In: Dediu, A.H., Ionescu, A.M., Martín-Vide, C. (eds.) LATA 2009. LNCS, vol. 5457, pp. 740–751. Springer, Heidelberg (2009). https://doi.org/10.1007/978-3-642-00982-2_63
23. Verwer, S., de Weerdt, M., Witteveen, C.: The efficiency of identifying timed automata and the power of clocks. Inf. Comput. **209**(3), 606–625 (2011)
24. Verwer, S., de Weerdt, M., Witteveen, C.: Efficiently identifying deterministic real-time automata from labeled data. Mach. Learn. **86**(3), 295–333 (2011). https://doi.org/10.1007/s10994-011-5265-4

Learning and Characterizing Fully-Ordered Lattice Automata

Dana Fisman[✉] and Sagi Saadon[✉]

Ben-Gurion University, Beersheba, Israel
dana@cs.bgu.ac.il, sagisaa@post.bgu.ac.il

Abstract. Traditional automata classify words from a given alphabet as either *good* or *bad*. In many scenarios, in particular in formal verification, a finer classification is required. Fully-ordered lattice automata (FOLA) associate with every possible word a value from a finite set of values such as $\{0, 1, 2, \ldots, k\}$. In this paper we are interested in learning formal series that can be represented by FOLA. Such a series can be learned by a straight forward extension of the $\mathbf{L}^*$ algorithm. However, this approach does not take advantage of the special structure of a FOLA. In this paper we investigate FOLAs and provide a Myhill-Nerode characterization for FOLAs, which serves as a basis for providing a specialized algorithm for FOLAs, which we term $\mathbf{FOL}^*$. We compare the performance of $\mathbf{FOL}^*$ to that of $\mathbf{L}^*$ on synthetically generated FOLA. Our experiments show that $\mathbf{FOL}^*$ outperforms $\mathbf{L}^*$ in the number of states of the obtained FOLA, the number of issued *value queries* (the extension of *membership queries* to the quantitative setting), and the number of issued *equivalence queries*.

1 Introduction

Automata, being a simple computational model on which many operations (such as union, intersection, complementation, emptiness, equivalence) can be efficiently computed, have found usages in many applications including pattern matching, syntax analysis, and formal verification. Traditional automata are *Boolean* in the sense that they associate with any given word one of two possible values. In many applications, such as biology, physics, cognitive sciences, control, and linguistics, it is desired to associate with any given word one of many possible values. These motivated the study of richer types of automata such as *weighted automata* in which a word is associated with a value from a given semiring over a large range of values [22].

Focusing on formal verification, of particular interests are semirings that form a (distributive) *lattice*. A lattice $\mathcal{L} = \langle A, \leq \rangle$ is a partially ordered set in which every two elements $a, b \in A$ have a least upper bound (a *join* b) and a greatest lower bound (a *meet* b). Lattices offer generalization for multi-valued logics, and as such arise in quantitative verification [6, 12, 15, 18, 21], abstraction methods [13], query checking [10, 16], and verification under inconsistent view-points [17, 29].

In recent years, *model learning* emerged as a useful technique in formal verification [30]. Model learning, roughly speaking, refers to the task of learning a black-box

D. Fisman and S. Saadon—This research was partially supported by the Israel Science Foundation (ISF) grant 2507/21.

system, implemented by some automaton, by querying it with sequences of input and observing the received sequences of outputs. Model learning can be achieved using learning algorithms that ask membership and equivalence queries, as does the classical $\mathbf{L}^*$ algorithm developed by Angluin for learning regular languages represented by DFAs [2]. To this aim, the verification community seeks for query leaning algorithms for the automata types in use. Angluin-style algorithms have been developed for many automata types such as tree-automata [27], non-deterministic and alternating finite automata [4,9], Mealy machines [28], I/O-Automata [1], modular visibly pushdown automata [19], ω-automata [5], symbolic automata [11], strongly unambiguous Büchi automata [3], and structurally unambiguous probabilistic grammars [25].

In this work we are interested in learning fully-ordered lattice automata. A *fully-ordered lattice automata* (FOLA) is a lattice automata over a fully-ordered set $\{0, 1, \ldots, k\}$ where min and max are the meet and join operations, respectively. Roughly speaking a FOLA extends a DFA by annotating the transitions and states with values from the given lattice, as shown for instance in Fig. 1. The value the FOLA gives an input word is computed as the meet of all the lattice values read along the run as well as the lattice value of the final state (a formal definition is provided in Sect. 2). Thus the FOLA $\mathcal{A}$ of Fig. 1 gives the word b the value $2 \wedge 1 = 1$, and the word ba the value $2 \wedge 2 \wedge 2 = 2$.

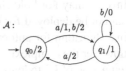

Fig. 1. A FOLA $\mathcal{A}$

We consider the active learning setting in which the algorithm can use *value queries* (VQ) (the extension of *membership queries* to the quantitative case) and *equivalence queries* (EQ). We focus on FOLAs, since besides nicely modeling multi-valued logics, they posses a polynomial minimization algorithm, while the minimization problem for general lattice automata is NP-complete [14]. Thus, assuming P$\neq$NP general lattice automata cannot be polynomially learned, since the learning algorithm can act as a minimization procedure.

In a FOLA, both transitions and states are annotated with values l from the given lattice $\mathcal{L}$. The value the automaton provides for a word depends on both the values traversed during the run, and the value of the state at the end of the run. If all transition values are the maximal value (thus do not affect the final value), the FOLA, is said to be a *simple* FOLA, abbreviated, SFOLA. A FOLA of size n over a lattice $\mathcal{L}$ can be simulated by an SFOLA of size $n \times |\mathcal{L}|$. This blowup is tight in the sense that there exists a family of languages $\{L_n\}_{n\in\mathbb{N}}$ over $\Sigma = \{a, b\}$ and lattice of size n which can be implemented by a FOLA with n states but there is no SFOLA with less than $n \times (n - 1)$ states. A FOLA for L_n is provided in Fig. 2 and an equivalent SFOLA is given in Fig. 10 in App.A.[1]

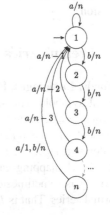

Fig. 2. A FOLA for L_n.

---

[1] The reason for the quadratic blowup can be understood by noticing that states of the SFOLA are required to record the traversal value up to that state (since all transitions values are $\top$), and for any $l \in \{2, 3, \ldots, n\}$ the FOLA needs to check whether an a will follow n consecutive b's (which requires of course n states), so in total $(n - 1) \times n$ states are required.

SFOLAs can be polynomially learned using a straight forward extension of the $\mathbf{L}^*$ algorithm.[2] It is therefore desired that the developed algorithm for FOLAs would perform better. However, we cannot expect the algorithm to have better worst-case complexity analysis since there are families of languages for which the minimal size of a FOLA is the same as the minimal size of a SFOLA. For instance this is the case for the family $\{L'_n\}_{n \in \mathbb{N}}$ over lattice $\mathcal{L} = \{0, \ldots, n-1\}$ which returns the size of the word modulo n. We do, however, expect a specialized algorithm can take into account the special structure of FOLAs and work better in practice.

In [8] an algorithm for learning *multiplicity automata*, an algebraic generalization of automata, that works with respect to a given *field* was developed. This algorithm was deployed by [7] to learn weighted automata, under the assumption that the semiring is a field. While a (distributive) lattice is a special case of a semiring, a lattice is not a field, since the property that every element $a \in A$ has an additive (and/or multiplicative) inverse may not hold. It follows that the algorithm for learning multiplicity automata cannot be deployed for learning lattice automata. FOLAs can be learned using a learning algorithm for automata based on a monoid action, called writer automata in [31], however the complexity of this algorithm for the case of FOLA is the same as using the extension of $\mathbf{L}^*$ to learn SFOLAs.

In order to obtain an algorithm that in practice would perform better on FOLAs than $\mathbf{L}^*$ for SFOLA, we must understand FOLAs better. To this aim, building on the work of Halamish and Kupferman [14] who studied minimization of FOLAs, we reveal: an equivalence relation for FOLAs; a canonical minimal FOLA; and a respective Myhill-Nerode characterization for FOLAs. Section 3 is devoted for this investigation.

The provided characterization and insights allow us to design a specialized algorithm for FOLAs; this is the topic of Sect. 4. Section 5 compares the performance of $\mathbf{FOL}^*$ with that of the $\mathbf{L}^*$ algorithm on synthetically generated FOLAs. The experiments shows a clear advantage to our algorithm, with up to an $|\mathcal{L}|$ blowup. Section 6 concludes. Due to space restrictions some proofs are deferred to the appendix of the full version.

2   Preliminaries

Words, Languages, Formal Series. We use Σ for an *alphabet* i.e. a finite non-empty set of symbols. The set of word over Σ is denoted Σ^*. The length of a word $w = \sigma_1 \sigma_2 \ldots \sigma_m$, denoted $|w|$ is m. The prefix of w up to position i, namely $\sigma_1 \sigma_2 \ldots \sigma_i$, is denoted $w[..i]$. Similarly the suffix of w starting at position i, namely $\sigma_i \sigma_{i+1} \ldots \sigma_m$, is denoted $w[i..]$. A *language* is a subset of Σ^*. A *formal series* f is a function $f : \Sigma^* \to A$ mapping each word to a value in A, where A is some set. Such a formal series f is sometimes called an A-language. Note that a language is a special case of a formal series. That is $L \subseteq \Sigma^*$ can be thought of as a formal series $f_L : \Sigma^* \to \mathbb{B}$ where

---

[2] In this extension, the observation table matrix holds values in the lattice instead of $\{0, 1\}$, that is, the entry (i, j) holds the result of the value query for the word $s_i \cdot e_j$ where s_i is the title of row i and e_j the title of row j. Two rows in the observation table are considered equivalent if they are exactly the same. These are the only changes required w.r.t. to $\mathbf{L}^*$ for DFAs.

$\mathbb{B} = \{0, 1\}$. In this work we are interested in formal series that map words to a value in a fully ordered set $\{0, 1, \ldots, k\}$.

Lattice. Let $\mathcal{L} = \langle A, \leq \rangle$ be a partially ordered set. An element $a \in A$ is an *upper bound* on A (denoted $\top$) if $b \leq a$ for all $b \in A$. An element $a \in A$ is a *lower bound* on A (denoted $\bot$) if $a \leq b$ for all $b \in A$. A partially (or fully) ordered set $\langle A, \leq \rangle$ is a *Lattice* if for every two elements $a, b \in A$ both the least upper bound, denoted as $a \vee b$, and the greatest lower bound, denoted as $a \wedge b$, of $\{a, b\}$ exist. A lattice is *complete* if for every subset $A' \subseteq A$ the least upper bound and the greatest upper bound exist. In a complete lattice $\top$ denotes the join of all elements in A and $\bot$ denotes their meet.

Lattice Automata. Lattice automata are a generalization of finite-state automata [20]. Their deterministic version is defined as follows. A *deterministic lattice automaton* (LDFA) $\mathcal{A}$ is a tuple $\langle \mathcal{L}, \Sigma, Q, q_0, \delta, \eta, F \rangle$ where $\mathcal{L}$ is a complete lattice; Σ is the alphabet; Q is a finite set of states; $q_0 \in Q$ is the initial state; $\delta : Q \times \Sigma \to Q$ is the state transition function; $\eta : Q \times \Sigma \to \mathcal{L}$ is the transitions value function associating with every transition (from a state q on letter σ) a value ℓ from the lattice; and $F : Q \to \mathcal{L}$ is the state-value function associating with each state a value form the lattice.

A run of $\mathcal{A}$ on a word $w = \sigma_1 \sigma_2 \cdots \sigma_n$ is a sequence $r = q_0 \ldots q_n$ of $n + 1$ states. The *traversal value* of r on w, denoted $trvl(w)$ is the meet of all transitions involved, i.e., if $\eta(q_{i-1}, \sigma_i) = \ell_i$ then $trvl(w) = \bigwedge_{i=1}^{n} \ell_i$. The value of r on w is defined as $val(w) = trvl(w) \wedge F(q_n)$. Namely it is the meet of the traversal value and the state-value of the last state of the run.[3] The extension of δ from letters to words is denoted δ^* (i.e., $\delta^*(q, \epsilon) = q$, and $\delta^*(q, u\sigma) = \delta(\delta^*(q, u), \sigma)$ for $u \in \Sigma^*$ and $\sigma \in \Sigma$). The formal series defined by $\mathcal{A}$ is denoted $[\![\mathcal{A}]\!]$, and $[\![\mathcal{A}]\!](w)$ denotes the value $\mathcal{A}$ gives to word w.

A *fully-ordered lattice automaton* (FOLA) is a lattice automaton over a fully-ordered set $\{0, 1, \ldots, k\}$ where min and max are the meet and join operations, respectively.

Example 1. Recall the FOLA $\mathcal{A}$ over the lattice $\mathcal{L} = \{0, 1, 2\}$ and the alphabet $\Sigma = \{a, b\}$ from Fig. 1. Consider the word $w = baa$. The run of $\mathcal{A}$ on w is the sequence $\rho = q_0 q_1 q_0 q_1$. Its traversal-value is $trvl(w) = \eta(q_0, b) \wedge \eta(q_1, a) \wedge \eta(q_0, a) = 2 \wedge 2 \wedge 1$. The value of $\mathcal{A}$ on w is $val(w) = trvl(w) \wedge F(q_1) = 1 \wedge 1 = 1$.

3 A Myhill-Nerode Characterization for FOLAs

For a language $L \subseteq \Sigma^*$, one defines the equivalence relation $\equiv_L \subseteq \Sigma^* \times \Sigma^*$ as follows $x \equiv_L y$ iff for every $z \in \Sigma^*$ it holds that $xz \in L \iff yz \in L$. The celebrated Myhill-Nerode theorem states that (i) L is a regular iff $\equiv_L$ has a finite index (i.e. $\equiv_L$ induces a finite number of equivalence classes), (ii) there is a one-to-one relation between the states of a minimal DFA for L and the equivalence classes of $\equiv_L$, and (iii) all DFAs with minimal number of states are isomorphic to each other, or put otherwise there is a unique minimal DFA [23,24]. Many automata learning algorithms, including $\mathbf{L}^*$, rely

---

[3] In non-deterministic lattice automata, there may be several runs on a given word, and each run may have a different value. In this case the value of the automaton on the word is the join of the values of all of its runs on that word.

on the correspondence between the equivalence classes and the states of the minimal representation. Therefore, we seek for a similar correspondence between an adequate equivalence relation for formal-series defined by FOLAs and minimal FOLAs.

3.1 No Unique Minimal FOLA

We first note that unlike the situation in regular languages, for formal series represented by FOLAs there may exists two FOLAs with a minimal number of states that are not isomorphic to each other. Figure 3 depicts two minimal distinct FOLAs, $\mathcal{A}_1$ and $\mathcal{A}_2$, implementing the formal-series $f : \{a\}^* \rightarrow \{0,1\}$ that gives 1 iff the length of the word is at most one.

Let us examine this closely. Let $\mathcal{A} = \langle \mathcal{L}, \Sigma, Q, q_0, \delta, \eta, F \rangle$ be a FOLA. It induces an equivalence relation $\equiv_{\mathcal{A}}$ between pairs of words, defined as follows. For $x, y \in \Sigma^*$ we have $x \equiv_{\mathcal{A}} y$ iff the run of $\mathcal{A}$ on x ends in the same state as the run of $\mathcal{A}$ on y. In the case of regular languages, if $\mathcal{A}_1$ and $\mathcal{A}_2$ are two minimal DFAs for the same language L, then $\equiv_{\mathcal{A}_1}$ and $\equiv_{\mathcal{A}_2}$ are exactly the same relation as $\equiv_L$.

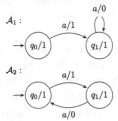

Figure 3 shows that in the case of languages accepted by FOLAs, this is not necessarily the case. Indeed, while the FOLAs $\mathcal{A}_1$ and $\mathcal{A}_2$ define the same function, and are both minimal in the number of states, the induced equivalence relations are different: for $\equiv_{\mathcal{A}_1}$ we have $E_0 = \{\epsilon\}$ and $E_1 = \Sigma^+$, whereas for $\equiv_{\mathcal{A}_2}$ we have $E_0 = \{w : |w| \bmod 2 = 0\}$ and $E_1 = \{w : |w| \bmod 2 \neq 0\}$ where E_i describes the equivalence class of state q_i.

Fig. 3. Two minimal FOLAs for the same formal series.

3.2 Difficulties in Defining $\equiv_f$

Investigating minimization of FOLAs, Halamish and Kupferman [14] explain the difficulty in finding an equivalence relation for FOLAs. Their first observation is that the natural extension $x \equiv_f^1 y$ iff for every $z \in \Sigma^*$ it holds that $f(xz) = f(yz)$ is too refined, as for the FOLA $\mathcal{B}$ over $\Sigma = \{a,b,c\}$ and $\mathcal{L} = \{0,1,2\}$ depicted in Fig. 4 it will consist of three equivalence classes, while one suffices. Yet, this definition holds under the assumption that all transition values are $\top$. As mentioned earlier, FOLAs admitting this restriction are called *simple FOLAs* or in short SFOLAs.

Fig. 4. A FOLA $\mathcal{B}$

Their second observation concerns the following definition $x \equiv_f^2 y$ which states that $x \equiv_f^2 y$ iff for every $z \in \Sigma^*$ exists $\ell_z \in \mathcal{L}$ such that $f(xz) = f(x) \wedge \ell_z$ and $f(yz) = f(y) \wedge \ell_z$. This definition seems intuitive for FOLAs for which all acceptance values are $\top$, however, it does not work in this case as well. The main problem with this definition is that it is not transitive and thus it is not an equivalence relation, as shown in Example 2.

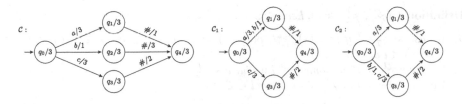

Fig. 5. The definition $\equiv_f^2$ breaks transitivity [14]

Example 2 ([14]). To see that transitivity does not hold for $\equiv_f^2$ consider the FOLA $\mathcal{C}$ given in Fig. 5. It defines a function from words over $\Sigma = \{a, b, c, \#\}^*$ to values in lattice $\mathcal{L} = \{0, 1, 2, 3\}$. The proposed definition satisfies that $a \equiv_f^2 b$ and $b \equiv_f^2 c$ yet $a \not\equiv_f^2 c$. Indeed the FOLAs $\mathcal{C}_1$ and $\mathcal{C}_2$, depicted in Fig. 5, are equivalent to $\mathcal{C}$ and each makes a different choice regarding equivalence of the string b.

3.3 Defining the Equivalence Relation

The relation $\equiv_L$ for a regular language L captures that two words reach the same state of the minimal DFA. The relation $\equiv_f$ for a formal series f should capture that two words reach the same state of a minimal FOLA. To define it we make use of the notion of a Hankel Matrix. With every formal series $f : \Sigma^* \to \mathcal{L}$ we can associate its *Hankel Matrix* $\mathcal{H}_f$. The Hankel Matrix has infinitely many rows and infinitely many columns. The entry (i, j) has the value $f(w_i \cdot w_j)$ where w_i and w_j are the i-th and j-th words in an agreed enumeration of Σ^*. Consider the Hankel Matrix for a regular language L and two words w_1, w_2. The rows of w_1 and w_2 in $\mathcal{H}_L$ are exactly the same iff $w_1 \equiv_L w_2$. This is since if $w_1 \not\equiv_L w_2$ then there exists a word $z \in \Sigma^*$ s.t. $w_1 z \in L$ and $w_2 z \notin L$ or vice versa, thus $\mathcal{H}_L(w_1, z) \neq \mathcal{H}_L(w_2, z)$. To define $\equiv_f$ we need to understand how do two rows of words w_1 and w_2 resemble if w_1 and w_2 reach the same state of a minimal FOLA. Clearly they need not be exactly the same, since $f(w_1 z)$ relies also on the values traversed while reading w_1.

We use the term *observation table* for any sub-matrix of $\mathcal{H}_f$. Two subsets S and E of Σ^* define the observation table $\mathcal{T} = (S, E, T)$ where $T : S \times E \to \mathcal{L}$ is defined as $T(s, e) = f(s \cdot e)$ for every $s \in S$ and $e \in E$. We will define relations for an arbitrary observation table; when applied to the full Hankel Matrix, it will convey the desired equivalence relation. The algorithm will use the definitions for a finite observation table.

We say that the *row-potential* of a row s (or simply its *potential*) is l if there exists a column $e \in E$ such that $T(s, e) = l$ and there is no $e' \in E$ such that $T(s, e') > l$. This means that the traversal value of the correct automaton on reading s cannot be smaller than l as otherwise for no extension the value l can be obtained. However, according to the observed data, there is no reason to assign it a value greater than l.

Definition 3 (Row Potential). *Let $\mathcal{T} = (S, E, T)$ be an observation table, and $s \in S$. The row-potential of s, denoted $\mathrm{pot}_{\mathcal{T}}(s)$, is $\max\{T(s \cdot e) : e \in E\}$.*

For every value $l \in \mathcal{L}$ and every pair of rows whose potential is at least l we would like to ask whether they should be distinguished according to the data. The following definitions make this precise.

Definition 4 ($\nsim_T^l$, $\napprox_T^l$, $\napprox_T$). *Let* $l \in \mathcal{L}$ *and* $s, s' \in S$.

1. *We use* $s \nsim_T^l s'$ *if* $\text{pot}_T(s) \geq l$, $\text{pot}_T(s') \geq l$ *and* $\exists e \in E$ *s.t.* $T(s, e) \geq l$ *and* $T(s', e) < l$ *or vice versa.*
2. *We use* $s \napprox_T^l s'$ *if for some* $l' \leq l$ *we have* $s \nsim_T^{l'} s'$.
3. *We use* $s \napprox_T s'$ *if* $s \nsim_T^l s'$ *for some* $l \in \mathcal{L}$.

It is easy to see that $x \approx_T^l y$ implies $x \approx_T^{l-1} y$ and that $x \approx_T y$ iff $x \approx_T^k y$ where $\mathcal{L} = \{0, 1, \ldots, k\}$.

The following claim states that if we have two rows s_1 and s_2 such that in one column e the entry for $T(s_1, e)$ is strictly bigger than $T(s_2, e)$ whereas in another column e' the entry for $T(s_1, e')$ is strictly smaller than $T(s_2, e')$, then $s_1 \napprox_T s_2$.

Claim 5. *Let* $T = (S, E, T)$. *Let* $s_1, s_2 \in S$ *and* $e_1, e_2 \in E$. *If* $T(s_1, e_1) < T(s_2, e_1)$ *while* $T(s_1, e_2) > T(s_2, e_2)$ *then* $s_1 \napprox_T s_2$.

We claim that if $s \napprox_T s'$ then strings s and s' cannot reach the same state of a FOLA for the respective formal series.

Lemma 6. *Let* $T = (S, E, T)$ *be an observation table for formal series* f, *and let* $s, s' \in S$. *If* $s \napprox_T s'$ *then in no FOLA for* f *the words* s, s' *reach the same state.*

Proof. From $s \napprox_T s'$ it follows that exists $l \in \mathcal{L}$ such that $s \nsim_T^l s'$. From the definition of $\nsim_T^l$ it follows that $\text{pot}_T(s) \geq l$, $\text{pot}_T(s') \geq l$ and $\exists e \in E$ s.t. $T(s, e) \geq l$ and $T(s', e) < l$ or vice versa. Let $\mathcal{A} = \langle \mathcal{L}, \Sigma, Q, q_0, \delta, \eta, F \rangle$ be a FOLA for f. The traversal value of s in $\mathcal{A}$ must be at least l, as otherwise for every z, $\mathcal{A}(sz) < l$ but $\text{pot}_T(s) \geq l$ implies there exists a $z \in E$ for which $T(s, z) \geq l$ so $\mathcal{A}_f$ disagrees with T. The same argument shows that the traversal value of s' in $\mathcal{A}$ must be at least l. Assume towards contradiction that $\mathcal{A}$ upon reading s or s' reaches the same state q_s. Let q_e be the state that $\mathcal{A}$ reaches upon reading se (or $s'e$ as this must be the same state). The traversal value of e starting from the state q must be at least l and $F(q_e)$ must be at least l as otherwise $\mathcal{A}$ will be wrong regarding $s \cdot e$. But if this is the case then $\mathcal{A}$ is wrong regarding $s' \cdot e$. Contradiction. □

While the relation $\approx_T$ differentiates words that do not reach the same state, it is not an equivalence relation. The reason is that it does not satisfy the transitivity requirement as shown by Fig. 6. The following claim will help us strengthen it to get the desired equivalence relation.

T	e_1	e_2	e_3
s_1	1	2	1
s_2	1	1	1
s_3	2	1	2

Claim 7. *Let* $s_1, s_2, s_3 \in S$. *If* $s_1 \approx_T s_2, s_2 \approx_T s_3$, $s_2 \napprox_T s_1$ *and* $s_2 \napprox_T s_3$ *then* $s_1 \approx_T s_3$.

Fig. 6. $s_1 \approx_T s_2$ and $s_2 \approx_T s_3$ but $s_1 \napprox_T s_3$

If we would like to pick one of a set of non-distinguishable words to be a representative, following Claim 7 it makes sense to choose one with the highest potential. Since there could be several such, we define an order between two rows in the table. We use the *shortlex* order between strings, denoted $\leq_{slex}$.[4]

---

[4] The *shortlex* order (aka the *length-lexicographic* order) stipulates that string w_1 is smaller than string w_2, denoted $w_1 <_{slex} w_2$ if $|w_1| < |w_2|$ or $|w_1| = |w_2|$ and w_1 precedes w_2 in the lexicographic order.

Definition 8 (Rows order). *Let $T = (S, E, T)$ be an observation table and s, s' rows in S. We say that $s \succeq_T s'$ if either [$pot_T(s) \geq pot_T(s')$] or [$pot_T(s) = pot_T(s')$ and $s \leq_{slex} s'$] (where $\leq_{slex}$ is the shortlex order).*

The representative for a set $S' \subseteq S$ of rows that cannot be distinguished from one another is chosen to be the minimal element in the shortlex order, among those in S' with the highest potential. That is, the set of representatives of an observation table T is defined as follows.

Definition 9 (*reps(T)*, *repT s*, $\equiv_T$). *Let $T = (S, E, T)$ be an observation table.*

- *The set of representatives of the table is defined as $reps(T) = \{s \in S \mid \forall s' \approx_T s.\ s \succeq_T s'\}$.*
- *For a row $s \in S$ we use $rep_T(s)$ for the row $s_* \in reps(T)$ such that $s \approx_T s_*$ and for every $s' \in reps(T)$ satisfying $s' \approx_T s$ we have $s_* \succeq_T s'$.*
- *Let s, s' be rows in S. We use $s \equiv_T s'$ to denote that $rep_T(s) = rep_T(s')$. That is, two rows are equivalent if they have the same representative.*

Given a formal series $f : \Sigma^* \to \mathcal{L}$ let $T_f = (\Sigma^*, \Sigma^*, T_f)$ be the Hankel Matrix for f. Let $reps(f)$, $rep_f(w)$ and $pot_f(w)$ abbreviate $reps(T_f)$, $rep_{T_f}(w)$ and $pot_{T_f}(w)$. Likewise, let $\sim^l_f$, $\approx^l_f$, $\approx_f$, and $\equiv_f$ abbreviate $\sim^l_{T_f}$, $\approx^l_{T_f}$, $\approx_{T_f}$, and $\equiv_{T_f}$.

We show that $\equiv_f$ is an equivalence relation on Σ^* and a right congruence relation.

Claim 10. *The relation $\equiv_f$ is an equivalence relation.*

Claim 11. *The relation $\equiv_f$ is a right congruence relation. That is, $x \equiv_f y$ implies $xz \equiv_f yz$ for all $z \in \Sigma^*$.*

Note that if s_* is the representative of s, then for every $e \in E$ we have that $T(se) \leq T(s_*e)$ and more precisely $T(se) = T(s_*e) \wedge pot_T(s)$.

Claim 12. *Let $T = (S, E, T)$ be an observation table, $s \in S$ and $s_* = rep_T(s)$. Then for all $e \in E$ (i) $T(s, e) \leq T(s_*, e)$ and moreover (ii) $T(s, e) = T(s_*, e) \wedge pot_T(s)$.*

Proof. Assume towards contradiction that $\exists e \in E$ s.t. $T(s, e) > T(s_*, e)$. Assume $T(s, e) = l$. Then $T(s_*, e) < l \leq pot_T(s) \leq pot_T(s_*)$. Therefore, according to Definition 4, $s \not\sim^l_T s_*$ which contradicts that s_* is the representative of s (Definition 9). This proves item (i).

For item (ii), assume toward contradiction that $\exists e \in E$ for which $T(se) \neq T(s_*e) \wedge pot_T(s)$. It is clear that $T(se) \leq pot_T(s)$ and from item (i) we know that $T(se) \leq T(s_*e)$. Applying these conclusions, we get that $T(se) < T(s_*e) \wedge pot_T(s)$, which implies that $T(se) < T(s_*e)$ and $T(se) < pot_T(s)$. Let $\ell \in \mathcal{L}$ be the minimal element for which $\ell > T(se)$. Hence, $pot_T(s), pot_T(s_*) \geq \ell$, and $T(s_*e) \geq \ell$, but $T(se) < \ell$. Thus, according to Definition 4, $s_* \not\equiv s$ reaching a contradiction. $\square$

3.4   The Correspondence Between $\equiv_f$ and a Minimal FOLA

Next we prove that for every formal series f defined by a FOLA the induced equivalence relation $\equiv_f$ has a one-to-one correspondence with a minimal FOLA for f.

Utilizing the provided definitions, we can associate with a given formal series $f : \Sigma^* \to \{0, 1, \ldots, k\}$, a specific FOLA which we denote $\mathcal{A}_f$.

Definition 13 (The FOLA $\mathcal{A}_f$). *Let $f : \Sigma^* \to \{0, 1, \ldots, k\}$ be a formal series. Let $reps(f) = \{r_0, r_1, \ldots, r_n\}$. The FOLA $\mathcal{A}_f = (\Sigma, Q, q_0, \delta, \eta, F)$ is defined as follows: $Q = reps(f)$, $q_0 = rep_f(\epsilon)$, $F(r_i) = f(r_i)$, $\delta(r_i, \sigma) = rep_f(r_i \cdot \sigma)$ and $\eta(r_i, \sigma) = pot_f(r_i \cdot \sigma)$.*

We claim in Theorem 17 that $\mathcal{A}_f$ recognizes the formal series f.

To prove it we associate with the formal series f a tree $\mathbb{T}_f$, whose nodes are set of words, defined as follows.

Definition 14 (The tree $\mathbb{T}_f$, the sets W_ℓ). *Let $f : \Sigma^* \to \{0, 1, \ldots, k\}$ be a formal series. Let $W_\ell = \{w \mid pot_f(w) \geq \ell\}$. The tree $\mathbb{T}_f$ has $k + 1$ layers. The set of nodes in layer ℓ consists of the equivalence classes of $\approx_f^\ell$ intersected with W_ℓ. There is an edge from node N in layer ℓ to node N' in layer $\ell + 1$ iff $N \supseteq N'$.*

Note that $W_0 = \Sigma^*$ and $\approx_\ell^0 = \sim_f^0$ has a single equivalence class. Thus, the first layer consists of a single node (the root) which is the set Σ^*. Note also that the nodes of layer ℓ partition the set W_ℓ (i.e. their union is this set, and they are pairwise disjoint). Moreover, if two words are in the same node of layer ℓ then they are also in the same node of layer $\ell - 1$ (since $x \approx_f^\ell y$ implies $x \approx_f^{\ell-1} y$). It follows that a node in layer $\ell + 1$ is connected to a single node in layer ℓ. Thus $\mathbb{T}_f$ is indeed a tree.

Example 15. Consider the FOLA $\mathcal{D}$ depicted in Fig. 7 implementing a formal series $f_\mathcal{D} : \{a, b\}^* \to \{0, 1, 2, 3, 4\}$. In Fig. 7 we show the tree $\mathbb{T}_{f_\mathcal{D}}$. The first layer, layer 0, of $\mathbb{T}_{f_\mathcal{D}}$, as always consists of a single node $W_0 = \Sigma^*$. Layer 1 of $\mathbb{T}_{f_\mathcal{D}}$ also consists of a single node Σ^* since according to $f_\mathcal{D}$ the potential of all words is at least one. That is, $W_1 = \Sigma^*$. Layer 2 of $\mathbb{T}_{f_\mathcal{D}}$ consists of two nodes $W_{2a} = \{\epsilon\}$ and $W_{2b} = a\Sigma^*$. Indeed the word ϵ is differentiated from all words in $a\Sigma^*$ by $\sim_f^2$ as evident by the word b. To see why note that the potential of both ϵ and a (for instance) is $4 \geq 2$ and $f(\epsilon \cdot b) = 1 < 2$ while $f(a \cdot b) = 3 \geq 2$. Observe that $W_2 = W_{2a} \cup W_{2b} = W_1 \setminus b\Sigma^*$, since no word starting with b has a potential of 2 or more. Layer 3 of $\mathbb{T}_{f_\mathcal{D}}$ consists of four nodes $W_{3a} = \{\epsilon\}$, $W_{3b} = a(ba^*b\Sigma)^*$, $W_{3c} = a(ba^*b\Sigma)^*ba^*$ and $W_{3d} = a(ba^*b\Sigma)^*ba^*b$. Note that $W_3 = W_2 \setminus a(ba^*b\Sigma)a\Sigma^*$, since once the a transition from q_2 to q_4 is taken the potential drops to 2. Layer 4 of $\mathbb{T}_{f_\mathcal{D}}$ consists of two nodes $W_{4a} = \{\epsilon\}$, and $W_{4b} = \{a\}$, since once the b transition from q_2 to q_3 is taken the potential drops to 3. The representatives are shown below the leaves.

Claim 16 connects $\equiv_f$ and the tree $\mathbb{T}_f$, and consequently the FOLA $\mathcal{A}_f$ and $\mathbb{T}_f$.

Claim 16. *Let L be a leaf in layer l of $\mathbb{T}_f$ and let u be the biggest word in L according to the $\succcurlyeq_f$ order. Then $L = \{u' \mid u' \equiv_f u\} \cap W_l$.*

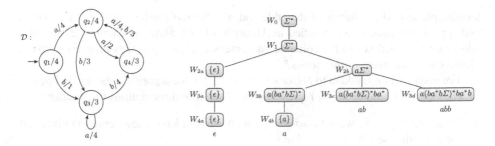

Fig. 7. A FOLA $\mathcal{D}$, and the tree $\mathbb{T}_{f_\mathcal{D}}$ induced by FOLA $\mathcal{D}$

Let $leaves(\mathbb{T}_f) = \{L_0, L_1, L_2 \ldots, L_n\}$ be the leaves of $\mathbb{T}_f$. It follows that there exists a one-to-one mapping $h : reps(f) \to leaves(\mathbb{T}_f)$ satisfying that $h(r_i) = L_i$ for $L_i = \{w \mid w \equiv_f r_i\} \cap W_{pot_f(r_i)}$. Since the states of $\mathcal{A}_f$ are $reps(f)$, this shows there is a one-to-one mapping between the states of $\mathcal{A}_f$ and the leaves of $\mathbb{T}_f$. Moreover, the representative of a word $u \in \Sigma^*$ can be found by searching for the deepest node N in the tree to which u belongs. This node is unique since nodes in the same layer are disjoint, and a node is subsumed by its parent. If N is a leaf, then the smallest word in N in the shortlex order is its representative. Otherwise let $L_1, \ldots, L_k$ be the deepest leaves in the sub-tree rooted by N. Then the smallest word in the shortlex order amongst $L_1, \ldots, L_k$ is its representative.

Theorem 17 states that the desired relation between $\mathcal{A}_f$ and f holds. Its correctness follows from the stronger inductive claim, Claim 18.

Theorem 17. *The FOLA $\mathcal{A}_f$ of Definition 13 correctly computes f. That is, $f(w) = \mathcal{A}_f(w)$ for every $w \in \Sigma^*$.*

Claim 18. *Let $f : \Sigma^* \to \{0, \ldots, k\}$ be a formal series, and let $\mathcal{A}_f$ be the FOLA from Definition 13. Let $u \in \Sigma^*$. Then $rep_f(u) = r_i$ iff $\delta^*(q_0, u) = r_i$ and $\mathcal{A}_f(u) = f(u)$.*

4   The Learning Algorithm

The learning algorithm **FOL*** tries to distinguish the equivalence classes of $\equiv_f$. It does so by maintaining an observation table which keeps track of queried words. Starting with $S = \{\epsilon\} \cup \Sigma$ and $E = \{\epsilon\}$ it fills the missing entries of the table using value queries. This is done by procedure *Fill*. To extract a FOLA from a table, it is necessary to have for every distinguished equivalence class s, and any letter σ of the alphabet, a row for $s \cdot \sigma$. When this criterion holds we say that the table is *closed* as defined next.

Definition 19 (Closed Table). *An observation table $T = (S, E, T)$ is termed closed if for every $s \in reps(T)$ and every $\sigma \in \Sigma$ there exists $s' \in reps(T)$ such that $s' \approx_T s\sigma$.*

After extracting a FOLA the algorithm asks an equivalence query (EQ).[5] If the answer is "yes" the algorithm terminates. Otherwise the algorithm adds all suffixes of the coun-

---

[5] An EQ receives as an argument a FOLA $\mathcal{A}$, and checks if $[\![\mathcal{A}]\!] = f$ where f is the target formal series. If so it returns "yes", otherwise, it returns "no" with a counterexample, a word w such that $[\![\mathcal{A}]\!](w) \neq f(w)$. A value query (VQ) receives as an argument a word w and returns $f(w)$.

terexample w to the columns of the table and fills the table using value queries (VQ) s and repeats the process as specified in Algorithm 1. We show in Theorem 22 that the addition of the suffixes to the columns guarantees the learner makes progress towards identifying the correct formal series.[6]

For each $s\sigma$ that is added to S (for $s \in S_*, \sigma \in \Sigma$), the algorithm checks (in lines 5-8) whether $s\sigma$ should be a new representative. There are three options to consider:

1. If for every $s' \in S_*$ we have $s\sigma \not\approx_T s'$, then $s\sigma$ is indeed a new representative, and the algorithm sets $S_* \leftarrow S_* \cup \{s\sigma\}$
2. If there exists $s' \in S_*$ such that $s' \succeq_T s\sigma$ and $s\sigma \approx_T s'$ then no update needs to be done (and practically the algorithm defines $rep_T(s\sigma) = s'$).
3. Otherwise, there exists $s' \in S_*$ such that $s\sigma \succ_T s'$ and $s\sigma \approx_T s'$. In this case $s\sigma$ replaces a current representative: $S_* \leftarrow (S_* \setminus \{s'\}) \cup \{s\sigma\}$. Note that there exists exactly one row s' as such in the current case, as we prove in Claim 20.

Algorithm 1. FOL*

1: $S := \{\epsilon\} \cup \Sigma$, $E := \{\epsilon\}$, $S_* = \{\epsilon\}$, $T := (S, E, T)$, $Fill(T)$
2: **while** *True* **do**
3:     **if** exists $s \in S_*$ and $\sigma \in \Sigma$ such that $s \cdot \sigma \notin S$ **then**
4:         $S := S \cup \{s \cdot \sigma\}$, $Fill(T)$
5:         **if** $s\sigma \not\approx_T s_*$ for all $s_* \in S_*$ **then**
6:             $S_* \leftarrow S_* \cup \{s\sigma\}$ ▷ a new equivalence class is discovered
7:         **else if** $s\sigma \approx_T s_*$ for some $s_* \in S_*$ and $s\sigma \succ_T s_*$ **then**
8:             $S_* \leftarrow (S_* \setminus \{s_*\}) \cup \{s\sigma\}$ ▷ the potential of an equivalence class increased
9:     $\mathcal{A} = ExtractAut(S, E, T)$ ▷ the procedure *ExtractAut* applies Definition 13 on $\equiv_T$
10:     **if** EQ$(\mathcal{A}) = ($"no"$, w)$ **then**   ▷ w is the counterexample
11:         $E := E \cup Suffs(w)$, $Fill(T)$
12:     **else**
13:         **return** $\mathcal{A}$

A running example is provided in App.C.

The following claim asserts that S_* never contains two representatives of the same class. Since the observation table T at every step of the algorithm is a subset of the Hankel Matrix $\mathcal{H}_f$ of the target series f, the size of S_* is bounded by n, the index of $\equiv_f$.

Claim 20. *In every step of the algorithm, $\forall s, s' \in S_*$ we have $s \not\approx_T s'$.*

The following lemma asserts that if the algorithm terminates, it returns a minimal FOLA.

Lemma 21. *Let $T = (S, E, T)$ be a closed observation table, and let $S_* = reps(T)$. Any FOLA consistent with T must have at least $|S_*|$ states.*

---

[6] The proof shows that Rivest and Schapire's optimization of adding just one of these suffixes [26] is possible here as well.

Termination follows from the following theorem, that guarantees that when a counterexample is received, the algorithm makes progress towards inferring the target series. It shows that either a new pair of rows is differentiated, namely a new equivalence class has been discovered, or the potential of one of the equivalence classes increases.

Theorem 22. *Let $T = (S, E, T)$ be an observation table, and let $T' = (S', E', T')$ be the table after processing the counterexample (i.e. after line 11). Then either $\exists s, s' \in S$ such that $s \equiv_T s'$ and $s \not\equiv_{T'} s'$ or $\equiv_{T'}$ is the same as $\equiv_T$ and $\exists s \in S$ for which $pot_{T'}(rep_{T'}(s)) > pot_T(rep_T(s))$.*

Proof. Let $w = \sigma_1 \sigma_2 \ldots \sigma_m$ be the counterexample received for a FOLA $\mathcal{A}$ extracted from the table T. Let $s_i = \delta(s_0, w[..i])$, that is, s_i is the state reached by the constructed FOLA $\mathcal{A}$ when reading the prefix of w of length i. Consider the following sequence (and recall that the states s_i of $\mathcal{A}$ are also strings).

$$r_0 = \text{VQ}(s_0 \cdot w[1..])$$
$$r_1 = pot_T(s_0 \cdot \sigma_1) \wedge \text{VQ}(s_1 \cdot w[2..])$$
$$r_2 = pot_T(s_0 \cdot \sigma_1) \wedge pot_T(s_1 \cdot \sigma_1) \wedge \text{VQ}(s_2 \cdot w[3..])$$
$$\vdots$$
$$r_m = pot_T(s_0 \cdot \sigma_1) \wedge pot_T(s_1 \cdot \sigma_2) \wedge \ldots \wedge pot_T(s_{m-1} \cdot \sigma_m) \wedge \text{VQ}(s_m \cdot \epsilon)$$

Note that r_0, the result of the first line in the sequence, is $f(w)$ since $s_0 = \epsilon$ and $w[1..] = w$, hence $r_0 = \text{VQ}(w)$. While r_m, the result of the last row, is $\mathcal{A}(w)$ because r_m corresponds exactly to the returned value of $\mathcal{A}$ on w. Since w is a counterexample $r_0 \neq r_m$. Consider the first i for which $r_i \neq r_0$. Let $r_0 = r_{i-1} = \ell$ and $r_i = \ell'$. I.e.

$$\ell = r_{i-1} = pot_T(s_0 \cdot \sigma_1) \wedge \ldots pot_T(s_{i-2} \cdot \sigma_{i-1}) \wedge \text{VQ}(s_{i-1} \cdot w[i..])$$
$$\ell' = r_i = pot_T(s_0 \cdot \sigma_1) \wedge \ldots pot_T(s_{i-2} \cdot \sigma_{i-1}) \wedge pot_T(s_{i-1} \cdot \sigma_i) \wedge \text{VQ}(s_i \cdot w[i+1..])$$

There are two cases to consider.

1. Case $\ell' > \ell$:
   Since all components of the row r_{i-1} but the last one are also components of the row r_i, their value must be at least ℓ' (as otherwise the value of r_i will be less than ℓ'). It follows that the value of the last component of r_{i-1}, namely $\text{VQ}(s_{i-1} \cdot w[i..])$, is exactly ℓ (since $\ell' > \ell$, and $\text{VQ}(s_{i-1}, \sigma_i)$ is the only component in r_{i-1} that is not in r_i). While the values of $pot_T(s_{i-1} \cdot \sigma_i)$ and $\text{VQ}(s_i \cdot w[i+1..])$ must be at least ℓ'. Consider the words $s = s_{i-1}\sigma_i$ and $s' = s_i$. In T the row s_i was the representative of $s_{i-1}\sigma$ (as per *ExtractAut*, namely Definition 13), i.e., $s_{i-1}\sigma_i \equiv_T s_i$. From $pot_{T'}(s_{i-1}\sigma_i) \geq \ell'$ and $rep_T(s_{i-1}\sigma_i) = s_i$ we get that also $pot_{T'}(s_i) \geq pot_T(s_i) \geq pot_T(s_{i-1}\sigma_i) \geq \ell'$. Recall that we added all suffixes of w as columns in T'. Considering the column $w[i+1..]$ we have that $T'(s_{i-1}\sigma_i, w[i+1..]) = T'(s_{i-1}, w[i..]) = \ell$ while $T'(s_i, w[i+1..]) \geq \ell' > \ell$. Therefore $s_{i-1}\sigma_i \not\equiv_{T'}^{\ell'} s_i$ proving $s_{i-1}\sigma_i \not\equiv_{T'} s_i$.

2. Case $\ell' < \ell$:

   Since all but the last two components of row r_i are also in row r_{i-1} their values must be at least ℓ (as otherwise the value of r_{i-1} will be less than ℓ). The value of the last two components must be at least ℓ', and at least one should be exactly ℓ'. We investigate both cases.

   (a) Case $\text{VQ}(s_i w[i+1..]) = \ell'$.

   Consider rows $s_{i-1}\sigma_i$ and s_i. From $\text{VQ}(s_{i-1}w[i..]) \geq \ell$ we get that $T(s_{i-1}\sigma_i, w[i+1..]) \geq \ell > \ell'$ while $T(s_i, w[i+1..]) = \ell'$. Since s_i is the representative of $s_{i-1}\sigma_i$ in T, we know from Claim 12 that for all columns $e \in E$ (before adding the suffixes of the counterexample) we have $T(s_i, e) \geq T(s_{i-1}\sigma_i, e)$.

   (i) If for one of the columns the relation is strict, namely $T(s_i, e) > T(s_{i-1}\sigma_i, e)$ then since in column $w[i+1..]$ we have the opposite relation by Claim 5 $s_i \not\approx_{T'} s_{i-1}\sigma_i$ so the claims hold since we separated states.

   (ii) Otherwise if the relation is $=$ in all columns $e \in E$ then $pot_T(s_i) = pot_T(s_{i-1}\sigma_i)$.
   – If $pot_T(s_{i-1}\sigma_i) = pot_T(\text{rep}_T(s_{i-1}\sigma_i)) < \ell$ then the potential increased since now $pot_{T'}(\text{rep}_{T'}(s_{i-1}\sigma_i)) \geq \ell$.
   – Otherwise $pot_T(s_{i-1}\sigma_i) \geq \ell$. Since $pot_T(s_i) \geq \ell$ we get that $s_i \not\approx_{T'}^{\ell} s_{i-1}\sigma_i$ (as evident by column $w[i+1..]$).

   (b) Case $\text{VQ}(s_i w[i+1..]) > \ell'$ and $pot_T(s_{i-1}\sigma_i) = \ell'$.

   Since s_1 is the representative of $s_0\sigma_1$ we get that $T(s_1, w[2..]) \geq \ell$. This in turn implies from the same reasoning that $T(s_1\sigma_2, w[3..]) \geq \ell$ and $T(s_2, w[3..]) \geq \ell$. If we keep going on this way we get that $T(s_i\sigma_{i-1}, w[i+1..]) \geq \ell$. The potential of $s_{i-1}\sigma_i$ in T is $\ell' < \ell$. If the potential of its representative s_i was also ℓ' then the potential of this equivalence class in T' increased since it is now at least $\ell > \ell'$. If the potential of s_i is more than ℓ' then $s_i \not\approx^{\ell'+1} s_{i-1}\sigma_i$ since the potential of both is at least $\ell' + 1$ and in column $w[i+1..]$ only one of them is less than $\ell' + 1$. □

Corollary 23. *Let* FOLA *be the class of languages represented by FOLAs. The algorithm* **FOL*** *terminates and correctly learns any target language $L \in$* FOLA.

Following Theorem 22 we can bound the number of equivalence queries, call it m_{EQ} by $n|\mathcal{L}|$, since every counterexample either reveals a new equivalence class, or provides evidence that the potential of a class is higher. The number of VQs is bounded by the size of the obtained table. The table has at most $n|\mathcal{L}| + n|\mathcal{L}||\Sigma|$ rows since a new row is added to S_* only if it revealed a new equivalence class or it increased the potential of a known class, and when a row is added to S_* all its one letter extensions are added to S. The number of columns is bounded by c times m_{EQ} where c is the size of the longest counterexample.[7] While these theoretical bounds are the same as **L*** for SFOLA, as discussed in page. 3 they cannot be better, and as we show in Sect. 5, in practice the number of EQ and VQ issued by our algorithm is significantly smaller than that by **L***.

---

[7] This can be strengthened to $\log(c)$ times m_{EQ} using the optimization that finds one suffix to add to the columns, as described in the proof of Theorem 22.

5   Empirical Results

We implemented the algorithm and compared its performance on randomly generated FOLAs against the straightforward extension of $\mathbf{L}^*$ to learn SFOLAs.[8] We compared them in terms of (a) the number of states obtained (b) the number of issued value queries and (c) the number of issued equivalence queries. We used a binary alphabet $\Sigma = \{a, b\}$, the number of states N was chosen uniformly at random amongst the values $\{1, ..., 70\}$ and the size of the lattice K was chosen uniformly at random amongst $\{2, ..., 70\}$ (i.e. $\mathcal{L} = \{0, ..., K\}$). For each state q and letter σ, the state to transit to was chosen uniformly at random amongst $\{1, ..., N\}$ and the transition value was chosen uniformly at random amongst $\{1, ..., K\}$. The initial state was fixed to be 1. Finally, for each state the state-value was chosen uniformly at random amongst $\{1, ..., K\}$.

Note that the generated automata may not necessarily be minimal in terms of the number of states, and may not utilize all the available $K + 1$ lattice values. We thus define n to be the number of states in the minimal FOLA for the formal series $f : \Sigma^* \rightarrow \{0, ..., K\}$ computed by the generated automaton, and k as the number of values that are possible outputs of this automaton, meaning $k = |Image(f)|$.[9] In addition, we define n_s to be the number of states in the minimal SFOLA for that language. The implementation of the algorithm and the tests are available in https://github.com/sagisaa/Learning_FOLA.

We generated 10334 automata as specified, and ran both algorithms $\mathbf{L}^*$ and $\mathbf{FOL}^*$ on the languages induced by these automata. A VQ for a word w was answered by running the word on the generated automata, and the EQs were answered using a complete equivalence check, as specified in [14]. The gray bars on the graphs show the number of samples for a certain x, (denoted 'Count') and their scale is placed on the right y-axis. Each point on the graphs indicates the average result of the samples with the same x.

The graphs are organized as three pairs, measuring number of states of the resulting automaton, number of issued VQ, and number of issued EQ. The upper row measures these with respect to the actual number of states (n), and the lower row with respect to the actual lattice size (k).

The first pair of graphs (a) and (d) provide the number of states of the resulting automaton in $\mathbf{L}^*$ vs $\mathbf{FOL}^*$ measured with respect to n and k, resp. Recall that the output of $\mathbf{L}^*$ is an SFOLA and the output of $\mathbf{FOL}^*$ is a FOLA, and both algorithms return the minimal one. These graphs show that the number of states in SFOLA is about k times bigger than the minimal FOLA. This conclusion is supported with regression testing on the relation between k and the number of states in each type given in App.D.

The second pair of graphs (b) and (e) provide the number of VQs issued by $\mathbf{L}^*$ vs $\mathbf{FOL}^*$ measured with respect to to n and k, resp. These graphs show that the relation between the number of states in the minimal matching representation and the number of VQs is roughly quadratic. This result is compatible with the structure of the algorithm,

---

[8] In this extension the observation table has answers to value queries (as in $\mathbf{FOL}^*$) but two rows are determined equivalent iff they are exactly the same. All transitions values are set to $\top$, and the state values are determined by the value of the respective row in the column ϵ.

[9] Note that k, the number of lattice values occurring in transitions or state-values, is bounded by $n + n|\Sigma|$ where n is the number of states. Thus, for a constant-size alphabet it is $O(n)$.

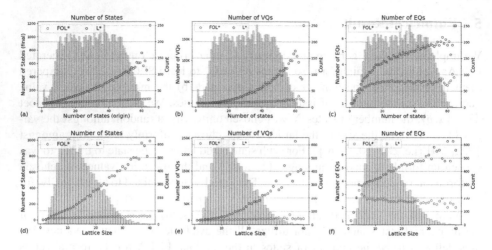

Fig. 8. L*and **FOL***comparison: Number of states, VQs, EQs

since the data of the VQs is organized in a table in which the number of rows and the number of columns are $O(n)$ each.[10]

Last important factor we looked at is the number of EQs required in order for the algorithm to converge. The third pair of graphs (c) and (f) provide the number of EQs issued by **L*** vs **FOL*** measured with respect to n and k, resp. These graphs show that the number of EQs required by the **FOL***algorithm *decreases* when the lattice size k increases. This can be explained by the fact that the higher the lattice size is, the easier it is to distinguish between rows.

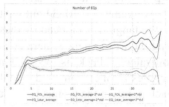

Fig. 9. EQs in relation to k

With that said, less EQs are needed since states are discovered sooner when closing the table. To make sure of that result, we use confidence interval method (CI) of 99% to distinguish between the 2 methods, see Fig. 9.

6   Conclusions

We provided a definition of equivalence classes for a formal series recognizable by a FOLA, which yields a canonical minimal FOLA and a Myhill-Nerode theorem, namely a one-to-one relation between the equivalence classes and the canonical FOLA. Based on it we designed a specialized learning algorithm that outputs the canonical FOLA and compared it against **L*** on synthetically generated FOLAs. Our experiments show a clear advantage to using **FOL*** as it outperforms **L*** in the number of states of the obtained FOLA, the number of issued VQs, and the number of issued EQs.

---

[10] The number of columns is bounded by nc where c is the size of the longest counterexample.

References

1. Aarts, Fides, Vaandrager, Frits: Learning I/O automata. In: Gastin, Paul, Laroussinie, François (eds.) CONCUR 2010. LNCS, vol. 6269, pp. 71–85. Springer, Heidelberg (2010). https://doi.org/10.1007/978-3-642-15375-4_6
2. Angluin, D.: Learning regular sets from queries and counterexamples. Inf. Comput. **75**(2), 87–106 (1987)
3. Angluin, D., Antonopoulos, T., Fisman, D.: Strongly unambiguous Büchi automata are polynomially predictable with membership queries. In: 28th EACSL Annual Conference on Computer Science Logic (CSL) (2020)
4. Angluin, D., Eisenstat, S., Fisman, D.: Learning regular languages via alternating automata. In: Proceedings of the 24th International Joint Conference on Artificial Intelligence (IJCAI) (2015)
5. Angluin, D., Fisman, D.: Learning regular omega languages. In: Proceedings of the 25th International Conference on Algorithmic Learning Theory (ALT) (2014)
6. Bakhirkin, A., Ferrère, T., Maler, O.: Efficient parametric identification for STL. In: Proceedings of the 21st International Conference on Hybrid Systems: Computation and Control (HSCC), pp. 177–186 (2018)
7. Balle, Borja, Mohri, Mehryar: Learning weighted automata. In: Maletti, Andreas (ed.) CAI 2015. LNCS, vol. 9270, pp. 1–21. Springer, Cham (2015). https://doi.org/10.1007/978-3-319-23021-4_1
8. Beimel, A., Bergadano, F., Bshouty, N.H., Kushilevitz, E., Varricchio, S.: Learning functions represented as multiplicity automata. J. ACM **47**(3), 506–530 (2000)
9. Bollig, B., Habermehl, P., Kern, C., Leucker, M.: Angluin-style learning of NFA. In: Proceedings of the 21st International Joint Conference on Artificial Intelligence (IJCAI), vol. 9, pp. 1004–1009 (2009)
10. Chan, William: Temporal-logic queries. In: Emerson, E. Allen., Sistla, Aravinda Prasad (eds.) CAV 2000. LNCS, vol. 1855, pp. 450–463. Springer, Heidelberg (2000). https://doi.org/10.1007/10722167_34
11. Drews, Samuel, D'Antoni, Loris: Learning symbolic automata. In: Legay, Axel, Margaria, Tiziana (eds.) TACAS 2017. LNCS, vol. 10205, pp. 173–189. Springer, Heidelberg (2017). https://doi.org/10.1007/978-3-662-54577-5_10
12. Easterbrook, S., et al.: /spl chi/Chek: a model checker for multi-valued reasoning. In: Proceedings of the 25th International Conference on Software Engineering, pp. 804–805. IEEE (2003)
13. Graf, Susanne, Saidi, Hassen: Construction of abstract state graphs with PVS. In: Grumberg, Orna (ed.) CAV 1997. LNCS, vol. 1254, pp. 72–83. Springer, Heidelberg (1997). https://doi.org/10.1007/3-540-63166-6_10
14. Halamish, S., Kupferman, O.: Minimizing deterministic lattice automata. ACM Trans. Comput. Log. **16**(1), 1–21 (2015)
15. Henzinger, T.A.: From Boolean to quantitative notions of correctness. In Proceedings of the 37th Annual ACM SIGPLAN-SIGACT Symposium on Principles of Programming Languages, pp. 157–158. POPL (2010)
16. Huang, Samuel, Cleaveland, Rance: Temporal-logic query checking over finite data streams. Int. J. Softw. Tools Technol. Transfer **24**(3), 473–492 (2022). https://doi.org/10.1007/s10009-022-00656-0
17. Hussain, A., Huth, M.: On model checking multiple hybrid views. Theor. Comput. Sci. **404**(3), 186–201 (2008)
18. Jakšić, S., Bartocci, E., Grosu, R., Ničković, D.: An algebraic framework for runtime verification. IEEE Trans. Comput.-Aided Des. Integr. Circuits Syst. **37**(11), 2233–2243 (2018)

19. Kumar, Viraj, Madhusudan, P.., Viswanathan, Mahesh: Minimization, learning, and conformance testing of Boolean programs. In: Baier, Christel, Hermanns, Holger (eds.) CONCUR 2006. LNCS, vol. 4137, pp. 203–217. Springer, Heidelberg (2006). https://doi.org/10.1007/11817949_14

20. Kupferman, Orna, Lustig, Yoad: Lattice automata. In: Cook, Byron, Podelski, Andreas (eds.) VMCAI 2007. LNCS, vol. 4349, pp. 199–213. Springer, Heidelberg (2007). https://doi.org/10.1007/978-3-540-69738-1_14

21. Mamouras, Konstantinos, Chattopadhyay, Agnishom, Wang, Zhifu: A compositional framework for quantitative online monitoring over continuous-time signals. In: Feng, Lu., Fisman, Dana (eds.) RV 2021. LNCS, vol. 12974, pp. 142–163. Springer, Cham (2021). https://doi.org/10.1007/978-3-030-88494-9_8

22. Mohri, M.: Finite-state transducers in language and speech processing. Comput. Linguist. **23**(2), 269–311 (1997)

23. Myhill, J.: Finite automata and the representation of events. WADD Tech. Rep. **57**, 112–137 (1957)

24. Nerode, A.: Linear automaton transformations. Proc. Am. Math. Soc. **9**(4), 541–544 (1958)

25. Nitay, D., Fisman, D., Ziv-Ukelson, M.: Learning of structurally unambiguous probabilistic grammars. In: Proceedings of the AAAI Conference on Artificial Intelligence, vol. 35, No. 10, pp. 9170–9178 (2021)

26. Rivest, R.L., Schapire, R.E.: Inference of finite automata using homing sequences. In: Proceedings of the Twenty-First Annual ACM Symposium on Theory of Computing, pp. 411–420 (1989)

27. Sakakibara, V.: Learning context-free grammars from structural data in polynomial time. In: Proceedings of the First Annual Workshop on Computational Learning Theory (COLT) (1988)

28. Shahbaz, Muzammil, Groz, Roland: Inferring Mealy machines. In: Cavalcanti, Ana, Dams, Dennis R.. (eds.) FM 2009. LNCS, vol. 5850, pp. 207–222. Springer, Heidelberg (2009). https://doi.org/10.1007/978-3-642-05089-3_14

29. Streb, J., Alexander, P.: Using a lattice of coalgebras for heterogeneous model composition. In: Proceedings of the MoDELS Workshop on Multi-Paradigm Modeling, pp. 27–38 (2006)

30. Vaandrager, F.W.: Model learning. Commun. ACM **60**(2) (2017)

31. van Heerdt, Gerco, Sammartino, Matteo, Silva, Alexandra: Learning automata with side-effects. In: Petrişan, Daniela, Rot, Jurriaan (eds.) CMCS 2020. LNCS, vol. 12094, pp. 68–89. Springer, Cham (2020). https://doi.org/10.1007/978-3-030-57201-3_5

Probabilistic and Stochastic Systems

Optimistic and Topological Value Iteration for Simple Stochastic Games

Muqsit Azeem⬛, Alexandros Evangelidis$^{(\boxtimes)}$⬛, Jan Křetínský⬛,
Alexander Slivinskiy⬛, and Maximilian Weininger⬛

Technical University of Munich, Munich, Germany
{muqsit.azeem,alexandros.evangelidis,jan.kretinsky,alexander.slivinskiy,
maximilian.weininger}@tum.de

Abstract. While value iteration (VI) is a standard solution approach to simple stochastic games (SSGs), it suffered from the lack of a stopping criterion. Recently, several solutions have appeared, among them also "optimistic" VI (OVI). However, OVI is applicable only to one-player SSGs with no end components. We lift these two assumptions, making it available to *general SSGs*. Further, we utilize the idea in the context of topological VI, where we provide an efficient *precise* solution. In order to compare the new algorithms with the state of the art, we use not only the standard benchmarks, but we also design a *random generator* of SSGs, which can be biased towards various types of models, aiding in understanding the advantages of different algorithms on SSGs.

1 Introduction

Stochastic games (SGs) are a standard model for decision making in the presence of adversary and uncertainty, by combining two (opposing) non-determinisms with stochastic dynamics. Thus, they extend both Markov decision processes (MDPs), the standard model for sequential decision making and probabilistic verification, and 2-player graph games, the standard model for reactive synthesis. *Simple stochastic games* (SSGs) [13] form an important special case where the goal is to reach a given state. In technical terms, an SSG is a zero-sum two-player turn-based game played on a graph by Maximizer and Minimizer, who choose actions in their respective vertices (also called states). Each action is associated with a probability distribution determining the next state to move to. The objective of Maximizer is to maximize the probability of reaching a given target state; the objective of Minimizer is the opposite. The interest in SSGs stems from two sources. Firstly, solving an SSG is polynomial-time equivalent to solving perfect information Shapley, Everett and Gillette games [1] and further important problems can be reduced to SSGs, for instance parity games, mean-payoff games, discounted-payoff games and their stochastic extensions [7]; yet,

The work has been partially supported by DFG projects 383882557 *Statistical Unbounded Verification (SUV)* and 427755713 *Group-By Objectives in Probabilistic Verification (GOPro)*.

the complexity of solving SSGs remains a long-standing open question, known to be in **UP** ∩ **coUP** [21], but with polynomial-time algorithm staying elusive. Secondly, the problem is practically relevant in verification and synthesis in stochastic environments, with many applications, e.g., [6,10,11,25], surveyed in detail in [28]. Consequently, heuristics improving performance of the algorithms for solving SSGs are also practically relevant.

Algorithms used to (approximately) solve SSGs can be divided into several classes, most notably quadratic programming (QP) and dynamic programming, the latter comprising strategy iteration (SI) and value iteration (VI). For their practical comparison, see the recent [22].

On the one hand, only when exact solutions are required, SI is mostly used. It provides a sequence of improving strategies and, accompanied by evaluation of Markov chains via systems of linear equations, can yield the precise result. On the other hand, approximate solutions (with a certain imprecision) are faster to compute and often sufficient. For this reason, VI is the technique used in practice the most, e.g., in PRISM-games [23], although not necessarily always the best. It gradually approximates (from below) the optimal probability to reach the target from each state. Interestingly, until very recently no means were known to determine the current precision, and so standard implementations terminating whenever no significant improvements occur can be arbitrarily wrong [18]. More surprisingly, this was even the case for MDPs, i.e., SSGs with a single player.

In 2014 [5,18], the first stopping criterion for MDPs was given, quantifying precision of the current approximation by providing also a sequence converging to the optimal probabilities from above. The difficulty to obtain such converging upper bound arises from cyclic dependencies of the optimal probabilities in so-called end components (ECs). For instance, an action surely self-looping on a state trivializes the equations, stating only that the probability in this state is simply equal to itself, yielding an infinity of solutions, not just the optimal one. This issue has been solved for MDPs [5,18] by "collapsing" these ECs into single states with no loops, which corresponds to identifying cyclically dependent variables into a single one.

In 2018 [17], the idea was finally extended to SSGs, giving rise to *bounded value iteration* (BVI) with the first stopping criterion for SSGs. Note that the MDP solution could not be directly used since the analog of ECs in SSGs is more complex: different states in an EC in an SSG can have different optimal probabilities and thus cannot be merged. Instead, *"deflating"* manipulates the values in smaller and dynamically changing "simple ECs".

Since the first VI stopping criterion was given for MDPs, several alternatives have been proposed, most notably *sound VI* (SVI) [27] and *optimistic VI* (OVI) [19]. However, the termination proofs of both require the MDP to contain no ECs. They achieve this by collapsing ECs, which is not applicable to SSGs.

Our Contribution. In this paper, we extend the idea of OVI in two ways so that we obtain algorithms for SSGs.

First Algorithm. The idea of OVI [19] is to run VI (converging from below) until changes are small, then to guess slightly larger values and check whether they form an upper bound. If not, the process continues. To overcome the requirement that there is no EC, we complement the procedure of [19] with the deflating of [17]. However, to ensure monotonicity of the Bellman operator, the so-called "simple" ECs must be computed differently from [17]. While the rest of the proof is analogous to [19], we try to make it simpler and more elegant by separating the core idea from the practical improvements. As a result, we obtain an OVI algorithm for SSGs.

Second Algorithm. We consider the classic *"topological"* optimization of VI [16], where the system is analyzed per strongly connected component (SCC) in the bottom-up order. While such decomposition often leads to savings in runtime and memory, also when expected accumulated rewards are considered [4], the imprecisions from lower SCCs propagate to the upper ones, yielding the method useless whenever the system is too deep (with as few SCCs in a row as 20) even for Markov chains, see Example 1. We fix this issue by precise *and* fast computations in each SCC as follows. First, we quickly obtain an approximate solution by VI, then we optimistically guess the solution, but in contrast to OVI which guesses values, we guess optimal strategies, which turns out to require orders of magnitude fewer guesses. If the guess is not correct, a step of SI can be cheaply performed. This version of OVI can thus be also seen as a possible warm start for SI.

Comparison and Model Generation. We compare the resulting approaches to BVI and a more recent SSG solution called "widest path" [26] (WP). While there is no clear winner, we provide insights as to which algorithm to use in different settings. As noticed already in [22], the performance of SSG algorithms is extremely sensitive to the structure of the models. Unfortunately, there are too few realistic case studies and thus a very limited number of model structures. Consequently, in order to be able to experimentally compare our algorithms in a reasonable way, we propose an approach for random SSG generation. While we prove that our approach can generate every SSG, it skews towards certain types of models. Hence we provide means for the user to skew towards model structures that they are interested in, e.g., increasing or decreasing the number of SCCs. This helps to find out which algorithms are sensitive to which model parameters, e.g., amount of SCCs. While this is only the first step towards filling this gap of random SSG (and MDP) generation, we hope to encourage more research on the topic through this effort.

Our contribution can be summarized as follows:

- We design an extension of OVI to SSGs. As a side effect, we extend OVI on MDPs, lifting the requirement of no ECs (Sect. 3).
- We extend the landscape by providing an efficient VI-based approach for precise solutions, using the OVI idea on strategies, rather than values (Sect. 4).
- We provide and evaluate a random generator of SSGs, which can be biased towards various types of models (Sect. 5).
- We compare the resulting methods to the state of the art (BVI, WP, SI) experimentally (Sect. 6).

Related Work. Closest to our work, in the case of SSGs, is the work of [17] where the first stopping criterion for VI was given. It extends both normal BVI [18] and its learning-based counterpart [5] from MDPs by incorporating the so-called deflating procedure as part of their computation. Recently, another BVI variant for SSGs was proposed which introduces a global propagation of upper bounds [26]. Also, the simpler case of an SSG with one-player ECs is discussed in [29].

In general, the tools which are available for solving SGs are limited. PRISM-games [23] implements the standard VI algorithms, and it also considers other objectives apart from reachability, such as mean-payoff and ratio reward. Further, GAVS+ [12] is an algorithmic game solver with support for solving SSGs, and GIST [9] allows for the qualitative verification of SGs.

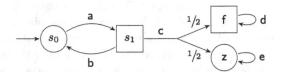

Fig. 1. An example of an SG with $S = \{s_0, s_1, f, z\}, S_\square = \{s_1, f\}, S_\bigcirc = \{s_0, z\}$, the initial state s_0 and set of actions $A = \{a, b, c, d, e\}$; $Av(s_0) = \{a\}$ with $\delta(s_0, a)(s_1) = 1$; $Av(s_1) = \{b, c\}$ with $\delta(s_1, b)(s_0) = 1$ and $\delta(s_1, c)(f) = \delta(s_1, c)(z) = \frac{1}{2}$. For actions with only one successor, we do not depict the transition probability 1.

2 Preliminaries

2.1 Simple Stochastic Games

A probability distribution on a finite set X is a mapping $\delta : X \rightarrow [0, 1]$, such that $\sum_{x \in X} \delta(x) = 1$. The set of all probability distributions on X is denoted by $Dist(X)$.

Definition 1. (Stochastic game (SG), e.g., [14]). *A stochastic turn-based two-player game is defined by a tuple* $\mathcal{G} = \langle S, S_\square, S_\bigcirc, s_0, A, Av, \delta \rangle$ *where* S *is a finite set of states partitioned into a set of* Minimizer ($S_\bigcirc$) *and* Maximizer ($S_\square$) *states, respectively.* $s_0 \in S$ *is the initial state.* A *is a finite set of actions.* $Av : S \rightarrow 2^A$ *assigns to every state a set of available actions. Finally,* $\delta : S \times A \rightarrow Dist(S)$ *is the transition function.*

Note that a Markov decision process (MDP) is a special case of an SG where either $S_\bigcirc = \emptyset$ *or* $S_\square = \emptyset$ *and a Markov chain is a special case of an MDP where in each state there is only one available action.*

Without loss of generality, we assume SGs to be non-blocking, i.e., for all $s \in S : Av(s) \neq \emptyset$. For convenience, we use the following notation: Given a state $s \in S$ and an action $a \in Av(s)$, the set of successor states is denoted as $Post(s, a) := \{s' \mid \delta(s, a, s') > 0\}$. For a set of states $T \subseteq S$, we use $T_\square = T \cap S_\square$

to denote all Maximizer states in T, and dually for Minimizer. Figure 1 shows an example SG.

Semantics: Paths, Strategies and the Value. Formally, an *infinite path* ρ is defined as $\rho = s_0 a_0 s_1 a_1 \ldots \in (S \times A)^\omega$, such that for every $i \in \mathbb{N}$, $a_i \in Av(s_i)$ and $s_{i+1} \in Post(s_i, a_i)$. The set of all paths in an SG $\mathcal{G}$ is denoted as $Paths_\mathcal{G}$. A finite path is a prefix of an infinite path ending in a state s.

A Maximizer *strategy* is a function $\sigma : S_\square \to A$ such that $\sigma(s) \in Av(s)$ for all s; Minimizer strategies τ are defined analogously. We restrict attention to *memoryless deterministic* strategies, because they are sufficient for the objective we consider [13]. By fixing both players' choices according to a pair of strategies (σ, τ), we turn an SG $\mathcal{G}$ into a Markov chain $\mathcal{G}^{(\sigma,\tau)}$ with state space S and the transition function $\delta^{\sigma,\tau}(s, s') = \delta(s, \sigma(s), s')$ for Maximizer states s and dually for Minimizer with σ replaced by τ. Given a state s, the Markov chain $\mathcal{G}^{(\sigma,\tau)}$ induces a unique probability distribution $\mathcal{P}_s^{\sigma,\tau}$ over the set of all infinite paths [3, Sect. 10.1].

Since we consider SSGs, we complement an SG with a set of goal states $F \subseteq S$ and formalize the objective of reaching F, as follows: we denote as $\Diamond F :=$ $\{\rho \mid \rho = s_0 a_0 s_1 a_1 \ldots \in Paths_\mathcal{G} \land \exists i \in \mathbb{N}.s_i \in F\}$ the (measurable) set of all paths which eventually reach F. We are interested in the *value* of every state s, i.e., the probability that s reaches a goal state if both players play optimally. Formally, for each $s \in S$, its value is defined as

$$V(s) := \sup_\sigma \inf_\tau \mathcal{P}_s^{\sigma,\tau}(\Diamond F) = \inf_\tau \sup_\sigma \mathcal{P}_s^{\sigma,\tau}(\Diamond F), \qquad (1)$$

where the equality follows from [13]. We use $V : S \to \mathbb{R}$ to denote the function that maps every $s \in S$ to its value. When comparing functions $f_1, f_2 : S \to \mathbb{R}$, we use point-wise comparison, i.e., $f_1 \le f_2$ if and only if for all $s \in S : f_1(s) \le f_2(s)$.

2.2   Value Iteration and Bounded Value Iteration

To compute the value function V for an SSG, the following partitioning of the state space is useful: firstly the goal states F, secondly the set of *sink states* that do not have a path to the target $Z = \{s \in S \mid \nexists \rho = s_0 a_0 s_1 a_1 \ldots \in Paths_\mathcal{G} : s_0 = s \land \rho \in \Diamond F\}$, and finally the remaining states $S^?$. For F and Z (which can be easily identified by graph-search algorithms), the value is trivially 1 respectively 0. Thus, the computation only has to focus on $S^?$.

The well-known approach of value iteration leverages the fact that V is the least fixpoint of the *Bellman equations*, cf. [8]:

$$V(s) = \begin{cases} 1 & \text{if } s \in F \\ 0 & \text{if } s \in Z \\ \max_{a \in Av(s)} \left(\sum_{s' \in S} \delta(s, a, s') \cdot V(s') \right) & \text{if } s \in S_\square^? \\ \min_{a \in Av(s)} \left(\sum_{s' \in S} \delta(s, a, s') \cdot V(s') \right) & \text{if } s \in S_\bigcirc^? \end{cases} \qquad (2)$$

Now we define[1] the Bellman operator $\mathcal{B} : (\mathsf{S} \to \mathbb{R}) \to (\mathsf{S} \to \mathbb{R})$:

$$\mathcal{B}(\mathsf{f})(s) = \begin{cases} \max_{a \in \mathsf{Av}(s)} \left(\sum_{s' \in \mathsf{S}} \delta(s, a, s') \cdot f(s') \right) & \text{if } s \in \mathsf{S}_{\square} \\ \min_{a \in \mathsf{Av}(s)} \left(\sum_{s' \in \mathsf{S}} \delta(s, a, s') \cdot f(s') \right) & \text{if } s \in \mathsf{S}_{\bigcirc} \end{cases} \tag{3}$$

Value iteration starts with the under-approximation

$$\mathsf{L}_0(s) = \begin{cases} 1 & \text{if } s \in \mathsf{F} \\ 0 & \text{otherwise} \end{cases}$$

and repeatedly applies the Bellman operator. Since the value is the least fixpoint of the Bellman equations and $\mathsf{L}_0 \leq \mathsf{V}$ is lower than the value, this converges to the value in the limit [8] (formally $\lim_{i \to \infty} \mathcal{B}^i(\mathsf{L}_0) = \mathsf{V}$).

While this approach is often fast in practice, it has the drawback that it is not possible to know the current difference between $\mathcal{B}^i(\mathsf{L}_0)$ and V for any given i. To address this, one can employ *bounded value iteration* (BVI, also known as interval iteration [5,17,18]) It additionally starts from an over-approximation U_0, with $\mathsf{U}_0(s) = 1$ for all $s \in \mathsf{S}$. However, applying the Bellman operator to this upper estimate might not converge to the value, but to some greater fixpoint instead, see [17, Sect. 3] for an example. The core of the problem are so called *end components*.

Definition 2 (End component (EC)). *A set of states T with $\emptyset \neq T \subseteq \mathsf{S}$ is an end component if and only if there exists a set of actions $\emptyset \neq B \subseteq \bigcup_{s \in T} \mathsf{Av}(s)$ such that:*

1. *for each $s \in T$, $a \in B \cap \mathsf{Av}(s)$ we have $\mathsf{Post}(s, a) \subseteq T$.*
2. *for each $s, s' \in T$ there exists a finite path $\mathsf{w} = s a_0 ... a_n s' \in (T \times B)^* \times T$.*

An end component T is a maximal end component (MEC) if there is no other EC T' such that $T \subseteq T'$.

Intuitively, ECs can be problematic, because the over-approximation U is higher in the EC than the value. Thus, Maximizer prefers staying in the EC and keeping the illusion of achieving the high U; it is an illusion, because staying will never reach a target, and Maximizer actually has to use some exit of the EC. The solution proposed in [17] explicitly identifies these situations and forces all states in the EC to decrease their U by making it depend on the best exit of the EC. This operation is called *deflating*, to evoke the impression of releasing the pressure in an EC that is bloated by having too high estimates. To define deflating more formally, we need two definitions from [17]:

---

[1] In the definition of $\mathcal{B}$, we omit the technical detail that for goal states $s \in \mathsf{F}$, the value has to remain 1. Equivalently, one can assume that all goal states are absorbing, i.e., only have self looping actions.

Definition 3 (Best exit). *Given a set of states* $T \subseteq S$ *and a function* $f : S \rightarrow \mathbb{R}$, *the best exit according to* f *from* T *is defined as:*

$$\text{bexit}_f(T) = \max_{\substack{s \in T_\square, a \in \text{Av}(s) \\ \text{Post}(s,a) \not\subseteq T}} \left(\sum_{s' \in S} \delta(s, a, s') \cdot f(s, a) \right),$$

with the convention that $\max_\emptyset = 0$.

Definition 4 (Simple end component (SEC)). *An EC* T *is a simple end component (SEC) if for all* $s \in T$, $V(s) = \text{bexit}_V(T)$

In SSGs, states in an EC can have different values. Thus, it is necessary to find the SECs. In these simple sub-parts of the EC all states have the same value, namely that of the best exit. By setting the over-approximation to $\text{bexit}_U(T)$ for each SEC T (additionally to applying $\mathcal{B}$), we ensure that it converges to the value [17]. As a final complication, computing SECs is difficult, since they depend on the value V that we want to compute. The solution of [17] is to use the current under-approximation L to guess which states form a SEC and as L converges to V in the limit, eventually we guess correctly.

Thus, we can augment the Bellman operator with additional deflating and define an operator $\mathcal{B}_L^D : (S \rightarrow \mathbb{R}) \rightarrow (S \rightarrow \mathbb{R})$. Note that it depends on an L to guess the SECs. Given a function U, it proceeds as follows:

- Apply a Bellman update $\mathcal{B}(U)$.
- Guess the SECs according to L by using [17, Algorithm 2].
- For each SEC T and all states $s \in T$, set $U(s) = \min(U(s), \text{bexit}_U(T))$. The min is only to ensure monotonicity.

In summary, BVI computes two sequences: the sequence of lower bounds $L_i = \mathcal{B}^i(L)$ for $i \in \mathbb{N}$ and an additional sequence of upper bounds $U_i = (\mathcal{B}_L^D)^i(U)$. Note that for the i-th application of $\mathcal{B}_L^D$, it uses the current lower bound L_i. Both sequences converge to the value V in the limit [17, Theorem 2]. This allows to terminate the algorithm when the difference between the lower and upper bound is less than a pre-defined precision ε and obtain an ε-approximation of the value.

3 Optimistic Value Iteration

The idea of optimistic value iteration (OVI, [19]) is to leverage the fact that classic VI (only from below) typically converges quickly to the correct value. Indeed, the following "naive" stopping criterion results in an approximation that is ε-close in all available realistic case studies: stop when for all $s \in S$ applying the Bellman update does not result in a big difference, i.e., $\text{diff}(L(s), \mathcal{B}(L)(s)) < \varepsilon$, where we use $\text{diff}(\text{old}, \text{new}) = \text{new} - \text{old}$ to denote the absolute difference between two numbers[2]. However, the naive stopping criterion can also terminate early when the estimate still is arbitrarily wrong [18].

OVI first performs classic VI with the naive stopping criterion, optimistically hoping that it will terminate close to the value. Additionally, it uses a *verification*

---

[2] One can also use the relative difference, i.e., $\text{diff}(\text{old}, \text{new}) = \frac{\text{new} - \text{old}}{\text{new}}$.

phase, where it checks whether the result of VI was indeed correct. If it was, OVI terminates with the guarantee that we are ε-close to the value. Otherwise, if the result of VI cannot be verified, OVI continues VI with a higher precision ε'. By repeating this, at some point ε' is so small that when VI terminates, OVI can verify that the result is ε-precise.

Our version of OVI for SSGs is given in Algorithm 1. Lines 2–3 are the classic VI, Lines 4–9 the verification phase. Concretely, in the verification phase we first guess a candidate upper bound U (Line 4), so that the difference between L and U is small enough that, if U indeed is an upper bound, we could terminate. Formally, for all $s \in \mathsf{S}$, $\mathsf{U}(s) = \mathsf{diff}^+(\mathsf{L}(s))$, where $\mathsf{diff}_\varepsilon^+(x) = \begin{cases} 0 & \text{if } x = 0 \\ x + \varepsilon & \text{otherwise} \end{cases}$

for absolute difference[3]. Then we apply the Bellman operator once (Line 6) and check whether $\mathcal{B}_\mathsf{L}^\mathsf{D}(\mathsf{U}) \leq \mathsf{U}$ (Line 7). If that holds, we know (by arguments from lattice theory) that $\mathsf{V} \leq \mathsf{U}$, i.e., that U is a valid upper bound on the value. Thus, since L and U are ε-close to each other and $\mathsf{L} \leq \mathsf{V} \leq \mathsf{U}$, we return an ε-approximation of the value (Line 8). **The key difference** between the original algorithm for MDPs and the extension to SSGs is that we do not use $\mathcal{B}$ in Line 6 any more, but the Bellman operator with additional deflating $\mathcal{B}^\mathsf{D}$. On MDPs, the termination of OVI relied on the assumption that there were no ECs. This is justified, since in MDPs one can remove the ECs by "collapsing" them beforehand, cf. [5,18]. On SSGs, collapsing is not possible [17], which is why we need the new operator.

We have addressed the case that the guessed U can indeed be verified as an upper bound. In the other case where we are not (yet) able to verify it, Algorithm 1 continues applying $\mathcal{B}_\mathsf{L}^\mathsf{D}$ for a finite number of times (we chose $\frac{1}{\varepsilon'}$, Line 5). If for all iterations we cannot verify U as an upper bound, the precision ε' for the naive stopping criterion is increased (we chose $\frac{\varepsilon'}{2}$) and we start over (Line 10).

Theorem 1. *Given an SSG $\mathcal{G}$ and a lower bound $\mathsf{L}_0 \leq \mathsf{V}$, $OVI(\mathcal{G}, \mathsf{L}_0, \varepsilon, \varepsilon)$ terminates and returns (L, U) such that $\mathsf{L} \leq \mathsf{V} \leq \mathsf{U}$ and $\mathsf{diff}(\mathsf{U}(s), \mathsf{L}(s)) \leq \varepsilon$ for all $s \in \mathsf{S}$.*

Our formulation of Algorithm 1 is simpler than [19, Algorithm 2], since we include only the key parts that are necessary for the proof of Theorem 1 (provided in [2, App. B]). Below we comment on three ways in which our algorithm can be changed, following the ideas of [19, Algorithm 2]. All these changes are not necessary for correctness or termination, but they can practically improve the algorithm.

1. We can include a check $\mathcal{B}^\mathsf{D}(\mathsf{U}) \geq \mathsf{U}$. It allows to detect whether $\mathsf{U} \leq \mathsf{V}$, i.e., U actually is a lower bound on the value. In that case, one can immediately terminate the verification phase and use U as the new L. We include this improvement in our implementation, and it is used in almost every unsuccessful verification phase.

---

[3] $\mathsf{diff}_\varepsilon^+(x) = x * (1 + \varepsilon)$ for relative difference.

Algorithm 1. Optimistic value iteration for SSGs.

Input: SSG $\mathcal{G}$, lower bound $L \leq V$, precision $\varepsilon > 0$ and naive precision $\varepsilon' > 0$
Output: (L, U) such that $L \leq V \leq U$ and $\mathrm{diff}(U(s), L(s)) \leq \varepsilon$ for all $s \in S$
1: **procedure** $\mathrm{OVI}(\mathcal{G}, L, \varepsilon, \varepsilon')$

    ▷ Classic VI with naive convergence criterion
2:    **while** for some state $s \in S$: $\mathrm{diff}(L(s), \mathcal{B}(L)(s)) > \varepsilon'$ **do**
3:        $L \leftarrow \mathcal{B}(L)$

    ▷ Verification phase
4:    $U \leftarrow \{s \mapsto \mathrm{diff}_\varepsilon^+(L(s)) \mid s \in S\}$ ▷ Guess candidate upper bound
5:    **for** $\frac{1}{\varepsilon'}$ times **do**
6:        $U' \leftarrow \mathcal{B}_L^D(U)$
7:        **if** $U' \leq U$ **then**
8:            **return** (L, U) ▷ Found inductive upper bound
9:        For all $s \in S^? : U(s) \leftarrow \min(U(s), U'(s))$ ▷ Ensure monotonicity
10:   **return** $\mathrm{OVI}(\mathcal{G}, L, \varepsilon, \frac{\varepsilon'}{2})$ ▷ Try again with more precision

---

2. The original version continues to update the lower bound during the verification phase. This is used for an additional breaking condition if the lower bound crossed the upper bound in some state. For clarity of presentation, we chose to separate concerns and only update the upper bound in the verification phase. This improvement never made a significant difference in our experiments.
3. The original version used Gauß-Seidel VI, cf. [19, Sect. 3.1], for both the lower and the upper bound. Our implementation allows the user to select whether to use classic or Gauß-Seidel VI.

4 Precise Topological Value Iteration

Topological value iteration (TVI, [16]) is a variant of VI that does not solve the whole game at once, but rather proceeds piece by piece. This can speed up convergence and help with memory issues. Concretely, it uses the insight that the strongly connected components (SCCs) of an SSG always form a directed acyclic graph. Thus, one can first solve the bottom SCCs, i.e., the last in the topological ordering, and then proceed backwards one SCC by the next, relying on the results of the already computed successor SCCs. This idea is not restricted to VI algorithms, but can also be used for other solutions methods like strategy iteration (SI) and quadratic programming [22].

The evaluation of [22] showed that this can be quite useful in some cases, but also much slower in other, possibly even running into time outs on models where the normal algorithms succeed. The reason for this is a complex problem that did not occur in the proof of correctness, as it is related to machine precision: SCCs are not solved precisely, but only with ε-precision. That means that SCCs which are considered later in the computation have suboptimal information about their exits. This not only slows down convergence, but can even aggregate and lead

---

Algorithm 2. Precise topological value iteration

Input: SSG $\mathcal{G}$
Output: The precise value V for all states in $\mathcal{G}$
 1: **procedure** PTVI($\mathcal{G}$)
 2:     **for** every SCC T in reverse topological ordering **do**
 3:         Select arbitrary ε
 4:         $L, U \leftarrow$ computed by some VI-algorithm with precision ε
 5:         Compute strategies σ, τ which are optimal according to L and U
 6:         Precisely compute the value $V_{\mathcal{G}^{(\sigma,\tau)}}$ of T in the Markov chain $\mathcal{G}^{(\sigma,\tau)}$
 7:         **if** For all $s \in T : \begin{cases} \sigma(s) \in \arg\max_{a \in A(s)} V_{\mathcal{G}^{(\sigma,\tau)}}(s,a) & \text{if } s \in S_\square \\ \tau(s) \in \arg\min_{a \in A(s)} V_{\mathcal{G}^{(\sigma,\tau)}}(s,a) & \text{if } s \in S_\bigcirc \end{cases}$ **then**
 8:             **Return** $V_{\mathcal{G}^{(\sigma,\tau)}}$ as value for T.
 9:         **else**
10:             Apply strategy iteration, using σ or τ as initial strategy.

---

to precision problems and non-termination when there is a chain of many SCCs, as we show in the following example.

Example 1. To exemplify TVI and show when its precision problems occur, we consider an SSG that is a chain of n SCCs, each with one state. Every state either loops or continues to the next state, both with probability 0.5. At the end of the chain, we go to the goal with 0.6 and to the sink with 0.4.

Formally, $S = S_\square = \{t, z, s_0, s_1, \ldots, s_n\}$, where s_0 is the initial state and $t \in F$ is the only goal state. There only is one action a, so $Av(s) = A = \{a\}$ for all states $s \in S$. For every s_i with $i < n$, we have $\delta(s_i, a, s_i) = \delta(s_i, a, s_{i+1}) = 0.5$ and for s_n, we have $\delta(s_n, a, t) = 0.6$ and $\delta(s_n, a, z) = 0.4$. Both states t and z are absorbing, so they loop with probability one.

Running topological bounded VI on this SSG, we first solve the bottom SCCs, i.e., t and z, and (by graph algorithms) infer their values of 1 and 0, respectively. Then we solve the SCC $\{s_n\}$ and set both its bounds to 0.6. Next, for the SCC $\{s_{n-1}\}$ bounded VI returns an ε-precise result, as with the self-loop the precise value is only obtained in the limit. Using precision of $\varepsilon = 10^{-6}$, the resulting interval is $[0.5999994277954102, 0.6000003814697266]$. Now the imprecisions start to add up: when solving the next SCC $\{s_{n-2}\}$, we depend on the imprecise bounds for $\{s_{n-1}\}$. Thus, the progress we make in every Bellman update is smaller. This not only slows down convergence, but it also leads to the first ε-precise interval being $[0.5999994099140338, 0.6000003933906441]$. So when BVI for the SCC $\{s_{n-2}\}$ terminates, both the lower and the upper bound are less precise than in the previous SCC. In state s_{n-19}, this imprecision has aggregated such that the computation is stuck at the interval $[0.5999994000000000, 0.6000004000000001]$, where the difference is larger than ε. Even though theoretically we make progress with a Bellman update, this progress is smaller than machine precision, so practically we can neither converge nor terminate.

Note that the SSG in this example is a Markov chain, so this problem occurs not only in SSGs, but already in Markov chains and MDPs. $\triangle$

We address this problem by introducing the precise-topological-optimization (PTVI, see Algorithm 2). The idea of PTVI is that, after an SCC has been solved with ε-precision (Line 4), we first extract the strategies for both players from the result (Line 5) and then compute the exact value of all states in the SCC under this pair of strategies (Line 6). Finally, we use a simple local check to verify that this is indeed the optimal value (Line 7). If it is, we return the precise values that the next SCCs can safely depend on (Line 8). If it is not, then we have to continue with some precise solution method (Line 10). Since we have just extracted near-optimal strategies, it makes sense to continue with SI, see e.g., [22, Sect. 3.2]. For details on the selection of the strategies and the proof of Theorem 2, see [2, App. B].

Theorem 2. *Algorithm 2 returns the precise solution* V.

The strength of PTVI is the simple local check that allows it to conclude that the estimates for an SCC are precise. It relies on guessing both strategies. This differs from guessing an upper bound, as OVI does; or guessing one strategy, as in SI with a warm start [22, Sect. 4.3]. We emphasize that even using the classical naive stopping criterion in Line 4, this local check succeeded on more than 99% of the case studies, and thus the additional steps of Line 10 are almost never necessary. Using bounded VI in Line 4, we immediately succeeded on all case studies. In contrast, the first verification phase of OVI—having the same estimates and thus "information" as PTVI has when performing the local check—succeeded only for 15% of the random case studies; in 85% of the random cases as well as several larger real case studies OVI had to perform additional verification phases.

Note that PTVI can be seen from different directions: (i) it is a practical fix of TVI [16]; (ii) it is a new way to make classical VI return a precise result, which is more efficient than running for an exponential number of steps and rounding as described in [8]; (iii) it is a warm start for SI, in the seldom case that the SI phase of the algorithm (Line 10) is necessary; and (iv) just like OVI, it optimistically iterates the lower bound and then uses guessing to verify this guess. However, unlike OVI it produces a precise result, albeit at the cost of solving a Markov chain precisely, and it uses the information available at the time of guessing more efficiently, succeeding on the first check more often than OVI.

5   Random Generation of Simple Stochastic Games

In order to properly evaluate and compare our algorithms, we need a diverse set of benchmarks. However, to the best of our knowledge, there are only 12 SSG case studies modelling real world problems and 3 handcrafted models for theoretical corner cases. Since the underlying structure of a model greatly affects the runtime of algorithms [22], only scaling these few models is insufficient. Thus, we propose an algorithm for random generation of SSG case studies, which enables us to test our algorithms on a broader spectrum of models.

Moreover, as we are interested in the relation between our verification algorithms and certain features of the model structure, our implementation also allows for skewing the probability distribution towards models that exhibit certain features. This is very useful, since it allows us to test our algorithms on models whose features were not considered before (e.g., large number of actions per state, etc.). In particular, we provide: **(i)** parameters to tune features that can be affected by parameters of single states (e.g., the size, percentage of Minimizer states, actions per state, etc.). For example, if for each state the probability of being a Maximizer or Minimizer state is equal, we get 50% Minimizer states on average. Similarly, by choosing a high probability of adding another action to a state during the generation, we obtain states with up to 90 actions and an average around 7; **(ii)** more involved guidelines to affect features which depend on the interactions of several states (e.g., the number and size of SCCs and ECs, etc.). Intuitively, to obtain an SCC or MEC of a certain size n, we have to restrict the choice of successors during the transition or action generation to ensure that there are n strongly connected states.

We provide a detailed description of our random generation algorithm in [2, App. C]. There, we prove that it can generate every possible SSG with positive probability, and also describe and discuss the aforementioned guidelines. Additionally, we give a detailed analysis of model features for all random case studies used in the evaluation, as well as a comparison to the features of the real case studies in [2, App. D].

6   Experiments

In this section we talk about the practical evaluation of our algorithms and the comparison to the state of the art. First, we describe the setup in Sect. 6.1. Then we give a general overview in Sect. 6.2 before analyzing the algorithms' performance in more detail in Sects. 6.3 and 6.4.

6.1   Experimental Setup

Algorithms. Our implementation is based on PRISM-games [23] and available at https://github.com/ga67vib/Algorithms-For-Stochastic-Games.

We compare to the following algorithms from related work: classical value iteration (VI, [8]), bounded value iteration (BVI, [17]) and the improvement of bounded value iterations based on widest paths (WP, [26]). Moreover, as a representative of a competitor yielding a precise result, we implemented a precise variant of strategy iteration (SI), which relies on linear programming for solving the opponent MDP.

The new algorithms are optimistic VI (OVI, Sect. 3) and the precise topological version of VI (Sect. 4). For the latter, we give two variants with different stopping criteria in Line 4 of the algorithm: PTVI uses the naive criterion and PTBVI the ε-guaranteed one. Finally, we consider several optimizations, but their analysis is delegated to [2, App. E.1] due to space constraints. Quite surprisingly, for all optimizations, their impact can be positive or negative on different models.

Case Studies. We consider case studies from three different sources: (i) all real case studies that were already used in [22], and are mainly part the PRISM benchmark suite [24]; (ii) several handcrafted corner case models: haddad-monmege (the adversarial example from [18]), BigMec and MulMec (a single big MEC or a long chain of many small MECs from [22]), as well as two new models to analyze the behavior of OVI and one large model with many SCCs; (iii) randomly generated models as discussed in Sect. 5. Note that throughout our experiments, we omitted models solved by pre-computations.

Technical Details. We conducted the experiments on a server with 64 GB of RAM and a 3.60 GHz Intel CPU running Manjaro Linux. We always use a precision of $\varepsilon = 10^{-6}$. The timeout was set to 15 min and the memory limit was 6 GB for all models except for large models ($\geq$1,000,000 states). For the large models, the timeout was set to 30 min and the memory limit to 36 GB.

6.2   Overview

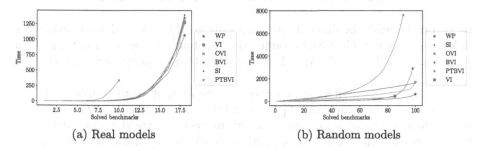

(a) Real models   (b) Random models

Fig. 2. Overview of the performance of the main algorithms on the *real* and *random* case studies. See Sect. 6.2 for a description.

Figure 2 gives an overview of the performance of the algorithms on the real and random case studies. The plots depict the number of solved benchmarks (horizontal axis) and the time it took to solve them (vertical axis). For each algorithm, the benchmarks are sorted in ascending order by verification time. A line stops when no further benchmarks could be solved. Intuitively, the further to the bottom right a line extends, the better. The algorithms shown in the legend on the right are sorted based on their performance, in descending order. Note that these plots have to be interpreted with care, as they greatly depend on the selection of benchmarks.

The precise algorithms provide harder guarantees, so we expect them to be slower. This is visible for PTBVI, which is slower and solves less benchmark than others. Still, PTBVI is optimal on certain kinds of models, as we detail in Sect. 6.3. Surprisingly, SI performed very well, even competing with the approximate algorithms BVI, OVI and WP. However, this comes from the model selection, particularly of the random models. Firstly, they exhibit very small transition probabilities, since we wanted the models to be hard for VI so that

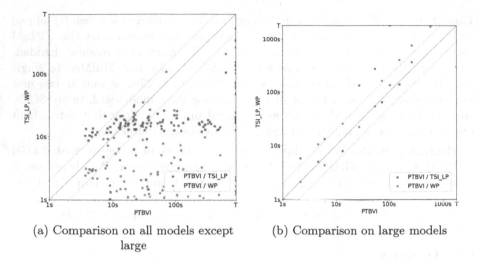

(a) Comparison on all models except large

(b) Comparison on large models

Fig. 3. PTBVI compared to SI and WP on all datasets.

we can distinguish the different stopping criteria. This slows down convergence of VI, but does not affect SI. Secondly, they contain few states, so using a linear program is feasible. In [2, App. E.4], we show that as model size increases, SI becomes less viable.

The algorithms giving ε-guarantees are overall quite comparable. This was also the case in the evaluation of [19], where the authors note that *"for probabilistic reachability, there is no clear winner"*. In Sect. 6.4, we give more details on how the performance of certain algorithms is affected by the structural features of a case study. Note that we included classical VI as a baseline, even though it gives no guarantees. It returned wrong results on two random models as well as the handcrafted haddad-monmege and MulMec.

Finally, it is important to note that random models of size 10,000 were already very hard for all algorithms, while some real models with more than 100,000 states could be solved quickly. This confirms the hypothesis of [22] that the graph structure of an SG (e.g., number of actions per state, depth of topological ordering, connectedness) is more important than its pure size.

6.3   Detailed Analysis of Precise Algorithms

PTVI and PTBVI are able to solve the chain of SCCs MulMec where normal topological VI [22] was stuck, so we achieved our original goal.

We use scatter plots to evaluate the algorithms' performance in detail. Each point in a scatter plot denotes a model. If a point is below the diagonal, the algorithm on the horizontal axis required more time to solve it than the corresponding algorithm on the vertical axis and vice versa. The two lines next to the diagonal mark the case where one algorithm was twice as fast as the other.

Figure 3 shows a scatter plot of PTBVI (which performed better than PTVI) versus the precise SI and the approximate, but very performant WP. While on

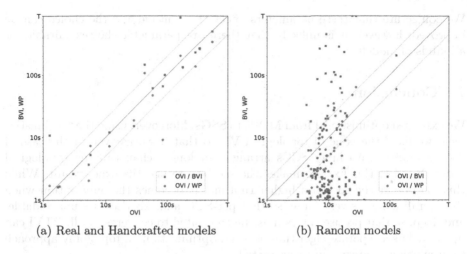

(a) Real and Handcrafted models   (b) Random models

Fig. 4. OVI compared to BVI and WP on all datasets.

smaller models PTBVI does not perform very well (Fig. 3(a)), on larger models
it often outperforms SI, in many cases halving the runtime or even reducing
it by an order of magnitude, as shown in Fig. 3(b). We conjecture that this
comes from the fact that SI has to solve a linear program multiple times, while
PTBVI only guesses the optimal strategies once and then solves a single Markov
chain. We emphasize that PTBVI never had to resort to actually performing
strategy iteration, because it guessed the correct strategies in all case studies.
Moreover, PTBVI even beats the best approximate method, WP, in sufficiently
large instances that contain multiple chained SCCs. In summary, PTBVI is a
promising alternative to SI when needing precise solutions, especially on large
models with chains of SCCs.

6.4 Detailed Analysis of Approximate (ε-Precise) Algorithms

All ε-precise algorithms perform similarly well. WP has the smallest accumulated runtime (Fig. 2), no models where it is significantly worse than BVI ([2,
App. E.2]) and only few models where it is significantly worse than OVI (Fig. 4).
As already observed in [26], it is particularly good when there are several or many
MECs (especially on the handcrafted MulMec). Thus, it is a valid initial choice
except when the models are large with a chain of big SCCs, where we concluded
in Sect. 6.3 that PTBVI is better.

We analyzed OVI in more detail to find our what features of the model
affect its performance. Details validating the following statements are provided
in [2, App. E.3]. Intuitively, OVI outperforms the other algorithms when the
lower bound quickly converges, but the upper bound does not. Dually, if the
lower bound converges slowly, this is problematic for OVI. Note that there are
many hyper-parameters of OVI, for example the number of steps in the verification phase or the modification of the precision after a failed verification phase.

We conjecture that these parameters affect the runtime and the choice can be improved; however, it is unlikely that there are parameter choices suitable for all kinds of models.

7   Conclusion

We extended optimistic VI from MDPs to SSGs. Moreover, using the "optimistic" idea, we fixed the issue of topological VI, so that it works even in the case of deeper models with more SCCs arranged in longer chains in the topological order. Besides, this fix also makes the method return the exact result. While this may be at the cost of a higher runtime, it becomes the only option when the overall model is very large, so that per-SCC analysis becomes unavoidable, and deep, so that precise values must be computed to converge at all. PTVI can be viewed as a separate algorithm or as an optimization on top of any approach from which a strategy can be extracted.

The experimental results show that the algorithms are of comparable performance, especially on real models from the standard benchmark sets. However, an in-depth analysis of the handcrafted and random models reveals that the performance of these algorithms is often sensitive to the underlying graph structure and, thus, their performance can vary accordingly. While we discuss some rules of thumb as to which algorithm is to be used for a particular benchmark, a part of the future work is to provide clearer and more algorithmic recommendations. An interesting direction here might also be to apply machine learning to recommend the most appropriate algorithm, as done for software model checkers already a few years ago, e.g., [15].

Moreover, we introduced a random generator, capable of producing various patterns even to extreme degrees. While this is very useful to find bugs and corner cases, many of the patterns need not be realistic. Consequently, we introduce a powerful set of tools to bias the generation. Nevertheless, future work shall amend this spectrum of tools with further hyper-parameters and approaches. We hope to hereby establish the platform for the community to contribute, complementary to benchmark sets [20,24].

References

1. Andersson, D., Miltersen, P.B.: The complexity of solving stochastic games on graphs. In: Dong, Y., Du, D.-Z., Ibarra, O. (eds.) ISAAC 2009. LNCS, vol. 5878, pp. 112–121. Springer, Heidelberg (2009). https://doi.org/10.1007/978-3-642-10631-6_13
2. Azeem, M., Evangelidis, A., Křetínský, J., Slivinskiy, A., Weininger, M.: Optimistic and topological value iteration for simple stochastic games. arXiv:2207.14417 (2022)
3. Baier, C., Katoen, J.P.: Principles of Model Checking. MIT Press, Cambridge (2008)

4. Baier, C., Klein, J., Leuschner, L., Parker, D., Wunderlich, S.: Ensuring the reliability of your model checker: interval iteration for Markov decision processes. In: Majumdar, R., Kunčak, V. (eds.) CAV 2017. LNCS, vol. 10426, pp. 160–180. Springer, Cham (2017). https://doi.org/10.1007/978-3-319-63387-9_8
5. Brázdil, T., et al.: Verification of Markov decision processes using learning algorithms. In: Cassez, F., Raskin, J.-F. (eds.) ATVA 2014. LNCS, vol. 8837, pp. 98–114. Springer, Cham (2014). https://doi.org/10.1007/978-3-319-11936-6_8
6. Cámara, J., Moreno, G.A., Garlan, D.: Stochastic game analysis and latency awareness for proactive self-adaptation. In: Proceedings of the 9th International Symposium on Software Engineering for Adaptive and Self-Managing Systems, pp. 155–164 (2014)
7. Chatterjee, K., Fijalkow, N.: A reduction from parity games to simple stochastic games. In: GandALF, pp. 74–86 (2011)
8. Chatterjee, K., Henzinger, T.A.: Value iteration. In: Grumberg, O., Veith, H. (eds.) 25 Years of Model Checking. LNCS, vol. 5000, pp. 107–138. Springer, Heidelberg (2008). https://doi.org/10.1007/978-3-540-69850-0_7
9. Chatterjee, K., Henzinger, T.A., Jobstmann, B., Radhakrishna, A.: GIST: a solver for probabilistic games. In: Touili, T., Cook, B., Jackson, P. (eds.) CAV 2010. LNCS, vol. 6174, pp. 665–669. Springer, Heidelberg (2010). https://doi.org/10.1007/978-3-642-14295-6_57
10. Chen, T., Forejt, V., Kwiatkowska, M.Z., Parker, D., Simaitis, A.: Automatic verification of competitive stochastic systems. Form. Methods Syst. Des. **43**(1), 61–92 (2013). https://doi.org/10.1007/s10703-013-0183-7
11. Chen, T., Kwiatkowska, M., Simaitis, A., Wiltsche, C.: Synthesis for multi-objective stochastic games: an application to autonomous urban driving. In: Joshi, K., Siegle, M., Stoelinga, M., D'Argenio, P.R. (eds.) QEST 2013. LNCS, vol. 8054, pp. 322–337. Springer, Heidelberg (2013). https://doi.org/10.1007/978-3-642-40196-1_28
12. Cheng, C.-H., Knoll, A., Luttenberger, M., Buckl, C.: GAVS+: an open platform for the research of algorithmic game solving. In: Abdulla, P.A., Leino, K.R.M. (eds.) TACAS 2011. LNCS, vol. 6605, pp. 258–261. Springer, Heidelberg (2011). https://doi.org/10.1007/978-3-642-19835-9_22
13. Condon, A.: The complexity of stochastic games. Inf. Comput. **96**(2), 203–224 (1992)
14. Condon, A.: On algorithms for simple stochastic games. Adv. Comput. Complex. Theory **13**, 51–72 (1993)
15. Czech, M., Hüllermeier, E., Jakobs, M., Wehrheim, H.: Predicting rankings of software verification tools. In: SWAN@ESEC/SIGSOFT FSE, pp. 23–26. ACM (2017)
16. Dai, P., Weld, D.S., Goldsmith, J.: Topological value iteration algorithms. J. Artif. Intell. Res. **42**, 181–209 (2011)
17. Eisentraut, J., Kelmendi, E., Křetínský, J., Weininger, M.: Value iteration for simple stochastic games: stopping criterion and learning algorithm. Inf. Comput. **285**, 104886 (2022)
18. Haddad, S., Monmege, B.: Interval iteration algorithm for MDPs and IMDPs. Theor. Comput. Sci. **735**, 111–131 (2018)
19. Hartmanns, A., Kaminski, B.L.: Optimistic value iteration. In: Lahiri, S.K., Wang, C. (eds.) CAV 2020. LNCS, vol. 12225, pp. 488–511. Springer, Cham (2020). https://doi.org/10.1007/978-3-030-53291-8_26
20. Hartmanns, A., Klauck, M., Parker, D., Quatmann, T., Ruijters, E.: The quantitative verification benchmark set. In: Vojnar, T., Zhang, L. (eds.) TACAS 2019.

LNCS, vol. 11427, pp. 344–350. Springer, Cham (2019). https://doi.org/10.1007/978-3-030-17462-0_20

21. Hoffman, A.J., Karp, R.M.: On nonterminating stochastic games. Manage. Sci. **12**(5), 359–370 (1966)

22. Křetínský, J., Ramneantu, E., Slivinskiy, A., Weininger, M.: Comparison of algorithms for simple stochastic games. EPTCS **326**, 131–148 (2020)

23. Kwiatkowska, M., Norman, G., Parker, D., Santos, G.: PRISM-games 3.0: stochastic game verification with concurrency, equilibria and time. In: Lahiri, S.K., Wang, C. (eds.) CAV 2020. LNCS, vol. 12225, pp. 475–487. Springer, Cham (2020). https://doi.org/10.1007/978-3-030-53291-8_25

24. Kwiatkowska, M.Z., Norman, G., Parker, D.: The PRISM benchmark suite. In: QEST 2012, pp. 203–204. IEEE Computer Society (2012)

25. LaValle, S.M.: Robot motion planning: a game-theoretic foundation. Algorithmica **26**(3–4), 430–465 (2000)

26. Phalakarn, K., Takisaka, T., Haas, T., Hasuo, I.: Widest paths and global propagation in bounded value iteration for stochastic games. In: Lahiri, S.K., Wang, C. (eds.) CAV 2020. LNCS, vol. 12225, pp. 349–371. Springer, Cham (2020). https://doi.org/10.1007/978-3-030-53291-8_19

27. Quatmann, T., Katoen, J.-P.: Sound value iteration. In: Chockler, H., Weissenbacher, G. (eds.) CAV 2018. LNCS, vol. 10981, pp. 643–661. Springer, Cham (2018). https://doi.org/10.1007/978-3-319-96145-3_37

28. Svorenová, M., Kwiatkowska, M.: Quantitative verification and strategy synthesis for stochastic games. Eur. J. Control. **30**, 15–30 (2016)

29. Ujma, M.: On verification and controller synthesis for probabilistic systems at runtime. Ph.D. thesis, University of Oxford, UK (2015)

Alternating Good-for-MDPs Automata

Ernst Moritz Hahn[1] (ORCID), Mateo Perez[2] (ORCID), Sven Schewe[3] (ORCID), Fabio Somenzi[2] (ORCID),
Ashutosh Trivedi[2] (ORCID), and Dominik Wojtczak[3(✉)] (ORCID)

[1] University of Twente, Enschede, The Netherlands
[2] University of Colorado Boulder, Boulder, USA
[3] University of Liverpool, Liverpool, UK
d.wojtczak@liverpool.ac.uk

Abstract. When omega-regular objectives were first proposed in model-free
reinforcement learning (RL) for controlling MDPs, deterministic Rabin automata
were used in an attempt to provide a direct translation from their transitions to
scalar values. While these translations failed, it has turned out that it is possible to repair them by using good-for-MDPs (GFM) Büchi automata instead.
These are nondeterministic Büchi automata with a restricted type of nondeterminism, albeit not as restricted as in good-for-games automata. Indeed, deterministic
Rabin automata have a pretty straightforward translation to such GFM automata,
which is bi-linear in the number of states and pairs. Interestingly, the same cannot
be said for deterministic Streett automata: a translation to nondeterministic Rabin
or Büchi automata comes at an exponential cost, even without requiring the target
automaton to be good-for-MDPs. Do we have to pay more than that to obtain a
good-for-MDPs automaton? The surprising answer is that we have to pay significantly less when we instead expand the good-for-MDPs property to alternating
automata: like the nondeterministic GFM automata obtained from deterministic
Rabin automata, the alternating good-for-MDPs automata we produce from deterministic Streett automata are bi-linear in the size of the deterministic automaton
and its index. They can therefore be exponentially more succinct than the minimal
nondeterministic Büchi automaton.

1 Introduction

Omega-automata [18, 27] have found renewed interest—often as the result of translat-
ing a formula in LTL [20]—as specifications of qualitative objectives in reinforcement
learning (RL) [26]. The acceptance condition of an ω-automaton determines the reward
whose cumulative return the learning agent strives to maximise. The relation between
the automaton and the reward signal should ensure that a strategy that maximises the
expected return also maximises the probability to realise the objective. This so-called
faithfulness requirement [10] restricts the type of ω-automaton that can be used to represent the objective, and this paper concerns how to find the right type of ω-automata.

This project has received funding from the European Union's Horizon 2020 research and innovation programme under grant agreements 864075 (CAESAR), and 956123 (FOCETA). This
work is supported in part by the National Science Foundation grant 2009022, by a CU Boulder
Research and Innovation Office grant, and by the EPSRC through grant EP/V026887/1.

A. Bouajjani et al. (Eds.): ATVA 2022, LNCS 13505, pp. 303–319, 2022.
https://doi.org/10.1007/978-3-031-19992-9_19

Deterministic automata with various types of acceptance conditions have been used in model checking and strategy synthesis [2]; notably, Büchi, parity, Rabin, and Streett. While deterministic Büchi automata—including generalised deterministic Büchi automata—do not accept all ω-regular languages, deterministic parity, Rabin, and Streett automata do; therefore, they are employed in the formulation of general solutions to synthesis problems. In addition, maximising the chance of meeting a parity and Rabin winning conditions in a game can be obtained using positional strategies, while Streett winning conditions require finite additional memory. This means that a positional strategy for a Markov decision process (MDP) or a stochastic game endowed with a parity or Rabin objective can be turned into a positional strategy to resolve nondeterministic choice. Strategy computation methods for both Rabin and Streett automata have been studied extensively [1,4,19]. These methods, however, are not applicable in RL. In order to apply RL to the computation of optimal strategies for ω-regular objectives, we have to devise a scheme for doling out rewards that, for generality, depend on the given ω-automaton, and perhaps on some hyperparameters of the learning algorithm, but not on the MDP—or the stochastic game—for which a control strategy is sought.

Two features of RL algorithms significantly affect the choice of translation from acceptance condition to rewards: 1) they require positional optimal strategies after the translation to rewards, as they learn values of states and transitions, and 2) the same transitions will always be optimal once a property is translated into scalar rewards. This appears to effectively exclude using Streett conditions directly [13], as optimal control requires memory for Streett objectives. This is regrettable, as Streett objectives do occur in practice. GR(1) [3] conditions, for example, translate smoothly into Streett objectives (in the pure original form, to one pair Streett objectives), such that a conjunction of GR(1) objectives will always have a natural representation as a deterministic Streett automaton. Likewise, each strong fairness requirement produces a Streett pair. Moreover, minimising the chance of satisfying a Rabin condition given as a deterministic Rabin automaton (DRA) is also equivalent to maximising the chance of satisfying the Streett condition given by its dual.

A natural way to move to simpler acceptance conditions requires some form of nondeterminism. Full recourse to nondeterminism, however, is not compatible with the computation of optimal strategies for MDPs or stochastic games. If we want to move away from using deterministic automata to describe the objective, we therefore need to impose restrictions on the automaton's nondeterminism. The precise nature of these restrictions depends on the type of environment interacting with the agent, whose control strategy we want to build. If the environment is a Markov decision process [21], the automaton needs to be good-for-MDPs (GFM) [11] (previously used automata [5,8,28] have this property) while, for stochastic games, with two strategic players, the stronger requirements of good-for-games automata [15] must be satisfied. GFM automata have the advantage that they can use simpler acceptance mechanisms. In particular, the GFM automata developed so far are nondeterministic Büchi automata, and being able to use a simple acceptance mechanism like Büchi is quite beneficial for RL [9,11]—though it is possible to use parity automata, using them comes at a cost [12].

When starting with a deterministic Streett automaton (DSA), a translation to a nondeterministic Büchi automaton (NBA) [23], or even to a nondeterministic Rabin automaton [23], comes at the cost of an exponential blow-up, even without the restriction to GFM automata. This raises the question of whether or not there is a different way to efficiently translate the DSA into a suitable automaton. Our main result is that **alternating GFM automata can be exponentially more succinct than general nondeterministic Büchi automata**.

Intuitively, this should not be possible: the reason for the exponential blow-up from DSAs to NBAs (and even NRAs) is that one will either need some form of memory, such as a latest appearance record (LAR [6,7]), or a nondeterministic guess as to which way each Streett pair is satisfied in. Recall that a Streett pair consists of a green and a red set of states or transitions, and it is satisfied if no entry of the red set *or* some entry of the green set occurs infinitely often; a nondeterministic automaton can guess, for each pair, to validate either of these conditions. The intuitive effect of this blow-up would be that starting with DSAs is something that efficient RL approaches will struggle with.

The key message of this paper is that one can trade-off *alternation* for memory in computing an optimal strategy by moving to *alternating* GFM automata instead of traditional nondeterministic ones. Here is the interesting bit: while we do, unsurprisingly, need a latest appearance record in the control strategy we develop, the blow-up due to the LAR is not necessary while learning the optimal strategy!

2 Preliminaries

A *probability distribution* over a finite set S is a function $d\colon S \to [0,1]$ such that we have $\sum_{s \in S} d(s) = 1$. Let $\mathcal{D}(S)$ denote the set of all probability distributions over S. We say a distribution $d \in \mathcal{D}(S)$ is a *point distribution* if $d(s) = 1$ for some $s \in S$. For $d \in \mathcal{D}(S)$ we write $supp(d)$ for $\{s \in S\colon d(s) > 0\}$.

2.1 Stochastic Game Arenas and Markov Decision Processes

A *stochastic game arena* $\mathcal{G}$ is a tuple $(S, s_0, A, T, S_{\mathrm{Max}}, S_{\mathrm{Min}}, AP, L)$, where S is a finite set of states, $s_0 \in S$ is the initial state, A is a finite set of *actions*, $T\colon S \times A \to \mathcal{D}(S)$ is the *probabilistic transition (partial) function*, $\{S_{\mathrm{Max}}, S_{\mathrm{Min}}\}$ is a partition of the set of states S, AP is the set of *atomic propositions*, and $L\colon S \to 2^{AP}$ is the *labeling function*. For $s \in S$, $A(s)$ denotes the set of actions enabled in s. For states $s, s' \in S$ and $a \in A(s)$ we write $p(s'|s, a)$ for $T(s,a)(s')$.

A *run* of $\mathcal{G}$ is an ω-word $\langle s_0, a_1, s_1, \ldots \rangle \in S \times (A \times S)^\omega$ such that $p(s_{i+1}|s_i, a_{i+1}) > 0$ holds for all $i \geq 0$. A finite run is a finite such sequence, that is, a word in $S \times (A \times S)^*$. For a *run* $r = \langle s_0, a_1, s_1, \ldots \rangle$ we define the corresponding labeled run as $L(r) = \langle L(s_0), L(s_1), \ldots \rangle \in (2^{AP})^\omega$. We write $Runs^{\mathcal{G}}$ ($FRuns^{\mathcal{G}}$) for the set of runs (finite runs) of the SGA $\mathcal{G}$ and $Runs^{\mathcal{G}}(s)$ ($FRuns^{\mathcal{G}}(s)$) for the set of runs (finite runs) of the SGA $\mathcal{G}$ starting from state s. We write $last(r)$ for the last state of a finite run r.

A game on an SGA $\mathcal{G}$ is played between two players, Max and Min, by moving a token through the states of the arena. The game begins with a token in an *initial state* s_0; players Max and Min construct an infinite run by taking turns to choose enabled actions when the token is in a state controlled by them, and then moving the token to a successor state sampled from the selected distribution. A strategy of player Max in

$\mathcal{G}$ is a partial function $\pi\colon FRuns \rightharpoonup \mathcal{D}(A)$, defined for $r \in FRuns$ if, and only if, $last(r) \in S_{\text{Max}}$, such that $supp(\sigma(r)) \subseteq A(last(r))$. A strategy σ of player Min is defined analogously. We drop the subscript $\mathcal{G}$ when the arena is clear from the context. Let $\Sigma_{\mathcal{G}}$ and $\Pi_{\mathcal{G}}$ be the sets of all strategies of player Max and player Min, respectively.

A memory structure for $\mathcal{G}$ is a tuple $\mathbf{M} = (M, m_0, \alpha_u)$ where M is a finite set of memory states, $m_0 \in M$ is the initial state, and $\alpha_u\colon M \times 2^{AP} \rightarrow M$ is the memory update function. The extended memory update $\hat{\alpha}_u\colon M \times (2^{AP})^* \rightarrow M$ can be defined in the usual manner. A finite memory strategy of player Max in $\mathcal{G}$ over a memory structure $\mathbf{M}$ is a Mealy machine $(\mathbf{M}, \alpha_x)$ where $\alpha_x\colon S_{\text{Max}} \times M \rightarrow \mathcal{D}(A)$ is the *next action function* that suggests the next action based on the SGA and the memory state. The semantics of a finite memory strategy $(\mathbf{M}, \alpha_x)$ is given as a strategy $\sigma \in \Sigma_{\mathcal{G}}$ such that for every $r \in FRuns$ with $last(r) \in S_{\text{Max}}$, we have that $\sigma(r) = \alpha_x(last(r), \hat{\alpha}_u(m_0, L(r)))$.

A strategy σ is *pure* if $\sigma(r)$ is a point distribution wherever it is defined; otherwise, σ is *mixed*. We say that σ is *stationary* if $last(r) = last(r')$ implies $\sigma(r) = \sigma(r')$ wherever σ is defined. A strategy is *positional* if it is both pure and stationary. We write $\overline{\Sigma}_{\mathcal{G}}$ and $\overline{\Pi}_{\mathcal{G}}$ for the sets of all *positional* strategies of player Max and player Min, respectively.

Let $Runs^{\mathcal{G}}_{\sigma,\pi}(s)$ denote the subset of runs $Runs^{\mathcal{G}}(s)$ starting from state s that are consistent with player Max and player Min following strategies σ and π, respectively. The behaviour of an SGA $\mathcal{G}$ under a strategy pair $(\sigma, \pi) \in \Sigma_{\mathcal{G}} \times \Pi_{\mathcal{G}}$ is defined on the probability space $(Runs^{\mathcal{G}}_{\sigma,\pi}(s), \mathcal{F}_{Runs^{\mathcal{G}}_{\sigma,\pi}(s)}, \Pr^{\mathcal{G}}_{\sigma,\pi}(s))$ over the set of infinite runs $Runs^{\mathcal{G}}_{\sigma,\pi}(s)$, where $\mathcal{F}_{Runs^{\mathcal{G}}_{\sigma,\pi}(s)}$ is the standard σ-algebra over them. Given a random variable $f\colon Runs^{\mathcal{G}} \rightarrow \mathbb{R}$ over the infinite runs of $\mathcal{G}$, we denote by $\mathbb{E}^{\mathcal{G}}_{\sigma,\pi}(s)\{f\}$ the expectation of f over the runs in the probability space $(Runs^{\mathcal{G}}_{\sigma,\pi}(s), \mathcal{F}_{Runs^{\mathcal{G}}_{\sigma,\pi}(s)}, \Pr^{\mathcal{G}}_{\sigma,\pi}(s))$.

We say that an SGA is a Markov decision process if $A(s)$ is a singleton for every $s \in S_{\text{Min}}$ and is a Markov chain if $A(s)$ is singleton for every $s \in S$. To distinguish an MDP from an SGA, we denote an MDP by $\mathcal{M}$ and write its signature $\mathcal{M} = (S, s_0, A, T, AP, L)$ by assigning the (choiceless) states of player Min to player Max. The notions defined for SGAs naturally carry over to MDPs.

2.2   Omega-Automata

An alphabet is a finite set of letters. We write $\mathbb{B}$ for the binary alphabet $\{0, 1\}$. A finite word over an alphabet Σ is a finite concatenation of symbols from Σ. Similarly, an ω-word w over Σ is a function $w\colon \omega \rightarrow \Sigma$ from the natural numbers to Σ. We write Σ^* and Σ^{ω} for the set of finite and ω-words over Σ.

An ω-automaton $\mathcal{A} = (\Sigma, Q, q_0, \delta, \alpha)$ consists of a finite alphabet Σ, a finite set of states Q, an initial state $q_0 \in Q$, a transition function $\delta\colon Q \times \Sigma \rightarrow 2^Q$, and an acceptance condition $\alpha\colon Q^{\omega} \rightarrow \mathbb{B}$. A *deterministic* automaton is such that $\delta(q, \sigma)$ is a singleton for every state q and alphabet letter σ. For deterministic automata, we write $\delta(q, \sigma) = q'$ instead of $\delta(q, \sigma) = \{q'\}$.

A *run* of an automaton $\mathcal{A} = (\Sigma, Q, q_0, \delta, \alpha)$ on word $w \in \Sigma^{\omega}$ is a function $\rho\colon \omega \rightarrow Q$ such that $\rho(0) = q_0$ and $\rho(i+1) \in \delta(\rho(i), w(i))$. A run ρ is *accepting* if $\alpha(\rho) = 1$. A word w is accepted by $\mathcal{A}$ if there exists an accepting run of $\mathcal{A}$ on w. The language of $\mathcal{A}$, written $\mathcal{L}(\mathcal{A})$, is the set of words accepted by $\mathcal{A}$. The set of states that appear infinitely often in ρ is written $\mathrm{inf}(\rho)$. A deterministic automaton $\mathcal{D}$ has exactly one run for each word in Σ^ω. We write $\mathrm{inf}^{\mathcal{D}}(w)$ for the set of states that appear infinitely often in the unique run of $\mathcal{D}$ on w; when clear from the context, we drop the superscript and simply write $\mathrm{inf}(w)$.

Several ways to give finite presentations of the acceptance conditions are in use. The ones relevant to this paper are listed below.

- A *Büchi* acceptance condition is specified by a set of states $F \subseteq Q$ such that

$$\alpha(\rho) = [\,\mathrm{inf}(\rho) \cap F \neq \emptyset\,].$$

- A *Rabin* acceptance condition of index k is specified by k pairs of sets of states, $\{(R_i, G_i)\}_{1 \leq i \leq k}$, and intuitively a run should visit at least one set of Red (ruinous) states finitely often and its corresponding Green (good) set of states infinitely often. Formally,

$$\alpha(\rho) = [\,\exists\, 1 \leq i \leq k.\, \mathrm{inf}(\rho) \cap R_i = \emptyset \text{ and } \mathrm{inf}(\rho) \cap G_i \neq \emptyset\,].$$

- A *Streett* acceptance condition of index k is specified by k pairs of sets of states, $\{(G_i, R_i)\}_{1 \leq i \leq k}$, and intuitively a run should visit each Red set of states finitely often or its corresponding Green set of states infinitely often. Formally,

$$\alpha(\rho) = [\,\forall\, 1 \leq i \leq k.\, \mathrm{inf}(\rho) \cap R_i = \emptyset \text{ or } \mathrm{inf}(\rho) \cap G_i \neq \emptyset\,].$$

We also allow for moving the acceptance condition from states to transitions. For a Büchi acceptance condition, this means defining a set $F \subseteq Q \times \Sigma \times Q$ of final transitions, where the ith transition for a run ρ of a word w is $t(i) = \big(\rho(i), w(i), \rho(i+1)\big)$, $\mathrm{inf}_t(\rho, w)$ is the set of transitions that occur infinitely often, and a run ρ is accepting for w if $\mathrm{inf}_t(\rho, w) \cap F \neq \emptyset$.

2.3 Semantic Satisfaction: Optimal Strategies Against ω-Automata

Given an MDP $\mathcal{M} = (S, s_0, A, T, AP, L)$ and an ω-automaton $\mathcal{A} = (2^{AP}, Q, q_0, \delta, \alpha)$, we are interested in strategies that maximise the probability that the labels of a run of $\mathcal{M}$ form an ω-word in the language of $\mathcal{A}$. A strategy $\sigma \in \Sigma_{\mathcal{M}}$ and initial state $s \in S$ determine a sequence X_i of random variables denoting the ith state of the MDP, where $X_0 = s$.

We define the optimal satisfaction probability $\mathrm{PSem}_{\mathcal{A}}^{\mathcal{M}}(s)$ as

$$\mathrm{PSem}_{\mathcal{A}}^{\mathcal{M}}(s) = \sup_{\sigma \in \Sigma_{\mathcal{M}}} \Pr{}_{\sigma}^{\mathcal{M}}(s)\,\{\langle L(X_0), L(X_1), \ldots \rangle \in \mathcal{L}(\mathcal{A})\}.$$

We say that a strategy $\sigma \in \Sigma_{\mathcal{M}}$ is optimal for $\mathcal{A}$ if

$$\Pr{}_{\sigma}^{\mathcal{M}}(s)\,\{\langle L(X_0), L(X_1), \ldots \rangle \in \mathcal{L}(\mathcal{A})\} = \mathrm{PSem}_{\mathcal{A}}^{\mathcal{M}}(s)$$

for all $s \in S$.

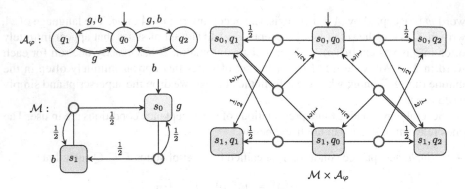

Fig. 1. Syntactic and Semantic Probabilities Differ. A nondeterministic Büchi automaton $\mathcal{A}_\varphi$ (top left) that recognises the language of infinitely many g's or infinitely many b's (which accepts all ω-words) and a Markov decision process $\mathcal{M}$, whose set of actions is a singleton (a Markov chain). Note that double edges mark accepting transitions. Notice that the MDP $\mathcal{M}$ satisfies the property with probability 1. Their product is shown on the right side, where there is no accepting end-component. Hence, the probability of reaching an accepting end-component (under any strategy) is 0.

2.4   Good-for-MDPs Automata

Given an MDP $\mathcal{M} = (S, s_0, A, T, AP, L)$ and automaton $\mathcal{A} = (2^{AP}, Q, q_0, \delta, \alpha)$, the *probabilistic model checking* problem is to find the optimal value $\mathsf{PSem}_\mathcal{A}^\mathcal{M}(s_0)$ and an optimal strategy in $\Sigma_\mathcal{M}$. An intuitive way to compute $\mathsf{PSem}_\mathcal{A}^\mathcal{M}(s_0)$ is to build the synchronous product $\mathcal{M} \times \mathcal{A}$ of $\mathcal{M}$ and $\mathcal{A}$ and compute the optimal probability to satisfy the acceptance condition in the product (we will name this syntactic satisfaction probability $\mathsf{PSyn}_\mathcal{A}^\mathcal{M}(s_0, q_0)$) and a strategy that maximises the probability of satisfying the acceptance condition. If these values $\mathsf{PSem}_\mathcal{A}^\mathcal{M}(s)$ and $\mathsf{PSyn}_\mathcal{A}^\mathcal{M}(s)$ coincide for all possible $\mathcal{M}$, then the automaton is said to be *good-for-MDPs* [11].

The synchronous product is an MDP $\mathcal{M} \times \mathcal{A} = (S \times Q, (s_0, q_0), A \times Q, T^\times, AP, L)$, where

$$T^\times((s, q), (a, q'))(s', q'') = \begin{cases} T(s, a)(s') & \text{if } q' \in \delta(q, L(s)) \text{ and } q'' = q' \\ 0 & \text{if } q' \in \delta(q, L(s)) \text{ and } q'' \neq q' \\ \text{undefined} & \text{otherwise .} \end{cases}$$

A strategy $\sigma \in \Sigma_{\mathcal{M} \times \mathcal{A}}$ and initial state $(s, q) \in S \times Q$ determine a sequence (X_i, Q_i) of random variables denoting the ith state of the product MDP, where $X_0 = s$ and $Q_0 = q$. The syntactic probability is defined to be

$$\mathsf{PSyn}_\mathcal{A}^\mathcal{M}(s, q) = \sup_{\sigma \in \Sigma_{\mathcal{M} \times \mathcal{A}}} \mathbb{E}_\sigma^{\mathcal{M} \times \mathcal{A}}(s)\{\alpha(\langle Q_0, Q_1, \ldots \rangle)\}.$$

An automaton is good-for-MDPs if $\mathsf{PSem}_\mathcal{A}^\mathcal{M}(s, q_0) = \mathsf{PSyn}_\mathcal{A}^\mathcal{M}(s)$ for all MDPs $\mathcal{M}$ and states $s \in S$. Figure 1 shows an example of an ω-automaton with Büchi acceptance

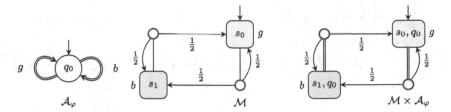

Fig. 2. Syntactic and Semantic Probabilities Agree. A deterministic Büchi automaton $\mathcal{A}_\varphi$ (left) that recognises the language of infinitely many g's or infinitely many b's (accepts all ω-words) and an MDP $\mathcal{M}$ (center), whose set of actions is singleton (a Markov chain). Again double edges mark accepting transitions. Notice that the MDP $\mathcal{M}$ satisfies the property with probability 1. Their product is shown on the right side where the whole MDP is one accepting end-component. Hence, the probability of reaching the end-component (under any strategy) is 1.

condition that is not GFM, while Fig. 2 shows an automaton that is GFM (since every deterministic ω-automaton is GFM.).

The advantage of being able to work on the syntactic product MDP is that the goal turns into reaching an accepting end-component (an end-component is a region of the MDP that, once entered, can be covered—each state visited infinitely often—almost surely while surely never leaving it; for Markov chains, these are the accepting leaf components) [11].

2.5 GFM Büchi Automata and Reinforcement Learning

The limit reachability technique [9] reduces the model checking problem for given MDP and GFM Büchi automaton to a reachability problem by slightly changing the structure of the product: one adds a target state t that can be reached with a given probability $1 - \zeta$ whenever visiting an accepting transition of the original product MDP. This reduction avoids the identification of accepting end-components and thus allows a natural integration to a wide range of model-free RL approaches. Thus, while the proofs do lean on standard model checking properties that are based on identifying winning end-components, they serve as a justification not to consider them when running the learning algorithm.

For any $\zeta \in (0, 1)$, the *augmented MDP* $\mathcal{M}^\zeta$ is an MDP obtained from $\mathcal{M} \times \mathcal{A}$ by adding a sink state t with a self-loop to the set of states of $\mathcal{M} \times \mathcal{A}$, and by making t a destination of each accepting transition τ of $\mathcal{M} \times \mathcal{A}$ with probability $1 - \zeta$. The original probabilities of all other destinations of an accepting transition τ are multiplied by ζ. An example of an augmented MDP is shown in Fig. 3. With a slight abuse of notation, if σ is a strategy on the augmented MDP $\mathcal{M}^\zeta$, we denote by σ also the strategy on $\mathcal{M} \times \mathcal{A}$ obtained by removing t from the domain of σ. The following result shows the correctness of the construction.

Theorem 1 (Limit Reachability Theorem [9,11]). *If $\mathcal{A}$ is GFM, then there exists a threshold $\zeta' \in (0, 1)$ such that, for all $\zeta > \zeta'$ and every state s, any strategy σ that maximises the probability of reaching the sink in $\mathcal{M}^\zeta$ is (1) an optimal strategy in*

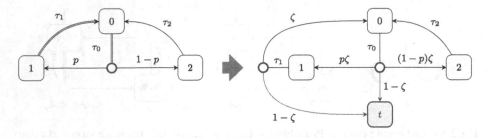

Fig. 3. Adding transitions to the target in the augmented product MDP.

$\mathcal{M} \times \mathcal{A}$ *from* s *and (2) induces an optimal strategy for the original MDP* $\mathcal{M}$ *from* s *with the objective to produce a run in the language of* $\mathcal{A}$. *Moreover,* $\mathcal{M}$ *produces such a run almost surely if, and only if, the sink is almost surely reachable in* $\mathcal{M}^{\varsigma}$ *for all* $0 < \varsigma < 1$.

Theorem 1 leads to a very simple model-free RL algorithm for GFM Büchi automata. The augmented product is not built by the RL algorithm, which does not know the transition structure of the environment MDP. Instead, the observations are used to drive the objective automaton. When the automaton reports an accepting transition, the interpreter tosses a biased coin to give the learner a reward with probability $1 - \varsigma$. The interpreter also extracts the set of actions for the learner to choose from. If the automaton is not deterministic and it has not taken the one nondeterministic transition it needs to take yet, the set of actions the interpreter provides to the learner includes the choice of special "jump" actions that instruct the automaton to move to a chosen accepting component. When the automaton reports an accepting transition, the interpreter gives the learner a positive reward with probability $1 - \varsigma$. When the learner actually receives a reward, the training episode terminates. Any RL algorithm that maximises this probabilistic reward is guaranteed to converge to a policy that maximises the probability of satisfaction of the objective.

3   Alternating GFM Automata

Before giving a translation from Deterministic Streett automaton (DSA) to a good-for-MDPs (GFM) alternating Büchi automaton (ABA), let us see how simple the translation is for its dual, a Deterministic Rabin Automaton (DRA). When we start with a DRA $\mathcal{R}$, the translation to a GFM Nondeterministic Büchi Automaton (NBA) [11] is straightforward as shown next.

Definition 1 (DRA to GFM NBA). *For a given deterministic Rabin automaton* $\mathcal{R} = (\Sigma, Q, q_0, \delta, \{\langle R_i, G_i \rangle \mid i \in \{1, \ldots, k\}\})$, *we construct a nondeterministic GFM automaton* $\mathcal{B} = (\Sigma, Q \times \{0, \ldots, k\} \cup \{\bot\}, (q_0, 0), \delta', F)$ *where:*

$$\delta'(\hat{q}, a) = \begin{cases} \{\delta(q, a)\} \times \{0, \ldots, k\} & \text{if } \hat{q} = (q, 0) \\ \{(\delta(q, a), i)\} & \text{if } \hat{q} = (q, i), i \neq 0, \text{ and } q \notin R_i \\ \bot & \text{otherwise.} \end{cases}$$

and $F = \{(q, i) \mid i \in \{1, \ldots, k\} \text{ and } q \in G_i\}$.

The resulting NBA makes only a single guess: it guesses when an accepting end-component is reached in the product MDP $\mathcal{M} \times \mathcal{R}$ (noting that the 0-copy is congruent to the original automaton), and then moves to a copy i, whose pair makes this end-component accepting. It is easy to see that this automaton is language equivalent to $\mathcal{R}$ and good-for-MDPs (e.g., it satisfies the simulation condition from [11]). For k pairs, this creates only $k+1$ copies, and thus a small overhead; and it allows one to then use standard reward translation techniques for Büchi acceptance conditions [9] in RL.

The question of how to maximise the probability to satisfy a Streett condition (or, likewise, how to minimise the probability to satisfy a Rabin condition) is more challenging. Broadly speaking, the translation of a Rabin acceptance condition is simplified by the fact that the nondeterministic choices of an NBA can easily handle the resolution of the disjunction of the acceptance condition on pairs, and resolving nondeterminism is something that always needs to be done when analysing an MDP. However, it is harder to accommodate for a conjunction of the acceptance condition on pairs, as in a Streett acceptance condition. As a consequence, the translation of a deterministic Streett automaton to a nondeterministic Rabin automaton (without a restriction to GFM) leads to a blow-up that results in $2^{\theta(n)}$ states [23], while a translation to an NBA requires $n2^{\theta(k)}$ states [23], even without the restriction to GFM.

Surprisingly, there is a way to exploit alternating good-for-MDPs automata with a small blow-up of $k+2$ for k pairs.

As Büchi games can be handled with similar techniques as for Büchi MDPs (Sect. 2.5) in model-free reinforcement learning (cf. [12]), the alternation itself does not create problems during learning; still, it is quite surprising that such a method works. This is partly because of the exponential memory requirement for Streett conditions, and partly because the acceptance player for the MDP would not have access to decisions the rejection player has made in the resulting game. However, while the automaton is small, the memory we infer from the winning strategy of this small automaton can be exponentially larger.

An optimal strategy in the resulting game does not in itself constitute a strategy for controlling the MDP for a given DSA. This is because different strategic choices of the antagonistic rejection player will lead to different positions in the game, and there is no guarantee that a consistent positional strategy for all of these positions exists. Moreover, the strategic choices of an antagonistic rejection player have no direct relation to the observable history. We show, however, that the history can be used to identify a state in the game, whose decisions the acceptance player should follow.

The need for memory is, therefore, not gone. Instead, the control strategy we construct in the correctness proof for the resulting alternating GFM Büchi automaton is only one part of the control strategy used for the MDP. The other is a latest appearance record (LAR), which is kept in addition to the constructed game. The LAR will determine the state, from a family of equivalent states, whose strategy will be followed.

3.1   Alternating GFM Automata

There is a number of mildly different definitions of alternating automata, and we can use the simplest one, where the states are partitioned into nondeterministic and universal states.

Definition 2. *An alternating ω-automaton $\mathcal{A} = (\Sigma, Q_n, Q_u, q_0, \delta, \alpha)$, with $Q = Q_n \cup Q_u$, is an automaton such that $(\Sigma, Q, q_0, \delta, \alpha)$ is a nondeterministic automaton, and Q_n and Q_u are disjoint sets of nondeterministic and universal states, respectively.*

A *run tree* of an alternating automaton $\mathcal{A} = (\Sigma, Q_n, Q_u, q_0, \delta, \alpha)$ on word $w \in \Sigma^\omega$ is a family of functions $\{\rho_j \colon \omega \to Q \mid j \in J\}$ for some non-empty index set J such that

- ρ_j is a run for all $j \in J$, and
- if ρ_j has a universal state q' at a position $i \in \omega$ ($\rho_j(i) = q' {\in} Q_u$), then, for all $q \in \delta(q', w(i))$, there is a $j_q \in J$ such that $\rho_{j_q}(k) = \rho_j(k)$ for all $k \leq i$, and $\rho_{j_q}(i + 1) = q$.

A run tree is accepting if all of the runs of $\{\rho_j \colon \omega \to Q \mid j \in J\}$ are accepting.

A minimal such family of runs can be viewed as a tree, where nondeterministic states have one successor, while universal states have many, namely all those defined by the local successor function. Alternatively, a family of runs can be viewed as a game, where an angelic acceptance player chooses the successor for a nondeterministic state, while an antagonistic rejection player selects the successor for a universal state. This way, they successively construct a run, and acceptance is decided by whether or not this run accepts.

We extend the product construction from Sect. 2.4 to produce a Büchi game from the product $\mathcal{M} \times \mathcal{A}$ of an MDP $\mathcal{M}$ with an alternating Büchi automaton $\mathcal{A}$, where the decisions of the rejection player are simply the decision to resolve the nondeterminism from the universal states, while resolving the nondeterminism from the MDP *and* resolving the nondeterminism from the nondeterministic automata states are left to the acceptance player. Both players have positional optimal strategies (where, for the rejection player, positionality includes the state and the choice made by the acceptance player[1]) in this game [17].

We refer to the probability, with which the acceptance player can win this product game from a product state (s, q) as

$$\mathsf{PSyn}_{\mathcal{A}}^{\mathcal{M}}(s, q) = \sup_{\sigma \in \Sigma_{\mathcal{M} \times \mathcal{A}}} \inf_{\pi \in \Pi_{\mathcal{M} \times \mathcal{A}}} \mathbb{E}_{\sigma, \pi}^{\mathcal{M} \times \mathcal{A}}(s, q) \left\{ \alpha(\langle X_0, X_1, \ldots \rangle) \right\} ,$$

where α is the Büchi condition and X_i is the random variable corresponding to the state of the automaton at the i-th step.

Definition 3 (Alternating GFM Automata). *An alternating automaton $\mathcal{A}$ is good-for-MDPs if, for all MDPs $\mathcal{M}$, $\mathsf{PSyn}_{\mathcal{A}}^{\mathcal{M}}(s_0, q_0) = \mathsf{PSem}_{\mathcal{A}}^{\mathcal{M}}(s_0)$ holds, where s_0 is the initial state of $\mathcal{M}$.*

---

[1] In a product of an MDP state with a universal automaton state, there needs to be a fixed order of who chooses first. It is common (and more natural) in RL to first resolve the choice of the action selected in the MDP.

3.2 Construction of the Alternating Büchi Automaton

The motivation for the translation of a deterministic Streett automaton to a GFM automaton is similar to that for Rabin: when having nondeterministic power, we can use it to guess when we have reached an accepting end-component that we plan to cover completely (i.e., we will almost surely visit every state and every transition in the end-component infinitely often).

While covering an accepting end-component may require memory (or randomisation), its properties with respect to the Streett condition are straightforward: for every Streett pair $\langle G, R\rangle$, if the end-component contains a red state $q \in R$ then it must also contain a green state $q' \in G$ from the same pair, which should (almost surely) be visited after every visit of q.

Definition 4 (DSA to Alternating GFM Büchi). *For a given deterministic Streett automaton $S = (\Sigma, Q, q_0, \delta, \{\langle G_i, R_i\rangle \mid i \in \{1, \ldots, k\}\})$, where we assume without loss of generality that $G_i \cap R_i = \emptyset$ for all $i = 1, \ldots, k$, we construct an alternating Büchi automaton $A = (\Sigma, Q, Q \times \{0, \ldots, k\}, q_0, \delta', F)$ where:*

- *First, for every state $q \in Q$, we let $I_q = \{0\} \cup \{i \mid q \in R_i\}$.*
- *We now define, for every state $q \in Q$ and letter $a \in \Sigma$, where $q' = \delta(q, a)$:*
  - $\delta'(q, a) = \{q', (q', 0)\}$ *and,*
  - *for all $i = 0, \ldots, k$, $\delta'((q, i), a) = \{q'\} \times (I_{q'} \setminus \{i\})$ if $q' \in G_i$ and $\delta'((q, i), a) = \{q'\} \times (I_{q'} \cup \{i\})$ if $q' \notin G_i$, using $G_0 = \emptyset$.*
- *Finally, we set the set of final transitions to $F = \{(q, i), a, (q', j) \mid i \neq j \text{ or } i = j = 0\}$.*

Note that the projection on the state of S is not affected by this translation.

The intuition for this translation is that the acceptance game starts in the original copy of the states—the nondeterministic states Q. From there, the acceptance player can *declare* when he has reached an accepting end-component, moving from the original copy to the 0-copy of the game. The rejection player can henceforth, whenever a state from the ith red set R_i is seen, move from a j-copy to the i-copy, which can be viewed as a claim that the requirement on the ith Streett pair is not fulfilled (finitely many R_i or infinitely many G_i states). She therefore *challenges* the acceptance player to visit a state from the ith green set G_i (an i-challenge for short). When the game is in the j-copy, the game moves back to the 0-copy when no new challenge is made and a state in G_j is visited. Otherwise, the game stays in the j-copy.

The acceptance player wins if the rejection player makes infinitely many challenges (the $i \neq j$ part of the final transitions) or if the game stays infinitely often in the 0-copy (the $i = j = 0$ part of the final states). The rejection player wins if the acceptance player never declares, or if she makes only finitely many challenges, and her last challenge is never met.

To keep the definition simple, we have allowed the rejection player to always withdraw a challenge by moving back to the 0-copy without reason. This is never an attractive move for her (so long as she has other options), and can therefore be omitted in an implementation.

An illustrative example can be found in the full version of this paper [14].

Before proving that the resulting automaton is good-for-MDPs in the next section, we would like to point out that it is *not* good-for-games in general. An example for this is provided again in [14].

4   Correctness of the Construction

In order to prove that this alternating Büchi automaton is good-for-MDPs, we first show that using this automaton provides at least the same syntactic probability to win as using the deterministic Streett automaton S.

Lemma 1. *Let S be a deterministic Streett automaton and A the alternating automaton from above constructed from S. Then, for every MDP M, $M \times A$ has at least the same winning probability as $M \times S$.*

Proof. We first observe that the acceptance player (as the Streett player in a finite state Streett game) has an optimal pure finite state memory strategy σ for $M \times S$. Let $(M \times S)_\sigma$ be the Markov chain obtained by using this optimal control.

In $(M \times S)_\sigma$, we will almost surely reach a leaf component, and the chance of winning is the chance of reaching an accepting leaf component (i.e., a leaf component where the Streett condition is almost surely satisfied).

For $M \times A$, we now define a pure finite state strategy τ for the acceptance player from σ and $(M \times S)_\sigma$ as follows. Outside the accepting leaf components, we follow σ and stay in the original copy. When entering an accepting leaf component, we move to the 0-copy, but otherwise make the same decision as for σ. Henceforth, we make the same decision that σ would make on the history obtained by ignoring in which i-copy we are. (Note that the decision on making an i-challenge, and hence on which i-copy should be visited, rests with the rejection player.)

As this was an accepting leaf component in $(M \times S)_\sigma$, if there is, for any pair $\langle G_i, R_i \rangle$, a (red) state in R_i in the leaf component, there is also a (green) state in G_i, and this state is almost surely visited infinitely often. Consequently, every challenge will, almost surely, eventually be met, and the acceptance player will win almost surely from these positions, regardless of how the rejection player plays. Thus, τ provides (at least) the same probability to win in $M \times A$ as σ provides for $M \times S$.   □

Different to the case of nondeterministic good-for-MDPs automata originally suggested in [11], we also have to show that the probability of winning for A cannot exceed that for S.

Lemma 2. *Let S be a deterministic Streett automaton and A the alternating automaton from above constructed from S. Then, for every MDP M, $M \times S$ has at least the same winning probability as $M \times A$.*

Before starting the proof, we define useful terminology, and make the assumption, for simplicity, that a positional optimal strategy σ for the acceptance player on $M \times A$ has been fixed.

We call two states of $M \times A$ *related*, if they refer to the same vertex of M and S, but possibly to different copies of this state in A. For such related states, it is obviously the case that the probability to win from the 0-copy is at least as high as the probability to win from any other i-copy, as the acceptance player can just play as if he started in that i-copy until the time where the first challenge is made. (The only difference with respect to acceptance from the i-copy is then that paths where no challenge is made become winning, such that the probability to win can only go up.) We further observe that the probability to win from the original copy is always at least as high as the probability to win from the 0-copy, as the acceptance player can always declare.

We therefore coin the term "good copy" of a state: a copy of a state is *good* if, and only if, the probability of winning from this copy is as high as the probability of winning from the original copy. A good copy is called *reachable* if it is reachable in $(\mathcal{M} \times \mathcal{A})_\sigma$. The *oldest* reachable good copy of a state (relative to a history) is the good copy i, for which the last visit to G_i is longest ago, where the higher number is given preference as a tie breaker. The 0-copy is only the oldest reachable copy, when it is the only reachable good copy different to the original copy. If no other reachable copy is good, the original copy is the oldest reachable good copy. Naturally, all σ-successors of a reachable good copy are reachable good copies.

Note that the property of being the oldest reachable good copy is relative to the history; a latest appearance record (also known as index appearance record) [7,16,24,25] is a standard memory structure of size $k!$ for keeping track of all information required for determining the oldest copy for a given history. Let $M_\mathcal{S}$ be such a memory structure.

Proof. Let σ be an optimal positional strategy of the acceptance player in the Büchi game $\mathcal{M} \times \mathcal{A}$, and let $\mathcal{S}' = \mathcal{S} \times M_\mathcal{S}$ be $\mathcal{S}$ equipped with a latest appearance record with $>$ as a tie breaker. We use this to construct the positional strategy τ for $\mathcal{M} \times \mathcal{S}'$ as the strategy that makes the same choice σ makes for the oldest reachable good copy of that state in the $\mathcal{S}$ projection of $\mathcal{S}'$.

It now suffices to show that the rejecting leaf components of $(\mathcal{M} \times \mathcal{S}')_\tau$ refer to states of $\mathcal{M} \times \mathcal{A}$, whose good copies have a winning probability of 0.

We first assume that there is a reachable leaf component that contains a state, where the oldest reachable good copy is the original copy. Note that this implies that the original copy is the only reachable good copy of that state. Naturally, the successor of a reachable good copy under σ is a reachable good copy, so every predecessor of the original copy, and by induction the complete leaf component, consists of states, where the original copy is the only good reachable copy. Thus, this leaf component in $(\mathcal{M} \times \mathcal{S})_\tau$ projects into an end-component in $(\mathcal{M} \times \mathcal{A})_\sigma$, where the rejection player has no decisions, and where no final transition occurs. The winning probability of all states in this end-component is 0.

We now assume that the rejecting leaf component contains only states with the same oldest reachable copy $i \geq 1$. Then the leaf component follows the positional strategy for the i-copy in $(\mathcal{M} \times \mathcal{A})_\sigma$; note that this entails that it does not contain a state in G_i. Therefore the rejection player surely wins in the i-copy of this end-component in $(\mathcal{M} \times \mathcal{A})_\sigma$ by never changing her challenge.

Let us finally turn to the case where a leaf component in $(\mathcal{M} \times \mathcal{S})_\tau$ contains only states, where all oldest reachable good copies are not the original copy, and that these copies are different, or all 0. We assume for contradiction that the leaf component is rejecting. Then there must be an index i such that there is a (red) state from R_i in the leaf component, but not a (green) state from G_i. Moreover, there must be an i^* with this property where, in the given history, the last occurrence of G_{i^*} is longest ago, using $>$ as tie breaker. Further, let us consider a path through this leaf component that visits states from all (green) sets $G_{i'}$ represented in this leaf component.

Let us now consider a (red) state in R_{i^*} in the leaf component. If the j-copy is not the i^*-copy, then, as the rejection player can make an i^* challenge, the i^*-copy (as a viable successor under the optimal strategy) must be a reachable good copy of the state, too, and therefore, by our assumption, the oldest reachable good state. Thus, we move on to the i^*-copy, and henceforth never leave it, contradicting the assumption that we are in a leaf component that contains different copies, or only the 0-copy, as oldest reachable states.

We have shown that we almost surely reach a leaf component, where the probability of winning all related states is 0 in $\mathcal{M} \times \mathcal{A}$, or where the chance of winning is 1. Together with the local consistency of the probabilities, we get the claim.   □

The two lemmas from this section imply that the syntactic and semantic probability to win are the same for all MDPs—in short, that $\mathcal{A}$ is good-for-MDPs. This in particular implies language equivalence on ultimately periodic words (which are a special case of Markov chains, where every state has only one successor), and therefore on all words, as two ω-automata that accept the same ultimately periodic words recognise the same language.

Moreover, we have provided a translation of an optimal strategy obtained for $\mathcal{M} \times \mathcal{A}$ into a strategy for $\mathcal{M} \times \mathcal{S}$ with (at least, and then with Lemma 1 precisely) the same optimal probability to win in the proof of Lemma 2.

Corollary 1. *The alternating Büchi automaton $\mathcal{A}$ that results from the construction of Sect. 3.2 from a DSA $\mathcal{S}$ is a good-for-MDPs automaton that recognises the same language as $\mathcal{S}$. Moreover, we can infer an optimal control strategy for the acceptance player for $\mathcal{M} \times \mathcal{S}$ from an optimal strategy of the acceptance player in $\mathcal{M} \times \mathcal{A}$.* □

An example of adding LAR memory can be found in [14].

We note that the memory we actually need is often smaller than the LAR we have mentioned, as the order can be mangled finitely often. That would, for example, allow us to only keep the order in some SCCs, namely those where we might get stuck in (with probability $\neq 0$)—and, of course, only for those indices that occur in states within these SCCs.

Note that the definition relative to reachability under σ is not required for correctness, but it provides the required connection to learning: when learning an optimal strategy in the game, the bit that is reachable under the optimal strategy we have learned is enough for constructing a pure finite state strategy.

Succinctness. Corollary 4 shows that the alternating Büchi automaton $\mathcal{A}$ that results from the construction of Sect. 3.2 from a DSA $\mathcal{S}$ is a good-for-MDPs automaton that recognises the same language as $\mathcal{S}$, and the number of states of $\mathcal{A}$ is merely $O(kn)$, where n and k are the number of states and Streett pairs of $\mathcal{S}$. At the same time, the translation of a deterministic Streett automaton to a nondeterministic Rabin automaton (without a restriction to GFM) leads to a blow-up that results in $2^{\theta(n)}$ states [23], while a translation to an NBA requires $n2^{\theta(k)}$ states [23], even without the restriction to GFM.

This immediately provides the following theorem.

Theorem 2. *Alternating GFM Büchi automata can be exponentially more succinct than (general) nondeterministic Büchi and Rabin automata.*   □

5 Discussion

When ω-regular objectives were first used in model checking MDPs, deterministic Rabin automata were used to represent the objectives. The same has been attempted by the reinforcement learning community: when they first turned to ω-regular objectives, they tried the tested route through deterministic Rabin automata [22], but that translation fails as shown in [9]. Of course, with the current state of knowledge of good-for-MDPs automata, it is not hard to translate deterministic Rabin automata to nondeterministic Büchi automata that are good-for-MDPs, and then to analyse the product of such a Büchi automaton and the MDP in question.

While MDPs with Büchi conditions are a (relatively) easy target for RL methods (like Q-learning [9,11]), a similar translation of Streett automata (or for minimising the chance of meeting a Rabin objective) appears prohibitive. This is because *every* translation from DSAs to nondeterministic Büchi (or even to Rabin) automata incurs an exponential blow-up in the worst case. Surprisingly, we found a way to allow even this accepting condition to be efficiently used in reinforcement learning by generalising the property of being good-for-MDPs to alternating automata, and by constructing an equivalent good-for-MDPs alternating Büchi automaton with linear overhead.

References

1. de Alfaro, L.: Formal Verification of Probabilistic Systems. Ph.D. thesis, Stanford University (1998)
2. Baier, C., Katoen, J.P.: Principles of Model Checking. MIT Press, Cambridge (2008)
3. Bloem, R., Jobstmann, B., Piterman, N., Pnueli, A., Sa'ar, Y.: Synthesis of reactive(1) designs. J. Comput. Syst. Sci. **78**(3), 911–938 (2012). https://doi.org/10.1016/j.jcss.2011.08.007
4. Buhrke, N., Lescow, H., Vöge, J.: Strategy construction in infinite games with Streett and Rabin chain winning conditions. In: Margaria, T., Steffen, B. (eds.) TACAS 1996. LNCS, vol. 1055, pp. 207–224. Springer, Heidelberg (1996). https://doi.org/10.1007/3-540-61042-1_46
5. Courcoubetis, C., Yannakakis, M.: The complexity of probabilistic verification. J. ACM **42**(4), 857–907 (1995)
6. Dziembowski, S., Jurdziński, M., Walukiewicz, I.: How much memory is needed to win infinite games? In: Symposium on Logic in Computer Science (LICS 1997), pp. 99–110 (1997)
7. Gurevich, Y., Harrington, L.: Trees, automata and games. In: Symposium on Theory of Computing (STOC 1982), pp. 60–65 (1982)
8. Hahn, E.M., Li, G., Schewe, S., Turrini, A., Zhang, L.: Lazy probabilistic model checking without determinisation. In: Concurrency Theory, pp. 354–367 (2015)

9. Hahn, E.M., Perez, M., Schewe, S., Somenzi, F., Trivedi, A., Wojtczak, D.: Omega-regular objectives in model-free reinforcement learning. In: Vojnar, T., Zhang, L. (eds.) TACAS 2019. LNCS, vol. 11427, pp. 395–412. Springer, Cham (2019). https://doi.org/10.1007/978-3-030-17462-0_27

10. Hahn, E.M., Perez, M., Schewe, S., Somenzi, F., Trivedi, A., Wojtczak, D.: Faithful and effective reward schemes for model-free reinforcement learning of omega-regular objectives. In: Hung, D.V., Sokolsky, O. (eds.) ATVA 2020. LNCS, vol. 12302, pp. 108–124. Springer, Cham (2020). https://doi.org/10.1007/978-3-030-59152-6_6

11. Hahn, E.M., Perez, M., Schewe, S., Somenzi, F., Trivedi, A., Wojtczak, D.: Good-for-MDPs automata for probabilistic analysis and reinforcement learning. In: TACAS 2020. LNCS, vol. 12078, pp. 306–323. Springer, Cham (2020). https://doi.org/10.1007/978-3-030-45190-5_17

12. Hahn, E.M., Perez, M., Schewe, S., Somenzi, F., Trivedi, A., Wojtczak, D.: Model-free reinforcement learning for stochastic parity games. In: CONCUR: International Conference on Concurrency Theory, pp. 21:1–21:16. LIPIcs 171 (2020)

13. Hahn, E.M., Perez, M., Schewe, S., Somenzi, F., Trivedi, A., Wojtczak, D.: An impossibility result in automata-theoretic reinforcement learning. In: ATVA: Automated Technology for Verification and Analysis (2022). (to appear)

14. Hahn, E.M., Perez, M., Schewe, S., Somenzi, F., Trivedi, A., Wojtczak, D.: Alternating good-for-MDP automata. arXiv preprint arXiv:2205.03243 (2022)

15. Henzinger, T.A., Piterman, N.: Solving games without determinization. In: Ésik, Z. (ed.) CSL 2006. LNCS, vol. 4207, pp. 395–410. Springer, Heidelberg (2006). https://doi.org/10.1007/11874683_26

16. Löding, C.: Methods for the transformation of ω-automata: complexity and connection to second order logic. Ph.D. thesis, Christian-Albrechts-University of Kiel (1998). Supervisor, Prof. Wolfgang Thomas

17. McIver, A.K., Morgan, C.C.: Games, probability, and the quantitative μ-calculus $qM\mu$. In: Baaz, M., Voronkov, A. (eds.) LPAR 2002. LNCS (LNAI), vol. 2514, pp. 292–310. Springer, Heidelberg (2002). https://doi.org/10.1007/3-540-36078-6_20

18. Perrin, D., Pin, J.É.: Infinite Words: Automata, Semigroups, Logic and Games. Elsevier (2004)

19. Piterman, N., Pnueli, A.: Faster solutions of Rabin and Streett games. In: Symposium on Logic in Computer Science, pp. 275–284 (2006)

20. Pnueli, A.: The temporal logic of programs. In: IEEE Symposium on Foundations of Computer Science, pp. 46–57 (1977)

21. Puterman, M.L.: Markov Decision Processes: Discrete Stochastic Dynamic Programming. John Wiley & Sons, NY (1994)

22. Sadigh, D., Kim, E., Coogan, S., Sastry, S.S., Seshia, S.A.: A learning based approach to control synthesis of Markov decision processes for linear temporal logic specifications. In: Conference on Decision and Control (CDC), pp. 1091–1096 (2014)

23. Safra, S., Vardi, M.Y.: On ω-automata and temporal logic. In: Proceedings of the Twenty-First Annual ACM Symposium on Theory of Computing, pp. 127–137. STOC 1989, ACM, NY (1989). https://doi.org/10.1145/73007.73019

24. Safra, S.: Exponential determinization for omega-automata with strong-fairness acceptance condition (extended abstract). In: Proceedings of the 24th Annual ACM Symposium on Theory of Computing, 4–6 May 1992, Victoria, British Columbia, pp. 275–282. ACM (1992). https://doi.org/10.1145/129712.129739

25. Safra, S.: Exponential determinization for omega-automata with a strong fairness acceptance condition. SIAM J. Comput. **36**(3), 803–814 (2006). https://doi.org/10.1137/S0097539798332518

26. Sutton, R.S., Barto, A.G.: Reinforcement Learning: An Introduction. Second edn. MIT Press (2018)
27. Thomas, W.: Automata on infinite objects. In: Handbook of Theoretical Computer Science, pp. 133–191. The MIT Press/Elsevier (1990)
28. Vardi, M.Y.: Automatic verification of probabilistic concurrent finite state programs. In: Foundations of Computer Science, pp. 327–338 (1985)

PET – A Partial Exploration Tool for Probabilistic Verification

Tobias Meggendorfer[(✉)] [ID]

Institute of Science and Technology Austria (ISTA), 3400 Klosterneuburg, Austria
tobias.meggendorfer@ist.ac.at

Abstract. We present PET, a specialized and highly optimized framework for *partial exploration* on *probabilistic systems*. Over the last decade, several significant advances in the analysis of Markov decision processes employed partial exploration. In a nutshell, this idea allows to focus computation on specific parts of the system, guided by heuristics, while maintaining correctness. In particular, only relevant parts of the system are constructed on demand, which in turn potentially allows to omit constructing large parts of the system. Depending on the model, this leads to dramatic speed-ups, in extreme cases even up to an arbitrary factor. PET unifies several previous implementations and provides a flexible framework to easily implement partial exploration for many further problems. Our experimental evaluation shows significant improvements compared to the previous implementations while vastly reducing the overhead required to add support for additional properties.

Keywords: Markov system · Markov decision processes · Probabilistic verification · Partial exploration

1 Introduction

Stochastic systems such as *Markov chains* (MC) [2] and *Markov decision processes* (MDP) [13] are a widely used formalism for modelling and analysing probabilistic processes, potentially involving non-determinism. Classical objectives such as *reachability* or *mean payoff* can be solved by a variety of approaches. From a theoretical perspective, linear programming (LP) is most appealing, since it yields precise answers in polynomial time. Yet, in practice, LP approaches often are only able to deal with small systems of at most a few hundred thousand states. In contrast, dynamic programming approaches such as *value iteration* (VI) and *strategy iteration* (SI) turn out to be quite performant, despite their exponential worst-case complexity. Indeed, (a variant of) value iteration is the default method of the widely used model checkers PRISM [9] and Storm [4].

However, systems with significantly more than a few billion states remain out of reach also for these approaches, not only due to timeouts but also simply because of memory constraints. In some cases, techniques such as *abstraction* or *symbolic representation* may mitigate these issues. Over the last decade, yet another technique gained popularity, namely to restrict computation to specific

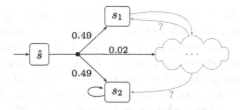

Fig. 1. Example system to motivate partial exploration.

Algorithm 1. PARTIALEXPLORATION
___

Input: MDP $\mathcal{M}$ with initial state $\hat{s}$, Query Q
Output: Answer to Q
1: **while** Q not answered by bounds for $\hat{s}$ **do**
2:     path $\leftarrow$ GETSTATES   ▷ Select states to update
3:     explored $\leftarrow$ explored $\cup$ path   ▷ Mark states explored
4:     UPDATEECS($\mathcal{M}$, explored)   ▷ Identify and collapse explored end components
5:     **for** s in path **do**
6:         Update / propagate lower and upper bounds for s
7: **return** Answer for Q

___

parts of the system. Inspired by asynchronous VI and the BRTDP algorithm [11], specialized techniques arose for reachability [3] and mean payoff [1]. In turn, these two works resulted in a more fundamental analysis of partial exploration, resulting in the notion of *cores* [7], which comprise the "relevant" part of a probabilistic system. For an intuitive example demonstrating partial exploration, consider Fig. 1. In order to determine that state s_1 can be reached with a probability between 0.49 and 0.51 in this system we do not need to construct the "cloudy" part of the system at all (which could comprise millions of states).

This idea of only considering relevant parts of the system lies at the heart of all mentioned partial exploration approaches: While the approaches of [1, 3, 7] all deal with different problems, their algorithms and, in particular, their implementation share a significant number of concepts. Indeed, all these algorithms essentially are adaptations of Algorithm 1. Intuitively, they work as follows: As long as we cannot yet answer the given query, we select parts of the system to update, e.g., by sampling a path, potentially guided by a heuristic. This may explore new parts of the system. Since end components introduce fix points of the value propagation, we repeatedly check if the part of the system explored so far contains problematic components and, if so, collapse them. Finally, the states along the sampled path are updated, using value iteration. In a nutshell, as long as GETSTATES repeatedly yields all "relevant" states and all end components which could cause issues are collapsed, the bounds of the initial state eventually converge due to classical results on value iteration and we can answer the query. Note that classical interval iteration [5] can essentially be obtained by letting GETSTATES always yield all states of the system.

PET unifies these previous approaches, providing a stable and correct foundation, and easing development of future partial exploration implementations.

Capabilities. At its heart, PET provides central concepts of partial exploration approaches as an extensible, efficient framework. The implementations of [1, 3, 7] each required several thousand lines of code. Through distilling the common concepts into suitable abstractions, each of these previous approaches can in contrast be implemented with a few dozen lines while being applicable to a much wider variety of problem instances as well as achieve a significant improvement in performance. Aside from efficient implementation, PET additionally comes with several "quality of life" and engineering improvements, easing development. Finally, we also fixed several subtle errors of previous implementations.

Availability. PET is written in Java and is continuously developed further, serving as the basis for several other projects. It is available under the MIT licence and can be obtained from the artefact [12] or the development GitLab[1].

2   Capabilities

In the interest of space, we only briefly highlight some key features of PET.

Models and Properties. PET supports parsing probabilistic models, reward structures, and properties given in PRISM's modelling language. The details of PRISM are abstracted, and the underlying `probabilistic-models` library can easily be extended to support other formalisms. For example, the generator for a model only needs to provide (i) the set of initial states and (ii) for a given state, the set of available actions and their respective successor distributions.

Currently, PET supports (discrete-time) Markov chains and Markov decision processes, as well as continuous time Markov chains (through embedding/uniformization). In terms of properties, PET currently supports (i) (un)bounded reachability, (ii) mean payoff queries, and (iii) (un)bounded cores.

On-the-fly Collapsing. A substantial technical contribution of [3] and elementary partial exploration in general is the so-called *on-the-fly* detection of end components and their collapsing, i.e. replacing them with a single representative state. PET provides an optimized implementation of Tarjan's SCC decomposition algorithm and custom end component detection, as well as an involved, tailored implementation of a dynamic quotient model.

Separation of Concerns. As mentioned above, a key goal of PET is to separate and abstract the elementary concepts of partial exploration. As hinted by Algorithm 1, obtain the states to update, i.e. GETSTATES, how (and when) to identify end components, how values are propagated, and when the bounds are sufficient to answer the query are all largely independent of each other, which is reflected in

---

[1] https://gitlab.lrz.de/i7/partial-exploration.

the abstractions of PET. For example, we completely isolate the sampling mechanism GetStates from the exact property or type of model being dealt with and vice versa. As such, a "naive" implementation of GetStates which returns all available options or selects a random one requires less than a dozen lines of code. Similarly, the partial exploration specific parts of [1,3,7], i.e. (unbounded) reachability, mean payoff, and cores, require approximately 60, 200, and 50 lines of code, respectively (excluding some boilerplate code for CLI etc.). Moreover, all implementations transparently support both qualitative queries (e.g. "is the value larger than threshold t?") and quantitative queries ("what is the optimal value up to a precision of 10^{-6}?") without additional effort.

Data Structures and Libraries. Aside from algorithm-specific improvements, PET leverages high-performance data structures and libraries, in particular naturals-util[2], a library for efficiently dealing with natural numbers initially designed for PET, backed by Roaring Bitmaps [10] and fastutil[3]. The model representation library probabilistic-models[4], which comprises the majority of the code, is agnostic of partial exploration and is available separately for reuse in other projects dealing with probabilistic systems. Further, we took care to perform computations in a numerically stable way without overly compromising performance, e.g. by using Kahan summation whenever applicable.[5]

Usability and Extensibility. PET comes with a descriptive CLI provided by picocli[6]. Additional "quality of life" features include a common output format (in JSON), utilities for analysing a given system, informative statistics during and after execution, a vast amount of assertions throughout the code, and extensible integration testing. A modern infrastructure, such as Gradle build scripts and static analysis tools, facilitates easy development. Finally, PET uses modern features of Java, e.g. lambdas, records, and sealed classes, improving readability.

3   Evaluation

In this section, we present a comparison of PET to the respective implementations of [1,3,7], which we denote by Learn[7], OVI, and Core. For completeness, we furthermore ran PRISM [9] (version 4.7) with both explicit and hybrid engine on applicable instances, denoted PRISMe and PRISMh, to demonstrate the overall performance of partial exploration (on suitable models).

---

[2] https://github.com/incaseoftrouble/naturals-util.
[3] https://fastutil.di.unimi.it/.
[4] https://gitlab.lrz.de/i7/probabilistic-models.
[5] Unfortunately, Java does not allow to specify the IEEE 754 rounding mode for floating point operations, which would further increase numerical stability, see [6].
[6] https://picocli.info/.
[7] The implementation is not available from the URL mentioned in [3], we obtained the sources from the authors and include it in our artefact.

Table 1. Comparison on selected benchmarks, with reachability on top, mean payoff bottom left, and cores bottom right. For each tool, we list the time until convergence (seconds) and required memory (megabytes). Timeouts are denoted by T/O and memouts by M/O. All properties were computed with a precision requirement of $\varepsilon = 10^{-6}$. The † symbol indicates a wrong result of the tool.

Model	Property	PRISMe	PRISMh	Learn	PET
firewire(36,200)	elected_max	4.4 (362)	13 (213)	1.3 (113)	0.9 (72)
firewire(36,200)	elected_min	5.5 (339)	12 (195)	M/O	34 (383)
pacman(20)	crash	25 (950)	84 (864)	5.3 (233)	2.0 (140)
pacman(40)	crash	M/O	T/O	M/O	22 (333)
wlan(6,6)	collisions	M/O	61 (263)	M/O	44 (370)
zeroconf(1000,14)	correct_max	M/O	271 (843)	5.0 (202)	1.1 (117)

Model	Rewards	OVI	PET		Model	Core	PET
mer(3)	grants	279 (355)†	6.6 (160)		mer(3)	12 (150)	5.7 (155)
mer(4)	grants	T/O	36 (308)		mer(4)	183 (227)	32 (258)
pacman(10)	default	4.4 (183)	1.7 (142)		sensors(2)	4.3 (162)	2.8 (137)
pacman(20)	default	M/O	7.3 (177)		sensors(3)	T/O	15 (224)
virus(3)	attacks	T/O	1.3 (126)		wlan(6,6)	33 (381)	29 (380)

Setup. We ran our experiments in a Docker container with an AMD Ryzen 5 3600 CPU, using Benchexec 3.11 [15] to obtain reliable measurements. Each run is restricted to a single core, 1000 MB of memory, and a 5 min time limit. (We deliberately chose reasonably sized models to ease evaluation.)

Models. We used a variety of PRISM models, picked from the PRISM benchmark suite, the examples provided with PRISM, and from the evaluation sets of the previous implementations. Due to space constraints, we omit a discussion of each model and refer the reader to the mentioned sources and our artefact for further information. For each comparison, we selected "sensible" models. For example, when computing cores, it is not informative to compare strongly connected / communicating models, as outlined in [7]: In this case, no non-trivial core exists.

Results. We present a subset of our evaluation results in Table 1, the full evaluation, further data, and replication instructions can be found in the artefact [12]. In summary, we observe that for all comparisons, our new implementation achieves significant savings in both time and memory compared to the previous implementations of [1,3,7]. We mention that performance of PET and Core is similar on a number of models. This is to be expected, since the codebase of Core actually forms the foundations of PET. Nevertheless, PET still achieves noticeable improvements on several shown models through, e.g., further optimizations in the computation and representation of end components.

We emphasize that the improvements are due to careful engineering and specialized data structures; the underlying theory remains the same. In particular, on some models, PET is outperformed by PRISM simply due to the particular model being unsuitable to partial exploration (see [7] for further discussion).

4   Conclusion and Future Work

We present PET, an efficient framework for partial exploration on Markov systems. PET implements several previous partial exploration approaches and provides significant improvements compared to their original versions, while drastically reducing the specific implementation effort. Moreover, PET transparently supports a wider range of inputs (both in terms of models and properties) and, due to carefully chosen abstractions, is easily extensible.

For future work, we plan to incorporate algorithms related to stochastic games. Moreover, for algorithmic improvements, specialized MEC decomposition algorithms could improve performance of the quotient model if applicable. Thirdly, we want to integrate Owl [8] for LTL model checking, essentially providing the features of MoChiBa [14] in combination with partial exploration. Finally, compilation to an executable through GraalVM may provide further speed ups.

Acknowledgements. We thank Pranav Ashok and Maximilian Weininger for their contributions to spiritual predecessors of PET as well as motivating the initial development of this tool.

References

1. Ashok, P., Chatterjee, K., Daca, P., Křetínský, J., Meggendorfer, T.: Value iteration for long-run average reward in markov decision processes. In: Majumdar, R., Kunčak, V. (eds.) CAV 2017. LNCS, vol. 10426, pp. 201–221. Springer, Cham (2017). https://doi.org/10.1007/978-3-319-63387-9_10
2. Baier, C., Katoen, J.: Principles of Model Checking. MIT Press, Cambridge (2008)
3. Brázdil, T., et al.: Verification of markov decision processes using learning algorithms. In: Cassez, F., Raskin, J.-F. (eds.) ATVA 2014. LNCS, vol. 8837, pp. 98–114. Springer, Cham (2014). https://doi.org/10.1007/978-3-319-11936-6_8
4. Dehnert, C., Junges, S., Katoen, J.-P., Volk, M.: A storm is coming: a modern probabilistic model checker. In: Majumdar, R., Kunčak, V. (eds.) CAV 2017. LNCS, vol. 10427, pp. 592–600. Springer, Cham (2017). https://doi.org/10.1007/978-3-319-63390-9_31
5. Haddad, S., Monmege, B.: Interval iteration algorithm for MDPs and IMDPs. TCS **735**, 111–131 (2018)
6. Hartmanns, A.: Correct probabilistic model checking with floating-point arithmetic. In: TACAS 2022. LNCS, vol. 13244, pp. 41–59. Springer, Cham (2022). https://doi.org/10.1007/978-3-030-99527-0_3
7. Kretínský, J., Meggendorfer, T.: Of cores: a partial-exploration framework for markov decision processes. LMCS **16**(4), 3:1-3:31 (2020)
8. Křetínský, J., Meggendorfer, T., Sickert, S.: Owl: a library for ω-words, automata, and LTL. In: Lahiri, S.K., Wang, C. (eds.) ATVA 2018. LNCS, vol. 11138, pp. 543–550. Springer, Cham (2018). https://doi.org/10.1007/978-3-030-01090-4_34

9. Kwiatkowska, M., Norman, G., Parker, D.: PRISM 4.0: verification of probabilistic real-time systems. In: Gopalakrishnan, G., Qadeer, S. (eds.) CAV 2011. LNCS, vol. 6806, pp. 585–591. Springer, Heidelberg (2011). https://doi.org/10.1007/978-3-642-22110-1_47

10. Lemire, D., Kai, G.S.Y., Kaser, O.: Consistently faster and smaller compressed bitmaps with roaring. SPE **46**(11), 1547–1569 (2016)

11. McMahan, H.B., Likhachev, M., Gordon, G.J.: Bounded real-time dynamic programming: RTDP with monotone upper bounds and performance guarantees. In: ICML 2005, vol. 119, pp. 569–576. ACM (2005)

12. Meggendorfer, T.: PET: partial exploration tool (2022). https://doi.org/10.5281/zenodo.6517820

13. Puterman, M.L.: Markov Decision Processes: Discrete Stochastic Dynamic Programming. Wiley Series in Probability and Statistics, Wiley, Hoboken (1994)

14. Sickert, S., Křetínský, J.: MoChiBA: probabilistic LTL model checking using limit-deterministic Büchi automata. In: Artho, C., Legay, A., Peled, D. (eds.) ATVA 2016. LNCS, vol. 9938, pp. 130–137. Springer, Cham (2016). https://doi.org/10.1007/978-3-319-46520-3_9

15. Wendler, P., Beyer, D.: sosy-lab/benchexec: Release 3.11 (2022)

STOMPC: Stochastic Model-Predictive Control with UPPAAL STRATEGO

Martijn A. Goorden[1]([⊠])(iD), Peter G. Jensen[1](iD), Kim G. Larsen[1],
Mihhail Samusev[1,2], Jiří Srba[1], and Guohan Zhao[2]

[1] Department of Computer Science, Aalborg University, Aalborg, Denmark
{mgoorden,pgj,kgl,srba}@cs.aau.dk
[2] Department of the Built Environment, Aalborg University, Aalborg, Denmark
{msam,guohanz}@build.aau.dk

Abstract. We present the new co-simulation and synthesis integrated-framework STOMPC for stochastic model-predictive control (MPC) with UPPAAL STRATEGO. The framework allows users to easily set up MPC designs, a widely accepted method for designing software controllers in industry, with UPPAAL STRATEGO as the controller synthesis engine, which provides a powerful tool to synthesize safe and optimal strategies for hybrid stochastic systems. STOMPC provides the user freedom to connect it to external simulators, making the framework applicable across multiple domains.

1 Introduction

Controller software has become increasingly dominant in cyber-physical systems. Functionality that previously was implemented by hardware is now being shifted towards software. Often cyber-physical systems are safety-critical, hence strong safety-related requirements are formulated for them. At the same time, quality objectives need to be considered, such as being as fast as possible or minimizing resource usage. Designing safe and optimal controller software manually is a challenge, and several formal methods have been developed to synthesize controller strategies automatically [1,14,15].

For stochastic hybrid systems, the tool UPPAAL STRATEGO [5,10] is the newly emerged branch of the leading tool UPPAAL that can automatically synthesize safe and near-optimal controller strategies. It combines statistical model checking, synthesis for timed games, and reinforcement learning. UPPAAL STRATEGO has been applied successfully to several case studies [3,6,8,11,12].

Within industry, model predictive control (MPC) is a widely adopted method for designing controllers [7]. MPC schemes are popular as they yield high-performing control systems without expert intervention over long periods of time. This is achieved by periodically using a model to predict the system's

---

This work is partly supported by the Villum Synergy project CLAIRE and the ERC Advanced Grant LASSO.

A. Bouajjani et al. (Eds.): ATVA 2022, LNCS 13505, pp. 327–333, 2022.
https://doi.org/10.1007/978-3-031-19992-9_21

future behavior and calculate an optimal control strategy for the next time-bounded period [4]. Therefore, MPC schemes are also called *online control*, as they can adapt control strategies while the system is running.

UPPAAL STRATEGO conceptually fits well within MPC designs. Yet it lacks the ability to periodically update the model's state and synthesize a new strategy. In previous work [11], bash scripts are created utilizing the command line interface of UPPAAL STRATEGO to do all the calculations periodically. Unfortunately, these bash scripts are very case specific and not well adaptable to other case studies. Furthermore, we noticed that for each new case study, researchers were repeatedly rediscovering MPC schemes for UPPAAL STRATEGO.

We present the co-simulation and synthesis integrated-framework STOMPC, which implements a basic MPC scheme using UPPAAL STRATEGO as the core engine for synthesizing the strategies. With this framework, we aim to greatly simplify the setup for different case studies by implementing standard functionalities for MPC schemes with UPPAAL STRATEGO in Python classes. Furthermore, STOMPC can be connected to external, domain specific, simulators (or in fact again UPPAAL STRATEGO) that represent the real world. This makes the framework applicable to cases from different domains. Our framework is accessible on GitHub[1], can be installed through pip, and its documentation is available[2]. An artifact for evaluation can be downloaded from Zenodo[3].

2   Framework Overview

MPC captures a particular way of designing controllers for a broad range of systems and processes. It has the following three characteristics [4]: a model, which is used to predict the future of the system within a certain horizon, the calculation of a control sequence (or strategy) that optimizes some objective, and a receding approach, where all calculations are repeated after executing the first control action from the sequence and observing the true state as a consequence of that.

Figure 1 provides a conceptual overview of the key ingredients of MPC that are implemented by STOMPC. Up to time $t = k$, we have observed the true state of the system x and provided control input u to it. Using a model of the system, we can predict the future state $\hat{x}_k$ within the control horizon. The evolution of the state depends on the control sequence being applied $\hat{u}_k$, where the applied control action can be switched after each control period. To determine which control sequence to choose, the objective is optimized. Often the objective is to minimize the difference between the state of the system and a reference signal.

Once the optimal control sequence is obtained, the first control action of this sequence is applied. When the end of the control period is reached, the process mentioned above is repeated. At time $t = k + p$, where p is the duration of the control period, the true value of the state of the system $x(k + p)$ is observed,

---

[1] https://github.com/DEIS-Tools/strategoutil.
[2] https://strategoutil.readthedocs.io/en/latest/.
[3] https://doi.org/10.5281/zenodo.6519909.

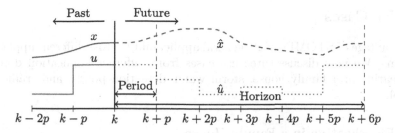

Fig. 1. Conceptual overview of model predictive control. In blue (dashed line) is the continuous evolution of the state in the past x and for the future $\hat{x}$, while red (dotted line) shows the periodically switched control signal in the past u and for the future $\hat{u}$. (Color figure online)

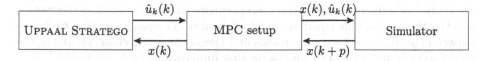

Fig. 2. Global architecture of STOMPC, where the MPC setup starts a new step at time $t = k$. After each step, k is replaced by $k + p$ and everything is repeated.

which, most likely, is different from the predicted state $\hat{x}_k(k + p)$. Repeating the calculation with the new true state $x(k + p)$ might result in a different control sequence $\hat{u}_{k+p}$ than the one calculated before $\hat{u}_k$.

STOMPC implements this MPC scheme using Python, hiding as much details as possible, such that a user can focus more on the application itself. Figure 2 shows the architecture of STOMPC. It provides the component MPC setup, which orchestrates the MPC scheme. At time $t = k$ for some k, it supplies the current true state of the system $x(k)$ to UPPAAL STRATEGO. It does this by inserting the state values into the UPPAAL STRATEGO model. Subsequently, the MPC setup runs UPPAAL STRATEGO with this model to calculate the optimal control strategy. From the report generated by UPPAAL STRATEGO, the MPC setup identifies the calculated control action $\hat{u}_k(k)$ for the next control period.

After this, the MPC setup switches to the simulator. This simulator can be again UPPAAL STRATEGO or an external, domain specific one (see Sect. 3 for examples), or the actual physical system. The MPC setup supplies the simulator with the calculated control action $\hat{u}_k(k)$ for the next control period and, for memory-less simulators, also the last recorded true state $x(k)$ from which the simulator should continue. Subsequently, the simulator returns the true state $x(k+p)$ at the end of the control period. After that, the above procedure repeats until the end of the experiment.

More information on the setup of the tool, including a detailed example, can be found in the tool's documentation[4].

---

[4] https://strategoutil.readthedocs.io.

3 Use Cases

An advantage of STOMPC is its general applicability across different application domains. We now discuss three use cases from different application domains: floorheating in a family house, storm water detention ponds, and traffic light control.

3.1 Floorheating in a Family House

The MPC scheme from Sect. 2 is in collaboration with the company Seluxit applied to controlling floor heating in a family house located in Northern Jutland, Denmark. Figure 3 shows a screenshot of a digital twin of the house, displaying all its 10 rooms and the water pipes supplying heat to the rooms. Each room has its individually controlled target temperature (the upper digits in the rooms) and the thermodynamic equations used in the model consider the heat exchange between the rooms, between the rooms and their outside envelope, as well as the heat exchange from the water pipes passing under rooms.

In each 15 min period, temperature sensors in each room report the current readings to the central control unit. During the following 15 min, the server gathers a 24-h weather forecast and computes an optimal control strategy for the next 75 min using UPPAAL STRATEGO. The computed strategy optimizes the comfort in each room.

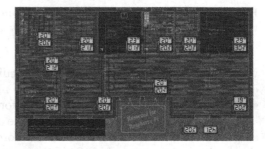

Fig. 3. Digital twin of a floor heating system

Simulations on the digital twin using the UPPAAL STRATEGO online controller (where the real house behavior is replaced by a Simulink model) show an average 40% improvement in comfort, compared to the controller that was used in the house before. As a side effect of the predictive control, the new UPPAAL STRATEGO control saves about 10% of energy. Further details about this concrete application of MPC can be found in [2,11].

3.2 Stormwater Detention Ponds

Stormwater Detention Ponds are critical real-time control assets in urban stormwater management systems. They reduce the considerable hydraulic impact towards the natural stream, as well as avoid significant pollutant loads being discharged. However, only passive control of the stormwater pond outlet valves is currently used in Danish engineering practice.

We implement a co-simulation by combining UPPAAL STRATEGO with the domain specific simulator EPA-SWMM [9], as shown in Fig. 4. EPA-SWMM is an open-source physical-based dynamic rainfall-runoff model that has been implemented for decades in the urban stormwater management [9].

Pyswmm [13], a python interface wrapper, is used for the interfacing of EPA-SWMM with STOMPC. In each 15 min control period, EPA-SWMM extracts the current water level in stormwater ponds, and feeds it towards UPPAAL STRATEGO. From thereon until the end of the upcoming control horizon (48 h), UPPAAL STRATEGO synthesizes the optimal control strategy for the outlet valves taking weather forecasting data into account. Two objectives are involved: guarantee the safe operation of the stormwater pond without any overflow and maximize the sedimentation process to

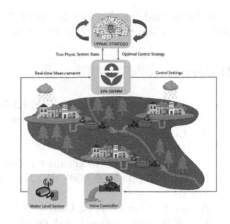

Fig. 4. Digital twin of an urban stormwater management system

improve the water quality. Our approach increased the control performance by 22%. Further details can be found in [8].

3.3 Traffic Light Control

The application of MPC is widespread in the domain of traffic control. Recently UPPAAL STRATEGO has been successfully used to minimize the delays, queue lengths, number of stops, and fuel consumption of vehicles traveling on the arterial street Hobrovej in Aalborg simulated in VISSIM [6]. The street consists of 4 signalized intersections as shown in Fig. 5. The original traffic light controllers are pre-timed or detector time-gap based.

Every second UPPAAL STRATEGO is called to solve a traffic light configuration sequence planning problem that minimizes the total intersection delay. The vehicle information communicated to UPPAAL STRATEGO are the estimated times of arrival extracted from VISSIM's area sensors for each vehicle within 200m of the

Fig. 5. Intersections optimized by UPPAAL STRATEGO at Hobrovej, Aalborg

intersection. The first step in the resulting optimal control sequence is then sent back to VISSIM. Compared to the original control, and considering an intersection with smallest improvements, the described MPC approach manages to reduce the delays by 27%, queue lengths by 42%, number of stops by 20% and fuel consumption by 19%.

In the original paper the data exchange between UPPAAL STRATEGO and VISSIM was established using a Python script. STOMPC can with minimal adjustments wrap the complexity of the communication between those two pieces of software and let the user focus on the more high-level problems such as the definition of input data, objective function, and MPC parameters.

References

1. Abadi, M., Lamport, L., Wolper, P.: Realizable and unrealizable specifications of reactive systems. In: Ausiello, G., Dezani-Ciancaglini, M., Della Rocca, S.R. (eds.) ICALP 1989. LNCS, vol. 372, pp. 1–17. Springer, Heidelberg (1989). https://doi.org/10.1007/BFb0035748

2. Agesen, M., et al.: Toolchain for user-centered intelligent floor heating control. In: IECON, pp. 5296–5301. IEEE (2016). https://doi.org/10.1109/IECON.2016.7794040

3. Ashok, P., Křetínský, J., Larsen, K.G., Le Coënt, A., Taankvist, J.H., Weininger, M.: SOS: safe, optimal and small strategies for hybrid Markov decision processes. In: Parker, D., Wolf, V. (eds.) QEST 2019. LNCS, vol. 11785, pp. 147–164. Springer, Cham (2019). https://doi.org/10.1007/978-3-030-30281-8_9

4. Camacho, E.F., Alba, C.B.: Model Predictive Control. Springer, Heidelberg (2013)

5. David, A., Jensen, P.G., Larsen, K.G., Mikučionis, M., Taankvist, J.H.: UPPAAL STRATEGO. In: Baier, C., Tinelli, C. (eds.) TACAS 2015. LNCS, vol. 9035, pp. 206–211. Springer, Heidelberg (2015). https://doi.org/10.1007/978-3-662-46681-0_16

6. Eriksen, A., Lahrmann, H., Larsen, K., Taankvist, J.: Controlling signalized intersections using machine learning. Transp. Res. Proc. **48**, 987–997 (2020). https://doi.org/10.1016/j.trpro.2020.08.127

7. García, C.E., Prett, D.M., Morari, M.: Model predictive control: theory and practice - a survey. Automatica **25**(3), 335–348 (1989). https://doi.org/10.1016/0005-1098(89)90002-2

8. Goorden, M.A., Larsen, K.G., Nielsen, J.E., Nielsen, T.D., Rasmussen, M.R., Srba, J.: Learning safe and optimal control strategies for storm water detention ponds. IFAC-PapersOnLine **54**(5), 13–18 (2021). https://doi.org/10.1016/j.ifacol.2021.08.467

9. Huber, W.C., Rossman, L.A., Dickinson, R.E.: EPA storm water management model, SWMM5. Watershed Models **338**, 359 (2005)

10. Jaeger, M., Jensen, P.G., Guldstrand Larsen, K., Legay, A., Sedwards, S., Taankvist, J.H.: Teaching stratego to play ball: optimal synthesis for continuous space MDPs. In: Chen, Y.-F., Cheng, C.-H., Esparza, J. (eds.) ATVA 2019. LNCS, vol. 11781, pp. 81–97. Springer, Cham (2019). https://doi.org/10.1007/978-3-030-31784-3_5

11. Larsen, K.G., Mikučionis, M., Muñiz, M., Srba, J., Taankvist, J.H.: Online and compositional learning of controllers with application to floor heating. In: Chechik, M., Raskin, J.-F. (eds.) TACAS 2016. LNCS, vol. 9636, pp. 244–259. Springer, Heidelberg (2016). https://doi.org/10.1007/978-3-662-49674-9_14

12. Larsen, K.G., Mikučionis, M., Taankvist, J.H.: Safe and optimal adaptive cruise control. In: Meyer, R., Platzer, A., Wehrheim, H. (eds.) Correct System Design. LNCS, vol. 9360, pp. 260–277. Springer, Cham (2015). https://doi.org/10.1007/978-3-319-23506-6_17

13. McDonnell, B.E., Ratliff, K., Tryby, M.E., Wu, J.J.X., Mullapudi, A.: PySWMM: the python interface to stormwater management model (SWMM). J. Open Sour. Softw. **5**(52), 2292 (2020). https://doi.org/10.21105/joss.02292

14. Pnueli, A., Rosner, R.: On the synthesis of an asynchronous reactive module. In: Ausiello, G., Dezani-Ciancaglini, M., Della Rocca, S.R. (eds.) ICALP 1989. LNCS, vol. 372, pp. 652–671. Springer, Heidelberg (1989). https://doi.org/10.1007/BFb0035790

15. Ramadge, P.J., Wonham, W.M.: Supervisory control of a class of discrete event processes. SIAM J. Control. Optim. **25**(1), 206–230 (1987)

Synthesis and Repair

Synthesis of Parametric Hybrid Automata from Time Series

Miriam García Soto[1]([✉])[iD], Thomas A. Henzinger[2][iD], and Christian Schilling[3][iD]

[1] Complutense University of Madrid, Madrid, Spain
miriamgs@ucm.es
[2] IST Austria, Klosterneuburg, Austria
tah@ist.ac.at
[3] Aalborg University, Aalborg, Denmark
christianms@cs.aau.dk

Abstract. We propose an algorithmic approach for synthesizing linear hybrid automata from time-series data. Unlike existing approaches, our approach provides a whole family of models with the same discrete structure but different dynamics. Each model in the family is guaranteed to capture the input data up to a precision error ε, in the following sense: For each time series, the model contains an execution that is ε-close to the data points. Our construction allows to effectively choose a model from this family with minimal precision error ε. We demonstrate the algorithm's efficiency and its ability to find precise models in two case studies.

Keywords: Synthesis · Hybrid automata · Time series

1 Introduction

Mathematical models are ubiquitous across all sciences [11], from systems biology [23] to epidemiology [43] to cyber-physical systems [25]. The construction of such models is a central challenge in science [38]. One main benefit of *mathematical* models is the clearly defined semantics, which make these models amenable to automatic analysis (such as simulation [9,22] and verification [1,6,34]). Another main benefit that is usually desired is interpretability for high-level reasoning.

Hybrid automata [2,17] are a prominent class of interpretable models with mixed continuous and discrete behavior. They are particularly suitable in biological domains [27,39], where systems typically evolve continuously but are subject to internal and external events, and in cyber-physical domains [21], where physical entities interact with digital devices. In a nutshell, the evolution of a hybrid automaton follows a differential equation associated with one of several locations (or modes), until a discrete event leads to a different location.

In this paper we address the problem of synthesizing a linear hybrid automaton (LHA) [2] from a set of time series. The informal goal of model synthesis is

A. Bouajjani et al. (Eds.): ATVA 2022, LNCS 13505, pp. 337–353, 2022.
https://doi.org/10.1007/978-3-031-19992-9_22

that the model *captures* the data well. What it means to "capture well" is difficult to formalize. Here we adopt the recent notion of ε *-capturing* from García et al. [12,13], which requires that, for each time series in the input data, the LHA must expose an execution that stays ε-close to all data points (see Fig. 2 for an illustration). In [12,13], the value of ε is fixed in the problem input. Here we consider ε a parameter, which we associate with a *family of parametric models*: LHA whose continuous dynamics are not fixed yet. Each possible fixation of the continuous dynamics corresponds to an instantiated LHA. All instantiated LHA associated with a concrete value of ε have the property that they ε-capture the data. We can then effectively search for an ε-capturing LHA with the minimal value of ε, whose behavior intuitively best resembles the data.

Our algorithm consists of two phases. In the first phase we synthesize the discrete structure of the LHA by fixing the set of locations and mapping data points in the time series to the locations. We propose an algorithm to obtain this mapping based on clustering. In the second phase we construct the parameter space, which is a polyhedron that associates ε to all possible instantiated LHA (i.e., fixations of continuous dynamics) that ε-capture the data. We select a concrete LHA by minimizing the value of ε, for which we solve a linear program.

We evaluate the algorithm in two case studies. In the first case study we investigate the scalability in terms of the different input parameters; we can synthesize a seven-dimensional model with 15 locations from 12,000 data points in 15 min, which shows that the algorithm is applicable in practice. In the second case study we use the algorithm to synthesize a model for a biological system (regulation of a cell cycle) in less than half a minute.

Related Work. Synthesizing models is known to different communities as *system identification*, *process mining*, or *model learning*. Models that are akin to hybrid automata have been studied extensively in control theory; while the main aim in control theory is to find a controller for a system, which is outside the scope of the present paper, there is still a large body of works on system identification [14,33]. Many of these approaches focus on input-output models, such as autoregressive exogenous (ARX) models and in particular the switched (SARX) [16,32] and piecewise (PWARX) [5,8,19,30,37] versions, and focus on single-input single-output (SISO) systems, but there are also works on multiple-input multiple-output (MIMO) systems [3,18,42]. SARX and PWARX models can be seen as restricted linear hybrid automata where the locations form a state-space partition and the switching behavior is deterministic. This allows to reduce the synthesis problem to a parameter-optimization problem. The second phase of our algorithm also uses a reduction to parameter optimization, but the parameter space is different and our model class is more general.

In computer science, several approaches learn hybrid automata from input-output traces or time series. Similar to our approach, the works in [4,29] first use clustering to learn the discrete structure, but they employ different techniques, such as Angluin's algorithm for learning a finite automaton, and do not provide minimality guarantees for the result. Other approaches construct automata whose discrete structure is acyclic [31] respectively cyclic [15], or a deterministic model with urgent transitions [24]. The work in [40] exhaustively constructs all possible models for optimizing a cost function, while in our approach the enumeration is only symbolic and we choose a model by solving a linear program, which scales favorably. A recent work shows that timed automata can be effectively learned from traces with a genetic algorithm [41]; learning timed automata has orthogonal challenges: they form a subclass of LHA where all variables are clocks with constant rate 1 and hence no continuous dynamics need to be learned, but the discrete dynamics are more complex than in this work. The work in [44] provides a framework for identifying deterministic models with affine dynamics from input-output traces, while we identify nondeterministic models. Our works in [12,13] proposed the notion of ε-capturing that we adopt here; those works synthesize a model from single traces online, but the algorithms are not scalable for offline usage of realistic dimension and size.

Outline. In Sect. 2 we fix the terminology. In Sect. 3 we formalize the synthesis problem and describe our solution on a high level. The low-level descriptions of the two phases of the algorithm follow in Sect. 4 and Sect. 5. We evaluate the algorithm in Sect. 6 and conclude in Sect. 7.

2   Terminology

Euclidean Sets. We write $\mathbf{x}$ for points $(x_1, \ldots, x_n)$ in $\mathbb{R}^n$ and consider the infinity norm $\|\mathbf{x}\| = \max_{x_i} |x_i|$. The *ball* of radius $\varepsilon \in \mathbb{R}_{\geq 0}$ around a point $\mathbf{x} \in \mathbb{R}^n$ is $\mathcal{B}_\varepsilon(\mathbf{x}) = \{\mathbf{y} \in \mathbb{R}^n : \|\mathbf{x} - \mathbf{y}\| \leq \varepsilon\}$. The ε-*bloating* of $\mathcal{X} \subseteq \mathbb{R}^n$ is $\mathcal{X} \oplus \mathcal{B}_\varepsilon(\mathbf{0}) = \{\mathbf{x} + \mathbf{y} : \mathbf{x} \in \mathcal{X}, \|\mathbf{y}\| \leq \varepsilon\}$. A *polyhedron* over $\mathbb{R}^n$ is a finite intersection of *constraints* $\mathbf{a}^T \mathbf{x} \leq b$ where $\mathbf{a} \in \mathbb{R}^n$ and $b \in \mathbb{R}$. Let $\mathbb{P}_n$ be the set of all n-dimensional polyhedra. An *interval* is written $[a, b] = \{x : a \leq x \leq b\} \subseteq \mathbb{R}$.

Functions. Given a function $f : A \to B$, let $\mathtt{dom}(f) \subseteq A$ denote its domain. Let $f\lfloor_D$ denote the restriction of f to set $D \subseteq \mathtt{dom}(f)$. A continuous function $f : [0, T] \to \mathbb{R}^n$ is a *piecewise-linear (PWL) function* with k pieces if there exists a triple $(I, M, \mathbf{x}_0)$ where I is a k-tuple of consecutive time intervals $[t_0, t_1], [t_1, t_2], \ldots, [t_{k-1}, t_k]$ with $[0, T] = \bigcup_{1 \leq i \leq k} [t_{i-1}, t_i]$, M is a k-tuple of slope vectors $\mathbf{m}_i \in \mathbb{R}^n$, and $\mathbf{x}_0 \in \mathbb{R}^n$ is the initial state $f(t_0) = \mathbf{x}_0$, such that each $f\lfloor_{[t_{i-1}, t_i]}$ is a solution of the differential equation $\dot{\mathbf{x}}(t) = \mathbf{m}_i$, for all $i = 1, \ldots, k$. We refer to the line segments $f\lfloor_{[t_{i-1}, t_i]}$ as the *pieces* of f. A *time-series* $s : D \to \mathbb{R}^n$ maps time points t from a finite set $D \subseteq \mathbb{R}_{\geq 0}$ to data points $s(t)$. There is a one-to-one correspondence between PWL functions and time series: A PWL function f over $I = ([t_0, t_1], [t_1, t_2], \ldots, [t_{k-1}, t_k])$ induces a time series as the restriction $s = f\lfloor_D$ to time points $D = \{t_0, t_1, \ldots, t_k\}$, and s induces f as the piecewise-linear interpolation of the data points. Thus we may refer to, e.g., the pieces of a time series. The *distance* between a PWL function f and a time series s with $\mathtt{dom}(f\lfloor_{\mathtt{dom}(s)}) = \mathtt{dom}(s)$ is $d(f, s) = \max_{t \in \mathtt{dom}(s)} \|f(t) - s(t)\|$.

Linear Hybrid Automata. An n-dimensional *linear hybrid automaton* (LHA) [2,17] is a tuple $\mathcal{H} = (Loc, E, Flow, Inv, Grd)$, where 1) *Loc* is the finite set of locations, 2) $E \subseteq Loc \times Loc$ is the transition relation, 3) $Flow : Loc \to \mathbb{R}^n$ is the flow function, 4) $Inv : Loc \to \mathbb{P}_n$ is the invariant function, and 5) $Grd : E \to \mathbb{P}_n$ is the guard function. Our LHA model does not have assignments along the transitions and is also called switched linear system [26]. We also consider partially defined hybrid automata without flows, invariants, or guards assigned. This *discrete structure* $\mathcal{H}_d = (Loc, E)$ only consists of locations and transitions.

The semantics of LHA are described by the set of executions. A *state* of an LHA is a pair $(\ell, \mathbf{x})$ of a location $\ell \in Loc$ and a point $\mathbf{x} \in Inv(\ell)$ in the invariant. An *execution* σ of an LHA evolves continuously according to the flow function in each location. The execution starts in some state $(\ell_1, \mathbf{x}_1)$ and the continuous evolution follows the constant differential equation $\dot{\mathbf{x}} = Flow(\ell_1)$ while satisfying the invariant $Inv(\ell_1)$ for some dwell time $\delta \in \mathbb{R}_{\geq 0}$. The execution can instantaneously switch locations, from a state $(\ell_1, \mathbf{x}_2)$ to another state $(\ell_2, \mathbf{x}_2)$, if there is a transition $(\ell_1, \ell_2) \in E$ and the guard $Grd(\ell_1, \ell_2)$ contains $\mathbf{x}_2$. The projection of an execution σ to the second component is a PWL function, which we denote by σ_π. We use the following compact notation for executions, where $\delta_i \in \mathbb{R}_{\geq 0}$ (for $i \geq 1$) denotes the duration of a dwell action and *jmp* denotes a switch:

$$\sigma \equiv (\ell_1, \mathbf{x}_1) \xrightarrow{\delta_1} (\ell_1, \mathbf{x}_2) \xrightarrow{jmp} (\ell_2, \mathbf{x}_2) \xrightarrow{\delta_2} (\ell_2, \mathbf{x}_3) \xrightarrow{jmp} (\ell_3, \mathbf{x}_3) \cdots$$

3 Synthesis of ε-Close Linear Hybrid Automata

In this section we formalize the synthesis problem that we address in this paper and give a high-level overview of our approach to solve it. Given a time series, we want to construct an LHA that captures the data up to a given precision. We first formalize the notion of capturing.

Definition 1 (ε-**capturing** [13]). *Given a time series s and a value $\varepsilon \in \mathbb{R}_{\geq 0}$, we say that an LHA $\mathcal{H}$ ε -captures s if there exists an execution σ of $\mathcal{H}$ such that $d(\sigma_\pi, s) \leq \varepsilon$. We also say that s and σ_π (resp. s and σ) are ε -close.*

Our goal is to construct an LHA that ε-captures several time series.

Problem 1 (ε-close synthesis [13]). Given a finite set of time series $\mathcal{S}$ and a value $\varepsilon \in \mathbb{R}_{\geq 0}$, construct an LHA $\mathcal{H}$ that ε-captures each s in $\mathcal{S}$.

As we observed in [13], it is straightforward to find a solution to the problem even for $\varepsilon = 0$ by simply introducing a fresh location for each piece of the time series. Such a model does not aggregate nor generalize the information in the data and is hence of little use. To obtain a reasonable model, one needs to add another bound to the problem, e.g., by fixing the discrete structure.

We address this observation in a two-phase algorithm. In the first phase we fix the discrete structure $\mathcal{H}_d$ of the LHA, where we try to reuse the locations for multiple time series (or pieces therein). In the second phase we instantiate the model for the smallest possible value of ε under the given discrete structure. Thus in this paper we consider a synthesis problem where we do not fix the value of ε and rather find a sufficiently small value for ε automatically.

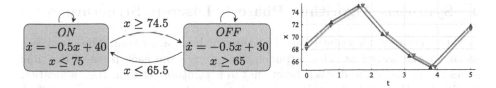

Fig. 1. Left: A hybrid automaton. Right: Two time series (triangle markers) obtained from sampling two executions of the automaton, and induced PWL functions.

Problem 2 (ε-minimal synthesis). Given a finite set of time series $\mathcal{S}$ and a discrete structure $\mathcal{H}_d$, find the minimal value $\varepsilon \in \mathbb{R}_{\geq 0}$ and an instantiation $\mathcal{H}$ of $\mathcal{H}_d$ such that $\mathcal{H}$ ε-captures each s in $\mathcal{S}$.

3.1 Synthesis Algorithm

In the next two sections we describe our algorithm to solve the above synthesis problem, but first we give a high-level overview of the algorithm. Our algorithm computes a parametric family of LHA that all ε-capture the given data. The LHA share the same discrete structure but differ in the continuous dynamics. Since ε itself is a parameter of that construction, we can then choose an LHA with a minimal value for ε (which is not necessarily unique) from that family.

Our goal is that the final LHA has an ε-close execution for each time series. To simplify the theoretical presentation, we will use the following conceptual view on our algorithm. Instead of synthesizing an LHA directly, we synthesize ε-close executions. These executions then induce an LHA.

As mentioned, our algorithm proceeds in two phases. In the first phase we fix the discrete structure of the executions (and thus of the resulting LHA). In the second phase we construct the space of continuous dynamics to be assigned to the locations, depending on the value ε. For LHA, this space is a polyhedron, which we call the *flow polyhedron*. We then choose concrete continuous dynamics from the flow polyhedron to instantiate concrete executions (and thus an LHA). We explain each step of the algorithm using the following running example.

Example 1 (running example). We consider two time series in one dimension:

$$t_1 = \quad (0.00, \quad 0.76, \quad 1.59, \quad 2.32, \quad 3.15, \quad 3.79, \quad 5.00)$$
$$d_1 = \quad (68.91, \quad 72.41, \quad 75.00, \quad 70.44, \quad 66.90, \quad 65.00, \quad 71.81)$$

$$t_2 = \quad (0.0, \quad 0.75, \quad 1.61, \quad 2.33, \quad 3.16, \quad 3.76, \quad 5.00)$$
$$d_2 = \quad (68.16, \quad 71.85, \quad 74.70, \quad 70.22, \quad 66.75, \quad 65.00, \quad 71.92)$$

We obtained the time series from two random trajectories of a hybrid automaton modeling a simple thermostat controller, all given in Fig. 1. Note that the original continuous dynamics are described by an affine differential equation, which cannot be expressed with an LHA. (We round all numbers to two digits, which explains small inconsistencies over the course of this running example.)   ◁

4   Synthesis Algorithm, Phase 1: Discrete Structure

In this section we describe Phase 1 of the synthesis algorithm. The input is a finite set of time series. The output is a mapping from each piece of the time series (resp. the induced PWL functions) to a *symbolic location* (i.e., a location label). Together with the order of the pieces in the time series, as we explain below, this mapping already fixes the discrete structure $\mathcal{H}_d$ of the LHA.

4.1   Simplification of the Time Series

In the first step of our algorithm, we preprocess the time series by removing some data points for better stability of the second step (we explain this connection later). Note that for Phase 2 we again use the original time series, so correctness is not affected. The goal is to merge consecutive pieces in the time series with similar slopes, i.e., such that the linear interpolation is a good approximation. In our implementation we use a variant of the Ramer-Douglas-Peucker algorithm [7, 36] where we consider time as another dimension. We shortly recall this algorithm but refer to the literature for details. Following a divide-and-conquer scheme, the algorithm starts with only the first and last point of the time series, connects them with a line segment, finds the point $\mathbf{x}$ with the largest distance from the line segment, and, unless this distance is small enough, repeats the process recursively for the corresponding two parts before and after $\mathbf{x}$.

4.2   Assignment of Symbolic Locations

The goal of the first phase is to determine the discrete structure $\mathcal{H}_d$ of the resulting LHA. For each time series with p pieces we synthesize a corresponding *symbolic execution* of the prospective LHA. These are executions that do not yet contain information about the continuous state, but the discrete state is already determined, i.e., we fix the sequence of visited locations $\ell_1, \ldots, \ell_p$ together with the points in time when the execution switches to a new location. (Here we restrict ourselves to switching in synchrony with the time series.) Thus each symbolic execution consists of a (timed) sequence of symbolic locations. It is easy to see that, by ignoring time, these sequences induce the discrete structure $\mathcal{H}_d$ of an LHA: the set of locations is the union of all locations occurring in the sequences, and there is a transition for each consecutive pair of locations. Formally, for a symbolic execution associated with a time series with p pieces, the discrete structure $\mathcal{H}_d = (Loc, E)$ is given by $Loc = \{\ell_1, \ldots, \ell_p\}$ and $E = \{(\ell_i, \ell_{i+1}) : i = 1, \ldots, p-1\}$, and the generalization to sets of symbolic executions consists of the union of these locations and transitions.

Given a time series with p pieces and a set of symbolic locations $\{\ell_1, \ldots, \ell_\lambda\}$, a symbolic execution as described above is merely a mapping from the pieces to location labels, which we call $\mathcal{M} : \{1, \ldots, p\} \to \{1, \ldots, \lambda\}$. Our algorithm is parametric in the concrete way to obtain this mapping. Typically we are interested in finding an LHA with a small number of locations. Thus the implicit requirement for the mapping is to share locations for multiple pieces.

Algorithm 1. Assignment of a symbolic location to each piece of a set of time series. Line 1 is optional and can be implemented with the identity. Line 2 can be implemented with k-means, which can also provide a good value for λ $(= k)$ if not specified in the input (as described in Sect. 4.2).

Input: A set of time series $\mathcal{S} = \{s_1, \ldots, s_r\}$ and optionally a number of locations λ
Output: A mapping from the pieces to symbolic locations and a number of locations
1: $\mathcal{S}' := \text{simplify}(\mathcal{S})$ {see Sect. 4.1}
2: $\mathcal{M}, \lambda := \text{assign\_location\_labels\_to\_pieces}(\mathcal{S}', \lambda)$ {see Sect. 4.2}
3: **return** $\mathcal{M}, \lambda$

In our implementation we obtain the mapping using a variant of the k-means clustering algorithm [28]. The input to the clustering algorithm are the slopes of the PWL functions induced by the time series. The k-means algorithm requires to specify upfront the number of clusters k, which corresponds to the number of locations in our setting. If the intended number of locations is already known in advance, this algorithm can be used directly. Otherwise, to find a good value of k automatically, we use a common refinement loop by starting with some value for k (e.g., $k = 1$) and then increasing k until the clustering error (which is defined as the sum of the squared Euclidean distance of each point to its associated cluster center) does not decrease substantially anymore.

The k-means algorithm is sensitive to the initial choice of the cluster centers. The preprocessing step proposed in Sect. 4.1 increases the stability in this regard. As initial candidates for the cluster centers we choose the first k slopes induced by the simplified time series. This choice results in candidates that are sufficiently different in practice and thus k-means yields more robust clusters.

We summarize the main steps of Phase 1 in Algorithm 1.

Example 2 (cont'd) . The input to the clustering algorithm are the slope values of the two time series. In the table below we list the clustering cost for different numbers of clusters k, together with the relative improvement compared to $k-1$:

Clusters (k)	1	2	3	4	5	6	7	8
Cost	259.76	17.07	11.80	2.46	0.78	0.09	0.04	0.01
Rel. [%]	–	0.93	0.31	0.79	0.68	0.89	0.60	0.61

The table suggests that good values for k are 2, 4, or 6. To obtain a small model, here we settle for $k = 2$ locations. The associated (one-dimensional) cluster centers (representing slopes) are 4.53 and -4.46. For both time series, the assigned clusters are $(1, 1, 2, 2, 2, 1)$, corresponding to the symbolic location ℓ_1 for the pieces 1, 2, 6 and symbolic location ℓ_2 for the other three pieces. $\lhd$

5   Synthesis Algorithm, Phase 2: Continuous Dynamics

In this section we describe Phase 2 of the synthesis algorithm. The input is a finite set of time series together with a discrete structure $\mathcal{H}_d$ obtained in Phase 1, which is represented by the mapping $\mathcal{M}$ assigning a symbolic location to each piece of the time series. The output is an LHA $\mathcal{H}$ and a value for ε such that $\mathcal{H}$ ε-captures the time series. As mentioned before, we describe how to obtain an ε-close *corresponding execution* for each time series.

5.1   Construction of the Flow Polyhedron

In the first step, we construct the flow polyhedron P, which represents the set of all possible continuous dynamics such that the corresponding executions are ε-close to the time series. Here ε itself is a dimension of P. For technical reasons, we construct a new flow polyhedron for each time series.

Assume that we have n-dimensional data in the form of r time series and we want to synthesize an LHA with λ locations. Say that we consider a time series with p pieces. Then P is a polyhedron with $\lambda n + rn + 1$ dimensions. The first λn dimensions represent the location slopes. The next rn dimensions represent the coordinates of the initial states $\mathbf{x}_0^{(j)}$ of the j-th execution. (These $\mathbf{x}_0^{(j)}$ are auxiliary dimensions which we are not interested in.) The last dimension is ε.

Next we describe the constraints of P. These constraints express that the distance between the time series and the execution is less than ε (and thus the execution ε-captures the time series). We need to express the symbolic value of the execution, $\mathbf{x}_k$, at each time point t_k of the time series. Let $\mathbf{q}_k$ be the k-th data point of the time series, starting at $k = 0$. For each data point we have $2n$ constraints (i.e., $2n(p+1)$ constraints in total) to express the requirement $\mathbf{x}_k \in \mathcal{B}_\varepsilon(\mathbf{q}_k)$. In $n = 1$ dimension, for each k we express the requirement with the two constraints $x_k - \varepsilon \leq q_k$ and $x_k + \varepsilon \geq q_k$. In $n > 1$ dimensions we have such constraints in each dimension.

It remains to explain how to express the term x_k. For $k = 0$ we represent $\mathbf{x}_0$ with the dedicated variables $x_0^{(\cdot)}$. For $k > 0$ we rewrite x_k using the following identity: $x_k = x_0 + \sum_{j=1}^{k}(t_j - t_{j-1})m^{(j)}$. The time points t_j are known constants and the $m^{(j)}$ are the slope variables for the j-th piece (recall that we have associated the pieces with locations in advance).

Below we formalize the flow polyhedron for $r = 1$ time series.

Definition 2. *Given a time series s with p pieces and an associated mapping $\mathcal{M} : \{1, \ldots, p\} \to \{1, \ldots, \lambda\}$, the* flow polyhedron P_s *is defined as*

$$\{(\mathbf{m}_1, \ldots, \mathbf{m}_\lambda, \mathbf{x}_0, \varepsilon) \in \mathbb{R}^{\lambda n + n} \times \mathbb{R}_{\geq 0} \mid \mathbf{x}_0 \in \mathcal{B}_\varepsilon(s(t_0)),$$
$$\mathbf{x}_0 + (t_1 - t_0)\mathbf{m}_{\mathcal{M}(1)} \in \mathcal{B}_\varepsilon(s(t_1)),$$
$$\mathbf{x}_0 + (t_1 - t_0)\mathbf{m}_{\mathcal{M}(1)} + (t_2 - t_1)\mathbf{m}_{\mathcal{M}(2)} \in \mathcal{B}_\varepsilon(s(t_2)),$$
$$\vdots$$
$$\mathbf{x}_0 + (t_1 - t_0)\mathbf{m}_{\mathcal{M}(1)} + \ldots + (t_p - t_{p-1})\mathbf{m}_{\mathcal{M}(p)} \in \mathcal{B}_\varepsilon(s(t_p))\}.$$

Example 3 (cont'd). Our example has $n = 1$ dimension, $\lambda = 2$ locations, and $r = 2$ time series. The flow polyhedron consists of five variables $(m_1, m_2, x_0^{(1)}, x_0^{(2)}, \varepsilon)$. Here m_1 and m_2 represent the slopes of the two locations, $x_0^{(1)}$ and $x_0^{(2)}$ represent the initial state of the first resp. second execution, and ε represents the allowed distance between the time series and the executions. Below we show the 14 constraints for the first execution:

$$
\begin{array}{ll}
x_0^{(1)} - \varepsilon \le 68.91 & -x_0^{(1)} - \varepsilon \le -68.91 \\
0.76m_1 \quad + x_0^{(1)} - \varepsilon \le 72.41 & -0.76m_1 \quad -x_0^{(1)} - \varepsilon \le -72.41 \\
1.59m_1 \quad + x_0^{(1)} - \varepsilon \le 75.00 & -1.59m_1 \quad -x_0^{(1)} - \varepsilon \le -75.00 \\
1.59m_1 + 0.72m_2 + x_0^{(1)} - \varepsilon \le 70.44 & -1.59m_1 - 0.72m_2 - x_0^{(1)} - \varepsilon \le -70.44 \\
1.59m_1 + 1.55m_2 + x_0^{(1)} - \varepsilon \le 66.90 & -1.59m_1 - 1.55m_2 - x_0^{(1)} - \varepsilon \le -66.90 \\
1.59m_1 + 2.20m_2 + x_0^{(1)} - \varepsilon \le 65.00 & -1.59m_1 - 2.20m_2 - x_0^{(1)} - \varepsilon \le -65.00 \\
2.80m_1 + 2.20m_2 + x_0^{(1)} - \varepsilon \le 71.81 & -2.80m_1 - 2.20m_2 - x_0^{(1)} - \varepsilon \le -71.81 \triangleleft
\end{array}
$$

Note that, for multiple time series, each flow polyhedron only constrains n dimensions of the rn dimensions reserved for the initial states $x_0^{(\cdot)}$. The need for the separate dimensions will become clear when we aggregate the different flow polyhedra in the next step. Any feasible point inside the polyhedron P represents a concrete execution in an LHA that ε-captures the time series. We formalize this statement after defining the corresponding LHA in the next step.

5.2 The Common Solution Space

In the first phase we implicitly fixed the discrete evolution of the executions, which also induced the discrete structure of the LHA we want to synthesize. In the previous step we obtained the flow polyhedra P_s, one for each time series s. In the next steps we combine these results to obtain concrete executions by assigning the continuous states. The concrete executions also induce the final LHA, i.e., we assign continuous dynamics, invariants, and guards.

Since we want to obtain one LHA to ε-capture *all* time series, we need to find compatible values for the dynamics and ε. For that purpose we can just intersect all flow polyhedra. Let $P_{\mathcal{H}} = \bigcap_{s \in \mathcal{S}} P_s$ be the polyhedron resulting from this intersection. Note that, since we used disjoint dimensions for the $\mathbf{x}_0^{(\cdot)}$ for different executions, the initial states are not shared in $P_{\mathcal{H}}$. (We note that intersecting polyhedra in constraint representation is a constant-time operation.)

5.3 Choice of Minimizing Parameters

Now we have to choose *any* feasible point $\mathbf{p}$ in $P_{\mathcal{H}}$. We argue that the most interesting points are those that minimize ε, since they correspond to executions that are closest to the original data. (In applications where further constraints should be considered, other choices are possible.) Minimizing a polyhedron in the dimension of ε means to solve the corresponding linear program with objective function ε, which is efficient in practice. We remark that $P_{\mathcal{H}}$ is bounded in the

---

Algorithm 2. Synthesis algorithm.

Input: A set of time series $\mathcal{S} = \{s_1, \ldots, s_r\}$, a number of locations λ, and a mapping
  from the pieces of each time series to symbolic locations $\mathcal{M}$
Output: An LHA $\mathcal{H}$ and a minimal value ε such that $\mathcal{H}$ ε-captures all elements of $\mathcal{S}$
  1: **for** $s \in \mathcal{S}$ **do**
  2:    $P_s :=$ flow_polyhedron$(s, \mathcal{M}, \lambda)$ {see Sect. 5.1}
  3: **end for**
  4: $P_\mathcal{H} := \bigcap_{s \in \mathcal{S}}^r P_s$ {see Sect. 5.2}
  5: *slopes*, $\varepsilon :=$ choose_minimizing_point$(P_\mathcal{H})$ {see Sect. 5.3}
  6: $\mathcal{H} :=$ construct_automaton$(\mathcal{S}, \mathcal{M}, slopes, \varepsilon)$ {see Sect. 5.4}
  7: **return** $\mathcal{H}, \varepsilon$

---

dimension of ε from below by 0, so this minimization always returns a proper solution $\mathbf{p} = (\mathbf{m}_1, \ldots, \mathbf{m}_\lambda, \mathbf{x}_0^{(1)}, \ldots, \mathbf{x}_0^{(r)}, \varepsilon)$. The point $\mathbf{p}$ contains a number for each dimension. The first λn numbers are the slope values for the locations, in the order they have been specified. The next rn numbers are the values of $\mathbf{x}_0^{(\cdot)}$ for the different executions (note again that we do not need these numbers). The last number is the corresponding value for ε.

5.4 Construction of the Final LHA

Next we describe, for a given time series s_i over time instants $t_0, t_1, \ldots, t_p$, the execution that is induced by the above point $\mathbf{p}$. Let $\mathbf{m}_1, \ldots, \mathbf{m}_\lambda$ be the slopes taken from the point and $\mathcal{M}$ be the mapping from the pieces of s_i to the associated location (e.g., $\ell_{\mathcal{M}(1)}$ is the location for the first piece, with slope $\mathbf{m}_{\mathcal{M}(1)}$) obtained in Algorithm 1. The execution is a PWL function whose pieces have the same duration as the pieces of s_i. As defined before, the execution starts at $\mathbf{x}_0 = \mathbf{x}_0^{(i)}$ and the end point of the k-th piece is $\mathbf{x}_k = \mathbf{x}_0 + \sum_{j=1}^p (t_j - t_{j-1}) \mathbf{m}_{\mathcal{M}(j)}$.

$$(\ell_{\mathcal{M}(1)}, \mathbf{x}_0) \xrightarrow{t_1 - t_0} (\ell_{\mathcal{M}(1)}, \mathbf{x}_0 + (t_1 - t_0)\mathbf{m}_{\mathcal{M}(1)})$$
$$\xrightarrow{jmp} (\ell_{\mathcal{M}(2)}, \mathbf{x}_0 + (t_1 - t_0)\mathbf{m}_{\mathcal{M}(1)})$$
$$\xrightarrow{t_2 - t_1} (\ell_{\mathcal{M}(2)}, \mathbf{x}_0 + (t_1 - t_0)\mathbf{m}_{\mathcal{M}(1)} + (t_2 - t_1)\mathbf{m}_{\mathcal{M}(2)})$$
$$\vdots$$
$$\xrightarrow{t_p - t_{p-1}} (\ell_{\mathcal{M}(p)}, \mathbf{x}_0 + \sum_{j=1}^p (t_j - t_{j-1})\mathbf{m}_{\mathcal{M}(j)})$$

We have not yet described the invariants and guards of the resulting LHA. We say that a data point in the time series is associated with a location if the preceding or the succeeding piece in the time series is assigned that location in the mapping from Algorithm 1. Similarly, a data point is associated with the transition (ℓ_i, ℓ_j) if the preceding piece is associated with ℓ_i and the succeeding piece is associated with ℓ_j. A sufficient condition for our construction to be correct is: define the invariant of each location as the ε-bloated convex hull around

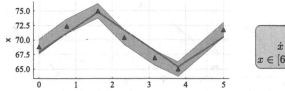 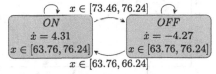

Fig. 2. Left: The first time series (triangle markers) inside an ε-tube (green) and the corresponding induced execution (red), for two locations. Right: The synthesized LHA. (Color figure online)

all data points associated with it, and define the guard of each transition as the ε-bloated union around all data points associated with it. In our implementation we use the ε-bloated interval hull in both cases. That is, we take the smallest box around all data points as defined above and then extend the box in each direction by ε. We summarize the main steps of Phase 2 in Algorithm 2.

Example 4 (cont'd). We intersect the two flow polyhedra and minimize the resulting polyhedron in the dimension of ε to receive the following point: $m_1 = 4.31, m_2 = -4.27, x_0^{(1)} = 67.90, x_0^{(2)} = 67.63, \varepsilon = 1.24$. Thus we have synthesized the following execution for the first time series: $(\ell_1, 67.90) \xrightarrow{0.76} (\ell_1, 71.18) \xrightarrow{jmp} (\ell_1, 71.18) \xrightarrow{0.84} (\ell_1, 74.80) \xrightarrow{jmp} (\ell_2, 74.80) \xrightarrow{0.72} (\ell_2, 71.72) \xrightarrow{jmp} (\ell_2, 71.72) \xrightarrow{0.83} (\ell_2, 68.18) \xrightarrow{jmp} (\ell_2, 68.18) \xrightarrow{0.64} (\ell_2, 65.44) \xrightarrow{jmp} (\ell_2, 65.44) \xrightarrow{1.21} (\ell_1, 70.66)$. The execution and the final LHA are depicted in Fig. 2. ◁

5.5 Correctness

We show that the algorithm produces an LHA that ε-captures the given data.

Lemma 1. *For every time series s that is input to Algorithm 2, the induced execution ε-captures s, where ε is obtained in Line 5.*

Proof. The constraints of the flow polyhedron P_s corresponding to s enforce that the induced execution is ε-close to all data points of s. This even holds for *any* point in P_s. Since the concrete choice of the point in Line 5 is taken from $P_{\mathcal{H}}$, which is a subset of P_s, the claim follows.

Theorem 1. *The LHA $\mathcal{H}$ synthesized in Algorithm 2 ε-captures all time series, where ε is obtained in Line 5. Furthermore, Algorithm 2 solves Problem 2 in polynomial time.*

Proof. Lemma 1 ensures that the induced executions ε-capture the time series. It remains to show that these induced executions belong to $\mathcal{H}$. This holds by construction of $\mathcal{H}$; we only sketch the main arguments. Each execution follows the slopes of the associated locations. For each location switch there exists a transition in $\mathcal{H}$. The executions always stay in ε-proximity to the data points, and

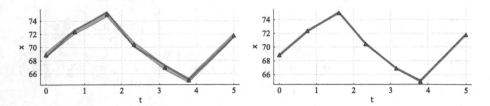

Fig. 3. The first time series (triangle markers) from Fig. 2 inside other ε-tubes (green) and the corresponding induced executions (red). Left: The result obtained for four locations ($\varepsilon = 0.38$). Right: The result obtained for six locations ($\varepsilon = 0.15$). (Color figure online)

hence they stay inside the invariants at all times. Similarly, since the executions change the location at time points of the data, the guards are satisfied. The solution to Problem 2 follows from the minimization of ε in Line 5. For the polynomial complexity, observe that the flow polyhedron's size is polynomial in the input and that the minimization can be implemented polynomially [20].

We remark that the number of locations λ and the sequence of locations obtained from Algorithm 1 influence the quality of the LHA resp. the size of ε but not the validity of the theorem (correctness of Algorithm 2). If these inputs are unsuitably chosen, the algorithm just returns a larger value for ε.

Example 5 (cont'd). Figure 3 shows the synthesized executions and corresponding values of ε for the first time series with $\lambda = 4$ and $\lambda = 6$ locations.   ◁

6   Evaluation

In this section we describe our implementation and present experimental results. Our implementation in the Julia programming language is available at https://github.com/HySynth/HySynthParametric. To generate time series, we implemented a simulator of hybrid automata based on the ODE toolbox Differential-Equations.jl [35]. For polyhedral computations we use LazySets.jl [10].

We evaluate our algorithm in two case studies. In the first case study we investigate the scalability. In the second case study we synthesize an LHA model on data obtained from a model of a biological system. We note that all experiments are fully automatic with no human involved in the annotation or modeling.

Scalability. In the first case study we measure the scalability of the algorithm in four different input dimensions: the data dimension n, the number of time series r, the number of data points per time series p, and the number of locations in the final automaton λ. Here we do not use the preprocessing from Sect. 4.1 for better comparability between different runs. The majority (>90%) of the run time is spent in solving the linear program (Line 5 in Algorithm 2).

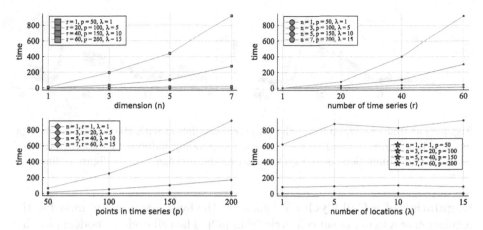

Fig. 4. Scalability in four different algorithm parameters. Each parameter varies between four values. In each of the four plots we vary one parameter and fix the remaining three. Each plot shows four graphs with indices $i = 1, \ldots, 4$, where for graph i we fix the parameters to their i-th value (which are also given in the legend).

To obtain the time series, we instantiate a parametric version of the thermostat model (our running example) with n independent thermostats running in parallel. We obtain r random simulations of time duration $T = 40$, which are represented as time series, and then choose the first p data points from them. Since we fix λ, we pass it to Algorithm 1, which then skips the refinement procedure for k-means clustering in Line 2 and directly uses λ clusters.

We consider the following combination of parameters: $n \in \{1, 3, 5, 7\}$, $r \in \{1, 20, 40, 60\}$, $p \in \{50, 100, 150, 200\}$, and $\lambda \in \{1, 5, 10, 15\}$. To examine the scalability in these four dimensions, we fix three parameters and plot the run time for varying only one of the parameters in Fig. 4.

From the results we observe that the input parameters n and r have the main influence on the complexity of the problem (the corresponding graphs have the steepest growth). The parameter p is less influential, and the parameter λ has almost no influence (the corresponding graphs barely grow and are not even monotonic). While λ influences the dimension of the flow polyhedron P, the different constraints are weakly coupled in these additional dimensions and thus the linear program is not substantially harder to solve.

In practice, when the data comes from experiments, the problem dimension n is fixed, and so is p if the data points are obtained from periodic measurements of fixed duration. Increasing r corresponds to additional experimental runs. The parameter λ can be freely chosen, but since a major benefit of hybrid automata is that they are interpretable models, we argue that λ should not be too large. Hence we believe that the algorithm is efficient enough to be used for real applications. We substantiate this claim in the next case study.

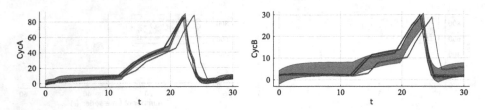

Fig. 5. The first two variables of the cell-cycle regulation with the ε-tube induced by the first time series ($\varepsilon = 3.15$, green), the corresponding induced execution (red), and three random simulations of the synthesized model (orange). (Color figure online)

Regulation of a Cell Cycle. We consider the hybrid-automaton model of the regulation of a mammalian cell cycle from [39]. The cell cycle is modeled in nine phases. The model has one location for each phase, affine differential equations ($\dot{\mathbf{x}} = A\mathbf{x} + \mathbf{b}$), and assignments associated with some transitions. There are three main dimensions (CycA, CycB, and CycE), one secondary dimension for the mass of the cell, and time as auxiliary dimension for time-triggered transitions.

We run our synthesis algorithm on 20 time series obtained from random simulations of the model proposed in [39]. In total these time series consist of 3,557 data points. Before passing them to the algorithm, we project out the time variable. Hence our model cannot reason about time-dependent behavior. We used the refinement process for choosing the number of locations (λ) automatically. After 26 s we obtain an LHA with nine locations and a precision value $\varepsilon = 3.15$. In Fig. 5 we show the ε-tube around the first time series together with three random simulations of the synthesized LHA. The ε-tube looks reasonably tight for the CycA dimension but wider for the CycB dimension, which is because the value of ε is the same in all dimensions, but the plot scales differ.

7   Conclusion

We have presented a synthesis algorithm to obtain a linear hybrid automaton from a set of time series. The algorithm uses two independent phases. In the first phase it constructs the discrete structure of the automaton. In the second phase it constructs the parameter space of all possible solutions and then selects an automaton by solving a linear program. The automaton is guaranteed to contain executions that are ε-close to the time series, where ε is minimal for the discrete structure chosen in the first phase. The algorithm is polynomial and scales to thousands of data points, but it also works with scarce data.

We see several directions for future work. The choice of the discrete structure in the first phase is important. We have proposed a heuristic implementation based on clustering that does not take the number of transitions into account. Reducing that number can remove unwanted behavior in the resulting model.

By minimizing ε we only minimize the maximum deviation of the executions from the data points. One can encourage the solver to find executions that stay close to the data points (the middle of the ε-tube in the plots). This can be encoded in the linear program by associating a cost to the sum of the deviation.

A more challenging extension is to use other classes of dynamics such as affine differential equations. The (exponential) solutions for such systems still have a closed form. Thus, instead of a linear program, we can solve a general optimization problem as in [12]. The difficult part is how to select the appropriate symbolic dynamics for the different parts of the time series.

Finally, in this paper we have only considered the automatic aspects of the algorithm. However, we believe that truly useful modeling ultimately requires interaction with a human in the loop. The separation of concerns – first finding a suitable discrete structure and formulating a parametric solution for finding suitable continuous dynamics – allows scientists to incorporate domain knowledge, e.g., by adding further modeling constraints beyond ε-capturing. A key question is how to refine the model if the results are not accepted.

Acknowledgements. This work was supported in part by the European Union's Horizon 2020 research and innovation programme under the Marie Skłodowska-Curie grant agreement no. 847635, by the ERC-2020-AdG 101020093, by DIREC - Digital Research Centre Denmark, and by the Villum Investigator Grant S4OS.

References

1. Althoff, M., Frehse, G., Girard, A.: Set propagation techniques for reachability analysis. Ann. Rev. Control Robot. Auton. Syst. **4** (2020)
2. Alur, R., Courcoubetis, C., Henzinger, T.A., Ho, P.-H.: Hybrid automata: an algorithmic approach to the specification and verification of hybrid systems. In: Grossman, R.L., Nerode, A., Ravn, A.P., Rischel, H. (eds.) HS 1991-1992. LNCS, vol. 736, pp. 209–229. Springer, Heidelberg (1993). https://doi.org/10.1007/3-540-57318-6_30
3. Bako, L., Vidal, R.: Algebraic identification of MIMO SARX models. In: Egerstedt, M., Mishra, B. (eds.) HSCC 2008. LNCS, vol. 4981, pp. 43–57. Springer, Heidelberg (2008). https://doi.org/10.1007/978-3-540-78929-1_4
4. Bartocci, E., Deshmukh, J., Gigler, F., Mateis, C., Nickovic, D., Qin, X.: Mining shape expressions from positive examples. Trans. Comput. Aided Des. Integr. Circuits Syst. **39**(11), 3809–3820 (2020)
5. Bemporad, A., Garulli, A., Paoletti, S., Vicino, A.: A bounded-error approach to piecewise affine system identification. Trans. Automat. Contr. **50**(10) (2005)
6. Clarke, E.M., Henzinger, T.A., Veith, H., Bloem, R. (eds.): Handbook of Model Checking. Springer, Cham (2018). https://doi.org/10.1007/978-3-319-10575-8
7. Douglas, D.H., Peucker, T.K.: Algorithms for the reduction of the number of points required to represent a digitized line or its caricature. Cartographica **10**(2) (1973)
8. Ferrari-Trecate, G., Muselli, M.: Single-linkage clustering for optimal classification in piecewise affine regression. In: ADHS, vol. 36, pp. 33–38. Elsevier (2003)
9. Fishwick, P.A.: Handbook of Dynamic System Modeling. CRC Press, Boca Raton (2007)
10. Forets, M., Schilling, C.: LazySets.jl: scalable symbolic-numeric set computations. In: Proceedings of the JuliaCon Conferences, vol. 1, no. 1, p. 11 (2021)

11. Frigg, R., Hartmann, S.: Models in science. In: The Stanford Encyclopedia of Philosophy. Metaphysics Research Lab, Stanford University (2020)
12. García Soto, M., Henzinger, T.A., Schilling, C.: Synthesis of hybrid automata with affine dynamics from time-series data. In: HSCC, pp. 2:1–2:11 (2021)
13. García Soto, M., Henzinger, T.A., Schilling, C., Zeleznik, L.: Membership-based synthesis of linear hybrid automata. In: Dillig, I., Tasiran, S. (eds.) CAV 2019. LNCS, vol. 11561, pp. 297–314. Springer, Cham (2019). https://doi.org/10.1007/978-3-030-25540-4_16
14. Garulli, A., Paoletti, S., Vicino, A.: A survey on switched and piecewise affine system identification. IFAC Proc. Vol. 45(16), 344–355 (2012)
15. Grosu, R., Mitra, S., Ye, P., Entcheva, E., Ramakrishnan, I.V., Smolka, S.A.: Learning cycle-linear hybrid automata for excitable cells. In: Bemporad, A., Bicchi, A., Buttazzo, G. (eds.) HSCC 2007. LNCS, vol. 4416, pp. 245–258. Springer, Heidelberg (2007). https://doi.org/10.1007/978-3-540-71493-4_21
16. Hashambhoy, Y., Vidal, R.: Recursive identification of switched ARX models with unknown number of models and unknown orders. In: CDC, pp. 6115–6121 (2005)
17. Henzinger, T.A.: The theory of hybrid automata. In: Inan, M.K., Kurshan, R.P. (eds.) Verification of Digital and Hybrid Systems. NATO ASI Series, vol. 170, pp. 265–292. Springer, Heidelberg (2000). https://doi.org/10.1007/978-3-642-59615-5_13
18. Huang, K., Wagner, A., Ma, Y.: Identification of hybrid linear time-invariant systems via subspace embedding and segmentation (SES). In: CDC (2004)
19. Juloski, A.L., Weiland, S., Heemels, W.P.M.H.: A Bayesian approach to identification of hybrid systems. Trans. Autom. Control. 50(10), 1520–1533 (2005)
20. Khachiyan, L.G.: A polynomial algorithm in linear programming. In: Doklady Akademii Nauk, vol. 244, pp. 1093–1096. Russian Academy of Sciences (1979)
21. Khaitan, S.K., McCalley, J.D.: Design techniques and applications of cyberphysical systems: a survey. IEEE Syst. J. 9(2), 350–365 (2015)
22. Klee, H., Raimondi, A.: Simulation of dynamic systems with Matlab and Simulink. J. Artif. Soc. Soc. Simul. 11(2) (2008)
23. Klipp, E., Liebermeister, W., Wierling, C., Kowald, A.: Systems Biology: A Textbook. Wiley, Hoboken (2016)
24. Lamrani, I., Banerjee, A., Gupta, S.K.S.: HyMn: mining linear hybrid automata from input output traces of cyber-physical systems. In: ICPS, pp. 264–269 (2018)
25. Lee, E.A., Seshia, S.A.: Introduction to Embedded Systems: A Cyber-Physical Systems Approach. MIT Press, Cambridge (2017)
26. Liberzon, D.: Switching in Systems and Control. Birkhäuser Boston (2003)
27. Liu, L., Bockmayr, A.: Formalizing metabolic-regulatory networks by hybrid automata. Acta. Biotheor. 68(1), 73–85 (2020)
28. Lloyd, S.P.: Least squares quantization in PCM. Trans. Inf. Theory 28(2) (1982)
29. Medhat, R., Ramesh, S., Bonakdarpour, B., Fischmeister, S.: A framework for mining hybrid automata from input/output traces. In: EMSOFT (2015)
30. Nakada, H., Takaba, K., Katayama, T.: Identification of piecewise affine systems based on statistical clustering technique. Automatica 41(5), 905–913 (2005)
31. Niggemann, O., Stein, B., Vodencarevic, A., Maier, A., Kleine Büning, H.: Learning behavior models for hybrid timed systems. In: AAAI (2012)
32. Ozay, N.: An exact and efficient algorithm for segmentation of ARX models. In: ACC, pp. 38–41 (2016)
33. Paoletti, S., Juloski, A.L., Ferrari-Trecate, G., Vidal, R.: Identification of hybrid systems: a tutorial. Eur. J. Control 13(2–3), 242–260 (2007)

34. Platzer, A.: Logical Foundations of Cyber-Physical Systems. Springer, Heidelberg (2018). https://doi.org/10.1007/978-3-319-63588-0
35. Rackauckas, C., Nie, Q.: DifferentialEquations.jl - a performant and feature-rich ecosystem for solving differential equations in Julia. JORS **5**(1) (2017)
36. Ramer, U.: An iterative procedure for the polygonal approximation of plane curves. Comput. Graph. Image Process. **1**(3), 244–256 (1972)
37. Roll, J., Bemporad, A., Ljung, L.: Identification of piecewise affine systems via mixed-integer programming. Automatica **40**(1), 37–50 (2004)
38. Silvert, W.: Modelling as a discipline. Int. J. General Syst. **30**(3) (2001)
39. Singhania, R., Sramkoski, R.M., Jacobberger, J.W., Tyson, J.J.: A hybrid model of mammalian cell cycle regulation. PLoS Comput. Biol. **7**(2) (2011)
40. Summerville, A., Osborn, J.C., Mateas, M.: CHARDA: causal hybrid automata recovery via dynamic analysis. In: IJCAI, pp. 2800–2806 (2017)
41. Tappler, M., Aichernig, B.K., Larsen, K.G., Lorber, F.: Time to learn – learning timed automata from tests. In: André, É., Stoelinga, M. (eds.) FORMATS 2019. LNCS, vol. 11750, pp. 216–235. Springer, Cham (2019). https://doi.org/10.1007/978-3-030-29662-9_13
42. Verdult, V., Verhaegen, M.: Subspace identification of piecewise linear systems. In: CDC, pp. 3838–3843 (2004)
43. Vynnycky, E., White, R.: An Introduction to Infectious Disease Modelling. OUP Oxford (2010)
44. Yang, X., Beg, O.A., Kenigsberg, M., Johnson, T.T.: A framework for identification and validation of affine hybrid automata from input-output traces. Trans. Cyber-Phys. Syst. **6**(2) (2022)

Optimal Repair for Omega-Regular Properties

Vrunda Dave[1], Shankara Narayanan Krishna[1], Vishnu Murali[2(✉)],
and Ashutosh Trivedi[2]

[1] Indian Institute of Technology Bombay, Mumbai, India
[2] University of Colorado Boulder, Boulder, USA
vishnu.murali@colorado.edu

Abstract. This paper presents an optimization based framework to
automate system repair against omega-regular properties. In the proposed formalization of *optimal repair*, the systems are represented as
Kripke structures, the properties as ω-regular languages, and the repair
space as *repair machines*—weighted omega-regular transducers equipped
with Büchi conditions—that rewrite strings and associate a cost sequence
to these rewritings. To translate the resulting cost-sequences to easily interpretable payoffs, we consider several aggregator functions to
map cost sequences to numbers—including limit superior, supremum,
discounted-sum, and average-sum—to define quantitative cost semantics. The problem of optimal repair, then, is to determine whether traces
from a given system can be rewritten to satisfy an ω-regular property
when the allowed cost is bounded by a given threshold. We also consider
the dual challenge of *impair verification* that assumes that the rewritings
are resolved adversarially under some given cost restriction, and asks to
decide if all traces of the system satisfy the specification irrespective of
the rewritings. With a negative result to the impair verification problem, we study the problem of designing a minimal mask of the Kripke
structure such that the resulting traces satisfy the specifications despite
the threshold-bounded impairment. We dub this problem as the *mask
synthesis* problem. This paper presents automata-theoretic solutions to
repair synthesis, impair verification, and mask synthesis problem for limit
superior, supremum, discounted-sum, and average-sum cost semantics.

1 Introduction

Given a Kripke structure and an ω-regular specification, the model checking
problem is to decide whether all traces of the system satisfy the specification.
Vardi and Wolper [17] initiated the automata-theoretic approach to model-
checking by reducing the ω-regular model checking problem to the language
inclusion problem. If the system violates the specification, this approach returns
a simple lasso-shaped counterexample demonstrating the violation. While these

This work was supported by the National Science Foundation (NSF) under Grant
ECCS-2015403 and NSF CAREER award CCF-2146563.

counterexamples often aid the designer in manually repairing the system, this repair process can be exhausting and error-prone. Moreover, different repair policies may incur different costs rendering the repair problem a non-trivial optimization problem. *This paper investigates a range of problems in synthesizing optimal repair policies against ω-regular specification.*

As a concrete motivation for various repair problems, we consider security issues (confidentiality and availability) in manufacturing. It is well documented [7] that acoustic side-channels leak valuable intellectual property information during the manufacturing process. Consider a 3D printer which can print either squares or triangles. Since the movement of the stepper motors of the printer vary based on the design, this difference in movement leads to the printer producing different sounds. Thus, an intruder may be able to discern the shape being printed by observing the audio output of the system as it acts as an acoustic side-channel. One can model such a system as a *Kripke structure*: a mockup of such systems is represented in Fig. 1a where the label corresponds to the state being idle (⊥), printing squares (□), or printing triangles (△).

Suppose that the system designer wishes to protect the information that a given printer prints only a fixed number of objects of one shape, or the sequence in which these shapes appear, from an eavesdropper. This specification, and a rich class of similar specifications on the observations, can be captured using ω-regular languages (see the Büchi automaton of Fig. 1b which requires that both shapes are printed infinitely often), and one can verify if the system satisfies such a specification using classical model checking. It is easy to see that our system does not satisfy this property for all traces. To repair this situation, we may wish to add spurious motor rotations to mimic the other shape, but adding such rotations comes with a cost (say energy or time overheads). The choices and cost available for repair can intuitively be expressed as a repair machine (a weighted nondeterministic transducer) given in Fig. 1c. For example, the label □|□△, 3 represents the situation where the repair machine modifies the observation corresponding to a square shape by appending a spurious rotation mimicking a triangle shape with an extra cost of 3 units.

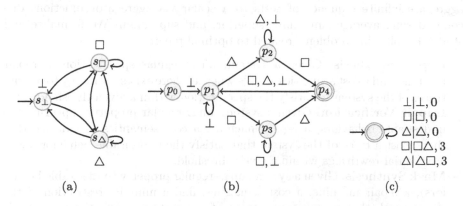

Fig. 1. (a) Krikpe structure representing the 3D printer system, (b) Büchi automaton B specifying the property, and (c) Repair machine

A key synthesis problem, then, is to compute a minimum cost repair strategy
to add these spurious rotations such that the system after repair satisfies the
specification. The cost of an ω-sequence can be aggregated using discounted-sum,
average-sum, liminf, limsup, inf, or sup. We call this problem the *repair synthesis*
where the goal is given an aggregator and cost threshold, design a strategy on the
nondeterministic transducer such that every trace of the system can be written
to satisfy the specification with cost bounded by the given threshold.

Example 1. Consider the repair machine T from Fig. 1c with the average-sum
cost semantics and a threshold of 2. For every spurious motor rotation, T incurs
a cost of 3 units of power. Note that a strategy of replacing every $\triangle$ with $\triangle\square$,
maps $\bot\triangle^\omega$ to $\bot(\triangle\square)^\omega$ which is accepted by B. The mean cost of this rewrite
is 3 and is above threshold. However, there exists a strategy that rewrites $\bot\triangle^\omega$
to $\bot(\triangle\triangle\square)^\omega$ that is accepted by B, with a mean cost equal to 1.

A related problem is that of *impair verification* that is connected to availability vulnerabilities. Consider an attack model in the aforementioned 3D manufacturing setting where an attacker with bounded capabilities controls the rewriting
process (by introducing subtle undetectable changes in the manufacturing process) and intends to rewrite the traces in such a way that the resulting trace
satisfy some undesirable behavior (to make the acoustic profile violate some
regulatory norms) with a cost bounded below a threshold. Such undesirable
rewritings may impair the capabilities of the system and render it unavailable
for normal use. The impair verification problem is to verify whether the system
is safe from such adversarial rewritings.

If the system is found to be vulnerable to impair and the system designer
has no control over the rewriting process, a viable mitigation approach is to
minimally restrict the behavior of the system to harden it against the adversarial
rewriting. We formalize this problem as the *mask synthesis* problem.

Contributions. We consider repair machines to be specified as weighted ω-transducers and study various optimal repair problems for different aggregator
functions. As we deal with reactive systems, we consider cost semantics that
aggregate infinite sequence of costs to a scalar via aggregator functions discounted sum, average sum, limit superior, and supremum. We formalize and
study the following problems related to optimal repair:

- **Repair Synthesis.** Given a system, an ω-regular specification, a repair
  machine, and a cost semantics, decide whether there exists a strategy to rewrite
  traces of the system to satisfy the specification within a given threshold.
- **Impair Verification.** Given a system, an ω-regular property capturing the
  undesirable behaviors, a repair machine, a cost semantics, decide whether
  there exist a trace of the system that satisfy the undesirable behavior under
  adversarial rewritings within a given threshold.
- **Mask Synthesis.** Given a system, an ω-regular property (undesirable behaviors), a repair machine, a cost semantics, find a minimal restriction of the
  system such that no remaining trace of the system satisfy the undesirable
  behavior under any adversarial rewritings within the threshold.

Our work is inspired by the idea of weighted transducers studied in [10] for finite strings. The notions of robust verification and kernel synthesis studied in [10] are templates for the impair verification and mask synthesis problems studied here, but the present setting requires extension of those results to the setting of ω-words: this is one of the secondary contributions of this paper.

Our results imply that the results presented in [10] carry over to the setting of ω-words for the discounted-sum and mean cost-semantics, the robust verification problem for both of these can be decided in P (cf. Theorems 5 and 6), while the robust kernel for discounted-sum cost-semantics is ω-regular if the language of the Kripke structure is a cut-point language (cf. Theorem 8). Furthermore, the notion of repair synthesis, to the best of our knowledge, is yet unexplored. We characterize the complexity of repair synthesis (Theorems 2–4) and impair verification problems (Theorems 5–7), and for the mask synthesis problem we discuss which aggregators allow ω-regular mask (Theorems 8–9).

Proofs of the theorems can be found in the technical report [9].

2 Preliminaries

Let Σ denote a finite alphabet. We write Σ^ω and Σ^* for the set of infinite and finite words over Σ. We denote an empty string by ϵ.

Kripke Structures. A *Kripke structure* is a tuple $K = (S, \hookrightarrow, S_0, AP, \mathcal{L})$ where S denotes a set of states, $\hookrightarrow \subseteq S \times S$ is the transition relation, $S_0 \subseteq S$ is the set of initial states, AP is the set of atomic propositions, and $\mathcal{L} : S \to 2^{AP}$ denotes the labeling function. An infinite sequence of states $\pi = s_0 s_1 \ldots \in S^\omega$ is said to be a path of the Kripke structure if $(s_i, s_{i+1}) \in \hookrightarrow$ for all $i \in \mathbb{N}$. Let $\Sigma = 2^{AP}$. The labeling function applied to a path $\pi = s_0 s_1 \ldots \in S^\omega$ defines traces $\mathcal{L}(\pi) = a_0 a_1 \ldots \in \Sigma^\omega$ of K where for each $i \geq 0$ we have that $a_i = \mathcal{L}(s_i)$. We use $\mathcal{T}_K$ to indicate the set of all traces of K.

Omega-Regular Specifications. A *non-deterministic Büchi automaton* (NBA) over Σ is a tuple $A = (Q, \Sigma, Q_0, Q_f, \delta)$, where Q is a finite set of states, $Q_0 \subseteq Q$ is the set of initial states, $Q_f \subseteq Q$ is the set of final states, Σ is the finite input alphabet, and $\delta \subseteq Q \times \Sigma \times Q$ denotes the transition relation. We define the extended transition relation $\widehat{\delta} \subseteq Q \times \Sigma^* \times Q$ in the standard fashion, i.e. $(q, \epsilon, q) \in \widehat{\delta}$ for $q \in Q$ and $ax \in \Sigma\Sigma^*$ we have $(q, ax, q') \in \widehat{\delta}$ if there exists $q'' \in Q$ such that $(q, a, q'') \in \delta$ and $(q'', x, q') \in \widehat{\delta}$.

A run ρ over a word $w = w_0 w_1 \ldots \in \Sigma^\omega$ is an infinite sequence of states $q_0, q_1 \ldots$ such that $(q_i, w_i, q_{i+1}) \in \delta$. A run ρ is accepting iff some final state from Q_f occurs infinitely often in ρ. The language defined by the automaton A, denoted as $L(A)$, is the set of words w over Σ^ω such that there exists an accepting run of w by A.

Cost Aggregation Semantics. An aggregator function $\oplus : \mathbb{N}^\omega \to \mathbb{Q}_{\geq 0}$ maps infinite sequences of numbers to a scalar. Let $\tau = \tau_1 \tau_2 \cdots \in \mathbb{N}^\omega$ with each $\tau_i \in \mathbb{N}$. We consider the following aggregators:

- $\mathsf{DSum}_\lambda \overset{\text{def}}{=} \overline{\tau} \mapsto \lim_{n\to\infty} \sum_{i=1}^n \lambda^{i-1} \tau_i$, with discount factor $0 \le \lambda < 1$,
- $\mathsf{Mean} \overset{\text{def}}{=} \overline{\tau} \mapsto \limsup_{n\to\infty} (1/n) \cdot \sum_{i=1}^n \tau_i$,
- $\mathsf{Sup} \overset{\text{def}}{=} \overline{\tau} \mapsto \sup\{\tau_i \mid i \in \mathbb{N}\}$, and
- $\mathsf{LimSup} \overset{\text{def}}{=} \overline{\tau} \mapsto \limsup\{\tau_i \mid i \in \mathbb{N}\}$.

Quantitative Games. A *game arena* $\mathcal{G} = (G, V_{\mathrm{Min}}, V_{\mathrm{Max}})$ consists of a graph $G = (V, E, w)$ where V is a finite set of vertices, $E \subseteq V \times V$ is the set of edges, $w : E \to \mathbb{N}$ is the weight function. The sets V_{Max} and V_{Min} characterize a partition of the vertex set V such that player Min controls the edges from vertices in V_{Min}, while Max controls the vertices in V_{Max}.

A play of the game $\mathcal{G}$ is an infinite sequence of vertices $\pi = \langle v_0, v_1, \ldots \rangle$ such that $(v_i, v_{i+1}) \in E$ for all $i \in \mathbb{N}$. A finite play is a finite such sequence, that is, a sequence in V^*. We denote by $\mathsf{last}(\pi)$ the final vertex in the finite play π. We write $\mathsf{Play}_\mathcal{G}$ and $\mathsf{FPlay}_\mathcal{G}$ for the set of infinite and finite plays of the game arena $\mathcal{G}$, respectively. A strategy of player Min in $\mathcal{G}$ is a partial function $\sigma : \mathsf{FPlay} \to V$ defined over all plays $\pi \in \mathsf{FPlay}$ with $\mathsf{last}(\pi) \in V_{\mathrm{min}}$, such that we have $(\mathsf{last}(\pi), \sigma(\pi)) \in E$. A strategy χ of player Max is defined analogously. We say that a strategy σ is *positional* if $\mathsf{last}(\pi) = \mathsf{last}(\pi')$ implies $\sigma(\pi) = \sigma(\pi')$. Strategies that are not positional are called *history dependent*. Let Σ_{Min} and Σ_{Max} be the sets of all strategies of player Min and player Max, respectively. We write Π_{Min} and Π_{Max} for the set of positional strategies of player Min and player Max, respectively. For a game arena $\mathcal{G}$, vertex v of $\mathcal{G}$ and strategy pair $(\sigma, \chi) \in \Sigma_{\mathrm{Min}} \times \Sigma_{\mathrm{Max}}$, let $\mathsf{Play}^{\sigma,\chi}(v)$ be the infinite play starting from v in which player Min and Max play according to σ and χ, respectively.

The weight function $w : E \to \mathbb{N}$ can be naturally extended from edges to plays as $w : \mathsf{Play}_\mathcal{G} \to \mathbb{N}^\omega$ as $\pi \mapsto c_0 c_1 \ldots$ where $c_i = w(v_i, v_{i+1})$ for all $i \in \mathbb{N}$. Given an aggregator function $\oplus \in \{\mathsf{DSum}_\lambda, \mathsf{Mean}, \mathsf{Sup}, \mathsf{LimSup}\}$, we define the payoff of player Min to player Max for a play π as $\oplus(w(\pi))$. Depending on the choice of the aggregator function $\oplus \in \{\mathsf{DSum}_\lambda, \mathsf{Mean}, \mathsf{Sup}, \mathsf{LimSup}\}$, we refer to the game as $\oplus$-game. In a $\oplus$-game, the goal of player Min is to choose her actions in such a way so as to minimize the payoff, while the goal of player Max is to maximize the payoff. For every vertex $v \in V$, define the *upper value* $\overline{\mathsf{Val}}_\oplus(\mathcal{G}, v)$ as the minimum payoff player Min can ensure irrespective of player Max's strategy. Symmetrically, the *lower value* $\underline{\mathsf{Val}}_\oplus(\mathcal{G}, v)$ of a vertex $v \in V$ is the maximum payoff player Max can ensure irrespective of player Min's strategy.

$$\overline{\mathsf{Val}}_\oplus(\mathcal{G}, v) = \inf_{\sigma \in \Sigma_{\mathrm{Min}}} \sup_{\chi \in \Sigma_{\mathrm{Max}}} \oplus(w(\mathsf{Play}^{\sigma,\chi}(v)))$$

$$\underline{\mathsf{Val}}_\oplus(\mathcal{G}, v) = \sup_{\chi \in \Sigma_{\mathrm{Max}}} \inf_{\sigma \in \Sigma_{\mathrm{Min}}} \oplus(w(\mathsf{Play}^{\sigma,\chi}(v))).$$

The inequality $\underline{\mathsf{Val}}_\oplus(\mathcal{G}, v) \le \overline{\mathsf{Val}}_\oplus(\mathcal{G}, v)$ holds for all two-player zero-sum games. A game is *determined* when, for every vertex $v \in V$, the lower value and upper value are equal. In this case, we say that the value of the game $\mathsf{Val}_\oplus$ exists with

$\mathsf{Val}_\oplus(\mathcal{G}, v) = \underline{\mathsf{Val}}_\oplus(\mathcal{G}, v) = \overline{\mathsf{Val}}_\oplus(\mathcal{G}, v)$ for every $v \in V$. For strategies $\sigma \in \Sigma_{\mathrm{Min}}$ and $\chi \in \Sigma_{\mathrm{Max}}$ of players Min and Max, we define their values Val^σ and Val^χ as

$$\mathsf{Val}^\sigma_\oplus : v \mapsto \sup_{\chi \in \Sigma_{\mathrm{Max}}} \oplus(w(\mathsf{Play}^{\sigma,\chi}(v))) \text{ and}$$

$$\mathsf{Val}^\chi_\oplus : v \mapsto \inf_{\sigma \in \Sigma_{\mathrm{Min}}} \oplus(w(\mathsf{Play}^{\sigma,\chi}(v))).$$

A strategy σ_* of player Min is called *optimal* if $\mathsf{Val}^{\sigma_*}_\oplus = \mathsf{Val}_\oplus$. Likewise, a strategy χ_* of player Max is optimal if $\mathsf{Val}^{\chi_*}_\oplus = \mathsf{Val}_\oplus$. We say that a game is *positionally determined* if both players have positional optimal strategies.

Theorem 1 [4,19]. *For* $\oplus \in \{\mathsf{DSum}_\lambda, \mathsf{Mean}, \mathsf{Sup}, \mathsf{LimSup}\}$, $\oplus$-*games are determined in positional strategies. The complexity of solving is in* NP ∩ co-NP *for* DSum_λ-*games and* Mean-*games, and, is in* P *for* Sup-*games and* LimSup-*games.*

The goal of the player Min in a Büchi game [6] over a game arena $\mathcal{G}$ and a set $F \subseteq V$ is to choose her actions in such a way that some vertex $v_f \in F$ occurs infinitely often in the play, while the goal of the Max player is to prevent this. We note from [4] that LimSup-games generalize Büchi games. For Theorem 1 it follows that the winning region, i.e. the set of vertices where the player Min has a strategy to win can be computed in P.

3   Problem Definition

Just as weighted transducers extend finite state automata with outputs and costs on transitions, NBAs can be extended to *weighted non-deterministic Büchi transducers* by adding an output word and costs to transitions. We define a repair machine as a weighted non-deterministic Büchi transducer equipped with a cost aggregation. We introduce repair machines and their computational problems.

Definition 1. *A* repair machine *(RM)* T *is a tuple* $(Q, \Sigma, Q_0, Q_f, \Gamma, \delta, \oplus)$ *where* Q *is a finite set of states,* $Q_0 \subseteq Q$ *is the set of initial states,* $Q_f \subseteq Q$ *is the set of final states,* Γ *is the output alphabet,* $\delta \subseteq Q \times \Sigma \times Q \times \Gamma^* \times \mathbb{N}$ *is the transition relation, and* $\oplus$ *is the cost aggregator function.*

For a given aggregator function $\oplus \in \{\mathsf{DSum}_\lambda, \mathsf{Mean}, \mathsf{Sup}, \mathsf{LimSup}\}$, we refer to a repair machine as DSum-RM, Mean-RM, Sup-RM, LimSup-RM.

A transition $(q, a, q', w, c) \in \delta$ indicates that, the transducer on reading the letter $a \in \Sigma$ in state q, transitions to state q', and outputs a word $w \in \Gamma^*$, incurring a cost c for rewriting a to w. We write $q \xrightarrow{a/w}_c q'$ if $(q, a, q', w, c) \in \delta$. A run ρ of T on $u = a_1 a_2 \cdots \in \Sigma^\omega$ is a sequence $\langle q_0, (a_0, w_0, c_0), q_1, (a_1, w_1, c_1), \ldots \rangle$ where for every $i \geq 0$ we have that $q_0 \in Q_0$ and $q_i \xrightarrow{a_i/w_i}_{c_i} q_{i+1}$. Let $\mathsf{Runs}(T, u)$ be the set of runs of T on u. We write $\mathcal{O}(\rho)$ and $\mathcal{C}(\rho)$ for the projection on the outputs and cost sequences, i.e. $\mathcal{O}(\rho) = w_0 w_1 \ldots$ and $\mathcal{C}(\rho) = c_0 c_1 \ldots$, of a run ρ of T. We say that a run of T is accepting if states from Q_f are visited infinitely often. We write $\mathsf{dom}(T)$ for the set of all words which have an accepting run.

We define three different semantics for T. The function $[\![T]\!](u)$ returns the set of all pairs of outputs and cost sequences over the word $u \in \Sigma^\omega$; the function $[\![T]\!]_*^\oplus(u, v)$ returns the optimal rewriting cost w.r.t the aggregator function $\oplus$ over T for a rewriting of u to v; and $[\![T]\!]_\tau^\oplus(u)$ returns the set of all rewritings of a word u with cost bounded by a threshold $\tau \in \mathbb{R}$.

$$[\![T]\!](u) = \{(\mathcal{O}(\rho), \mathcal{C}(\rho)) \; : \; u \in \mathrm{dom}(T) \text{ and } \rho \in \mathrm{Runs}(T, u)\} \,,$$

$$[\![T]\!]_*^\oplus(u, v) = \inf\{\oplus(\mathcal{C}(\rho)) \; : \; \rho \in \mathrm{Runs}(T, u) \text{ and } \mathcal{O}(\rho) = v\} \,,$$

$$[\![T]\!]_\tau^\oplus(u) = \{\mathcal{O}(\rho) \; : \; \rho \in \mathrm{Runs}(T, u) \text{ and } [\![T]\!]_*^\oplus(u, \mathcal{O}(\rho)) \leq \tau\} \,.$$

Problems of Optimal Repair. Given the Kripke structure K representing the system, the ω-regular specification specified by the language $L \subseteq \Gamma^\omega$, a RM T, a cost semantics $\oplus \in \{\mathsf{DSum}_\lambda, \mathsf{Mean}, \mathsf{Sup}, \mathsf{LimSup}\}$, and a threshold $\tau \in \mathbb{Q}_{\geq 0}$, the *repair synthesis* problem asks if there exists a strategy of rewriting every trace $t \in \mathcal{T}_K$ to some word $w \in L$ using T such that cost is at most τ.

We restrict the repair policies where Player Min is restricted to rewrite a letter of the trace based on history and not to rely on a lookahead. We give a game semantics to the repair synthesis problem as a turn-based two player game between players Min and Max that proceeds as follows. The game begins with player Max selecting the initial state $s_0 \in S_0$ of the Kripke structure and ends her turn. Player Min, starts from the initial state q_0 of the RM and then selects a valid rewriting w_i of $\mathcal{L}(s_0)$ such that $(q_0, \mathcal{L}(s_0), q_i', w_i, c) \in \delta$ is a valid transition for some $c \in \mathbb{N}$ and changes the state of the RM to q_i', she then ends her turn. The game continues in this fashion, where player Max selects the next state s_i' of the Kripke structure and Player Min selects a valid rewriting and thus the next state of the repair machine. This turn based game proceeds indefinitely and results in Player Max selecting a trace $t \in \mathcal{T}_K$ and player Min selecting a word $w \in \mathbb{N}^\omega$. Player Min wins the game if $w \in [\![T]\!]_\tau^\oplus(t)$, and $w \in L$, otherwise player Max wins the game. The existence of a winning strategy for Player Min implies the existence of a repair strategy.

Definition 2 (Repair Synthesis). *Given a Kripke structure K representing the system, an ω-regular specification L, a repair machine T, a cost semantics $\oplus \in \{\mathsf{DSum}_\lambda, \mathsf{Mean}, \mathsf{Sup}, \mathsf{LimSup}\}$, and a threshold τ decide whether there exists a strategy to rewrite every trace $t \in \mathcal{T}_K$ to some word $w \in L$ with a cost of at most τ, and if so synthesise this strategy.*

We also consider the dual challenge of *impair verification* where the system is subjected to adversarial rewritings. This setting has applications in, among others, availability vulnerability detection. We consider an attack model where the rewritings given by the repair machine are resolved adversarially but are restricted to be within a given cost. The verification problem is to decide if there exists traces of the system that satisfy an ω-regular property capturing the undesirable behaviors for some such rewritings. The game semantics for the impair verification problem are similar to that of repair synthesis, however in the case of impair verification the player Max not only controls the selection of the next state s_i', but also decides the rewriting by selecting the word w_i' as well.

Definition 3 (Impair Verification). *Given a structure K representing the system, an ω-regular language L capturing the undesirable behavior given as an NBA A, repair machine T, a cost semantics $\oplus \in \{\mathsf{DSum}_\lambda, \mathsf{Mean}, \mathsf{Sup}, \mathsf{LimSup}\}$, and a threshold $\tau \in \mathbb{Q}_{\geq 0}$, the impair verification problem fails if there exists a trace $t \in \mathcal{T}_K$ that can be rewritten to some word $w \in L$ with a cost of at most τ under an adversarial strategy.*

When one may not be able to pass the impair verification problem, it may be desirable to design a way to minimally mask the Kripke structure such that the resulting system satisfies the specifications despite the threshold-bounded impairment. In such a case, we wish to find the maximal subset N' of traces which, even under adversarial rewrites, satisfy the ω-regular specification L.

Definition 4 (Mask Synthesis). *Given a Kripke structure K representing the system, an ω-regular language L capturing the undesirable behavior given as an NBA A, repair machine T, a cost semantics $\oplus \in \{\mathsf{DSum}_\lambda, \mathsf{Mean}, \mathsf{Sup}, \mathsf{LimSup}\}$, and $\tau \in \mathbb{Q}_{\geq 0}$, the problem of mask synthesis is to find a maximal subset $N' \subseteq \mathcal{T}_K$ such that all traces $t \in N'$ pass the impair verification.*

The next three sections present our results on these three problems.

4   Repair Synthesis

To solve the problem of repair synthesis, we reduce it to a related problem of *threshold synthesis*. Threshold synthesis asks for a partition of the rational numbers $\mathbb{Q}_{\geq 0}$ into sets $\mathbb{G}$ (good) and $\mathbb{B}$ (bad) sets such that the repair synthesis problem can be solved for all good thresholds $\tau \in \mathbb{G}$. Given a system K, the specification $L \subseteq \Gamma^\omega$ represented by an NBA B, a repair machine T, and a cost semantics $\oplus \in \{\mathsf{DSum}_\lambda, \mathsf{Mean}, \mathsf{Sup}, \mathsf{LimSup}\}$, we focus on the threshold synthesis problem: find a partition of $\mathbb{Q}_{\geq 0}$ into two sets $\mathbb{G}$ and $\mathbb{B}$ such that the policy synthesis can be solved for all $\tau \in \mathbb{G}$. We note that in the case of policy synthesis, the sets $\mathbb{G}$ and $\mathbb{B}$ are upward and downward closed respectively. If player Min has a winning strategy for some $\tau \in \mathbb{Q}_{\geq 0}$ then she may use the same strategy for all $\tau' \geq \tau$. Let the infimum value τ for which player Min wins be denoted as τ^*, then $\mathbb{G} = [\tau^*, \infty)$ and $\mathbb{B} = [0, \tau^*)$. We call this value τ^* the optimal threshold.

4.1   Solving the Büchi Games

Our approach to compute the optimal threshold is to first restrict the choice of player Min to those where she has a strategy to win with respect to the Büchi objective, irrespective of the choices of Player Max on the Kripke structure. If Player Min has no valid strategy to rewrite a trace of the system to satisfy the Büchi objective, then the optimal threshold $\tau^* = \infty$. We thus consider the case when $\tau^* \neq \infty$ by playing a Büchi game on a game arena and then pruning it.

To construct the game arena, we first construct the synchronized product $K \times T \times B$ of K, T, and B. Intuitively, $K \times T \times B$ accepts those traces of the system, which have some rewriting that is in L.

Definition 5. *The synchronized product $K \times T \times B$ of the Kripke Structure $K = (S, \hookrightarrow, S_0, \mathcal{L})$, the repair machine $T = (Q, \Sigma, Q_0, Q_f, \Gamma, \Delta, C)$ and the NBA $B = (P, \Gamma, P_0, P_f, \delta)$ is a weighted (directed) graph $G^\times = (V, E, W, V_I, V_F)$, where:*

- $V = S \times Q \times P \times \{1, 2\}$ *is the set of vertices consisting of states of the system K, repair machine T, and NBA B, and a counter that tracks the visitation of accepting states of T and B (like the degeneralization construction for the generalized Büchi automata)*
- $E \subseteq V \times V$ *is such that $((s, q, p, i), (s', q', p', i')) \in E$ if $(s, s') \in \hookrightarrow$ is a transition in K, for some $w \in \Gamma^*$ and $c \in \mathbb{N}$ transition $(q, \mathcal{L}(s), q', w, c) \in \Delta$ is in T, and $(p, w, p') \in \widehat{\delta}$ is a transition in B, and one of the following holds:*
  - $i = i' = 1$ *and* $q' \notin Q_f$
  - $i = i' = 2$ *and* $p \notin P_f$
  - $i = 1$ *and* $i' = 2$ *and* $q' \in Q_f$
  - $i = 2$ *and* $i' = 1$ *and* $p \in P_f$
- $W : E \to \mathbb{N}$ *is the weight function such that*

$$W((q, s, p, i), (q', s', p', i')) = \min \{c : (q, \mathcal{L}(s), q', w, c) \in \Delta\};$$

- $V_I \subseteq V = Q_0 \times S_0 \times P_0 \times \{1\}$ *is the set of initial vertices; and*
- $V_F \subseteq V = Q \times S \times P_f \times \{2\}$ *is the set of final vertices.*

To distinguish the choice of player Max and Min, we define a game structure $\mathcal{G}^\times$ on the product graph $G^\times$ by introducing intermediate states by appending another layer to the track counter. The formal construction is shown next.

The game graph $\mathcal{G}^\times = ((\overline{V}, \overline{E}, \overline{W}, V_I, V_F), \overline{V}_{\text{Min}}, \overline{V}_{\text{Max}})$ for product $G^\times = (V, E, W, V_I, V_F)$ is such that:

- $\overline{V} = S \times Q \times P \times \{1, 2, 3\}$;
- $\overline{E}$ is such that for $e = ((s, q, p, i)(s', q', p', i')) \in E$ we have two edges to separate the choice of the RM and the NBA from the Kripke structure:
  - $e_1 = ((s, q, p, i), (s, q', p', 3)) \in \overline{E}$ and
  - $e_2 = ((s, q', p', 3)(s', q', p', i')) \in \overline{E}$;
  with the weights $\overline{W}(e_1) = W(e)$ and $\overline{W}(e_2) = 0$;
- $\overline{V}_{\text{Min}} = S \times Q \times P \times \{1, 2\}$; and
- $\overline{V}_{\text{Max}} = S \times Q \times P \times \{3\}$.

Note that the first choice is made by player Max in choosing the starting state of the Kripke structure, and in the subsequent transitions player Min reads those states and makes a choice over the rewrites. For this reason, the choice of player Max appear to be lagging by one.

We play the Büchi-game on $\mathcal{G}^\times$ with the set of accepting states as V_F. We then prune the arena to contain only those states that are in the winning region of player Min with respect to the Büchi objective, that is, the set of states where player Min has a strategy to enforce visiting Büchi states irrespective of the strategy chosen by the player Max. We denote this pruned game arena as $\mathcal{G}$.

4.2   Optimal Threshold for DSum-RM

We reduce the problem of finding the optimal threshold τ^* for a DSum-RM to the problem of finding the value of a DSum-game on the game arena $\mathcal{G}$. As such we reduce the choices of selecting a trace by player Max and that of selecting a rewriting by player Min in the context of repair synthesis to choices made by the players in a DSum-game over an arena $\mathcal{G}$. In particular, we have the following.

Theorem 2. *The optimal threshold τ^* for the DSum-RM can be computed in NP $\cap$ co-NP via solving a DSum-game on $\mathcal{G}$.*

Proof (Sketch). We solve the DSum$_\gamma$ game on $\mathcal{G}$ with $\gamma = \sqrt{\lambda}$, the value of this game corresponds to the optimal threshold τ^*, as each edge of the synchronized product is captured by a pair of edges in $\mathcal{G}$. For any $\varepsilon > 0$, Player Min has a strategy of following this DSum strategy, and then following the strategy of the Büchi-game such that the cost of this rewriting is $\tau^* + \varepsilon$.

4.3   Optimal Threshold for Mean-RM

Similar to the case of the DSum-RM, in the case of the Mean-RM, we reduce the problem of finding the optimal threshold τ^* to the problem of finding the value of a Mean-game on a game arena $\mathcal{G}$. However we note that unlike the case of the DSum-RMs we also need to ensure that the mean cost cycle is co-accessible from the accepting vertices. In particular we have the following result.

Theorem 3. *The optimal threshold τ^* for the Mean-RM can be computed in NP $\cap$ co-NP via solving a Mean game on $\mathcal{G}$.*

Proof (Sketch). The proof of this theorem is similar to that of Theorem 2. Here, we first find a least cost mean cycle that is co-accessible by Player Min from the winning strategy of the Büchi-game on $\mathcal{G}$ (either a cycle following some Mean-game or the Büchi cycle itself). To do so we determine vertex that is co-accessible along the Mean-game over $\mathcal{G}$ as well as the Büchi-game. Player Min then alternates between two strategies in rounds, the first, where she follows the strategy of the Mean-game and the second to where she follows the strategy of the Büchi-game. At any round i, she follows the strategy of the Mean-game until she cycles on the co-accessible vertex 2^i many times and then follows the strategy of the Büchi-game once to return to this vertex. As the least cost-cycle has twice the number of edges of the synchronized product we divide the value of the Mean-game by two to determine the optimal threshold. We note that the above strategy relies on infinite memory, however Player Min can restrict the number of rounds for any $\varepsilon > 0$, and so she has a finite memory policy to guarantee repair for any threshold of $\tau^* + \varepsilon$.

4.4   Optimal Thresholds for Sup-RMs and LimSup-RMs

In the case of the Sup aggregator function we first order the edges of $G^\times$ in the descending order of their weights and remove them in stages from the largest to the smallest. If, at any stage, the removal of edge e, leads to a failure of satisfying the Büchi condition, we infer that e is necessary to satisfy the Büchi condition for some state in G. We claim that the weight of the edge e is τ^*.

Similar to the Sup aggregator function, we start removing edges of $G^\times$ in the descending order of their weights only if they are present in an accepting cycle in the case of theLimSup aggregator function. Then, if at any stage, the removal of edge e, leads to a failure of satisfying the Büchi condition, we infer that the $\tau^* = W(e)$ and conclude that we can safely remove edges with a higher weight.

Theorem 4. *Computing optimal threshold τ^* for Sup and LimSup-RMs is in P.*

Proof (Sketch). Note that the removal of any edge e from the synchronized product that causes the Büchi-objective to no longer be satisfied guarantees that all the rewrite strategies for at least one trace do not satisfy the Büchi objective. Hence the removal prevents the satisfaction of either the acceptance of RM T or the NBA B, and in either case, leads to a trace of the Kripke structure that cannot be rewritten to some word that is accepted by the NBA B.

5 Impair Verification

Given the Kripke structure K representing the system, the ω-regular language L capturing undesirable behavior, represented as an NBA B, a repair machine T, and a cost semantics $\oplus \in \{\mathsf{DSum}_\lambda, \mathsf{Mean}, \mathsf{Sup}, \mathsf{LimSup}\}$, we reduce the impair verification problem to the threshold verification problem. The threshold verification problem is to find a partition of $\mathbb{Q}_{\geq 0}$ into two sets $\mathbb{G}$ and $\mathbb{B}$, such that none of the traces to system can be rewritten to a word that is in the language of B for all $v \in \mathbb{G}$. Let τ^* denote the infimum value for which a trace $t \in \mathcal{T}_K$ can be rewritten to some word $w \in \Gamma^\omega$ such that $w \in L$. Then, the threshold verification problem is solved for any $\tau < \tau^*$, as $[\![T]\!]_\tau^\oplus(t) \not\subseteq L$ for every trace $t \in \mathcal{T}_K$. Thus the set $\mathbb{G} = (0, \tau^*)$ and the set $\mathbb{B} = [\tau^*, \infty)$ and problem reduces to finding the optimal threshold τ^*.

In order to find the optimal threshold τ^*, we construct the synchronised product $G^\times = K \times T \times B$ as detailed in Definition 5. We prune $G^\times$ to keep only those states from where player Max has a winning strategy against the Büchi objective. The construction is similar to Büchi games, except that the opponent has no choice. In the following, we refer to this pruned graph as G.

5.1 Optimal Threshold for DSum-RM

In the case of a DSum-RM, we show that the optimal threshold τ^* is the minimum infinite discounted cost path in G. While it may not be possible to achieve this cost, for any $\varepsilon > 0$ we show the existence of a finite memory strategy of player Max that guarantees that some rewriting with threshold of $\tau^* + \varepsilon$ is in L.

We claim that the optimal threshold τ^* is the minimum discounted cost in G. To find this value, we associate a variable $\mathcal{V}_s$, to each vertex $v \in V$, characterizing minimum discounted cost among all paths starting from the state s. The minimum discounted values can then be characterized as [15]:

$$\mathcal{V}_v = \min_{(v,v')\in E} \{W(v,v') + \lambda \cdot \mathcal{V}_{v'}\}$$

This equation can be computed by solving the following LP.

$$\max \sum_{v\in V} \mathcal{V}_v \text{ subject to:} \qquad \mathcal{V}_v \le W(v,v') + \lambda \mathcal{V}_v \text{ for all } (v,v') \in E.$$

A positional discount-optimal strategy can be computed from the solutions of these equations simply by picking a successor vertex minimizing the right side of the optimality equations. Observe, however, that the 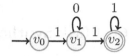 resulting path may not satisfy the Büchi condition. Consider the graph shown in the inset (right). In order to satisfy the Büchi objective, a run must visit the state v_2, while to minimize the discounted cost the strategy is to cycle in the state v_1 getting a discounted sum of 1. While it is possible to achieve an ε-optimal discounted cost and satisfy the Büchi objective by looping on v_1 for an arbitrary number of steps before moving to the state v_2, no strategy satisfying the Büchi objective can achieve a DSum cost of 1.

Theorem 5. *The optimal threshold τ^* for DSum-RMs can be computed in P.*

5.2 Optimal Threshold for Mean-RM

In the case of the Mean aggregator function, we note that only those edges that are visited infinitely often have an effect on the cost. We say that a cycle is accepting if there exists some vertex $v \in V_F$ that occurs in the cycle. We let C_1 denote the least average cost cycle that can be reached and is reachable from some accepting cycle C_2. We use d_1 and d_2 to denote the total cost of these cycles and n_1 and n_2 to be the number of edges in each of them respectively. We then show that τ^* is the mean value of cycle C_1. We observe that a strategy to determine this optimal threshold requires infinite memory. However for any $\varepsilon > 0$, there exists a finite memory strategy that is ε close to τ^*. Consider the graph shown in the inset (right) and the following strategy adopted by Player Max. Player Max cycles between v_0 and v_1 in rounds. At any given round i, Player Max cycles on v_0 for 2^i times, and then moves and cycles once in v_1 and returns to v_0. Observe this strategy ensures that the Büchi objective is satisfied while also ensuring the Mean cost to be 0 but requires infinite memory to keep track of the rounds. However, Player Max can achieve a ε-optimal mean cost by limiting the number of rounds.

Theorem 6. *The threshold τ^* for Mean-RMs can be computed in P.*

5.3 Optimal Thresholds for Sup-RMs and LimSup-RMs

For the Sup aggregator function, let S be the set of values c_i such that c_i is the supremum of the cost of some lasso that starts from some $v_i \in V_I$ and cycles in a loop containing some $v_f \in V_F$. Let k be the least element in S. We claim $\tau^* = k$. Similar to the Sup aggregator function, we consider the set S to contain the values c_i such that c_i is the supremum of the costs of the edges in the cycles that visit some $v_f \in V_F$ in the case of the LimSup aggregator function. We then take the least of these to be the optimal threshold for the LimSup-RMs.

Theorem 7. *The threshold τ^* for* Sup *and* LimSup-*RMs can be computed in P.*

6 Mask Synthesis

Given a Kripke structure K representing the system, an ω-regular language L capturing the undesirable behavior given as an NBA B, repair machine T, a cost semantics $\oplus \in \{\mathsf{DSum}_\lambda, \mathsf{Mean}, \mathsf{Sup}, \mathsf{LimSup}\}$, and $\tau \in \mathbb{Q}_{\geq 0}$, the problem of *mask synthesis* is to find a maximal subset $N' \subseteq T_K$ such that all traces $t \in N'$ pass the impair verification.

It is well known that every Kripke structure admits an ω-regular language N such that a word $u \in N$ if and only if $u \in T_K$. Let the ω-regular language of K be N. To solve the mask synthesis problem, we restrict the domain of the repair machine T to N by constructing a repair machine T' using product construction and give our results on the repair machine T'.

6.1 Mask Synthesis for *DSum*-RMs

We show that the maximal subset N' for isolated cut-point languages [3] is ω-regular. Given a threshold $\tau \in \mathbb{Q}$, the maximal subset N', is the set of all words $u \in \mathrm{dom}(T')$, such that for every word $w' \in [\![T]\!]_\tau^{\mathsf{DSum}}(u)$ we also have $w \notin L$. A threshold τ is ε-isolated for RM T', if for $\varepsilon > 0$ and all accepting runs r of T',

$$[\![T']\!]_*^{\mathsf{DSum}}(r, w) \in [0, v - \varepsilon] \cup [v + \varepsilon, \infty).$$

It is isolated if it is isolated for some ε. To prove that N' is ω-regular for such thresholds, we first note that isolated-cut point languages are ω-regular in the context of weighted automata [11]. We follow a similar strategy to [10], and slowly unroll our synchronous product. We note that since the repair machine is over ω strings, there must exist some n such that

$$\mathsf{DSum}(w_0 w_1 \ldots) \leq \mathsf{DSum}(w_0 \ldots w_n) + B_n,$$

where $B_n = V \frac{\lambda^n}{1 - \lambda}$, where V is the largest cost that is not ∞. Therefore if $\mathsf{DSum}(w_0, w_1, \ldots) \leq v - \varepsilon + B_n$ we can conclude that $\mathsf{DSum}(w_0, \ldots, w_n) \leq v - \varepsilon$.

Lemma 1. *Let T' be a* DSum *repair machine and $\tau \in \mathbb{Q}$. If τ is ε-isolated for some ε, then there is $n^* \in \mathbb{N}$ such that any partial run r of length at least n^* satisfies one of the following properties:*

1. $\mathsf{DSum}(r) \leq \tau - \varepsilon$ and $\mathsf{DSum}(rr') \leq \tau - \varepsilon$ for every infinite continuation r' of r.
2. $\mathsf{DSum}(r) \geq \tau + \frac{\varepsilon}{2}$ and $\mathsf{DSum}(rr') \geq \tau + \varepsilon$ for every infinite continuation r' of r.

Here, for finite r, $\mathsf{DSum}(r)$ is defined in the usual fashion except that the summation will be upto the length of r.

Theorem 8. *Let T' be a DSum repair machine, $v \in \mathbb{Q}$, and L an ω-regular language given by an NBA. For all n, we can construct an NBA A_n such that $L(A_n) \subseteq L(A_{n+1})$ and $L(A_n) \subseteq \overline{N'} \cap \mathrm{dom}(T')$. Moreover, if τ is ε-isolated, there exists n^* such that $L(A_{n^*}) = \overline{N'} \cap \mathrm{dom}(T')$.*

For the construction of A_n in Theorem 8, a notion of bad and dangerous runs are defined. Intuitively, The bad runs are all those runs which are accepting with cost $\leq \tau$, such that the output word is not in L. The dangerous runs are the finite partial runs which can be extended to bad runs. The idea for construction of A_n is to identify all the finite partial runs r of length n which can later be extended to bad runs. This way we can construct a sequence of Büchi automata that better under approximate the automata for the non-robust words in the domain. Thanks to Lemma 1, we can assure that there exists a fixed point at n^* such that A_{n^*} recognizes all the non-robust words from T'.

6.2 Mask Synthesis for Mean-RMs

The mask synthesis problem for Mean-RMs is already undecidable for finite words [10, Theorem 17] and this result carries over to the case of ω-words.

6.3 Mask Synthesis for Sup-RMs and LimSup-RMs

For the Sup-RMs, we can construct an NBA recognizing all output words with a cost greater than τ and show that the maximal subset N' is ω-regular. The results for Sup-RMs can be extended carefully to only account the costs occurring in accepting loops and be used for the LimSup-RMs as well.

Theorem 9. *Let T' be a Sup-RM, $\tau \in \mathbb{Q}$ and L be a ω-regular language. The language of N' is ω-regular and we can effectively construct an NBA for it.*

7 Related Work

Our work is closest to the idea of weighted transducers as studied in [10] for finite strings. We extend the known results of [10] in the context of robust verification and kernel synthesis from finite strings to infinite strings.

D'Antoni, Samanta, and Singh [8] presented QLOSE, a program repair approach with quantitative objectives. The QLOSE approach permits rewriting syntactical expressions with arbitrary expressions while keeping the control structure of the program intact. In comparison, our approach permits modification of the control structure albeit with a finite set of expressions (encoded as a finite alphabet) considered for rewriting. Consequently, our setting remains decidable as opposed to repair with QLOSE that is, in general, undecidable, and for tractability it restricts the correctness criterion to being correct over a given set of input-output examples. Similarly Samanta, Olivo, and Emerson [16], considered cost-aware program repair for Turing-complete programs through the use of predicate abstraction. However, their cost function is dependent only on the program location as opposed to more general ω-traces as proposed in our work.

Jobstmann, Griesmayer, and Bloem [13], and von Essen and Jobstman [18], studied program repair as a two-player game with qualitative ω-regular objectives. Our work, in contrast, allows quantitative notions of repair costs.

Cerny and Henzinger [2] championed for the need of partial program synthesis, which can be thought of as a repair, though its aim is to complete the given partial program, with respect to the specification. Although not directly related to repair, the framework of model measuring [12] presents a notion of distance between models; it studies the problem that given a model M and specification find the maximal distance such that all models within that distance from M satisfy the specification. Bansal, Chaudhuri, and Vardi [1] study comparator automata that read two infinite sequences of weights and relate their aggregate values to compare such quantitative systems. Kupferman and Tamir [14] consider the problem of cheating, where they use weighted automata and a penalty function to determine if the environment is cheating. The penalty function considered is again a map from a pair of letters to a value and so the environment is only permitted letter-to-letter rewritings. In contrast, our models permits more general letter-to-string rewritings constrained with ω-regular objectives.

Chatterjee et al. [5] consider the problem of solving both quantitative and qualitative objectives and define the notion of implication games where the objective is to solve both. While we provide direct proofs, Theorems 2 and 3 can also be recovered from results on implication games.

8   Conclusion

This paper presented a generalization of fundamental problems on weighted transducers and robustness threshold synthesis for ω-words. We proposed and solved the problem of minimal cost repair formulated as two player games on weighted transducers. We note that this problem is similar to multi-objectives optimization where the goal of the players is to satisfy an ω-regular property while optimizing a quantitative payoff. We also considered a related problem of impair verification that is related to availability problem where an attacker intends to rewrite the observations of the system to make it satisfy some undesirable behavior. We believe that the repair problem may find application in designing mitigation policies against side-channel vulnerability where some confidential property of the system is leaking in the output trace, and the goal is to find a minimum-cost repair to make the system opaque.

References

1. Bansal, S., Chaudhuri, S., Vardi, M.Y.: Comparator automata in quantitative verification. In: Baier, C., Dal Lago, U. (eds.) FoSSaCS 2018. LNCS, vol. 10803, pp. 420–437. Springer, Cham (2018). https://doi.org/10.1007/978-3-319-89366-2_23
2. Cerný, P., Henzinger, T.A.: From boolean to quantitative synthesis. In: International Conference on Embedded Software, EMSOFT 2011, pp. 149–154 (2011)
3. Chatterjee, K., Doyen, L., Henzinger, T.A.: Quantitative languages. In: Kaminski, M., Martini, S. (eds.) CSL 2008. LNCS, vol. 5213, pp. 385–400. Springer, Heidelberg (2008). https://doi.org/10.1007/978-3-540-87531-4_28
4. Chatterjee, K., Doyen, L., Henzinger, T.A.: A Survey of stochastic games with limsup and liminf objectives. In: Albers, S., Marchetti-Spaccamela, A., Matias, Y., Nikoletseas, S., Thomas, W. (eds.) ICALP 2009. LNCS, vol. 5556, pp. 1–15. Springer, Heidelberg (2009). https://doi.org/10.1007/978-3-642-02930-1_1
5. Chatterjee, K., Henzinger, T.A., Otop, J., Velner, Y.: Quantitative fair simulation games. Inf. Comput. **254**, 143–166 (2017)
6. Chatterjee, K., Henzinger, T.A., Piterman, N.: Algorithms for Büchi games. arXiv preprint. arXiv:0805.2620 (2008)
7. Chhetri, S.R., Canedo, A., Faruque, M.A.A.: Confidentiality breach through acoustic side-channel in cyber-physical additive manufacturing systems. ACM Trans. Cyber-Phys. Syst. **2**(1), 1–25 (2017)
8. D'Antoni, L., Samanta, R., Singh, R.: QLOSE: program repair with quantitative objectives. In: Chaudhuri, S., Farzan, A. (eds.) CAV 2016. LNCS, vol. 9780, pp. 383–401. Springer, Cham (2016). https://doi.org/10.1007/978-3-319-41540-6_21
9. Dave, V., Krishna, S., Murali, V., Trivedi, A.: Optimal repair for omega-regular properties (2022). arxiv.org/abs/2207.13416
10. Filiot, E., Mazzocchi, N., Raskin, J., Sankaranarayanan, S., Trivedi, A.: Weighted transducers for robustness verification. In: International Conference on Concurrency Theory, CONCUR 2020, pp. 17:1–17:21 (2020)
11. Henzinger, T.A., Doyen, L., Chatterjee, K.: Expressiveness and closure properties for quantitative languages. In: Logic in Computer Science, Symposium on, pp. 199–208 (2009)
12. Henzinger, T.A., Otop, J.: From model checking to model measuring. In: D'Argenio, P.R., Melgratti, H. (eds.) CONCUR 2013. LNCS, vol. 8052, pp. 273–287. Springer, Heidelberg (2013). https://doi.org/10.1007/978-3-642-40184-8_20
13. Jobstmann, B., Griesmayer, A., Bloem, R.: Program repair as a game. In: Etessami, K., Rajamani, S.K. (eds.) CAV 2005. LNCS, vol. 3576, pp. 226–238. Springer, Heidelberg (2005). https://doi.org/10.1007/11513988_23
14. Kupferman, O., Tamir, T.: Coping with selfish on-going behaviors. Inf. Comput. **210**, 1–12 (2012)
15. Puterman, M.L.: Markov Decision Processes: Discrete Stochastic Dynamic Programming, 1st edn. John Wiley & Sons Inc., USA (1994)
16. Samanta, R., Olivo, O., Emerson, E.A.: Cost-aware automatic program repair. In: Müller-Olm, M., Seidl, H. (eds.) SAS 2014. LNCS, vol. 8723, pp. 268–284. Springer, Cham (2014). https://doi.org/10.1007/978-3-319-10936-7_17

17. Vardi, M.Y., Wolper, P.: An automata-theoretic approach to automatic program verification. In: Proceedings of the First Symposium on Logic in Computer Science, pp. 322–331. IEEE Computer Society (1986)
18. von Essen, C., Jobstmann, B.: Program repair without regret. Formal Methods Syst. Des. **47**(1), 26–50 (2015). https://doi.org/10.1007/s10703-015-0223-6
19. Zwick, U., Paterson, M.: The complexity of mean payoff games on graphs. Theoret. Comput. Sci. **158**(1), 343–359 (1996)

Repairing Real-Time Requirements

Reiya Noguchi[1,2], Ocan Sankur[3(✉)], Thierry Jéron[3], Nicolas Markey[3],
and David Mentré[2]

[1] Mitsubishi Electric Corporation, Tokyo, Japan
`noguchi.reiya@ah.MitsubishiElectric.co.jp`
[2] Mitsubishi Electric R&D Centre Europe, Rennes, France
`{r.noguchi,d.mentre}@fr.merce.mee.com`
[3] Univ Rennes, Inria, CNRS, Rennes, France
`{ocan.sankur,thierry.jeron,nicolas.markey}@inria.fr`

Abstract. We consider the problem of repairing inconsistent real-time requirements with respect to two consistency notions: non-vacuity, which means that each requirement can be realized without violating other ones, and rt-consistency, which means that inevitable violations are detected immediately. We provide an iterative algorithm, based on solving SMT queries, to replace designated parameters of real-time requirements with new Boolean expressions and time constraints, so that the resulting set of requirements becomes consistent.

1 Introduction

Requirements play an important role in the design of real-time systems. These allow one to specify desired properties for the system under development at an early stage, and can be used to guide testing and formal verification [26]. While basic requirements focus on the relation between the inputs and outputs of the system, extrafunctional properties such as timing constraints are crucial for describing the behaviors of real-time systems.

It is thus important to design formal requirements that are *consistent*, that is, that avoid contradictions and admit implementations. Several works have focused on providing tools to define, combine, and study specifications [8]; others have defined various notions of *consistency*, *e.g.* [1,14,27,28], which are used to detect conflictual requirements that are impossible to satisfy in an implementation according to given criteria.

While several works have focused on checking the consistency of requirement sets, or applying formal verification on requirements, we are interested in *repairing* a given requirement set that is inconsistent, in order to turn it into a consistent set. Repairing an unsatisfactory model or program is an active research area. It consists in building expressions that fit a given data set to fill unknown expressions in programs. Various techniques such as constraint solving, decision tree learning, or search algorithms are used for repairing programs [3,16]. We believe that requirements are a good target for repair algorithms as they can

---

This work was partially funded by ANR project Ticktac (ANR-18-CE40-0015).

A. Bouajjani et al. (Eds.): ATVA 2022, LNCS 13505, pp. 371–387, 2022.
https://doi.org/10.1007/978-3-031-19992-9_24

assist the user in correcting unsatisfactory requirement sets in an early stage. In this paper, we provide repair algorithms tailored for the consistency of real-time requirements.

We consider two consistency notions from the literature. The first one is the *non-vacuity* of a requirement set, studied in temporal logic model checking [22] but also in requirement verification [28]. This line of work was inspired by the observation that formulas of the form $a \to b$ might hold in a given model simply because a never becomes true. Thus, such a formula is *vacuously* satisfied, which indicates an error, either in the design of the model or in the specification. Intuitively, when all requirements are such implications, a requirement set is *non-vacuous* if the premise of each requirement is satisfied by some execution which does not fail the other requirements.

We consider requirements expressed as Simplified Universal Patterns (SUPs for short) [9,29], which are patterns defining real-time temporal properties, and are in the form of a logical implication with time constraints: in each requirement, completing a given *trigger* phase implies the realization of a corresponding *action* phase. Moreover, the action phase must start after a given time interval following the trigger, and phases are given durations with time intervals. Due to this form, non-vacuity is easy to define and to interpret: the trigger phase of each requirement must be realized by some execution which does not fail other requirements. SUPs can be expressed as timed automata, and our algorithms can be easily extended to general timed automata [2] as in [18]. We do focus on SUPs here for their simplicity, and because non-vacuity can be defined naturally due to their form. They are expressive enough to write complex specifications, including the benchmarks we consider in Sect. 4.

The second consistency notion we consider is *rt-consistency* [27]. This requires that all finite executions that satisfy all requirements (*i.e.*, do not violate any of them) admit infinite extensions that still satisfy all the requirements. Put differently, this means that if an implementation produces a finite execution whose all continuations necessarily lead to the failure of some requirement, then there must be a requirement that already fails at the said finite execution: the inevitability of an error must be anticipated by the set of requirements. It can be shown that rt-consistency is not a linear-time property; it was expressed using a CTL formula in [18]. It can be observed that adding a requirement to the set can remove rt-inconsistencies, since, intuitively, the new requirement can be made to imediately fail whenever the error is inevitable in the future. However, this must be done with care since adding a requirement might also introduce new rt-inconsistencies and render some other requirements vacuous.

Our main result is an algorithm that, given a requirement set and some designated parameter set M (time constraints and/or Boolean expressions that appear in requirements), attempts to compute new values for the parameters in M such that the new requirement set is rt-consistent and non-vacuous. Our algorithm is iterative: at each iteration, we solve an SMT query to compute candidate values for the parameters, and check whether non-vacuity and rt-consistency hold. When this is not the case, we derive a new constraint to add to the SMT query and start again. The new constraint either forces one of the requirements to be satisfied non-vacuously, or it excludes a counterexample to rt-consistency.

We apply our algorithm to several benchmarks including four case studies that have appeared in the literature, and anonymized benchmarks from [23]. In each case, we considered manually-introduced rt-inconsistencies and focused on two uses: repairing the requirement set by adding a fresh requirement; and repairing the set by modifying the parameters of a designated requirement.

Related Works. Verification algorithms for non-vacuity and rt-consistency were given in [23] based on a reduction of the problems to a safety verification problem, and using a software model checker. Due to efficiency constraints, the presented results are obtained using a partial check: the rt-consistency is checked only for pairs of real-time requirements; nonetheless, the method can also be applied to consider the whole set.

Our approach is similar to program repair [3,16] where some techniques are also based on using solvers to find expressions subject to given constraints. The main difference of such lines of work with ours is that correctness is defined based on non-vacuity and rt-consistency rather than on the acceptance of given test cases, or on the model checking of the program w.r.t. a specification.

Repairing real-time systems has been considered recently. In [19,20], the authors provide an iterative algorithm that finds a timed diagnostic trace in a timed automaton using a model checker, and use an SMT solver to compute modifications in the guards of the automaton. To ensure that the new automaton is satisfactory, they check for untimed language equivalence (which is EXPSPACE-complete [13]). Their tool enumerates all possible repairs until one passes this equivalence test. In [4], the authors use parameter synthesis to find new values of guards and validate with testing. Guard relaxation for ensuring a reachability property is studied in [7].

Several algorithms for temporal logics rely on a given labeling of input signals: the goal is to compute parameter values so as to reject some set of inputs signals, and accept some others; see [11,15,21] for signal temporal logic. The problem of synthesizing parameters for metric temporal logic formulas for a given hybrid system was studied in [30]; see also [5] for a statistical learning procedure. In [25], the goal is to compute a formula that accepts a given set of positive traces, and rejects given negative traces. The algorithm also uses a SAT solver to guess the formula as a DAG of size n, and increases n until a solution is found. In our case, we restrict to requirements with propositional formulas in conjunctive form, which simplifies their encodings.

2   Preliminaries

Traces. We fix a set AP of atomic propositions that represent Boolean inputs and outputs of the system. A *valuation* of AP is a mapping $v_{AP} \colon AP \to \{\top, \bot\}$ (or equivalently an element of 2^{AP}). We write $\mathcal{B}(AP)$ for the set of Boolean combinations of atomic propositions in AP. That a valuation v_{AP} satisfies a formula $\phi \in \mathcal{B}(AP)$, denoted by $v_{AP} \models \phi$, is defined in the usual way.

A (finite) *trace* σ is a sequence of valuations, and its length is denoted by $|\sigma|$. Traces are seen as elements of $(2^{AP})^*$. The *prefix of length* i of the trace $\sigma = \sigma_1\sigma_2\ldots\sigma_n$ is denoted by $\sigma_{1\ldots i} = \sigma_1\sigma_2\ldots\sigma_i$.

Timed Automata. We use timed automata (here with a discrete-time semantics) to model and reason about timed requirements.

Let $\mathcal{X} = \{c_i \mid 1 \le i \le k\}$ be a set of variables called *clocks*. We consider integer-valued clocks. For a valuation $v_{\mathcal{X}}\colon \mathcal{X} \to \mathbb{N}$ (equivalently an element of $\mathbb{N}^{\mathcal{X}}$), an integer $d \in \mathbb{N}$, and a subset of clocks $R \subseteq \mathcal{X}$, we define $v_{\mathcal{X}} + d$ as the valuation $(v_{\mathcal{X}} + d)(c) = v_{\mathcal{X}}(c) + d$ for all $c \in \mathcal{X}$, and $v_{\mathcal{X}}[R \leftarrow 0]$ as $v_{\mathcal{X}}[R \leftarrow 0](c) = 0$ if $c \in R$, and $v_{\mathcal{X}}[R \leftarrow 0](c) = v_{\mathcal{X}}(c)$ otherwise. Let $\mathbf{0}$ be the valuation mapping all variables to 0.

The set of *clock constraints* over $\mathcal{X}$ is defined by the grammar: $g ::= c \sim n \mid g \wedge g$, where $c \in \mathcal{X}$, $n \in \mathbb{N}$, and $\sim \in \{<, \le, =, \ge, >\}$. Let $\mathcal{C}(\mathcal{X})$ denote the set of all clock constraints over $\mathcal{X}$. The semantics of clock constraints is defined in the expected way: given a clock valuation $v_{\mathcal{X}}\colon \mathcal{X} \to \mathbb{N}$, a constraint $g \in \mathcal{C}(\mathcal{X})$ is true at $v_{\mathcal{X}}$, denoted $v_{\mathcal{X}} \models g$, if the formula obtained by replacing each occurrence of c in g by $v_{\mathcal{X}}(c)$ holds.

We consider timed automata over the alphabet 2^{AP} of valuations of AP, thereby generating (discrete-time) traces. Transitions are labelled with Boolean constraints on AP.

A *timed automaton* (TA) is a tuple $\mathcal{A} = \langle S, s_0, AP, \mathcal{X}, T, F \rangle$ where S is a finite set of states, $s_0 \in S$ is the initial state, AP is a finite set of atomic propositions, $\mathcal{X}$ is a finite set of clocks, $T \subseteq S \times \mathcal{B}(AP) \times \mathcal{C}(\mathcal{X}) \times 2^{\mathcal{X}} \times S$ is a finite set of transitions, and $F \subseteq S$ is the set of accepting states.

We endow timed automata with a discrete-time semantics, as follows. With a timed automaton $\mathcal{A}$, we define the infinite-state automaton $\mathcal{S}(\mathcal{A}) = \langle Q, q_0, D, Q_F \rangle$ over 2^{AP} where $Q = S \times \mathbb{N}^{\mathcal{X}}$, $q_0 = (s_0, \mathbf{0})$, $Q_F = F \times \mathbb{N}^{\mathcal{X}}$ is the set of accepting configurations, and transitions in D are combinations of a transition of the TA and a one-time-unit delay. Formally, given a valuation $v_{AP} \in 2^{AP}$ and two configurations $(s, v_{\mathcal{X}})$ and $(s', v'_{\mathcal{X}})$, there is a transition $((s, v_{\mathcal{X}}), v_{AP}, (s', v'_{\mathcal{X}}))$ in D if, and only if, there is a transition (s, ϕ, g, r, s') in T such that $v_{AP} \models \phi$ and $v_{\mathcal{X}} \models g$, and $v'_{\mathcal{X}} = (v_{\mathcal{X}}[r \leftarrow 0]) + 1$.

Our semantics thus makes it compulsory to take a transition of the TA (possibly a self-loop) at each time unit. This can be used to emulate invariants in states. The automaton $\mathcal{S}(\mathcal{A})$ can be rendered finite by bounding the clocks since the exact values of clock variables above a threshold do not matter (see [2]).

A *run* of $\mathcal{A}$ is a run of its associated infinite-state automaton $\mathcal{S}(\mathcal{A})$. It can be represented as a sequence along which configurations and actions alternate: $(s_0, v_0) \cdot \sigma_1 \cdot (s_1, v_1) \cdot \sigma_2 \cdots (s_n, v_n) \cdots$. A finite run is *accepting* if it ends in Q_F. A trace $\sigma = (\sigma_i)_{1 \le i \le n}$ is accepted by $\mathcal{A}$ if there is an accepting run $(s_0, v_0) \cdot \sigma_1 \cdot (s_1, v_1) \cdot \sigma_2 \cdots (s_n, v_n)$ in $\mathcal{A}$.

We only consider *safety* TAs, *i.e.*, TAs in which there are no transitions from $S \setminus F$ to F. Under such a condition, a run is accepting if, and only if, it never visits any non-accepting state. This simplifies the presentation but a richer set of properties could be handled as in [18].

Simplified Universal Patterns. Simplified Universal Patterns (SUPs) [9,29] are a simple and convenient formalism for expressing requirements. They are more intuitive, but less expressive, than TAs.

An SUP requirement has the following form:

$$(\text{TSE}, \text{TC}, \text{TEE})[\text{Tmin}, \text{Tmax}] \xrightarrow{[\text{Lmin}, \text{Lmax}]} (\text{ASE}, \text{AC}, \text{AEE})[\text{Amin}, \text{Amax}],$$

where $\mathcal{F}_b = \{\text{TSE}, \text{TC}, \text{TEE}, \text{ASE}, \text{AC}, \text{AEE}\}$ is the set of *Boolean parameters* (See Fig. 1 for the meaning of acronyms), which are Boolean formulas on AP, and $\mathcal{F}_t = \{\text{Lmin}, \text{Lmax}, \text{Amin}, \text{Amax}, \text{Tmin}, \text{Tmax}\}$ is the set of *time parameters*, which are integer time bounds. Their union is $\mathcal{F} = \mathcal{F}_b \cup \mathcal{F}_t$. We only consider bounded intervals.

Figure 1 illustrates the intuitive semantics of SUPs. A *trigger phase* (left) is realized, if TSE occurs and is confirmed within a duration in [Tmin, Tmax], that is, if TC holds until TEE occurs; otherwise the trigger is *aborted*. For the SUP instance to *succeed*, following each realized trigger phase, an *action phase* must be realized: an action phase starts with ASE within [Lmin, Lmax] time units after the end of the trigger phase, and AC must hold until AEE occurs within [Amin, Amax] time units. Otherwise, the SUP is *failed*.

The semantics of (generic) SUPs can be encoded using timed automata [6]. These automata are defined over states $Q_{\text{SUP}} = \{\text{init}, \text{trig}, \text{delay}, \text{act}, \text{err}\}$ with err the only state not in F. Intuitively, the execution starts at init, it is at trig if the trigger phase is being checked; at delay if the trigger was realized but the subsequent action has not started yet; at act if the action phase is being checked; from delay or act, either err is reached and the SUP is failed, or init is reached and the SUP succeeds. Note that similar automata definitions were previously given [6].

An SUP instance can be defined as a valuation P of parameters in $\mathcal{F}$, *i.e.*, a valuation of each Boolean parameter of $\mathcal{F}_b$ by a formula in $\mathcal{B}(\text{AP})$, and each time parameter of $\mathcal{F}_t$ by an integer. We then write $\text{SUP}(P)$ for the SUP with parameters defined by P, and $\mathcal{A}_{\text{SUP}(P)}$ for the timed automaton corresponding to $\text{SUP}(P)$. Given such a P and $f \in \mathcal{F}$, P_f refers to the value of the parameter f in P.

The sets of SUP requirements we consider will always be assumed to be indexed, and will be written in the form $(\text{SUP}(P^i))_{1 \leq i \leq n}$. Thus P_f^i will refer

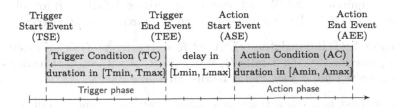

Fig. 1. Intuitive semantics of SUPs

to the value of the parameter f in P^i. We will also consider subsets of *indexed parameters* $\{(f,i) \mid f \in \mathcal{F}, 1 \leq i \leq n\}$ to refer to a subset of the parameters.

Example 1. Consider a flashing light which can blink with a period of 20 time units. The variable `blink` determines whether the blinking mode is active, and `on` indicates that the light is currently on.

$$R_1: \qquad (\mathsf{on}, \mathsf{true}, \mathsf{true})[0,0] \xrightarrow{[0,0]} (\mathsf{true}, \mathsf{on}, \neg\mathsf{on})[10,10]$$

$$R_2: \qquad (\neg\mathsf{on}, \neg\mathsf{on}, \neg\mathsf{on} \wedge \mathsf{blink})[9,9] \xrightarrow{[1,1]} (\mathsf{true}, \mathsf{true}, \mathsf{on})[0,0]$$

R_1 means that when the light turns on, it will remain on for 10 time units, and then turn off. R_2 states that if the light has been off for 9 time units, and the blinking mode is active, then it should turn on at the next time unit.

If we write $R_1 = \text{SUP}(P^1)$ and $R_2 = \text{SUP}(P^2)$, then for instance, P^2_{TSE} is the formula $\neg\mathsf{on}$, and $P^1_{\text{Amax}} = 10$.

In the rest of the paper, we only consider timed automata that correspond to SUPs; and the term *requirement* interchangeably refers to an SUP or to its timed-automaton representation.

A trace σ is said to *trigger* an SUP requirement $\text{SUP}(P)$, if the trigger phase is realized by reading σ, that is, if TSE is observed and, within a period in [Tmin, Tmax], TC holds until a point where TEE is true.

A finite or infinite trace σ *satisfies* the SUP if the state `err` is never reached in $\mathcal{A}_{\text{SUP}(P)}$ by reading σ; this is denoted by $\sigma \models \text{SUP}(P)$. If `err` is reached, then σ *fails* $\text{SUP}(P)$ and we write $\sigma \not\models \text{SUP}(P)$. For a set of requirements $\mathcal{R} = (\text{SUP}(P^i))_{1 \leq i \leq n}$, we write $\sigma \models \mathcal{R}$ if σ satisfies *all* requirements in $\mathcal{R}$. Symmetrically, we write $\sigma \not\models \mathcal{R}$ if σ fails *at least one of* the requirements in $\mathcal{R}$. Note that since we consider bounded time intervals, when a trace triggers a requirement R, all extensions will eventually either realize the action phase or fail R.

RT-Consistency. We recall rt-consistency, introduced in [27] and further studied in [18]. Put simply, a set $\mathcal{R}$ of requirements is rt-consistent if all finite traces that do not fail $\mathcal{R}$ admit infinite continuations that satisfy $\mathcal{R}$. In other terms, at any finite trace where failure is inevitable, some requirement must already be failed.

For a requirement set $\mathcal{R}$, and trace σ, we write σ **I-fails** $\mathcal{R}$ if for all infinite traces σ', $\sigma \cdot \sigma' \not\models \mathcal{R}$. RT-consistency can then be expressed as follows:

Definition 1 (RT-consistency). *A set $\mathcal{R}$ of requirements is* rt-consistent *if, for any finite trace σ, if σ **I-fails** $\mathcal{R}$, then $\sigma \not\models \mathcal{R}$. A witness to rt-inconsistency then is a finite trace σ such that σ **I-fails** $calR$ and $\sigma \models \mathcal{R}$.*

Thus a witness is a finite trace that satisfies all requirements but whose all infinite continuations fail some of the requirements.

A simpler characterization of rt-inconsistency was proven in [18]:

Theorem 1 [18]. *A set $\mathcal{R}$ of requirements is* rt-inconsistent *if, and only if there exists a trace σ such that $\sigma \models \mathcal{R}$, and for any valuation $a \in 2^{AP}$, $\sigma a \not\models \mathcal{R}$.*

Example 2. We consider the requirements R_1 and R_2 from Example 1. We add an atomic proposition lowBattery, and consider the new requirement

$$R_3 \colon (\text{lowBattery}, \text{true}, \text{true})[0, 0] \xrightarrow{[0,0]} (\text{true}, \neg\text{on}, \text{true})[50, 50],$$

which requires to switch off the lights for 50 time units if the battery is detected to be low. The set $\mathcal{R} = \{R_1, R_2, R_3\}$ of requirements is rt-inconsistent. In fact, the finite trace $\sigma = \{\text{lowBattery}\} \cdot \emptyset \cdot \ldots \cdot \emptyset \cdot \{\text{blink}\}$ of length 9 does not fail any of the requirements, so $\sigma \models \mathcal{R}$. But all extensions of σ fail $\mathcal{R}$. In fact, by R_2, on must be true in the next state; while by R_3, on must be false. Thus, σ is a witness to the rt-inconsistency of $\mathcal{R}$. One could repair this rt-inconsistency by forcing the value of blink to false for 50 time units whenever lowBattery is true: $R_4 \colon (\text{lowBattery}, \text{true}, \text{true})[0, 0] \xrightarrow{[0,0]} (\text{true}, \neg\text{blink}, \text{true})[50, 50]$, so that $\mathcal{R} \cup \{R_4\}$ is rt-consistent.

Non-vacuity. We define the *non-vacuity* of a set of requirements, which states that each requirement must be triggered by some trace without failing any requirement. This notion is closely related to non-vacuity in temporal logic, where an implication of the form $a \to b$ is said to be satisfied *vacuously* if a is never satisfied in the given system [22]. SUP requirements are similar to implications since the realization of a trigger phase implies the non-violation of the action phase. Intuitively, a requirement that is impossible to trigger points to a bug in the set of requirements, and a good set of requirements must be non-vacuous.

For $R \in \mathcal{R}$, we say that R is *non-vacuous in* $\mathcal{R}$ if there exists a trace that satisfies $\mathcal{R}$ and triggers R; otherwise R is *vacuous* in $\mathcal{R}$.

Definition 2 (Non-vacuity). *A set $\mathcal{R}$ of SUP requirements is* non-vacuous *if for each $R \in \mathcal{R}$, there exists a trace that satisfies $\mathcal{R}$ and triggers R.*

Example 3. Consider again requirements R_1, R_2. Assume that the designer wants to allow a user to maintain the light on manually by pushing a button, but wants blinking to be deactivated if the user has been pushing the button for 20 time units, expressed as

$$R_3' \colon (\text{on}, \text{on}, \text{on})[20, 20] \xrightarrow{[0,0]} (\text{true}, \text{true}, \neg\text{blink})[0, 0].$$

However, the set $\{R_1, R_2, R_3'\}$ is vacuous: in fact, R_3' can never be triggered since according to R_1, maintaining on for 10 time units switches the light off. Thus, R_3' is useless. To fix this issue, the designer can introduce a predicate button determining whether the button is being pushed, require R_1, R_2 under condition $\neg$button, and trigger R_3 if button $\wedge$ on has been true for 20 time units.

Conjunctive Formulas and Substitutions. Although we allow the parameters of SUP requirements to be arbitrary Boolean expressions, we will only synthesize parameters that are conjunctive formulas when repairing requirements. We show here how synthesizing a conjunctive formula can be seen as choosing an integer valuation for a set of fresh variables. This will allow us to use an SMT solver for finding repairs.

Let us fix a requirement set $\mathcal{R} = (\text{SUP}(P^i))_{1 \leq i \leq n}$, and a subset of *modifiable* indexed parameters $M \subseteq \{(f, i) \mid 1 \leq i \leq n, f \in \mathcal{F}\}$. For $(f, i) \in M$, define $\text{AP}_{f,i}$ as the set of fresh integer variables $x_{f,i}$ for $x \in \text{AP}$ as follows:

- For $f \in \mathcal{F}_b$, the value of $x_{f,i}$ encodes how x should appear in the conjunctive formula for f in P^i: as a positive literal (1), as a negative literal (-1), or absent (0). We define the *template* for (f, i) as

$$\text{tmp}(f, i) = \wedge_{x \in \text{AP}}([x_{f,i} = 1] \Rightarrow x) \wedge ([x_{f,i} = -1] \Rightarrow \neg x).$$

  A substitution $\xi : \text{AP}_{f,i} \to \{-1, 0, 1\}$ simplifies this formula into a conjunctive formula over AP, so looking for such a conjunctive formula is reduced to looking for a valuation over the variables in $\text{AP}_{f,i}$. The conjunctive formula thus obtained is denoted $\text{tmp}(f, i)[\xi]$. Conversely, any conjunctive formula over AP can be obtained from a template formula by such a substitution.
- For $f \in \mathcal{F}_t$, we define $\text{tmp}(f, i) = x_{f,i}$, and consider substitutions which replace variables $x_{f,i}$ with natural numbers.

Let us define $\text{AP}_M = \bigcup_{\{(f,i) \in M\}} \text{AP}_{f,i}$. Given $\mathcal{R}$ and M, a substitution will refer to a function that is the union of substitutions for all parameters in M (including both timed and Boolean). We denote by $\text{tmp}_M(\mathcal{R})$ the *template requirement set* in which each parameter value P^i_f with $(f, i) \in M$ is replaced with $\text{tmp}(f, i)$; and for a substitution ξ, $\text{tmp}_M(\mathcal{R})[\xi]$ denotes the requirement set obtained by applying the given subtitution to all templates.

Example 4. Consider the following requirements $\mathcal{R} = \{R_1, R_2\}$.

$$R_1: \qquad (\text{on}, \text{true}, \text{true})[0, \square] \xrightarrow{[0,0]} (\text{true}, \text{on}, \square)[10, 10]$$

$$R_2: \qquad (\neg\text{on}, \neg\text{on}, \square)[9, 9] \xrightarrow{[1,1]} (\text{true}, \text{true}, \text{on})[0, 0]$$

with $\text{AP} = \{\text{on}, \text{blink}\}$, and consider $M = \{(\text{AEE}, 1), (\text{TEE}, 2), (\text{Tmax}, 1)\}$ (*i.e.*, AEE and Tmax in R_1 and TEE in R_2). Placeholders for parameters in M are shown as $\square$. We have, for instance,

$$\text{tmp}(\text{AEE}, 1) = ([\text{on}_{\text{AEE},1} = 1] \Rightarrow \text{on}) \wedge ([\text{on}_{\text{AEE},1} = -1] \Rightarrow \neg\text{on})$$
$$\wedge ([\text{blink}_{\text{AEE},1} = 1] \Rightarrow \text{blink}) \wedge ([\text{blink}_{\text{AEE},1} = -1] \Rightarrow \neg\text{blink})$$

The substitution defined by $\xi(\text{on}_{\text{AEE},1}) = -1$, $\xi(\text{blink}_{\text{AEE},1}) = 0$, $\xi(\text{on}_{\text{TEE},2}) = -1$, $\xi(\text{blink}_{\text{TEE},2}) = 1$, and $\xi(t_{\text{Tmax},1}) = 0$, yields $\text{tmp}(\text{AEE}, 1)[\xi] = \neg\text{on}$ and tmp(TEE, 2)$[\xi]$ = $\neg$on $\wedge$ blink and tmp(Tmax, 1)$[\xi]$ = 0. Thus, tmp$_M(\mathcal{R})[\xi]$ is the following:

$$R_1: \qquad (\text{on}, \text{true}, \text{true})[0,0] \xrightarrow{[0,0]} (\text{true}, \text{on}, \neg\text{on})[10,10]$$

$$R_2: \qquad (\neg\text{on}, \neg\text{on}, \neg\text{on} \wedge \text{blink})[9,9] \xrightarrow{[1,1]} (\text{true}, \text{true}, \text{on})[0,0]$$

3   Repair Algorithm

Let $\mathcal{R} = (\text{SUP}(P^i))_{1 \leq i \leq n}$ denote a set of SUP requirements and suppose that it is either vacuous or rt-inconsistent. Given $M \subseteq \{(f, i) \mid 1 \leq i \leq n, f \in \mathcal{F}\}$ of indexed parameters of $\mathcal{R}$, we want to render $\mathcal{R}$ rt-consistent *and* non-vacuous by replacing the parameters in M by fresh conjunctive formulas or time bounds.

Definition 3 (ReqFix). *Given a set $\mathcal{R} = (\text{SUP}(P^i))_{1 \leq i \leq n}$ of requirements, and a subset $M \subseteq \{(f, i) \mid 1 \leq i \leq n, f \in \mathcal{F}\}$, find a substitution ξ such that $\mathcal{R}' = \text{tmp}_M(\mathcal{R})[\xi]$ is non-vacuous and rt-consistent.*

Thus, our goal is to repair the given requirements by modifying the allowed set M of parameters. The most general use of the algorithm is to let the user identify the set M. This can be based on their expertise, while we discuss automatizing the choice of M using rt-inconsistency or vacuity proofs in Sect. 5.

We will also consider a particular use of the algorithm. Notice that some rt-inconsistencies can be repaired by adding a new requirement as we saw in Example 2. The ReqFix problem can be instantiated to add a new requirement as follows. Let trivial denote the SUP requirement where all Boolean parameters are $\top$, and all time parameters are 0. This requirement is trivially satisfied. We add the trivial requirement to $\mathcal{R}$, and let M be the set of all parameters of trivial. Note however that vacuity cannot be repaired by a new requirement, so this only applies to rt-inconsistency.

3.1   Checking Non-vacuity and rt-Consistency

For a finite trace $\sigma \in (2^{\text{AP}})^*$, let $\text{trig}_\sigma(R)$ denote a propositional formula that is true if, and only if, σ has triggered R. This formula guesses the execution of the SUP automaton on the trace σ and constrains it to visit the state delay. Similarly, a propositional formula can be built for $\sigma \models \mathcal{R}$ (as well as for $\sigma \not\models \mathcal{R}$) by guessing an execution on the automata corresponding to each $R \in \mathcal{R}$ and constraining these to end outside of err (resp. at err).

We perform non-vacuity checking for a requirement $R \in \mathcal{R}$ as a bounded search for a trace that triggers R without failing $\mathcal{R}$.

Definition 4. *For a given set of requirements $\mathcal{R}$, $R \in \mathcal{R}$, and bound $\alpha > 0$, define* nonvac$(R, \mathcal{R})$ *as* $\exists \sigma \in (2^{\text{AP}_1} \cdot \ldots \cdot 2^{\text{AP}_\alpha})$. $\text{trig}_\sigma(R) \wedge \sigma \models \mathcal{R}$.

Notice that each 2^{AP_i} defines the valuation at the i-th step. This is thus a partial check since the bound α needs to be fixed. Notice that even though σ triggers R and $\sigma \models R$, it might be that no infinite extensions of such a σ satisfy R; nonetheless, since we also ensure that R is rt-consistent, such an extension will be guaranteed to exist. If nonvac(R, R) is true, then one can query the solver for a witness trace σ triggering R and satisfying R.

We will use template variants of the above formulas: $\mathsf{trig}_\sigma(\mathsf{tmp}_M(R))$, $\sigma \models \mathsf{tmp}_M(R)$, $\sigma \not\models \mathsf{tmp}_M(R)$, nonvac$(\mathsf{tmp}_M(R), \mathsf{tmp}_M(R))$. These simply consist in replacing formulas corresponding to parameters in M by templates. The set of free variables of the latter formulas is AP_M. As in Sect. 2, applying a substitution for AP_M determines the truth value of each formula.

This allows us to constrain substitutions ξ we want to compute. For instance, if we want ξ to define a new requirement set $\mathsf{tmp}_M(R)[\xi]$ that is satisfied by a given trace σ, and in which $R \in R$ is non-vacuous, we can check the satisfiability of $\sigma \models \mathsf{tmp}_M(R) \wedge \mathsf{nonvac}(\mathsf{tmp}_M(R), \mathsf{tmp}_M(R))$, and choose ξ as a model of this formula. We generalize this idea into an algorithm in the next section.

To check rt-consistency, one can use, as a black box, any algorithm given in [18,23,27]. Here, we consider a bounded model checking approach and look for an rt-inconsistency witness of bounded length using an SMT solver, following the formulation of Theorem 1. This approach only gives partial guarantees, it improves the performance while ruling out any counterexample of a given length. A sound and complete algorithm from [18,23] can be used instead to make the check complete.

3.2   Algorithm for ReqFix

Consider $R = \mathrm{SUP}(P_i)_{1 \leq i \leq n}$ and a subset M of indexed parameters. Let $R_M \subseteq R$ be the subset of requirements with parameters in M, and $\overline{R}_M = R \setminus R_M$. That is, only R_M has modifiable parameters.

The algorithm consists in guessing conjunctive formulas for parameters in M, that is, a substitution ξ that satisfies a set of constraints C that we iteratively build. If the guessed substitution ξ yields a non-vacuous and rt-consistent requirement set, then we return $\mathsf{tmp}_M(R)[\xi]$ as the new requirement set. Otherwise, the algorithm derives new constraints to add to C and iterates.

Assume that R is vacuous, that is, there exists $R \in R$ which cannot be triggered. Then, the substitution ξ we are looking for must be such that $\mathsf{tmp}_M(R)[\xi]$ is non-vacuous in $\mathsf{tmp}_M(R)[\xi]$, that is, we must add the following formula to C: nonvac$(\mathsf{tmp}_M(R)[\xi], \mathsf{tmp}_M(R)[\xi])$.

Assume that R is rt-inconsistent, σ is an rt-inconsistency witness.

1. If σ is an rt-inconsistency witness for $\overline{R}_M$, since we can only modify R_M, then we need $\mathsf{tmp}_M(R_M)[\xi]$ to rule out σ, that is, σ must fail $\mathsf{tmp}_M(R_M)[\xi]$. We thus add $\sigma \not\models \mathsf{tmp}_M(R_M)$ to the constraint set C.
2. If σ is not an rt-inconsistency witness for $\overline{R}_M$, then σ can be extended without failing $\overline{R}_M$, but these extensions lead to failure in R_M. In order to rule out the witness σ, $\mathsf{tmp}_M(R_M)[\xi]$ must be such that either σ is rejected (*i.e.*, $\sigma \not\models$

$\mathsf{tmp}_M(\mathcal{R}_M)[\xi])$, or σ admits a one-step extension that satisfies $\mathsf{tmp}_M(\mathcal{R})[\xi]$. This constraint on ξ is written as $\sigma \not\models \mathsf{tmp}_M(\mathcal{R}_M) \vee \mathsf{ext}_\sigma(\mathsf{tmp}_M(\mathcal{R}))$, where $\mathsf{ext}_\sigma(\mathsf{tmp}_M(\mathcal{R})) = \exists a \in 2^{\mathsf{AP}}. \; \sigma \cdot a \models \mathsf{tmp}_M(\mathcal{R})$.

The following lemma shows that the constraints added in the two cases described above are necessary in order to rule out the rt-inconsistency witness.

Lemma 1. *Let σ be an rt-inconsistency witness for $\mathcal{R}$.*

1. *If σ is an rt-inconsistency witness in $\overline{\mathcal{R}}_M$, then for all requirement sets $\mathcal{R}'$ with $\sigma \models \mathcal{R}'$, σ is an rt-inconsistency witness in $\overline{\mathcal{R}}_M \cup \mathcal{R}'$.*
2. *If σ is not an rt-inconsitency witness in $\overline{\mathcal{R}}_M$, then for all requirement sets $\mathcal{R}'$ with $\sigma \models \mathcal{R}' \wedge \neg\mathsf{ext}_\sigma(\overline{\mathcal{R}}_M \cup \mathcal{R}')$, σ is an rt-inconsistency witness in $\overline{\mathcal{R}}_M \cup \mathcal{R}'$.*

Algorithm. The full procedure is described in Algorithm 1. Its inputs are a set $\mathcal{R}$ of requirements, and a subset M of indexed parameters of $\mathcal{R}$. For any propositional formula Φ, we denote by $\mathsf{SAT}(\Phi)$ the satisfiability check which returns either true and a model for Φ, or false.

The algorithm starts with a vacuity check inside the set $\overline{\mathcal{R}}_M$ on line 2: if $\overline{\mathcal{R}}_M$ itself is vacuous, then $\mathcal{R}$ cannot be repaired and the algorithm rejects. We maintain a set of constraints $\mathcal{C}$, which contains non-vacuity constraints of the form $\mathsf{nonvac}(\mathsf{tmp}_M(R), \mathsf{tmp}_M(\mathcal{R}))$ and constraints of the forms $\sigma \not\models \mathsf{tmp}_M(\mathcal{R}_M)$, $\sigma \models \mathsf{tmp}_M(\mathcal{R}_M)$ and $\sigma \not\models \mathsf{tmp}_M(\mathcal{R}_M) \vee \mathsf{ext}_\sigma(\mathsf{tmp}_M(\mathcal{R}))$. Recall that the set of free variables of these formulas is AP_M, so a model for the query on line 5 defines a substitution ξ, and thus a new requirement set $\mathsf{tmp}_M(\mathcal{R})[\xi]$.

On line 7, we check if $\overline{\mathcal{R}}_M \cup \mathcal{R}'_M$ is vacuous, and then identify a requirement R that cannot be triggered without violating $\overline{\mathcal{R}}_M \cup \mathcal{R}'_M$. We necessarily have $R \in \overline{\mathcal{R}}_M$, since all requirements in $\mathcal{R}'_M$ are non-vacuous as they satisfy $\mathcal{C}$. We find a trace σ that triggers R while satisfying $\overline{\mathcal{R}}_M$. Such a trace σ exists by line 2, but necessarily violates $\mathcal{R}'_M$. We add $\sigma \models \mathsf{tmp}_M(\mathcal{R}_M)$ to $\mathcal{C}$, which ensures that subsequent iterations will make sure that σ triggers R without violating $\mathcal{R}'_M$.

If $\overline{\mathcal{R}}_M \cup \mathcal{R}'_M$ is non-vacuous, then we check its rt-consistency. If it is rt-consistent, then the algorithm has succeeded, and we return $\overline{\mathcal{R}}_M \cup \mathcal{R}'_M$. Otherwise, we consider a witness σ to rt-inconsistency. We distinguish two cases as above: On line 13, we check if σ is already a witness to the rt-inconsistency of $\overline{\mathcal{R}}_M$, in which case we add the constraint $\sigma \not\models (\mathsf{tmp}_M(\mathcal{R}_M))$. Otherwise, we add $\sigma \not\models \mathsf{tmp}_M(\mathcal{R}_M) \vee \mathsf{ext}_\sigma(\overline{\mathcal{R}}_M \cup \mathsf{tmp}_M(\mathcal{R}))$.

Observe that if the query on line 5 is unsatisfiable, then the algorithm returns "Unknown", in which case the result is inconclusive. In fact, since the choice of the non-vacuity constraints on Line 8 is arbitrary, the unsatisfiability of the query does not imply the absence of solution. The algorithm could be rendered complete using backtracking although we have not explored this direction.

Minimizing Distance. It may be desirable to compute a solution $\mathsf{tmp}_M(\mathcal{R})[\xi]$ that is syntactically close to $\mathcal{R}$, so as to make a minimal number of changes during the repair. To formalize this, let us define a distance between conjunctive formulas. Let

$$d(\ell_1 \wedge \ldots \wedge \ell_m, \ell'_1 \wedge \ldots \wedge \ell'_n) = |\mathsf{Supp}(\{\ell_1, \ldots, \ell_m\} \oplus \{\ell'_1, \ldots, \ell'_n\})|,$$

Input: A set $\mathcal{R}$ of SUP requirements, and parameter set M
1 Let $\mathcal{R}_M \subseteq \mathcal{R}$ the set of those requirements that contain parameters in M,
  and $\overline{\mathcal{R}}_M = \mathcal{R} \setminus \mathcal{R}_M$
2 **if** $\exists R \in \overline{\mathcal{R}}_M.\ \neg\mathsf{nonvac}(R, \overline{\mathcal{R}}_M)$ **then**
3 | **return** Reject
4 $\mathcal{C} \leftarrow \bigwedge_{R \in \mathcal{R}_M} \mathsf{nonvac}(\mathsf{tmp}_M(R), \mathsf{tmp}_M(\mathcal{R}))$
5 **while** $\mathsf{SAT}(\bigwedge_{\phi(M) \in \mathcal{C}} \phi(M))$ **do**
6 | Let ξ be a model of this formula, and let $\mathcal{R}'_M = \mathsf{tmp}_M(\mathcal{R}_M)[\xi]$
7 | **if** $\overline{\mathcal{R}}_M \cup \mathcal{R}'_M$ *is vacuous* **then**
8 | | Choose $R \in \overline{\mathcal{R}}_M$ which cannot be triggered
9 | | Let σ be a trace that triggers R and satisfies $\overline{\mathcal{R}}_M$
10 | | $\mathcal{C} \leftarrow \mathcal{C} \cup \{\sigma \models \mathsf{tmp}_M(\mathcal{R}_M)\}$
11 | **else if** $\overline{\mathcal{R}}_M \cup \mathcal{R}'_M$ *is rt-inconsistent* **then**
12 | | Let σ be an rt-inconsistency witness
13 | | **if** σ *is an rt-inconsistency witness for* $\overline{\mathcal{R}}_M$ **then**
14 | | | $\mathcal{C} \leftarrow \mathcal{C} \cup \{\sigma \not\models \mathsf{tmp}_M(\mathcal{R}_M)\}$
15 | | **else**
16 | | | $\mathcal{C} \leftarrow \mathcal{C} \cup \{\sigma \not\models \mathsf{tmp}_M(\mathcal{R}_M) \vee \mathsf{ext}_\sigma(\overline{\mathcal{R}}_M \cup \mathsf{tmp}_M(\mathcal{R}_M))\}$
17 | **else**
18 | | **return** $\overline{\mathcal{R}}_M \cup \mathcal{R}'_M$
19 **return** Unknown

Algorithm 1: Algorithm for ReqFix.

where $\oplus$ denotes the symmetric difference, and Supp is the set of variables appearing in the given set of literals. For instance, $d(\neg\mathsf{on}, \mathsf{on}) = 1$, and $d(\mathsf{on} \wedge \mathsf{blink}, \mathsf{on}) = 1$. For two time bounds T, T', we extend this definition to $d(T, T') = |T - T'|$. The distance between two SUPs with parameters P and P' is the weighted sum of the distances of their parameters: $d(P, P') = w_b \cdot \sum_{f \in \mathcal{F}_b} d(P_f, P'_f) + w_t \cdot \sum_{f \in \mathcal{F}_t} d(P_f, P'_f)$ for given weights $w_b, w_t \geq 0$. Furthermore, given two SUP requirement sets of the same size, $\mathcal{R} = (\mathsf{SUP}(P^i))_{1 \leq i \leq n}$ and $\mathcal{R}' = (\mathsf{SUP}(P'^i))_{1 \leq i \leq n}$, define $d(\mathcal{R}, \mathcal{R}') = \sum_{i=1}^n d(P^i, P'^i)$.

In order to find the substitution that minimizes the distance between the original requirement set and the new one, we use MaxSMT [10]. The query on line 5 is considered a *hard* formula (that must be satisfied), and the following are *soft* formulas (that may be satisfied or violated):

$$ w_b \cdot \sum_{(f,i) \in M: f \in \mathcal{F}_b} (\text{if } (x_{f,i} \neq \bar{x}_{f,i}) \text{ then 1 else 0}) + w_t \cdot \sum_{(f,i) \in M: f \in \mathcal{F}_t} |x_{f,i} - \bar{x}_{f,i}| \leq k, $$

for all $0 \leq k \leq m$, for an appropriately chosen m, and weights $w_b, w_t \geq 0$, where $x_{f,i} \in \mathsf{AP}_M$ and the $\bar{x}_{f,i}$ are constant values defining the substitution that yields the original requirement set $\mathcal{R}$. The MaxSMT solver returns a model that satisfies the hard formulas, and satisfies a maximal number of soft formulas; which means minimizing $d(\mathcal{R}, \mathsf{tmp}_M(\mathcal{R})[\xi])$.

4   Experiments

We implemented our techniques in Python and applied it to four case studies from the literature [12,17,24] as well as to a set of anonymized benchmarks from [23]. We manually introduced rt-inconsistencies by removing a requirement, or by modifying the parameters of a requirement. The summary of the results are shown in Table 1. We considered two applications of our algorithm. In the first case, starting from an rt-inconsistent set, we looked for a repair by *generating* a new requirement with the minimal number of literals and the least time bounds. We call this the *generation variant* of our program. Notice that this consists in minimizing the distance of the generated requirement to the trivial requirement. In the second case, we selected the parameters of a requirement as the set M to be *modified*, and looked for a repair that minimizes the distance of the new requirement with the old one. We call this the *modification variant* of our program. While the generation variant allowed us to find very simple repairs, these were not always satisfactory. The second one yields repairs that are syntactically very similar to the initial requirement, and were closer to the intended behavior in the considered case studies. We provide a focus on two case studies below.

Blinking System. This case study corresponds to the behaviour of the turning light indicator in a car [17]. The pitman arm can be moved up or down to a first position (5°) to turn the indicator on for only 3 cycles; in each direction (up and down), it can also be moved to a second position (7°) where the indicator remains on until the arm is moved back. We analyzed a set of 7 requirements, including the following one.

$$R : (\text{down5}, \text{down5}, \neg\text{down5})[0, 3] \xrightarrow{[5,5]} (\neg\text{down5} \wedge \neg\text{down7}, \text{true}, \text{true})[0, 0],$$

which states that if the pitman arm is maintained down for less than 3 time units, then it will automatically be on neutral position 5 time units later. We modified this, by introducing a typo, into the following requirement in order to introduce an rt-inconsistency:

$$R' : (\text{down5}, \text{down5}, \neg\text{down5})[0, 3] \xrightarrow{[5,5]} (\neg\text{down5}, \text{true}, \text{true})[0, 0],$$

and ran the modification variant of the algorithm to find a repair by modifying the parameters of R'. A solution was found after 3 iterations and 12 s:

$$R_{\text{fix}} : (\text{down5}, \text{down5}, \neg\text{down5})[0, 3] \xrightarrow{[5,5]} (\neg\text{down5}, \text{true}, \neg\text{down7})[0, 0],$$

which is semantically equivalent to R.

When we ran the generation variant of the algorithm to find a repair to the set obtained by removing R altogether, we obtained the following requirement:

$$R'_{\text{fix}} : (\text{true}, \text{true}, \text{true})[0, 0] \xrightarrow{[0,0]} (\text{true}, \text{down7}, \neg\text{blink})[0, 6].$$

This requirement enforces that the blinking must be disabled every 6 time units, while in the meantime, the pitman arm kept down by 7°. While this intuitively

Table 1. Results of the benchmarks for two variants of the algorithm: the generation variant repairs requirement sets by adding a fresh requirement; the modification requirement repairs by modifying the parameters of a designated requirement. The former minimizes the number of literals and the size of the time bounds introduced, while the latter minimizes the distance between the designated requirement and the new one. The size column shows the number of requirements; the time column is execution time, and %iter. column shows the number of iterations. A bound of $\alpha = 30$ was used for non-vacuity and rt-consistency checks.

Case study	Size	Modification		Generation	
		Time	#iter.	Time	#iter.
Carriage line [24]	12	24 s	4	38 s	11
Landing gear [12]	10	14 s	2	21 s	6
Car light blink. [17]	6	13 s	4	13 m 47 s	44
Cruise ctrl. [17]	7	9 s	4	12 s	6
part1–04	13	29 s	11	21 s	9
part1–05	14	19 s	4	47 s	17
part1–06	16	17 s	4	21 s	10
part2–06	18	32 s	11	48 s	16
part2–07	24	43 s	5	58 s	12
part2–08	27	51 s	4	1 m 8 s	13
part2–10	80	3 m 47 s	2	2 m 39 s	1
part3–02	26	45 s	5	1 m 3 s	13
part3–04	13	24 s	8	21 s	8
part3–05	26	1 m 6 s	9	1 m 7 s	13
part3–08	27	1 m 52 s	10	1 m 32 s	19
part3–14	24	3 m 8 s	3	10 m 55 s	18
part3–16	22	TO	–	TO	–

does not correspond to a desirable requirement, it does ensure the rt-consistency and non-vacuity. In practice, one would perhaps need to allow the user to inspect the repair and accept or reject, add constraints and ask for a new repair. This could yield more satisfactory repairs for the generation variant.

Carriage Line Control. This example from [24, Appendix 4.20] represents a carriage in charge of bringing a piece of material from a container to a conveyor. When the carriage receives the piece of material, it moves forward to a place where an arm will push the piece onto the conveyor, and then moves back to its original location.

We described the behaviour of this system using 12 SUP requirements, of which 6 involved timing constraints. As an example, we have the following SUP:

$R : (\mathtt{fwd}, \mathtt{true}, \mathtt{true})[0,0] \xrightarrow{[1,1]} (\neg\mathtt{bckwd}, \neg\mathtt{bckwd}, \neg\mathtt{bckwd}\wedge\mathtt{right})[0,20)$, stating that when the carriage is at its forward position, then at the next step, it should not be at the backward position until it starts moving right. This requirement is used to model the physical environment: the carriage cannot be both on the forward and backward limits, and it must start moving right before it can reach the backward limit.

Modifying this requirement by introducing a typo as follows leads to an rt-inconsistency. R' : $(\mathtt{fwd}, \mathtt{true}, \mathtt{true})[0,0] \xrightarrow{[1,1]} (\neg\mathtt{bckwd}, \neg\mathtt{bckwd}, \mathtt{true})[0,20)$,

The modification variant of our tool computed the following repair: R'_{fix} : $(\mathtt{fwd}, \mathtt{true}, \mathtt{true})[0,0] \xrightarrow{[1,1]} (\neg\mathtt{bckwd}, \neg\mathtt{bckwd}, \neg\mathtt{push})[0,20)$, which says that the carriage cannot be in the backward position until the arm stops pushing the object. This is slightly different than the original requirement R but it does constrain the environment in a similar way. In fact, the idea of the system is that the carriage must move right when the arm stops pushing, and R'_{fix} says that only then can the carriage reach the backward limit.

5 Conclusion

We believe that the practical application of requirement repair would be a tool that assists the designer by suggesting repairs. The designer should be able to either pick a suggested repair, suggest additional constraints and request different repairs. Our program is currently a proof of concept and many additional features would be required to turn it into such a tool.

One of the possible directions is to be able to choose the set M automatically. This is possible in some cases, for instance, if $\mathsf{nonvac}(R, \mathcal{R})$ is not true, then one can determine the set of parameters involved in its unsatisfiability proof, which can be included in M (we know that at least one such parameter must be in M). The choice of M with a similar method is less obvious for rt-consistency and will be the subject of future work.

Another important direction would be the computation of solutions that are close to the original requirement set *semantically*, for instance, minimizing the number of traces that are accepted by one but not the other set.

References

1. Aichernig, B.K., Hörmaier, K., Lorber, F., Ničković, D., Tiran, S.: Require, test, and trace IT. Int. J. Softw. Tools Technol. Transf. **19**(4), 409–426 (2016). https://doi.org/10.1007/s10009-016-0444-z
2. Alur, R., Dill, D.L.: A theory of timed automata. Theoret. Comput. Sci. **126**(2), 183–235 (1994)
3. Alur, R., et al.: Search-based program synthesis. Commun. ACM **61**(12), 84–93 (2018)
4. André, É., Arcaini, P., Gargantini, A., Radavelli, M.: Repairing timed automata clock guards through abstraction and testing. In: Beyer, D., Keller, C. (eds.) TAP 2019. LNCS, vol. 11823, pp. 129–146. Springer, Cham (2019). https://doi.org/10.1007/978-3-030-31157-5_9

5. Bartocci, E., Bortolussi, L., Sanguinetti, G.: Data-driven statistical learning of temporal logic properties. In: Legay, A., Bozga, M. (eds.) FORMATS 2014. LNCS, vol. 8711, pp. 23–37. Springer, Cham (2014). https://doi.org/10.1007/978-3-319-10512-3_3

6. Becker, J.S.: Analyzing consistency of formal requirements. In: Automated Verification of Critical Systems (AVoCS) (2019)

7. Bendík, J., Sencan, A., Gol, E.A., Černá, I.: Timed automata relaxation for reachability. In: TACAS 2021. LNCS, vol. 12651, pp. 291–310. Springer, Cham (2021). https://doi.org/10.1007/978-3-030-72016-2_16

8. Benveniste, A., et al.: Contracts for system design. Found. Trends Electron. Des. Autom. **12**(2–3), 124–400 (2018)

9. Bienmüller, T., et al.: Modeling requirements for quantitative consistency analysis and automatic test case generation. In Workshop on Formal and Model-Driven Techniques for Developing Trustworthy Systems (2016)

10. Biere, A., Heule, M., van Maaren, H.: Handbook of Satisfiability. IOS press, Amsterdam (2009)

11. Bombara, G., et al.: A decision tree approach to data classification using signal temporal logic. In: Hybrid Systems: Computation and Control (HSCC), pp. 1–10, Vienna, Austria, April (2016)

12. Boniol, F., Wiels, V.: Landing gear system (2014). https://www.irit.fr/ABZ2014/landing_system.pdf

13. Brenguier, R., Göller, S., Sankur, O.: A comparison of succinctly represented finite-state systems. In: Koutny, M., Ulidowski, I. (eds.) CONCUR 2012. LNCS, vol. 7454, pp. 147–161. Springer, Heidelberg (2012). https://doi.org/10.1007/978-3-642-32940-1_12

14. Ellen, C., Sieverding, S., Hungar, H.: Detecting consistencies and inconsistencies of pattern-based functional requirements. In: Lang, F., Flammini, F. (eds.) FMICS 2014. LNCS, vol. 8718, pp. 155–169. Springer, Cham (2014). https://doi.org/10.1007/978-3-319-10702-8_11

15. Ergurtuna, M., Yalcinkaya, B., Aydin Gol, E.: An automated system repair framework with signal temporal logic. Acta Informatica **59**, 1–27 (2021). https://doi.org/10.1007/s00236-021-00403-z

16. Goues, C.L., Pradel, M., Roychoudhury, A.: Automated program repair. Commun. ACM **62**(12), 56–65 (2019)

17. Houdek, F., Raschke, A.: Adaptive exterior light and speed control system (2021). https://abz2021.uni-ulm.de/resources/files/casestudyABZ2020v1.17.pdf

18. Jéron, T., Markey, N., Mentré, D., Noguchi, R., Sankur, O.: Incremental methods for checking real-time consistency. In: Bertrand, N., Jansen, N. (eds.) FORMATS 2020. LNCS, vol. 12288, pp. 249–264. Springer, Cham (2020). https://doi.org/10.1007/978-3-030-57628-8_15

19. Kölbl, M., Leue, S., Wies, T.: Clock bound repair for timed systems. In: Dillig, I., Tasiran, S. (eds.) CAV 2019. LNCS, vol. 11561, pp. 79–96. Springer, Cham (2019). https://doi.org/10.1007/978-3-030-25540-4_5

20. Kölbl, M., Leue, S., Wies, T.: TARTAR: a timed automata repair tool. In: Lahiri, S.K., Wang, C. (eds.) CAV 2020. LNCS, vol. 12224, pp. 529–540. Springer, Cham (2020). https://doi.org/10.1007/978-3-030-53288-8_25

21. Kong, Z., et al.: Temporal logic inference for classification and prediction from data. In: 17th International Conference on Hybrid Systems: Computation and Control (HSCC), pp. 273–282, New York, NY, USA. ACM (2014)

22. Kupferman, O., Vardi, M.Y.: Vacuity detection in temporal model checking. Int. J. Softw. Tools Technol. Transf. **4**(2), 224–233 (2003). https://doi.org/10.1007/s100090100062

23. Langenfeld, V., et al.: Scalable analysis of real-time requirements. In: International Requirements Engineering Conference (RE), pp. 234–244. IEEE (2019)

24. Mitsubishi Electric Corporation. Mitsubishi programmable controller - Training manual (2012). https://dl.mitsubishielectric.com/dl/fa/document/manual/school_text/sh081123eng/sh081123enga.pdf

25. Neider, D. Gavran, I.: Learning linear temporal properties. In: 2018 Formal Methods in Computer Aided Design (FMCAD), pp. 1–10. IEEE (2018)

26. Pohl, K.: Requirements Engineering: Fundamentals, Principles, and Techniques. Springer, Heidelberg (2010)

27. Post, A., Hoenicke, J., Podelski, A.: rt-Inconsistency: a new property for real-time requirements. In: Giannakopoulou, D., Orejas, F. (eds.) FASE 2011. LNCS, vol. 6603, pp. 34–49. Springer, Heidelberg (2011). https://doi.org/10.1007/978-3-642-19811-3_4

28. Post, A., Hoenicke, J., Podelski, A.: Vacuous real-time requirements. In: IEEE International Requirements Engineering Conference (RE), pp. 153–162 (2011)

29. Teige, T., Bienmüller, T., Holberg, H.J.: Universal pattern: formalization, testing, coverage, verification, and test case generation for safety-critical requirements. In: 19th GI/ITG/GMM Workshop Methoden und Beschreibungssprachen zur Modellierung und Verifikation von Schaltungen und Systemen (MBMV'16), pp. 6–9. Albert-Ludwigs-Universität Freiburg (2016)

30. Yang, H., Hoxha, B., Fainekos, G.: Querying parametric temporal logic properties on embedded systems. In: Nielsen, B., Weise, C. (eds.) ICTSS 2012. LNCS, vol. 7641, pp. 136–151. Springer, Heidelberg (2012). https://doi.org/10.1007/978-3-642-34691-0_11

Verification of Neural Networks

An Abstraction-Refinement Approach to Verifying Convolutional Neural Networks

Matan Ostrovsky[1], Clark Barrett[2], and Guy Katz[1(✉)]

[1] The Hebrew University of Jerusalem, Jerusalem, Israel
matan.ostrovsky@mail.huji.ac.il, guykatz@cs.huji.ac.il
[2] Stanford University, Stanford, USA
barrett@cs.stanford.edu

Abstract. Convolutional neural networks (CNNs) have achieved immense popularity in areas like computer vision, image processing, speech proccessing, and many others. Unfortunately, despite their excellent performance, they are prone to producing erroneous results — for example, minor perturbations to their inputs can result in severe classification errors. In this paper, we present the CNN-ABS framework, which implements an abstraction-refinement based scheme for CNN verification. Specifically, CNN-ABS simplifies the verification problem through the removal of convolutional connections in a way that soundly creates an over-approximation of the original problem; it then iteratively restores these connections if the resulting problem becomes too abstract. CNN-ABS is designed to use existing verification engines as a backend, and our evaluation demonstrates that it can significantly boost the performance of a state-of-the-art DNN verification engine, reducing runtime by 15.7% on average.

1 Overview

Deep neural networks (*DNN*s) have demonstrated a remarkable ability to solve extremely complex tasks [4,11]. However, they are also notoriously opaque to human engineers, and various errors have been demonstrated in real-world, state-of-the-art DNNs [12]. Such errors are a hindrance to the adoption of DNN-based methods in critical systems and have sparked great interest in DNN verification (e.g., [1,2,5,6,9,10,13], among many others). Unfortunately, the DNN formal verification problem is NP-complete even for simple neural networks and specifications [5], and emperically, it appears to become exponentially harder as the network size increases — making scalability a key challenge for DNN verification tools.

Here, we contribute to the ongoing effort to address this challenge with a new framework called CNN-ABS, which uses an *abstraction-refinement* based approach for verifying *convolutional neural networks* (*CNN*s). A CNN is a particular type of DNN that uses *convolutions*: constructs that allow for a very compact representation of the DNN, and consequently enable engineers to overcome memory-related bottlenecks. CNNs have been shown to perform well in image processing and computer vision tasks [4,11] and are in widespread use. Existing verification tools can verify CNNs, but typically only by reducing them to the general, *fully connected* case, thus failing to leverage the built-in compactness of CNNs. Because the size of the DNN slows down its verification, such transformations are costly. In contrast, our proposed framework aims to utilize the special properties of a CNN in expediting its verification.

At a high level, given a verification query over a CNN, CNN-ABS first creates an *abstract* network, with significantly fewer neurons, with the property that if the query can be proved for this smaller network, then it also holds for the original network. Notably, the abstract network that we construct is fully connected, and can thus be verified using existing technology. Further, because the verification complexity depends on the number of neurons and edges in the DNN, verifying this smaller network is faster than transforming the CNN into an equivalent, fully connected network and verifying it. Due to the abstraction procedure, verifying the smaller network might produce a spurious counterexample, in which case our framework refines the network and repeats the process.

The overall flow of CNN-ABS is depicted in Fig. 1. Initially, CNN-ABS applies bound propagation [10,13] to compute lower and upper bounds for all hidden neurons within the network. Then, it selects a set of neurons and *abstracts* them by removing their incoming edges and treating them as input neurons — which can take on values within the previously-computed range. Any other neurons that become disconnected from the network's outputs as a result are *pruned* entirely; the number of such neurons tends to be high, due to the nature of convolutional layers, where each neuron is only connected to a small number of neurons in following layers. A small illustrative example appears in Fig. 2. For a more thorough and precise description of the technique, as well as a proof of its soundness, see the full version of this paper [8].

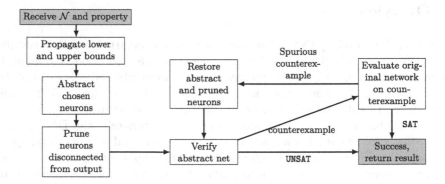

Fig. 1. The suggested abstraction-refinement scheme.

Related Work. Abstraction-refinement techniques have been successfully applied in DNN verification [1,3,9], though these attempts were not particularly aimed at CNNs. Specific approaches to CNN verification have also been

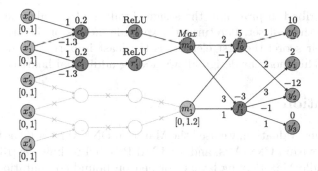

Fig. 2. A toy CNN, abstracted by disconnecting the edges leading to m_1 and pruning the neurons no longer connected to the output neurons (in gray). m'_1 is now treated as an input neuron, bounded by its computed bounds $0 \leq m'_1 \leq 1.2$.

proposed (e.g., [2,14]), but these do not focus on abstraction/refinement. For a more thorough discussion, see [8].

2   Design of Cnn-Abs

We implemented CNN-ABS as a set of Python modules, available online.[1] CNN-ABS currently accepts CNNs stored in Tensorflow format as input. The tool's main module, *CnnAbs.py*, implements the abstraction and refinement principles described in Sect. 1 and currently supports five different heuristics for iteratively applying refinement steps when spurious counterexamples are detected (see [8]). CNN-ABS can be used in verifying arbitrary CNN properties, although it contains a specialized interface for verifying adversarial robustness properties [12], which are the most common kinds of properties in currently available verification benchmarks. The central classes in CNN-ABS are:

The *CnnAbs* class, which implements CNN-ABS's main functionality, and manages solving, logging, and heuristic configurations. It includes the following methods: (i) *solveAdversarial(model, abstractionPolicy, sampleIndex, distance)*: solves an adversarial robustness query on *model*, allowing input perturbations in an $\|\|_{\infty}$-ball of radius *distance* around an input sample whose index is *sampleIndex* in the data-set, using *abstractionPolicy* as the abstraction policy; (ii) *solve(model, modelTF, abstractionPolicy, property)*: solves *model*, which encodes both a network and a property, using the abstraction policy *abstractionPolicy*. For technical reasons, this method also receives a property object *property* and a Keras sequential model *modelTF*; and (iii) *propagateBounds(model)*: propagates lower and upper bounds for all neurons in the network and properties encoded in *model*. CNN-ABS includes a novel technique for bound propagation across Max-Pooling layers — see [8] for details.

Policy Classes: Abstraction policies are implemented as classes inheriting from the *PolicyBase* class. Every child class is required to implement the *rankAbsLayer(model, prop, absLayerPredictions)* function. Its arguments are *model*, a

---

[1] https://drive.google.com/file/d/1En8f_I8LWFWQ6LFMHF9SSajszfOEKWF4.

property described in *prop*, and the assigned values of the abstracted layer for each point in the test-set. It returns the variable indices of the layer's neurons, sorted by their score: the first element is the least important and will thus be refined last. This modular design allows adding additional heuristics easily.

3   Evaluation

Setup. For our evaluation, we used the Marabou DNN verifier [6] as the backend DNN verifier within CNN-ABS, and used MILP-based techniques [13] (enhanced to better handle Max-Pooling layers) for neuron bound computation.

We trained three convolutional networks on the MNIST digit recognition data-set [7]. The first network, network A, has two *convolution blocks* (a convolution layer followed by a ReLU layer and a max-pooling layer), another block consisting of a weighted-sum layer and a ReLU layer, and a final weighted-sum layer. When transformed into an equivalent, fully-connected model, it has a total of 2719 neurons and achieves a test-set accuracy of 93.7%. The second network, B, has the same layer sequence as A, but its convolution kernels are larger; consequently, it has 4564 neurons and achieves an accuracy of 96.2%. Network C is similar but has three convolution blocks instead of two; it has 4636 neurons and achieves an accuracy of 86.6%. Additional details appear in Appendix B of [8].

For specifications, we focused on adversarial robustness properties [12], which have become the de-facto standard for DNN verification benchmarks [10,13]. An adversarial robustness query consists of input x^0 and some $\varepsilon > 0$, and its goal is to prove that perturbations to x_0 within a ball of radius ε do not result in a change in the classification. For simplicity, we consider *targeted* adversarial robustness, where the goal is to prove that some perturbation cannot result in the input being classified as some target label l. We select l as the label that received the second-highest score when the DNN is evaluated on x_0.

Experiments. We ran a comprehensive comparison between vanilla Marabou and CNN-ABS (with Marabou as a backend). All experiments were run with a 1-hour timeout, and individual verification queries on abstract networks were limited to 800 s. Our benchmarks consisted of our three CNNs and robustness properties with varying values of ε, 0.01, 0.02, and 0.03, over 100 input points, resulting in nine combinations and a total of 900 experiments. The results are depicted in Fig. 3. Excluding the $(C, 0.03), (B, 0.03), (A, 0.01)$ queries, in every category the abstraction-enhanced version solved more instances than vanilla and required a shorter total runtime. In the $(A, 0.01)$ category, both

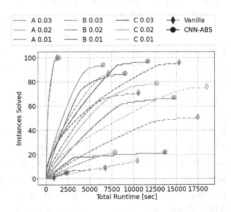

Fig. 3. Performance over different networks and ε values. Each query was ran in vanilla Marabou (dash-dotted line), and with CNN-ABS (solid line).

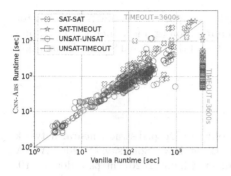
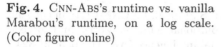

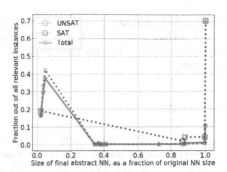

Fig. 4. CNN-ABS's runtime vs. vanilla Marabou's runtime, on a log scale. (Color figure online)

Fig. 5. The size of the abstract network when CNN-ABS terminates, compared to the size of the original network.

frameworks performed similarly; and in $(C, 0.03), (B, 0.03)$, CNN-ABS solved more instances, but at the cost of additional runtime. Aggregating the results over all instances solved by both frameworks, CNN-ABS's average runtime was 84.3% that of vanilla Marabou's runtime, and its median runtime 75.4% that of vanilla Marabou's. Additionally, CNN-ABS solved 1.13 times as many instances as vanilla Marabou. The exact numbers of instances solved, average runtimes, and median runtimes all appear in Appendix C.2 of [8]. This experiment clearly indicates the superior performance of CNN-ABS compared to the vanilla version.

Figure 4 depicts the runtime of CNN-ABS vs. vanilla Marabou for every query solved by at least one of the verifiers. There are 526 UNSAT points (green) and 49 SAT points (red). The results show that for SAT instances, the frameworks achieve similar performance; whereas for UNSAT instances, CNN-ABS performs significantly better, solving 61 instances that the vanilla version timed out on. We thus conclude that the CNN-ABS is particularly effective on UNSAT instances, presumably because SAT instances require multiple refinement steps.

In Fig. 5, we measure the number of refinement steps needed by CNN-ABS before arriving at an answer. Specifically, it depicts the size of the DNN in the final iteration of the abstraction/refinement algorithm, as a fraction of the size of the original DNN. The results differ significantly between UNSAT queries, which terminate with small networks and few refinement steps, and SAT queries, which often require the network to be refined back to the original DNN. The corollary is that slow, gradual refinement is ineffective; and that CNN-ABS performs better on UNSAT queries, as these can often be solved on small, abstract networks.

Conclusion. We presented a novel scheme for CNN verification, which uses abstraction-refinement techniques to effectively reduce network sizes and facilitate verification. Our tool, CNN-ABS, can be used with various existing DNN verifiers as backends. We regard this effort as a step towards more effective verification of real-world CNNs.

Acknowledgements. This work was partially supported by the Semiconductor Research Corporation, the Binational Science Foundation (grant numbers 2017662 and 2020250), the Israel Science Foundation (683/18), and the National Science Foundation (1814369).

References

1. Ashok, P., Hashemi, V., Křetínský, J., Mohr, S.: DeepAbstract: neural network abstraction for accelerating verification. In: Hung, D.V., Sokolsky, O. (eds.) ATVA 2020. LNCS, vol. 12302, pp. 92–107. Springer, Cham (2020). https://doi.org/10.1007/978-3-030-59152-6_5
2. Boopathy, A., Weng, T.W., Chen, P.Y., Liu, S., Daniel, L.: CNN-Cert: an efficient framework for certifying robustness of convolutional neural networks. In: Proceedings of the 33rd AAAI Conference on Artificial Intelligence (AAAI), pp. 3240–3247 (2019)
3. Elboher, Y.Y., Gottschlich, J., Katz, G.: An abstraction-based framework for neural network verification. In: Lahiri, S.K., Wang, C. (eds.) CAV 2020. LNCS, vol. 12224, pp. 43–65. Springer, Cham (2020). https://doi.org/10.1007/978-3-030-53288-8_3
4. He, K., Zhang, X., Ren, S., Sun, J.: Deep residual learning for image recognition. In: Proceedings of the IEEE Conference on Computer Vision and Pattern Recognition (CVPR), pp. 770–778 (2016)
5. Katz, G., Barrett, C., Dill, D.L., Julian, K., Kochenderfer, M.J.: Reluplex: an efficient smt solver for verifying deep neural networks. In: Majumdar, R., Kunčak, V. (eds.) CAV 2017. LNCS, vol. 10426, pp. 97–117. Springer, Cham (2017). https://doi.org/10.1007/978-3-319-63387-9_5
6. Katz, G., et al.: The marabou framework for verification and analysis of deep neural networks. In: Dillig, I., Tasiran, S. (eds.) CAV 2019. LNCS, vol. 11561, pp. 443–452. Springer, Cham (2019). https://doi.org/10.1007/978-3-030-25540-4_26
7. LeCun, Y.: The MNIST database of handwritten digits (1998). http://yann.lecun.com/exdb/mnist/
8. Ostrovsky, M., Barrett, C., Katz, G.: An abstraction-refinement approach to verifying convolutional neural networks (full version). Technical report. arxiv.org/abs/2201.01978
9. Prabhakar, P., Afzal, Z.: Abstraction based output range analysis for neural networks (2020). Technical report. arxiv.org/abs/2007.09527
10. Singh, G., Gehr, T., Puschel, M., Vechev, M.: An abstract domain for certifying neural networks. In: Proceedings of the 46th ACM SIGPLAN Symposium on Principles of Programming Languages (POPL) (2019)
11. Szegedy, C.: Going deeper with convolutions. In: Proceedings of the IEEE Conference on Computer Vision and Pattern Recognition (CVPR), pp. 1–9 (2015)
12. Szegedy, C., et al.: Intriguing properties of neural networks (2013). Technical report. arxiv.org/abs/1312.6199
13. Tjeng, V., Xiao, K., Tedrake, R.: Evaluating robustness of neural networks with mixed integer programming (2017). Technical report. arxiv.org/abs/1711.07356
14. Xu, J., Li, Z., Zhang, M., Du, B.: Conv-Reluplex: a verification framework for convolution neural networks. In: Proceedings of the 33rd International Conference on Software Engineering and Knowledge Engineering (SEKE) (2021)

Prioritizing Corners in OoD Detectors via Symbolic String Manipulation

Chih-Hong Cheng[1]([✉]), Changshun Wu[2], Emmanouil Seferis[1],
and Saddek Bensalem[2]

[1] Fraunhofer IKS, Munich, Germany
{chih-hong.cheng,emmanouil.seferis}@iks.frauhofer.de
[2] Univ. Grenoble Alpes, Verimag, Grenoble, France
{changshun.wu,saddek.bensalem}@univ-grenoble-alpes.fr

Abstract. For safety assurance of deep neural networks (DNNs), out-of-distribution (OoD) monitoring techniques are essential as they filter spurious input that is distant from the training dataset. This paper studies the problem of systematically testing OoD monitors to avoid cases where an input data point is tested as in-distribution by the monitor, but the DNN produces spurious output predictions. We consider the definition of "in-distribution" characterized in the feature space by a union of hyperrectangles learned from the training dataset. Thus the testing is reduced to finding corners in hyperrectangles distant from the available training data in the feature space. Concretely, we encode the abstract location of every data point as a finite-length binary string, and the union of all binary strings is stored compactly using binary decision diagrams (BDDs). We demonstrate how to use BDDs to symbolically extract corners distant from all data points within the training set. Apart from test case generation, we explain how to use the proposed corners to fine-tune the DNN to ensure that it does not predict overly confidently. The result is evaluated over examples such as number and traffic sign recognition.

Keywords: OoD monitoring · Test case prioritization · Neural network · Training

1 Introduction

To cope with practical concerns in autonomous driving where deep neural networks (DNNs) [7] are operated in an open environment, out-of-distribution (OoD) monitoring is a commonly used technique that raises a warning if a DNN receives an input distant from the training dataset. One of the weaknesses with OoD detection is regarding inputs that fall in the OoD detector's decision boundary while being distant from the training dataset. These inputs are considered

---

The first two authors contributed equally to this work.

A. Bouajjani et al. (Eds.): ATVA 2022, LNCS 13505, pp. 397–413, 2022.
https://doi.org/10.1007/978-3-031-19992-9_26

"in-distribution" by the OoD detector but can impose safety issues due to extensive extrapolation. In this paper, we are thus addressing this issue by developing a disciplined method to identify the weakness of OoD detectors and improve the system accordingly.

Precisely, we consider OoD detectors constructed using boxed abstraction-based approaches [3, 10, 24], where DNN-generated feature vectors from the training dataset are clustered and enclosed using hyperrectangles. The OoD detector raises a warning over an input, provided that its corresponding feature vector falls outside the boxed abstraction. We focus on analyzing the corners of the monitor's hyperrectangle and differentiate whether a corner is *supported* or *unsupported* depending on having some input in the training dataset generating feature vectors located in the corner. However, the number of *exponentially many corners* in the abstraction reveals two challenges, namely (1) how to enumerate the unsupported corners and (2) how to prioritize unsupported corners to be analyzed.

- For (1), we present an encoding technique that, for each feature vector dimension, decides if an input falls in the border subject to a closeness threshold δ. This allows encoding for each input in-sample as a binary string and storing the complete set compactly via Binary decision diagrams (BDDs) [2]. With an encoding via BDD, one can compute all unsupported corners using set difference operations.
- For (2), we further present an algorithm manipulated on the BDDs that allows filtering all corners that are far from all training data subject to a minimum constant Hamming distance (which may be further translated into Euclidean distance). This forms the basis of our corner prioritization technique for abstractions characterized by a single hyperrectangle. For multiple boxed-abstraction, we use a lazy approach to omit the corners when the proposed corner from one box falls inside another box.

With a given corner proposal, we further encounter practical problems to produce input images that resemble "natural" images. We thus consider an alternative approach: it is feasible to have the DNN generate a prediction with low confidence for any input whose feature vectors resemble unsupported corners. This requirement leads to a DNN fine-tuning scheme as the final contribution of this paper: The fine-tuning freezes parameters for all network layers before the monitored layer, thereby keeping the validity of the OoD monitor. However, it allows all layers after the monitored features to be adjusted. Thus the algorithm feeds the unsupported corners to the fine-tunable sub-network to ensure that the modified DNN reports every class with low confidence, while keeping the same prediction for existing training data.

We have evaluated our proposed techniques in applications ranging from standard digit recognition to traffic sign detection. For corners inside the monitor while distant from the training data, our experiment indicates that the DNN indeed acts over-confidently in the corresponding prediction, which is later adjusted with our local training method. Altogether the positive evaluation of the technique offers a rigorous paradigm to align DNN testing, OoD detection, and DNN repair for safety-critical systems.

The rest of the paper is structured as follows: After reviewing related work in Sect. 2, we present in Sect. 3 the basic notation as well as a concise definition on abstraction-based monitors. Subsequently, in Sect. 4 we present our key results for prioritized corner case proposal in a single-box configuration and its extension to a multi-box setting. In Sect. 5 we present how to use the discovered corners in improving the DNN via local training. Finally, we present our preliminary evaluation in Sect. 6 and conclude in Sect. 7.

2   Related Work

Systematically testing of DNNs has been an active research scheme, where readers may reference Sect. 5.1 of a recent survey [12] for an overview of existing results. Overall, the line of attack is by first defining a coverage criterion, followed by concrete test case generation utilizing techniques such as adversarial perturbation [23], constraint solving [13], or model-based exploration [21]. For white box coverage criteria, neuron coverage [20] and extensions (e.g., SS-coverage [22] or neuron combinatorial testing [18]) essentially consider the activation pattern for neurons and demand the set of test inputs to satisfy a pre-defined relative completeness criterion; the idea is essentially motivated by classical software testing coverage (e.g., branch coverage) as used in safety standards. For black-box coverage criteria, multiple results are utilizing combinatorial testing [1,4], where by first defining the human-specified features in the input space, it is also possible to argue the relative completeness of the test data. For the above metrics, one can apply coverage-driven testing, i.e., generate test cases that maximally increase coverage. Note that the above test metrics and the associated test case prioritization techniques are not *property-oriented*, i.e., prioritizing the test cases does not have a direct relation with dependability attributes. This is in contrast to our work on testing the decision boundary of a DNN monitor, where our test prioritization scheme prefers corners (of the monitor) that have no input data being close-by. These corners refer to regions where DNN decisions are largely extrapolated, and it is important to ensure that inputs that may lead to these corners are properly tested. The second differentiation is that we also consider the subsequent DNN repair scheme (via local training) to incorporate the distant-yet-uncovered corners.

In this paper, we are interested in testing the monitors built from an abstraction of feature vectors from the training data, where the shape of the abstraction is a union of hyperrectangles [3,10,24]. There exist also other types of monitors. The most typical runtime monitoring approach for DNNs is to build a logic on top of the DNN, where the logic inspects some of the DNN features and tries to access the decision quality. Popular approaches in this direction are the baseline of Hendrycks et al. [9] that looks at the output softmax value and flags it as problematic if lower than a threshold, or the ODIN approach that improves on it using temperature scaling [17]. Further, [16] looks at intermediate layers of a

DNN and assumes that their features are approximately Gaussian-distributed. With that, they use the Mahanalobis distance as a confidence score for adversarial or OoD detection. The work of [16] is considered the practical state-of-the-art in the domain. In another direction, researchers have attempted to measure the uncertainty of a DNN on its decisions, using Bayesian approaches such as drop out at runtime [6] and ensemble learning. Deep Ensembles [14] achieve state-of-the-art uncertainty estimation but at a large computational overhead (since one needs to train many models), thus recent work attempts to mitigate this with various ideas [5,8]. Although the above results surely have their benefits, for complex monitoring techniques, the decision boundary is never a single value but rather a complex geometric shape. For this, we observe a strong need in systematic testing over the decision boundaries (for rejecting an input or not), which is reflected in this work by testing or training against unsupported corners of a monitor.

3   Preliminaries

Let $\mathbb{N}$ and $\mathbb{R}$ be the sets of natural and real numbers. To refer to integer intervals, we use $[a \cdots b]$ with $a, b \in \mathbb{N}$ and $a \leq b$. To refer to real intervals, we use $[a, b]$ with $a, b \in \mathbb{R} \cup \{-\infty, \infty\}$ and if $a, b \in \mathbb{R}$, then $a \leq b$. We use square bracket when both sides are included, and use round bracket to exclude end points (e.g., $[a, b)$ for excluding b). For $n \in \mathbb{N} \backslash \{0\}$, $\mathbb{R}^n \overset{\text{def}}{=} \underbrace{\mathbb{R} \times \cdots \times \mathbb{R}}_{n \text{ times}}$ is the space of real coordinates of dimension n and its elements are called n-dimensional vectors. We use $\mathbf{x} = (x_1, \ldots, x_n)$ to denote an n-dimensional vector.

Feedforward Neural Networks. A neuron is an elementary mathematical function. A *(forward) neural network* $f \overset{\text{def}}{=} (g^L, \ldots, g^1)$ is a sequential structure of $L \in \mathbb{N} \backslash \{0\}$ layers, where, for $i \in [1 \cdots L]$, the i-th layer comprises d_i neurons and implements a function $g^i : \mathbb{R}^{d_{i-1}} \to \mathbb{R}^{d_i}$. The inputs of neurons at layer i comprise (1) the outputs of neurons at layer $(i-1)$ and (2) a bias. The outputs of neurons at layer i are inputs for neurons at layer $i+1$. Given a network input $\mathbf{x} \in \mathbb{R}^{d_0}$, the output at the i-th layer is computed by the function composition $f^i(\mathbf{x}) \overset{\text{def}}{=} g^i(\cdots g^2(g^1(\mathbf{x})))$. Therefore, $f^L(\mathbf{x})$ is the output of the neural network. We use $f^i_j(\mathbf{x})$ to extract the j-th value from the vector $f^i(\mathbf{x})$.

Abstraction-Based Monitors Using Boxes [3,10,24]. In the following, we present the simplistic definition of abstraction-based monitors using multiple boxes. The definition is simplified in that we assume the monitor operates on all neurons within a given layer, but the technique is generic and can be used to monitor a subset of neurons across multiple layers.

For a neural network f whose weights and bias related to neurons are fixed, let $\mathcal{D}_{train} \overset{\text{def}}{=} \{(\mathbf{x}, \mathbf{y}) \mid \mathbf{x} \in \mathbb{R}^{d_0}, \mathbf{y} \in \mathbb{R}^{d_L}\}$ be the corresponding training dataset. We call $B \overset{\text{def}}{=} [[a_1, b_1], \cdots, [a_n, b_n]]$ an n-**dimensional box**, where B is the set of points $\{(x_1, \ldots, x_n)\} \subseteq \mathbb{R}^n$ with $\forall i \in [1 \cdots n] : x_i \in [a_i, b_i]$. Given a neural network f and the corresponding training dataset, let k be a positive integer constant and $l \in [1 \cdots L]$. Then $\mathcal{B}_{k,l,\delta} \overset{\text{def}}{=} \{B_1, \ldots, B_k\}$ is a **k-boxed abstraction monitor over layer l with buffer vector** $\delta \overset{\text{def}}{=} (\delta_1, \ldots, \delta_{d_l})$, provided that $\mathcal{B}_{k,l,\delta}$ satisfies the following properties.

1. $\forall i \in [1 \cdots k]$, B_i is a d_l-dimensional box.
2. $\forall (\mathbf{x}, \mathbf{y}) \in \mathcal{D}_{train}$, there exists $i \in [1 \cdots k]$ such that $f^l(\mathbf{x}) \in B_i$.
3. $\forall i \in [1 \cdots k]$, let B_i be $[[a_1, b_1], \cdots, [a_{d_l}, b_{d_l}]]$. Then
   - for every $j \in [1 \cdots d_l]$, there exists $(\mathbf{x}, \mathbf{y}) \in \mathcal{D}_{train}$ such that $a_j \leq f_j^l(\mathbf{x}) \leq a_j + \delta_j$, and
   - for every $j \in [1 \cdots d_l]$, there exists $(\mathbf{x}', \mathbf{y}') \in \mathcal{D}_{train}$ such that $b_j - \delta_j \leq f_j^l(\mathbf{x}') \leq b_j$.

The three conditions stated above can be intuitively explained as follows: Condition (1) ensures that any box is well formed, condition (2) ensures that for any training data point, its feature vector at the l-th layer falls into one of the boxes, and (3) the construction of boxes is relatively tight in that for any dimension, there exists one training data point whose j-th dimension of its feature vector is close to (subject to δ_j) the j-th lower-bound of the box; the same condition also holds for the j-th upper-bound.

Monitoring. Given a neural network f and the boxed abstraction monitor $\mathcal{B}_{k,l,\delta}$, in runtime, the **monitor rejects an input** $\mathbf{x}'$ if $\nexists i \in [1 \cdots k] : f^l(\mathbf{x}') \in B_i$. That is, the feature vector of $\mathbf{x}'$ at the l-th layer is not contained by any box. As the containment checking $f^l(\mathbf{x}') \in B_i$ simply compares $f^l(\mathbf{x}')$ against the box's lower and upper bounds on each dimension, it can be done in time linear to the number of neurons being monitored.

Example 1. Consider the set $\{f^l(\mathbf{x}) \mid (\mathbf{x}, \mathbf{y}) \in \mathcal{D}_{train}\} = \{(0.1, 2.9), (0.3, 2.6), (0.6, 2.3), (0.8, 2.8), (0.9, 2.1), (2.1, 0.1), (2.2, 0.7), (2.3, 0.3), (2.6, 0.6), (2.9, 0.2), (2.7, 0.9)\}$ of feature vectors obtained at layer l that has only two neurons: Fig. 1 shows $\mathcal{B}_{2,l,\delta} = \{[[0, 1], [2, 3]], [[2, 3], [0, 1]]\}$, a 2-boxed abstraction monitor with $\delta = (0.15, 0.15)$. The area influenced by δ is visualized in yellow.

Corners Within Monitors. As a monitor built from boxed abstraction only rejects an input if the feature vector falls outside the box, the borders of the box actually serve as a proxy for the boundary of the operational design domain (ODD) - anything inside a box is considered acceptable. With this concept in mind, we are interested in **finding test inputs that can lead to corners** of these boxes. As shown in Fig. 1, for the box $[[0, 1], [2, 3]]$, the bottom left corner is not occupied by a feature vector produced from any training data point.

We now precise the definition of corners.

Given a box $B_i = [[a_1, b_1], \cdots, [a_{d_l}, b_{d_l}]] \in \mathcal{B}_{k,l,\delta}$, **the set of corners associated with B_i is** $C_{B_i} \overset{\text{def}}{=} \{[[\alpha_1, \beta_1], \cdots, [\alpha_{d_l}, \beta_{d_l}]]\}$ where $\forall j \in [1 \cdots d_l]$, either

- $[\alpha_j, \beta_j] = [a_j, a_j + \delta_j]$, or
- $[\alpha_j, \beta_j] = [b_j - \delta_j, b_j]$.

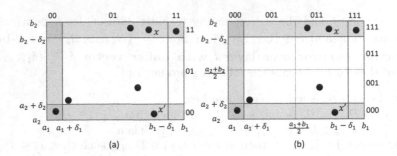

Fig. 2. Partition the boxed monitor and encode every region using BDDs. A black dot represents a feature vector generated from a training data point.

Without surprise, the below lemma reminded us the well known problem of *combinatorial explosion*, where the number of corners, although linear to the number of boxes, is exponential to the number of dimensions.

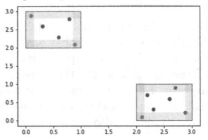

Lemma 1. *Given* $\mathcal{B}_{k,l,\delta}$, $\sum_1^k |C_{B_i}|$, *i.e., the total number of corners associated with the monitor, equals* $k \cdot 2^{d_l}$.

Fig. 1. An example of two-boxes, where corners are deep-yellow areas. (Color figure online)

Given the set C_{B_i} of corners associated with B_i, define $C_{B_i}^s \subseteq C_{B_i}$ to be the **(training-data) supported corners** where for each $[[\alpha_1, \beta_1], \cdots, [\alpha_{d_l}, \beta_{d_l}]]$ in $C_{B_i}^s$, exists $(\mathbf{x}, \mathbf{y}) \in \mathcal{D}_{train}$ such that $\forall j \in [1 \cdots d_l] : f_j^l(\mathbf{x}) \in [\alpha_j, \beta_j]$. The set of **(training-data) unsupported corners** $C_{B_i}^u$ is the set complement, i.e., $C_{B_i}^u \stackrel{\text{def}}{=} C_{B_i} \backslash C_{B_i}^s$. As an example, consider the box B_i in Fig. 2(a). The set of unsupported corners $C_{B_i}^u$ is $\{[[a_1, a_1+\delta_1], [b_2-\delta_2, b_2]], [[b_1-\delta_1, b_1], [a_2, a_2+\delta_2]]\}$, i.e., the top-left corner and the bottom-right corner.

An unsupported corner reflects the possibility of having an input $\mathbf{x}_{op}$ in operation time, where the DNN-computed l^{th}-layer feature vector $f^l(\mathbf{x}_{op})$ falls into that corner of the monitor. It reflects additional risks, as we do not know the prediction result, but the monitor also will not reject the input. The consequence of Lemma 1 implies that when we only have a finite budget for testing unsupported corners, we need to develop methods to **prioritize** them, as detailed in the following sections.

4   Unsupported Corner Prioritization Under Single-Boxed Abstraction

We first consider the special case where only one box is used in the monitoring. That is, we consider $\mathcal{B}_{1,l,\delta} = \{B\}$ where $B = \{(x_1, \ldots, x_{d_l}) \mid x_1 \in$

$[a_1, b_1], \ldots, x_{d_l} \in [a_{d_l}, b_{d_l}]\}$. The workflow is to first consider encoding feature vectors at the l-th layer into fixed-length binary strings, in order to derive the set of unsupported corners. Subsequently, prioritize the unsupported corners via Hamming distance-based filtering. The algorithm stated in this section serves as the foundation for the general multi-boxed monitor setting detailed in later sections.

4.1 Encoding Feature Vectors Using Binary Strings

Given a finite-length Boolean string $\mathbf{b} \in \{0,1\}^*$, we use $\mathbf{b}_{[i \ldots j]}$ to denote the substring indexed from i to j. For a single-boxed monitor $\mathcal{B}_{1,l,\delta} = \{B\}$ constructed from $\mathcal{D}_{train}$, let the ϕ-bit encoding ($\phi \geq 2$) be a function $\text{enc}^\phi : \mathbb{R}^{d_l} \to \{0,1\}^{\phi \cdot d_l}$ that, for any $\mathbf{x} \in \mathcal{D}_{train}$, translates the feature vector $f^l(\mathbf{x})$ to a Boolean string $\mathbf{b}$ (with length $\phi \cdot d_l$) using the following operation: $\forall j \in [1 \cdots d_l]$,

- if $f_j^l(\mathbf{x}) \in [\alpha_j, \alpha_j + \delta_j]$, then $\mathbf{b}_{[\phi(j-1)+1 \cdots \phi j]} = \underbrace{0 \cdots 0}_{\phi \text{ times}}$;

- else if $f_j^l(\mathbf{x}) \in [\beta_j - \delta_j, \beta_j]$, then $\mathbf{b}_{[\phi(j-1)+1 \cdots \phi j]} = \underbrace{1 \cdots 1}_{\phi \text{ times}}$;

- otherwise, $\mathbf{b}_{[\phi(j-1)+1 \cdots \phi j]} = \underbrace{0 \cdots 0}_{\phi - \tau \text{ times}} \underbrace{1 \cdots 1}_{\tau \text{ times}}$ when

$$f_j^l(\mathbf{x}) \in [a_j + \delta_j + \frac{(\tau-1)(b_j - a_j - 2\delta_j)}{\phi - 1}, a_j + \delta_j + \frac{(\tau)(b_j - a_j - 2\delta_j)}{\phi - 1})$$

The ϕ-bit encoding essentially considers $f_j^l(\mathbf{x})$ in dimension j, assigns the substring with all 0s when $f_j^l(\mathbf{x})$ falls in the corner reflecting the lower-bound, assigns with all 1s when $f_j^l(\mathbf{x})$ falls in the corner reflecting the upper-bound, and finally, splits the rest interval of length $b_j - a_j - 2\delta_j$ into $\phi - 1$ equally sized intervals and assigns each interval with an encoding. Figure 2 illustrates the result of 2-bit and 3-bit partitioning under a 2-dimensional boxed monitor. For point $\mathbf{x}$ in Fig. 2(b), $\text{enc}^3(\mathbf{x}) = 011111$. The first part "011" comes as when $\tau = 2$, $f_1^l(\mathbf{x}) \in [a_1 + \delta_1 + \frac{(2-1)(b_1 - a_1 - 2\delta_1)}{3 - 1}, a_1 + \delta_1 + \frac{(2)(b_1 - a_1 - 2\delta_1)}{3 - 1})$. The second part "111" comes as $f_2^l(\mathbf{x}) \in [\beta_2 - \delta_2, \beta_2]$. Given an input $\mathbf{x}$ and its computed feature vector $f^l(\mathbf{x})$, the time required for performing ϕ-bit encoding is in low degree polynomial with respect to d_l and ϕ.

4.2 BDD Encoding and Priortizing the Unsupported Corners

This section presents Algorithm 1, a BDD-based algorithm for identifying unsupported corners. To ease understanding, we separate the algorithm into three parts.

A: Encode the Complete Training Dataset. Given the training dataset $\mathcal{D}_{train}$ and the DNN function f, one can easily compute $\{\mathbf{b} \mid \mathbf{b} = \text{enc}^\phi(f^l(\mathbf{x}))$ where $\mathbf{x} \in \mathcal{D}_{train}\}$ as be the set of all binary strings characterizing the complete training

---

Algorithm 1. Priortizing unsupported corners using BDD

Input: Dataset $\mathcal{D}_{train}$, DNN f, 1-box monitor $\mathcal{B}_{1,l,\delta} = \{B\}$, ϕ, distance metric Δ

Output: The set $\{\mathbf{b}^u\}$ of binary strings represented in BDD, reflecting unsupported corners C_B^u for box B, with each $\mathbf{b}^u$ distant to all training data encodings by at least $\Delta + 1$ bits.

1: Declare BDD variables $\mathsf{bv}_1, \ldots, \mathsf{bv}_{\phi d_l}$.
2: $S_{train} \leftarrow$ BDD.false   (* Initialize to empty set *)
3: **for all** $\mathbf{x} \in \mathcal{D}_{train}$ **do**
4:     $\mathbf{b} \leftarrow enc^{\phi}(f^l(\mathbf{x}))$
5:     $S_{\mathbf{b}} \leftarrow$ BDD.true
6:     **for all** $m \in [1 \cdots \phi d_l]$ **do**   (* Refine the set to contain only $\mathbf{b}$ *)
7:         **if** $\mathbf{b}_{[m \cdots m]} = 1$ **then** $S_{\mathbf{b}} \leftarrow$ BDD.and($S_{\mathbf{b}}, \mathsf{bv}_m$)
8:         **else** $S_{\mathbf{b}} \leftarrow$ BDD.and($S_{\mathbf{b}}$, BDD.not(bv_m))
9:     $S_{train} \leftarrow$ BDD.or(S_{train}, S_b)   (* Add S_b to the set *)
10: $S_{all.corners} \leftarrow$ BDD.true
11: **for all** $j \in [1 \cdots d_l]$ **do**
12:     $S_{j0s} \leftarrow$ BDD.true; $S_{j1s} \leftarrow$ BDD.true
13:     **for all** $m \in [1 \cdots \phi]$ **do**
14:         $S_{j0s} \leftarrow$ BDD.and(S_{j0s}, BDD.not($\mathsf{bv}_{\phi(j-1)+m}$))
15:         $S_{j1s} \leftarrow$ BDD.and($S_{j1s}, \mathsf{bv}_{\phi(j-1)+m}$)
16:     $S_{all.corners} \leftarrow$ BDD.and($S_{all.corners}$, BDD.or(S_{j0s}, S_{j1s}))
17: $S_{unsup} \leftarrow S_{all.corners} \backslash S_{train}$ (* BDD.setminus($\cdot, \cdot$) operation *)
18: $S_{train}^{\leq \Delta} \leftarrow S_{train}$
19: **for all** $n \in [1 \cdots \Delta]$ **do**
20:     $S_{local} \leftarrow S_{train}^{\leq \Delta}$
21:     **for all** $m \in [1 \cdots \phi d_l]$ **do**
22:         $S_{train}^{\leq \Delta} \leftarrow$ BDD.or($S_{train}^{\leq \Delta}$, BDD.exists(S_{local}, bv_m))
23: **return** $S_{unsup} \backslash S_{train}^{\leq \Delta}$

---

dataset. As each element in the set is a fixed-length binary string, the set can be compactly stored using Binary Decision Diagrams.

Precisely, as the length of a binary string $\mathbf{b} = enc^{\phi}(f^l(\mathbf{x}))$ equals $\phi \cdot d_l$, in our encoding we use $\phi \cdot d_l$ BDD variables, denoted as $\mathsf{bv}_1, \ldots, \mathsf{bv}_{\phi d_l}$, such that $\mathsf{bv}_i = \mathsf{true}$ iff $\mathbf{b}_{[i \cdots i]} = 1$. Line 1 of Algorithm 1 performs such a declaration. Lines 2 to 9 perform the BDD encoding and creation of the set S_{train} containing all binary strings created from the training set. Initially (line 2) S_{train} is set to be an empty set. Subsequently, generate the binary string (line 4), and encode a set $S_{\mathbf{b}}$ which contains only the binary string (line 5–8). Finally, add $S_{\mathbf{b}}$ to S_{train} (line 9).

B: Derive the Set of Unsupported Corners. Lines 10 to 17 of Algorithm 1 computes S_{unsup}, where each binary string in S_{unsup} corresponds to an unsupported corner. The set is computed by a set difference operation (line 17) between the set of all corners $S_{all.corners}$ and S_{train}. Following the encoding in Sect. 4.1, we know that the set of all corners corresponds to $\{\underbrace{0 \cdots 0}_{\phi \text{ times}}, \underbrace{1 \cdots 1}_{\phi \text{ times}}\}^{d_l}$. As an example, in Fig. 2(b), the set of all corners equals $\{000000, 000111, 111000, 111111\}$. Lines 10 to 16 of Algorithm 1 describe how such a construction can be done symbolically using BDD, where the number of BDD operations being triggered is linear to $\phi \cdot d_l$. The set S_{j0s}, after the inner loop (line 13–15), contains the set of all possible Boolean words with the restriction that $\mathbf{b}_{[\phi(j-1)+1\cdots\phi j]}$ equals $\underbrace{0\cdots0}_{\phi\ \text{times}}$ (similarly S_{j1s} for having 1 s). The "BDD.or" operation at line 16 performs a set union operation between S_{j0s} and S_{j1s}, to explicitly allow two types of possibilities within $\mathbf{b}_{[\phi(j-1)+1\cdots\phi j]}$.

C: Filter Unsupported Corners that are Close to Training Data. Although at line 17 of Algorithm 1, all unsupported corners are stored compactly inside the BDD, the implication of Lemma 1 suggests that the number of unsupported corners can still be exponential. Therefore, we are interested in further filtering out some unsupported corners and only keeping those unsupported corners that are distant from the training data.

Consider again the example in Fig. 2(b), where S_{unsup} is the symbolic representation of two strings, namely

- 000111 reflecting the top-left corner, and
- 111000 reflecting the bottom-right corner.

The algorithm thus should keep 000111 and filter 111000, as the bottom-right corner has a training data $\mathbf{x}'$ being close-by.

The final part of Algorithm 1 (starting at line 18) describes how to perform such an operation symbolically by utilizing the Hamming distance on the binary string level. Consider again the example in Fig. 2(b), where for training data $\mathbf{x}'$, $\mathrm{enc}^3(f^l(\mathbf{x}')) = 011000$. The Hamming distance between "011000" and the bottom-right corner encoding "111000" equals 1. For the top-left corner having its encoding being 000111, there exists only data points whose encoding (e.g., $\mathbf{x}$ has an encoding of 011111) has a Hamming distance of 2. Therefore, by filtering out the elements with Hamming distance 1, only the top-left corner is kept.

Within Algorithm 1, line 18 maintains $S_{train}^{\leq \Delta}$ as a BDD storing every binary string that has another binary string in S_{train} such that the Hamming distance between these two is at most Δ. Initially, $S_{train}^{\leq \Delta}$ is set to be S_{train}, reflecting the case of Hamming distance being 0. The loop of Line 19 is executed Δ times to gradually increase $S_{train}^{\leq \Delta}$ to cover strings with Hamming distance from 1 up to Δ.

Within the loop, first a local copy S_{local} is created (line 20). Subsequently, enlarging the set by a Hamming distance 1 can be done by the inner loop within line 21–22: for each variable index m, perform existential quantification over the local copy to get the set of binary strings that is insensitive at variable bv_m. As an example, if $S_{local} = \{011000\}$, then performing existential quantification on the first variable generates a set "$\{\theta 11000 \mid \theta \in 0,1\}$", and performing existential quantification on the second variable generates another set "$\{0\theta 1000 \mid \theta \in 0,1\}$".

A union over all these newly generated sets returns the set of strings whose Hamming distance to the original "011000" is less or equal to 1.

Finally, line 23 performs another set difference to remove elements in S_{unsup} that is present in $S_{train}^{\leq \Delta}$, and the resulting set is returned as the output of the algorithm.

4.3   Corner Prioritization with Multi-boxed Abstraction Monitors

In the previous section, we focus on finding corners within a box, where the corners are distant (by means of Hamming distance) to DNN-computed feature vectors from the training dataset. Nevertheless, when the monitor uses multiple boxes, is it possible that the corner being prioritized in one box has been covered by another box? An example can be found in Fig. 3, where the monitor contains two boxes B_1 and B_2. If the algorithm applied on B_1 proposes corner c_1 to be tested, it would be a waste as c_1 lies inside B_2.

We propose a lazy approach to mediate this problem - whenever a corner proposal is created from one box, use a strengthened condition and check if some part of the corner is deep inside another box (subject to δ). Precisely, given $\mathcal{B}_{k,l,\delta}$, provided that Algorithm 1 applied on $B_i = [[a_1, b_1], \cdots, [a_{d_l}, b_{d_l}]] \in \mathcal{B}_{k,l,\delta}$ suggests an unsupported corner $c \in C_{B_i}^u$ whose corresponding binary string equals $\mathbf{b}$, conduct the following:

1. Given $\mathbf{b}$, find a vertex $\mathbf{v} = (v_1, \ldots, v_{d_l})$ in box B_i that is also in the proposed corner c. Precisely, for $\forall j \in [1 \cdots d_l]$,
   - if $\mathbf{b}_{[\phi(j-1)+1 \cdots \phi j]} = \underbrace{0 \cdots 0}_{\phi \text{ times}}$, set v_j to be a_j.
   - Otherwise, set v_j to be b_j.
2. Discard the corner proposal on c, whenever there exists $B_{i'} = [[a_1', b_1'], \cdots, [a_{d_l}', b_{d_l}']] \in \mathcal{B}_{k,l,\delta}$, $i' \neq i$, such that the following holds: $\forall j \in [1 \cdots d_l] : a_j' + \delta_j < v_j < b_j' - \delta_j$.

The time complexity for rejecting a corner proposal is in low degree polynomial:

- For step (1), assigning each v_j sums up the time $\mathcal{O}(d_l)$.
- For step (2), the containment check is done on every other box (the number of boxes equals k) over all dimensions (size d_l), leading to the time complexity $\mathcal{O}(k \cdot d_l)$.

5   Improving the DNN Against the Unsupported Corners

As unsupported corners represent regions in the monitor where no training data is close-by, any input whose feature vector falls in that corner will not be rejected by the monitor, leading to safety concerns if the prediction is incorrect. For classification tasks, one possible mediation is to explicitly ensure that any input whose feature vector falls in the unsupported corner does not cause the DNN to generate a strong prediction over a particular class.

Algorithm 2. DNN modification against unsupported corners under 1-boxed abstraction monitor (classification network with one-hot output encoding)

Input: Dataset $\mathcal{D}_{train}$, DNN $f = (g^L, \ldots, g^1)$, 1-boxed monitor $\mathcal{B}_{1,l,\delta}$, $S \subset S_{unsup} \backslash S_{train}^{\leq \Delta}$ created from Algorithm 1, the number of samples ρ per unsupported corner.

Output: Updated DNN f'.

1: Create dataset $\mathcal{D}_{modify} \stackrel{\text{def}}{=} \{(f^l(\mathbf{x}), \mathbf{y})) \mid (\mathbf{x}, \mathbf{y}) \in \mathcal{D}_{train}\}$
2: **for all** $\mathbf{b} \in S$ **do**
3:     Let $\mathbf{c} \stackrel{\text{def}}{=} [[\alpha_1, \beta_1], \cdots, [\alpha_{d_l}, \beta_{d_l}]] \in \mathbb{R}^{d_l}$ be the corresponding corner of $\mathbf{b}$.
4:     Sample ρ points $\mathbf{p}_1, \ldots, \mathbf{p}_\rho$ from $\mathbf{c}$.
5:     **for all** $i \in [1 \cdots \rho]$ **do**
6:         $\mathcal{D}_{modify} \leftarrow \mathcal{D}_{modify} \cup \{(\mathbf{p}_i, (\frac{1}{d_L}, \ldots, \frac{1}{d_L}))\}$
7: Improve $g^L, \ldots g^{l+1}$ to $\hat{g}^L, \ldots \hat{g}^{l+1}$ by training against $\mathcal{D}_{modify}$
8: Return $f' \stackrel{\text{def}}{=} (\hat{g}^L, \ldots \hat{g}^{l+1}, g^l, \ldots, g^1)$

As an example, if the DNN f is used for digit recognition and d_L equals 10 with each $f_i^{(L)}$ indicating the possibility of the character being $i-1$, it is desirable to let an input $\mathbf{x}$, whose feature vector falls inside the unsupported corner, to produce $f_1^{(L)}(\mathbf{x}) \cong f_2^{(L)}(\mathbf{x}) \cong \ldots \cong f_{10}^{(L)}(\mathbf{x}) \cong 0.1$, i.e., the DNN is not certain on which class this input belongs to. One can naively retrain the complete DNN against such an input $\mathbf{x}$. Nevertheless, if the DNN is completely retrained, the created monitor $\mathcal{B}_{k,l,\delta}$ is no longer valid, as the parameters before layer l have been changed due to re-training.

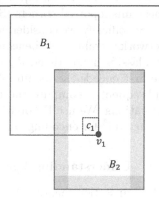

Fig. 3. Two overlapping boxes.

Towards this issue, Algorithm 2 presents a local DNN modification scheme[1] where the re-training is only done between layers $l+1$ and L. As the new DNN share the same function with the existing one from layer 1 to layer l, previously constructed 1-boxed monitor remains applicable in the new DNN.

As re-training is only done over a sub-network between layers $l+1$ and L, the input for training the sub-network is the output of layer l. Therefore, reflected at line 1, one prepares a new training dataset where the input is $f^l(\mathbf{x})$. The input for Algorithm 2 also contains S, which is a subset of unsupported corners derived from Algorithm 1. Lines 2 to 6 translate each binary string in S into an unsupported corner (line 3) and sample ρ points (line 4) to be added to the new training dataset. As stated in the previous paragraph, we wish the result of these points to be unbiased for any output class. Therefore, as stated at line 6, the corresponding label, under the assumption where $\mathcal{D}_{train}$ uses one-hot encoding, should be $(\frac{1}{d_L}, \ldots, \frac{1}{d_L})$.

---

[1] For simplicity, we only show the algorithm for 1-boxed abstraction monitors, while extensions for multi-boxed abstraction monitors can follow the same paradigm stated in Sect. 4.3.

Table 1. Hyper-parameter setting in the experiments

dataset	# of monitored neurons	m :# unsupported corners	ρ: # collected samples per corner
MNIST	40	1000	10
GTSRB	84	1000	10

6 Evaluation

This section aims to experimentally answer two questions about the unsupported corners generated by the method in Sect. 4. The first question is regarding the behavior of feature vectors in the unsupported corners reflected in the output (Sect. 6.1). The second question is regarding generating inputs that can lead to these unsupported corners (Sect. 6.2).

Specifically, we consider monitors built on the penultimate layer of two neural networks, trained on benchmarks MNIST [15] and GTSRB [11], respectively, to classify handwritten digits (0–9) and traffic signs. Following Algorithm 1, we first encode the monitors' supported corners using the BDD representation. Subsequently, compute the unsupported corners using symbolic set difference operations. We use Pytorch[2] to train the DNN and use the python-based BDD library dd[3] for encoding the binary strings into the BDD.

6.1 Understanding Unsupported Corners

This subsection focuses on understanding the output softmax (probability) values for the feature vectors from unsupported corners. We take m unsupported corners and from each of them uniformly pick ρ samples in the corresponding corner. The hyper-parameters used in the experiments are shown in Table 1.

We first examine if the DNN can output overconfident softmax values for these samples. From the statistical results, as shown in the left part of Fig. 4, one can find that samples from many unsupported corners (with Hamming distance larger than 3 from the training dataset) are assigned a high softmax value. This confirms our conjecture that additional local training is needed to suppress high-confident outputs against unsupported corners. After applying Algorithm 2 for fine-tuning the after-monitored-layer sub-network, these unsupported cases are all assigned an averaged softmax value of $\frac{1}{10}$, as shown in the right part of Fig. 4. Interestingly, the fine-tuning does not deteriorate the accuracy of the neural network on the original training and test sets: We observe a shift from the original accuracy of 99.34% (98.8%) on the training (test) dataset to a new one of 99.24% (98.84%).

---

[2] https://pytorch.org/.
[3] https://github.com/tulip-control/dd.

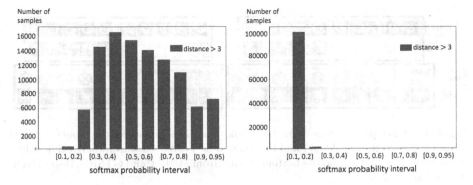

Fig. 4. Statistics of numbers of samples (picked from unsupported corners) per softmax value interval on MNIST (left: before re-training; right: after re-training).

Remark 1. The repair of the sub-network essentially equips the original network with an additional ability of identifying out-of-distribution samples (around the area of unsupported corners) by observing whether the softmax value of prediction is close to $\frac{1}{d_L}$ or not.

6.2   From Test Case Proposal to Test Case Generation

This subsection explores two possibilities for generating inputs that yield features in specific unsupported corners of the monitored layer.

- The first method is to verify whether the maximum or minimum activation value of each monitored neuron is responsible for a particular segment or local area of the input, hereafter referred to as Neuron-Wise-Excited-Input-Feature (NWEIF). If such a connection exists, since a corner is a combination of the maximum/minimum activation values of each neuron, then a new input can be formed by combining the NWEIFs of each neuron.
- The second is to apply optimization techniques. Given an image in the training dataset, perform gradient descent to find a modification over the image such that the modified image generates a feature within a given unsupported corner.

Neuron-Wise Excited Input-Feature Combination. We applied the layer-wise relevance propagation (LRP) [19] technique to interpret the images that reach the maximum and minimum five values of a neuron. LRP is one of the back-propagation techniques used for redistributing neuron activation values at one layer to its precedent layers (possible up to the input layer). In a nutshell, it explains which parts of the input contribute to the neuron's activation and to what extent.

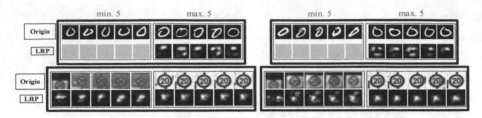

Fig. 5. LRP interpretation example: each bold-black block contains the inputs reaching the minimum 5 (red sub-block) and the maximum 5 (blue sub-block) activation values of a neuron; the top two and the bottom two are from MNIST and GTSRB, respectively. (Color figure online)

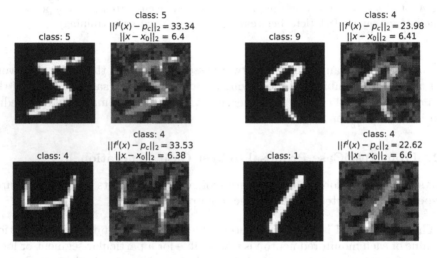

Fig. 6. Using adversarial testing to generate images whose feature vectors fall into a particular corner. The original images are shown on the left, and the perturbed ones on the right. We also show the predicted classes, and for the perturbed images additionally the distance of their features from the corner point, as well as the distance from the unperturbed image.

Discussion. The results in Fig. 5 show that it is difficult for humans to compose new inputs based on NWEIF. The first and second rows in each bold-black block are the original images and corresponding heat maps interpreted by LRP. Although LRP can help us identify regions or features, it is very difficult to precisely associate one neuron with one specific input-feature. We can observe in Fig. 5 that for the 20km/h speed sign, the area that leads to maximum activation has considerable overlap with the area that leads to minimum activation. This makes a precise association between neurons and features difficult, justifying the need of using other methods such as optimization-based image generation for testing and Algorithm 2 for local training over unsupported corners.

Optimization-Based Test Case Generation. Finally, we create images corresponding to corners by using an optimization method, similar to the ones used for adversarial example generation [23]. Overall, the generated test case should allow the DNN to (1) fall inside the box of the unsupported corner and to (2) be confident in predicting a wrong class. In our implementation, the previously mentioned two objectives are integrated as a loss function, which is optimized (by minimizing the loss) with respect to the input image. We refer readers to an extended version[4] for details regarding how such a method is implemented. Figure 6 illustrates examples of original and perturbed images, where for the bottom-right example, the perturbed images not only falls into a particular corner, but the resulting prediction also changes from the initially correct "1" to the incorrect "4". We observe that when the buffer δ around the box is small, it can be difficult for the adversarial testing method to generate images that fall into a specific corner. However, we are unable to state that it is impossible to generate such an input; the problem can only be answered using formal verification. This further justifies the need for local DNN training.

7   Concluding Remarks

In this paper, we address the issue of testing OoD monitors built from boxed abstractions of feature vectors from the training data, and we show how this testing problem could be reduced to finding corners in hyperrectangle distant from the available training data in the feature space. The key novelty lies in a rigorous method for analyzing the corners of the monitors and detecting whether a corner is supported or not according to the input in the training data set, generating feature vectors located in the corner. To the best of our knowledge, it is the first approach for testing the decision boundary of a DNN monitor, where the test prioritization scheme is based on corners (of the monitor) that have no input data being close-by. The other important result is the DNN repair scheme (via local training) to incorporate the distant-yet-uncovered corners. To this end, we have developed a tool that provides technical solutions for our OoD detectors based on boxed abstractions. Our experiments show the effectiveness of our method in different applications.

This work raises a new research direction on rigorous engineering of DNN monitors to be used in safety-critical applications. An important future direction is the refinement of boxed abstractions: By considering the unrealistic corners, we can refine the abstraction by adding more boxes to remove them. Another direction is to use some probability estimation method to prioritize corners rather than using Hamming distance.

Acknowledgement. This work is funded by the Bavarian Ministry for Economic Affairs, Regional Development and Energy as part of a project to support the thematic development of the Fraunhofer Institute for Cognitive Systems. This work is also supported by the European project Horizon 2020 research and innovation programme under grant agreement No. 956123.

---

[4] Available at https://arxiv.org/abs/2205.07736.

References

1. Abrecht, S., Gauerhof, L., Gladisch, C., Groh, K., Heinzemann, C., Woehrle, M.: Testing deep learning-based visual perception for automated driving. ACM TCPS **5**(4), 1–28 (2021)
2. Bryant, R.E.: Symbolic Boolean manipulation with ordered binary-decision diagrams. CSUR **24**(3), 293–318 (1992)
3. Cheng, C.-H., Huang, C.-H., Brunner, T., Hashemi, V.: Towards safety verification of direct perception neural networks. In: DATE, pp. 1640–1643. IEEE (2020)
4. Cheng, C.-H., Huang, C.-H., Yasuoka, H.: Quantitative projection coverage for testing ML-enabled autonomous systems. In: Lahiri, S.K., Wang, C. (eds.) ATVA 2018. LNCS, vol. 11138, pp. 126–142. Springer, Cham (2018). https://doi.org/10.1007/978-3-030-01090-4_8
5. Dusenberry, M., et al.: Efficient and scalable Bayesian neural nets with rank-1 factors. In: ICML, pp. 2782–2792. PMLR (2020)
6. Gal, Y., Ghahramani, Z.: Dropout as a Bayesian approximation: representing model uncertainty in deep learning. In: ICML, pp. 1050–1059. PMLR (2016)
7. Goodfellow, I., Bengio, Y., Courville, A.: Deep Learning. MIT Press, Cambridge (2016)
8. Havasi, M., et al.: Training independent subnetworks for robust prediction. arXiv preprint arXiv:2010.06610 (2020)
9. Hendrycks, D., Gimpel, K.: A baseline for detecting misclassified and out-of-distribution examples in neural networks. arXiv preprint arXiv:1610.02136 (2016)
10. Henzinger, T.A., Lukina, A., Schilling, C.: Outside the box: abstraction-based monitoring of neural networks. arXiv preprint arXiv:1911.09032 (2019)
11. Houben, S., Stallkamp, J., Salmen, J., Schlipsing, M., Igel, C.: Detection of traffic signs in real-world images: the german traffic sign detection benchmark. In: IJCNN, pp. 1–8. IEEE (2013)
12. Huang, X., Kroening, D., Ruan, W., Sharp, J., Sun, Y., Thamo, E., Wu, M., Yi, X.: A survey of safety and trustworthiness of deep neural networks: verification, testing, adversarial attack and defence, and interpretability. Comput. Sci. Rev. **37**, 100270 (2020)
13. Katz, G., Barrett, C., Dill, D.L., Julian, K., Kochenderfer, M.J.: Reluplex: an efficient SMT solver for verifying deep neural networks. In: Majumdar, R., Kunčak, V. (eds.) CAV 2017. LNCS, vol. 10426, pp. 97–117. Springer, Cham (2017). https://doi.org/10.1007/978-3-319-63387-9_5
14. Lakshminarayanan, B., Pritzel, A., Blundell, C.: Simple and scalable predictive uncertainty estimation using deep ensembles. arXiv preprint arXiv:1612.01474 (2016)
15. LeCun, Y., Cortes, C., Burges, C.: MNIST handwritten digit database (2010)
16. Lee, K., Lee, K., Lee, H., Shin, J.: A simple unified framework for detecting out-of-distribution samples and adversarial attacks. In: NeurIPS, vol. 31 (2018)
17. Liang, S., Li, Y., Srikant, R.: Enhancing the reliability of out-of-distribution image detection in neural networks. arXiv preprint arXiv:1706.02690 (2017)
18. Ma, L., et al.: Combinatorial testing for deep learning systems. arXiv preprint arXiv:1806.07723 (2018)
19. Montavon, G., Binder, A., Lapuschkin, S., Samek, W., Müller, K.-R.: Layer-wise relevance propagation: an overview. In: Samek, W., Montavon, G., Vedaldi, A., Hansen, L.K., Müller, K.-R. (eds.) Explainable AI: Interpreting, Explaining and Visualizing Deep Learning. LNCS (LNAI), vol. 11700, pp. 193–209. Springer, Cham (2019). https://doi.org/10.1007/978-3-030-28954-6_10

20. Pei, K., Cao, Y., Yang, J., Jana, S.: DeepXplore: automated whitebox testing of deep learning systems. In: SOSP, pp. 1–18. ACM (2017)
21. Riccio, V., Tonella, P.: Model-based exploration of the frontier of behaviours for deep learning system testing. In: FSE, pp. 876–888. ACM (2020)
22. Sun, Y., Huang, X., Kroening, D., Sharp, J., Hill, M., Ashmore, R.: Structural test coverage criteria for deep neural networks. ACM TECS **18**(5s), 1–23 (2019)
23. Szegedy, C., et al.: Intriguing properties of neural networks. arXiv preprint arXiv:1312.6199 (2013)
24. Wu, C., Falcone, Y., Bensalem, S.: Customizable reference runtime monitoring of neural networks using resolution boxes. arXiv preprint arXiv:2104.14435 (2021)

POLAR: A Polynomial Arithmetic Framework for Verifying Neural-Network Controlled Systems

Chao Huang[1](✉), Jiameng Fan[2], Xin Chen[3], Wenchao Li[2], and Qi Zhu[4]

[1] University of Liverpool, Liverpool, UK
chao.huang2@liverpool.ac.uk
[2] Boston University, Boston, USA
{jmfan,wenchao}@bu.edu
[3] University of Dayton, Dayton, USA
xchen4@udayton.edu
[4] Northwestern University, Evanston, USA
qzhu@northwestern.edu

Abstract. We present POLAR (The source code can be found at https://github.com/ChaoHuang2018/POLAR_Tool. The full version of this paper can be found at https://arxiv.org/abs/2106.13867.), a **POL**ynomial **AR**ithmetic-based framework for efficient time-bounded reachability analysis of neural-network controlled systems. Existing approaches leveraging the standard Taylor Model (TM) arithmetic for approximating the neural-network controller cannot deal with non-differentiable activation functions and suffer from rapid explosion of the remainder when propagating TMs. POLAR overcomes these shortcomings by integrating TM arithmetic with *Bernstein polynomial interpolation* and *symbolic remainders*. The former enables TM propagation across non-differentiable activation functions and local refinement of TMs, and the latter reduces error accumulation in the TM remainder for linear mappings in the neural network. Experimental results show POLAR significantly outperforms the state-of-the-art tools on both efficiency and tightness of the reachable set overapproximation.

1 Introduction

Neural networks have been increasingly used as the central decision makers in a variety of control tasks [17,21]. However, the use of neural-network controllers also gives rise to new challenges on verifying the correctness of the resulting closed-loop control systems especially in safety-critical settings [29,30]. In this paper, we consider the reachability verification problem of neural-network controlled systems (NNCSs). The high-level architecture of a simple NNCS is shown in Fig. 1 in which the neural network senses the system state $\vec{x}$ at discrete time

---

C. Huang—Part of the work was done when the author was in Northwestern University, US.

© The Author(s), under exclusive license to Springer Nature Switzerland AG 2022
A. Bouajjani et al. (Eds.): ATVA 2022, LNCS 13505, pp. 414–430, 2022.
https://doi.org/10.1007/978-3-031-19992-9_27

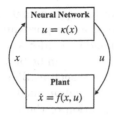

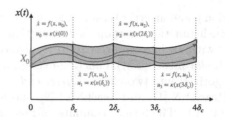

Fig. 1. A typical NNCS model.   **Fig. 2.** Executions over 4 control steps.

steps, and computes the corresponding control values $\vec{u}$ for updating the system dynamics which is defined by an ordinary differential equation (ODE) over $\vec{x}$ and $\vec{u}$. The *time-bounded reachability analysis problem* of an NNCS is to compute a state set that contains all the trajectories of a finite number of control steps from a given initial set. The initial set may represent uncertainties in the starting state of the system or error (e.g. localization error) bounds in estimating the current system state during an execution of the system. Figure 2 shows an illustration of reachable sets for 4 steps, where the orange region represents the reachable set, and the two red, arrowed curves are two example trajectories starting from two different initial states in the initial set X_0 (blue).

Reachability analysis of general NNCSs is notoriously difficult due to nonlinearity in both the neural-network controller and the plant. The difficulty is further exacerbated by the coupling of the controller and the plant over multiple control steps. Since exact reachability of general nonlinear systems is undecidable [2], current approaches for reachability analysis largely focus on computing a tight overapproximation of the reachable sets [1,6,10]. Verisig [14] leverages properties of the sigmoid activation function and converts an NNCS with these activation functions to an equivalent hybrid system. Thus, existing tools for hybrid system reachability analysis can be directly applied to solve the NNCS reachability problem. However, this approach inherits the efficiency problem of hybrid system reachability analysis and does not scale beyond very small NNCSs. Another line of approach is to draw on techniques for computing the output ranges of neural networks [12,16,24,26–28] and directly integrating them with reachability analysis tools designed for dynamical systems. NNV [25], for instance, combines star set analysis on the neural network with zonotope-based analysis of the nonlinear plant dynamics from CORA [1]. However, such approaches have been shown to be ineffective for NNCS verification due to the lack of consideration on the interaction between the neural-network controller and the plant dynamics [8,11,13]. In particular, since the primary goal of these techniques is to bound the output range of the neural network instead of approximating its input-output function, they *cannot track state dependencies across the closed-loop system and across multiple time steps in reachability analysis.*

More recent advances in NNCS reachability analysis are based on the idea of *function overapproximation* of the neural network controller. A function overapproximation of a neural network κ has two components: an approximated function p and an error term I (e.g. an interval) that bounds the approximation error. Such function overapproximation that produces a *point-wise* approximation of κ with an interval error term (typically called a remainder) is also known as a *Taylor model* (TM). Function-overapproximation approaches can be broadly categorized into two classes: *direct end-to-end approximation* such as Sherlock [8], ReachNN [11] and ReachNN* [9], and *layer-by-layer propagation* such as Verisig 2.0 [13]. The former computes a function overapproximation of the neural network end-to-end by sampling from the input space. The main drawback of this approach is that it does not scale beyond systems with more than a few input dimensions. The latter approach tries to exploit the neural network structure and uses *Taylor model arithmetic* to more efficiently obtain a function overapproximation of κ by propagating the TMs layer by layer through the network (details in Sect. 3). However, due to limitations of basic TM arithmetic, these approaches *cannot handle non-differentiable activation functions and suffer from rapid growth of the remainder* during propagation. For instance, explosion of the interval remainder would degrade a TM propagation to an interval analysis.

In this paper, we propose a principled POLynomial ARithmetic framework (POLAR) that enables precise layer-by-layer propagation of TMs for general feed-forward neural networks. Basic Taylor model arithmetic cannot handle ReLU that is non-differentiable (cannot produce the polynomial), and also suffers from low approximation precision (large remainder). POLAR addresses the key challenges of applying basic TM arithmetic through a novel use of *univariate Bernstein polynomial interpolation* and *symbolic remainders*. Univariate Bernstein polynomial interpolation enables the handling of non-differentiable activation functions and local refinement of Taylor models (details in Sect. 3.1). Symbolic remainders can taper the growth of interval remainders by avoiding the so-called wrapping effect [15] in linear mappings. The paper has the following novel contributions: (I) A polynomial arithmetic framework using both Taylor and univariate Bernstein approximations for computing NNCS reachable sets to handle general NN controllers; (II) An adaptation of the symbolic remainder method for ODEs to the layer-by-layer propagation for neural networks; (III) A comprehensive experimental evaluation of our approach on challenging case studies that demonstrates significant improvements of POLAR against SOTA.

2 Preliminaries

A *Neural-Network Controlled System (NNCS)* is a continuous plant governed by a neural network controller. The plant dynamics is defined by an ODE of the form $\dot{\vec{x}} = f(\vec{x}, \vec{u})$ wherein the state variables and control inputs are denoted by the vectors $\vec{x}$ and $\vec{u}$ respectively. We assume the function f is at least locally Lipschitz continuous such that its solution w.r.t. an initial state and constant control inputs is unique [20]. We denote the input-output mapping of the neural network controller as κ. The controller is triggered every δ_c time which is called the *control stepsize*. A system *execution (trajectory)* is produced as follows: starting from an initial state $\vec{x}(0)$, the controller senses the system state at the beginning of every control step $t = j\delta_c$ for $j = 0, 1, \ldots$, and updates the control inputs to $\vec{v}_j = \kappa(\vec{x}(j\delta_c))$. The system's dynamics in that control step is governed by the ODE $\dot{\vec{x}} = f(\vec{x}, \vec{v}_j)$.

Given an initial state set $X_0 \subset \mathbb{R}^n$, all executions from a state in this set can be formally defined by a *flowmap* function $\varphi_\mathcal{N} : X_0 \times \mathbb{R}_{\geq 0} \to \mathbb{R}^n$, such that the system state at any time $t \geq 0$ from any initial state $\vec{x}_0 \in X_0$ is $\varphi_\mathcal{N}(\vec{x}_0, t)$. We call a state $\vec{x}' \in \mathbb{R}^n$ *reachable* if there exists $\vec{x}_0 \in X_0$ and $t \geq 0$ such that $\vec{x}' = \varphi_\mathcal{N}(\vec{x}_0, t)$. The *reachability problem* on NNCS is to decide whether a state is reachable in a given NNCS, and it is *undecidable* since NNCS is more expressive than two-counter machines for which the reachability problem is already undecidable [2]. Many formal verification problems can be reduced to the reachability problem. For example, the safety verification problem can be reduced to checking reachability to an unsafe state. In the paper, we focus on computing the reachable set of an NNCS over a bounded number K of control steps. Since flowmap $\varphi_\mathcal{N}$ often does not have a closed form due to the nonlinear ODEs, we seek to compute *state-wise overapproximations* for it over multiple time segments, that is, in each control step $[j\delta_c, (j+1)\delta_c]$ for $j = 0, \ldots, K-1$, the reachable set is overapproximated by a group of flowpipes $\mathcal{F}_1(\vec{x}_0, \tau), \ldots, \mathcal{F}_N(\vec{x}_0, \tau)$ over the N uniformly subdivided time segments of the time interval, such that $\mathcal{F}_i(\vec{x}_0, \tau)$ is a *state-wise overapproximation* of $\varphi_\mathcal{N}(\vec{x}_0, j\delta_c + (i-1)\delta + \tau)$ for $\tau \in [0, \delta_c/N]$, i.e., $\mathcal{F}_j(\vec{x}_0, \tau)$ contains the exact reachable state from any initial state $\vec{x}_0$ in the i-th time segment of the j-th control step. Here, τ is the local time variable which is independent in each flowpipe. A high-level flowpipe construction algorithm is presented as follows, in which $\hat{X}_0 = X_0$ and $\delta = \delta_c/N$ is called the *time step*.

1: **for** $j = 0$ to $K-1$ **do**
2:    Computing an overapproximation $\hat{U}_j$ for the control input range $\kappa(\hat{X}_j)$;
3:    Computing the flowpipes $\mathcal{F}_1(\vec{x}_0, \tau), \ldots, \mathcal{F}_N(\vec{x}_0, \tau)$ for the continuous dynamics $\dot{\vec{x}} = f(\vec{x}, \vec{u}), \dot{\vec{u}} = 0$ from the initial set $\vec{x}(0) \in \hat{X}_j, \vec{u}(0) \in \hat{U}_j$;
4:    $\mathcal{R} \leftarrow \mathcal{R} \cup \{\mathcal{F}_1(\vec{x}_0, \tau), \ldots, \mathcal{F}_N(\vec{x}_0, \tau)\}$;
5:    $\hat{X}_{j+1} \leftarrow \mathcal{F}_N(\vec{x}_0, \delta)$;

Notice that $\vec{x}(0)$ denotes the local initial set for the ODE used in the current control step, that is the system reachable set at the time $j\delta_c$, while the variables $\vec{x}_0$ in a flowpipe are the symbolic representation of an initial state in X_0. Intuitively, a flowpipe overapproximates not only the reachable set in a time step, but also the *dependency* from an initial state to its reachable state at a particular time. For settings where the plant dynamics of an NNCS is given as a difference equation in the form of $\vec{x}_{k+1} = f(\vec{x}_k, \vec{u}_k)$, we can obtain *discrete* flowpipes which are the reachable set overapproximations at discrete time points by repeatedly computing the state set at the next step using TM arithmetic.

Dependencies on the Initial Set. As we mentioned previously, the reachable state of an NNCS at a time $t > 0$ is *uniquely determined* by its initial state if there is no noise or disturbance in the system dynamics or on the state measurements. If we use X_j to denote the exact reachable set $\{\varphi_\mathcal{N}(\vec{x}_0, j\delta_c) \mid \vec{x}_0 \in X_0\}$ from a given initial set X_0, then the control input range is defined by the set $U_j =$

$\{\kappa(\vec{x}_j) \mid \vec{x}_j = \varphi_\mathcal{N}(\vec{x}_0, j\delta_c) \text{ and } \vec{x}_0 \in X_0\}$. More intuitively, the set U_j is the image from the initial set X_0 under the mapping $\kappa(\varphi_\mathcal{N}(\cdot, j\delta_c))$. *The main challenge in computing NNCS reachable sets is to control the overapproximation, which requires accurately tracking the dependency of a reachable set on the initial set across multiple control steps.* In this paper, we present a polynomial arithmetic framework for tracking such dependencies using Taylor models.

Taylor Model Arithmetic. Taylor models are originally proposed to compute higher-order overapproximations for the ranges of continuous functions (see [4]). They can be viewed as a higher-order extension of intervals [22], which are sets of real numbers between lower and upper real bounds, e.g., the interval $[a, b]$ wherein $a \leq b$ represents the set of $\{x \mid a \leq x \leq b\}$. A *Taylor model* *(TM)* is a pair (p, I) wherein p is a polynomial of degree k over a finite group of variables $x_1, \dots, x_n$ ranging in an interval domain $D \subset \mathbb{R}^n$, and I is the remainder interval. The range of a TM is the Minkowski sum of the range of its polynomial and the remainder interval. Thereby we sometimes intuitively denote a TM (p, I) by $p + I$ in the paper. TMs are closed under operations such as addition, multiplication, and integration (see [19]). Given functions f, g that are overapproximated by TMs (p_f, I_f) and (p_g, I_g), respectively, a TM for $f + g$ can be computed as $(p_f + p_g, I_f + I_g)$, and an order k TM for $f \cdot g$ can be computed as $(p_f \cdot p_g - r_k, I_f \cdot B(p_g) + B(p_f) \cdot I_g + I_f \cdot I_g + B(r_k))$, wherein $B(p)$ denotes an interval enclosure of the range of p, and the *truncated part* r_k consists of the terms in $p_f \cdot p_g$ of degrees $> k$. Similar to reals and intervals, TMs can also be organized as vectors and matrices to overapproximate the functions whose ranges are multidimensional. Notice that *a TM is a function overapproximation and not just a range overapproximation like intervals or polyhedra.*

3   Framework of POLAR

In this section, we describe POLAR's approach for computing a TM for the output range of a neural network (NN) when the input range is defined by a TM. POLAR uses the layer-by-layer propagation strategy, and features the following key novelties: (a) A method to compute univariate Bernstein Polynomial (**BP**) overapproximations for activation functions, and selectively uses Taylor or Bernstein polynomials to *limit the overestimation produced when overapproximating the output ranges of individual neurons.* (b) A technique to symbolically represent the intermediate linear transformations of TM interval remainders during the layer-by-layer propagation. The purpose of using Symbolic Remainders (**SR**) is to *reduce the accumulation of overestimation in composing a sequence of TMs.*

3.1   Main Framework

We begin by introducing POLAR's propagation framework that incorporates only (a), and then describe how to extend it by further integrating (b). Although using TMs to represent sets in layer-by-layer propagation is already used in [13], the method only computes Taylor approximations for activation functions, and

Algorithm 1. Layer-by-layer propagation using polynomial arithmetic and TMs

---

Input: Input TM $(p_1(\vec{x}_0), I_1)$ with $\vec{x}_0 \in X_0$, the $M+1$ matrices $W_1, \ldots, W_{M+1}$ of the weights on the incoming edges of the hidden and the output layers, the $M+1$ vectors $B_1, \ldots, B_{M+1}$ of the neurons' bias in the hidden and the output layers, the $M+1$ activation functions $\sigma_1, \ldots, \sigma_{M+1}$ of hidden and output layers.

Output: a TM $(p_r(\vec{x}_0), I_r)$ that contains the set $\kappa((p_1(\vec{x}_0), I_1))$.

  1: $(p_r, I_r) \leftarrow (p_1, I_1)$;

  2: **for** $i = 1$ to $M+1$ **do**

  3:    $(p_t, I_t) \leftarrow W_i \cdot (p_r, I_r) + B_i$;   # Using TM arithmetic

  4:    Computing a polynomial approximation $p_{\sigma,i}$ for σ w.r.t. the domain (p_t, I_t);

  5:    Evaluating a conservative remainder $I_{\sigma,i}$ for $p_{\sigma,i}$ w.r.t. the domain (p_t, I_t);

  6:    $(p_r, I_r) \leftarrow p_{\sigma,i}(p_t + I_t) + I_{\sigma,i}$;   # Using TM arithmetic

  7: **return** (p_r, I_r).

---

the TM output of one layer is propagated by the existing arithmetic for TM composition to the next layer. Such a method has the following shortcomings: (1) the activation functions have to be differentiable, (2) standard TM composition is often the source of overestimation even if preconditioning and shrink wrapping are used. Here, we seek to improve the use of TMs in the above two aspects.

Before presenting our layer-by-layer propagation method, we describe how a TM output is computed from a given TM input for a single layer. The idea is illustrated in Fig. 3. The circles in the right column denote the neurons in the current layer which is the i-th layer, and those in the left column denotes the neurons in the previous layer. The weights on the incoming edges to the current layer is organized as a matrix W_i, while we use B_i to denote the vector organization of the biases in the current layer. Given that the output range of the neurons in the previous layer is represented as a TM (vector) $(p_i(\vec{x}_0), I_i)$ wherein $\vec{x}_0$ are the variables ranging in the NNCS initial set. Then, the output TM $(p_{i+1}(\vec{x}_0), I_{i+1})$ of the current layer can be obtained as follows. First, we compute the polynomial approximations $p_{\sigma_1,i}, \ldots, p_{\sigma_l,i}$ for the activation functions $\sigma_1, \ldots, \sigma_l$ of the neurons in the current layer. Second, interval remainders $I_{\sigma_1,i}, \ldots, I_{\sigma_l,i}$ are evaluated for those polynomials to ensure that for each $j = 1, \ldots, l$, $(p_{\sigma_j,i}, I_{\sigma_j,i})$ is a TM of the activation function σ_j w.r.t. z_j ranging in the j-th dimension of the set $W_i(p_i(\vec{x}_0) + I_i) + B_i$. Third, $(p_{i+1}(\vec{x}_0), I_{i+1})$ is computed as the TM composition $p_{\sigma,i}(W_i(p_i(\vec{x}_0) + I_i) + B_i) + I_{\sigma,i}$ wherein $p_{\sigma,i}(\vec{z}) = (p_{\sigma_1,i}(z_1), \ldots, p_{\sigma_l,i}(z_k))^T$ and $I_{\sigma,i} = (I_{\sigma_1,i}, \ldots, I_{\sigma_l,i})^T$. Hence, when there are multiple layers, starting from the first layer, the output TM of a layer is treated as the input TM of the next layer, and the final output TM is computed by composing TMs layer-by-layer.

We give the whole procedure by Algorithm 1, where the polynomial approximation $p_{\sigma,i}$ and its remainder interval $I_{\sigma,i}$ for the vector of activation functions σ in the i-th layer can be computed in the following two ways.

Taylor Approximation. When the activation function is differentiable in the range defined by (p_t, I_t). The polynomial $p_{\sigma,i}$ can be computed as the order k Taylor expansion of σ (in each of its dimension) at the center of (p_t, I_t), and the remainder is evaluated using interval arithmetic based on the Lagrange remainder form. More details are described elsewhere [19].

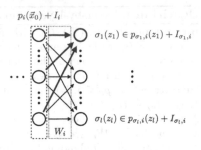

Fig. 3. Single layer propagation

Bernstein Interpolation. The use of Bernstein approximation only requires the activation function to be continuous in (p_t, I_t), and can be used not only in more general situations, but also to obtain better polynomial approximations than Taylor expansions (see [18]). Intuitively, an order k Taylor approximation can only guarantee to have the same value as the approximated function at the expansion point, while an order k Bernstein interpolation has the same value as the approximated function at $k + 1$ points. We give the details of our Bernstein overapproximation method as follows.

Bernstein Approximation for $\sigma(\vec{z})$ w.r.t. $\vec{z} \in (p_t, I_t)$. Given (p_t, I_t) computed in Line 3, the j-th component of the polynomial vector $p_{\sigma,i}$ is the order k Bernstein interpolation of the activation function σ_j of the j-th neuron. It can be computed as $p_{\sigma_j,i}(z_j) = \sum_{s=0}^{k} \left(\sigma_j(\frac{\overline{Z}_j - \underline{Z}_j}{k} s + \underline{Z}_j)\binom{k}{s} \frac{(z_j - \underline{Z}_j)^s (\overline{Z}_j - z_j)^{k-s}}{(\overline{Z}_j - \underline{Z}_j)^k} \right)$, such that $\overline{Z}_j$ and $\underline{Z}_j$ denote the upper and lower bounds respectively of the range in the j-th dimension of (p_t, I_t), and they can be obtained by interval evaluating TM.

Evaluating the Remainder $I_{\sigma,i}$. The j-th component $I_{\sigma_j,i}$ of $I_{\sigma,i}$ is computed as a conservative remainder for the polynomial $p_{\sigma_j,i}$, and it can be obtained as a symmetric interval $[-\epsilon_j, \epsilon_j]$ such that

$$\epsilon_j = \max_{s=1,\cdots,m} \left(\left| p_{\sigma_j,i}(\frac{\overline{Z}_j - \underline{Z}_j}{m}(s - \frac{1}{2}) + \underline{Z}_j) - \sigma_j(\frac{\overline{Z}_j - \underline{Z}_j}{m}(s - \frac{1}{2}) + \underline{Z}_j) \right| + L_j \cdot \frac{\overline{Z}_j - \underline{Z}_j}{m} \right)$$

wherein L_j is a Lipschitz constant of σ_j with the domain (p_t, I_t), and m is the number of samples that are uniformly selected to estimate the remainder. The soundness of the error bound estimation above has been proven in [11] for multivariate Bernstein polynomials. Since univariate Bernstein polynomials is a special case of multivariate Bernstein polynomials, our approach is also sound.

The following theorem states that a TM flowpipe computed by our approach is not only a range overapproximation of a reachable set, but also a function overapproximation for the dependency of a reachable state on its initial state.

Theorem 1. *If $\mathcal{F}(\vec{x}_0, \tau)$ is the i-th TM flowpipe computed in the j-st control step, then for any initial state $\vec{x}_0 \in X_0$, the box $\mathcal{F}(\vec{x}_0, \tau)$ contains the actual reachable state $\varphi_{\mathcal{N}}(\vec{x}_0, (j - 1)\delta_c + (i - 1)\delta + \tau)$ for all $\tau \in [0, \delta]$.*

3.2   Selection of Polynomial Approximations

Since an activation function is univariate, both of its Taylor and Bernstein approximations have a size which is linear in the order k. Then we investigate the accuracy produced by both approximation forms. Since the main operation in the TM layer-by-layer propagation framework is the composition of TMs, we study the *preservation of accuracy* for both of the forms under the composition with a given TM. We first define the *Accuracy Preservation Problem*.

When a function $f(\vec{x})$ is overapproximated by a TM $(p(\vec{x}), I)$ w.r.t. a bounded domain D, the approximation quality, i.e., size of the overestimation, is directly reflected by the width of I, since $f(\vec{x}) = p(\vec{x})$ for all $\vec{x} \in D$ when I is zero by the TM definition. Given order k TMs $(p_1(\vec{x}), I_1)$ and $(p_2(\vec{x}), I_2)$ which are overapproximations of the same function $f(\vec{x})$ w.r.t. a bounded domain $D \subset \mathbb{R}^n$, we use $(p_1(\vec{x}), I_1) \prec_k (p_2(\vec{x}), I_2)$ to denote that the width of I_1 is smaller than the width of I_2 in all dimensions, i.e., $(p_1(\vec{x}), I_1)$ is a more accurate overapproximation of $f(\vec{x})$ than $(p_2(\vec{x}), I_2)$.

Accuracy Preservation Problem. Assume $(p_1(\vec{x}), I_1)$ and $(p_2(\vec{x}), I_2)$ are overapproximations of $f(\vec{x})$ with $\vec{x} \in D$, and $(p_1(\vec{x}), I_1) \prec_k (p_2(\vec{x}), I_2)$. Another function $g(\vec{y})$ is overapproximated by a TM $(q(\vec{y}), J)$ whose range is a subset of D, does $(p_1(q(\vec{y})+J), I_1) \prec_k (p_2(q(\vec{y})+J), I_2)$ hold by order k TM arithmetic?

We give the following counterexample to show that the answer is **no**, i.e., although $(p_1(\vec{x}), I_1)$ is more accurate than $(p_2(\vec{x}), I_2)$, the composition $p_1(q(\vec{y})+J)+I_1$ might not be a better order k overapproximation than $p_2(q(\vec{y})+J)+I_2$ for the composite function $f \circ g$. Given $p_1 = 0.5+0.25x-0.02083x^3$, $I_1 = [-7.93e-5, 1.92e-4]$, and $p_2 = 0.5+0.24855x-0.004583x^3$, $I_2 = [-2.42e-4, 2.42e-4]$, which are both TM overapproximations for the sigmoid function $f(x) = \frac{1}{1+e^{-x}}$ w.r.t. $x \in q(y) + J$ such that $q = 0.1y - 0.1y^2$, $J = [-0.1, 0.1]$, and $y \in [-1, 1]$. We have that $(p_1, I_1) \prec_3 (p_2, I_2)$, however after the compositions using order 3 TM arithmetic, the remainder of $p_1(q(y) + J) + I_1$ is $[-0.0466, 0.0477]$, while the remainder of $p_2(q(y) + J) + I_2$ is $[-0.0253, 0.0253]$, and we do not have $(p_1(q(y) + J), I_1) \prec_3 (p_2(q(y) + J), I_2)$.

Since the accuracy is not preserved under composition, we do not decide which approximation to choose directly based on the their remainders. Instead, we integrate an additional step in Algorithm 1 to replace line 4–6: for each activation function, we compute both Taylor and Bernstein overapproximations, and choose the one that produces the smaller remainder interval I_r after composition.

3.3   Symbolic Remainders in Layer-by-Layer Propagation

We describe the use of symbolic remainders (SR) in the layer-by-layer propagation of computing an NN output TM. The method was originally proposed in [7] for reducing the overestimation of TM flowpipes in the reachability computation for nonlinear ODEs, we adapt it particularly for reducing the error accumulation in the TM remainders during the layer-by-layer propagation. Unlike the BP technique whose purpose is to obtain tighter TMs for activation functions, the use of SR only aims at reducing the overestimation accumulation in the composition of a sequence of TMs each of which represents the input range of a layer.

Algorithm 2. TM output computation using symbolic remainders, input and output are the same as those in Algorithm 1

```
1: Setting Q as an empty array which can keep M + 1 matrices;
2: Setting J as an empty array which can keep M + 1 multidimensional intervals;
3: J ← 0;
4: for i = 1 to M + 1 do
5:     Computing the composite TM (p_{σ,i}, I_{σ,i}) using BP;
6:     Evaluating q_i(x̄_0) + J_i based on J and Q[1]I_1;        # Q[1]I_1 = I_1 when i = 1
7:     J ← J_i; Φ_i ← Q_i W_i;
8:     for j = 1 to i − 1 do
9:         Q[j] ← Φ_i · Q[j];
10:    Adding Φ_i to Q as the last element;
11:    for j = 2 to i do
12:        J ← J + Q[j] · J[j − 1];
13:    Adding J_i to J as the last element;
14: Computing an interval enclosure I_r for J + Q[1]I_1;        # interval evaluation
15: return q_{M+1}(x̄_0) + I_r.
```

Consider the TM composition for computing the output TM of a single layer in Fig. 3, the output TM $p_{\sigma,i}(W_i(p_i(\vec{x}_0) + I_i) + B_i) + I_{\sigma,i}$ equals to $Q_i W_i p_i(\vec{x}_0) + Q_i W_i I_i + Q_i B_i + p_{\sigma,i}^R(W_i(p_i(\vec{x}_0) + I_i) + B_i) + I_{\sigma,i}$ such that Q_i is the matrix of the linear coefficients in $p_{\sigma,i}$, and $p_{\sigma,i}^R$ consists of the terms in $p_{\sigma,i}$ of the degrees $\neq 1$. Therefore, the remainder I_i in the second term can be kept symbolically such that we do not compute $Q_i W_i I_i$ out as an interval but keep its transformation matrix $Q_i W_i$ to the computation for the subsequent layers. Given the image S of an interval under a linear mapping, we use $\underline{S}$ to denote that it is kept symbolically, i.e., we keep the interval along with the transformation matrix, and $\overline{S}$ to denote that the image is evaluated as an interval.

Then we present the use of SR in layer-by-layer propagation. Starting from the NN input TM $(p_1(\vec{x}_0), I_1)$, the output TM of the first layer is computed as

$$\underbrace{Q_1 W_1 p_1(\vec{x}_0) + Q_1 B_1 + p_{\sigma,1}^R(W_1(p_1(\vec{x}_0) + I_1) + B_1) + I_{\sigma,1}}_{q_1(\vec{x}_0) + J_1} + \underline{Q_1 W_1 I_1}$$

which can be kept in the form of $q_1(\vec{x}_0) + J_1 + \underline{Q_1 W_1 I_1}$. Using it as the input TM of the second layer, we have the following TM

$$p_{\sigma,2}(W_2(q_1(\vec{x}_0) + J_1 + \underline{Q_1 W_1 I_1}) + B_2) + I_{\sigma,2}$$

$$= \underbrace{Q_2 W_2 q_1(\vec{x}_0) + Q_2 B_2 + p_{\sigma,2}^R(W_2(q_1(\vec{x}_0) + J_1 + \overline{Q_1 W_1 I_1}) + B_2) + I_{\sigma,2}}_{q_2(\vec{x}_0) + J_2}$$

$$+ Q_2 W_2 J_1 + \underline{Q_2 W_2 Q_1 W_1 I_1}$$

for the output range of the second layer. Therefore the output TM of the i-th layer can be obtained as $q_i(\vec{x}_0) + J_i + \underline{Q_i W_i \cdots Q_1 W_1 I_1}$ such that $J_i = J_i + Q_i W_i J_{i-1} + \underline{Q_i W_i Q_{i-1} W_{i-1} J_{i-2}} + \cdots + \underline{Q_i W_i \cdots Q_2 W_2 J_1}$.

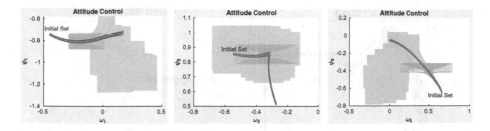

Fig. 4. Comparison between reachable sets of the 6-dimensional attitude control benchmark produced by POLAR (dark green), Verisig 2.0 (gray) and NNV (yellow). The red curves are simulated trajectories. (Color figure online)

We present the SR method by Algorithm 2 in which we use two lists: $Q[j]$ for $Q_i W_i \cdots Q_j W_j$ and $\mathcal{J}[j]$ for $\mathbb{J}_j$ to keep the intervals and their linear transformations. The symbolic remainder representation is replaced by its interval enclosure I_r at the end of the algorithm.

Time and Space Complexity. Although Algorithm 2 produces TMs with tighter remainders than Algorithm 1 because of the symbolic interval representations under linear mappings, it requires (1) two extra arrays to keep the intermediate matrices and remainder intervals, (2) two extra inner loops which perform $i-1$ and $i-2$ iterations in the i-th outer iteration. The size of $Q_i W_i \cdots Q_j W_j$ is determined by the rows in Q_i and the columns in W_j, and hence the maximum number of neurons in a layer determines the maximum size of the matrices in $\mathcal{Q}$. Similarly, the maximum dimension of J_i is also bounded by the maximum number of neurons in a layer. Because of the two inner loops, time complexity of Algorithm 2 is quadratic in M, whereas Algorithm 1 is linear in M.

Sizes of the TMs. All the TMs computed in the layer-by-layer propagation are over the same variables $\vec{x}_0$ which are symbolic representation for the NNCS initial set, i.e., $\vec{x}_0 \in X_0$. Therefore, the maximum size of an order k TM over n variables is bounded by $\binom{n+k}{n}$, and *hence the TM sizes are independent from the total number of neurons in the hidden layers of the NN controller.*

4 Experiments

We perform a comprehensive empirical study of POLAR against state-of-the-art (SOTA) techniques. We first demonstrate the performance of POLAR on two examples with high dimensional states and multiple inputs, which are far beyond the ability of SOTAs (Sect. 4.1). A comprehensive comparison over the full benchmarks in [11,13] is then given (Sect. 4.2). Finally, we present ablation studies, scalability analysis, and the ability to handle discrete-time systems (Sect. 4.3). More detailed results can be found in the full version of the paper.

All our experiments were run on a machine with 6-core 2.90 GHz Intel Core i5 and 8 GB of RAM. POLAR is implemented in C++. We present the results for POLAR, Verisig 2.0 and Sherlock using a single core without parallelization.

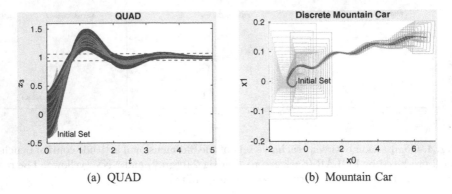

(a) QUAD   (b) Mountain Car

Fig. 5. (a) Results of QUAD. POLAR for 50 steps (dark green sets), Verisig 2.0 for 3 steps (grey sets), and simulation traces for 50 steps (red curves). It took POLAR 1533 s seconds to compute the flowpipes for 50 steps. On the other hand, it took Verisig 2.0 more than 5 h to compute the flowpipes for the first 3 steps, and the TM remainders computed in the 4th step are already of the size 10^{15}. NNV crashed with out-of-memory errors when computing the 1st step. (b) Results of Mountain Car. POLAR for 150 steps (dark green sets), Verisig 2.0 for 150 steps (grey sets), ReachNN* for 90 steps (light green sets), NNV for 65 steps, and simulation traces for 150 steps (red curves). (Color figure online)

The results of ReachNN* were computed on the same machine with the aid of GPU acceleration on an Nvidia GeForce RTX 2060 GPU.

State-of-the-Art Tools. We compare with SOTA tools in the NNCS reachability analysis literature, including Sherlock [8] (only works for ReLU), Verisig 2.0 [13] (only works for sigmoid and tanh), NNV [25], and ReachNN* [9][1].

4.1   High Dimensional Case Studies: Attitude Control and QUAD

We consider an attitude control of a rigid body with 6 states and 3 control inputs [23], and quadrotor (QUAD) with 12 states and 3 control inputs [3] to evaluate the performance of POLAR on difficult problems. The complexity of these two example lies in the combination of the numbers of the state variables and control inputs. For each example, we trained a sigmoid neural-network controller and compare POLAR with Verisig 2.0 and NNV. The detailed setting of these two examples can be found in the full version of the paper.

The result for the attitude control benchmark is shown in Fig. 4, and the result for the QUAD benchmark is shown in Fig. 5a. In the attitude control benchmark, POLAR computed the TM flowpipes for 30 control steps in 201 s. From Fig. 4, We can observe that the flowpipes computed by POLAR are tight w.r.t. the simulated traces. As a comparison, although Verisig 2.0 [13] can handle this system in theory, its remainder exploded very quickly and the tool crashed after only a few steps. NNV computed flowpipes for 25 steps by doing extensive splittings on the state space and crashed with out-of-memory errors. In the

---

[1] The results of ReachNN* are based on GPU acceleration.

Table 1. V: number of state variables, σ: activation functions, M: number of hidden layers, n: number of neurons in each hidden layer. For each approach, we give the runtime in seconds if it verifies the property. 'Unknown': the property is not verified. '–': the approach cannot be applied due to the type of σ.

#	V	NN Controller			**POLAR**	ReachNN* [9]	Sherlock [8]	Verisig 2.0 [13]
		σ	M	n				
1	2	ReLU	2	20	**12**	26	42	–
		sigmoid	2	20	**17**	75	–	47
		tanh	2	20	**20**	Unknown	–	46
		ReLU+tanh	2	20	**13**	71	–	–
2	2	ReLU	2	20	**2**	5	3	–
		sigmoid	2	20	9	13	–	**7**
		tanh	2	20	**3**	73	–	Unknown
		ReLU+tanh	2	20	**2**	Unknown	–	–
3	2	ReLU	2	20	**16**	94	143	–
		sigmoid	2	20	**36**	146	–	44
		tanh	2	20	**26**	137	–	38
		ReLU+sigmoid	2	20	**15**	150	–	–
4	3	ReLU	2	20	**2**	8	21	–
		sigmoid	2	20	**3**	22	–	11
		tanh	2	20	**3**	21	–	10
		ReLU+tanh	2	20	**2**	12	–	–
5	3	ReLU	3	100	**13**	103	15	–
		sigmoid	3	100	76	**27**	–	190
		tanh	3	100	**76**	Unknown	–	179
		ReLU+tanh	3	100	**10**	Unknown	–	–
6	4	ReLU	3	20	**16**	1130	35	–
		sigmoid	3	20	**21**	13350	–	83
		tanh	3	20	**19**	2416	–	70
		ReLU+tanh	3	20	**15**	1413	–	–
ACC	6	tanh	3	20	**343**	Unknown	–	3344
QMPC	6	tanh	2	20	**61**	–[a]	–	652
Attitude Control	6	sigmoid	3	64	**201**	–[a]	–	Unknown
QUAD	12	sigmoid	3	64	**1533**	–[a]	–	Unknown

[a] This example has multi-dimensional control inputs. ReachNN* only supports NN controllers that produce single-dimensional control inputs.

QUAD benchmark, POLAR computed the TM flowpipes for 50 control steps in 1533 s, while Verisig 2.0 and NNV took hours to compute flowpipes just for the first few steps.

4.2 Comparison over a Full Set of Benchmarks

We compare POLAR with the SOTA tools mentioned previously, including Sherlock, Verisig 2.0, NNV, and ReachNN* over the full benchmarks in [11,13]. We refer to [11, 13] for more details of these benchmarks. The results are presented in Table 1 where NNV is not included since we did not successfully use it to prove any of the benchmarks likely because it is designed for linear systems. Similar results for NNV are also observed in [13]. We can see POLAR successfully verifies all the cases and the runtime is **on average 8x and up to 94x faster**[2] compared with the tool with the second best efficiency. The "Unknown" verification results either indicate the overapproximation was too large for verifying the safety property or the tool terminated early due to an explosion of the overapproximation. POLAR achieves the best performance among all the tools.

We remark that the hyperparameter settings used by all of the three tools for the benchmarks in Table 1 were set to be the same for a fair, lateral comparison. However, they are not the best settings for POLAR. For example, POLAR finishes in **0.5 s** for the benchmark #1 with an integration stepsize that is same as the control stepsize and a TM order of 4.

4.3 Discussion

POLAR demonstrates substantial performance improvement over existing tools. In this section, we seek to further explore the capability of POLAR. We conduct several experiments for the QUAD benchmark to better understand the limitation and scalability of POLAR. We also include a mountain car example to show that POLAR is able to handle discrete-time systems.

Ablation Studies. To explore the impact of the two proposed techniques, namely Bernstein polynomial interpolation (BP) and symbolic remainder (SR) on the overall performance, we conduct a series of experiments on the QUAD benchmark with different configurations. Table 2 shows the performance of POLAR with and without the proposed techniques SR and BP in the NN propagation: 1) TM: only TM arithmetic is used; 2) TM+SR: SR is used with TM arithmetic; 3) BP is used with TM arithmetic; and 4) Both BP and SR are used with TM arithmetic. Based on the results, we can observe that SR significantly improves the accuracy of the reachable set overapproximation. Finally, the combination of basic TM with BP and SR not only achieves the best accuracy, but also is the most efficient. While the additional BP and SR operations can incur runtime overhead compared with basic TM, they help to produce a tighter overestimation and thus reduce the state space being explored during reachability analysis. As a result, the overall performance including runtime is better.

The following further observations can be obtained from Table 2. (i) Both of the independent use of BP and SR techniques significantly improves the performance of reachable set overapproximations. (ii) When the BP technique is used, Bernstein approximation is often not used on activation functions, but the few times for which they are used significantly improve the accuracy. The reason of having this phenomenon is that Taylor and Bernstein approximations are similarly accurate in approximating activation functions with small domain.

---

[2] These are lower bounds on the improvements since other tools terminated early for certain settings due to explosion of their computed flowpipes.

Table 2. Ablation Studies for POLAR on the QUAD benchmark. We compare the width of TM remainder on x_3 at the 50th step under different settings. For settings with BP, we also list the percentage of times where BP is used among 9600 neurons. If a setting cannot compute flowpipes for all 50 steps, it is marked as *Unknown*. X_0 is the radius of the initial set. k is the order of the TM.

X_0	k	TM		TM+SR		TM+BP			TM+BP+SR		
		Width	Time (s)	Width	Time (s)	Width	Time (s)	BP %	Width	Time (s)	BP %
0.05	2	7.5e−04	229	1.3e−04	233	6.8e−04	228	5.79%	1.2e−04	231	1.34%
	3	5.2e−04	273	6.5e−05	251	5.0e−04	274	3.62%	6.5e−05	251	0%
	4	4.9.e−04	332	6.2e−05	270	4.7e−04	336	3.57%	6.2e−05	270	0%
0.1	2	*Unknown*	–	2.3e−03	319	1.0e−02	325	9.68%	1.1e−03	289	4.80%
	3	1.8e−03	352	2.2e−04	287	1.7e−03	349	6.85%	2.2e−04	287	0%
	4	1.6e−03	431	1.9e−04	304	1.5e−03	427	6.70%	1.9e−04	304	0%
0.2	2	*Unknown*	–	*Unknown*	–	*Unknown*	–	–	*Unknown*	–	–
	3	9.0e−03	721	1.9e−03	412	7.8e−03	670	4.03%	1.6e−03	394	0.77%
	4	5.0e−03	761	9.2e−04	403	4.7e−03	728	4.38%	8.1e−04	396	0.07%
0.4	2	*Unknown*	–	*Unknown*	–	*Unknown*	–	–	*Unknown*	–	–
	3	*Unknown*	–	*Unknown*	–	*Unknown*	–	–	*Unknown*	–	–
	4	*Unknown*	–	*Unknown*	–	*Unknown*	–	–	3.7e-02	1533	3.25%

However, the Lagrange form-based remainder evaluation in Taylor polynomials performs better than the sample-based remainder evaluation in Bernstein polynomials in those cases. It can also be seen that for each X_0, the use of Bernstein approximation becomes more frequent when the TMs has larger remainders. (iii) When both BP and SR techniques are used, the approach produces the tightest TMs compared with the other columns in the table even though the use Bernstein approximation is less often. The reason is that the remainders of the TMs are already well-limited and most of the activation functions handled in the reachability computation are with a "small" TM domain.

Scalability Analysis. Table 1 shows that POLAR can handle much larger NNCSs compared with the current SOTA. To better understand the scalability of POLAR, we further conduct scalability analysis on the size of the NN controller and the width of the initial set using the QUAD benchmark. The experiment results in Fig. 6 for the neural networks with different widths and depths show that POLAR scales well on the number of layers and the number of neurons in each layer in the NN controller. On the other hand, the time cost grows rapidly when the width of the initial set becomes larger. Such a phenomenon already exists in the literature for reachability analysis of ODE systems [5]. The reason for this is that when the initial set is larger, it is more difficult to track the state dependencies and requires keeping more terms in a TM flowpipe.

Discrete-Time NNCS. Finally, we use Mountain car, a common benchmark in Reinforcement Learning literature, to show that POLAR also works on discrete-time systems. The comparison with Verisig 2.0, ReachNN* and NNV is shown in Fig. 5b. POLAR also outperforms these tools substantially for this example.

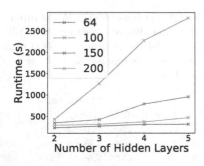 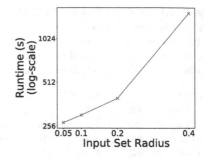

Fig. 6. Scalability analysis for POLAR on the QUAD benchmark. We present the runtime of QUAD for 50 steps reachability analysis. Under all settings, POLAR can verify that the system reaches the target set at the 50th step. Left figure: Runtime on different neural network architectures with the input set radius as 0.05. We study neural-network controllers with different number of layers (2, 3, 4, 5) and neurons (64, 100, 150, 200). Right figure: Runtime on the different input set radius of the QUAD benchmark. We use the same network in Fig. 5 which has 3 hidden layers with 64 neurons in each layer.

5   Conclusion

In this paper, we propose POLAR, a polynomial arithmetic framework, which integrates TM flowpipe construction, Bernstein overapproximation, and symbolic remainder method to efficiently compute reachable set overapproximations for NNCS. Empirical comparison shows POLAR performs significantly better than SOTAs on both computation efficiency and tightness of reachable set estimation. Our future work includes parallelization of POLAR on GPUs to further improve computation efficiency.

Acknowledgement. We gratefully acknowledge the support from the National Science Foundation awards CCF-1646497, CCF-1834324, CNS-1834701, CNS-1839511, IIS-1724341, CNS-2038853, ONR grant N00014-19-1-2496, and the US Air Force Research Laboratory (AFRL) under contract number FA8650-16-C-2642.

References

1. Althoff, M.: An introduction to CORA 2015. In: International Workshop on Applied veRification for Continuous and Hybrid Systems (ARCH). EPiC Series in Computing, vol. 34, pp. 120–151 (2015)
2. Alur, R., Dill, D.L.: A theory of timed automata. Theoret. Comput. Sci. **126**(2), 183–235 (1994)
3. Beard, R.: Quadrotor dynamics and control rev 0.1 (2008)
4. Berz, M., Makino, K.: Verified integration of ODEs and flows using differential algebraic methods on high-order Taylor models. Reliable Comput. **4**, 361–369 (1998). https://doi.org/10.1023/A:1024467732637
5. Chen, X.: Reachability analysis of non-linear hybrid systems using taylor models. Ph.D. thesis, RWTH Aachen University (2015)

6. Chen, X., Ábrahám, E., Sankaranarayanan, S.: Flow*: an analyzer for non-linear hybrid systems. In: Sharygina, N., Veith, H. (eds.) CAV 2013. LNCS, vol. 8044, pp. 258–263. Springer, Heidelberg (2013). https://doi.org/10.1007/978-3-642-39799-8_18
7. Chen, X., Sankaranarayanan, S.: Decomposed reachability analysis for nonlinear systems. In: Proceedings of RTSS 2016, pp. 13–24 (2016)
8. Dutta, S., Chen, X., Sankaranarayanan, S.: Reachability analysis for neural feedback systems using regressive polynomial rule inference. In: Proceedings of HSCC 2019, pp. 157–168. ACM (2019)
9. Fan, J., Huang, C., Chen, X., Li, W., Zhu, Q.: ReachNN*: a tool for reachability analysis of neural-network controlled systems. In: Hung, D.V., Sokolsky, O. (eds.) ATVA 2020. LNCS, vol. 12302, pp. 537–542. Springer, Cham (2020). https://doi.org/10.1007/978-3-030-59152-6_30
10. Frehse, G., Le Guernic, C., Donzé, A., Cotton, S., Ray, R., Lebeltel, O., Ripado, R., Girard, A., Dang, T., Maler, O.: SpaceEx: scalable verification of hybrid systems. In: Gopalakrishnan, G., Qadeer, S. (eds.) CAV 2011. LNCS, vol. 6806, pp. 379–395. Springer, Heidelberg (2011). https://doi.org/10.1007/978-3-642-22110-1_30
11. Huang, C., Fan, J., Li, W., Chen, X., Zhu, Q.: ReachNN: reachability analysis of neural-network controlled systems. ACM Trans. Embed. Comput. Syst. 18(5s), 106:1-106:22 (2019)
12. Huang, C., Fan, J., Li, W., Chen, X., Zhu, Q.: Divide and slide: layer-wise refinement for output range analysis of deep neural networks. IEEE Trans. Comput.-Aided Des. Integr. Circ. Syst. (TCAD) 39(11), 3323–3335 (2020)
13. Ivanov, R., Carpenter, T., Weimer, J., Alur, R., Pappas, G., Lee, I.: Verisig 2.0: verification of neural network controllers using Taylor model preconditioning. In: Silva, A., Leino, K.R.M. (eds.) CAV 2021. LNCS, vol. 12759, pp. 249–262. Springer, Cham (2021). https://doi.org/10.1007/978-3-030-81685-8_11
14. Ivanov, R., Weimer, J., Alur, R., Pappas, G.J., Lee, I.: Verisig: verifying safety properties of hybrid systems with neural network controllers. In: Proceedings of HSCC 2018, pp. 169–178. ACM (2019)
15. Jaulin, L., Kieffer, M., Didrit, O., Walter, É.: Interval Analysis. Applied Interval Analysis, Springer, Cham (2001). https://doi.org/10.1007/978-1-4471-0249-6_2
16. Katz, G., Barrett, C., Dill, D.L., Julian, K., Kochenderfer, M.J.: Reluplex: an efficient SMT solver for verifying deep neural networks. In: Majumdar, R., Kunčak, V. (eds.) CAV 2017. LNCS, vol. 10426, pp. 97–117. Springer, Cham (2017). https://doi.org/10.1007/978-3-319-63387-9_5
17. Levine, S., Finn, C., Darrell, T., Abbeel, P.: End-to-end training of deep visuomotor policies. J. Mach. Learn. Res. 17(1), 1334–1373 (2016)
18. Lorentz, G.G.: Bernstein Polynomials. American Mathematical Society (2013)
19. Makino, K., Berz, M.: Taylor models and other validated functional inclusion methods. Int. J. Pure Appl. Math. 4(4), 379–456 (2003)
20. Meiss, J.D.: Differential Dynamical Systems. SIAM publishers (2007)
21. Mnih, V., et al.: Human-level control through deep reinforcement learning. Nature 518(7540), 529–533 (2015)
22. Moore, R.E., Kearfott, R.B., Cloud, M.J.: Introduction to Interval Analysis. SIAM (2009)
23. Prajna, S., Parrilo, P.A., Rantzer, A.: Nonlinear control synthesis by convex optimization. IEEE Trans. Autom. Control 49(2), 310–314 (2004)
24. Singh, G., Ganvir, R., Püschel, M., Vechev, M.T.: Beyond the single neuron convex barrier for neural network certification. In: Proceedings of NeurIPS 2019, pp. 15072–15083 (2019)

25. Tran, H.-D., et al.: NNV: the neural network verification tool for deep neural networks and learning-enabled cyber-physical systems. In: Lahiri, S.K., Wang, C. (eds.) CAV 2020. LNCS, vol. 12224, pp. 3–17. Springer, Cham (2020). https://doi.org/10.1007/978-3-030-53288-8_1

26. Wang, Z., Huang, C., Zhu, Q.: Efficient global robustness certification of neural networks via interleaving twin-network encoding. In: Proceedings of DAT2 2022 (2022)

27. Weng, T.W., et al.: Towards fast computation of certified robustness for relu networks. In: Proceedings of ICML 2018 (2018)

28. Zhang, H., Weng, T.W., Chen, P.Y., Hsieh, C.J., Daniel, L.: Efficient neural network robustness certification with general activation functions. In: Proceedings of NeurIPS 2018, pp. 4944–4953 (2018)

29. Zhu, Q., et al.: Safety-assured design and adaptation of learning-enabled autonomous systems. In: Proceedings of ASPDAC 2021 (2021)

30. Zhu, Q., et al.: Know the unknowns: addressing disturbances and uncertainties in autonomous systems. In: Proceedings of ICCAD 2020 (2020)

Author Index

Printed in the United States
by Baker & Taylor Publisher Services